Urban Affairs in Alberta

Urban Affairs in Alberta

by David G. Bettison
John K. Kenward and
Larrie Taylor

This is Volume II of a 2-volume work on Urbanization in Canada. Volume I appears under the title *The Politics of Canadian Urban Development.*

Published for the Human Resources Research Council of Alberta by The University of Alberta Press
1975

First published by
The University of Alberta Press,
Edmonton, Alberta, Canada

1975

ISBN 0-88864-009-9

ERRATA

Pages 55 to 60 inclusive should be
read in the following order
55, 58, 59, 56, 57, 60

Printed in Canada by
Printing Services of The University of Alberta

Table of Contents

List of Tables

List of Figures

Foreword

In November of 1969, the Alberta Human Resources Research Council sponsored an Urban Studies Symposium which took stock of the process of urbanization in Alberta and sought to identify areas where research would be required in order to guide urban development policies in the future. The papers given at this Symposium were edited by Gordon McIntosh, Ian Housego, and Glenda Lamont and published by HRRC in 1970 under the title *Urbanization and Urban Life in Alberta.*

Out of this Symposium, as Dr. Bettison and his colleagues make clear in their Preface to the present work, there evolved the research program which has resulted in this book, *Urban Affairs in Alberta.*

Urbanization is one of the most prominent features of life in Alberta today. In this, Alberta is merely sharing in a world-wide process. But because the cities of Alberta are, as cities, very recent, Alberta has the chance to avoid many of the mistakes and problems suffered by other areas, both in Canada and outside it which are undergoing urbanization. This possibility informs the work of Dr. Bettison and his colleagues, and both they and the Council hope that these problems and mistakes may be avoided. Certainly *Urban Affairs in Alberta* is a major contribution to our understanding of the Alberta scene.

While the Human Resources Research Council is therefore pleased to present this work to the public, the Council would like to emphasize that the opinions and conclusions expressed in this book are those of the authors, and should not be construed to be the view of the Council.

Human Resources Research Council
Edmonton, Alberta
August 1972

Preface

This study originated with Lorne Downey, Director of the Human Resources Research Council (HRRC), and his staff in November, 1969, when they called together a variety of persons interested in the urban affairs of the province of Alberta for a symposium at The University of Alberta. This symposium explored the prospect of developing a research capacity in urban studies in Alberta. Papers from the symposium were edited by Gordon McIntosh, Ian Housego, and Glenda Lamont and published in 1970 under the title *Urbanization and Urban Life in Alberta.*

The Human Resources Research Council moved cautiously in developing such a complex research area and requested that a year be spent on identifying appropriate research problems before launching a major project on the urban affairs of the province. The idea that the most prosperous of the prairie provinces should commit resources to the study of urban phenomena was novel. Subsequent events, such as Premier Harry Strom's "Task Force on Urbanization and the Future," under Peter Boothroyd as co-ordinator, and the imminent "Urban policy for Canada" bear witness to the foresight of the council and its staff in this regard. We regret to note, however, that, following the change of government in Alberta, in January, 1972, the government announced that both the Human Resources Research Council and the Task Force were to be phased out of existence.

An advisory committee on Urban Studies was struck in early 1970 to assist the authors. Our thanks are due to Erwin Adderley, Executive Director of the Oldman River Regional Planning Commission, Bruce Proudfoot, Professor of Geography at The University of Alberta, Jack Snary, Director of Industrial Development, Department of Industry and Tourism, and R. W. Wright, Dean of Arts and Science at The University of Calgary for their advice and generously given time during the study and its subsequent writing. The opinions expressed in this study, however, are not necessarily their own either individually or collectively.

The advisory committee agreed in early 1970 to grant limited financial support to a study of migration and migrants to some of the smaller towns of the province. This had been a forgotten research topic amid the rush of migrants to the metropolitan centres of Calgary and Edmonton in recent decades. Under the guidance of Professor Proudfoot, Glenda Lamont undertook this study which was presented as a report to HRRC in 1972 under the title "Migration and small towns in Alberta." We would also acknowledge the assistance of Frank Jankunis of the Department of Geography at The University of Lethbridge for a tour he undertook in the summer of 1970 to gather data on a wide variety of small towns and villages in the province. This study has been made available through the Department of Geography, The University of Lethbridge.

The three authors of this study were asked to undertake a year of inquiry into appropriate research problems. The team was carefully chosen to represent a variety of perspectives. John Kenward is a political scientist with particular interests in community political processes; Larrie Taylor is an architect and town planner with experience in England, Sweden, and Canada; and David Bettison is a sociologist and anthropologist with experience of urban affairs in South Africa, Australia, and elsewhere. The three authors shared their criticism and advice over the whole book; but the task of collecting the evidence and preparing the early drafts was divided so that Larrie Taylor concentrated on Edmonton and the planning facilities of the province; John Kenward on Calgary, the Crowsnest Pass, and other small towns; and David Bettison on the more general nature of federal and provincial matters.

During the writing of this book, the assistance of Lija Bane was obtained to catalogue and put order into the array of research material procured. Throughout most of the work the secretarial and machine calculating duties were willingly performed by Jean Rigaux. Betty Dahl prepared the final draft of the report for submission to HRRC. The co-operation and constructive criticism of all members of the team are warmly acknowledged.

Through generous, continued financial support by the HRRC, it was possible to extend the time of inquiry beyond the initial year. The field work was conducted from April, 1970 to May, 1971, and the writing of this report was extended to the close of 1971. We would like to thank the council for its extended support of our efforts, and The University of Lethbridge for granting David Bettison three-fifths of his time free from teaching duties to undertake the job.

Acknowledgement of the help given us by numerous officers of the provincial administration and many local authorities of the province is little compensation to them for their assistance. Their frankness and honesty bear witness to the openness of governmental institutions in Alberta. Though we cannot say we were given everything we asked for, the co-operation we received was heartening. To many individuals of the province, from Crowsnest Pass to Grande Prairie, we express our gratitude for the many hours spent in discussion with us during field work. Without their interest and support this study would have been impossible because we aimed to discover the situation on the ground, as far as time permitted, as well as to appreciate what official statistics and reports indicated the situation might be. Whatever misinterpretation there may remain in this study is our responsibility, though sorting opinion from fact was not easy. Needless to say, however, this is precisely the situation with which Albertans themselves are concerned, particularly in the development of Alberta's urban culture.

Thanks are due finally to the Government of Alberta for supporting the publication of this book both financially and morally, to The University of Alberta Press for publishing it, and to Stuart Piddocke for editing the manuscript.

David G. Bettison
John K. Kenward
Larrie Taylor
August 1972.

Chapter 1
The Past and the Generation of Basic Issues, 1880 to 1935

A Glimpse at the Distant Past: Setting the Pattern for the Future

Since its founding on September 1, 1905 Alberta has had only four changes of political party. The victory of the Progressive Conservatives under Mr. Peter Lougheed in August, 1971 was the first victory for this party in Alberta. From 1905 to 1921 the Liberal Party held uninterrupted office; from 1921 to 1935 the United Farmers of Alberta (UFA) held power; and from 1935 to September, 1971 the Social Credit League of Alberta formed the government. The Commonwealth Co-operative Federation (CCF), later the New Democratic Party (NDP), have not held office. For 50 years, from 1921 to 1971, the province has had what might be construed as a one-party government, though oppositions have come and gone.

This tendency to one party government and the relative ineffectiveness of left-wing ideologies reflects Albertans' stoic recognition of the value of individual rights, coupled to their consciousness that they have been the subject of thoroughly exploitive policies imposed upon them from elsewhere and especially from eastern Canadian companies.[1] As will be discussed later, the UFA and especially the Social Credit movement were a response in non-socialist terms to the evils that were seen to lie in the exploitation of the public and its collective amenities by privately organized capital. To a great extent this radical reaction was a response to the events that preceded the First World War and to the depressions of the early 1920s and the 1930s.

Radical thought of the 1920s and 1930s in Alberta differed from left-wing thought in industrial Europe because Albertans themselves were title holders to agricultural land with obviously immense potential, or were owners of businesses in urban centres with equal potential. What was seen to be wrong was the world system outside Alberta. In every slump this system had let these potentials fall away while tying Albertans to debt at very high rates of interest to persons in the outside world. Outside companies and political parties to whom their interests were tied had immorally crashed the economic system while still holding Albertans handcuffed to interest rates on borrowed money for Albertan exploitation. This in turn restricted Albertan capacities to take effective remedial action even inside their own province. By the mid-

1930s Albertans were satisfied that they knew what economic system the world should have in order to avoid the evils of depression. They were angry that they were unable to make this system work even in their own province and Albertans very quickly became a group of self-conscious, proud, liberally-oriented frontiersmen who felt themselves to be the exploited tools of misguided powers in distant places. This world view perhaps increased the ease with which disparate immigrant groups from all parts of Europe so easily and successfully identified with the greater Albertan culture of which they were a part.[2] Social Credit philosophy in the 1920s and 1930s was offered not only as an example for others to follow, but as the saviour of Canada from the troubles it was continually running into through "faulty" public finance policies. This, and similar philosophies which preceded it, have had their impact on Alberta's urban affairs no less than on the integration of its immigrant ethnic minorities.

The way in which privately organized eastern capital served its own convenience and involved Albertans in unnecessary work and expense — quite apart from dashing their hopes of speculative gain from early and wise local decisions — can be seen as early as 1880 in the affairs of the Canadian Pacific Railway (CPR). Pierre Berton, in his recent excellent account of the building of the trans-Canada railway, has suggested that the explanation for the change of route from the North Saskatchewan River through Edmonton to the relatively dry and less agriculturally rewarding southern route through Calgary was taken because of the advantages to the CPR which would accrue from siting the urban centres of the prairies on land which the CPR had been granted by right of contract with the dominion government.[3] The change of route was decided in 1881 soon after the formation of the CPR (in 1880). It was not chosen for engineering reasons: the Kicking Horse Pass was 1,600 feet higher than the Yellowhead Pass with more difficult grades, and the route via the Kicking Horse Pass was known to involve probable difficulties in British Columbia in getting over the Selkirk range.[4] The company could benefit financially from two main sources — the sale of land it obtained from the dominion government under contract to build the railway and from the freight it carried both to the developing prairies and from the prairies to the coasts.

Pierre Berton argues that the situation as seen by the CPR management was probably as follows:

> On the other hand, that line (the northern route) ran through country where some settlement already existed and where real estate speculators — at Battleford and Prince Albert, for example — expected to make profits out of land adjacent to the right of way. It undoubtedly occurred to the railway company that it would be easier to control an area that had never known a settler and where there were no established business interests of any kind.

Why should the road increase the value of other men's property?[5]

The CPR therefore took the agricultural land to which it was entitled, not from the dry areas of the Palliser Triangle, but from the richer areas of the north; and took the urban land to which it was entitled in the dry Palliser Triangle. Here the future cities of the prairies would be established at the company's instigation. The company also developed policies favouring land settlement on irrigated land thereby ensuring its traffic in freight from the dryer southern lands as well. It benefited from higher priced land sales on good agricultural northern land and from freight traffic to and from the cities and irrigated farms of the south.

Settlers had moved into the Edmonton and St. Albert areas and along the North Saskatchewan River prior to 1881 partly for agricultural reasons, but also to take advantage of the railway when it eventually came that way. Land values were bound to rise. The foothills south of Calgary had been found suitable for cattle ranching, but before the arrival of the CPR in August, 1883, the early settlers were tied to a north-south route ending in Montana. In 1881 the Calgary settlement on the east bank of the Bow River, which was later to be moved to the west bank under CPR intimidation, had some 75 people. Silver City's supposed silver deposits in the vicinity of Castle Mountain near Banff boosted population in the Calgary area. A sawmill was set up just below the junction of the Bow and Elbow Rivers in 1882 and had more business than it could cope with when the rail approached the city. In the same year a detachment of police was assigned to the Calgary area and a $35,000 contract to erect new barracks on the west bank of the Bow River was awarded.[6] The first construction train entered the Calgary settlement in August, 1883 after a record-breaking laying of track from Medicine Hat. This made the Calgary centre the most important in the far west and reduced the settler's dependence on the north-south axis to Montana and Edmonton.

The established Calgary centre on the east bank of the river, however, was on Section 14. The CPR had rights only to odd-numbered sections. Section 15 was across the river where the police post was located. Immediately on reaching Calgary, the company's land agents attempted to purchase Section 14, but the owners asked too high a price for the company's liking. The company thereupon asked the dominion government to release Section 15 to it in terms of its contract to build the railway. The police post had to be relinquished in consequence. The company built the Calgary railway station on the west bank on Section 15 over which it had rights. By 1884, the very year following the rail's arrival, the settlement on the east bank was obliged to move to the west bank in order to be near the station. The inhabitants accepted lots of land on the Company's terms. [7]

Pierre Berton has described in detail how the same tactics were used at Grand Valley and Brandon in Manitoba, west of

Winnipeg.[8] He remarks "The company arbitrarily determined its location in the interests of real estate profit, and the company totally controlled it."[9] The CPR, an eastern-based private company, dictated both the location and the shape of the centres which it decided to sponsor. Pierre Berton comments, "With a scratch of the pen the company could, and did, decide which communities would grow and which would stagnate; the placing of divisional points made all the difference."[10] When other railway interests moved into Alberta to provide feeder line services for settler produce, they also were granted land rights to pay for construction and similarly determined the site of urban centres. As some 800 villages, towns and cities were set up in the three prairie provinces by the CPR alone "the advantages of total control were inestimable."[11]

The "total control" of the CPR, however, referred more to the siting of towns in general than to control over the allocation of land in lot size planning. For example, the attempt to buy Section 14 on the east bank of the Bow River in Calgary, and the eventual siting of the station on its own land over the river on Section 15, put the CPR in a position of controlling the general growth of Calgary on the west bank only. Had it bought Section 14 at the price the inhabitants demanded, the CPR could have controlled both sides of the river. The company was no doubt short of capital to engage in such a "total control" of urban development, but its unwillingness or inability to do so had immense consequences for the laying-out and planning of the urban centres it stimulated.

Pierre Berton has well described the extraordinary speculation in land that occurred in Winnipeg from June 1881 to mid-April 1882. He remarks, "For all of those eleven months, the business section of the city resembled nothing so much as a giant carnival, which seemed to run day and night."[12] Brandon was not very different and even Medicine Hat had its real estate boom after the arrival of the railway. One of the first acts of W.C Van Horne, after being made general manager of the CPR and arriving in Winnipeg to take up the job in December, 1881, was to place an advertisement in the Winnipeg newspaper "cautioning the public against buying lots at prospective stations along the line until he had officially announced their locations."[13] The company intended to decide on the location of future townsites "without regard to any private interest whatever."[14]

It was fair warning. But it does not explain why the immense speculation in land and urban lot sites which accompanied the building of the CPR line across the prairies was largely an urban phenomenon. Though agricultural land changed hands or was allotted by government or was sold by the company and its subsidiaries, the paper boom was typical of the embryonic urban centres.[15] Urban dwellers of the time envisaged their centres growing into new Chicagos. They apparently acted on the assumption that the development of the agricultural potential would follow and that the urban centres would grow as transit connection points in consequence. We have not had the opportunity to enquire in greater detail into this apparently important point in Alberta's history; but it is significant that the boom in the earliest years was an urban one based upon immense speculation and imagined potential. The opening of a frontier by railway caused the urban emphasis. Anything seemed possible if only the market and opportunities could be captured and harnessed to the control of amenities that "ownership" implied, and if other towns or individuals would be prevented from seizing an advantage. Concentration was the key both to control and to ease of business opportunity. The developmental process occurred almost entirely under conditions of capitalist ownership in its purest, most uncontrolled form. The Northwest Territories government was involved in the responsibilities of land survey and also in the provision of police whom they effectively co-ordinated from the centre of power, not subject to locally elected officials. The CPR across the prairies was built under conditions of prohibition, and this law and order meant more in Canada than it ever did during the opening up of the prairies south of the border.[16]

The first issue of the *Calgary Herald, Mining and Ranch Advocate and General Advertiser* appeared on August 31, 1883.[17] The police post at Fort Macleod similarly attracted a population, and the discovery of coal on the Belly River established Lethbridge. When the rail was completed to Calgary in 1883 the trail to Edmonton was rapidly improved for horse transport, and later, in 1891, a line of rail was laid. The stopping places for horse transport — Red Deer Crossing, Battle River Crossing to the north and High River to the south of Calgary, became the places where towns grew up. Pincher Creek in 1883 was a settlement of 80 people, based largely on cattle ranching. Medicine Hat was first established to serve forestry and agricultural interests in the Cypress Hills, and grew with the railway from 1881. Mormon settlers from Utah moved onto land south of Lethbridge and later formed Cardston. By 1887 German families had settled west of Red Deer and, later, others moved to the Stony Plain district around Edmonton. In 1892 some 3,134 settlers took up land along the Calgary-Edmonton railway. French colonists moved into St. Albert in 1891 and were followed by others within a few years. In May, 1892 the CPR offered for sale odd-numbered sections in the townships around Edmonton at prices from $3 to $15 an acre. John Blue reports that one firm in Edmonton sold 10,000 acres in two weeks.[18] The company opened land offices in Calgary, Red Deer, and Edmonton the same year.

By 1893 a new policy of homesteading, whereby settlers took up lots of 160 acres, increased the density of settlement and guaranteed the CPR both rail traffic and a means of disposing of its land for its eventual benefit. Extensive cattle ranches were threatened by the new policy, but available land was taken up in most parts of the province as eager towndwellers and newcomers took up the chance of gaining title to land and trying agriculture. In 1894 a topographical and hydrographical survey was set up, and in 1896 the St. Mary and Lethbridge plains and the Bow River were surveyed for irrigation. Irrigation companies were established to exploit them. The growth of the beef industry up to 1902 in southern Alberta assisted foothill towns in the area and contributed to Calgary's pre-eminence. Calgary was incorporated as a town in 1884 and was also the first city to be incorporated in Alberta, in 1893. Edmonton was incorporated as a city in 1904. It was declared the capital of the province by an Act of the Legislature in 1905, although Calgary hotly objected.[19]

The area of initial settlement was spread over an area almost 600 miles north-south and 200 miles east-west with the railway forming the essential links.[20] The nodes of concentrated settlement served both as depots for interprovincial trade and as centres for Alberta-based farmers. A series of regional centres sprang up concurrently either to service local agricultural interests or to provide construction and maintenance amenities for the railways. The government was faced with the problem of servicing widely scattered villages and settler concentrations and of providing marketing outlets for agricultural exports from the new province. It is important to note that the settlement policy was inspired by the dominion government in concert with the CPR and other eastern interests. Even after 1905 it was not a provincially inspired program, though there is no evidence to suggest that established settlers generally resisted the arrival of newcomers. The dominion inspiration, however, had the effect of obliging the newly formed Albertan provincial government to generate the public services required by the settlers. Though this was subsidized by dominion grants, the province regularly expended more on public works than it received.

Unlike the older Canadian provinces joining Confederation, Alberta entered without autonomy over public lands. This situation continued until 1931 despite repeated requests from Alberta for an amendment to the Alberta Act of 1905. The federal government in order to get a trans-Canada railway built, had granted to the CPR land subsidies across the prairies to an extent of 25,000,000 acres, valued at $1 an acre, and an additional cash subsidy of a further $25 million. This grant was later reduced to about 18 million acres as a consequence of a settlement made between the dominion and the railway. Other benefits were conferred upon the company, including a perpetual exemption from taxation of its mainline properties and tax exemption of its land and mineral rights for 20 years. The provincial government and particularly the local authorities of Alberta suffered severely in later years from this arrangement by the dominion government. As increased rail construction continued on the prairies, some 55 million acres were granted in part payment to different railway companies.

The reasons for the reluctance of the dominion government to hand over control of public lands to the new provincial government vary from source to source. The old established provinces objected to Alberta being granted rights to public lands unless compensation was paid and a readjustment of the public debt covering the $25 million cash subsidy to the railways arrived at. A grant, in lieu of revenues received from public lands by the federal government based on a variable per capita assessment, was paid instead.[21] Thus though public money became available for expenditure by the provincial government on the network of services required by a growing rural and urban population, a major source of taxation available to the government — the landed property of railway and settlement companies — was denied to the province until the companies chose to sell the land to settlers and homesteaders. By 1938[22] the Alberta government had begun to see the dominion government's reluctance in terms of its keeping control over immigration on the prairies thereby guaranteeing its concession to the CPR and maintaining demand for manufactured goods for the benefit of the "mechanics and artisans" of eastern Canada.

In 1905 Alberta was very much the junior province. It was the remotest of all the prairie provinces from eastern Canada and its gross agricultural income was not much over 10 percent of the total for the prairie provinces.[23] Due in part to its lack of control over public lands, its revenue base was very narrow. One of the first steps of the new Alberta provincial government was to legislate taxation on CPR property, but this was declared *ultra vires* in the courts except for the taxation of branch lines. These in turn were sorely needed for the development of the province and from 1907 to 1914 the provincial government assisted branch-line construction all over the province by guarantees to various railway companies. Similarly there was an attempt in 1907 to take over the operation of the Bell Telephone Company in the province by negotiation. This was unsuccessful, and the government therefore legislated to build rural and trunk lines to protect the public from what the government alleged was the monopoly of the Bell Telephone Company.[24] Municipalities were also empowered to erect and operate telephone services.

Though these attempts at takeovers and taxation may appear to be socialist in character, they rather reflect the struggle of the provincial government for greater power in its own house. It was a Liberal government until 1921. It was also a government caught in a squeeze. It was pressed from below by continuous demands for expenditure on public services derived from opening up the province and from the expectations of immigrants from eastern Canada, Europe, and the United States who were intent as much upon easy gains as upon hard work. It was also pressed from above by the dominion government's intent to disperse the immigrants and spread the settlement over Alberta as widely as circumstances permitted. The government was therefore forced to adopt a policy of extensive borrowing.[25] The protectionist tariffs which supported central Canadian industry added costs to the western primary producers. The Alberta farmer felt that he was caught on both sides — by monopoly on the services supplied him from interests centred in eastern Canada and by national tariffs supporting eastern industries whose commodities he had to buy. His own government seemed unable to cope with the situation he was in. Eastern financiers had benefited from land speculation, and real estate offices blossomed in many parts of the province. An account from Medicine Hat illustrates the climate of the times:

> During the boom years of 1911 to 1914 the boundaries of the city were extended and subdivisions were laid out in several directions. People hoped all these areas would be required for building lots. Real estate offices were opened wherever there was a vacant space and people from as far away as England bought lots by cable. Some people were convinced that there was nothing to justify such expansion. The Editor of the *Medicine Hat News* opposed concessions being given to a group who proposed to start a street railway. He also doubted the good intentions of some who were promising to start industries. There was considerable resentment to his attitude and he was thrown into the South Saskatchewan River, fortunately in effigy.[26]

These times contrasted markedly with the lean years to come.

The farm communities were heavily dependent upon the array of small villages and towns which had grown up wherever settlement had taken place. Settlement was scattered in the province and this added to the costs of local public works. Towns served as vital service centres to the agricultural export industry, then based on animal transport and railways. The importance of these centres varied. Central place theory has offered an explanation for the changes in importance, the distribution and the size of these towns, but by 1930 there was general evidence that those off the railway and without grain elevators were disappearing.[27] Farmers had the means to travel further, or less often; and the centres with a greater variety of services, with mechanical workshops or distributor agencies, had the competitive edge over nearer but less responsive villages. The towns and villages were linked through a variety of larger towns such as Lethbridge, Medicine Hat, Red Deer, and Lloydminister, and in turn to Calgary or Edmonton.

Before the onset of the First World War therefore, the pattern of urban distribution and the hierarchy of importance of Alberta's cities and towns had become entrenched. Apart from developments in the Peace River area and the relative collapse of the south-eastern portion of the province, this general pattern has been maintained. Only the rapid and continuous growth of Calgary and Edmonton after 1945 has tended to upset the original hierarchy of importance by exaggerating the dominance of these metropolitan centres.

Early Local Government

Among the earliest problems of a scattered prairie region was the proper founding of local government. Settlers could not expect, nor were they particularly disposed to accept, provincial responsibility for local services. Organized local activity, first by voluntary labour, then by permitting exemption from service if a cash payment was made (an essential option for large railway companies who preferred to pay tax in cash rather than labour) and later by cash taxation, was an essential component of provincial development. Such local activity was related, however, to the provincial (or prior to 1905, the territorial) government in three important ways.

First, local authority boundaries, delineated in terms of generally stated provincial regulations as to size and population, became seriously confused and overlapping. Educational authorities frequently had different boundaries from governmental (road and civic) authorities, etc. So jealously were such boundaries guarded, and so respectful was the provincial government of local authorities, that it was only in the 1950s, and after the establishment of a Royal Commission in 1947 and a special committee in 1953, that boundaries were finally co-ordinated.[28] The provincial government was very reluctant to determine and impose a clearer system of local boundaries.

Secondly, the provincial government prescribed by general statutes for villages, towns, hamlets, and rural municipalities, and by particular charters for cities, the official powers and duties of the local authorities. In Alberta a local authority has only such powers as are prescribed to it by the authority creating it, which authority may also prescribe procedures and responsibilities. It is not a case of a local authority having power to act except in such matters as are expressly denied it. In a sense the provincial government is theoretically always in a position to know what its local authorities are doing but, as in all such relationships, the facts tend to be different.

Thirdly, the dynamic of events within the boundaries and within the terms and duties legally prescribed to a local authority tend to occur irrespective of either local or provincial governments. This is particularly the case when this dynamic is closely associated with privately organized capital empowered to come and go, to make profits or incur losses, to employ local or foreign citizens, and to report in secret its affairs to authorities outside and beyond the boundaries of the local government territory within which it is located. For example, once a retail business has been licenced by a local authority to operate from a prescribed address within its jurisdiction, that business may grow in terms of its profits without further regulation by the local authority.[29] If it improves or expands its property and buildings, however, the local authority is concerned both as an approver of building plans and as an assessor of tax potential. There is a range of activities which is the concern of the local government and a range which is not. These ranges vary from time to time, and most of the conflicts that surround the interaction of governments within Alberta are concerned with varying the powers of different levels and units of government.

The provincial government is a party to all aspects, but the influence it has over them varies markedly and has varied also in time.

The system of local government introduced in Alberta has been described by Eric J. Hanson in his book, *Local Government in Alberta.*[30] In many respects local government typifies the character of the people of a province more clearly than anything else. The relation of the provincial government to local government in Alberta has been critically important in the evolution of the province's urban affairs. Our enquiries during 1970 showed that the stoic independence of mind of the local residents in the smaller cities and towns concerning their rights in local government had not diminished from what the historical record suggests it was before the turn of the century. The concurrent problems of the co-ordination of governmental activity, of provincial policy having influence over local decision, and of offering incentives to influence local government decisions rather than giving direction, are much as they ever were. With companies and corporations having the right to choose their locality of operation, the independence of local authorities was, and still is, a major difficulty confronting provincial authorities in the implementation of any policy affecting the direction or distribution of town and city growth. Such policy seems to be little more effective today than at the turn of the century.

Even before the founding of the province in 1905 the powers granted to local authorities were extensive. By-laws to raise revenue and to expend public monies on roads, bridges, lighting, drainage, public health, and nuisance control were introduced from the start. Municipalities were also empowered to build, own, and operate grist mills, grain elevators, and manufacturing establishments.

Provincial controls became most pronounced over the debts incurred by local authorities. Loans that could not be paid off within a year required the approval of the Lieutenant-Governor. After 1897 the local councils were limited in their borrowing to 10 percent of the assessed value of assessable property, and a two-thirds majority of ratepayers had also to approve borrowings lasting longer than a year. Excess borrowing by local authorities has been perhaps the most guarded-against feature of local government in Alberta over the years. The inspectorate branch of the Department of Municipal Affairs in 1970 considered this aspect of its work to be of great importance. The province was seen largely as the guardian of the money invested in the potential of the local communities.

The early system was therefore one whereby local developmental public works were assigned to local authorities. Where private initiative did not take up an opportunity, local authorities could provide the needed service, subject to debt control. The scene was set at this early stage for competition between private and public investment in every community in the province. Although the inability of urban authorities to tax CPR mainline land holdings reduced their base, Edmonton and Calgary at least were able to offer the railways incentives to run their tracks through parts of these cities and to build repair sheds within the cities. These two cities could even grant tax holidays to railway companies (on the limited property remaining that was subject to tax) in order to gain advantages from having the railways serve them or use their facilities.[31] By establishing themselves as entrepots for both local and transcontinental activities, these two centres assured their futures. Private investment capital quickly recognized the added security of this assured future. The control of public debt, in the light of this speculative attitude, was important, but the higher rates of interest payable in western Canada over eastern Canada added to the difficulties of local authorities to service it.

Hanson has delightfully described the heated nature of debate that occurred when local authorities were first confronted with an obligation to help finance education.[32] The move from mission-sponsored education to a state system (plus a separate, denominational school system) was not an easy one. All persons, rather than just those making gifts to religious and benevolent institutions, became involved. In 1884 when the first school ordinance was passed which provided for both public and separate schools, the local tax levies to support them were hotly contested. It is reported that major land-holding companies, including the Hudson's Bay Company and the CPR, took whatever measures were at their disposal (such as the temporary transfer of employees) to vote against the measure.[33] A hotel keeper, perhaps with a large family to educate, brought along his guests to vote *for* the measure! School boards were at first independent of other forms of local government and their boundaries often crossed a number of other governmental boundaries. The provincial government was often asked to collect school tax arrears for fear of local officials upsetting their neighbours and friends in attempting to collect it. A more systematic mode of collection through local authorities emerged only gradually. Teachers' salaries were modest, but many had to wait for their salaries until the government grant arrived; rural districts in particular had little ready cash for regular payments. Teachers often "boarded around" with their children's families, and many taxpayers contributed their dues in this way.

Education was imposed on local authorities by the provincial administration, but the local authorities could decline to make the additional levy if a majority of local taxpayers voted against it. Education was supported by the dominion government in the first instance, and had as well territorial and provincial support, so the incentive existed for local taxpayers to support it. In the 1890s a pronounced acceptance of school boards and school levies emerged in what is now Alberta. However, the boundaries of local authorities and school divisions were not co-ordinated from the start. School divisions and rural municipal districts usually overlapped, and in some cases a school division included four municipal districts.[34] This led to difficulties in administering both types of local authority, as well as requiring parents to pay taxes to both, frequently in disparate centres. Yet these administrative difficulties continued until late in the 1950s. The Co-Terminous Boundaries Commission was set up on March 2, 1953 to make a systematic co-ordination of local government and local school administrative boundaries. It was only done, however, after the 1952 annual conventions of both the Alberta School Trustees Association and the Alberta Association of Municipal Districts had formally passed resolutions requesting the provincial government to deal with the matter.

Herd and fire districts were instituted on application by two-thirds of the voters in not less than four townships. Fire guardians could be appointed by the Lieutenant-Governor. Stray animals and fires had to be dealt with collectively, as also did grazing pasture on commonage for stock on the trails. Similarly, when the need for roads emerged, to get children to school, produce to local markets, congregations to church, and supporters to local social events, the sparsely settled areas of the province were organized under the 1890 Statute Labour and Fire Ordinance. Again, although districts were proclaimed by the Lieutenant-Governor under this legislation, local residents had to petition to have it apply, or, where imposed, could vote to disallow it. The ordinance provides for elected local overseers to arrange for regular labour from settlers — based upon their proportion of land holdings[35] — to build and maintain needed roads and services. The area which settlers thus had to serve was limited — not more than 144 square miles — and it had to be outside of a regular municipal district. Payments in cash at the rate of $1.50 a day in lieu of service were allowed, and the big land-holding companies used this device. Some assistance was given by the provincial authority, again as an incentive. After 1897 the overall management of the scheme in the province fell under the local improvement branch of the Commissioner for Public Works, and locally elected councillors in each district decided on the priorities of local matters with the elected overseers responsible for their execution and the organization of the labour force. Also in 1897 the statutory labour districts were changed to local improvement districts. By 1903 general dissatisfaction had arisen over the quality of local roads. Farmers were said to be incompetent and unskilled. A larger unit of construction was proposed and by the use of taxation obtained in cash, a better job could be done by professional persons employed by the local ratepayers. The more progressive districts had voted in a plebiscite to move towards the more efficient system at the cost of greatly increased assessments for local improvements.[36] The territorial government was disinclined to undertake the work as a public responsibility and was strongly in favour of strengthening local government as a developmental instrument of local services. The government, as early as 1899, had organized large-area improvement districts where settlement was so sparse that the local improvement districts could not be applied. Its Public Works Department was directly involved in road construction in these large areas, and it was unwilling to become involved in rapidly developing areas where development could be undertaken by local initiative.

Later amendments provided for an ongoing institution of elected councillors to fix the rate and to manage local affairs and removed the need for an annual meeting of ratepayers to fix the coming year's program. The senior government continued to assist in collecting arrears. New boundaries were created and the old districts abolished. The large-area, sparsely populated improvement districts have continued to be managed by the provincial government. The influence of the Department of Municipal Affairs remains prominent in these districts, since the minister, aided by local advisory committees, retains the right of final decision on local matters within them. They are also supported more prominently by the provincial administration than are other forms of local government.

Hanson concludes his analysis of this era of local government development by explaining that though dissatisfaction with the system continued, district organization continued rapidly, "for it had come to be regarded as a means of asking for assistance for public services from the provincial government. The trick was to elect a council and then send councillors to Edmonton to make representation to the province."[37] As each district moved into prominence for one reason or another — a group of settlers newly arrived, a new railway line built, or just for political reasons — the strength of its case improved in Edmonton; but the amount of provincial assistance that could be offered to each and every locale of settlement and development was clearly limited. The provincial government in the meantime was becoming increasingly concerned with financial backing for railways, with the funding of civic buildings and a university, and with the general growth of amenities in the towns and cities. The early, primitive form of local development by local initiative was being increasingly superseded by province-wide considerations. Public and private investment in the local community were becoming increasingly subordinate to the system of relations which governed the larger political unit.

The Early Rural-Urban Conflict, 1881-1920

The policy of the dominion government was to settle the prairies as speedily as possible in order to stimulate demand for tariff-protected manufacturing production in Ontario and Quebec, to support the traffic of the Canadian Pacific Railway in its risky endeavour to build the line of rail across Canada, and to guarantee the continued existence of a united Canada including British Columbia, which had threatened secession from confederation if the line was not built. Settlement increased the economic potential of the prairies and also of the increasingly industrial areas of eastern Canada. It increased Canada's exports and holdings of foreign currency. For several decades it also helped to generate boom conditions on the prairies. Settlers already established benefited from the added trade, the sale of developed land holdings, the speculation, and the improved claims for added public expenditure on the services which they needed. There were clear advantages to a greater and a more concentrated population.

Faced with the inhospitable terrain of the Rocky Mountains to the west, and the distance of Winnipeg, Regina, Moose Jaw, and Saskatoon in the east, it was inevitable that centres of inter-provincial activity would be generated in Alberta. The role of Calgary and Edmonton as entrepots for the CPR favoured their early growth. The security which this growth and concentraton offered to private financiers made these cities a natural place for the favouring of investment. The concentration of services, whether to local farmers and traders or to the province or the nation in general, was inevitable for sound economic reasons in the frontier situation of the time. By 1911 Calgary had a recorded population of 43,700 and Edmonton-Strathcona combined had some 31,000. The smaller cities recorded populations of: Lethbridge 9,035; Medicine Hat 5,608; Wetaskawin 2,411, and Red Deer 2,118. Thus, in the first 30 years of the growth of urban settlement in Alberta, Calgary and Edmonton had established a clear pre-eminence. They were attracting economic facilities that supported populations from four to seven times those of their next smallest competitors.

The growth of trade in Alberta's urban centres, that followed from the opening up and settlement of the province by a railway, took an unusual form. Business tended to be started not by small-scale impoverished landholders forced off the land to try something else, but by substantial men from the east or by companies relying on eastern finance. Lawrence Bussard, in concluding his thesis written in 1935, wrote:

> Middle-aged men from Ontario and the Central States came in to take up free homesteads or to engage in the business life of the towns so that their sons might have those opportunities which the East did not provide. Most of these men had money and they gave the west a stability which it would not otherwise have had ... The increase of wealth and population resulted in well-defined social classes replacing the more democratic life of the frontier town. The relative proportion of women to men increased and more attention was paid to education and the other niceties of civilization.[38]

They brought with them to Alberta not only their Liberal political persuasion but also a dedicated interest in the arts and learning. The arts and learning, however, had to be funded at public expense along with the feeder railway tracks, roads, and public amenities required to transport agricultural products out of the province and provide the economic infrastructure.

As early as 1903 the Northwest Territory assembly resolved to set up a university. A School Ordinance providing for the formation of school districts had been passed only as recently as

1884. A dominion grant for secondary education was provided in 1886. Considerable attention was given to the problems of higher education and to the training of teachers as early as 1887. By 1889 the Board of Education, which met in Regina, was pressing the dominion government to set aside university land grants in each of the provincial districts of Alberta, Assiniboia and Saskatchewan.[39] In 1891 the board invited all the graduates residing in the Northwest Territories to meet at Regina to consider the advisability of organizing a university and to draft an ordinance to give effect to it. This invitation was, however, not acted upon until 1903. In the election of November, 1905 which followed the Alberta Act of September, the main issues separating the parties were the rights of minorities to establish separate schools, and the provincial ownership of public lands.[40] The Alberta Act had provided for the rights of minorities over separate schools, but the interpretation of the Act led to political differences.[41] In 1906 a normal school for the training of teachers was opened in Calgary, and a second in 1912 in Camrose.

The decision taken in 1905 to make Edmonton the capital of Alberta virtually guaranteed the investment of public money in that city to meet the cultural interests of the population. The 1903 assembly resolution to set up a university was largely a response to persistent requests from religious denominations to set up degree-granting colleges of their own. In the first sitting of the Alberta legislature in 1906, the premier and minister of education, the Honourable A.C. Rutherford, introduced a bill providing for The University of Alberta. It was opposed by businessmen who were aware of the likely implications for them by way of taxation.[42] It was sited in the city of Strathcona in south Edmonton. Land speculation immediately followed the identification of the site.[43] Dr. Henry Marshall Tory was appointed by the provincial government as the first president in January, 1908, and the first building, Athabasca Hall, was built in 1911. Assiniboia Hall was completed in 1913, Pembina Hall in 1914, and the main Arts and Science building of that time in 1915. Since then, the university has developed within it the major professional schools in the province, as well as most of the graduate programs.

Pressure for a university in Calgary started at the same time. A petition from Calgary citizens was presented to the Legislative Assembly in 1910. But the Assembly passed an Act incorporating not a university, but the Calgary College, and withheld from the College degree-granting powers and powers to control examinations governing admission to the professions. The provincial government decided to leave these critically important elements with The University of Alberta in Edmonton. Despite gifts to the College and a grant of 575 acres of land, requests in 1911 and 1913 for university status for Calgary College were denied. The College proposal was eventually abandoned under wartime pressures. An Institute of Technology and Art, with power to grant certificates and diplomas in technical subjects, was recommended for

Calgary after the war; but though used for the training of ex-servicemen, it was given its own buildings only in 1923.[44] Only in the late 1940s were steps taken to develop the present University of Calgary.

Hospitals, public library buildings, government offices, and other amenities were built in many urban centres before the First World War. The Legislative Building in Edmonton was opened in 1913. While the province was booming after 1906 from the steady arrival of settlers, the demand for wheat and cattle, and the growing speculation over land helped the cities to become the nub of both community services and of private businesses. The construction industry in particular, for both urban buildings and railway extensions, guaranteed the continued growth of the cities. J.G. MacGregor reports that during 1907-8 Edmonton's population increased by almost 30 percent. The Board of Trade boasted about the city's growth, "But the city council and its treasurer worried about it." Some fifteen thousand people, barely established themselves, were called upon to provide streets, sewers, sidewalks, and telephones, and a host of other services for the thousands who were coming in or would be living in Edmonton three or four years hence.[45]

As early as 1898 the City of Calgary gave the CPR a bonus of $25,000 to locate its repair shops in the city. By 1912 these had become the largest in western Canada. MacGregor describes how Edmonton City Council "fell for the bait dangled before all cities and towns in Canada by all railways" when it subsidized the entry into the city of the proposed Grand Trunk Pacific Railway in 1906.[46] Edmonton put up $100,000 and benign tax exemptions for a number of concessions on the railway's part. Edmonton was busy competing with Calgary for railway advantages, and the use of taxpayers' money for the purpose was considered to be to the cities' ultimate advantage. Concurrently, the deals that major cities were able to make with large, usually eastern-based companies were, especially in the formative years, the critical issues that guaranteed their pre-eminence over their competing peers. This competition, however, inevitably played into the hands of eastern capitalists who became skilled at negotiation among the competing urban centres to their private advantage. This in turn ensured the company's success vis a vis the competitive relation it had with other companies. The symbiotic relation between organized private capital and organized public government, from the municipal to the dominion level, was ensuring the growth of Alberta's cities.

At the same time a number of genuinely economic developments were being undertaken in Alberta by privately organized capital. The CPR turned to irrigated agriculture around Calgary, based on the Bow River. This agriculture stimulated their freight traffic. Extensive stockyards were also established in Calgary along the rail.[47] In 1910, the city's first industrial sites were purchased, electrical power plants were renovated, and two additional railways negotiated to serve the city. The Hudson Bay

Company and the CPR erected large buildings in the city centre soon aftwards, and natural gas was piped to the city from Bow Island by 1912. So significant was the manufacturing growth of Calgary that a "made in Calgary" industrial show was staged in 1913 and a sum of $350,000 was authorized for the city to purchase the site and to build municipal abattoirs. Calgary's industrial base was expanding in depth and variety. Police barracks, military barracks during the war, and later the construction of an aerodrome, added to the public services.[48]

During the boom years of 1911-13 the provincial government was obliged to start regulating the growth and activities of urban centres. The urban inhabitants had shown a marked cohesiveness of sentiment for two decades. They were conscious of the competitive game with which they were involved. The coercion which the provincial government had employed to get rural local government established did not apply to the urban centres.[49] Their inhabitants had anticipated that many towns would soon grow into prosperous cities. Land developers had long discovered the rewards from laying out on paper their lots for future development and sale to non-Albertan residents. Speculation was endemic. Town boundaries were disregarded if the opportunity arose to sell laid-out lots in the rural periphery. The status of centres, as reflected in their titles — village, town, or city — became important for sales purposes, though it provided no particular administrative advantage over other designations.[50] The charter or ordinance any city could negotiate with the government came to be important, though the Municipal Ordinance of 1883 tended to set the general pattern of urban government. By the time Red Deer obtained city status in 1913 a varied pattern of city privilege and arrangement had come about.

In 1912 the government set up the Department of Municipal Affairs "to promote municipal organization and superintend municipal administration."[51] Town organization was now to be separated from rural municipal organization. The legislation of 1912 provided for a Town Act, a Rural Municipal Districts Act, a Village Act, and an Improvement Districts Act. The emphasis of the new department was, however, to regulate the keeping of municipal books and records and the auditing function of municipal government. A "systematic and uniform conduct of the affairs" of local authorities had become necessary.[52] A body of visiting inspectors was built up for this purpose. It was a function that limited the autonomy of local authorities only in so far as their bookkeeping and records were involved.

Control of the physical lay-out of cities had been implemented by council by-laws from the earliest times. Prior to granting city status to Edmonton in 1904 the grid system of street alignment had been introduced. Some public control of subdivision was introduced in 1906 to facilitate the provision of water mains and sewers, fire access, and telephone pole erection.[53] Streets and lanes had also to be included as part of the subdivision. The same by-law required that each subdivision within the city had to be approved by the city engineer. The Land Titles Act of 1906 further stipulated that the width of streets had to be 60 feet, and lanes 20 feet; access to the rear of every lot had to be given by lanes, etc.[54] City control of its physical development, in terms of privately initiated subdivisions, was a feature of early urban planning in Alberta.

In 1913, however, the Town Planning Act was passed. This was an attempt to control the speculative land boom by statute, but it also had much wider implications. The Act was based on the English model of 1909. MacGregor records that 1912 was Edmonton's all-time boom year with new subdivisions in all directions.[55] It was also the year that Edmonton amalgamated with Strathcona. What was going on in Edmonton was likely to be closest to the eye of the minister.

The Act was administered by the Minister of Municipal Affairs, but it was double-edged in being permissive in the right it afforded a local authority to prepare a Town Planning Scheme — such a scheme "*may* be prepared in accordance with the provisions of this Act."[56] However, should a local authority have failed to take the requisite steps to have a scheme prepared and approved "in a case where a town planning scheme ought to be made"; or if a local authority "failed to adopt a scheme proposed by owners of any land in a case where ... (it) ought to be adopted"; or if it unreasonably refused to consent to a modification imposed by the minister, then the minister after a public hearing could act without the local authority being involved.[57] Similarly, if a local authority did not reasonably carry out an approved scheme, the minister could act on its behalf.

The approval of the minister was required to have a proposed scheme put into effect, or have any part of that scheme put into effect. Without such approval the scheme was void. Similarly, the minister could authorize a local authority to prepare and execute a scheme "in the neighbourhood of the area over which it has municipal control." In this sense the Act had something of a regional planning character, but the measure was primarily a means of regulating extra-boundary subdivisions. The minister could also require modifications of schemes put up both by local authorities and by "all or any owners of land."[58] Thus, from the start in Alberta, the provincial government had a theoretical interest in planning both within and outside municipal boundaries despite the practical purpose of the 1913 Act to control subdivision and use. The 1909 British model proved to be far ahead of the realities of Alberta, but it is important to recognize that the minister and the provincial government were prepared in 1913 to take a pretty tough line in the control of urban growth. The fact that such a bill passed the Legislature is significant in itself. It is also significant in relation to the appeasement of rural and farm interests in the province that typified the Liberal administration from 1913 to the end of the war. This will be described below.

The Act used the expression "land likely to be used for

building purposes" and meant by that phrase land "likely to be used as or for the purpose of providing open spaces, roads, streets, parks, pleasure or recreation grounds, or for the purpose of executing any work upon or under the land incidental to a town planning scheme, whether in the nature of a building work or not."[59] The decision of the minister as to whether land was likely to be used for building purposes was final. Similarly, the minister could authorize the inclusion in a scheme of land already built upon, "if it be made to appear to him that such land is so situated that it ought to be included."[60] He could also provide for the demolition or alteration of any building as may be necessary to the implementation of the scheme. Once a municipal authority or land owner moved to have a scheme accepted, or even part of a scheme, then the minister had wide powers. He could "refuse to approve any such scheme except with such modifications and subject to such conditions as he may think fit to impose" provided that before approving any scheme a notice was published in *The Alberta Gazette* for at least a month and if within 21 days after its publication any interested person or authority filed notice of objection, such objection had to be adjudicated upon by the minister "or by such board or boards of commission as may be appointed by the minister . . ." to deal with the dispute.[61]

Local authorities could amend or redraft a scheme already approved and seek to have the new scheme approved. The local authority under whose jurisdiction the scheme fell was awarded the necessary power to execute it; where the scheme involved more than one local authority it could be executed by one or both authorities together or parts of the scheme administered by each; alternatively a body constituted specifically for the purpose could be awarded the necessary powers and duties. To facilitate the last mentioned option, the Act provided for a commission of not less than five persons approved by the minister. The commission had powers both to prepare and execute a scheme. Such commissions, however, were local rather than provincial authorities. The Act made no provision for a provincial planning authority — a step that was to come only in 1928.

The 1913 Act further envisaged provincial-wide regulations "for carrying out ... the general objects of town planning schemes" and in particular for dealing with such matters as streets and roads, buildings, open spaces, the preservation of historical sites and points of natural beauty, sewerage and drains, water supply, private and public easements, disposal of land by public authorities, powers of inspection, regulations and by-laws. For this purpose the Lieutenant-Governor in Council had prescriptive powers. The regulations could be either province-wide or separate sets of provisions provided "for areas of any special character."[62] The authority responsible for administering both the general and special area provisions was to be defined by the Lieutenant-Governor in Council, but it was inevitably local as there was no province-wide board. Similarly, special provision could be made as part of any scheme to indicate the way in which the funds required to prepare and execute it were to be raised, subject to the approval of the local authorities concerned. Expenses incurred in preparing any town planning scheme could be paid out of current revenue by the local authority or out of proceeds of a special tax up to $20,000 by a city, $10,000 by a town, and $5,000 by other municipalities.

The minister was empowered to regulate the procedures for preparing and adopting a scheme. The Act envisaged such regulations as obliging the local authority to secure co-operatively from land owners and others interested in the land to be affected by a scheme their concurrence in it. Conferences "and such other means as may be provided by the regulations" were envisaged as the means of achieving this.[63] Affected parties had to be given timely notice — "at the earliest stage possible" — as well as the opportunity to object prior to the submission of the scheme and estimates of expenditure to the minister. Compensation to owners suffering injury to property as a result of a scheme was complex. Implicit in it were the difficult questions of "individual rights" and "public interest," of "the real estate market" as an immediate allocator of sites of land and the "best land use pattern" in the overall interest of the community over the long run. As Hans Blumenfeld has emphasized,[64] land-use planning and development decisions do not occur independently of each other nor of the political necessity to balance the trade-offs and compromises necessary to protect both "individual rights" and the "public interest." Compensation to the holder of rights in land when the local authority acted in the public interest, therefore, was crucial.

The Act permitted a local authority or responsible authority to revoke or vary the town planning scheme by the preparation or adoption of a subsequent scheme which was to be approved by the minister. The Act contained provisions for compensation to any person whose property was injuriously affected by the implementation of a town planning scheme, or who had incurred expenses which were required in order to comply with the scheme but which were "rendered abortive by reason of revocation of the scheme" (Section 5 and 6). However, no compensation was to be paid if the provisions of the scheme "if or so far as the provisions are such as would have been enforced if they had been contained in by-laws made by the local authority" (Section 4). The conditions for eligibility for compensation were more clearly articulated in later Acts, but the principle that compensation could not be claimed because of the consequences of passing certain municipal by-laws was established in this original Act.

Section 6.2 of the Act stated:

> Property shall not be deemed to be injuriously affected by reason of the making of any provisions inserted in a town planning scheme, which with a view to securing the amenity of the area included in the scheme or any part thereof, prescribe the space about buildings or limit the

space about the buildings to be erected or prescribe the height or character of buildings or the amount of vacant land to be taken for parks or open spaces not to exceed five (5) percent of the total area and which the Minister having regard to the nature and situation of the land affected by the provisions considers reasonable for the purpose.

Although not so labelled, this section would appear to be the forerunner of zoning. In this original Act such public control over development was considered not confiscatory and, therefore, not eligible for compensation. All subsequent Acts were to retain this municipal protection under zoning.

The Act also contained provisions for 'betterment' by which if any property was increased in value by the making of any town planning scheme, the responsible authority was entitled to recover one-half of the amount of the increase. The Act did not set out how 'betterment' was to be made operational — e.g., could the value be recovered upon completion of the scheme or when the value was actually realized?

Similarly, in the event of the minister revoking an approved scheme a property owner had a right to compensation if he had incurred expenditure in terms of furthering the provisions of that scheme. Disputes under these provisions were to be settled through provisions of The Arbitration Act, unless some other means was agreed to by the parties.

This was comprehensive and powerful legislation. Although it gave lip service to local authority autonomy, the Act made clear in Section 8 that if a local authority was tardy about a scheme, the minister had the power to get the job done.[65] It is also important that the Act recognized three levels of planning — the urban centre itself, the region, and the province. The Minister of Municipal Affairs was clearly the instrument through which the Lieutenant-Governor in Council was to set up standards for the province as a whole, as well as for peculiar parts of regions of it. The Act might be seen as intending to centralize authority for planning in the provincial government, but leaving local authorities considerable latitude in the implementing of local policy. There being no provision for any province-wide planning authority, the onus of administration rested on the Department of Municipal Affairs — a fact which could have contributed to the apparent neglect of its provisions in the political climate of the 1913-1921 era. Though local authorities were obliged to co-operate with private land owners in the developments which the latter might sponsor, the critical point of there being no compensation available due to the consequences of passing municipal by-laws, provided the local council with some opportunity for initiative in the development process. In this respect, the Act was attempting to cope with the problems confronting many present-day authorities, and currently thought of in terms of land assembly.

The events of 1912 in Edmonton, which no doubt helped to persuade the provincial government of the merits of the 1913 legislation, have been well described by MacGregor.[66] The Act of Amalgamation which brought together Edmonton and Strathcona also provided for the annexation of land to the north. The new city's boundaries now contained 23.21 square miles. MacGregor writes:

> But even that was not enough. Annexation was in the air, and the people of North Edmonton put their heads together with those of Edmonton's city council and on July 22nd, 1912, the city absorbed the small town. Then a little later, on October 14th, the growing city annexed another 380 acres lying mainly east of what had been North Edmonton. Once these acquisitions were legalized Edmonton occupied an area of 24.80 square miles.[67]

When the villagers in North Edmonton petitioned the City of Edmonton to be annexed to the city in 1912, the city imposed a condition that "the Village should encourage and group the meat packing and allied industries, including tanneries and varnishing factories, into one locality."[68] The city's interest in its hinterland was already clear, though at this point in time its policy was to annex. The villagers acceded to the condition of the city and agreed that:

> annexation be made providing the City of Edmonton give assurance that water, electric light, sewers, police protection and other City conveniences will be given as soon as the development of this part of the city will warrant.[69]

It is clear from the conditions imposed by each party to this negotiation, that the city's concern was the planning of noxious industries on its boundary and the concern of the village's inhabitants was the city services which they wanted but could not afford. The McNally Commission in 1954-56 was to grapple with the same problem in both Calgary and Edmonton some forty years later.

The boom of 1910-13 was largely based on land speculation. Subdivisions in and around Edmonton were largely on virgin land.[70] Its consequences were to be paid for by way of some 70,000 lots reverting to the city between 1918 and 1920 in tax arrear forfeitures. Each subdivision was obliged to donate 5 percent of the land to the city for public parks — in Edmonton. This led later to difficulties with the City of Edmonton when adjacent fringe communities that had not applied the provision sought annexation with the city.

But the blow that hit Edmonton hardest, from the point of view of industrial promotion, was a 1913 amendment to the city charter. Before this time, Edmonton and Calgary had had power to provide by way of industrial incentive lump sum bonuses, periodical payments, exemption from local taxation, guarantee of debentures issued by any person, syndicate or corporation in respect of industrial, commercial or engineering undertakings, and the supply of public utilities free or at reduced rates. A negotiating company could hardly go wrong! Councillors were now threatened by a fine of up to $100 and disqualification from holding office for two years if they promoted or supported such city subsidization of private industry.[71] The city could, however, still sell its land at cost plus interest at 6 percent from date of purchase or acquisition. The establishment of the Department of Municipal Affairs in 1912 seems to have been soundly based from this perspective, for inter-city competition to attract industry under the pre-1913 terms could readily have led to municipal bankruptcy.

Though we have not examined the extent to which the Planning Act was used, or the extent to which its provisions affected growing urban centres in the province through the powers it gave the minister, the circumstances that surrounded its effective implementation were very adverse. There were signs of a slump in 1913. The 1911-13 boom immediately preceded the First World War. The war generated financial embarrassment in all the urban centres of Alberta. There was a sudden depreciation in land values in every municipality as immigration ceased and the capital that had sustained the early speculation was switched to other purposes, especially in eastern Canada. Construction activity fell off quickly, and unemployment was prevalent in the cities.[72] Unemployed persons in the surrounding areas moved to Edmonton and Calgary. The rural areas, however, benefited from the higher agricultural prices that resulted from war demand. It was the urban communities, lacking the manufacturing emphasis of those in eastern Canada, which suffered from wartime depression. The income of the province as a whole tended to rise through the war years.[73] Commerce in urban centres reaped vicarious benefits from agricultural activity and prices, but the mainstay of urban prosperity — construction — was almost halted. Though railway construction continued to grow during the early war years, it had little effect on the urban centres.

Following the end of the 1906-13 boom, Alberta's villages, towns, and cities got into increasing difficulties. Urban local government expenditure dropped by more than half in 1913-15.[74] Bond selling and deficit financing became almost impossible until after the war. Urban centreeres became dependent upon revenue, which was itself difficult to collect as tax arrears increased. The collapse of urban land valuulues particularly hit the urban centres because the provincial government had adopted a policy whereby urban centres taxed land values only, leaving buildings and improvements exempt. This may have been wise policy in times of boom when the object of city government management was to stimulate building and improvement to secure the value of further speculation and to ensure their position in the competitive race with their peers. But in the slump, urban centreeres were faced with highly valued assessments on land whether or not the land carried improvements capable of earning money sufficient to pay the tax. As arrears increased so the urban local authorities became owners of large tracts of undeveloped land from which h no revenue could be obtained.[75] They had been obliged, however, to provide services in terms of them. Concurrently, interest charges aaanpnd redemption of capital borrowed in the boom had to be paid off. The yearly budget to cover running expenses had to be cut to pay for interest and redemption on the existing capital plant. Municipaaal services were poorly maintained.

In 1916, the provincial government permitted the tax base to be broadened in the urban centres by including buildings and improvements up to 60 percent of their assessed value. Local authorities were also permitted the right to levy a business tax which was not to exceed 10 percent of the rental value of the premises. The provincial government moved increasingly between 1915 and 1920 to set up province-wide boards and commissions to cope with one or other aspect of municipal finance. In 1915 a Board of Public Utility Commissioners was established to supervise the issue and repayment of municipal debt. This board also had wide powers to regulate prices charged by public utilities from telephone charges to urban tramways when "the tolls demanded by any public utility exceed what is just and reasonable."[76] The provincial government was moving rapidly into the control of public affairs in so far as companies related to local authorities. To exploit natural resources, the major cities had been contracting with a variety of companies over the supply of electricity, the exploitation of natural gas, and the like, as amenities for themselves and to attract further potential. The commission was set up originally, and has remained to the present, an agency independent of the provincial government but within the Department of Municipal Affairs. It is among a number of agencies which stand between the government and the local authorities and whose political purpose is discussed in a later chapter.

Some smaller towns got into such financial difficulties due to excessive debt by 1920 that several special municipal finance enquiries were set up by the provincial government to examine their financial affairs and assessments in detail.[77] This could not have been done by the department's municipal inspectors because their job was to check more on the proper keeping of accounts than to question the wisdom of local decisions about finance. The most important of these enquiries were those conducted by the Municipal Finances Commission consisting of three judges of the Supreme Court of Alberta and an Edmonton citizen, and an Assessment Equilization Board consisting of two senior officials from the Department of Municipal Affairs. These special commissions were a direct intrusion into the autonomy of local decision, and it is important to note that this step was taken only after certain towns had got into a crippling financial condition. It was the beginning of the right of the Department of Municipal Affairs to step in and manage the affairs of a local authority when these got out of hand. But the step was taken in 1920 only by special, *ad hoc* authorities, not as a matter of regular, routine administration. What was in existence in terms of the rights of local authorities tended to be viewed as sacred, not to be touched. The special municipal finance commission also negotiated with bond holders to reorganize the debt, but, true to its policy on local autonomy, the provincial government did not itself make any advances to assist the stricken local authorities.[78] Only new initiatives, such as were regulated by the 1913 Town Planning Act, could become the subject of new provincial government direction. Even this approach, however, was not to last for long.

The war years imposed a personal strain on farmers who were short of labour and this hindered in developing the expansionary potential which they saw in steadily rising prices. School enrolment continued to rise, from 89,910 in 1914 to 111,109 in 1918, bringing many women teachers and others back to the classroom.[79] There was a growing shortage of medical personnel, and the rural areas felt this lack first and most sorely. The United Farmers of Alberta (UFA), a local community association formed in 1909 and which was a pressure group and not a political party during the war, increased its organizational capacity and influence. Agricultural prosperity facilitated the trend. The immediate post war years were times of great difficulty for the Liberal Party, whose term ended in 1921.

The Later Rural-Urban Conflict, 1914-1935

Though the First World War forced major changes on Alberta, a grass-roots reform movement within the province itself had emerged during the boom of 1911-13. This was eventually to take direct political form, but initially it was expressed as a morality-provoking pressure group, first in respect of women's rights and then prohibition. In its moral, agricultural nature it was not unlike similar movements elsewhere on the American continent about this time, but it had unique qualities in Alberta.

John Blue has extolled the virtues of women in their contribution to a settled agricultural life in Alberta.[80] Women had organized into several well-known associations prior to the First World War. Many national associations had locals in the main centres of Alberta and rural women were organized through the United Farm Women of Alberta. According to Blue, it was generally recognized throughout the dominion "that the position of the women in Alberta is farther advanced than in any other province."[81] Alberta's women were said to "participate in a greater degree in the economic and political life of the province than in most provinces of Canada, and are rapidly taking their places beside the men in the conduct of public affairs."[82] Though he may have come to this conclusion after the success of the UFA at the polls in 1921 — his book was published in 1924 — there is other evidence to suggest that a rurally-based popular movement to put right the evils of society in general, and particularly those of the towns and cities, was associated with the influence of women. Women were granted suffrage in 1916 without any opposition from Alberta men.

The toil of getting the frontier farm into production contrasted markedly with the speculative attributes and good luck with paper developments which typified the "fortunes" changing hands in the urban areas. The former real, in sweat and work, the latter artificial, contrived, and partly parasitic. Blue quotes Mrs. Henrietta Edwards[83] in these terms:

> To no one woman or group of women . . . is due the splendid legal position of women in Alberta. It is due to the Alberta women, who, by their courage, endurance and ability did team work with their husbands and brothers in all that has made for the development of the Province. The present legal position of Alberta women was gained not by militant methods, nor denunciation and accusations of men, but by measuring up to the requirements of new surroundings and new duties; and also to the generous appreciation of Alberta men who have placed the women on an absolute equality in all the responsibilities and duties of full citizenship.[84]

Women's rights, both those to suffrage in 1916, and those earlier recognized in the passing of the Married Women's Relief Act and the Dower Act by the provincial government, were supported by the men and the press in Alberta.[85]

The Liberal government from 1913 onwards was conscious of the political implications of this social trend. Though agriculturally based, the trend had its supporters in the urban elites in so far as it represented a steadying, consolidating influence on Alberta affairs.[86] The Liberal government had had to cede direct legislation by referendum to the voters in 1913 to assuage the grass-roots nature of this sentiment.[87] In 1914 Premier Sifton received a delegation claiming to represent 40,000 people demanding the suffrage. Women were already playing a prominent part in a movement that led to prohibition in 1916, and were demanding a vote in the referendum of July, 1915 that was to approve it. In April, 1916 the Liberals passed a bill providing women with equality with men on all matters pertaining to provincial, school and municipal elections. Thus, though women did not vote in the successful prohibition referendum, they achieved both their original demands nonetheless. Also in 1916 Edmonton was entertained by Katherine Stimson, a Texan aviatrix who engaged in stunt flying. Most Edmontonians of the time saw their first aeroplane piloted by a 20-year-old woman![88]

Professor L.G. Thomas has summed up the Liberal dilemma in these terms:

> The course of the struggle for prohibition reveals how far the Liberal government was prepared to relinquish control over legislation to a well organized pressure group . . . The

fact was that there was a substantial coincidence between those interested in moral causes such as prohibition and political innovations such as direct legislation and women suffrage and those who gave a sympathetic ear to criticisms of the traditional parties for their failure to take bold action in the cause of progress.[89]

The churches and temperance unions were behind prohibition. Organized labour generally was unenthusiastic over prohibition, but the cities tended to support it in the referendum of July, 1915. Only the coal mining centre of Lethbridge rejected it.[90] But when publicans and other vested interests in liquor were challenged on having contributed to political party funds — the government was rather non-commital over the whole question and was known to derive revenue from liquor — the grass-roots movements viewed the Liberals with suspicion. By a straight party vote Premier Sifton declined a request for a commission of enquiry.[91] Though this was not the final straw which led in 1921 to the collapse of the Liberals, it did a great deal to undermine confidence in them.

The Liberals came piece by piece to surrender the initiative in government — "The Legislature increasingly implemented policies that originated outside the party caucus and outside the cabinet."[92] The farmers in particular were setting the pace through the UFA. Farm credit legislation in 1917 was put to the annual convention of the UFA before being submitted to the Legislature. Cheaper money than could be obtained on the open market was provided to Albertan farmers with the tacit concurrence of both old-line political parties in the provincial Legislature. The Alberta Farm Loan Board was established and empowered to make loans up to $5,000 on farm lands secured by a 30 year mortgage. Co-operative credit societies were also set up. Albertan farmers and women voters had a tame and interested government throughout the years of the First World War. In general the Liberals enjoyed the support of the UFA, though both Conservatives and Liberals recognized its potential influence.[93] In the 1917 election the Conservatives tended to collect urban votes and the Liberals the rural votes. The Conservatives returned 19 members to the Liberals 34, though the latter were helped by the unequal distribution of seats which favoured rural areas and the northern portions of the province. The period 1917-20 was typified by divided allegiances over provincial and federal policies, and uncertain leadership within both the main parties.[94] Party and provincial uncertainty existed at the very time when the difficulties of post-war reconstruction faced the province.

Professor Thomas has argued that neither the Liberal nor Conservative Parties had clearly differentiated policies.[95] This may have been the case, but there is evidence to suggest that the Liberals were compromised over services to farmers and that they looked more kindly upon legislation which favoured the cities. The Public Highways Act, 1918, classified the highways of the province into

"Main Highways," "District Highways," and "Local Highways." The Lieutenant-Governor in Council had discretion as to which routes would be classified "Main Highways." The principal criterion for this discretion was the "trunk channels of communication between the more important cities and towns of the province . . ."[96] The Act also determined the extent of provincial contribution to the construction and maintenance of each type of highway. In the case of "Main Highways" the province paid 75 percent and local authorities affected by the route paid 25 percent. Maintenance costs and control of construction were 100 percent provincial responsibilities. This was a further instance of the provincial governement's influence on the essentials of urban development.

Similarly, under the Alberta Government Employment Bureau Act, 1919, a branch of the public service was set up to assist job placement, to co-operate with the dominion authorities "for the inter-provincial distribution of labour," to collect statistics, and to:

> Inquire and report as to the establishment of new industries in Alberta in any case where, by reason of the production of raw materials for such industries in the province or of the immigration of persons skilled in such industries or other circumstances, it appears that such industries can profitably be carried on.[97]

While devoted to the regulation of labour, this Act was the forerunner of incentives legislation affecting industry.

The railways of the province were in financial difficulties and lack of maintenance had made several feeder lines inoperative. Returned ex-servicemen were unemployed in the cities, and the cities were demanding assistance for relief measures. The Winnipeg general strike of 1919 and the One Big Union launched in Calgary in the same year brought fear of a Canada-wide revolution. In Edmonton the publication of the "Soviet" and a general strike were symptomatic. The motor car had made an appearance by 1919; 34,000 cars were registered in that year. Roads needed attention, and farmers were demanding action on irrigation projects, rural telephones, and more farm credit. In 1918 a Dominion-Provincial conference discussed industry and planning, and in 1919 the dominion government introduced a $25 million loan to the provinces to help municipalities cope with post-war unemployment through the construction industry. Alberta and Saskatchewan, however, either did not seek or were not granted loans, though Ontario took up $9.35 million, Quebec $7.4 million, and Manitoba almost $2 million.[98] This was the start of a series of occasions when Alberta would not benefit, for one reason or another, from federal hand-outs to the provinces.

In 1919 the farmers of the province, represented by the UFA, came to the conclusion that it was necessary to "supervise political organization in Federal and Provincial constituencies."[99] City graft, the complex relation of provincial to federal political parties, the exploitation of eastern-based companies usually associated with the railways, and the increasing rapport of urban centres with the provincial government under the Liberals, had gone too far. Membership of the UFA grew rapidly, aided by the energetic organization of the United Farmers Women's Association which provided the movement with a fundamental community spirit. The government was embarrassed by the liquor question when the Conservative opposition called attention to maladministration of the government's limited outlets in liquor stores,[100] and to the fact that the government's profit from liquor was $300,000 with sales of over $2 million in 1919.[101] The government explained that the success of the law rested on the willingness of people to uphold it. There is no doubt that illicit stills, doctors and druggists making fortunes on questionable permits, and similar happenings, helped to discredit the government. The UFA was firmly set against repeal of the legislation, however, and the Liberal Party had to take the consequences of legislation by referendum. The decision of 1919 whereby the UFA moved directly into politics set off the "movement" from the "parties." The Cochrane by-election of November 1919 was won by the UFA. The critical issue was not the support the government had given the farmers, for that had been exemplary throughout the war, but the right of recall of members of the legislature to determine the thinking and attitude of the electorate. The farmers and not the urban centres had carried the province through the war years. The UFA was a people's movement, not a party of politicians. The depression of 1920-21 had hit agriculture hard and this helped the growth of popular support.

The UFA contested every rural constituency in the 1921 election, and obtained 39 seats. Fourteen seats went to the Liberals, four to Labour, three to Independents, and one to Conservatives. Premier Greenfield formed the new government. The old-line parties and Ottawa, it seemed, had ended their influence over the province. Provincial farmers and the grass roots were thoroughly in control. The type of legislation passed in 1922 was very different in its rural and agricultural emphasis from that of the Liberals from 1916 to 1921.[102]

C.B. MacPherson, in his classic study *Democracy in Alberta,* has aptly described the UFA as "a popular movement broader than a political party" and as involving a novel theory of democratic government.[103] The farmers' complaints concerned the economic exploitation which they had experienced. This exploitation, they felt, was aided by the government through the close association of eastern capital with the national policies covering western Canadian development. To regulate this exploitation, they thought, a changed system of government was required; namely, a government which took its direction from the people less by representative membership than by regular consultation and policy formation at the membership level itself. Recall of elected members to account to their local association over their actions in the Assembly became a reality, if not common. The will of the people had to prevail, and if an Athenian type of democracy was impracticable due to distance, the next best type had to be used. They accepted the need to be governed by representatives and used instructed delegation as the means. This attitude to the governmental process was common in agrarian communities elsewhere in North America at the time, and all suffered from the inherent difficulty of preventing a formal party system and cabinet mode of decision-making from growing.

These inherent difficulties arose from the same source as those which had diminished the efforts of most radically-inclined ideological movements of history, namely, the inability to isolate themselves from the trends of world-wide cultural changes. The necessity to concentrate power in the hands of its leaders to cope with the confrontation of "reactionary" elements in its midst, such as the urban culture of Alberta and the old-line party political interests, typified the UFA administration of the 1920s as much as it did the early Social Credit League government under William Aberhart in the late 1930s. Isolation was impossible due to the position of Alberta and Saskatchewan as provinces of the Dominion of Canada.

Henry Wise Wood, who was president of the UFA from 1916 to 1931, developed a social theory based on the dialectic of competition and co-operation. As MacPherson summed it up, "competition compelled co-operation for survival, but co-operation made competition fiercer."[104] The farmers of Alberta were obliged, according to this belief, to co-operate increasingly to compete with alien interests. The philosophy was evolved to include a theory of man, nature, natural determinism and proper social conduct; and by 1918 had the essential ingredients of a popular belief and movement with political potential, despite a very varied outlook on almost every issue on the part of its membership in Alberta. Its political expression, in MacPherson's words, took the form of belief that:

> . . . in the prevailing competitive economic order there was a necessary and increasing opposition of interest between "the masses" and "the plutocratic classes," that this opposition was becoming more conscious and open as the mass of the people organized themselves in occupational groups, and that it would come to a head in a final conflict in which the defeat of the plutocratic forces would put an end to the competitive order and establish a harmonious co-operative society.[105]

Though there is a tinge of Marxist philosophy in this doctrine, its practical expression was not intra-societal class conflict, for Alberta was predominantly a land and business owning society, but rather a unified and self-conscious Alberta against its alien exploiters. It was a philosophy which resembles the opposition of neo-national colonialists to foreign imperialism, rather than the industrial class conflict of the Marxian tradition. The conflict was to be brought to a head by building up the organization of the masses, in their local occupational groups and communities, and by their involvement in local and provincial trade and production, confronting the plutocratic and autocratic forces threatening them from outside. These forces had been engendered by the abuse of trade — an abuse that led to the evolution of nations and war, as Germany was demonstrating in 1918 by her aspiration for commercial supremacy of the world — an abuse that led to the evolution of monopolies and omnipotent manufacturers' associations. Deterministically, these monopolies had turned on both the primary producer and the consumer and would "eventually reduce the great masses of the people to abject poverty, unless the people can build up a counter strength equal to or greater than that which has already been built up by the plutocratic classes . . ."[106] A producers' co-operative economy was thereby the practical answer to the Alberta farmers' problems with eastern Canadian monopolies. This idea won for the UFA its electoral victory of 1921, and sustained it as a political force in the province until 1935.

The contradictions inherent in this philosophy, such as the support of Britain in the First World War (which was itself the principal world trading nation and the fastest evolving monopolistic trading association) and the idea that trade was the basis of intercommunity strength and economic growth (but was subject to abuse rather than containing an inherent dynamic of growth in its own organizational requirements) need not concern us at this time.[107] The philosophy was sufficient to win political power in Alberta and, although modified by the Social Credit movement of the mid-1930s, has remained the basic world view of sufficient Albertan voters to retain a political expression up to 1971. This expression, in the case of both the UFA and the Social Credit movement, came as a grass-roots popular movement fructified by thoughtful speakers who articulated personal visions and identified the demons elsewhere who were thwarting the attainment of a good life. The role of political leaders was seen as being merely the running of the business side of government in such a way as to ensure fair treatment for the masses and circumstances to enable them to conduct their productions, occupations, and un-abused use of trade to maximum effectiveness and self-realization. The leadership prior to 1919 had felt that in a democracy it was possible to accomplish these things within the normal party system without actually taking over the government in the name of the new philosophy. But, in practice, in both 1919 and 1933, the groundswell of pressing public opinion obliged the leadership of both movements to stand for office. To turn dreams into the reality of organization was as much desired by men in Alberta as anywhere else, but in 1919 the UFA leadership was opting for "group government" rather than party government, saying that the latter only became an instrument of the moneyed classes to divide and rule the masses and that it was therefore inherently wrong — this had been proven by the experience of Albertan farmers with the in-line federal parties. Political organization as such, said the UFA leaders, was needed only to stamp out the influence of earlier party exploitation, and thereby radically transform the whole social and political system. In this sense, the 1921 election was the expression of a radical revolution in the political affairs of Alberta in relation to the general dominion situation.

The theory of "group government" was that occupational groups, each looking after their own interests, would nominate and elect representatives to the Legislature. These groups would be democratic within themselves and free of any party machine or disciplinary control. Within the Legislature issues would be decided on their merits as judged by the various representatives instructed from below by their various groups. The cabinet, in turn, would be composed of the representatives in proportion to their respective weight in the community at large. There would therefore be no need for the resignation of a government, as no party as such would be represented. Only unresisted power was selfish, and it was necessary to build up resistance to selfish power to achieve the true ends of democracy. Resistance was to be generated both among peers in the Legislature and between the delegated representatives and their grass-roots membership — the latter being the means by which the power-hungry drive of ambitious men would be regulated. Recall of delegates would become a reality under UFA administration. This theory imputed the role of maintaining democratic equality to competition and in this sense contrasted with the tenets of socialism which tended to assume the maintenance of democratic equality by the removal of competition. The long-extant competitive relation of local authorities, and particularly that of the cities in Alberta, would be guaranteed under this philosophy.

The theory had its merits when viewed from the perspective of farmers, whose base of operations was limited to the land they farmed, whose interests were limited to the sale of primary products, and whose human relations were confined to the limited differential implicit in family farm organization and local face-to-face relations.[108] It was quite another matter to apply it to the conditions of Alberta's towns and cities whose social system was, even by the 1920s, much more complex and differentiated than it was on the farms. Territorial representation was quite inappropriate to urban centres where the range of interest groups already included the local offices of eastern based companies, local independent business owners, civil servants, skilled artisans, and unskilled workers. The urban occupations were not represented in proportion to their respective numbers. The minutes of the 1928 UFA convention contain reference to Alberta's "urban element," in terms of "we've been pleading with them to do the same thing [elect representatives by class] and they won't do it."[109] Labour as a distinct class had apparently been able to go along with UFA representational theory, but urban business interests had not — "There is nothing to hinder them from doing it. Of course they have one representative from Edmonton. I don't see that you can facilitate voting by industrial classes much more."[110]

The issue, however, was much more complex than just voting and representation. Encapsulated as Alberta was in the Canadian economy, the modes of price-fixing and the costs of production were in fact determined by decisions beyond Alberta's control. The imposition of tariffs by the federal government, the determination of interest rates on Albertan loans, the costs of transporting Alberta's exports, and the activities of agents and middlemen lay beyond the powers of Albertan farmers and labour interests to command by their domestic provincial politics. These matters were essentially urban decisions, and as such were linked to the decisions made in other urban centres of Canada and to national policy. These centres, whether within Alberta or not, were operating, and intended to continue operating, on their own system of political interest, leaving the UFA to carry on in its domain as best it may. At the same time, the influence of these urban forces, being primarily on price, transport, and finance, eventually affected the farmer and labourer who could not get by without these urban services. As MacPherson remarks "As a provincial political organization the UFA could only seek to ameliorate, not to replace the existing economic order."[111]

Perhaps the best illustration of this ameliorating role is given by the steps taken by the UFA, after they had taken power in 1921, to deal with the poverty of farmers in southern Alberta. From 1918 to 1922 agricultural relief had been granted to the majority of municipal and improvement districts in the south. Drought had hit them hard, and between 1920 and 1924 economic depression added to their woes. Settlers had begun to move from these marginal areas and to leave the province. They had not turned to local manufacturing as this was not considered by either the provincial or dominion governments as an answer to Alberta's settler problem. The rehabilitative measure adopted by the provincial government in 1922 was The Drought Area Relief Act, which sought to give to settlers in the southern part of Alberta some measure of protection against their creditors. This initial legislation embodied many of the features to be built into western Canada-wide legislation later on. In 1923 this Act was repealed, but its principles were re-enacted in the form of the Debt Adjustment Act. These measures were intended to protect settlers from the effects of the rights of foreclosure held by Canadian finance and lending institutions, mainly in the east, but the provincial government was either unwilling or unable to set up financial machinery of its own within the province to take over the role that these lending institutions had been playing. In 1927 the government had to relieve many settlers of the heavy load of relief and arrears of taxes which had by then accumulated. A board was set up under the 1927 Tax Consolidation Act to hear applications for cancellation of arrear taxes and relief support. The dominion government became party to this facility in regard to arrears on seed grain advances. Over $20 million was written off from all sources under these measures.[112] A special Municipal Areas Board had later to be set up to deal with the finances of local authorities whose tax revenues had been virtually cut off by cancellation of tax and school arrears. In 1935 the dominion enacted the Prairie Farm Rehabilitation Act to deal more widely with the problems arising from settlement on marginal land and the depressed state of the general economy.

The Advantages of Urban Concentration

Up to the slump of 1920-24 the series of booms and depressions that swept into Alberta had had different consequences for the rural and the urban areas. From this time onward this was much less the case, though the phenomenon continued. Calgary and Edmonton had already reached the point where their extra-provincial relations coupled to their intra-provincial services ensured slow but steady growth. This was much less the case in the secondary cities and towns whose dependence on intra-provincial agricultural activity, and the economic state of the province in general, tended to determine their development or even existence.

The cities were far from booming between 1920 and 1930. Eric Hanson has shown that the expenditures of urban municipalities in Alberta increased only from $19.3 million to $24.4 million from 1920 to 1930. Their gross debenture debt rose from $67.4 million to $87.0 million.[113] But the scale of these figures compares markedly with those of rural local governments in Alberta. In that case the expenditures rose from $9.0 million to $10.7 million and gross debenture debt from $1.3 million to $4.5 million between 1920 and 1930. Urban local government was spending the money despite there being only 25 percent in 1921 and 27 percent in 1931 of Alberta's population resident in urban areas of 1,000 inhabitants or more (see Tables below). Rural local government had increased its revenue and expenditure considerably between 1913 and 1920, while urban local government expenditure dropped from $36.5 million to $19.3 million over these years. Urban revenue, however, picked up from $14.6 million to $20.3 million between 1913 and 1920.[114] The cities were consolidating their position at this time after the excesses of 1906-1913.

The First World War provided the impetus to evolve a series of technical changes which in the post-war years were to change Alberta's cities profoundly. The car and tractor had brought changes in the relation of country to city and then Edmonton opened its first radio station CJCA in 1922 and its first airport — the forerunner of the currently contentious Industrial Airport — in 1927.[115] Radio, particularly in Calgary where William Aberhart first gave his Sunday afternoon talks to Albertans in November 1925, was eventually to play a more significant role than merely entertainment. Similarly, by connecting Edmonton to the north and east, the aeroplane was to provide the cities with an additional transport link to facilitate their eventual industrial expansion. An airmail service to the east via Calgary was established in 1928. The province reversed its 1916 prohibition law in 1923 and Alberta's cities came to possess the best drinking and entertainment resorts on the prairies. The 1926 census showed Edmonton to have recouped its wartime population loss and the city was already attracting rural residents to work in its service industries — movies, radio shops, gasoline outlets, and garages.[116] The registration of vehicles in the province exceeded 65,000 in 1926. The good crop year of 1925, with wheat at $1.19 a bushel, gave Edmontonians greatly added trade. Some 11,311 tractors were already working on Alberta farms. By 1927, with a record acreage under the plow, farm incomes reached $168 million, a figure not to be exceeded for another 18 years. By 1929 building permits in Edmonton alone exceeded $5½ million. The cities benefited from every expansion in agriculture and at the same time were benefiting from the increasingly mechanical mode of production that was engaging the people in industrialized cities elsewhere on the continent.

An example of the relatively advantageous situation of the cities is what happened in Edmonton during the slump of 1920-24. J.G. MacGregor writes: "Economic conditions, however, were by no means disastrous, because even in the midst of what was after all a minor recession, everyone felt reasonably secure."[117] In spite of the recession Edmontonians saw a few minor buildings constructed, a new library provided, and the city supplied with natural gas from the Viking field. The gas line had been completed by International Utilities of New York under the name of a new subsidiary, Northwestern Utilities Ltd., set up for the purpose, and financed to the tune of $4 million. Coal mines closed down. The price of wheat dropped from $2.31 a bushel in the spring of 1920 to 65 cents in 1924. Agriculture and small towns were sorely hit, but the variety of activity already centred in the cities shored up their economies and even permitted limited growth. International corporations were able to take advantage of reduced prices for urban development. In Calgary the first substantial development of the oil industry by private enterprise occurred in 1922 when Imperial Oil's two and one-half million dollars refinery started up. Its Royalite No. 4 well was then producing 500 barrels a day. The Alberta Wheat Pool was established in Calgary in 1923. The discovery of natural gas in Medicine Hat had encouraged the settlement of industries there for a long time prior to 1914.

Following these diversifying and consolidating years for the cities, the UFA provincial government had to cope with debt adjustment legislation for the farmers in the southern part of the province. Relief and seed and feed grain advances to farmers and relief to the unemployed in the towns was a municipal responsibility. The rural municipal districts had had to meet the crisis of drought in 1918-19. They borrowed from the provincial government and banks to meet these emergencies. But, unlike the urban governments, rural local government remained limited in its tax base to assessed land value, ignoring buildings and improvements. Poor crop years in 1921 and 1922 coupled to declining produce prices made it impossible for many rural local authorities to provide relief at all. Several municipal districts had to revert to improvement district status where the influence of the provincial government could be more warmly felt. The cities of southern Alberta fared only slightly better. Lethbridge's population increased only from 11,097 to 13,489 during the ten years (1921-31); Medicine Hat had even less increase and Taber experienced a decline of population.

Paradoxically, the UFA government after obtaining office in 1921 and in the face of its avowed philosophy to support local involvement in province-wide decisions, had to become increasingly involved in handling extra-provincial pressures on Albertan affairs. Agricultural prices dropped sharply in 1922, and the province as a whole had difficulty in paying the debts incurred in previous years and in financing and reorganizing the ownership of local railways.

The UFA leadership's relations with the annual convention of the movement, held each January before the sitting of the provincial Legislature, became increasingly strained as the theory of participatory democracy turned in practice to a more regular form of party government. The technique used to hold down embarrassing convention resolutions was usually the threat of dissolution. The provincial government was dependent on the general money market to carry on provincial business. C.B. MacPherson cites the remarks of John Brownlee, who was Attorney-General in 1923, as warning that if a resolution was passed that the government should issue bonds to liquidate the debts of all the farmers in the province, it would probably prevent his obtaining a refunding loan of $13 million necessary to carry on provincial business. Mr. Brownlee is cited as saying that "owing to the close relationship between the UFA and the government, it might seriously injure the credit of the province if unsound financial resolutions were published abroad as coming from the convention."[118] A provincial bank was requested in the 1924 convention, but UFA leadership managed to quell it. At the 1932 convention a resolution for a moratorium of debts was narrowly defeated in a similar way.[119] The constituency associations which had originally been the theoretical strength of the UFA movement were made largely impotent by threats to the convention both by the Premier and the party leadership. Members of the Legislature were similarly placed relative to the cabinet. The demands derived from governing the province — in its financial complexity,[120] in the overwhelming problems involved in urban affairs, and in inter-provincial and provincial-federal relations — had brought to little the ideas, originally contained in UFA policy, of constitutency autonomy and participatory democracy. The UFA did not, however, put itself at the disposal of outside interests; it retained a fundamental honesty in the handling of its affairs and in its accountability to the farmers of Alberta.

In 1925 the Alberta provincial government took the initial step towards giving industry certainty over its local taxation obligations. It will be recalled that prior to 1913 cities had had considerable freedom to contract terms with private industrialists. The restraining of this freedom had been done in the interests of municipal viability and checking the competitive attractiveness of the cities in the province. By 1929 some incentives to encourage industry to the province were deemed necessary. The Industries Assessment Act provided for a city, town, or village to fix "the assessment of the property of any person carrying on or proposing to carry on, within the area of the municipality, any industrial establishment or manufacturing, on such terms and conditions as the council may deem proper."[120] The fixed assessment was to apply for no longer than 20 years and was not renewable. It was not to apply to any tax on land apart from the value of the improvements. The fixed assessment could not be less than 10 percent of the actual value of improvements or their actual cost as worked out between the company and the council. The agreement between the company and the council had to be approved by three-quarters of the councillors and two-thirds of the voting electors.

This was a direct incentive to industry, and provided for some limited negotiation between industrial companies and the council. However, it was expressly forbidden to contract with a company whose business was established elsewhere in Alberta, or which had moved from one municipality to another in Alberta. The competitive attractiveness of councils was not to be started all over again! The Act also provided for municipally-owned land to be transferred or leased to an industrial establishment. Similarly, water, light, power, and other services could be supplied "at a price, rental or rate determined by the Board of Public Utility Commissioners as being the fair market value or fair rental value of the land, or a fair wholesale rate for the said supply ..." (Section 6). It had particular advantage for a company considering the move to Alberta, or for one already established. The legislaton was amended frequently, in 1927, 1928, and 1929, and a new draft was prepared in 1937 under Social Credit administration.[121] Edmonton in 1925 also moved to establish clearly defined industrial areas by means of by-laws. Railway locations and stimulus from railway companies were involved.[122]

Wall Street collapsed on October 29, 1929, and farm prices in Alberta started to tumble by Christmas. The growing "scarcity of money" threatened everyone, and those in debt became held more closely to their repayments.

The ambivalent position of the UFA as broker between the demands and expectations of farmers and the stranglehold of urban interests through control of credit, transport and essential services, lost for the UFA leadership the interest of its membership. In the election of August, 1935 the UFA lost every seat. The failure of the UFA was a dramatic example of how inconsequential provincial decisions were in relation to outside forces, and in so far as the UFA reflected the will of the voting majority. The people of Alberta, however, were not about to give up faint-heartedly.

A brief analysis of population distribution between the

cities of the province and the rural areas illustrates clearly the advantageous position of the urban areas. While it was true in an absolute sense that the economy of Alberta depended on its agricultural exports, the urban centres came increasingly to benefit from them, in so far as population distribution reflects this fact.

The major urban centres of Alberta, whether Calgary and Edmonton or elsewhere, have shown an erratic but consistently expanding population since their founding. The recorded metropolitan population of Calgary and Edmonton increased as shown in Table 1.

Table 1. Metropolitan populations of Calgary and Edmonton, 1883-1966, and percentage increases over the previous Census

Year	*Calgary*	*Percent increase*	*Edmonton*	*Percent increase*
1883	300			
1901	4,400		2,600	
1906	13,600	209	14,000	438
1911	43,700	221	24,900	78
1921	63,300	45	58,800*	136
1931	83,900	33	79,200	35
1941	88,900	6	93,809	18
1951	142,300	60	176,800	88
1961	279,100	96	337,600	91
1966	330,600	18	401,300	19

*With Strathcona.

Figures derived from the Census of Canada, *Canada Year Book,* and John Blue's *Alberta: Past and Present,* Chicago, 1924, Pioneer Historical Publishing House. The city and metropolitan areas of Calgary became coincident in 1961 with the annexation by the city of Bowness, Forest Lawn, Montgomery, and parts of the municipal districts of Foothills and Rocky View. The metropolitan area of Edmonton includes the city (whose 1966 population was 376,925), St. Albert (9,736), parts of the municipal districts of Strathcona and Stony Plain, and the county of Sturgeon.

The city and metropolitan areas of Calgary became coincident in 1961 with the annexation by the city of Bowness, Forest Lawn, Montgomery, and parts of the municipal districts of Foothills and Rocky View. The metropolitan area of Edmonton includes the city (whose 1966 population was 376,925), St. Albert (9,736), parts of the municipal districts of Strathcona, and Stony Plain, and the county of Sturgeon. Over the 55 year period 1911-1966, the average annual rate of growth has been 4.25 percent in Calgary and 4.6 percent in Edmonton. Though Edmonton's increase is somewhat larger in percentage and absolute terms, this increase is, in relative significance to the two areas taken as a whole, much greater. Whereas Calgary has deliberately maintained a policy of incorporating small settlements beyond its boundaries into the city, and of concentrating new growth within its boundaries,

Table 2. Population and percentage increases of ten subsidiary centres, 1911-1966 (arranged in descending order of 1966 population)

	1911	*1921*	%	*1931*	%	*1941*	%	*1951*	%	*1961*	%	*1966*	%	*Annual percentage increase*
Lethbridge	9,035	11,097	23	13,489	22	14,612	8	22,947	57	35,454	55	37,186	5	3.6
Red Deer	2,118	2,328	10	2,344	1	2,924	25	7,575	159	19,612	159	26,171	33	4.8
Medicine Hat	5,608	9,634	72	10,300	7	10,571	3	16,364	55	24,484	50	25,574	4	3.5
Grande Prairie		1,061		1,464	38	1,724	18	2,664	55	8,352	214	11,417	37	4.9*
Camrose	1,586	1,892	19	2,258	19	2,598	15	4,131	59	6,939	70	8,362	21	3.1
Wetaskwin	2,411	2,061	-15	2,125	3	2,318	9	3,824	65	5,300	39	6,008	13	2.8
Taber	1,400	1,705	22	1,279	-25	1,331	4	3,042	129	3,951	30	4,584	16	1.8
Ponoka	642	1,594	148	836	-48	1,306	56	2,574	97	3,938	53	4,421	12	4.0
Vegreville	1,029	1,479	44	1,659	12	1,696	2	2,223	31	2,908	31	3,598	24	2.4
Stettler	1,444	1,416	-2	1,219	-14	1,295	6	2,442	89	3,638	49	3,088	-15	1.1

From *Canada Year Book*
*Calculated for the years 1921-1966.

greater Edmonton has had the characteristic of a dispersed centre with identifiable satellite communities whose population is not always recorded as part of metropolitan Edmonton itself. Such communities as Spruce Grove, Leduc, and Fort Saskatchewan, might, for relative purposes, be identified with greater Edmonton. Calgary does not have this concentration in its hinterland, and only High River and Okotoks could readily be considered as urban concentrations in the Calgary area.[123]

The population and its percentage increases for ten major subsidiary towns and cities are recorded in Table 2. These centres have been chosen by no strict criteria, but represent a scattered distribution over the province.

The average annual percentage increase for these 10 towns as a whole is 3.2 percent. The range is wide, from 1.1 percent to 4.9 percent, as the last column of the table shows. None of these centres, however, have recorded a decline in population since 1941, and the growth rate of some has been considerable, particularly over the period 1941-1961.

The population of Calgary and Edmonton combined, the population of the 10 major subsidiary centres combined, and the population of all 12 of these centres combined is given in Table 3 to the total population of Alberta over the period 1911-1966.

These three tables show the pre-eminence of Calgary and Edmonton over all other towns in Alberta from the turn of the century. Their rate of growth, though erratic, has been larger than major subordinate centres and the proportion of the total Alberta population they represent has increased steadily from 15 percent in 1906 to 50 percent in 1966. These twelve urban areas combined represented 59 percent of the Alberta population in 1966 as against only 25 percent as recently as 1921.

The tables also show that the twelve centres mentioned contained 25 percent of the province's population as early as 1911. If the standard definition of an "urban community" is accepted as one having 1,000 population or more, then the percentage of the province's total population considered "urban" is as shown in Table 4.

In 1911 over the whole province, only 29.4 percent of persons resided in urban areas, as against the 25 percent contained in the 12 centres of Table 3. There has been, therefore, a fairly clear hierarchy of cities and towns in Alberta, at least since 1911 and probably since 1883. Their importance as centres of population has grown steadily since the turn of the century, though from 1911 to 1941 the percentage of population resident in urban areas increased only from 29.4 percent to 31.5 percent. Agricultural settlement in the province was pronounced during this time.

However, in absolute numbers of persons resident in urban areas over this thirty years, the figures increased from 109,936 to 250,605. The difference between these two sets of numbers is 140,669. Table 3 shows that the combined population of Calgary and Edmonton increased during 1911-41 from 68,600 to 182,700, an

Table 3. Percentage of various urban populations as an expression of the population of Alberta, 1911-1966.

Years	*Calgary and Edmonton combined*	*Percentage of Alberta population*	*10 major centres combined*	*Percentage of Alberta population*	*12 centres combined*	*Percentage of Alberta population*	*Total Alberta population*
1881							18,100*
1891							25,300*
1901							73,000*
1906	27,600	15					185,400*
1911	68,600	18	25,300	7	93,900	25	374,700*
1921	112,105	19	34,300	6	146,400	25	588,500*
1931	163,100	22	37,000	5	200,000	27	731,600
1941	182,700	23	40,400	5	223,100	28	796,200
1951	319,100	34	67,800	7	386,900	41	939,500
1961	616,700	46	114,600	9	731,200	55	1,332,000
1966	731,900	50	130,400	9	862,300	59	1,463,200

*Figures for Alberta as a whole are derived from John Blue's *Alberta: Past and Present,* p. 217. The remainder are from the *Canada Year Book.*

Table 4. Number and percentage of Alberta population described as "urban," 1901-1966

	Number urban	*Number rural*	*Percentage of total population urban*
1901	11,851	61,171	16.2
1911	109,936	264,359	29.4
1921	177,170	411,284	30.1
1931	227,882	503,723	31.1
1941	250,605	545,564	31.5
1951	430,088	509,413	45.8
1961	851,576	480,368	63.9
1966	1,007,407	455,796	68.8

Source: *Alberta Industry and Resources,* Alberta Bureau of Statistics, Edmonton, 1970, p. 133.

increase of 114,100. This increase represents 81 percent of the 140,669 increase in the same period for the urban population of the province as a whole. Calgary and Edmonton were building up their populations during the period 1911-1941 at a much faster rate than the other urban areas of the province.[124] Thus while the economy of Alberta was predominantly rural in character, Calgary and Edmonton were expanding much faster than the middle-range towns which were in closer and more intimate contact with the farms. Edmund Dale has documented the enormous incidence of land transfers that occurred in Edmonton between 1920 and 1945. Over half the land in the city was claimed under tax arrears. Donations of land to the city to relieve tax obligations by individuals and large corporations, such as Hudson's Bay Company, and land transfers that re-arranged individual, company and city holdings, etc., were common in the 1930s.[125] The city was engaging in a massive reorganization of space-use and revenue resource during the depression. The Fortin Refunding Plan was introduced in 1937 which lightened the annual load on the city of its $37.8 million gross debt and interest rate of over 5 percent, by extending the term of debt to 30 years, reducing the interest rate, and providing for a call feature. Interest charges were reduced by this measure from $1.9 million to $559,000 a year, and the city was freed to start its expansion with the onset of the Second World War.

L.O. Stone found that by 1931 the percentage of Canadian population considered urban had passed 50 percent.[126] At the same time, in Alberta, as Table 4 shows, the percentage was only slightly above 31 percent, and it remained at about this level until sometime between 1941 and 1951. The prairies, and particularly Alberta, became increasingly urban after 1951 and had approached the Canadian average by 1966. In the meantime, however, Alberta was to remain relatively insecure due to the primary product nature and specialization of its economic base.

Thus, although farming was the characteristic economy of

Alberta up to about 1951, the significance of its urban areas, both as a place of residence for the population and as a contributor to its economy, was erratically but persistently increasing from the earliest years. The UFA was in consequence faced with an increasingly difficult long-term problem with the urban areas unless it could arrange its affairs to meet their needs in addition to those of farmers and labour.[127]

As farming became increasingly mechanized, furthermore,[128] and the horse plow gave way to the tractor and the size of the economic farming unit increased, the dependence of farmers on urban skills and services increased also.[129] The competitive relations in which the farmers were enmeshed were world-wide. So long as Albertan agriculture was dependent upon exporting to meet the demand for food in industrialized nations such as Britain, this competitive relation obliged the farmers to increasingly mechanize or lose the market. However well the UFA organized local, rural political co-operation, the forces it confronted in the form of world urbanization and industrialization and world competitive prices for primary products, far exceeded its local capacities.

The net income of the Alberta population was subject to large fluctuations. The international market for agricultural products was highly sensitive to booms and depressions, and price fluctuations occurred in sympathy. In Alberta these factors were exaggerated by extreme and unreliable weather. In 1938 the Alberta government saw the solution to this problem in these terms:

> The only lasting solution would be to develop a more balanced economy in Western Canada under a reformed financial system, which will protect both consumers and producers in the dominion until similar steps are taken by other countries to remove the vagaries of world markets.[130]

This was, in essence, the hope of the Social Credit Movement which took power in 1935.

Town-Planning and the Basic Issues to 1935

The decisions of the CPR and other railway companies in relation to stopover and collection points, and the distribution of land settlement, determined the sites of urban centres in the early years. The delineation of lot size by surveyors in order to register land with what was called the Land Titles Office — thereby making land a legally saleable commodity, and the subject of intense speculation — was the sum total of early planning efforts in Alberta. The rectangular grid is part of the early surveyors' legacy to the prairies.

The 1913 Town Planning Act, already described in a previous section of this Chapter, proved to be more idealistic than practical in all it set out to do; but it did contain many proposals and opportunities to get planning on a provincial and local scale underway in Alberta. Its introduction coincided, however, with the onset of serious slump conditions in urban areas, with the start of the Liberal Party's "back to the people by referendum" policy, and with the general moral reform movement which continued through the war years. Paradoxically, the 1913 Act was introduced at the very time when its authority was hardly needed. Rapid expansion of towns and cities had ceased and the next twenty years were to be largely consolidatory, with slow but steady development in selected urban areas. The 1913 Act, significantly, remained unamended until 1929, though the revision of 1922 gave a clearer statement of it.

In 1918 the Liberals moved towards controlling and stimulating the highways and roads of the province through the Public Highways Act. Similarly, the Employment Bureau Act of 1919 placed in provincial government hands some control over manpower. The Public Highways Act also introduced the concept of a provincial board (the Good Roads Board) and a Highway Commissioner. It was administered by the Minister of Public Works. The board, significantly, consisted of five members with the Highway Commissioner as chairman, the Deputy Minister of Public Works as a statutory member, and three other persons nominated by the Lieutenant-Governor in Council.[131] The Highway Commissioner was under "the general direction" of the minister, but it was the commissioner's reports which the board had to deliberate over and agree to in respect of: (a) which roads would be classified in terms of the classes enunciated in the Act; (b) the suitable methods of road construction and maintenance; (c) the allocation of public monies voted by the Legislative Assembly over the roads of the province, after the approval of the allocation had been given by the minister; and (d) the use of highways and roads by type of vehicle, speeds, safety, and other criteria. The board was obliged to take into consideration "the financial conditions of the local authorities" affected by the roads and who, except for main highways, had to contribute a fixed proportion to construction and maintenance costs.

This legislation, as was typical of much other legislation after it, placed the onus of decision over some very difficult political matters not directly on the government department, and therefore with the minister responsible and with the party in power by way of the cabinet, but on an *ad hoc* committee set up to deal with it. It was a useful political technique to avoid the public identifying the party in power as being responsible for decision, and at the same time to give practical demonstration to the voters of the "decentralized" nature of public decision, of the non-involvement of politics in public decision, and of the rectitude, the "objectivity", of decisions taken in the public interest. The technique gave the appearance of removing from party influence the decisions handed to *ad hoc* specialist boards. At the same time it permitted the government to exercise a co-ordinatory function, not a control function in terms of its public image (although the practical possibility of control, as against mere co-ordination, was never far from being a possibility), and the government could be seen to be the guardian of the public interest, but not its determiner. It was an illusion in a practical sense, a useful public relations technique, and also the philosophy through which powerful private investment was later to handle the problem of its advantageous settlement and location in the province.

The administrative means of provincial control of roads and highways was by way of subsidy for their construction and maintenance. The 1918 Act defined the classes of road as follows:

(a) *Main Highways,* recognizable as such by their interconnection of cities and towns. It was their "prime importance" in this that set them off from other classes (Section 7). The provincial government covered the full cost of construction and maintenance on them and could, therefore, relatively speaking, ignore the local authorities through which they passed. This was one of the first clear examples of urban provincial interests being paramount over local government interests. As the Act did not apply to the cities, which had their own charters, the province was free to act in their, or any other interest, by way of transport facilities between them, if it wished.

(b) *Market Roads,* which were defined as "of less general importance" than Main Highways, but "of outstanding local importance in the marketing of the produce of the area ..." (Section 12). The classification of general and local importance implicit in this legislation symbolizes the growing identification of Alberta as a collective in relation to other provinces and to the dominion government. It also symbolizes the impact of public expenditure involved in matters of local advantage. That this occurred in wartime, when Alberta sent its own military units to the front and was short of money for local needs, may be significant. Market roads were supported by the provincial government in both construction and maintenance in a complex way laid down in a Schedule to the Act.[132]

(c) *Local Roads,* which were defined as a class not included in the other types — a catch-all category — were to be funded by local authorities, but the board retained the right to approve them.

(d) *Colonization Roads,* which were "temporarily established as such for the development of newly settled districts or for other good reasons" (Section 21). They were funded entirely by the provincial government, which thereby held control over the success or failure of new settlement schemes. The Lieutenant-Governor in Council was assigned the final right of decision over this matter as he had to approve work to be done under this class of road (Section 23). The province was not, therefore, to be left with further public expenditure for servicing settlers on land sold to the profit of private companies who could conveniently ignore the costs of public facilities.

The importance of this legislation is in its marking of the turning point at which provincial, collective expenditure carried with it the right of provincial decision and authority over the province as a whole. Local advantage, whether public or private, had to be tempered to the considerations implicit in the province as a whole.

Though railway financing, and the taking over of privately financed railways by the provincial government, involved the same principle of collective necessity or collective advantage, public works expenditure on a planned, provincially designed basis for highways symbolized the change in the provincial scale of organization and therefore of responsibility. In this sense Alberta was becoming a "province," rather than a geographic boundary containing within it a host of interacting local authorities and private companies each seeking to use the provincial government for local advantage. This principle was less apparent in the 1913 Planning Act, which tended to provide for local commissions with the approval of schemes and the initiative for action (if local authorities failed to act) resting with the minister. Provincial and regional standards for planning purposes could be set, but this differed from the funding of a planned scheme of highways and roads directly from provincial government initiative.

When the UFA government took office in 1921 it was inevitably involved in the scale of organization and consequent authority that had already emerged, despite the UFA's principle of grass-roots decision-making. It was caught in a situation which it could not go back on. It tended to work increasingly through the Department of Public Works. In 1924 The Main Highways Loan Act authorized the Lieutenant-Governor in Council to raise, by way of loan, up to $3.5 million for highway construction.[133] A sinking fund was set up to redeem the loan. Main highways had clear advantages for the urban centres, with their increasing interdependence with the other urban centres of Canada, as well as for local farmers using vehicles to get to the cities. Highway construction was also a useful unemployment relief measure for farmers in times of drought. Surplus labour in agriculture could be used to build a provincial amenity, which happened, in fact, to promote metropolitan concentration and relative rural depopulation. About this time also Edmonton was increasing its links with the North.[134]

The province was becoming increasingly conscious of itself as a province. Public interest in planning and beautification, no less than in industrialization, was running high. In 1927 the Edmonton Local Council of Women petitioned the City Council to appoint a Civic Plan Committee with membership from various local organizations and with the duty of advising the council. The petition also called for "a dignified and attractive approach from the proposed Canadian National Railway Station to Jasper Avenue and the Macdonald Hotel."[135] A scheme of development was called for, backed by a publicity campaign, and the renovation of unsightly structures in the city centre was also recommended. The City Council, financially unable to meet all the requests, moved, however, to establish a Civic Plan Committee with membership for no less than 35 organizations.[136] In the following year, 1928, the council itself moved to request a revision of the Town Planning Act. The British Columbia model was thought to be more appropriate to the times. Something to preserve the beauty of the province was needed. The women of Alberta through their UFA women's organization were concerned with "the vulgar onslaught of the symbols of commercialism — billboards and boardings."[137] The 1928 and 1929 Planning Acts followed in quick succession.

From 1927 to 1929 the UFA administration undertook a thorough revision of local government administration, with the exception of the cities which continued their long-established series of almost annual provincial approval of amendments to their particular charters until 1951.[138] The cities were left alone in the 1927 Village Act and in the Town Act of the same year. The Village Act had some 381 sections to it, and the Town Act some 491 sections.[139] These were consolidating Acts covering about every aspect of local government with the exception of town planning. The Town Act did refer to annexation procedures, compensation, etc., but the concept of planning, whether as an organic process or as a right to control and regulate, appears to have been kept scrupulously distinct from the consolidated legislation. The 1913 Town Planning Act was still in force, but apparently it was not considered an aspect of practical administration. It would seem that planning was thought of as a local matter — a scheme put up by local authorities for provincial approval — rather than a matter in which the province as a collective, and as the responsible administrative authority, had an important say. Such decentralization would have been congruent with UFA political philosophy, and intra-provincial planning was not a topic that forced itself upon the government as did highways or lent itself to the support of farmers by way of public works.

During the sessions of 1928 and 1929, two pieces of legislation directly concerned with planning were introduced. The 1928 Town Planning and Preservation of Natural Beauty Act came under the administration of the Department of Public Works, except in Improvement Districts where the Minister of Municipal Affairs was inevitably involved.[140] This Act was repealed, and reintroduced in an amended form, in the 1929 Town Planning Act.[141] The 1929 Act was administered by the Minister of Municipal Affairs and repealed the 1913 Act. The circumstances surrounding this sequence of legislation and the transfer of administrative responsibility have not been ascertained. The 1928 Act gives the appearance of being hasty legislation. Its major contribution was to provide the administrative instrument the 1913 Act had omitted, a province-wide planning authority. But this authority was carefully removed from urban planning in the consolidating Act of 1929.

It may also be significant that, just as had been the case in 1913, the provincial government moved to amend town planning legislation in 1929 at precisely the time when the urban economic expansion of 1928-29 was coming to a sudden halt. The 1929 legislation was assented to on March 20, 1929, and the New York stock exchange slumped in October, 1929, to start the great depression of the 1930s. In both 1913 and 1929, the provincial government acted to improve its legislation at the peak of a splurge of urban activity. The 1929 Act was used by the cities in the depression, however.

The 1928 Act, under Public Works, provided for a Town and Rural Planning Advisory Board consisting of three or more members appointed by the Lieutenant-Governor in Council; only one member was to be paid. There was no statutory provision for a chairman, and the board conferred with and advised the minister, at his request, over any regulations covering subdivision under the Public Works Act.[142] The term "local authority" was defined to mean the council of any city or town, and one of the board's duties was "to co-operate with any local authority in formulating and carrying into effect any town planning scheme" (Section 4(a)). This measure would have involved local planning commissions under the Minister of Municipal Affairs dealing with a province-wide board reporting to the Minister of Public Works. The question of co-operation and consultation with affected local authorities was part of the 1913 Act and has reappeared in all Albertan planning legislation. If anything can be described as contrary to sound planning practice, it is this attribute of the legislation. It is also, however, the very essence of government by consultation, of respect for the autonomy of local government, and of respect for the interests of individuals which has been characteristic of Albertan urban affairs from the beginning.

The 1928 Act seems to have been an over-hasty provision to regulate provincially what had come to the notice of public works personnel and the United Farmers' Women's Association. The board's duties included assisting local authorities in preserving beauty spots and regulating buildings in their vicinity, and promoting community pride in the amenities of the neighbourhood. The board was also "to collect and collate information as to town planning schemes" (Section 4(e)).

The board was also to make regulations governing building lines on each side of highways, the design, location, and construction of buildings adjacent to highways — such as filling stations and cafeterias — the regulation of advertising boards, the acquisition of land for and the control of parks, and the licensing of gasoline stations on highways.

The 1928 legislation was a measure designed to regulate an activity outside the jurisdiction of towns and cities, namely, the ribbon development characteristic of the time. It was concerned also with trade and commerce along the highways and with recreational facilities to be provided in rural areas by means of provincial parks. In this sense, provision for a province-wide administrative facility was wise if only because the provincial government had virtually assumed responsibility for main highways. Local authorities were only consultatively involved. However, the board did not have quite the independence of action that had been awarded to the Good Roads Board in 1918. The 1928 Planning Advisory Board was essentially advisory to the minister, and in respect of regulations it advised and conferred with him only at his request (Section 4(b)). In 1928 the Planning Advisory Board was not envisaged as an executive instrument, but rather as a technical service to the administration though its membership had no statutory guarantee of technical competence.

"The Town Planning Act, 1929" kept in its long title reference to the "preservation of Natural Beauty," and incorporated into Part I much of the 1928 provisions. It also kept the title of the board (Town and Rural Planning Advisory Board) but added a Director of Town Planning as a statutory position if set up by the Lieutenant-Governor in Council. The board itself was subject to the will of this authority.[143] The director was to serve as "the executive member of the Board" (Section 65(2)). In this capacity the director made an annual report to the minister on the transactions of the board.

The 1929 Act is a peculiar document in many respects. Though making provision for a province-wide board and a Director of Town Planning (who could more easily be seen as a secretary to the board than as an expert planner with professional executive capacities), the Act clearly separated the board and the director's terms of reference from the planning instruments designed to apply to the urban centres. Urban planning instruments — which included local authorities, town planning commissions, regional planning commissions, an official town plan, official schemes, zoning by-laws and zoning districts, appeals, and compensation procedures — were scrupulously arranged to refer not to the board, but to the minister direct. The board's powers were limited to the adjudication of appeals which had first gone to local town or rural planning commissions; but in the general run of by-law regulation and control of planning the board was kept out of local matters. The director does not enter the urban instruments in any way except, possibly, in his annual report to the minister over the board's duty "to collect and collate information as to town planning schemes."[144]

The above separation of planning instruments and planning functions, with the Director of Town Planning having virtually no formal, statutory duties, and divorced from the mechanisms of urban planning, is of critical significance. Apparently Public Works in 1928 had seen the need for some province-wide articulatory advisory board, as well as for the need to control ribbon development along highways (service stations, etc.). When in 1929 Municipal Affairs took over this 1928 provision, it very carefully set off the board and the director as instruments coping with rural Alberta and its highways, from the planning machinery of urban centres which were granted autonomy subject only to approval direct from the minister, and the right of an aggrieved party to appeal to the board. The UFA government was, in effect, giving tacit recognition to the independence and autonomy of urban centres in comparison with the possibility of generating a province-wide planning instrument effective in the planning of both urban and rural areas as an integral whole. Although seeming to regulate and control the details of city growth and development, in its wider significance the 1929 Act very largely freed the cities from control by the provincial government and freed them almost entirely from control by the Town and Rural Planning Advisory Board and the Director of Town Planning. There could be scarcely a better case of names and titles conveying false impressions! The 1929 Act set the administrative seal on the independent growth of urban areas relative to the province as a whole. In this sense it reversed — unbeknownst no doubt to the provincial leaders of the time who were not anticipating the increased urban concentration of population or the industrialization of the province in future years — the trend towards provincial responsibility for publicly important decisions that had appeared in the 1918 Public Highways Act, the Employment Bureau Act 1919, and the 1928 Town Planning and Preservation of Natural Beauty Act.

One of the amendments to the 1928 Act, on its inclusion in the consolidated 1929 Act, was the removal of the restriction of the 1928 board to concern itself with regulations affecting only land "contiguous with any main highway." The removal of this restriction expanded the board's powers to all areas of the province not already covered by city, town, or village administrations, with which it still had to co-operate. The board in this sense became truly province-wide, but its powers in such areas were still limited to filling stations, cafeterias, billboards, licencing, tourist camps, and parks. It was therefore not given unrestricted power under Part I of the Act to plan the rural areas of the province.

In its control of parks, both existing and in the purchase of land for new parks, however, the board was empowered to serve an increasingly useful purpose as the concentration of people in urban centres increased and the motor car became more widely used. At the time this phenomenon was not as significant as it is today, but the legislation did recognize the inability of urban authorities to plan for rural recreational facilities for their populations in areas beyond their jurisdiction.

The machinery of urban planning set up under the 1929 Town Planning Act followed in outline that of 1913, but added a number of new controls and opportunities for effective planning. A local authority, which meant the council of any city or town could, by a by-law approved by the Minister of Urban Affairs, appoint a Town Planning Commission consisting of either three, six, or nine members. The council could delegate to the commission such powers as it chose with the exception of power to raise money or to expropriate land (Section 17). The exceptions remained with the council was in a position to control much of the expenxe that the duties could include advice on town planning matters, preparing and carrying into effect "an official town plan or scheme," and preparing and administering a zoning by-law. Membership of the commission was to be staggered so that one-third of the membership resigned each year. It had powers to "appoint such town planning engineers, consultants or other officers as may be necessary ... and may expend such funds as may be furnished by the Council" (Section 17(5)).

With the minister's approval, the councils of two or more adjoining municipalities, which meant cities, towns, villages, municipal districts, or improvement districts, could together establish a regional planning commission. Membership was to be arranged so that not more than three members were appointed from each jurisdiction. Its powers were delegated to it by the councils concerned with the same exceptions as for town planning commissions. It also had power to appoint a professional staff. The expenses of rural commissions, however, were to be borne "by the councils in the proportions which the total values of the assessable property in their respective municipalities as shown on the assessment rolls bear to one another, but shall not exceed the appropriation made by the councils" (Section 18(4)). No financial assistance was given by the province. There is little doubt that the greater contribution of wealthy centres to expenses could have influenced the decisions of the Rural Commission even if the majority of voting strength was even, or favoured the outlying, non-urban municipalities. The independence of local councils was respected in their right to determine the size of their appropriation, but again this principle favoured the higher assessed centre whose council was in a position to control much of the expenses that the rural commission might incur. This method of administration enhanced the cardinal principle of co-operation in getting planning undertaken; but it tended to load the basis on which co-operation would be achieved in favour of urban centres.

"The Official Town Plan" was a document any unit of local government, urban or rural, could prepare or have prepared "for the purpose of providing for the development of its municipal territory or any part thereof, in an orderly and convenient manner . . ." (Section 19(a)). Details of the plan for development, or any part of it, could be endorsed on the document or added by way of a Schedule. The plan or the details could be altered or extended. In distinction to The Official Town Plan, the Act provided for "Official Schemes" which referred to the plans and schemes of any unit of local government prepared "for specific public improvements not inconsistent with the official town plan (if any)" (Section 19(c)). Official schemes therefore refer to those which local governments were themselves undertaking, as distinct from Official Town Plans that provided for all types of investment within the general, planned context of local administration.

The Act, in the following sub-section, then proceeded to make perfectly explicit the powers of any local or rural authority to cope with public utilities, whether privately or publicly controlled. The subsection refers to plans covering the development "of railway and rapid transit and street railway and airport facilities." The local or rural authorities had power:

> to recommend plans so prepared to any Railway Board or public authority having jurisdiction in the matter, and to any railway or other company concerned therewith, and to

use all lawful measures to secure the adoption of such plans and the due co-ordination of terminal, transportation, and other facilities of commerce and traffic within and about the municipality (Section 19(d)).

The means of coping provided to a local or rural authority were limited to recommendation and the "use of all lawful measures" to secure the adoption of the plan. Local governments were not given power to enforce the requirements of their plan over public utilities wishing to utilize local amenities; but the provision throws into relief the changed status of local government relative to companies like the CPR and electricity concerns that had hitherto been subject to much less local influence. Co-operation in this case took the form of persuasion and legal rights, but it tended to load the basis on which co-operation would be achieved in favour of the utilities. It is perhaps important that the Act did not oblige a local government to "co-operate" with public utilities as it did with other local governments. Co-operation with public utilities was clearly far more legalistic and formal. In this sense the Act tacitly recognized the potential for domination, the aggressive thrust, of large private companies.

The Act further enhanced local governments' powers by affording them rights to enforce street widening programs, the reservation of land for public roads and parks, and the supply of light, water, sewerage, and street transit, to areas covered in the plan, to prescribe the order in which any part of the plan should be carried out, and to provide for a method of financing any works and expenses associated with the development provided for in the plan.

To safeguard local councils themselves with respect to developmental activities proposed in their own official plan or official schemes, they were not committed "to undertake any of the projects therein suggested or outlined" (Section 20). But any developmental activities they did undertake within the scope of the plan, or any scheme, had to conform to it. A plan or scheme once adopted by a local council came into effect only when approved by the minister who had the right to refuse approval until any modifications he required were made. Thus local governments were given an inalienable right to generate plans, but only on terms to which the minister would agree. Similarly, a plan or scheme could be amended or revoked by a local government only if the minister agreed (Section 21). Under Section 37, the minister could after proper enquiry oblige a council in the public interest to adopt a plan, scheme or zoning by-law. If this was declined he had the authority, as in 1913, to act on the council's behalf.

The practical consequence of Section 21, therefore, was to tie the hands of local governments to the plan and schemes they formulated at the time of their approval by the minister. They could not manoeuvre within the terms of their own planning proposals without ministerial consent.

This situation contributed its part to the decision of the

metropolitan councils to use only zoning by-laws as the means of controlling city development. The constraint of having themselves to operate within the terms of a genuine town plan, approved by the minister through complex ritual — as against a zoning by-law under their own control and specific in its terms of reference — led them to assume that developmental planning could be achieved through zoning by-laws unsupported by the concepts implicit in a town plan approved of and supported by the public at large and sanctified by the authority of the minister. As will be seen later, the strength of arguments in support of applications and appeals by private investors over zoning controls proved too powerful at a time when depression was seriously affecting city coffers. Only the near disasters, and imminent collapse of development control which occurred in the metropolitan centres in 1948, brought home to these councils the necessity of supporting zoning by-laws with professionally prepared, factually supported plans, backed up in turn by popular and ministerial support.

The 1929 Act also introduced the concept of a "replotting scheme." This involved the right of a local authority to report the layout of subdivisions it had previously approved. The Provincial Board, with the consent of the cabinet, was empowered to specify the procedures required to safeguard the interests of all concerned. These included the notification of affected parties, the rules to be observed, surveys, etc. In turn, a local council, by a two-thirds vote of all its members and with the concurrence of 60 percent of the owners of land parcels affected (and including 60 percent of the assessed value of the land affected), could by resolution move to redesign the subdivision. Stringent though the controls over replotting might appear, the high turnover of city land during the depression — a turnover due to tax arrears, gifts to avoid taxation, and land transfers between individuals and the city — enabled councils to use replotting provisions to some effect.[145]

Where owners could identify an improvement emerging from a redesign — for example, from circular drives instead of a grid iron layout — or where a council was itself a major land owner in the affected area, a considerable rearrangement of frontages and general design was accomplished. Lots were redistributed to the original owners after replotting. The compensation provisions, as well as the distribution of cost between owners and the council, had to be published at the time the intended scheme was announced. If more than 60 percent of plot owners objected, the council could not proceed. If a person felt aggrieved after the implementation of the replotting, he could appeal to the public utilities commissioners, who were then called The Compensation Board. After a hearing, this board could determine the compensation. But compensation could not be awarded for costs incurred by the action of replotting itself or for "any actual or anticipated loss, damage or inconvenience suffered in common by all or the greater part of the owners of replotted lands" (Section 58(c)). Thus, a local authority was empowered, in the public interest to change the speculative potential of subdivided land if it could lure the majority of owners into accepting the idea of replotting in principle.

This part of the Act, which was elaborated through re-enactment under very different circumstances in the 1953 amendments to the Planning Act, was a grand attempt by the provincial government to assist mainly the metropolitan centres in undoing some of their past mistakes. The provincial government, in the meantime, was directly involved with the activities of public utilities in the province — over which local government had influence but no planning control and was itself involved with main highway construction and maintenance. The minister, in consequence, held power over local governments by excerising his authority on issues that existed beyond local jurisdiction, but which were also the life-blood of urban centres and their development. In this respect the provincial government stood in the same relation to its local governments as did the federal government to provincial governments, except that federal-provincial relations were regulated by the 1867 BNA Act and provincial-local government relations were the consequence only of provincial prerogatives.

The significance of the 1929 Town Planning Act, in so far as it relates to the question of tri-level governmental powers, is in the rights it afforded local governments to generate development within the terms of the official plan or scheme once it had been approved by the provincial minister. Though the provincial minister had final authority at the point of approving a plan, or any alteration to it, his power was attenuated in terms of regulating the process of development within the context of the plan. He was also strategically placed with respect to the activities of public utilities and highway construction in the province and therefore capable of determining the major issues affecting the growth of an urban centre. But such a centre's council was left free to pursue any policy it might choose to develop itself within the terms of the official plan once approved. This freedom became a jealously guarded right for it served both as the means of growth when in competition with other urban centres, and of handling the provincial government in the political relationship which emerged as urban areas assumed greater importance in Alberta. When in 1935 the federal government opted to pursue its housing policy through private lending institutions rather than through co-operation with provincial governments, the local authorities were already some way towards developing their urban centres largely removed from the direct presence and influence of the provincial government. Private lending institutions and developers, when established within the city, were in an ideal position to work with the local council and planning commissions in terms of the plan. The province had largely to look on and interpret what it all meant only at the point of amendment to the official documents. Though this legislation was passed in 1929, it was only towards the close of the 1939-45 war that it became effective.

Besides the powers outlined above, a council could pass regulations by by-law covering zoning in any "district" the council wished to designate. The "district" was definable at the discretion of council within the area of its own jurisdiction, but where a commission had been established it was empowered to recommend the area and standards required of a "district." This it did by way of a report, but the council had the last word. The official status of a zoning by-law was obtained, as in the case of a plan or scheme, by it being forwarded with relevant reports for the minister's approval. The minister's act of approval of zoning by-laws, of amendments to official plans, and the approval of plans and schemes facilitated not only provincial interests as they came to be reflected in urban centres, but also identified local political issues influencing the planning process. The Act provided for the advertisement of all proposals and regulations, the handling of objections, and the forwarding of such matters to the minister if "such objections have not been withdrawn or acceded to" (Section 26(d)). But local political issues reached the minister usually only when there was fierce conflict. It was clearly in their own interests for local governments to compromise and bargain among the conflicting interests.

The criteria for zoning of a district were various. Land use was prominent regarding the type of activity to be carried on and the type of building to be erected. Population density and space densities could also be used as criteria by a council. The architectural design, character, and appearance of proposed building as well as the right to prohibit construction until utilities had been provided were also part of the council's new powers. Any person or member of a council could seek amendment to or repeal of a zoning by-law. The council was obliged to seek a report from a commission if such had been set up. If a protest by 20 percent of owners directly affected by the proposed change was received by the council, the council could approve the change only by a three-fifths affirmative vote of council members (Section 32(3)). A right of appeal on any specific case still rested with an aggrieved party, first to the town planning commission if such existed, and thence to the provincial board. In considering appeals, the board had to adhere to the spirit of the by-law. It "may make such regulations as *special cases* seem to it to call for and shall endeavour to see that substantial justice is done and that the interests of any individual are not unduly or unnecessarily sacrificed for the benefit of the community" (authors' emphasis). The appeal had to be dealt with on its merits (Section 36). The emphasis on the limited power of the board — limited to "special cases" and the pursuit of justice — rather than on the province-wide application of principles and regulations capable of influencing the planning of the province's urban centres, is typical of the 1929 legislation in so far as it applied to urban centres.

The principles and regulations implicit in plans, schemes, and zoning by-laws needed the approval of the minister who received all the documents and notes on any objections that had not been withdrawn or acceded to. He then had the right to require his amendments to be accepted. The treatment of *particular cases* of aggrieved parties over the application of principles and regulations concentration of population in the cities added to the costs of relief and make-work programs, but these were partly subsidized. The make-work programs in the cities contributed to their amenities while the rural districts had far less advantage in this respect.

Calgary and Edmonton city councils were far from inactive in the depression. In 1930 Calgary obtained an amendment to its charter allowing for a vote to be given to locally established companies for any money by-law. Debentures for public works were raised in limited amounts despite the depression, particularly in Edmonton.[151] By 1934 that city owed the Imperial Bank some $2.5 million.[152] Edmonton's assessments dropped from $66.5 million in 1931 to $53.5 million in 1938, but the mill rate rose to 54.0 in 1938 as the cities' financial obligations increased. The thousands of empty lots in Edmonton did not help its short-term finances as the city came increasingly to take over property in lieu of tax arrears.

The cities and towns of Alberta particularly moved ahead with their planning between 1929-31, i.e., during the very depths of the depression. Notes from a report by Horace L. Seymour (the province's first Director of Town Planning), headed "Town Planning Progress in Alberta up to December 31st, 1931," shows that some 20 planning commissions had been appointed under the 1929 Planning Act.[153] Calgary, Drumheller, Edmonton, and Wetaskawin were the four cities with commissions. In all, some 52 municipalities in Alberta were reportedly interested "in a program of development." Plans and maps showing contours, street grades and surfaces, and areas served by water and sewers, were in preparation in many urban centres. Zoning by-laws were prepared or in preparation in five cities and 11 towns, and building by-laws had been passed in one city and three towns. Mr. Seymour's final comment on this planning development was ". . . in general it may be stated that the work of town planning is proceeding at a rate that might be entirely unexpected in a year of financial depression."

On the other hand, Edmund Dale is most critical of the way Edmonton City Council used zoning by-laws in the absence of a general master plan.[154] The volunteer planning commission was denied both funds and technical competence to produce the master plan, and even the Street Plan it did produce was not forwarded for the minister's sanctification and authority. When passing a zoning by-law in 1933 covering the height and bulk of buildings, land use, and population densities, the council had to establish a Zoning Appeal Board. This instrument was used to control the development of Edmonton from 1933 to 1950; but the concept and the control mechanism were far from being a general plan of the type envisaged after the Second World War. The Zoning Appeal Board was caught in the trap so common to administrative instruments unsupported by general plans. In 1937 no less than 75 appeals were made to it, most of which were granted. The zoning by-law in effect became redundant and led to 27 amendments to it up to 1945. In times of depression the incentive of private enterprise to contribute to local tax revenues can be very influential. The council's omission of a general plan was to lead to its embarrassment in the spate of development that occurred in 1947-48 which, in turn, led to the council asking Professors Bland and Spence-Sales to report in 1948.

MacGregor has outlined the slow but steady increase in Edmonton's public amenities.[155] The mileage of street paving, water mains, and sewers completed increased presistently — "a block at a time ... as outlying homes obtained this service." Similarly, he records how some householders moved to points outside city limits in order to escape urban tax rates. Jasper Place got onto the map by this process. In 1932 the provincial government enacted The Corporations Temporary Additional Taxation Act which added 10 percent to the tax normally payable.[156] In the same year, under the Cities and Towns Emergency Borrowing Powers Act, urban councils were empowered to borrow money to meet the current expenditures of the city, pending the collection of taxes.[157] Sinking funds to repay past debentures had to be maintained intact, but beyond this additional powers to borrow against arrears and penalties were awarded. The banks had money to lend at low interest rates. The cities were the securest investment they could obtain until the federal government offered its assurance on loans under the 1935 Dominion Housing Act.

A number of public works of major proportions were also undertaken in the cities during the depression. In Calgary the Glenmore Reservoir was started in 1930. The Currie Military Barracks were planned in 1934 and were commenced in 1935, as also was the present airport. Edmonton expanded its air links with the North during the '30s, particularly with respect to mining interests.[158] Private capital was invested in sugar beet interests in Taber, Canada Packers opened a new plant in Edmonton in 1936, the Hudson's Bay and T. Eaton Companies established new buildings. The cities were dull and depressed but by no means inactive. Edmonton's building permits reached $2.8 million in 1938, but fell back again thereafter.

Urban centre governments moved fast in procuring approval of plans and we suspect, though we cannot document it, that the relation of planning to the obtaining of finance for a project had something to do with this matter. If by 1929 lending institutions had come to expect a loan they made to be covered by the added security of approved public plans covering the area in which the loan was to be made, then city councils would have had to act speedily. We know that this is the case in recent times covering loans for proposals in the rural residential parcels surrounding the metropolitan centres, but we have been unable to research the point in respect of the smaller cities in 1929-1935.

On the other side of the coin, the series of amendments to the 1929 Planning Act which were legislated between 1930 and 1935 were heavily weighted towards improving the appeal procedures. We also note that the apparent struggle between Public Works and Municipal Affairs continued; in fact in the 1934 amendment the administration of the Planning Act was handed to the Minister of went not to the minister — where political issues could easily be stirred up — but to the planning commission and then to the provincial board. It was a case of government by ideas but politics by quasi-governmental institutions set up outside of the formal political institutions of the province and given an aura of technical expertise and apparent objectivity in the issue at stake. It was an attribute of the one-party system which has typified Alberta; it was also a convenience for local governments and private companies to arrange their affairs through negotiation and co-operation without obliging the formal political instruments to become involved in disputes affecting aggrieved individuals. Quasi-governmental bodies, *ad hoc* committees, and boards were used to handling difficult matters apparently outside of and beyond the formal politics of government. In these respects the 1929 legislation set a pattern which was used increasingly over the years ahead.

Prior to the passing of the 1929 Planning Act, the cities had been using by-laws to achieve control of matters of city interest. Available records at the Provincial Planning Branch, Department of Municipal Affairs, indicate that to this time no municipality had adopted a town planning scheme or had established a local town planning commission. Thus, the main provisions of the 1913 legislation, in particular the provision for "betterment," had never been used. Edmonton, in 1923, passed a by-law prescribing the space to be left vacant around buildings to "provide light and ventilation directly from the outside." Certain parts of the city had restrictions on the number and nature of buildings to be erected on any lot. Certain streets were classified as "residential." Similarly, a by-law in 1925 delineated certain northern and southern parts of the city as areas for noxious industry.[146]

The passing of the 1929 Planning Act led to the setting up of Edmonton's first Town Planning Commission in August, 1929. Three industrial districts, a central, a southern, and a northeastern, were identified.

In conjunction with city policy the railway companies had encouraged industrial use adjacent to the tracks, and spur lines to industrial neighbourhoods. Edmund Dale remarks:

> Residential areas of varying densities could be distinguished, and a very distinct park system was emerging. The advent of the Town Planning Act of 1929, which was most timely, gave the council a further opportunity to channel land development in the direction determined by its overall policy. What was needed, then, was an official comprehensive plan similar to that which had just been prepared for the city of Vancouver.[147]

However, Edmonton City Council did not appoint a professional planner to generate an overall plan, but a draftsman designated as "City Town Planning Assistant." [148] The newly appointed commission was also instructed to prepare a major street plan and zoning by-law before preparing a general plan. However, the council was under pressure because of numerous construction proposals during the boom of 1929, and the more leisurely requirements of overall concepts had to be put aside.

Almost immediately following the passing of the 1929 legislation the depression hit Alberta. It was accompanied by drought. Together they forced many farmers off the land, especially in southern Alberta. The depression as a personal disaster for people has been well described elsewhere. But the questions concerning who fared the easiest and why still remained to be asked. It may be taken as a general rule that the local authority or individual with the least debt and with the most cash in hand fares the best in a depression. Thus some of the rural local authorities which had not incurred capital borrowing prior to 1930 managed to come through the depression intact, i.e. those in the Peace River area, in central Alberta, and in the northeast of the province.[149] Where the farmers could afford to pay their taxes because of high quality land, the local authority could fall behind in its salaries to teachers and secretary treasurers, knowing that it was only a matter of time before tax arrears came in. Other local authorities, particularly in the southeast of the province, had to revert to the status of improvement districts where the provincial government could be directly benevolent. By reverting in status the local authority became "peculiar" and thereby did not contravene the "equal treatment for all local authorities" which became a cardinal principle of government policy as local government pressures mounted for assistance from the province. The price of wheat fell to an average of 43 cents a bushel over the period 1930-34, and averaged only 72 cents over the period 1934-39. Rural roads were maintained by farmers in lieu of tax payments in cash. Provincial grants were increasingly relied upon for education as the number of children attending school continued to rise in the early 1930s. In the early stages of the depression local authorities were responsible for relief payments, but by agreement between the provincial and federal governments a system of subsidy to local authorities for relief and unemployment measures was enacted in 1931.

In the cities the queues awaiting relief lengthened. Construction fell off to insignificant amounts and even skilled workers were obliged to accept relief. Building permits in Edmonton amounted to less than half-a-million dollars in 1933 as private enterprise became reluctant to invest. Paradoxically, Edmonton's population increased by some 10,000 between 1931 and 1936. Calgary fared less well. Similarly, in 1936 the number of people living on farms increased by 7 percent over 1931 to almost 100,000, a record never exceeded before or since.[150] Urban dwellers with relatives on the farm moved out to share accommodation with them and thereby save the cash needed for urban taxes, rental, or mortgage payments. The urban centres received the population with no rural connections or from areas where no living could be obtained — such as parts of Saskatchewan. The increase and

Public Works.[159] The amendments of 1930-35 convey the impression of the provincial government urgently trying to cope with manoeuvres in city affairs. The 1930 Amendment Act limited appeal on a specific case to the provincial board only if the board granted the right to appeal.[160] It was, apparently, a measure aimed at coping with frivolous appeals, though it also granted to the board the option of whether or not to get involved in difficult and contentious local issues. The same amendment granted both planning commissions and the board the right to delegate to their members the right to hear appeals rather than the entire membership. In fact, the board was empowered to delegate "such of its powers as may seem to it proper, to any person or persons ..." (Section 7). It was further empowered to "make regulations calculated to effect the objects of this Act" (Section 8). It seems that the right of appeal was being taken very seriously by persons affected in the urban areas, and the administrative machinery was overtaxed.

The apparent struggle between Public Works — which had a particular interest in the board — and Municipal Affairs appeared in 1930 in terms of the new power of the board generally to make regulations. This was apparently a direct challenge to the autonomy of cities coupled to their relation to the Minister of Municipal Affairs over planning and zoning matters. It was also a step in the direction of making the board a regulative instrument, as well as an appeal instrument, and thereby tended to transfer the previous authority of the minister to the board as a quasi-governmental body.

The 1931 Amendment Act set up a Zoning Appeal Board which enabled an aggrieved party to appeal a "by-law, or any regulations made by the minister."[161] The Zoning Appeal Board tended to be composed of one or more persons so appointed by a local planning commission, but if none existed then the board could so appoint and act as a Zoning Appeal Board. The order disposing of an appeal was final. This amendment set off the local city council and the minister as the makers of by-laws and from the quasi-governmental instruments whose disposition of an appeal became final. In effect it diminished the authority of the centres of community political power, the city council and the minister, and enhanced that of the appeal mechanisms under the final authority of the board.

The 1934 Amendment Act, while transferring the administration of the Town Planning Act to the Minister of Public Works, tended to counter the powers previously ascribed to the board.[162] By providing a clause that obliged appeals against the provisions of a zoning by-law to go through the minister before the council could proceed to approve and pass an amendment, some of the board's 1931 powers were passed to the minister. The minister, however, had only to certify "by writing under his hand that any proposed amendment is not contrary to the fundamental principle of the scheme of the by-law or of this Act and involves no injustice to anyone concerned" (Section 8). This was, perhaps, little more than a formal notification to the minister and an assurance that all local squabbles, such as had been aroused by an appeal, had been amicably dealt with at the council level. This is a further instance of the growing ability of city councils to reconcile local conflicts without having to draw matters to the attention of provincial authorities. The 1934 Act also made the Director of Town Planning unambiguously the executive instrument of the board. The director now had power to issue the notification of the board and to sign its directions (Section 3).

While the politics of city planning were being arranged through the 1930-34 Amendment Acts, the provincial government was busy setting up new industrial promotion machinery. In 1934 the Act to set up the Department of Trade and Industry was passed.[163] The new department had several functions, many of which concerned standards for the trades in the province and the control of prices. But it was explicitly empowered to survey the natural resources of the province and "to formulate plans for their useful, economical and orderly development" (Section 4). It could also attend and promote conferences, form associations, and provide systematic information on the trades and natural resources of the province. It could also advise any interested parties. Thus, in the midst of the depression, Alberta made its first formal moves towards providing incentives to induce industry to settle in the province. In the same year an Act covering the Marketing of Natural Products and the appointment of a marketing board was passed.[164] Government was moving concertedly into the field of regulated marketing and industrial incentives that was to set the stage for Calgary's and Edmonton's industrial development.

In the following year the Department of Municipal Affairs Amendment Act was passed.[165] This Act enabled the minister to act as necessary whenever it appeared "that affairs of a municipality are in such a state or are being conducted in such a manner that immediate action by the council or any officer of the Municipality is necessary in the public interest but is not being undertaken." He could dismiss a council and call for the election of a new one or dismiss an officer and appoint a new one. He could also appoint an official administrator with the powers of a council. The system of local government in the smaller centres and rural areas of the province was under severe strain. Its management was causing the minister concern.

One of the last pieces of legislation enacted by the UFA during the spring of 1935 was the Alberta Municipal Assessment Commission Act.[166] It was administered by the Department of Municipal Affairs. It set up an elaborate machinery involving a Director of Assessments and a corps of inspectors coupled to a three-person Alberta Assessment Commission. Its purpose was to introduce uniformity across the province in the assessments made of land, buildings, and improvements in urban areas, and of land in the rural areas. It struck at the very heart of local government finance. It had power to hear and determine all appeals on assessments from a court of revision set up under the various local authority acts. It was "to establish equalized assessments for all municipalities," and to recommend to the minister standards and methods of assessment that could be applied province wide. The concept of equalized assessment was introduced by the UFA administration as part of its reform of local government finance, a matter that was increasingly to take up the attention of the incoming Social Credit government that September.

Thus, paradoxically, it was the UFA, the political arm of Alberta's farmers, that introduced the basic legislation governing town and rural planning, the Department of Industry and Trade, marketing board legislation, direct provincial control of local authorities if it appeared necessary, fixed industrial assessments, and equalized assessment machinery. The paradox illustrates the growing influence of urban areas, and particularly of Calgary and Edmonton in the province. The hidden but crucial services of urban centres were determining the course of public policy irrespective of the sentiments of the men in political office. It was into this predicament that the Social Credit government under William Aberhart came to power in 1935. The dominion government changed its policies in the same year by introducing the Prairie Farm Rehabilitation Act and in the urban areas, the Dominion Housing Act.

Notes
Chapter 1

1. See W.A. Mackintosh's "The economic background of dominion-provincial relations" being Appendix 3 to the *Report of the Royal Commission on Dominion-Provincial Relations,* Ottawa:1939, p.24. For an indication of the way in which settlement in Alberta and Saskatchewan was to serve the interests of eastern Canadian based business and of the way in which the dominion government's policy supported this, see *The Case for Alberta,* Government of the Province of Alberta, 1938, pp. 45-48.
2. This is a fascinating research subject that appears to have been ignored in Alberta, though its relevance to minorities and assimilating processes all over the world is obvious.
3. Berton, Pierre. *The National Dream: The Great Railway 1871-1881,* Toronto/Montreal: 1970, McClelland and Stewart Ltd., analyzes the evolution of the northern route to the Pacific. In the second volume, *The Last Spike: The Great Railway 1881-1885,* Toronto/Montreal: 1971, McClelland and Stewart Ltd., there is an account of the process whereby the CPR turned the change of route to its own benefit. (Excerpts printed here with the kind permission of the Canadian publisher.)
4. Berton, *The Last Spike,* pp.15-18.
5. Ibid., p.19.
6. Bussard, Lawrence H. "Early history of Calgary," unpublished MA thesis, Department of History, The University of Alberta, April, 1935, p.41.
7. Ibid., p.65.
8. Berton, *The Last Spike,* pp.23-30.
9. Ibid., p.19.
10. Ibid.
11. Ibid.
12. Ibid., p.58.
13. Ibid., p.52.
14. Ibid.
15. There is some indication in Pierre Berton's analysis that land speculation was of a variety of kinds. Certain well-placed wealthy eastern men bought up large tracts of land. One such was Henry Cochrane of Quebec, who purchased 100 square miles near Calgary as soon as the Kicking Horse Pass route was announced. Elsewhere Berton implies that other types of people engaged in other types of speculation. See *The Last Spike,* pp.52-64.
16. Ibid., pp.237-243.
17. Bussard, "Early history of Calgary," p.54.
18. Blue, John. *Alberta: Past and Present,* vol.1. Chicago: 1924, Pioneer Historical Publishing Co., p.211.
19 MacGregor, J.G. *Edmonton: A History,* Edmonton, 1967: M.G. Hurtig, Publishers, p.134. (Excerpts printed here with the kind permission of the publisher.)
20. For a discussion of the consequence on settlement dispersion of the right granted the CPR to own odd-numbered sections anywhere within 20 miles of the railroad throughout the province, see *The Case for ALberta,* pp. 48-51.
21. Blue, *Alberta: Past and Present,* Chapter IX.

22. *The Case for Alberta,* pp.45-48
23. Hanson, Eric J. *Local Government in Alberta,* Toronto: 1956, McClelland and Stewart, p.17.
24. Blue, *Alberta: Past and Present,* p.121.
25. Hanson, *Local Government in ALberta,* p.19. It is often assumed in the literature on the subject that the immigrants to Alberta were a wealthy class. The Introduction to *The Case for Alberta* addressed to the Sovereign People of Canada in 1938, p.8., mentions that "The rapid growth of the population in the earlier years — many settlers bringing with them considerable sums for investment — caused the inevitable expansion boom..." is an example of this opinion. There is also evidence in the literature that this may not be the complete situation. Our enquiries thus far have not resolved this point and it would be a useful thesis for a student of history as it concerns directly the question of investment in Alberta from local residents as against that from the east, with the consequences this has had on the political affairs of the province.
26. Gershaw, F.W. *Saamis: The Medicine Hat,* Medicine Hat: undated, printed by Val Marshall Printing Ltd., pp.162-3. Many parts of MacGregor's *Edmonton: A History,* especially Chapters 11 to 13, illustrate the same point.
27. See, for example, James Anderson's "Change in a central place system: trade centres and rural service in central Alberta," unpublished MA thesis, Department of Geography, The University of Alberta, 1967, Chapter 8. Post-office closures are a fair index of the process.
28. Even in 1971 the boundaries of many important regional agencies, sponsored by both the provincial and federal governments, formed a confused and disorderly pattern. It would appear that each sponsoring government delineates the boundaries it wishes to create with its own particular purposes in mind rather than the needs of the people to be serviced or the relation of that service to the situation of the inhabitants in the area. Political considerations enter into boundary delineations as much as, if not more than, functional or rationally administrative considerations.
29. This is the case only in recent times. Income tax rights were vested in local authorities until removed by the provincial government.
30. McClelland and Stewart, Ltd., 1956.
31. MacGregor, *Edmonton: A History,* p.155.
32. Hanson, *Local Government in Alberta,* pp.9-12.
33. Ibid., p.10.
34. *The Interim First Report of the Co-terminous Boundary Commission,* Government of the Province of Alberta, Edmonton, 1953, p.1.
35. Blue, *Alberta: Past and Present,* p.116, reports that each resident was assessed one day, and each farmer on the scale of two days for 160 acres, three days for 160 to 320 acres, four days for the next 320 acres, five days for 1,280 acres, and one day extra for every additional 640 acres. The principle of contribution by proportional property holding was well established from this point on.
36. Hanson, *Local Government in Alberta,* p.129, footnote 3.
37. Ibid., p.23.
38. Bussard, "Early history of Calgary," p.145.
39. Blue, *Alberta: Past and Present,* p.282.
40. Ibid., p.117.
41. For details see Ibid., pp.117-18.
42. MacGregor, *Edmonton: A History,* p.170.
43. Ibid., p. 165.
44. Blue, *Alberta: Past and Present,* pp. 297-298.
45. MacGregor, *Edmonton: A History,* p.163.
46. Ibid., p.155.
47. Gibson, John, "The impact of the railroad on urban patterns . . . an Alberta example," *The Albertan Geographer,* No. 1, 1964-65, Department of Geography, The University of Alberta, pp.41-46.
48. The above data were obtained from *The Municipal Manual,* City of Calgary, 1920, pp.130-34.

49. Hanson, *Local Government in Alberta,* p.27. Much of this rural reluctance arose from fear of increased taxation.
50. At first a centre with not less than 2,000 population could seek incorporation as a city.
51. Blue, *Alberta: Past and Present,* p.168.
52. Ibid., p. 152.
53. Dale, Edmund H., "The role of successive town and city councils in the evolution of Edmonton, Alberta, 1892 to 1966," unpublished PhD thesis, Department of Geography, The University of Alberta, 1969, p.113.
54. *Statutes of Alberta,* 1906, Chapter 24.
55. MacGregor, *Edmonton: A History,* p.189.
56. An Act Relating to Town Planning, Chapter 18, 1913, *Statutes of the Province of Alberta,* Section 1.
57. Ibid., Section 8(a), (b), and (c).
58. Ibid., Section 1(3).
59. Ibid., Section 1(4).
60. Ibid., Section 1(5).
61. Ibid., Section 1(6).
62. Ibid., Section 2(3).
63. Ibid., Section 3(2)(a).
64. Blumenfeld, Hans, *The Modern Metropolis,* New York: 1967, Harvest House, p.300.
65. Calgary, for example, employed its first city planner, Mr. Thomas R. Mawson, in 1912, and a plan was drawn up shortly after. The Mawson plan, for various reasons was, however, largely ignored.
66. MacGregor, *Edmonton: A History,* Chapter 14.
67. Ibid., p.196. Further annexations, to a total city area of 39.88 square miles, were made in 1913. Ibid., p.200.
68. Dale, "Successive town and city councils," p.108.
69. Cited by Dale, ibid.
70. See the map following p.115 in Dale,"Successive town and city councils."
71. Ibid., p.266.
72. Hanson, *Local Government in Alberta,* p.129, footnote 8, shows that the value of building permits in Calgary and Edmonton rose from $3 million in 1906 to a peak of $34.8 million in 1912, and by 1915 had dropped to $0.5 million.
73. Ibid., p. 129, footnote 9, shows that provincial income rose from $14 million in 1906 to $168 million in 1912, then declined slightly but rose during the war years. It reached $365 million in 1920.
74. Ibid., p.39. Some authorities have explained the ineffectual application of the 1913 Planning Act as due to a lack of professional personnel to implement it. In our view, the slump of 1913 and the war were more likely reasons.
75. In February, 1917, Edmonton advertised the sale of 20,114 lots in tax arrears. Dale, "Successive town and city councils," p.158.
76. *Statutes of Alberta,* 1915, Chapter 6, Section 20(b).
77. In 1919 The Tax Recovery Act and The Arrears of Taxes Act were passed. The first provided for the immediate sale of land on which taxes were in arrears on July 1 each year, beginning in 1920. Though sensibly applied, and amended in later years, such provisions did encourage the payment of arrear taxes. In Edmonton the collected portion of the tax levy rose from 49 percent in 1916 to 73 percent in 1920. Dale, "Successive town and city councils," p.162.
78. Hanson, *Local Government in Alberta,* p.40.
79. Thomas, L.G. *The Liberal Party in Alberta,* Toronto: 1959, University of Toronto Press, p.155.
80. Blue, *Alberta:Past and Present,* Chapter XXIV.
81. Ibid., p. 419.
82. Ibid. The same opinion is held by Thomas, *The Liberal Party in Alberta,* p. 165.
83. This lady was later to become one of the "famous five" who fought for

the right of women to be appointed to the Canadian Senate. The legal fight was taken to the Privy Council in 1929. In 1939 a tablet was unveiled to them in the lobby of the Canadian Senate.

84. Blue, *Alberta: Past and Present,* pp. 419-420.

85. These Acts amended the male prerogative incipient in the Torrens System of land title. Under the Relief Act a widow of a man leaving a will who received less than she would if he died intestate could apply to the Supreme Court for relief from its terms. Under the Dower Act a widow was entitled to a life interest in the homestead of the deceased husband. In rural areas a homestead meant one quarter section of land and in towns and cities it was construed to mean not more than four adjoining lots in one block in which the house occupied by the deceased husband was situated. The Acts were an early form of social welfare provisions using capital rather than allowances as its means.

86. Johnson and MacNutt in *Aberhart of Alberta,* Institute of Applied Art, Co-op Press Ltd., 1970, p.3, argue that the influence of women in the emerging social conscience was evident in 1910 when Aberhart first arrived in Calgary.

87. Thomas, *Liberal Party in Alberta,* p.157.

88. MacGregor, *Edmonton: A History,* p.218.

89. Thomas, *Liberal Party in Alberta,* p.157.

90. Ibid., p. 160.

91. Ibid., p. 161. Prohibition was eventually lifted, paradoxically by the UFA government, after a referendum in 1923.

92. Ibid., p. 166.

93. Ibid., p. 171 and p. 177. The Liberal party enjoyed considerable control over the machinery of government. The Lieutenant-Governor himself was a staunch Liberal. Ministers kept direct contact with various departments of the civil service whose heads tended to be Liberal. Patronage was unblushingly exercised, conforming to the tradition of the times. Ibid., p.172-173.

94. See Thomas's account of the period, *Liberal Party in Alberta,* Chapter 8.

95. Ibid.

96. *Statutes of Alberta,* Chapter 14, 1918, Section 4.

97. *Statutes of Alberta,* Chapter 14, 1919, Section 9(e).

98. *House of Commons Reports, Special Committee on Housing,* Ottawa: 1935, p.93.

99. Blue, *Alberta: Past and Present,* p.140.

100. The 1916 Act had reference only to consumption of liquor within the province. The manufacture, import, and export of liquor was still legal. The liquor stores were concerned with the sale of liquor for mechanical, scientific, medicinal, and sacramental purposes, for which a special permit had to be obtained.

101. Thomas, *Liberal Party in Alberta,* p.193.

102. Compare the list of enactments in the *Statutes of Alberta* for 1921 and 1922.

103. MacPherson, C.B. *Democracy in Alberta: Social Credit and the Party System,* 2nd edition, Toronto: 1962, University of Toronto Press, p.3.

104. Ibid, p.30.

105. Ibid.

106. Cited by MacPherson, *Democracy in Alberta,* p.33, from "The significance of democratic group organization," published in *The UFA,* 1922.

107. The contradiction in the concept of class is well analyzed by MacPherson, ibid, p.35. Similarly William Irvine's philosophy and its contradictions are well described by MacPherson in this section of his excellent book.

108. The proportion of owner-operated farms in Alberta was 80 percent in 1921, but only 64 percent in 1946. Similarly the amount of full-time employed labour on Albertan farms has always been small, though casual farm labour has been significant. See MacPherson, ibid, pp.10-20.

109. Cited in ibid, p.50.

111. Ibid. p.60.
112. *The Case for Alberta,* 1938, pp. 58-59.
113. Hanson, *Local Government in Alberta,* p.41.
114. Ibid. Dale, "Successive town and city councils," p.166, has shown that tax-forfeited land between 1920 and 1929 amounted to 43 percent of the total area of the City of Edmonton. The city had been using the technique of public sale of forfeited land for two years by 1920, and the proportion of tax levy collected rose 88 percent in 1928.
115. An excellent account of Edmonton's airport development is contained in Dale, "Successive town and city councils," Chapter VIII.
116. Both world wars had an adverse effect on Alberta's city populations if their relative significance to eastern industrial cities is taken as the measure. In the First World War Alberta's cities even lost population in absolute numbers, while in the Second World War their increase nowhere equalled that of the east. In Toronto and other eastern cities industrial wartime expansion generated serious housing and overcrowded conditions.
117. Most of the above information was obtained from MacGregor's *Edmonton: A History,* pp.223-241. The tables and appendices of *The Case for Alberta* contain a variety of factual data of this type up to the mid-1930s.
118. Macpherson, *Democracy in Alberta,* p.88.
119. Edmonton's bonded debt was $29.3 million in 1924, and it rose to 36.4 million by December, 1925. Dale, "Successive town and city councils," p.182.
120. *Statutes of Alberta,* 1925, Chapter 10, Section 3(1).
121. *Statutes of Alberta,* 1937, Chapter 61.
122. Dale, "Successive town and city councils" p. 285.
123. This modern situation contrasts with the regional distribution of cities. Particularly during the early years of modern Edmonton it benefited from being the only city in northern Alberta, while Clagary in the south was competing with Lethbridge and Medicine Hat as well as other smaller communities. The significance of their relative positions, isolation, and competition are not developed in this study. MacGregor remarks on p.177 of his *Edmonton: A History* that its solitary position was of advantage to Edmonton. Edmonton's relations with the Canadian north are well known, and in the past decade the advantage of Calgary's airport vis-a-vis the distance from the city of Edmonton's international airport at Leduc have been other significant geographical phenomena influencing the importance and growth of these cities.
124. The 10 major centres represented in Table 23 had a combined increase of population from 1911 of 24,300 to 40,400 or an increase of 1.6 times. Calgary and Edmonton increased 2.7 times.
125. Dale, "Successive town and city councils," Chapter 5.
126. Stone, L.E. *Urban Development in Canada,* 1961 Census Monograph, Dominion Bureau of Statistics, Ottawa, 1967, p.33.
127. There was one Labour member in the first UFA Cabinet but after later elections the Cabinet consisted only of UFA members.
128. See pp. 34 and 35 this Chapter.
129. In 1938 the officially estimated size of economic farms for most parts of Alberta had grown from the original 160 acre homestead to between 320 and 400 acres. This was particularly noticeable in the southern part of the province and has occurred elsewhere since 1921. *The Case For Alberta,* pp.55 and 56.
130. Ibid, p.92.
131. *Alberta Revised Statutes,* 1922, Chapter 45.
132. *Alberta Revised Statutes,* 1922, Chapter 45, Schedule.
133. *Statutes of Alberta,* 1924, Chapter 30.
134. MacGregor, *Edmonton: A History,* pp.236-239. Airmail became of increasing importance as regular schedules became established.
135. Dale, "Successive town and city councils," p.212.
136. A list of these is given in Dale, Ibid., p.213.
137. Ibid., p.215.
138. The series of amendments to city charters is an aspect of historical

research sorely lacking in the province. The series could be useful index of the issues which arose in city government and for which legislation became necessary.
139. *Statutes of Alberta,* 1927, Chapters 54 and 55 respectively.
140. *Statutes of Alberta,* 1928, Chapter 48, Section 2(c) and 2(d).
141. *Statutes of Alberta,* 1929, Chapter 49.
142. *Statutes of Alberta,* 1928, Chapter 48, Section 4(b). The Act does not mention subdivision under the 1913 Town Planning Act.
143. Section 65(2) refers to the Lieutenant-Governor in Council who "may appoint a Board...," and "may appoint a Director."
144. We have not had time to examine these reports to check if the director in fact included this topic in his reports. He was obliged, under Section 65(4), only to report on "the transactions of the Board."
145. See the discussion in Dale, "Successive town and city councils," pp.336-340, concerning Edmonton's use of replotting provisions.
146. Ibid., pp.210-211.
147. Ibid., p.216.
148. Ibid., p.217.
149. Hanson, *Local Government in Alberta,* p.42.
150. MacGregor, *Edmonton: A History,* p.244.
151. See the Edmonton Charter amendments for 1932. *Statutes of Alberta,* 1932.
152 MacGregor, *Edmonton: A History,* p.247.
153. The report may be inspected in the files of the Provincial Archives, Edmonton.
154. MacGregor, *Edmonton: A History,* p.247.
155. Ibid., p.248.
156. *Statutes of ALberta,* 1932, Chapter 62.
157. Ibid., Chapter2.
158. MacGregor, *Edmonton: A History,* pp.254-55.
160. The 1931 amendment repealed the right of the board to acquire land for provincial parks or to preserve places of natural beauty and historic interest.
160. *Statutes of Alberta,* 1930, Chapter 50.
161. *Statutes of Alberta,* 1931, Chapter 59.
162. In 1938 the licencing of service stations along highways was removed from the jurisdiction of the Planning Act.
163. *Statutes of Alberta,* 1934, Chapter 33.
164. Ibid., Chapter 34.
165. *Statutes of Alberta,* 1935, Chapter 64.
166. Ibid., Chapter 63.

Chapter 2
Social Credit and Urban Policy, 1935 to 1953

The General Scene

Between 1935 and 1971 the centralization of the population, the growth and concentration of secondary productive processes, and the pre-eminence of Calgary and Edmonton as the province's metropolitan centres moved perhaps faster than similar processes in any other province of Canada. The proportion of population classified as "urban" moved from the low 30 percent range to the 75 percent mark. The consumer purchasing power of each of the metropolitan centres came to exceed that of any one of all of the smaller cities combined by many fold. The paradox of this situation lies in the fact that it occurred under the Social Credit administration whose voting support rested broadly in the smaller cities and towns and in the rural areas of the province. This illustrates the point that a rurally supported administration can co-exist very amicably with the process of rapid metropolitan growth, and vice-versa.

It has often been assumed that Alberta's rapid industrialization can be accounted for by the development of oil and natural gas industries following the Leduc discovery in 1947, and the postwar demand for hydro-carbons. The royalties obtained by the provincial government did increase enormously between 1946 and 1955. Revenues of the provincial government from all sources moved from \$44.6 million to \$204.7 million over these years.[1] Natural resource revenues alone moved from \$3.3 million to \$85.8 million during this time. Yet, though there is no denying the advantage that this revenue gave the province, it does not in itself account for the growth and pre-eminence of the metropolitan centres. The philosophy and administrative practices of the government, the behaviour of the local authorities within these practices, and the investment policies of private enterprise (plus many other factors) collectively contributed to the development of Alberta and the changes this brought with it. In many respects Alberta's cities benefited very little from wartime activity, while the manufacturing cities in the east, the provinces with oceanic ports, and those strategically placed for war expenditures did very well. In this sense, the oil royalties acted as a catch-up benefit after the war had ended.

The situation of the province from 1935 to 1939 was

peculiar in many respects. Though having a predominantly rural labour force, it had some of the most advanced town planning legislation in all of Canada; it had introduced administrative instruments to achieve an equalized assessment of property; and it had a Department of Trade and Industry and a proven system of local government. Calgary and Edmonton continued a slow but steady expansion of population and amenities throughout the worst of the depression, though there were not many centres which did.

When the Social Credit administration took over, Alberta was among the top three provinces of Canada in the amount of net interest per capita paid on debts incurred through public ownership commitments. After a revision in the method of calculation, the Finance Branch of the Dominion Bureau of Statistics arrived at the distribution shown in Table 5.

Table 5. Net interest paid per capita on debts under public ownership by province, 1936 (in millions of dollars).

Province	*Gross interest paid*	*Interest received*	*Net interest paid*	*Net interest paid per capita*
British Columbia	8.3	0.4	7.9	10.47
Alberta	6.6	0.9	5.6	7.28
New Brunswick	3.1	0.1	3.0	6.81
Manitoba	5.9	2.0	4.0	5.53
Ontario	30.0	11.4	18.9	5.12
Nova Scotia	3.6	0.9	2.6	4.91
Saskatchewan	6.6	2.5	4.0	4.33
PEI	0.3		0.3	2.92
Quebec	6.1	1.0	5.0	1.63

From *The Canada Year Book,* 1938, p. 879, where the complete figures are given.

Interest on debts covering the continuing organization of the provinces fell particularly heavily on British Columbia and Alberta relative to their population. Alberta had a gross bonded debt (exclusive of treasury bills) in 1936 of $128.1 million; only Ontario, Quebec, and British Columbia had greater amounts.[2] Provincial government expenditure per head of population in 1936 was $23.69 which was exceeded only by British Columbia, $35.20, and Ontario with $28.09. The weighted national provincial average was $22.50.[3]

Pursuant to Social Credit philosophy and in view of the province's own vulnerability to external creditor demands, William Aberhart, on assuming the premiership in 1935 and with no previous parliamentary experience, undertook to cope with provincial debt. The political problems he encountered have been well described by John Irving and Professor C.B. MacPherson in texts already referred to. It is intended only to give the briefest outline here of the philosophy.

William Aberhart was the product of intellectual urban culture.[4] Unlike his UFA predecessors he was not the product of rural farm culture alone. Though Aberhart was born and spent his childhood on his father's western Ontario farm, he used education as the means of moving into an urban culture. In this respect he was using, at the turn of the century in Ontario, the same instruments of social and occupational mobility as later generations of farmers' sons and daughters would use in Alberta. He was justly proud of his BA degree earned through extramural study.[5] He did well at the village school in all subjects, but preferred mathematics. He was good at sports and enjoyed music. The epitaph considered most appropriate to him was that "he served his fellow man" with devotion and sincerity. Not all would agree with this in purely altruistic terms, though the remarks of the press at his death in 1943 would not belie it.

John A. Irving, in his excellent account of Mr. Aberhart as the prophet who stimulated the Social Credit movement in Alberta during the depression, emphasizes his intellectual and scholastic achievements.[6] After graduating from the Seaforth Collegiate Institute, Aberhart spent a year at the Chatham Business College and received a diploma in 1897. He was awarded a teaching certificate in 1898 from the Hamilton Normal School and was awarded numerous other qualifications in geometry, advanced drawing, a military cadet instructorship, and a commercial specialist's certificate with honours from the Ontario Department of Education between 1899 and 1905. He was awarded a Bachelor of Arts by extramural study from Queen's University in 1910. Concurrently he served with the YMCA and was also engaged in Sunday school work. As late as 1941 his intellectual interests continued as he started to learn French, German, and Spanish. He had a long-standing but unfulfilled ambition to be a lawyer. After teaching in rural and small towns of Ontario, including a principalship, he moved to Calgary in the spring of 1910 to take up a teaching appointment. He remained in Calgary as teacher and headmaster until he was obliged, more by circumstances than his own volition, to assume the premiership of Alberta.

From his early youth Aberhart used his considerable intellectual talents to work out an answer to the world's problems as he perceived them. As a youth he was interested in the teachings of itinerant evangelists rather than those of the Presbyterian church of his traditional up-bringing.[7] He marvelled at the power of the preacher over his audience, and at the power of human ideas and imagination contrasted with that of social institutions. He remarked: "I had discovered the power of words and gestures over people, and I have never forgotten the power of that preacher (seen in his youth) to dominate those people."[8] In Calgary he became a recognized Bible scholar and organized the Calgary Prophetic Bible Conference following the success of his teaching and preaching at the Westbourne Baptist Church. Interest in his Sunday afternoon teaching and particularly in its prophetic aspects, led him in 1920 to hold classes in local theatres to obtain sufficient seating for his audiences. In 1924 he expanded his mode of communicating with people and established the bi-monthly magazine, *The Prophetic Voice*. In November, 1925 he gave his first Sunday afternoon broadcast over CFCN radio in Calgary and became known as "The Voice of the Prairies." In 1926 he was invited to give guest lectures on prophetic topics in small towns around Calgary, and rural residents were pressing for a Radio Sunday School. Immediately before this he had had the idea of organizing a biblical study group which trained its adherents systematically in an almost seminary fashion. Although this study group was entirely voluntary, Aberhart generated an organizational form to accommodate it; it became known as the Bible Institute, and he assumed the title of Dean. This soon attracted students from adjacent provinces and the Westbourne Church was inadequate to accommodate it. A campaign for funds was started to erect a large building, which later came to be known as the Calgary Prophetic Bible Institute. By 1929 Aberhart was obliged to separate more clearly than before his role as a public school headmaster and his spare-time interest in the Bible Institute.[9]

The relation of funds to the execution of a project was always carefully worked out by Aberhart. He was nervous of using the radio lest people should not attend the classes being given at the theatre and that the classes' finances would suffer thereby. The way out was a radio club through which those who listened could contribute a dollar to defray expenses.[10] Earlier, at school, he had obtained a projector by issuing shares to pupils who not only received preferential rates on admission, but had their share returned to them with due ceremony plus interest. His means of funding the Bible Institute building is another well-known example.[11] Aberhart had a keen awareness of the necessity for an organization to pay its own way, funded by its users and beneficiaries rather than by loans obtained from outside. That way the benefits by way of interest would be returned to the organization or to those who used it. This became a critical feature of later Social Credit policy in Alberta.

Aberhart had known for some time of the works of C.H. Douglas, the Englishman who first proposed the principles of Social Credit, because UFA leaders were discussing it during the 1920s.[12] It was only during the early 1930s when the depression was bearing down on both the rural and urban dwellers of Alberta that Aberhart decided to apply his mathematical and financial skills to the adaptation of its principles to the Albertan scene.

Social Credit, whether in Britain or Alberta, combined a vision of a new and just society with solutions to obvious current problems. When man was so clearly master of the machinery to produce what he needed and master of the fertility of the soil, as had been shown in Alberta by the level of wheat exports prior to the depression, it was obvious that "society" — the way people organized their collective life — was responsible for the sadness and stupidity of human poverty and debt obligation. Economists and politicians had continued to press for harder and harder work and greater and greater productivity yet in the face of a lack of consumer demand. The methods of distributing what industry and the soil could so clearly provide had broken down. The interpretation given the message in Alberta was that Albertans were bound hand and foot to alien financial interests; they were the victims of gross human selfishness and debased moral values. Mr. Aberhart's biblical teaching, with its emphasis on prophetics and fundamentalist values, was not lost on a clear-thinking, grass-roots type of agricultural mind. He began injecting Social Credit ideas into his broadcasts in the fall of 1932, but by no means for personal political purposes at that time.

> The basic premise, as Aberhart himself wrote it, was as follows: It is the duty of the State through its government to organize its economic structure in such a way that no bona fide citizen, man, woman, or child, shall be allowed to suffer for lack of the bare necessities of food, clothing, and shelter, in the midst of plenty or abundance.[13]

He was convinced that the Province of Alberta was wealthy enough to put that premise into practice. Aberhart had announced in December, 1934 that Social Credit would contest the 1935 election,[14] but not as a political party. It is significant that he said "reliable, honourable, bribe-proof business men who have definitely laid aside their party political affiliations, will be asked to represent Social Credit in every constituency."[15] Canvassers visited every city block as well as farms. The election campaign itself opened in Edmonton with 5,000 people attending a picnic rally.[16]

The popularity of Social Credit in 1935 can be judged from its winning 89 percent of the seats. Its appeal lay as much in urban as rural areas, though powerful segments of the metropolitan centres who were later to feel the brunt of the Social Credit "reform" of lending institutions, were always opposed. The depression had heightened the urban citizens' awareness of the symbiotic nature of urban centre and agricultural production just as it reduced awareness of the nexus of relations among the metropolitan centres of Canada, and North America generally.[17] The development of Alberta's potential in the service of Albertans, demanded, it seemed to Social Credit thinkers, only honesty and integrity.

The circumstances of many Albertans in the depression was a violent contradiction of the work they had put into their farms and properties. This contradiction spoke to them of fraud. It did violence to their aspirations and hopes as a pioneer community and to their self respect as a people who had fed the industrialized world with export grain for three decades. MacPherson writes:

> It drew attention to the growing centralization of power in the state, in trade unions, and in business enterprise, and pointed to the suppression of individuality which this must

> entail. It argued that parliamentary democracy had become unreal, since successive governments, empowered by popular franchise, had given the people the opposite of what the people wanted.[18]

Though Communist sympathizers and activities were prominent in parts of Alberta during the depression, and though the CCF gained a substantial hearing, the Albertan voter became increasingly interested in the potential of Social Credit which did not denigrate the value of private enterprise and the autonomy of the individual. Under Aberhart's religious and moral teaching, the voter saw a clearer answer in Social Credit than in any of the socialistic doctrines of the time.[19]

The similarities and contrasts of Social Credit both in Alberta and Britain, and between Social Credit and UFA philosophies, have been well analyzed by Professor MacPherson and they will not be developed here.[20] Social Credit adopted a new perspective in its criticism of the existing, immoral order. It was no longer a matter of farmers as producers, and labour as consumers getting the raw end of an economic process dominated by monopolies. "The root cause of the malaise was an error in the accounting system of industry, an error which had become entrenched in the pricing mechanism and had made it impossible for people as consumers to buy back the goods they had created as producers."[21] By this mechanism, finance had gained control of the productive process and, in turn, of government. Financiers gained their power by manipulating other people's property. Their money was not strictly their own property, but in the loans they made and the interest they charged, they were capable of influencing the property of borrowers. There was nothing inherently wrong with industry and manufacturing, with the private ownership of production, with technological invention or science. Social Credit was not a fundamentalist belief in the evils of modern civilization in any form; on the contrary it was progressive and innovative. Finance had perverted the existing system by control of credit and the expropriation of man's productive capacities both as an individual and as a collective. The control of credit by the people would be sufficient to remedy the existing system, guarantee that system's rewards to the people rather than to the financiers, and generate the consumer power needed to provide economic stability and human tranquility. It was a simple and appealing message that could be understood by many classes of depressed townsmen no less than by the province's farmers.

Technology and its productive capacity had provided wealth that every member of the community had a right to share in. Inventions applied as man's cultural tools — "the progress of the industrial arts" — created new wealth as an unearned increment to human effort; but no one individual or class had a particular right to it as it was a consequence of collective endeavours and the division of labour. This was the nature of *social* credit; the unearned increment would not be inherently inflationary if applied to its proper owner — the community at large — rather than being kept by a few in order to generate an artificial scarcity.

Aberhart was given a clear eighteen months after taking office to begin the implementation of the philosophy in Alberta. The method whereby it was to be done was not, in theory, to be the concern of the electorate nor even of members of the Legislature.[22] Concurrently, he was concerned with the day-to-day administration of the province's affairs — the quality of which came to be of particular importance for vote-getting from 1929 to 1971, after the first flush of enthusiasm for the new philosophy had been wrecked against the rocks of federal government and judicial actions to thwart its implementation. Pride in the quality of this administration became part of Social Credit electioneering, and contributed time after time to Social Credit success at the polls. It did contribute substantially to the growth of urban Alberta during this time. The appointment of Mr. Charles Cochcraft both as Provincial Treasurer and as Minister of Municipal Affairs was not, perhaps, entirely coincidental.

On taking office in September, 1935 Aberhart found the provincial treasury held insufficient funds to pay the civil servants' salaries in October. There was an accumulated deficit of $250,000 for teachers' salaries. He went immediately to Ottawa to seek federal help.[23] He needed $18 million in loans to support the province in its obligations, but received much less.[24] While in eastern Canada searching for money, Aberhart visited the heads of banking institutions and manufacturers, and while in the U.S.A. visited Henry Ford.[25] He also recruited the first of the financial "experts" who were required to handle the technical aspects of the application of Social Credit policy. His recruit was R.J. Magor who had previously helped Newfoundland in financial problems and was known to be close to banking circles. However, Magor resigned in June, 1936. Aberhart was searching for expertise which would not alienate the sympathies of orthodox financiers while the province's finances were in such difficulties, and who could at the same time apply financial principles within the terms of Social Credit philosophy.

In 1935 The Prairie Farm Rehabilitation Act was passed in Ottawa, and Aberhart was obliged to act in rural and agricultural reform immediately. Rural land-use planning was an immediate necessity, particularly in the southeast of the province where distress was serious. The Special Areas Act of Alberta, 1938, eventually placed some 10,000 square miles under direct provincial administration and provided for farmer resettlement elsewhere.[26]

But Aberhart was not idle in starting the process of gearing the province's administrative facilities to the needs of new urban development. In 1936, only a year after taking office, he introduced the Provincial Industries Development Act to be administered by the Minister of Trade and Industries.[27] The Act was to encourage industry to process and manufacture the natural products of the province. The Provincial Treasurer was authorized "to guarantee on behalf of the Province the securities, obligations and financial undertakings of any company incorporated under any act of the Province which has for its object the development of any natural resource of the Province . . ." (Section 4). It limited the amount of assistance and also selected the type of company in terms of the size of its authorized capital, but it was a direct incentive to industrial production.

A further indication of the emphasis given to urban employment can be determined from the industrial training provided by Mr. Aberhart, who was also Minister of Education. The Departmental Annual Report for 1938 shows that commercial, technical, general shop, and home economics courses were being strengthened. That year 19 diplomas were issued in Industrial Electricity, 17 in Automobile Mechanics, four in Aeronautics, etc., from the Provincial Institute of Technology and Art in Calgary.[28] In 1948, a decade later, the Institute of Technology offered "a comprehensive programme of evening courses" for the upgrading of persons engaged in various industries. Some 506 diplomas were issued for the day courses alone, including 50 in welding, 50 in industrial electricity, 63 in agricultural mechanics, 42 in automobile mechanics, etc.[29] Aberhart himself initiated the reform in technical education, and did so during the early years of his administration.

The Dominion Housing Act, 1935, was taken seriously by the provincial government. In the 1936 legislative program The Dominion Housing Act Mortgages Act was passed.[30] This brief Act gave prior claim to mortgages made under the Dominion Housing Act in any judicial settlement in the province. Section 3 made reference to "every such mortgage shall have priority over every claim, lien, charge or encumbrance of any kind or nature whatsoever filed or registered subsequent to the due registration of any such mortgage, except only in respect of taxes due to a city, town . . . or to the Crown." The dominion government was demanding its pound of flesh in the security it sought. It must have been a bitter pill for Aberhart to swallow, though it was not entirely contrary to Social Credit philosophy in that it was government lending in the interests of the people. It was the life insurance company aspect of the federal Act that was to be resented. As events turned out, between 1935 and July 31, 1938, the distribution of money under the Act, by province, was as shown in Table 6; Alberta received no money at all.

Table 6. Use, by province, of the Dominion Housing Act, 1935-38*

Province	*Units built*	*Amount $'000*
Ontario	2,552	10,070
Quebec	1,200	5,492
British Columbia	908	2,841
Manitoba	150	639
New Brunswick	98	417

PEI	10	54
Saskatchewan	2	8
Alberta	Nil	Nil

*Extracted from A.E. Graver's *Housing, a study prepared for the Royal Commission on Dominion-Provincial Relations,* Ottawa, 1939, p. 40.

Thus, though the provincial government was prepared to have the Act apply in Alberta, the lending institutions with their right of selection of mortgages and locality of investment brought its facilities to nought. Just as Alberta had failed to gain from the dominion's 1919 disbursement to municipal areas to cope with urban unemployment through public works, the 1935 Act gave the province nothing.

On the other hand, the Home Improvement Plan of 1937, which was planned to work largely through chartered banks on a local, small-scale level, was well used by Albertans. From the initiation of the Act in January, 1937, to April 30, 1939, the distribution of use and amount of loans made by provinces was as shown in Table 7.

Table 7. Use, by province, of the Dominion Home Improvement Plan Act, 1937*

Province	*Number of loans*	*Amount $'000*
Ontario	30,986	12,612
Quebec	10,186	5,184
British Columbia	6,995	2,188
Alberta	5,018	2,154
Nova Scotia	5,159	1,560
Manitoba	4,025	1,541
New Brunswick	2,566	856
Saskatchewan	1,345	460
PEI	647	167

*Graver, *Housing,* p. 42. (See table 6.)

Farm houses in Alberta took up not less than 1,143 of the total of 5,018 loans, valued at $412,537. The non-farm houses of Alberta benefited under this Act in the ratio of 4.4:1. In this distribution the Home Improvement Plan Act decidely benefited the urban areas.

Among the provinces of Canada, Alberta did not do particularly well from these early federal initiatives. Against Ontario's allocation over both facilities of $22.7 million, Alberta obtained $2.15 million. From the very beginning of federal schemes, Ontario picked up the lion's share — a matter reflecting both population concentration, the problems inherent in urban centres, and the decisions of life insurance companies, which at that time were virtually the only lending institutions operating under the federal scheme.

The Dominion 1938 Municipal Improvements Assistance Act was eagerly taken up in Alberta, but did not produce much money. It involved the province in a lengthy enabling Act.[31] During 1939 the province stood surety for almost $130,000 of loans to local authorities, and by 1941 the figure had risen to almost $900,000.[32] This sum was distributed over cities, towns, and municipal hospital debentures roughly in the ratio of 7:2.6:1. In Alberta, therefore, the cities obtained the lion's share. It may be recalled that the dominion legislation was aimed at assisting local authorities to modernize their income earning utilities. It was the self-liquidating aspect of the loans which appealed to Social Credit philosophy — it was public money being used for public purposes that paid for themselves.

The provincial enabling legislation involved the provincial government at two principal points in the loans to be negotiated by local authorities with the federal government. First, the local authorities of Alberta were empowered by by-law to borrow "from the Minister of Finance of Canada moneys which he is authorised to lend" and to enter into agreements and provide for debentures, mortgages and other security instruments he may require.[33] Municipal councils had to pass a money by-law with its corresponding restrictions and obtain the approval of the Board of Public Utility Commissioners, which was a provincial institution. Secondly, applications by municipalities had to be forwarded to the Clerk of the Executive Council for submission to the Lieutenant-Governor in Council, who had the authority to approve or refuse any application. The Minister of Public Health was involved in any applications affecting water or sewerage works, but the Minister of Municipal Affairs was not formally brought into the control machinery at all.[34]

The symbolic significance of this omission is important. Local authorities were borrowing from the federal government for public facilities without the formal involvement of Municipal Affairs. The Public Utility Commissioners were seen as involved, and also the Provincial Treasurer, in terms of the guarantee the province had to provide. Apart from the need to obtain cabinet approval, local authorities were independent of provincial direction in the modernization of their utilities.

In general terms, therefore, the Social Credit government from 1935 to 1939 was not disposed to interfere with the autonomy and decisions of local governments. The principle of specialist, *ad hoc* boards and commissions, inherited from the UFA administration, was maintained. During this period, however, the tax structure of the province came increasingly to fall on urban institutions and urban dwellers. There was also a tightening up of local authority administration.

Aberhart moved quickly to impose a series of taxes on predominantly urban phenomena, while limiting the rate of interest which local authorities were obliged to pay on their debts. Under the 1936 Retail Sales Tax Act a 2 percent sales tax was imposed on retailers. A fuel oil tax of 11 cents a gallon was imposed in the same year, as was a $50 tax on each grain elevator operated by a company "which stores or distributes grain."[35] Similarly every investment company transacting business in Alberta had to pay one-quarter percent on the gross receipts of the company on its Albertan business. There were maximum tax amounts set for such companies depending upon the size of their paid-up capital.[36] Under the Municipal Securities Interest Act, 1936, the interest payable on bonds or debentures "issued for the purpose of securing the repayment of any monies borrowed by a municipality" was to be limited to 3 percent per annum.[37] Thus the banks and other lenders were not to be allowed to use the financial difficulties of local authorities to charge exorbitant interest.

To further support provincial revenues, the 1936 Social Services Tax Act was imposed. This Act used the equalized assessments of urban and rural municipalities as the basis of imposing a three mills levy, payable to the General Revenue Fund of the province through the local authority. Rural local authorities used their land assessments while cities and towns could choose whether to levy on rateable land only or against all the property in the municipality, retaining anything in excess of the three mills required by the General Revenue Fund for their own costs on social services. A Bureau of Relief and Public Welfare was established by separate Act in the same year which, typical of the mode of administration of the time, set up a commissioner and bureau specifically outside the routine of departmental administration. Its main purpose was to handle the politically sensitive matter of municipal responsibility for relief to its own citizenry, versus providing for the transient indigent for whom no municipality could be held responsible.

The legislative program of 1937-39 was as thoroughly oriented towards the cities as was the UFA 1922-24 program towards agriculture. A Debt Adjustment Board, complete with a clerk to administer it, oil refining and price determination legislation, the Provincial Guaranteed Securities Interest Act (which cut by half the interest payable on securities guaranteed by the province), and corporation income tax, were typical measures. Three Acts passed between 1937 and 1939 are of particular interest however. An amendment to the Town Planning Act in 1937 was aimed specifically at controlling land subdivision.[38] Any subdivision plan containing more than ten lots for sale could not be registered with the Land Titles Office until the owner obtained an order from the provincial board authorizing its registration. Before such authorization was given, the owner had to satisfy the board "that such land will be or may reasonably be expected to be required for building purposes within a reasonable period of time . . . " (Section 43(7)). The board was empowered to require such evidence as it deemed proper. The legislation was aimed directly at the preparations being made for speculative, large-scale control of land. It did not limit subdivision needed for building immediately and hence introduce an element of board control over expansion, but it did control speculative subdivision which would inevitably have had an influence in determining the future of expansion. It is difficult to know if the Act was intended to control unwarranted subdivision because such subdivision tended to predetermine land use in the expansion of the city, or whether the rise in land prices which were a consequence of planning was found objectionable.[39] Both factors could have been the interest of the legislation. The provision remained until it was relaxed in 1945 to cope with the needs of post-war reconstruction.

The second Act, the 1936 version of the 1925 Industries Assessment Act discussed in the previous chapter, kept the 1925 provisions almost intact, but raised from 10 percent to 25 percent of the actual value of improvements as the figure below which the fixed assessment could not be set.

This legislation might be seen as the start of the process that guaranteed the industrialization of certain, select localities in the province and provided further inter-provincial incentives to attract industry across Canada. However, this was hardly the case. The McNally Commission found that the fixed assessment principle provided through any legislation had been most sparingly used by the two metropolitan cities up to 1956.[40] The only notable instances were two in Calgary, i.e. an agreement with the CPR over the Ogden Shops and the Palliser Hotel, and one in Edmonton, i.e. an early agreement with Canada Packers and with the CNR concerning the MacDonald Hotel. The commissioners considered "The record of the cities is thus very good, despite strong pressures from time to time . . ." The controls in the legislation had certainly proved effective. In general perspective, the Act was typically enabling legislation passed by the provincial government to its cities, towns, and villages without in any way providing for provincial direction of that industry within the province as a whole. It was tantamount to a capitulation on the part of the province to become involved with those aspects of planning that go beyond mere subdivision control, zoning, plans, and the general layout and conditions of any growth a local authority could engender through its own initiatives.

This Act also empowered a municipality to transfer or lease land to any industry with the approval of the Public Utility Commissioners.

Thus, though a local council was not entrusted to settle the price of its land and utilities with an industry, and a province-wide commission was awarded the task, the principle of preferential rates was established. That such preferential rates were likely to have repercussions on the provincial treasury, in the supply of additional capital and guarantees for local debentures, or of increased supply of such utility services, does not appear to have occurred to the legislators in 1937. The pattern was set by this Act for the eventual command of the metropolitan centres over much of the services and finance of the province when prosperous times returned.

The third of this series of critical enactments has more to do with the politics of provincial-federal relations than with urban centres specifically. Much has been written about the conflict between the Social Credit administration and the federal government concerning provincial control of lending institutions, and the matter will not be elaborated needlessly here. However, The Treasury Branches Act, 1938, has some interesting features.[41] This Act established the Treasury Branches, still so typical of the towns and cities of Alberta. The legal ruse that facilitated this step was taken from the same principle as enabled the dominion government, in 1935 under the Dominion Housing Act, and again in 1938 under the first National Housing Act, to circumvent the rights of the provinces over housing. The sacred right to contract with whomsoever one pleased, and having so contracted to act as the other party required in terms of that contract, was used in Alberta to circumvent the powers of lending institutions and the constitutionally entrenched right of the federal government over financial matters.

The Treasury Branches Act defined a "depositor" as a person who entered into a contract with the Provincial Treasurer of Alberta providing for the making of deposits in a Treasury Branch. Each contract had to provide for either the payment of interest, if any, as may be agreed to between the contracting parties, or the transfer of a portion of a deposit "used in the purchase of specified goods from merchants who have entered into contracts with the minister . . . " (Section 6(3)(b)). So long as merchants, who were defined as any person, firm, or corporation engaged in the business of the sale of any goods, wares, or merchandise to the consumer, contracted with the minister they could use the Treasury Branches pretty well as a commercial bank. At the same time, using the prerogative of a minister of state under proper authority, the minister could "invest any deposits received under the provisions of this Act in such securities as he may prescribe . . . " (Section 6(4)). An amendment in 1940 further empowered the minister to lend any deposits "to persons, firms or corporations . . . "[42] In consequence, therefore, the Provincial Treasurer was empowered to act largely with the same influence on borrowers of money as lending institutions possessed. The local authorities of the province were empowered also to enter into contracts as depositors in the same way as anyone else. The provincial government was therefore coming to control a significant amount of the finances of the province.

Though the finances of the province were limited throughout the depression, the essential *modus operandi* was established for the better years to come. In terms of urban concentration, the critical feature of Social Credit policy was the autonomy afforded local government, in almost every direction, to man its own ship and make its own decisions regulated largely by *ad hoc* boards separated formally from the daily routine of governmental, departmental administration. When powerful economic development recurred in Alberta, it did so within this already established framework of municipal initiative.

The Decentralization of Decision

To make Social Credit philosophy a reality, the provincial government had to adopt such measures as would bring the lending institutions under its control. Aberhart had been unable to act effectively through 1936 in this direction. When faced with what became known as an "insurgency" within his own party, which arose also from feelings of impotence and nonparticipation by members of the Legislature, Aberhart moved to set up a Social Credit Board and a number of commissioners.[43] Besides its financial aspects (the Act set up credit houses for the distribution and transfer of the people's social credit, as well as payment of subsidies to producers and distributors in support of a system of price discounts) the Act decentralized from the cabinet to the board the details of administrative policy.[44] It was a hasty measure to cope with the demands of the "insurgents" within the party, and the cabinet disclaimed responsibility for it. In their mind, it was theoretically proper that a measure in the nature of a bill from the floor of the House should be enacted. On the other hand, the procedure implicit in the legislation — namely, decentralization to an *ad hoc* administrative board in the execution of policy — was not different from what had become common practice in both UFA and Social Credit administrations. It was also to be increasingly used as the complexity of provincial administration increased with rapid urbanization and industrialization. Thus, though it was a useful political means of coping with an "insurgency" within the party, it was only typical of common practice in other areas of provincial administration.

The Board of Public Utilities Commissioners, in particular, was granted enormous powers. The Municipal Affairs Department was concerned largely with the inspection and legal control of municipal finance. As the province stood behind the financial borrowing of cities for utilities, as well as for general development, close links existed between the commissioners and the department, but no administrative unit either singly or concertedly imposed a direction over the decisions of city councils. Within the limits of financial adequacy, the councils had more or less free reign to develop policy and generate initiative.

The bitter confrontation between the provincial and federal governments over the right to control financial institutions, and over other aspects of Social Credit legislation, has tended to obscure the significance of a battery of administrative measures introduced during the war.[45] Urban economic activity increased after 1940, in part due to war production but also from rising agricultural prices. The province's urban population increased by only a little over 7 percent during 1941 to 1946, which hardly compared with the industrial centres of eastern Canada, or with what happened in Alberta after the war. Local authorities which accumulated surpluses, due to restriction on spending within their jurisdiction, were empowered to invest it in war bonds.

After seeking unsuccessfully to establish an Alberta Bank

in 1940, the Legislature next enacted The Building Associations Act.[46] Its purpose was to finance the construction of houses costing less than $3,500 inclusive of land by private associations of three or more people, recognized as having most of the powers of a company, including limited liability. Typically, the Act established the Building Association Advisory Board, which reported in turn to the Minister of Trade and Industry. All associations formed under the Act were first approved by the minister before being registered by the Registrar of Joint Stock Companies. A 5 percent limit was imposed on the rate of interest allowed to be paid on preference shares, debentures could be issued at 3 percent, and the interest chargeable to a borrower or purchaser of a house could not exceed 4 percent, with a 20 year limit and 20 percent of the cost of the building had to be put down (Section 25). It was an attempt to establish a provincial type of Housing Act by individuals "with the general object of promoting the better housing of the people of the Province" (Section 4). The Provincial Treasurer was empowered to guarantee on behalf of the province the due payment of principal sum with interest on any debentures provided that, among several other clauses, "the association employs Alberta labour exclusively and Alberta materials were suitable in all construction of housing properties" (Section 23). It is understandable why the legislation was promoted by Trade and Industry, but it constitutes the first attempt in Alberta of the governmental stimulation of residential building.[47] According to the McNally Report (Chapter 4, p. 23) by 1956 only 25 to 30 houses in Calgary and a very few in Edmonton had been built under the Act. The province had not guaranteed any debentures.

In 1945, however, the provincial government passed the full-blown, province-wide "Alberta Housing Association Act".[48] We have not attempted to examine the relevant official argument surrounding the introduction of this legislation, but it may be recalled that in August, 1944, the federal Minister of Finance introduced the 1944 National Housing Act (NHA) placing its provisions directly under The National Housing Administration of the Department of Finance in Ottawa, and which, in the following year, led to the creation of the Central Mortgage and Housing Corporation (CMHC). The 1944 NHA also exposed more clearly than ever before the fundamental political issues surrounding the financing by lending institutions of the NHA relative to the possibility of using the provincial government and their local authorities.[49]

Viewed in the context of what the federal government was virtually ramming through in Ottawa, the Alberta Housing Association of 1945 has obvious significance. The Alberta legislation was a final attempt to apply the very essence of the economic (as distinct from financial) qualities of Social Credit philosophy, namely, that publicly controlled wealth should be used for the advantage of citizens without them having to be bound to private lending institutions on matters of important public concern. It is also significant that the Act though passed by the Legislature, was never put into effect. The Act remains on the Statute Books but was not brought forward into the 1970 *Revised Statutes* where it is denoted as "omitted but not repealed."[50]

Under the legislation, the Minister of Municipal Affairs and such cities, towns, villages, and municipal districts as voluntarily took up shares, were, as shareholders in the association, constituted a body corporate and politic with perpetual succession and a common seal (Section 3(1)). The association was not deemed "to be an agency or emanation of the Crown", and could sue and be sued in courts as could any other corporation (Section 3(2)). In this manner the provincial government attempted through law to make the association the equivalent of any finance companies which might seek approval from the federal Minister of Finance to use the provisions of the NHA. Among the powers of the association was one "to apply to the Minister of Finance of Canada for approval of the association as a lending institution under the terms of the Nation Housing Act, 1944" (Section 6(h)).

This, however, was far from being its sole purpose. The Act resembles in many ways the Municipal Financing Corporation legislation of 1956. It was the first of a number of Acts involving local authorities and the provincial government in shareholding capacities in *ad hoc* corporations to service the needs of urban centres. Each was an elaboration of the earlier principles of decentralized administration, i.e., outside of the formal departmental administration, but powerfully linked to it through the department's officers as responsible members directing the affairs of the *ad hoc* organ of administration.

The association was awarded capital stock of $2 million, divided into 20,000 shares of $100 each. The shares were allotted for cash with no liability on the shareholders for debts, were non-profit bearing, and were non-transferable except as the statute provided. Each share entitled its holder to one vote in the affairs of the association. The Provincial Treasurer, on behalf of the province, subscribed to 5,000 shares, or 25 percent of the total shares issued, which were to be held by the Minister of Municipal Affairs, thus making him the principal shareholder of the association. Debentures worth $500,000 were to be issued on behalf of the province through the Treasury Branches and held in the minister's name. Cities, towns, villages, and municipal districts, collectively known as "municipalities" under the Act, could, at their discretion and without submitting to the ratepayers, apply for "not less than the number of shares the par value of which is an amount equal to one dollar for each resident of the municipality" as shown in the 1941 census (Section 8(a)). The number of shares was rounded off upwards to the nearest 500 residents. Municipalities could also apply for debentures and pay for them from revenues or their sinking funds. The shareholding municipality then had a right to appoint a voting member to shareholders' meetings, casting the number of votes for which the municipality had shares.

The board of directors of the association consisted of not

less than five nor more than eleven directors appointed in the following way: the Lieutenant-Governor in Council on behalf of the province could appoint not more than six; Calgary and Edmonton city councils, if they became shareholders, could appoint one each, cities other than Calgary and Edmonton could jointly appoint one director; towns and villages could jointly appoint one director; and the municipal districts could jointly appoint one director. The chairman was the Minister of Municipal Affairs.

The powers ascribed to the association were varied. It could "carry on the business of lending money upon the security of mortgages upon real estate in the Province for the purpose of assisting in the erection of dwelling houses" (Section 6(a)); it could accept other securities than mortgages; and it could purchase land and property, enter into arrangements with any governments or authorities, and raise money by debentures up to a value of $2 million bearing interest at 3 1/2 percent over 20 years. Municipalities were to be given a specific time to take up their shares and buy debentures, after which the books of the association "shall be closed for the purpose of allocating for loans in the municipalities which are then shareholders the moneys available for loans from shares and debentures subscribed for up to that time" (Section 15(1)).

The allocation of resources among the municipal shareholders was regulated in terms of the proportion of their share and debenture contributions, plus a proportionate share of the province's financial contribution and of any debentures taken up by citizens or companies within the municipality concerned. In other words, those who contributed most received most. Any additional funds, such as those obtainable from the federal government under NHA provisions, were to be apportioned among housing applicants within the municipalities at the discretion of the directors. The association could not make any loan on a dwelling in excess of $5,000, the interest rate could not exceed 4 1/2 percent, and the value of the dwelling to be assisted by the association had to be less than $7,500.

This ingenious legislation, which was more comprehensive than the above outline suggests, related very closely the interests of local and provincial governments to the citizenry seeking low cost housing. It was typically a measure that related the collective funds of the community to the needs for housing the citizenry at rates of interest the latter could afford. It used the principles of company organization for a public service. It also continued the tradition of local autonomy, as the discretion over joining was left to the municipality, and the rights of its citizens to benefit by way of housing finance was roughly in proportion to the amount of capital subscribed by that municipality. It did not interfere, therefore, with the equal terms on which municipalities were competing for growth, though the directors had certain discretionary powers to favour municipalities hard-pressed for housing through surplus funds made available to their citizens.

Concurrently with the introduction of the Alberta Housing Association Act, the provincial Legislature passed the National Housing Loans Act (Alberta).[51] This was the enabling act covering the activities of the federal 1944 NHA in Alberta. The provincial government, therefore, did not exclude the application of the NHA in preference to its own association, and clearly hoped to use the association as the instrument of applying NHA funds in Alberta. That the Alberta Housing Association Act was never enforced seems significant in the face of the federal government's determination in 1944 to have the private lending institutions finance mortgages across Canada. Though greater detail than we have is necessary to prove the point, it would appear that the 1945 Alberta Act marks the point where the provincial government finally ceded to the demands of Ottawa on the principle of local authority control over the financing of residential urban construction. We also note that 1945 was the time when NHA mortgage financing started to pick up rapidly in Alberta.[52]

As early as 1941, some six years before the Leduc oil discovery, the provincial government, through the Oil and Gas Fields Public Service Utilities Act, provided the Lieutenant-Governor in Council the right to grant to one or more corporations an exclusive right to construct, maintain, and operate natural gas or oil plants.[53] Legislation governing pipe lines, water, gas, electricity, and telephone company operations had been in force for several years. The new legislation was specific to the activities of the oil industry. The Board of Public Utilities Commissioners had administrative responsibility for the Act, with the cabinet retaining the right to grant the exclusive facility in the first instance.

In 1944 the administrative control of oil and natural gas was transferred to a special Natural Gas Utilities Board consisting of two members.[54] The chairman of the new board was to be the Chairman of the Public Utilities Commissioners, and the second member the Chairman of the Petroleum and Natural Gas Conservation Board. The reason for this concentration of administrative authority into the hands of two powerfully placed civil servants has not been determined, but the Act was streamlining the decision-making process over vital urban and provincial interests in a way that was hardly within the tradition of the province, yet preserved the principle of administration outside the political party structure.

Also in 1944, by means of The Power Commission Act, the provincial government set up a commission of not more than three members appointed by the Lieutenant-Governor in Council, and with rights to appoint its own technical staff, to examine and investigate water facilities for hydro-electricity, the present distribution of electricity, and other relevant matters.[55] The commission reported its findings directly to the cabinet. The Act was very specific about the membership of the commission, which could carry on with less than three members. The commission was further empowered, at the discretion of the cabinet, to use and develop any water power, apply to the appropriate authority to divert and use water, to purchase property on which water was to be stored, and to construct dams, etc., for electricity generating purposes. It could also contract with any municipality over the supply of electricity, by the commission or otherwise. It was the start of a province-wide system of electrical reticulation and generation from which both rural and urban interests were to benefit. Private electrical interests, though entitled to compensation if taken over, had to negotiate with the commission over their mutual affairs and were placed in a competitive relation to a public authority. Under Section 9, any person or company "manufacturing or distributing power in Alberta" who refused or neglected to obey an order of the board could have its affairs taken over by the board.

In 1945, also, the provincial government by statute called The Provincial Debt Reorganization Act (Chapter 1) undertook a total reorganization of the province's public debt. It also repaid outstanding interest in full, and defaulted bonds were redeemed. Almost the whole debt was refunded at an average coupon rate of 3.4 percent as against the 5 percent of 1936 when the province was obliged on default to cut interest rates in half. In response to this provincial measure the federal government paid retroactive subsidies covering the 1937-46 period. The measure cost the provincial treasury some $11 million, but Alberta was again standing on its feet with its debts paid.[56] It is significant that this step was taken two years before the Leduc oil discovery. It was not this discovery, and the royalties it brought in, that enabled Alberta to achieve it.

Thus, by 1946 the provincial government had honoured its debts. Administratively it had passed through the phase of influencing urban centres through highways and public works, to that of control over the major financial resources, the growing petroleum industry, and the generation of electrical power.[57] Though such authority was centralized in the provincial cabinet it was decentralized administratively to an array of *ad hoc* boards. Behind these boards and commissions, and influencing them through a variety of powers and financial measures, was the cabinet or a minister. Many appeals from aggrieved persons or local authorities ended at the board level rather than at the level of the party in power. The manoeuvres and compromises of business, the local affairs of urban politics, and the relations of business, local authorities, and the various boards were handled below the party level. The cabinet ministers were indirectly involved in their outcome and were able to sit back to regulate by amendment, when necessary, the powers enacted and regulations approved that governed local activities.

An item of major provincial concern at this time, and which took a more powerful turn after Leduc in 1947, was a way of ensuring that all local authorities paid a fair share of their running costs and, conversely, after 1947, that they were in turn paid on a fair basis, the revenues received by the province. The first of these involved equalized assessments and the second the mode of making provincial grants to local authorities. In practice many of the provincial grants came to be based on equalized assessments, so the two aspects of the same problem were linked. Local authorities were left free to fix the mill rate each year to be charged against local property to raise the revenue they required. The equalized assessments came to be the standard measure whereby the province's contributions to local revenues would be determined. A Royal Commission reporting in 1948, recommended that the province institute a number of assessors, under the control of a director, to perform the property assessing function in all municipalities except the cities, which were to be left to use locally appointed assessors if they wished. This was implemented on a voluntary basis in 1949 and an incentive to accept it was added in the form of the province paying 25 percent of assessing costs. To ensure that assessment was as equal across the province as could humanly be achieved, provincial and city assessors met from time to time to check their decisions, and an elaborate appeal procedure was instituted.

Provincial-municipal grants will be discussed in the following section for they became particularly important when oil royalities to the province, after Leduc in 1947, were to be distributed to local authorities by a means that could be identified as being "fair and equal." This was the setting within which the rapid urbanization process took place. The system of administration introduced between 1935 and 1947 brought very rapid results thereafter.

Metropolitan Pre-eminence, 1945-1950

Calgary and Edmonton had not experienced the industrial boom during the Second World War that was typical of Ontario's manufacturing centres. MacGregor has recorded the pathetic state of Edmonton, with 11,000 of its 28,000 dwellings built before 1920, few new office buildings, and only 70 miles of its 400 miles of roads sealed.[58] The Mayor had managed to attract some industry during the war and a greater diversity was apparent.[59] It had benefited from the construction of the Alaska Highway and from large numbers of aircraft using its services. Calgary too had diversified its industry and benefited from pilot training schemes. Its population rose by about 13,000, to 100,000, between 1941 and 1946.

The return of ex-servicemen coupled with the new expectations of peace, led to the recognition of overcrowding in these cities. The Town Planning Act was amended to raise from 10 to 50 lots the special approval required for residential subdivisions not required immediately for house construction. A special Act was passed permitting the provincial government and Edmonton City Council, who together had come to "realize that the serious housing shortage . . . required immediate measures to be taken to provide emergency living accommodation . . . for returned veterans . . .", to purchase buildings from a firm known as C.C.C. Construction situated in Dawson Creek, British Columbia. This was a War Assets

Corporation, a Dominion Crown Company. It was intended to transport them to Edmonton as the "impossibility of obtaining at the present time certain materials" made this necessary. To do this the Act provided for the suspension of the Town Planning Act, city zoning and building by-laws, and the ordinary inspection procedures of the local authority.

At the federal level, the Central Mortgage and Housing Corporation (CMHC) was established in 1945 and a regional office was opened in Alberta in 1946. The incidence of loans made in Alberta during the first six months of 1945 and 1946 respectively was 116 and 425, involving $521,000 and $1,925,000 respectively.[60] The federal provisions were coming to be accepted in Alberta some 10 years after Social Credit came to power and under the difficult circumstances following from the war.

At a province-wide level in 1945, the provincial government enacted a bill providing for a Department of Economic Affairs with its own minister.[61] The minister was charged with encouraging "orderly economic, cultural and social development for the betterment of the people of the Province in accordance with the principles and requirements of a democracy . . . " (Section 6). The Act was in part a response to veteran rehabilitation, but it was also to encourage research into the economic potential of the province. In 1948, for this purpose, an Economic Research Bureau was also established.

The Alberta Industrial Corporation Act was passed in 1946 to promote the industrial incentives provided for a decade earlier.[62] This followed the same administrative pattern as the Alberta Housing Association Act of 1945; it was a body corporate, not to be deemed an agency or emanation of the Crown, etc. The corporation had wide powers, including lending "to any person, firm or corporation carrying on or proposing to carry on in the Province of Alberta, any manufacturing, processing or industrial business of any nature whatsoever . . . " (Section 5(a)). The corporation could also enter into business with an industrial company. It was regulated by the cabinet having to approve any loan made, and the Provincial Treasurer provided $100,000 initially under terms agreed to by the cabinet. The corporation could also issue debentures up to a total of $5 million. The councils of cities, towns, villages, municipal districts, school divisions and school districts could by by-law invest surplus funds in the corporation (Section 9). The board of directors had from three to five members nominated by the Lieutenant-Governor in Council. It could establish branches and agencies, and surplus funds were to be returned to the General Revenue Fund.

The value of building permits issued in Calgary in 1940 was $2.7 million, in 1945 it was $7.3 million and by 1950 it reached $25.9 million. This rate of increase continued. In 1955 it reached $58.9 million and a record of $101.6 million was reached in 1958.[63] This figure was exceeded again only in 1965 and in the subsequent years. Edmonton's building permits jumped from $15 million in 1946 to $46.5 million in 1950 and showed spectacular growth thereafter.

The Turner Valley Oilfield, some 24 miles south-west of Calgary, had been discovered in 1914. After 1940 an expansion of oil search activity took place all round Calgary. Then the Leduc strike some 17 miles south-west of Edmonton, in February, 1947, sealed the inevitable pre-eminence of these two cities. Even by 1940 there was little doubt about their importance, as they had epitomized the concentration of population and facilities in Alberta for over half a century. The oil discoveries so close to them made the likelihood of other urban competitors, based on different resources and activities, small beyond question.

By 1947 the provincial government had become increasingly concerned over the administration of municipal-provincial affairs. Between 1947 and 1954 three important commissions dealing with boundaries and developmental processes of local authorities were set up. In 1947 Mr. J.W. Judge, Deputy Minister of Municipal Affairs, was made a Royal Commissioner to investigate provincial-municipal relations.[64] One of his recommendations was the setting up of a further commission to determine co-terminous boundaries for municipal districts and school divisions.[65] In 1954 the five-man Royal Commission on the Metropolitan Development of Calgary and Edmonton, under Dr. G.F. McNally as chairman, was appointed. This commission has had a lasting and almost daily effect on the affairs of the metropolitan centres and its report will be discussed more fully in a later section. At this point it is convenient to describe further the series of provincial enactments that stimulated, regulated, and espoused the form of growth which local authorities, and particularly the metropolitan centres, came to enjoy.

Two years after the end of the Second World War the provincial Legislature passed the Real Estate Agents' Licencing Act, which restricted dealings in real estate to licenced persons and companies. Legislation governing the commission chargeable on real estate transactions had been introduced as early as 1906, and an Act in 1929 had led to the licencing of agents. The 1947 legislation was thorough and strict in its terms and has since formed the basis of all real estate business in the province. Also, the Industrial Assessment Amendment Act 1947, asserted that the approval of the Minister of Municipal Affairs was essential to any agreement made between a council and an industry, and that it had to be obtained prior to the by-law being submitted to the ratepayers. The amendment was back-dated to January 1, 1946.[66]

The year 1948 was one of severe strain for the province. Leduc had blown out in 1947, the metropolitan centres were described by the newspapers as "bursting at the seams," and the carefully prepared administrative instruments of the previous 12 years were being severely tested.

The provincial government moved to set up two new departments, i.e. the Department of Lands and Forests, and the Department of Mines. It is significant that in Alberta the

Department of Trade and Industry was set up well over a decade ahead of Lands and Forests and the Department of Economic Affairs preceded Mines by three years. The latter was likely to have been a consequence of the Leduc discovery. The Town Planning Act was transferred back to the Department of Municipal Affairs from Public Works that year and the Life Insurance Company Act of Alberta was also brought into being.[67] This Act provided for the Lieutenant-Governor in Council to appoint five directors. Its administrative powers resembled those of the Alberta Housing Association in that perpetual succession was provided for and it was not an emanation of the Crown, etc. It also provided for policy holders with a $1,000 policy or more to vote at general meetings and to elect a policy holders' director to the board. As Life Insurance was at that time the principal lending institution for mortgages, its benefits to the cities were assured.

The dilemma confronting the provincial government, and which led to the Judge Royal Commission, was on what basis provincial revenues should be used in support of local authority services. The commissioner noted:

> The burden of Taxation on real property is becoming onerous and relief is being sought through contributions from the Provincial Government. The rising cost of education, administration, public works etc. is alarming to the local authorities and it is contended the Provincial Government with its wider tax base can levy taxes not available to the municipalities. The municipalities are generally not in favour of being granted the right to levy new taxes.[68]

A municipal right to levy a local sales tax was particularly objectionable because, unless it was province-wide, it would only drive out local business. The commission held the view "that the responsibility of the municipality should be limited as little as possible."[69] The devolvement of responsibility on local authorities for the provision of services, and the provision of a tax base which recognized such responsibility, was, to the commission, a desirable end in itself.

The commissioner remarked:

> Local government and an equitable tax structure are ends in themselves. The arrangements between the Province and local governments should be such as to support these ends.
>
> The Commission therefore visualizes a situation in which the area of responsibility, that is, the specific services to be provided by the municipality, is legally defined and prescribed . . . but . . . rather than hold the municipality responsible for raising all the revenue necessary to support these services, it should receive revenues collected by the Province through a generally equitable tax system.[70]

This distribution from a provincial pool of revenue to local authorities to meet the services the people of Alberta expected, was to become increasingly prominent in the years ahead. In 1948 the justification was seen in terms of financial equity between local authorities and tax bases to pay for services; but the relation of each municipality to its peers was not to be disturbed. The commissioner remarked in emphatic print:

> Any system of grants must be devised to provide something less than total financial support of municipalities; but the aggregate amount received by each municipality should leave all municipalities in a comparable position (having in mind local needs and ability to raise revenue out of the sources remaining) to raise the necessary balance of revenue.[71]

The theory of fair and equal treatment for all local authorities was to remain a cardinal premise.

Following the report of the Royal Commission on Taxation the provincial government enacted the Alberta Corporation Income Tax Act.[72] This lengthy legislation reviewed the whole corporation taxation procedure and structure. Corporations already interested in Alberta's oil and gas potential, and those likely to follow with secondary activities, knew just where they stood with regard to taxation. Alberta's public debt had been corrected in 1945; the province clearly held vast natural resources and the structure of taxation gave organized private enterprise clearly defined terms of reference for the separation of taxation from profits, and indicated an acceptable mode of taxation avoidance procedures.

The administrative test came, not unexpectedly but significantly for this study, in the provisions of the Town Planning Act.[73] Private investment had identified Calgary and Edmonton, both through oil and gas potential and through prospects of capital gain on land development, as the place to be. The surge of speculative investment, subdivision, and high expectations which followed forced the provincial government in 1948 to transfer extraordinary powers to the Minister of Municipal Affairs and the Director of Town Planning. Edmonton particularly had trouble in controlling the plans of private investment managers.

The amendment attempted to give the provincial planning administration the means of imposing by temporary and drastic measures, control over subdivision while city planning administrations were preparing zoning by-laws, plans, and other official means of getting their own houses in order. Developers were purchasing land and proposing projects in areas beyond that already zoned and regulated. Local authority boundaries meant little. The minister was awarded power to make regulations covering zoning, etc., and to order their application to particular places.[74] The Director of Town Planning was empowered to prepare and sign what was called a "Zoning Caveat," which "set out the zones or districts into which any such proposed subdivision is divided and the regulations made by the Minister applicable thereto." The Provincial Planning Advisory Board was not formally brought into the picture.[75] The professional competence of the director and the authority of the minister were adequate. The owner of the proposed subdivision, or his agent, had to sign the zoning caveat before a witness who was obliged to swear an affidavit of execution that was to be attached to the caveat (Section 29(a)(3)). This in turn had to be lodged with the Land Titles Office at the time of registering the subdivision plan. It was an offence not to comply with this procedure. It was also an offence for any lot purchaser within the subdivision to act contratry to the provisions of the caveat.

The stringency of these measures (the executive use of the minister, the director, and the Titles Office, and the transfer of local authority responsibility to the provincial administration) illustrates how seriously the threat to orderly urban development was felt to be. It also illustrates the reserve power of the provincial administration when needed, though it is important to note that these measures required special amendment to the Town Planning Act to make them effective. The 1948 legislation also provided for the city council to take over again the powers of control devolved upon the province, whereupon "the zoning regulations and the zoning caveat shall cease to have any force and effect" (Section 29 (e)(1)).

A further provision of the 1948 amendment required that in cases where "an unsubdivided parcel of land is occupied by two or more occupiers of separate premises thereon," a plan of subdivision must be prepared and registered (Section 35(a)(1)). The erection of dwellings on communally owned land, so to speak, was to be brought under proper control and under the terms of individual title!

Following these emergency measures, in 1949 the City of Edmonton initiated the Bland, Spence-Sales Study. This study examined the failure of the then-current planning mechanisms. Its recommendations greatly influenced the 1950 amendments to the Planning Act.[76]

It was a time of immense emphasis on the outward development of suburban residential land in all of Canada. Edmonton in particular, but Calgary also, had for decades emphasized the expansion of the city outwards from the centre. The Edmonton council's preference for zoning by-laws and a street map instead of an official town plan in 1929 had led to compromising its control of planning. By 1933 Edmonton council had dispensed with the services of the secretary of its planning commission and reduced its budget to $500.[77] At the provincial level, the depression had led to the demise of the newly established Provincial Planning Branch of the Department of Municipal Affairs and it was not easily resuscitated when finances allowed. Yet the depression was precisely the time when urban centres were reorganizing their affairs through land transfers, consolidation, and volunteer planning commissions.

Edmonton's Zoning Appeal Board was inundated with

appeals in the mid-1930s. By 1936 the council was trying to cope with non-conforming businesses in residential areas. Edmund Dale comments:

> To deny the promoters of these business concerns the privilege of continuing or establishing in these areas was, the Council feared, to postpone Edmonton's development at a time when it should be encouraged . . . and yet, to acede to all the requests would be to defeat the purpose of the By-Law. Invariably the Council's action achieved the latter effect."[78]

Throughout the war years Edmonton council was rearranging the residential lots still available for development by widening small frontaged lots and standardizing others. There was persistent fringe development beyond the jurisdiction of the city council. Private developers purchased land adjacent to the city boundary, subdivided it, and then pressed to have the subdivision incorporated into the city after residential and industrial sites had been sold, and this added to the council's concern over the control of its hinterland. These developers escaped municipal taxation and defeated subdivision controls. Edmonton eventually took steps to cope with fringe development and, with the help of the provincial government, the Regional Planning Board was set up in 1950. But the extent of Edmonton's difficulties can be judged from the fact that the council was obliged to amend its 1933 zoning by-law six times in 1946, thrice in 1947, seven times in 1948 and 19 times in 1949.[79] Private investment was beginning to dominate the city. The feeling "that decisions about major matters affecting the plan of the city were taken without the knowledge of the Commission," led to its chairman's resignation and to the Edmonton Local Council of Women again petitioning the council,[80] this time, to establish a Department of Town Planning with competent professional direction.

Professors Bland and Spence-Sales of McGill University identified a major difficulty as being the unwillingness of Edmonton council to plan the city within the full provisions of the 1929 Planning Act. An "official town plan" had not been formulated, nor had any scheme. Interim development control was the only means available to cope with the existing situation.[81] Following receipt of the report in 1949 the Edmonton council made representations to the provincial government for amendments to the Planning Act to permit it to implement the recommendations of the report. As had happened so often in the past, Edmonton's initiative led to important changes in provincial legislation affecting the province's urban areas.

The amendments, *inter alia,* intended to bring the rather autocratic measures of 1948 into more democratic and local focus. It provided for a local authority, "upon the passage of a resolution providing for the preparation of a general plan," to advise the minister of the area to which it was to apply and request the minister to make "an interim development order."[82] This order suspended the operation of any existing zoning by-law and authorized "the local or rural authority to exercise control over such development as may take place within the described area prior to the coming into effect of the general plan" (Section 12(a)(2)). The interim development order had to prescribe the powers to be exercised by the local authority, prescribe the manner in which the order was to be administered with respect to the control of interim development, and to prescribe the provisions for appeal to the provincial board "against any decision of the local or rural authority" (Section 12(a)(3)).

The 1950 amendment was a fundamental reversal of the 1948 policy, though the 1948 provision was not repealed. It is worth analysis for several reasons, not the least of which is that the principle of interim development, enunciated first in 1950, was being used in certain areas by the City of Calgary in 1971. While it may be claimed that the 1948 measures were temporary, i.e., effective only while the local authority was getting its own house in order, and that the emergency nature of the situation made it necessary to give the Director of Town Planning and the minister the powers it conferred, the 1950 amendment in turn apparently gave the local authority unusual power to negotiate with developers over plans to subdivide or plan an area. While the minister in making an interim development order was required to prescribe the powers of the local authority and the manner in which the order was to be administered — thereby imposing limits to the actions, and giving decorum to the negotiations of the local authority — the new procedure nevertheless superseded the principle implicit in zoning by-laws. The principle of zoning was to set out in advance by public notice, for all to see and abide by, the standards applicable to and the uses to which a given portion of the city was to be subject. Thus a developer knew in advance what he might or might not do. If he wished to exceed or differ from the standards or uses prescribed, he had formally to request an amendment to the zoning by-law. The council was in turn obliged to take formal measures in approving or disapproving the request. The negotiations implicit in an interim development order by-passed almost the entire formality and the public nature of zoning by-law principles. Though the minister's order could require the publication of regulations, etc., the publication had by its very nature to be a *post hoc* situation, i.e., after the negotiation on the development proposals were concluded, or at least after some likelihood of agreement was in sight. This contrasted with the "before the situation" nature of zoning by-law administration. An interim development order provided the city authorities with much greater flexibility in their control over urban development than did zoning techniques.[83] [It would be a useful research exercise to determine the incidence and nature of any appeals made to the provincial board under this legislation.]

It is important to remember that interim development orders were a technique to cope with emerging, emergency, and unplanned situations. They were not considered a standard and enduring form of administration, and the situations in which it was foreseen that they would most likely be applied were those in the rapidly expanding metropolitan centres. Where growth was smaller in scale and less intense the formal zoning mechanisms would be adequate. It is ironic, therefore, that the flexibility in handling rapid growth afforded a local authority by an interim order offered precisely the ideal conditions required for attracting *further* growth. Negotiation is more attractive to the management of privately organized capital in its problems of location than conforming to previously prescribed standards or engaging in a public ritual over by-law amendment, and the metropolitan centres had a clear advantage over other smaller and less-rapidly growing urban centres. If the alternative approach to urban planning problems had been used — that of prescribing a freeze on further development until the local authority's house had been put in order and development could continue in an orderly fashion — the smaller cities might have benefited accordingly.

The 1950 amendments also made major revisions to the titles and concepts of administrative units in the planning process. It emphasized particularly the regional attribute of urban planning. The Act was renamed The Town and Rural Planning Act. It removed the phrases: "official town plan" and substituted "general plan," "town planning commission" was changed to "technical planning board," "Town and Rural Planning Advisory Board" was replaced by "Provincial Planning Advisory Board," "Director of Town Planning" became "Director of Town and Rural Planning," and "town plan" became merely "plan" and "town planning" became "planning." The 1950 Act, as the above changes show, generalized the concept of planning at the local level, while introducing a clearer and more centralized role for the provincial government. It also greatly enhanced the contribution of technical expertise to the planning process. In particular, the membership of the provincial board was changed to include the Director of Town and Rural Planning as the executive member, and "such representatives of Departments of the Provincial Government concerned with any aspects of urban and rural development within the Province as may be appointed by the Lieutenant-Governor in Council" (Section 15(2)(b)). The Act, therefore, placed administrative officers four-square in control of provincial planning, subject to the authority of the cabinet and the Minister of Municipal Affairs.

By deleting reference to the "Preservation of Natural Beauty" and generalizing the function of the board, Part 1 of the 1950 amended Act gave the Provincial Planning Advisory Board the power of general surveillance of planning in the province. The 1950 Act, in effect, did away with the compromise between the roles of Public Works and Municipal Affairs which had surrounded the 1928 and 1929 versions of the Planning Act. The provincial board's powers, however, remained similar to those of 1929. The new Act did not give it such powers and funds as could lead directly to the preparation of a planning document likely to determine planning at a provincial level of a kind similar to that provided for under a general plan prepared by a municipality. Even in 1971 no such provincial plan was in existence, though the need for it was spoken of freely in several planning offices throughout the province.

At the local level, a municipal council was given a choice of the type of planning instrument it wished to have. With neither type was it empowered to raise money or expropriate land. Under Section 10, the council could appoint "a commission representative of the citizens at large to be known as a Planning Advisory Commission," which advised the council on "general planning matters." Alternatively, under Section 11, by by-law approved by the minister, a board known as a Technical Planning Board could be appointed and have delegated to it such powers "as may be necessary for the purpose, of —

> (a) preparing a general plan or scheme of development and a zoning by-law or any plan or official scheme authorized . . .;
> (b) acting in an advisory capacity in matters pertaining to planning;
> (c) promoting public interest in planning.

Planning engineers, consultants, and other officers could be appointed, and such funds as the council provided could be expended. The Act did not prohibit a local authority from setting up both types of instrument, but apart from delegating to a local authority the powers of its instruments, it did not indicate the way in which they were to be connected.

Upon the recommendation of the provincial board and on a resolution being passed by two or more councils, the Lieutenant-Governor in Council could establish a district planning commission and designate the district planning area of its jurisdiction.[84] The order-in-council setting it up designated "the number of members to be appointed by and to represent each of the municipalities." It also designated "the proportion in which any funds required to meet the expenses of the Commission shall be contributed by the represented municipalities and the Province" (Section 11(b)(3)(a)). The 1950 Act no longer relied upon compromise and the fair bargaining of local authorities with equal membership, but on power made effective through a differential in the influence of member municipalities by the amount of their contribution to its funds. The province was now itself to make a financial contribution. Similarly the new Act provided for "not more than three members representing the Province and appointed by the Provincial Planning Advisory Board" (Section 11(b)(2)(b)). Already the competitive nature of local authority relations over planning had led to direct provincial representation on district planning commissions, and a financial contribution. The McNally Commission was appointed four years later.

The amendments of 1950 are particularly important in illustrating the intrusion of provincial authority, by both funds and membership, into the relations between local authorities when planning, urban development, and growth were at stake. The competition of municipal peers was seriously compromising effective and orderly planning. This has been one of the most critical issues in Albertan urban affairs over the past twenty years. Its nature and consequence will be described and discussed in subsequent chapters.

The powers ascribed to district planning commissions in 1950 were largely advisory to the councils, or to any one council, they served. All powers were discretionary, not obligatory. The commissions could also advise the provincial government. They were empowered to "prepare and recommend to each council represented a general plan and a zoning by-law." Similarly any official scheme of development which was of common concern to member municipalities or to one member could be prepared and recommended. Commissions had power to appoint planners and spend monies provided to them, but although a majority of the members formed a quorum "no business relating to any matter of special concern to a particular municipality shall be transacted at any meeting which is not attended by at least one representative of that municipality" (Section 11 c(2)). The problems inherent in joint municipal membership of planning commissions were well known to the provincial government by 1950. Should any additional municipality wish to join an established commission, then its membership and the membership of municipalities already represented on the commission were to be re-determined by the order-in-council, as were also to be the various financial contributions. In the event of a municipality failing or neglecting to comply with an order in council, the minister, after due publication of intent, could "authorize the Commission to act on behalf of the defaulting municipality" (Section 11(d) and (e)).

The province was starting to bring some pressures to bear on local authorities to ensure their co-operation but, as later events were to show, they proved only partially effective. The absence of a clear-cut directive as to how municipal planning controls were to be linked to those of the district as a whole was major omission. The assumption of the government at the time — following from the support it gave to Edmonton city council in preparing the 1950 planning amendment — was that:

> These Commissions would be set up chiefly in the metropolitan areas where planning for future city development will affect and require the co-operation of the Province and adjacent municipalities.[85]

The cities, therefore, were seen as setting the pace leaving the province and adjacent municipalities to co-operate. There could hardly be a clearer demonstration of the order of priority with which the provincial government was content to live!

The Bland, Spence-Sales study of 1949 had been commissioned partly because surplus development land within Edmonton city had been used up and the towns of Jasper Place and Beverly, and the municipal districts of Stony Plain, Sturgeon, Morinville, and Strathcona hemmed in the city. The study envisaged these surrounding rural municipalities and small urban centres as becoming independent urban centres, rather than being made part of Edmonton itself.[86] But the city was unable at that time to envisage such a process. It only saw as its immediate interest, the necessity for incorporation. Refining and petro-chemical industries had located in the municipal district of Strathcona, to the south-east of the city, because the oil pipe lines converged there and Edmonton already lacked sufficient land for their purposes.

The Mayor of Edmonton, Mr. William Hawrelak, in his evidence to the McNally Commission in October, 1954, stated the problem of the city in these terms:

> A man who works in one of the plants in the Municipal District of Strathcona, may live in Jasper Place, send his children to a school in Jasper Place, do his shopping at an Edmonton store and travel to and from his work by the streets of Edmonton and Beverly. Such a man votes only in Jasper Place. The taxes on his home go to Jasper Place, the taxes on his place of work go to Strathcona, the taxes on the store where he shops go to Edmonton. This is given by way of illustration but the situation is that employees in the plants in the Municipal District of Strathcona establish their homes in Jasper Place, Beverly and Edmonton with the result that the normal incidence of taxation as between business and residential property is thrown seriously out of balance, particularly in Jasper Place and Beverly.[87]

The city of Edmonton envisaged a wide extension of Edmonton's boundaries as the only solution.

By 1950 the city had become aware of a potential shortage of residential land within its boundaries. The city moved in 1951 to acquire the Holt Farm, and then in 1954 to take over River Lot 33, mainly to obtain residential land.[88] Private developers were concerned at the city's purchases of land outside the city limits. It threatened their interests in fringe development. The council was therefore caught in the cross-fire of speculative developers anxious to encourage city boundary expansion by slow, orderly and "appropriate" steps, and the need of the city, as the Mayor envisaged it, to greatly expand its boundaries in the interests of order and a unitary approach to city expansion. The provincial government, by its 1950 Planning Act amendment, saw itself co-operating with adjacent municipalities through the District Planning Board in ameliorating for the city the consequences of the selective investment and speculative thrust of privately organized capital. The city's charter was amended in 1955 whereby the city had to obtain the permission of the Lieutenant-Governor in Council "before acquiring any land situated outside the boundaries of the city or any interest in such land."[89] Real estate interests had achieved action via the provincial Legislature to inhibit the city's attempts to acquire residential land as one means of keeping residential prices down under conditions of limited supply.

Over 1950 and 1951, attention was turned powerfully to local government administration. The County Act of 1950 established the County as a new unit of local government. It was introduced experimentally at first because it involved the deliberate integration of school divisions, municipal governments of various types, and the redrawing of boundaries to make them co-terminous, etc. It was not just an enlargement of rural local government but, as Hanson described it, the setting up of an "omnibus authority," based on the English model.[90] Local citizens were expected to get a better overall view of their local problems, and to proceed thereby to rationalize the interconnectedness of the various items towards which their tax dollar was paid. Higher mill rates charged after 1945, to cover the costs of development and services, had led to an increasing local awareness by the individual of the processes occurring around him.

In response to the financial difficulties of rapidly expanding cities, the Act to Assist Municipalities in Financing Self-Liquidating Projects, 1950 (Chapter 67), was introduced. The principle of direct assistance to municipalities had given the Social Credit administration some difficulty. In the Budget Speech of 1951, Premier Ernest Manning commented:

> The Government's program is predicated on three major premises . . .
> (1) It is essential to the good and welfare of our people and to the progress of our Province generally that municipal and other local governments be assured sufficient financial resources to properly discharge their responsibilities without resorting to oppressive taxation and/or excessive borrowing.
> (2) The costs of local government have increased rapidly during recent years and in many cases have reached a level which cannot be maintained within the framework of their presently available local sources of revenue without inviting serious consequences.
> (3) Increased provincial financial assistance to local governments should not be provided merely to make possible still greater local expenditures but should be used, at least in part, to afford an actual easement in the heavy burden of taxation presently born by ratepayers in Municipalities, Improvement Districts and the Special Areas.[91]

It is clear from these comments, that the Premier envisaged the assistance to local authorities to be transferred, at least in part, to the individual taxpayer. This was conscientiously attempted in the early legislation, but by 1955 had become rather unrealistic. Local government, as such, was from this point on to be the beneficiary, and the taxpayer was to continue to shoulder the burden.

The Act to Assist Municipalities contained the principle of direct loan assistance from the provincial government to municipalities, with no board mandatorily placed between them in respect of the loans.[92] Significantly, its administrative minister was not the Minister of Municipal Affairs, but the Provincial Treasurer. Self-liquidating projects were those which, when completed, would on a conservative basis of estimate "increase the annual net revenue of the municipality either by reduction in the annual operating and maintenance charges . . . or by increase of revenues by persons using the services of . . . the project sufficient to pay the annual charges for interest on and amortization of the loan to be made by the Minister" (Section 2(c)). Municipal water works, gas plants, and electricity systems, were envisaged as the most likely areas of support, but any self-liquidating project could be proposed. With the approval of cabinet, the minister could enter into an agreement with any municipality or public board or commission over a loan or loans.

The onus was on the municipality to submit detailed financial estimates, to demonstrate to the minister's satisfaction the self-liquidating nature of the project, and to show that the project was "necessary or advisable in the public interest" (Section 3(2)(b)). The minister could call on the Public Utilities Commissioners for an opinion and recommendation. The interest rate was to be 2 percent and the amortization period to be fixed by the cabinet, but it was not to exceed the estimated useful life of the project. The municipality was expected to secure the loan by debenture or other security, or by first mortgage.

The aggregate of loans to be made by the minister was limited to $5 million, though it was increased greatly in later years, and the amount any one municipality could borrow was to be determined by the cabinet. The minister was obliged to report to the Legislature each year on the administration of the Act. Under this Act, from 1950 to 1954, loans were made as shown in Table 8.

Over the five years, 1950-1954, somewhat over $22 million were distributed over 101 cities, towns, and villages of the province. There was no regular or fixed allocation by population or equalized assessment, though both these criteria corresponded broadly to the distribution as the loans were related to the ability of the local authority to repay them on the self-liquidating basis. The sum of one million dollars appears to have been a guideline for the maximum loan awarded in any distribution year, as Calgary received this sum in July of each of 1950, 1951, and 1952. Edmonton also received this amount in 1950 and in 1952, but in 1951 received three separate loans amounting in all to $1.9 million. The loans were taken up

Table 8. Loans under the Self-liquidating Projects Act, 1950-54

Cities	*$'000*	*Towns*	*$'000*	*Villages*	*$'000*
Edmonton*	5,003	Taber	420	1 village with over 150	
Calgary	3,000	Pincher Creek	310	10 villages with 100-149	
Lethbridge	1,490	Devon	300	10 villages with 50- 99	
Medicine Hat	800	Vegreville	248	5 villages less than 50	
Red Deer	371	St. Paul	246		
Lloydminster	145	Picture Butte	242	26 villages received	
Grande Prairie	90	High Prairie	241		$2,217,940
7 cities received	$10,898,700				
		6 towns with 200-240			
		9 towns with 150-199			
		20 towns with 100-149			
		16 towns with 50- 99			
		10 towns less than 50			
		68 towns received	$8,897,070		

*Including Beverly and Jasper Place which received $533,000 and $570,000 respectively in 1953.
Derived from information in the Treasury Department Ledger, Edmonton.
Through this Act and the Municpal Capital Expenditure Loans Act of 1953, Calgary was able by 1955 to have 78 percent of its debentures held by the provincial government. Its debenture debt in 1955 was $50.49 million, of which $39.53 million was held by the province. *McNally Commission Report,* Chapter 6, p. 10.

fairly evenly over the cities, towns, and villages in each financial year.

If the cities of Calgary, Edmonton, and Lethbridge are considered as the basis on which a regional distribution of money was made, then the results show how Edmonton and Lethbridge, with the network of towns and villages surrounding them, benefited very greatly over Calgary. Within a 35 miles radius of these cities, and ignoring the loans made to these cities themselves, the Edmonton region received $1,178,700, Lethbridge $1,086,550, and Calgary $601,250. Lethbridge's regional figure is influenced by Taber's $420,000, but despite this, the significance for Calgary of an impoverished hinterland is marked on the basis of loans awarded to hinterland urban centres. Viewed on a broader regional basis than a 35 miles radius, the advantages would accrue to Edmonton considerably faster as many considerable loans in the wider hinterland around Edmonton were made. The McNally Commission recommended that the metropolitan centres receive a higher grant than the formula provided. The commission's argument rested on "The disproportionate rise in city costs due to (a) unusually rapid growth, and (b) large size, should be recognized."[93] Rapid growth and large size became the rationale for greatly increased metropolitan assistance in later years.

In 1953 the Municipal Capital Expenditure Loans Act was introduced with rather broader purposes than its predecessor. Loans would now be made for a wider variety of capital expenditures than "self-liquidating" utilities. The debt changes were to fall on the general mill rate, rather than on utility account. Municipalities other than urban could qualify, and in 1954 municipal hospital districts became eligible. Rural authorities could acquire road building equipment and capitalize homes for the aged. The 1953 legislation opened up to all local authorities the means of capital acquisition at below market interest rates. Many local authorities hitherto unable to float debentures on the open market now had available a source of capital from within Alberta itself. But it was the start of an escalating capital debt in the metropolitan areas whose tax payers contributed a substantial proportion through the mill rate (as much as 16 mills within a few years).

Thus, within the five years immediately following the war a network of institutions sponsored by the provincial government had been developed which permitted a variety of administrative initiatives and controls.[94] The province had instituted both incentives to attract industry to the province and clear taxation laws affecting its profits, and it had handed to local authorities a variety of planning instruments backed eventually by zoning caveats or interim development orders to cope with the nature of metropolitan land speculation and development if it threatened to get out of control. The province's financial resources had improved greatly both from royalities and higher per capita and corporate taxes. A system of local authority loans had been introduced. The question for the future would be the ability of the metropolitan centres to afford the costs which this growth involved.

"Orderly development"

As part of a review of local authority statutes the provincial government in 1951 legislated a uniform code of administration for the cities. This code was administered by Municipal Affairs, a decision that contrasted with a series of enactments, profoundly influencing the cities in the years to come, which were ascribed to other provincial departments. The role of the Department of Municipal Affairs was clearly to be linked to that of municipal government, while financial incentives to cities and towns, tax subsidies, municipal grants, etc., came to be administered elsewhere. These arrangements of twenty years ago conformed to the Social Credit philosophy of delegating responsibility to the local level. But, in turn, they have contributed to the provincial government's difficulties in maintaining control over the influence of Calgary and Edmonton in provincial affairs.

The City Act of 1951 was an enormous piece of legislation running to over 740 sections.[95] Every detail of city administration was covered, with sufficient options to enable the hitherto unique charters of each city to be fitted into its terms with a minimum of inconvenience. Among its terms was one empowering the council, by by-law, to require every tentative plan of subdivision to be submitted to the City Engineer and the Town Planning Commission before being submitted to the Provincial Planning Advisory Board (Section 318). The council was thereby able to forestall any proposed subdivision that might compromise it over the supply of services for which the city was responsible, or which might hinder the development of proposed highway or transit routes. On the surface this provision seemed to guarantee a city council the final right of decision but, as will be described in a later chapter, its actual effect was to lead to no end of political manoeuvring within the various levels and specialized departments of increasingly large municipal bureaucracies. The legislation assumed a unity of decision-making capacity within city hall, but the mix of technical, professional, political, and public interests was to make this assumption very questionable.

The Act further permitted by by-law, assented to by two-thirds of voting electors, the improvement of housing conditions in a city "by providing for the construction of dwelling houses at a reasonable cost for sale or lease to persons of moderate income" (Section 319(1)). Thus, cities were empowered to utilize the appropriate provisions of the National Housing Act(NHA), and could consider themselves to be a "local authority" or a "lending institution" as required by the NHA "with all the powers, rights, duties and remedies necessary or incidental thereto." Cities, therefore, could enter into any agreement with the federal government or with the provincial government involving "assistance to municipalities in the undertaking of a housing scheme." These general powers were to be made more specific under the Alberta Housing Acts of the following three years, largely in response to the demands of the federal government as expressed in the annually amended NHA, and particularly the 1954 NHA. The federal government was determined to by-pass the provincial governments even in low-cost housing. Although provincial governments had to make a financial contribution along with the federal government, the latter preferred to work directly through local authorities or limited-dividend corporations.

The Alberta Housing Act of 1952, as amended in 1953 and 1954, and consolidated in the Revised Statutes of 1957, was as much related to the amendments of the NHA in Ottawa as it was to provincial needs.[96] This was a time when Ottawa's conscience was moving away from the urgent post-war claims of individuals needing houses to problems of a collective nature, such as slum clearance, housing the poor, and the provision of serviced city land. The Alberta Housing Act was explicitly intended "to provide means whereby low-cost housing may be made available in the cities and towns of the Province" (Section 3). To do this, the Act provided machinery: (a) to execute agreements between the provincial and federal governments, (b) to acquire and develop land for low-cost housing, and (c) to construct low-cost housing for sale or rent. The legislation broadened the provisions of the 1951 City Act and extended the right to arrange with Ottawa for NHA facilities for Alberta's towns.

A local council, with the assent of the proprietory electors and the approval of the Board of Public Utilities Commissioners, was empowered to raise money for low-cost housing by the issue and sale of debentures. Alternatively or additionally, it could pay into a Housing Fund, established by the Provincial Treasurer, "such amounts as it desires to make available for a housing fund" (Section 5(2)). This deposit with the fund then enabled the provincial government to enter into an agreement with the federal government, CMHC, or other federal authority for a housing project "the capital cost of which shall not exceed four times the amount deposited by the municipality in the "Housing Fund" (Section 6(1)). However, the council's deposit with the fund could be expended by the province under any agreement under section 36 of the NHA (1954), and "shall be deemed to be the twenty-five per cent share of the capital cost of the housing project required to be borne by the Province" under the NHA's provisions (Section (2)(b)).

Though this provision would appear to save the provincial government from the obligation to contribute its share to the cost of housing the poor, it conformed consistently with Social Credit philosophy. As the province had arranged to distribute a part of its revenues to the local authorities of the province through municipal grants, or by loans at low interest, when a city or town council was afforded the opportunity by federal legislation and the NHA to obtain public money it could not again expect the province to meet an additional amount. What was fairly distributed downwards was not to carry obligations upwards! Concurrently, as the terms of the NHA required provincial participation in the cost of housing the poor, the provincial government was both giving the legal blessing required and was paying its share. On the face of it, it was admirably reasoned legislation. But the purpose behind the terms of the NHA was the need to establish incentives whereby local councils would move towards solving the national problems of the poor and the degraded areas of cities. The incentives were supposed to be handed down by the two senior governments, the federal and provincial. In Alberta, however, the incentive had to come directly from the conscience and concern of city and town councils, although the federal government was volunteering 75 percent of the capital investment.

This attribute of Albertan legislation does not necessarily explain the relative lack of interest and initiative in low-cost housing which has typified Albertan, as well as Canadian, cities for decades. As will be shown in a later chapter, low-cost housing, land development, and land use for this purpose serve a variety of purposes for both city hall and developers. Nevertheless, when city councils apply priorities in the face of rapid growth, high expenditures, and continued expectations, low-cost housing is rarely high on the list. By 1956 Albertan cities had taken no action under the NHA provisions.

In a very generally worded section, the Lieutenant-Governor in Council was empowered to constitute bodies corporate to plan, construct, and manage housing projects (Section 8). Also, apparently to obviate delays in getting low-cost housing underway, the same authority could authorize a municipality "in which a housing project is wholly or partly undertaken pursuant to this Act to do or not to do such acts or things as deemed expedient. . ." (Section 11). Apparently to cope with the variety of situations being generated annually in Ottawa, the Act provided for the Lieutenant-Governor in Council "to make such regulations as are considered necessary or advisable" to carry into effect the provisions of the Act or to meet any deficiency in its provisions (Section 13).

Thus, consistently since the 1935 Dominion Housing Act, the Alberta government had provided the provincial legislation necessary to have the NHA apply in the province. Its own Alberta Housing Association Act, passed in 1945, was held in abeyance. The ideas implicit in its measures were to re-emerge only in 1967 on the introduction of the Alberta Housing and Urban Renewal Corporation, but by then the relation to Ottawa's legislation was very differently envisaged.

By 1950 the provincial government had begun to consider the ways in which it might return to local authorities and invididual citizens some of the increasing revenue it had been receiving. Professor Hanson has remarked, "The Alberta government, like most senior governments, tends to regard its revenues as belonging essentially to the provincial government — any slices dispensed to the localities being regarded as allowances to children or as loans for performing functions which are regarded as being peculiarly local."[97] Provincial to local authority transfers moved from $42.6 million in 1947 to $118.2 million in 1951 and to $133.1 million by 1954.[98] As a percentage of current provincial revenue, the figure moved from 11.0 percent to 15.8 percent to 26 percent over these years respectively.

In 1951 the provincial government introduced its first attempt to distribute by way of local authority tax subsidy and unconditional municipal grants, the substantially increasing revenues it was receiving from fuel oil (gasoline) revenues.[99] The 1951 attempt was not particularly successful and a new measure was introduced in 1953. But the early efforts illustrate particularly well the principles held by the Social Credit administration in its relation to municipal authorities.

The Municipal Assistance Act[100] was intended:

(a) to benefit taxpayers by enabling a reduction in their municipal taxes, and

(b) to benefit municipalities by providing them with additional revenue (Section 3).

The separation of "taxpayers" from "municipalities" is significant in that the Act explicitly recognized the possibility of their interests being potentially dissimilar. Provincial revenues were to be used at the local level to subsidize taxation through reducing the mill rate, and also to provide local councils with a sum of money to be spent unconditionally.

The mechanisms to implement the intent of the Act were complex. A Municipal Assistance Fund was created, to be administered, however, by the Provincial Treasurer and not the Minister of Municipal Affairs. Each year the Provincial Treasurer paid into the fund a portion of the Fuel Oil Tax "equivalent to the net receipts from four cents per gallon for each gallon of fuel oil on which tax was collected during the immediately preceeding calendar year" (Section 4(2)). Each year out of the fund was to be paid to each municipality:

(a) a tax reduction subsidy, and
(b) an unconditional municipal revenue grant.

The tax reduction subsidy was based on the actual assessment for taxation purposes of each municipality on the last day of the preceding year. Land was assessed everywhere at 100 percent, buildings and improvements in the cities at up to 60 percent, while in other municipalities it was up to 100 percent. The 1942 value of assessment was taken to apply everywhere. Having determined these assessed values of property the Provincial Treasurer established a "basic mill rate" which was decided in terms of the highest mill rate levied in any year by a municipality after 1949 — in effect over the three years before the coming-into-force of the Act in 1951. A subsidy was then paid out of the fund to the municipality which enabled it to reduce the mill rate charged to the ratepayers by an amount, up to a maximum of three mills, which kept the mill rate below the "basic" mill rate. If a municipality had suffered a disaster, or was involved in unusually high expenditure such as the coming to completion of a new hospital in 1951, and was thereby unable to reduce the mill rate below the "basic" rate in order to benefit from the subsidy, it was entitled to make a special plea to the Provincial Treasurer, whose decision as to a "fair subsidy" was final.

The tax subsidy could therefore be interpreted as an incentive to local councils to keep down the cost of local government. But in this it proved to be a failure.[101] The fast growth centres had been raising mill rates in order to keep abreast of rising costs. By fixing the assessed value of city buildings and improvements at 60 percent and that of other municipalities at 100 percent, the Act tended to affect Calgary and Edmonton more than others, though the smaller cities of the province were similarly affected relative to the towns of equal population size who, because of their "town" status, could use 100 percent of assessed value of buildings and improvements. By sticking stoically to the general classification of "cities," instead of naming the metropolitan centres which the provincial government wished to single out for greater control, the legislation adversely affected the small cities of the province. Fair and equal treatment to all classes of municipality had to be maintained as a matter of policy, irrespective of its fairness in the practical situation. Strong representation from the municipalities had led to its eventual relaxation.[102]

The Municipal Revenue Grant was also computed in a complex way. Villages were selected as requiring special consideration as their computation was based on 110 percent of land assessment as against 100 percent for all other types of municipality. Buildings and improvements were further broken down such as to provide 60 percent in the case of cities, and 100 percent for all other types of local authority except villages, which again used 110 percent of assessed value.

Every year, after the fund had covered the benefits for tax reduction subsidy, the balance remaining in the fund was distributed to the municipalities as an "unconditional municipal revenue grant" (Section 11). The basis of distribution of such grant was "the same percentage of the total of all municipal revenue grants in that year as the percentage that its assessment is of the total of all municipal assessments" (Section 12). The councils could use the grants received as they wished (Section 18).

The thinking behind the legislation is certainly complex. It would seem that it was intended to ensure to everyone in the province both a measure of tax reduction in proportion to the value of property owned, and access to a minimum of public facilities. Villages were favoured slightly, possibly to ensure that the grant they received was large enough to do something useful, and possibly because the relative deprivation of their inhabitants in terms of basic amenities required it.[103] The legislation used complex, technical machinery in an attempt to guarantee the fair and equal treatment of all citizens and all municipalities. In this, it was the antithesis of a policy that set out to use provincial revenues as the instrument of guiding local authority development within a province-wide plan. The legislation was deliberately intended to check the existing processes of growth and the existing differentials among the urban centres.[104] As the metropolitan centres continued to attract investment and increase the value of their property, however, so too the grant increased. The relative size of the metropolitan grant over that of smaller centres inherently gave their councils a means to enhance the amenities the city could offer. The scale of village communities tended to ensure that basic human needs came first, whilst in the cities councils saw their needs in abstract terms — growth, roads, industrial serviced land, and a host of non-human but "essential needs" according to the judgement they made at the scale of their organization.

The Act was undeniably orderly in the "fairness" of its provisions, but the development to which it could lead might be quite different in practice. In 1953 the mechanisms to achieve a "fair" distribution over the province were totally revised.[105] The idea of a fund was retained, but the law distinguished between "urban" and "rural" municipalities. Urban meant a city, town, or village, while rural included municipal districts, counties, improvement districts, and special areas. The fund was now to be supplied by "one-half of the net receipts of taxes from each gallon of fuel oil, other than fuel oil used for industrial or agricultural purposes, on which tax was collected" over the previous calendar year (Section 3(2)). The fund was to be divided into two parts based on the dominion census returns of 1951 "respecting the ratio of the total population of all cities, towns and villages and that of rural municipalities to the total population of all municipalities in the Province" (Section 4). Thus, by 1953, a clear-cut basis of differential between urban and rural had been established. It was done at a time when the rate of urban population increase was the fastest in Alberta's history. The percentage of the population classified "urban" moved from 41 percent to 55 percent between 1951 and 1961, involving a total population jump from 430,000 to 852,000.[106]

The distribution of the respective parts of the fund was designed to give each urban municipality that portion of the urban municipalities' fund as was represented by its population to the population of all urban municipalities. To make sure that the rapidly growing centres were not handicapped by having to remain on the distribution shown in the 1951 census, the Act provided for the use of the Department of Municipal Affairs' census return. This return was collected annually by sworn affidavit "of the proper municipal officer that the population figure contained in the census return has been obtained as a result of an actual census having been taken of the persons bona fide residing in the municipality" (Section 7(2)). The mode of arriving at the annual census figure was most elaborate, but if the Provincial Treasurer had "reason to believe that an appreciable decline in the population has occurred", he could waive the annual return and apply the 1951 census figure.

Rural municipalities received grants on a much more complex basis. An equalization grant was paid to all rural municipalities that, in all, took up 40 percent of the rural part of the fund. The equalization grant appropriate for any rural municipality was calculated by the Provincial Treasurer on a formula "based on such factors as are necessary to establish in an equitable manner the need of each rural municipality for economic assistance" (Section 8(2)). The factors he had to consider were area, population, average assessment per acre, real property industrial assessment, personal property assessment, real property assessment; total assessment, "and such other factors as are relevant." The remaining 60 percent of the rural part of the fund was distributed "in the proportion that the assessment of the land, buildings and improvements in each rural municipality bears to the total assessment . . . of all rural municipalities in the Province" (Section 9(1)). However, if the total grant calculated by the above two formulae provided a rural municipality with more than $130,000 that figure was fixed as the maximum it could receive. If there was a surplus left in the fund as a result of this ceiling then it was to be divided among other rural municipalities of the same "class."

The Act then defined the classes (Section 10(3)), and the formula for this distribution; but enough has been described to show the enormous lengths to which provincial legislation by 1955 was obliged to go to determine, with hopelessly unreal precision, the amount to which a local authority was entitled. The irony of this lay in the Provincial Treasurer's powers to determine a formula usable in ascertaining the size of the equalization grant that in turn was to relate to "the need of each rural municipality for economic assistance." Though the legislation recognized very clearly in its splitting of urban from rural, in its use of population statistics for urban and property assessments for rural municipalities, and in the idea of an equalization grant in the rural context, the necessity to use provincial funds for socio-economic developmental purposes it did the job by way of hiding behind a barrage of complex arithmetic formulae (themselves based on largely subjective judgements in the field situation). Fair treatment had to be seen to be given to all. Figures, formulae, assessments, population numbers etc., rather than human decision taken within the context of planning policy for the province's development, were to be the guarantee both of local autonomy over policy decision and the establishment of orderly relations between provincial and local authorities.

The Municipal Assistance Acts of the early 1950s illustrate most clearly the three features which typified the provincial government's relations with its local authorities. First, no favouritism or particular direction could be shown to any one local authority, which came to mean in effect that the regulation of provincial development was undertaken in such a way as permitted the most powerful local authorities to determine what that development would be. The split of urban from rural in the assistance fund, and the use of population in determining the split, are indicative of the type of local authority which could call the tune, as early as 1953. Secondly, each local authority was to be treated as a semi-autonomous kingdom, such that its council was left free to determine the policy appropriate to its own development. There was no regional or provincial emphasis. There was no conception at the provincial level of developing Alberta's collective affairs in terms of a strategy which linked what was occurring in the world outside the province to the attributes and potential of the local authorities, at the grass-roots level, within the province. It was left to local councils to attract and negotiate with extra-provincial business and professional personnel about the terms of their settlement within the local jurisdiction. The local authorities became the link between national and international investment and grass roots local affairs. Thirdly, the interest of the individual Albertan taxpayer was not to be ignored in the management of local authority affairs. In the Budget Speech of 1952, Premier Manning outlined the ideas behind the Municipal Assistance Fund proposals in these terms:

> By permitting an adjustment of the basic mill rates on the basis proposed, it is hoped that all Municipalities, including the Cities, will secure for their ratepayers the full advantage of the tax reduction subsidy provided under the Act.[107]

Later in the same speech, the Premier emphasized the monetary reforms needed at the federal level "to make possible the distribution of additional purchasing power directly to consumers . . ." under conditions of inflation, rising prices and full employment.[108] The fundamental monetary reforms necessary in terms of Social Credit philosophy at the national level of organization could not be achieved; but the onus remained on the provincial legislature "to do everything in our power to secure for the people we are privileged to represent the effective control of their own credit resource . . ."[109] The ultimate goal was "a debt-free Province in which every citizen will have an unfettered opportunity to attain through his own initiative and enterprise a share of the material abundance our vast resources make physically possible."[110]

To cope with the high cost of interest on open market debentures, the provincial government initiated the Municipal Loans Revolving Fund in 1953.[111] It provided a $25 million fund to be made available to municipalities by loans for five to 25 years at interest rates ranging from two and one-half percent on a five year serialized debenture rising by one quarter percent for each additional five years of maturity to three and one-half percent. The fund was expected to be sufficient to provide for all capital borrowings of municipalities in the fiscal year. Repayments were expected to replenish it over time, but in the interim further provincial additions were to be made. Its revolving character was to provide local councils with the guaranteed source of low interest money for their capital development.

The metropolitan centres in particular stood to benefit. They were able to play the role of initiating and directing development which the provincial government itself declined to assume. The point is illustrated in the opening remarks of Premier Manning in the 1953 Budget Speech (page 3). He announced that in 1953, notwithstanding record expenditures on social services and capital development, Alberta had become the first Canadian province to accumulate cash surpluses and investments in excess of its total indebtedness. He then went on to add:

> The next step in the Government's program is to institute practical measures to assist municipal governments in attaining a comparable measure of financial independence and stability. Accordingly, the budget I am privileged to present today embodies substantially increased appropriations for direct municipal assistance and a program under which the total estimated necessary municipal borrowings for the ensuing year will be advanced by the Provincial Government from a revolving fund . . .

The paradox of Social Credit administration in its first twenty years was that its belaboured attempts at coping with inter-provincially and internationally flexible private capital, and the policies of the federal government, led to the usurpation of its provincial prerogative to plan and develop at the scale of organization. Its philosophy of fair and equal treatment of local authorities, its techniques of population criteria, and equalized assessment coupled to complex and abstract formulae, led to the domination by Calgary and Edmonton of the urban developmental process of the province.

Development could be seen to be orderly in every provincial statute and at the level of *ad hoc* boards and commissions supported by cabinet approved regulations. What happened on the ground, at the level of local authorities themselves, was a very different matter. The 1953 Town and Rural Planning Act illustrates at one level the type of provincial aid which had to be given urban planning to maintain control, not to mention direction of development or the implementation of a provincial plan. In the next chapter we discuss some findings of the Royal Commissions about the local situation; but first the 1953 Planning Act must be described.

The failure of urban planning controls in 1948 had led to the extreme centralization of decision in the minister and Director of Planning through zoning caveats and interim development orders. Edmonton started to use interim development by-laws in 1950 and Calgary in 1952. The long title referred to "A Means of Obtaining Orderly Development of Municipalities in the Province by Planning the Development and the Use of Land."[112] Cheap and largely unregulated development on and beyond the boundaries of the metropolitan centres was compromising control of development and also leading to vexatious conflict between metropolitan and adjacent local authorities. The Act was divided into three parts: Provincial Planning, Municipal Planning, and Miscellaneous. The responsible minister was left undesignated, but to be "that member of the Executive Council for the time being charged with the administration of this Act" (Section 2(j)).

At the provincial level, the membership of the Planning Advisory Board remained intact but provided the Director of Town and Rural Planning with a staff. In 1956 membership of the board included the Minister of Municipal Affairs, the Deputy Minister, and the Director of Town and Rural Planning. The board's duties were to advise and assist local councils on planning and orderly development, to collect information and do research, to act as a board of final appeal, and to "pay moneys and make grants to any municipality or district planning commission for such purposes and within such amounts as may be specified by the Lieutenant-Governor in Council from time to time" (Section 8(c)). The provincial board therefore became a potential monetary provider for all planning purposes. The planning board also replaced the minister in the making of regulations covering zoning caveats and interim development orders. The Act gave the director discretionary power over the division or classification of land in any proposed subdivision operating under this procedure. The minister, however, was given the same powers of enforcement of the regulations as was a council over its zoning by-laws (Section 23). The director and provincial board, therefore, became technical and regulatory instruments with the power of enforcement resting with the minister. The appeal function rested with the board, as before. Between 1951 and 1954, it decided 48 cases from Calgary and Edmonton, mainly dealing with subdivisions, parking lots, drive-in theatres, basement suites, etc.

The second tier of provincial planning organization in Part 1 of the Act was made up of District Planning Commissions. These were to be established in much the same way as in earlier legislation, except that the cabinet was left free to prescribe the membership without reference to any statutory number of representatives from participating local authorities. Once the number of members from each local authority was determined, the councils had the right to appoint its members to the commission by resolution. The council could also delegate to a commission the administration of the provisions of a by-law or general plan (Section 87(3)(b)). The district commissions in 1953 also had unambiguous right to "study the resources and development of the district planning area with a view to preparing a general plan for the area" (Section 14(a)). In the 1950 legislation this power had been couched in such terms as "prepare and recommend to each council represented a general plan . . ." (Section 11(c)(b) of the 1950 Act). In 1953 it was more a matter of a general plan in its own right for the area concerned and on terms appropriate to a professional staff, though the obligation to recommend the general plan to the member councils remained (Section 14(c)). Similarly, the decision as to whether to permit a subdivision in the peri-urban fringe of the cities continued to rest with elected councils, not with the technical commissions at a district level of planning. Two important exceptions to this general principle were introduced by Order-in-Council June 6, 1953.[113] The District Planning Commissions of Calgary and Edmonton were given some teeth by being made the "approving authority" over their areas of jurisdiction in matters of land subdivision. A similar right was extended to the Technical Planning Boards of the two cities in respect of the city itself. Thus, in theory, by close co-operation between the planning professionals within the city and those in the region, some co-ordination of subdivision was introduced. But if a council felt obstructed by the district commission there was nothing to prevent it withdrawing from membership of the commission and altering its zoning by-laws on its own terms. The effective instrument remained the council-approved by-law.

In addition to the section covering zoning caveats, Part 1 of the Act, under Provincial Planning, contained reference to "Transfers." This referred to the sale, lease, mortgage or charge concerned with the voluntary transfer of an interest in a "small parcel" of land, i.e., a piece of land of less than five acres adjoining a main highway situated within the boundaries of a city, town, or village, or within two miles of a city boundary or one mile of a town, village or hamlet boundary. It was directed at ribbon development and any transaction over a "small parcel" required the approval of the provincial board, if the subdivision was not already on record in the Land Titles Office. Any transfer of title of a "small parcel" adjoining a main highway had to be approved by the Minister of Highways in addition. With this multiplicity of approvals becoming legislatively entrenched, the problem emerged of which authority had final rights of decision. The law assumed common agreement of all authorities, but it also provided for appeals against decisions of particular authorities. The McNally Commission, by way of illustration, told of the way an auto mart obtained permission to locate a used car lot half a mile northwest of Edmonton. They got the Department of Highways to grant a permit without referring the matter to the local council, who had in turn upheld an appeal from an adverse decision of the Edmonton District Planning Commission.[114]

The substantive section of the Act covering Municipal Planning authorized a council to prepare a general plan "based on surveys of land use, population, transportation, communication, services and social services within the municipality" (Section 65(1)). The authority for its preparation had to indicate "the manner in which the council considers the development of the municipality should be carried out within a defined period of time, having regard to considerations of orderliness, economy and convenience . . ." (Section 64(1)). The maps and details of type of land use, public areas, the nature and content of zoning by-laws, etc., had to be prepared and made available to ensure that private development would take place in accordance with it. The 1953 amendment provided for the general plan to include proposals as to how the nature and content of zoning by-laws were to relate to it (Section 66(e)). It was to be a professionally prepared plan, based as far as possible on empirically derived evidence, and providing the skeleton to which private enterprise could contribute the flesh and blood. Once adopted, after advertisement and public hearings (Section 84), and approval by the minister, the council was obliged not to commence any undertaking "inconsistent with or at variance with the general plan" (Section 68(2)). There was provision for its amendment after appropriate ritual had been gone through and publicity given to it; but the general plan was the formal document that provided the certainty within which private investment could safely be made. It removed, in theory, the vagaries of public decision that could compromise the potential of private investment or threaten its value. The close disaster which had threatened the ability of metropolitan councils in 1948 to regulate their development — when the management of private capital decided to swing their resources into Calgary and Edmonton — and their necessity to fall back on provincial zoning caveats and ministerial decisions, had made the councils aware of the necessity of gaining public support and official sanction for their attempts at control. The days of *ad hoc,* convenient measures, easy manoeuverability, and attention to the idiosyncratic requests of particular companies and developers, had gone. Private investers too had been hurt by the uncertainties and their inability to negotiate with local authority officials during the era of zoning caveats and ministerial orders. A new mode of coping had been required by both parties in the development process. This mode, respecting the wishes of both levels of government and of private companies, had been placed again at the local authority level.

It is also interesting to observe the emphasis given to survey data and the use of empirical evidence in the preparation of a general plan. The professional planners were assigned the task, in effect, of determining the future through evidence gained of the nature of the present and the trends of the past. By extrapolation of trends (the planners' crystal ball) and their specialized intuition of the urban dynamic gained from local and comparative experience, they were to regulate the daily round of applications for development, and handle the local politics of council and its committees, through the dictates of a publicly known general plan. There was no future city beautiful, agreed upon by public consensus, and requiring both public and private investment to contribute to its creation. The future city was to evolve in terms of the trends implicit in its past statistics, the outcome of political manoeuvres, business competition and any new technology that might be fitted into the confines of the General Plan and its regulations.

"Orderly development" was therefore conceived in terms of the affairs of local authorities rather than those of the province. It was seen as a way of regulating the aberrant proposals of both private and public investment in relation to the fixed general plan of the area, and in the expectation that "investment" would become "development" because of the constrained and orderly nature of the urban dynamic as required by that general plan. "Development" was not just a more respectable word than "growth," it contained clearer emphasis on the orderly transition of the potential of the past into the amenities and status of the future. The development of growth was to be professionally and empirically determined, subjected to the wisdom of amendment if circumstances required it, and made to provide for the ultimate and enduring welfare of all the city's inhabitants and financial interests. In its conception the legislation was simple and magnificent. Land use and land development was a fixed and surveyable commodity being subjected to the determinable intentions of men. Clearly defined authority and duties had been provided to councils, boards, commissions and ministers, to ensure a self-regulating process within an explicit structure which would ensure the future of urban centres. But the 1953 legislation also reflects that provincial officials and legislators were conscious of the potential for schism that such orderliness inevitably imposes in conditions of competitive and volatile relations.

While the council of any municipality, urban or rural, could establish a Planning Advisory Commission to advise and assist the council with the planning and orderly development of the municipality, only a city council could establish a Technical Planning Board (Section 88(1)).[115] A technical planning board advised and assisted the council, and co-ordinated the planning and development activities of the various departments and agencies of the city. It was not unlike the specialized branch envisaged for the federal Department of Urban Affairs and Housing vis-a-vis CMHC in 1970. A technical board consisted of officials of the city, whether planners or administrators, appointed by the council. The technical board set up in Edmonton in 1950 consisted of the Mayor, a City Commissioner, the City Solicitor, the City Engineer, the Medical Officer of Health, the Town Planner, the Building Inspector, the City Architect, the Superintendent of Parks and Playgrounds, and such councillors as could be added from time to time.[116] It was a body of concerned officials rather than professional planners. The Calgary board was, with minor differences, similarly constituted; but it included the City Assessor and the Land Superintendent, and *ex officio* without vote, the superintendent of each of the city's utilities. The power-through-knowledge potential of these technical boards is explicit in their membership. Only major urban centres were entitled to have them.

The technical boards were delegated such powers as the council determined, except those of raising money and expropriating land. The board was statutorily required to keep minutes of its meetings and to record matters concerning its organization and the transaction of its business (Section 88(5)). It was clearly administrative and technical. It epitomized the entrenchment within the city's administration of expertise bound politically to the interest of the council and the city. It could facilitate both the handling of problems derived from development applications within the city's jurisdiction and those concerning local authorities and the provincial government beyond the city's jurisdiction. Knowledge could mean power in both directions. It was the start of the city bureaucracy that was to become increasingly pronounced over the years ahead, and which eventually brought into question the clear differentiation between political decisions and those of the professional and technical administration at the local level.

A Planning Advisory Commission, such as was set up in Calgary following the 1953 Planning Act, was made up of councillors and citizens at large.[117] It was public rather than technical, and introduced to the planning process that essential element of local public concern that was later to evolve into citizen participation encouraged officially at all levels of government. Its role was important during the early stages of planning when the overall scheme was under review. In Calgary this advisory commission also served as the body to whom appeals could be made concerning the rulings of the technical board, and such appeals were held in public. The power of the advisory commission to alter a decision of the technical board was however limited, as it required unanimity on the part of the advisors to overrule the board.[118]

Edmonton's appeal mechanism was a little different as, instead of an advisory commission, it used an Interim Development Appeal Board with the same appeal function as to development schemes, permits, and subdivisions. In Edmonton, however, when an appeal concerning the use of land for business purposes in a business zone was denied at the Interim Development Board level, a further appeal was possible to the city council. The McNally Report records that between November, 1950 and the end of December, 1954, Edmonton's Interim Development Appeal Board heard some 803 appeals, of which 492 were granted with or without conditions, and 200 refused. The remainder were withdrawn. Only 25 appeals during this time went to the Provincial Planning Advisory Board.[119]

Thus were the cities coping with the vast majority of appeals. The advisory, citizen-representing mechanism was having the final say on matters raised on appeal. Just how often and over what issues these appeals were made, concerning what ecological zones of the metropolitan areas, and what type of arguments were used by the technical and professional mechanisms, are all important research issues which we were unable to examine. Their importance lies in their revealing the clearly unhappy relation between professional and lay interests, between the interests of the community collectively considered and those of private developers, and especially in their revealing the consequences which the winning of an appeal would have for the effective application of the General Plan. In Chapter 5 we describe cases of this nature dealt with in Calgary in 1971-72.

Theoretically the interim development provisions and zoning caveats were introduced to give local authorities time to prepare general plans. These provisions assumed that once the plan was formulated then something fixed would exist, even if it was only a guideline; but the to and fro of appeal decisions and the opportunities they provided for further exploitation by private investors could well compromise the "fixed" quality implicit in a general plan. The constantly adjusting relation among technical and professional planners, the interests of elected officials and the citizenry, and the interests of organized capital involves a precarious balance which, under conditions of such rapid expansion as Calgary and Edmonton experienced after 1945, was very difficult to achieve.

Notes
Chapter 2

1. Hanson, E.J., *Local Government in Alberta,* Toronto: 1956, McLelland and Stewart, p.46.
2. *The Canada Year Book* 1938, p.877.
3. Ibid., p.876.
4. See C.B. MacPherson's *Democracy in Alberta, Social Credit and the Party System,* Toronto: 1962, University of Toronto Press, for a succinct analysis of the political issues. For a biography of William Aberhart see L.P.V. Johnson and Ola J. MacNutt's *Aberhart of Alberta,* Edmonton: 1970, Institute of Applied Art, Co-op Press Ltd. Aberhart was born in Egmondville, a village attached to Seaforth, Huron County, Ontario December 30, 1878, and died in Vancouver May 23, 1943.
5. Johnson and MacNutt, *Aberhart of Alberta,* p.29.
6. Irving, John A., *The Social Credit Movement in Alberta,* Toronto: 1959, University of Toronto Press. (Paperback edition, 1968.)
7. Ibid., p.11.
8. Ibid., p.12.
9. The above and most of the following factual data are derived from Chapter 2 of Irving's *Social Credit Movement.*
10. At the height of his fame the broadcasting station CFCN estimated that 350,000 people were listening to his broadcasts; not all paid their dollar, but the club was a financial success.
11. See Irving, *Social Credit Movement,* pp.34-35 for details.
12. See MacPherson, *Democracy in Alberta,* pp. 93-94 and 144-45.
13. Contained in Johnson & MacNutt's *Aberhart of Alberta,* p.204. This premise was published in July, 1935. A legal statement of the Social Credit position, as passed by the Legislature, is contained in *The Statutes of Alberta,* 1936, Chapter 5.
14. *Alberta Social Credit Chronicle,* December 1, 1934.
15. Quoted in Johnson and MacNutt's *Aberhart of Alberta,* pp.124-25.
16. Ibid., pp.131-33
17. MacPherson in *Democracy in Alberta,* pp. 230-250, has argued for the "quasi-party" nature of Social Credit political organization and has questioned the concept of "agrarian consciousness" as an adequate explanation of political support for Social Credit. We do not challenge this argument, but rather suggest that the urban centres' population was influential and also that Aberhart was obliged to serve urban interests particularly favourably.
18. MacPherson, *Democracy in Alberta,* p.96.
19. In the 1935 election the Communist vote totalled 5,771 and the Labour 5,986 against Social Credit 163,700 Liberals 69,845, UFA 33,063 and Conservatives 19,358. A full list of returns is provided in Johnson and MacNutt's *Aberhart of Alberta,* p.139.
20. MacPherson, *Democracy in Alberta,* Chapters 6 and 7. Also Johnson and MacNutt, op cit., Chapters 14 and 15.
21. MacPherson, op cit., p.97. It is not our intention to describe Douglas's notorious A + B theorem. Readers may refer to MacPherson pp.107-112 for a description and critical analysis.

22. See MacPherson, op cit., Chapter 7.
23. See Johnson and MacNutt, op cit., pp.141-42.
24. In 1936 the province defaulted on bonds totalling $3.2 million and legislated to cut in half the interest rate on its outstanding bonds.
25. Johnson and MacNutt, op cit., pp.142-43.
26. Gertler, Leonard O., "Some economic and social influences on regional planning in Alberta" in *Planning the Canadian Environment,* Montreal: 1968, Harvest House, p.87.
27. *Statutes of Alberta,* 1936, Chapter 71.
28. Thirty-third *Annual Report* of the Department of Education, 1938, p.72.
29. Forty-third *Annual Report* of the Department of Education, 1948, p.77.
30. *Statutes of Alberta,* 1936, Chapter 105.
31. *Statutes of Alberta,* 1939, Chapter 24, "The Municipal Improvements Assistance (Alberta) Act," assented to March 31, 1939, its provisions having become effective August 1, 1938 (Section 19).
32. *Public Accounts of the Province of Alberta,* Statement 22 or 23 depending on the year.
33. *Statutes of Alberta,* 1939, Chapter 24, Section 3.
34. It should be noted, however, that the Provincial Treasurer was also the Minister of Municipal Affairs.
35. *Statutes of Alberta,* 1936, Chapter 11, Corporation Taxation Amendment Act.
36. Ibid., Section 3.
37. *Statutes of Alberta,* 1936, Chapter 12, 2nd Session.
38. *Statutes of Alberta,* 1937, Chapter 61.
39. In England the 1947 Town and Country Planning Act deliberately made returns from higher prices derived from the mere act of planning and subdivision payable to the state.
40. *Report of the Royal Commission on the Metropolitan Development of Calgary and Edmonton,* Edmonton: 1956, Queen's Printer, Chapter 10, p.29. (See no.1 in the Notes following Chapter 3 of this volume)
41. *Statutes of Alberta,* 1938, Chapter 3.
42. *Statutes of Alberta,* 1940, Chapter 14.
43. MacPherson, *Democracy in Alberta,* pp. 169-75. See *Statutes of Alberta,* 1937, Chapter 10 for details of the Alberta Social Credit Act.
44. MacPherson, op cit., p.193.
45. The activities of the federal government in disallowing legislation such as the Alberta Social Credit Act, the Alberta Bank Act of 1940, and the litigation over the Debt Adjustment Act in the case of the North American Life Assurance Co., plaintiff, and Minnie Helen McLean, defendant, that was appealed to the Supreme Court and eventually to the Privy Council, had virtually squashed by 1940 the attempt to introduce Social Credit philosophy. See MacPherson, op cit., p.194. Government now became increasingly a matter of sound administration.
46. *Statutes of Alberta* 1940, Chapter 8. The Alberta Bank project was revived in 1944 by the passing of the Alberta Banking Powers Act, 1944, Chapter 7, which also repealed the 1940 Act but the 1944 attempt also failed.
47. There is an important historical research problem concerned with the administration and course of events of this Act and the Act that follows in the next paragraph of the text. As far as we can determine The Building Associations Act was at one time adminstered by the Department of Agriculture. Its present legislative provision is Chapter 36 of the 1970 *Revised Statutes of Alberta.* The Director of Co-operative Activities is named as the Director, which is under the Department of Industry.
48. *Statutes of ALberta,* 1945, Chapter 7. Assented to April 6, 1945.
49. See vol.1. of this work: *The Politics of Canadian Urban Development,* Chapter 2.
50. We would like to acknowledge the help of Mr. A.W. Morrison, Deputy Minister, Department of Municipal Affairs, for his advice on this point.
51. *Statutes of Alberta,* 1945, Chapter 6. Assented to March 28, 1945.
52. See p. 89, this Chapter.

53. *Statutes of ALberta,* 1941, Chapter 68.
54. *Statutes of Alberta,* 1944, Chapter 4.
55. Ibid., Chapter 5.
56. Hanson, *Local Government in Alberta,* p.135, footnote 7.
57. The separation of the Department of Highways from Public Works took place in 1951, presumably as a result of the federal interest in the TransCanada Highway project.
58. MacGregor, J.G. *Edmonton: A History, Edmonton: 1967, H.G. Hurtig, Publishers,* p.270.
59. The city benefited from expanding utility revenues during the war. The Fortin Refunding Plan, started in 1937, had reduced the burden of capital debt and the city was reluctant to engage in new capital expenditure in wartime. A $6 million reserve was invested in Victory Bonds. The mill rate was held at 49.50 from 1942 to 1950.
60. See vol.1. of this work: *The Politics of Canadian Urban Development,* Table 51.
61. *Statutes of Alberta,* 1945, Chapter 2.
62. *Statutes of Alberta,* 1946, Chapter 7.
63. *Municipal Manual,* City of Calgary, 1970, p.144.
64. *The Report of the Royal Commission on Taxation,* Sessional Paper No.71, 1948. Government of the Province of Alberta, Edmonton, February 12, 1948.
65. The Co-terminous Boundary Commission submitted a series of reports in 1953-54.
66. *Statutes of Alberta,* 1947, Chapter 51, Section 7.
67. *Statutes of Alberta,* 1948, Chapter 10.
68. *Report of the Royal Commission on Taxation,* Sessional Paper No.71, 1948, p.31.
69. Ibid., p.32.
70. Ibid.
71. Ibid.
72. *Statutes of Alberta,* 1949, Chapter 6.
73. We would like to acknowledge the assistance offered us by Mr. Noel Dant in giving us access to his unpublished paper "A brief history of the planning statutes in Alberta" for the elucidation of several points on this topic.
74. *Statutes of Alberta,* 1948, Chapter 54.
75. The minister functioned as the Zoning Appeal Board.
76. In addition to Dale, "Successive town and city councils" (see Note 77), see also Wah May Winnie Chan's "The impact of the Technical Planning Board on the morphology of Edmonton," unpublished MA thesis, Department of Geography, The University of Alberta, 1969.
77. Dale, "The role of successive town and city councils in the evolution of Edmonton, Alberta, 1892-1966," unpublished PhD thesis, Department of Geography, University of Alberta, 1969, p.222.
78. Ibid., pp.223-24.
79. Ibid., p.324. There were 55 applications for rezoning in 1948 and 75 in 1949.
80. Ibid.
81. See an excellent study by F.A. Laux, "The zoning game—Alberta style: part II, development control," *in Alberta Law Review,* 1972, 10:1, pp.1-37.
82. *Statutes of Alberta,* 1950, Chapter 71.
83. Laux, "The zoning game." Under interim development control, decisions tend to be made at the administrative and professional level, whereas under zoning procedures the rules are established at the political level and applied at the adminstrative level.
84. The 1929 legislation had provided for regional planning commissions but these had not been used. This was an additional illustration of the unwillingness of metropolitan centres to use the long-established provisions of the law.
85. Explanation on a Bill to Amend the Town Planning Act, Bill No.58 of 1950, p.ii.
86. Dale,"Successive town and city councils,"p.301.

87. Ibid.
88. Ibid., p.297.
89. Revised Statutes of Alberta, 1955, Chapter 42, Section 294(3).
90. Hanson, *Local Government in Alberta,* p.63.
91. Speech to the Legislature, March 5, 1951. Queen's Printer, Edmonton, p.19.
92. The legislation was similar in principle to the 1938 federal Municipal Improvements Assistance Act, but initiated for a different purpose.
93. *Royal Commission on the Metropolitan Development of Calgary and Edmonton,* Chapter 6, p.80.
94. Minor amendments to the Planning Act were made in 1951.
95. *Statutes of Alberta,* 1951, Chapter 9.
96. *Revised Statutes of Alberta,* 1957, Chapter 149.
97. Hanson, E.J. "Provincial grants in Alberta," *The Canadian Tax Journal,* September-October, 1953, p.480.
98. Ibid., p.479.
99. The tradition of the Social Credit administration at this time was to use revenues derived from oil royalties and the sale of crown reserves and development leases to retire the provincial public debt. When this was achieved in 1953, some of this revenue was switched to municipal debt retirement. The sale of oil leases, etc., between 1947 and 1954 had provided revenue in the order of $272 million. Budget speech 1954, p.27.
100. *Statutes of Alberta,* 1951, Chapter 54.
101. Hanson, "Provincial grants in Alberta," p.475.
102. Ibid.
103. Hanson, ibid., p.476, has argued that the purpose was essentially to check the rise in the level of property taxation and local expenditures.
104. The urban areas had to be given special concessions to qualify for the subsidy in 1951. Ibid., p.477.
105. The following description is taken from Chapter 212 of the 1957 *Revised Statutes of Alberta* and contains additional amendments made to the 1953 Act, namely, 1955, Chapter 55.
106. Premier Manning reported in the 1952 Budget speech, p.8, that there were "750 Alberta companies, representing an authorized capital of $176,572,000, incorporated during 1951, and 211 extra provincial companies were registered."
107. Budget speech to the Legislature, March 7, 1952, Queen's Printer, Edmonton, p.17.
108. Ibid., p.23.
109. Budget speech 1953, p.24.
110. Ibid., p.25.
111. *Statutes of Alberta,* 1953, Chapter 81.
112. *Statutes of Alberta,* 1953, Chapter 113. Assented to April 2, 1953.
113. Order in Council no. 969-53.
114. *Report of the Royal Commission on the Metropolitan Development of Calgary and Edmonton,* 1956, Chapter 5, p.9. 115. In 1960 only those municipalities with a population of over 15,000 were permitted to establish a technical planning board. Statutes of Alberta, 1960, Chapter 10, Section 14(c).
116. *Report of the Royal Commission of the Metropolitan Development of Calgary and Edmonton,* 1956, Chapter 5, p.14.
117. It too was empowered to appoint a professional staff.
118. Ibid., p.15.
119. Ibid., p.16.

Chapter 3
Disorderly Practice Within Social Urban Policy, 1950 to 1972

The Metropolitan Periphery

The census of 1951 showed that over the previous decade the metropolitan area of greater Edmonton had increased its population by 76 percent, and greater Calgary by 49.5 percent. These areas had the highest percentage increase of population in Canada. The McNally Commission Report pointed out that their problems were not caused by depression, but by expansion and prosperity.[1] Net immigration rather than natural increase accounted for about 70 percent of the increase. Their population problems, therefore, were of a kind that reflected an inadequate control of migration from country to city and from smaller city to metropolis. The McNally Report tended to take for granted the socioeconomic components of this migration; it tended to seek solutions to its consequence rather than to pinpoint its cause. The report nevertheless shows most clearly the processes occurring within the metropolitan centres, and the study is well documented by empirical evidence.

The report first examined the fringe areas beyond the city boundaries. Their rate of population growth had been even greater than that of the cities, and they were uniformly marked by the lower income status of the residents, the larger size of their families, and the apparent preference for home ownership rather than renting. In all these fringe communities, the standard of public services was lower than in the cities and the services were often more expensive. The local councils were in financial difficulties and heavily dependent on provincial grants for many types of amenities, and particularly for education. The fringe areas were different from selfstanding towns in Alberta's countryside due to their excessive dependence on residential property as a source of tax revenue, the high proportion of their inhabitants who worked in the city but resided in the fringe area, and the high percentage of consumer goods expenditure that took place in the city rather than in the local fringe area. Retail business could not, therefore, successfully establish itself in the fringe areas except on the major through-roads, and many of these areas could not attract industrial enterprise. The tax base was particularly narrow, the residential property poorer in quality, and the assessments were low but possibly higher assessed than equivalent standard city properties. The vicious circle of community degradation was being hedged off largely by provincial grants. The McNally Report showed that "low or medium cost housing cannot support a full range of municipal services at modern standards" and this was the case in almost every fringe area around both Calgary and Edmonton.[2] Local councillors knew that an answer was to be found in increasing the amount of commercial and industrial property to strengthen the tax base, but the limited services they could afford and their unequal competitive situation with the adjacent cities made any solution impossible.

The report identified a number of techniques which had been used to encourage the population to settle on the fringe rather than in the city itself. Though local governments had attempted to make construction conform to zoning by-laws and standards, and had attempted to provide what services they could afford by way of water, sewage, garbage disposal, gas, electricity and roads, the direct incentive to the individual home seeker was not derived from local government initiative. The local governments of the fringes were coping with the *fait accompli,* rather than with encouraging further settlement. The rapid rate of fringe settlement had occurred because of advantages to would-be house owners and to privately organized capital in relation to public regulations. On the fringe, home owners and contractors were permitted to build on unserviced lots, while in the cities they were not so permitted. NHA loans were applicable only to serviced lots, but on the fringe the builders arranged for low down-payments on smaller-sized houses than the NHA permitted with high cost Lease Options or Agreement of Sale at heavy discounts. The term of purchase was usually not more than 10 years. Thus, high monetary returns permitted the quick recovery of capital on sub-standard houses. The report comments:

> To the extent that this method of financing enabled low-income families to establish a small home in the fringes, the housing pressure in the entire area was relieved. But the purchaser of the house pays a high price in terms of the property he receives. He does get, on the whole, inferior or substandard housing that is too small. For the same outlay he could almost certainly purchase a better dwelling in the city, if the financing could be arranged.[3]

It is important to identify the type of person who had decided to live on the fringe because, although the process involves the exploitation of the relatively poor and disadvantaged, the tenets of Social Credit philosophy argued for the freedom of individuals and local authorities to make their own way in life, and to be publicly supported only in the public interest or in the case of a clearly identified handicap.

The fringe dwellers were mainly people with large families (with about 3.8 persons per family as against 3.3 in the city). The wages they received were lower than the average for the city, and their collective income was lower also. Yet their clear preference was for a single detached dwelling, with space and privacy. Many had had the initiative to build their own dwelling; they were prepared to put up with lower standards of public and personal amenity if this meant less money outlay and the freedom of uncompromised self-respect and privacy. In Jasper Place studies found that many inhabitants had lived in Edmonton for a year or two after first moving into the urban context from the farms. Only later had they chosen to move to the fringe.[4] It was a deliberate choice after weighing up the two situations, and was not entirely a matter of the physical inability to obtain city accommodation. They were not on the fringe entirely out of necessity, but by preference for a particular situation. They were not poor people merely pushed hither and yon by necessity, but persons intent on determining their own situation within the general constraints in which they were enmeshed. Private finance had provided the means of achieving it without any government assurance on the loan. The NHA had not directly helped the fringe residents despite the greater volume of money made available through the banks in 1954. The risks were not too high under NHA government assurances, but the down payments and the inadequacy of income to meet the NHA's formula of not more than 23 percent of income to be spent on mortgages and local taxes amounted to a possible technical exclusion. The right of decision afforded lending institutions under the NHA as to where their money be invested had ensured neglect of the fringe residents.

In discussing the causes of problems typical of the fringe, the McNally Report is content to leave explanations at the level of "the basic fact of rapid population growth." Immediate reasons are identified as "the trend common thoughout the province and country towards urban living," and "the special factor of the expanding Alberta economy" centred on the two large cities.[5] In failing to go beyond this, the report fails to identify the provincial government's possible power to amend the causative processes. The recommendation of the commission was as follows:

> That in the event that city boundaries are greatly enlarged, subject to the proviso that at least sewer and water are provided, some relaxing of the city building codes, in appropriate zones, is preferable to having new fringe development outside the enlarged city limits. Such a step would be the lesser of two evils.[6]

The basic issue, which the report did not notice, lay not in enlarging city boundaries and relaxing building codes, but in the unquestioned right of private investors to create job opportunites within the metropolitan centres rather than elsewhere in the province's towns and cities whose tax base was more varied and substantial, with the result that the latters' potential for expansion, though considerable, remained unused. The fact that a majority of fringe dwellers expressed a desire for incorporation of their community into the city, and also themselves expressed a wish to live in the city rather than on the fringe should perhaps not be taken as its face value. These were the wishes of the people clearly conscious of the constraints of their situation although they had opted to live on the fringe rather in the urban situation. Due to the absence of rapid expansion in most of the towns of Alberta, apart from some small urban centres affected by the oil industry, and to the failure of the provincial government to act effectively through deliberate policy, the fringe dwellers' opportunities were limited to the quasi-metropolitan symbiotic relation they were obliged to endure — "the fringes were chosen for the most part because there was no practicable alternative."[7]

After considering the legislative incentives for low cost housing, and finding none — either provincial or federal — to be satisfactorily providing this type of housing, the commission found that "the evidence was that the cities are unable with their other commitments to attempt any housing scheme under present conditions."[8] This situation was recognized as conducive to the continued growth of fringe settlements. The report aptly observes, however, that the settlement of the low-income persons (possessing both tolerance and initiative) on the fringes reduced the obligation of the cities to provide low-cost housing. It thereby saved them the expense this would have involved them in under provincial policy.[9] As the fringes were largely dormitory suburbs, their councils argued that they should be reimbursed by a share of the city's industrial tax revenues. The city planners, however, saw the fringes as a potential threat to orderly development, their health authorities saw them as involving a potentially threatening situation, and their city accountants saw them as serious potential liabilities.

Annexation to the city was no solution for, inevitably, city boundaries were only pushed out further and expanded the circumference of boundaries where fringe development could start up again. In the 1950s, and right into the 1970s, this was one of the perennial problems of local governments.

The converse of this situation may be seen from the position of the Municipal District of Strathcona in 1954. The Municipal District (MD) borders Edmonton city on three sides, from the south to the northeast and, at that time, had an area of 562 square miles. A giant petrochemical plant was established in a small part of this area in 1947, only two miles beyond Edmonton's eastern boundary. The total assessment of the Strathcona MD increased from $7.211 million in 1947 to $37.461 million in 1954, or an increase of 420 percent. The assessment for one plant alone was $14.553 million, and other plants had settled with it. The Royal Commission recognized Strathcona as being unique and made a detailed analysis of it.[10]

In addition to this industrial investment, the MD was largely a mixed farming area with a council of five elected members. The council included in its staff a secretary-treasurer, an assessor and assistant assessor, and a graduate civil engineer who happened also to be a land surveyor. Private consultants were also retained. The Commissioners remarked that "The evidence discloses a high degree of efficiency on the part of the Council and its staff."[11] As early as 1951 Strathcona had had plans to establish a 30,000 population centre on a townsite called Campbelltown, now Sherwood Park, but Edmonton had expressed concern at the establishment of a city of this size (Lethbridge then had a population of only 28,000) only a few miles beyond its boundary. Conflicts had emerged between the City and the MD, and Strathcona withdrew from the Edmonton District Planning Commission.[12] Subsequently, in June 1955, Strathcona submitted a new set of plans to the provincial Director of Town and Rural Planning and these were approved by him in respect of part of the total proposal. The 1956 program called for the completion of 1,000 homes and a 15 acre shopping centre. After considering further details the Commissioners concluded:

> Thus, it seems clear, that Strathcona has definite plans for the creation of a very large urban community within close distance of Edmonton's crowded east boundary . . . This then, stripped of all its trappings, represents the total Campbelltown proposals approved by the Council when it was not a member of the Edmonton District Planning Commission, and without regard for the effect such urban centre would have on the Edmonton Metropolitan Area, and on the city in particular.[13]

Later, in summing up its argument for the amalgamation of most of the industrial and developed area of the MD with Edmonton, the Commission remarked:

> And finally, of paramount importance, and perhaps transcending even a combination of all other reasons given, the Commission has reached a fifth conclusion. It is, that it would constitute nothing short of a metropolitan tragedy to permit a second city to grow up on Edmonton's east boundary completely independent of, and duplicating the existing city.[14]

The MD claimed that it was providing residential accommodation for the workers in the industrial complex, and the Edmonton Council therefore could not reasonably claim that it would be housing Strathcona's workers but not receiving a share of the MD's industrial assessment revenue. But in the Commission's view, because of the siting of residential and industrial areas, "the Campbelltown subdivision was ill-advised having regard to the larger interest of the whole Metropolitan Area."[15]

The autonomy that Strathcona had been demonstrating with regard to its independence of action, and its truculence from the point of view of Edmonton city whose assessed tax base was adversely affected, were based on its fortunate industrial development. The per capita assessment of Edmonton, the MD of Strathcona, and the degraded towns of Jasper Place and Beverly were from 1951 to 1954 as shown in Table 9.

Table 9. Assessment per capita of four local authorities in the Edmonton Metropolitan Area, 1951-54

Year	*Edmonton*	*MD Strathcona*	*Jasper Place*	*Beverly*
1951	$ 850	$2,220	$480	$490
1952	$1,060	$2,825	$490	$720
1953	$ 990	$2,725	$510	$630
1954	$1,000	$4,570	$540	$650

McNally Commision Report, Chapter 11, p. 13.

On a per capita basis, therefore, MD Strathcona had an assessment by 1954 some four-and-a-half times that of Edmonton, almost nine times that of Jasper Place and seven times that of Beverly. Strathcona's mill rate had dropped from 45 mills in 1948 to 30 in 1955. Edmonton's mill rate at that time was 48, after being 56 as recently as 1951. The Commission observed:

> The evidence disclosed that Edmonton's industrial and commercial assessment as a proportion of the total has been dropping steadily until the recent re-assessment; and, as more residences are built in Edmonton and more industries are established in Strathcona just outside the boundaries, the disparity will increase, and the City's percentage of assessment for industry will drop and that of Strathcona will increase.[16]

Though it might appear that Edmonton had a strong case for the amalgamation of such prime industrial assets into itself — in the interests of preventing the "metropolitan tragedy" — it is also noticeable how reluctant it had been to afford the same consideration to degraded peripheral centres.

The McNally Commission's task was in part to assess the extent to which amalgamations of both degraded and affluent centres should be mixed. Viewed in terms of local government finance, it would be ideal if they counterbalanced each other and the city were thereby enabled to bring greater uniformity of service to the inhabitants of the degraded centres. The amalgamation of industrially assessed land would obviate any excessive drain on city finances in servicing the degraded centres. But such reasoning reduces a final judgement to a matter of dollars and cents. There were planning and "orderly development" arguments in addition. The city's claim to interest in its periphery rested on both planning and financial considerations. It was an interest of an egocentric rather than an altruistic nature, however, for it was aimed at denying to the residents of the MD Strathcona the excellent position they had achieved through industrial location. The city attitude was that of "help myself," rather than of assisting the interests of people affected by the city's own policy of industrial concentration and unwillingness to provide the kind of housing required by the large but poorer families typical of peripheral centres. When the domination of the city over its hinterland is taken into account, a provincial policy resting on the concept of "fair and equal" treatment for all local authorities is seen to be something of a farce.

The Social Credit government supported the autonomy of Strathcona MD in respect of its refining and industrial complex as well as its Sherwood Park (Campbelltown) development. It did so against the recommendation of the Royal Commission. The provincial government was in a very difficult position. In terms of metropolitan expansion — and suburban sprawl rather than downtown high-rise was the expansionary fashion of the time — , the case for a greater Edmonton was substantial. The provincial government recognized that the degraded centres and their inhabitants were generally keen on amalgamation with Edmonton, so that amalgamation could proceed if the city agreed. Strathcona, however, was dead set against the loss of its industry, though it did express a willingness to cede residential land to the city.

The industries themselves generally declined to give evidence to the Commission — only two appeared and the remainder were silent. The Commission did not think it likely that if their interests were seriously affected by amalgamation they would have been content for the MD to plead their case. The Commission then commented:

> It is aware there may be some disadvantages to industry being brought within the city boundaries, but there are none which the City Council or the Legislature cannot rectify. These largely have to do with taxation and the cost of electricity and gas.[17]

The provincial government, through such instruments as the Industrial Assessment Act, could arrange with the City Council and the industries terms which would not be a disadvantage to them on account of amalgamation. The government's dilemma arose, however, more from assumptions about the sanctity of local government *per se,* than from a desire to be in industry's good books. In the Commission's view, and probably correctly, industry in general is not particularly concerned about taxation as a factor affecting its locational decision. This would particularly be the case where taxation and public utilities costs were largely negotiable.

The assumption about the sanctity of local government was a matter the Commission had to consider. Strathcona in arguing its case had had to raise the question of its rights to autonomy against the threat of Edmonton city's case for its amalgamation. It is on these formal occasions, like the Royal

Commission's hearings, that such conflicts are elucidated. The case of Brantford, Ontario, had been used by Strathcona MD to defend its position.[18] But in that instance a board had found that growth in the jurisdiction of an adjacent local authority was "part and parcel of the growth of Brantford and on the evidence there was no basis for the contention that it was or is an independent phenomenon." The Royal Commission considered Edmonton-Strathcona to be the same situation, where a labour force in Edmonton and the conjunction of pipe lines had led industry to settle in Strathcona. Growth dependent on the presence of a city should not, in effect, be allowed to occur under the aegis of independent, separate local authority. If this argument is pursued, it would be difficult to deny the right of Calgary and Edmonton to determine Alberta's affairs once these centres could demonstrate the dependence of other minor centres on them.[19]

The Ontario board had also referred to the serious error of assuming that municipal boundaries were fixed and determined for all time. The existing expansion of the cities themselves, over a long time, had shown the error of this view. The Royal Commission supported the Ontario board's view that the basic principle was that:

> a municipal corporation does not exist for its own sake. It is created primarily to provide and maintain essential local services required by the area which, for the time being, is included in its boundaries. It has no claim to the lands within its boundaries which is comparable to an owner. The Commission agrees this reasoning applies with equal force to Alberta.[20]

This reasoning, and the evaluation of the rights of inhabitants in their organized political community or local authority vis a vis the rights "of an owner" of land, goes to the very essence of the conflict between individual and public interests. It is a problem endemic to all western societies, and particularly to town planning.

Individual rights have been of particular importance to the Social Credit movement, and to the UFA administration before it. It would appear from the ubiquitous nature of this problem, from its long-standing presence in Alberta, and from the conflict it gives rise to in the relations of local authorities surrounding the metropolitan centres and in their internal city planning problems, that the provincial government can ill afford not to become directly party to the major issues where this matter is so frequently raised. In its control of provincial assets the provincial government is the only instrument available to ameliorate the financial consequences on cities and their adjacent local authorities of the upholding of one or other aspect of the dilemma.

Metropolitan Planning and Finance

While the fringe communities had managed to get along in part by provincial grants and in part by failing to provide high-standard services, the cities could not cope in this way. Though they received enormous sums by the way of provincial grants, the high standards, variety of service, regional responsibilities, and the demands and expectations of managers of private investment placed their administrations in a different complex of problems. Their competitors for the attention of business and industrial investors were other expanding metropolitan centres, and their stumbling block to being "properly serviced" with money was not a scarcity of locally-settled business and industrial property to tax, but the failure of the senior levels of government to distribute public money in the amount and the way they would prefer.

Up to the 1950s, city councils had absorbed some of the public costs associated with new housing by using the general "local improvement" debt, but by 1956 they were tending to pass these costs increasingly onto the builder and in consequence onto the homeowner. The city's public money was being required increasingly for more general and more abstract matters than residential servicing. So long as the rate of immigration kept up, the demand for housing was sustained; and so long as the NHA kept lowering its equity requirement to the homeowner, city councils could afford to ignore providing incentives to individuals to house themselves in the city. Apart from fringe possibilities, people had to settle within city boundaries because their jobs were in the cities. The lending institutions were unlikely to reverse their selective tendencies, and individual home purchasers could confidently expect to benefit from capital gains as the cities expanded. The stage was being set in the early 1950s, by the process of passing on to the homeowner the full cost of residential development schemes, for the scene, familiar by the end of the 1960s, in which an ever-decreasing proportion of Canadians could afford new housing. The cost of building sites and interest rates on mortgages contributed substantially more than any other cost factors to this process. Simultaneously, the ever-increasing expansion of metropolitan areas became thought of as a necessary part of their nature. The fact of metropolitan growth became as much a part of the battery of unquestioned assumptions implicit in metropolitan planning as was the autonomy and right of local authorities to make decisions, as provided by provincial government policy. The two together have ensured the continuation both of the phenomena associated with high rates of city growth and of the problems these have generated for the past twenty years.

Coupled to the increase in scale and the continued speed of growth, the mechanisms of control have become increasingly complex. The array of intramunicipal committees, of district commissions, provincial boards, ministers, etc. specialists—(lawyers, administrators, and planners)—which are involved both in getting applications for new activity approved and in stopping or directing them according to the General Plan, has reached dismaying proportions. Calgary moved in 1950 to set up a Town Planning Department and other planning machinery, replacing the earlier town planning commission and an inadequate zoning by-law.[21] In Edmonton, following the 1948 Bland Spence-Sales Report, a Town Planning Department was organized in 1949. Its staff was kept distinct from that of the Edmonton District Planning Commission. The problem confronting the provincial government in acknowledging, on the one hand, the contribution of professional planners and technical boards to planning, the preparation of official plans, and "orderly development"; and on the other, the right of popularly elected councillors to determine the future of their urban areas, came to be which of them should have priority and the right to make the final decision. The 1953 Planning Act clearly gave the local council the right to decide the outline of the future, subject to hearings on and advertisement of the proposal. But any application for a new subdivision was an indication of future potential investment and higher local tax returns. Unless very clear and good reasons for its prohibition could be provided by the District Planning Commission in terms of the "general plan" and the by-laws of the local authority itself, the tendency was that the wishes of the elected council would be upheld. The provincial board had power to disapprove and enforce its disapproval, and the district commission could only disapprove! The McNally Report comments:

> The enforcement of a general plan, whether inter- or intra-municipal, thus depends entirely on the willingness of the municipality or the Provincial Planning Board to enforce it. Since the policy of the Board is not to overrule the municipality, in practice the control of the spread of subdivisions into rural areas depends entirely on the willingness of the individual municipality.[22]

This practical situation conformed to Social Credit philosophy at the point where local authority autonomy remained paramount. The "experts" to be used at the provincial level of administration in 1935, were in reality employed and used by 1955 in the powerful metropolitan centres.[23] Their situation was set, however, not by provincial affairs and the application of Social Credit principles, but by elected councils and their committees, provincial boards of public officials supported by a minister (the Planning Board, the Public Utilities Commissioners and the Highways Department), and above all the interests and intrigues of local authorities intent upon furthering their own tax base or thwarting the plans and intentions of neighbouring authorities.

The immense significance of local authority boundaries, the right of councils to decision, the variety of local authorities existing in metropolitan regions, and the increasing complexity of the law, all bear witness to the competition, manoeuvering, intrigue, and jealousy typical of local government both in Alberta and elsewhere. The day-to-day situation was anything but "orderly development" in human affairs, though it did result in the increasing use of concrete and pavement of which the metropolitan areas came to be composed. In part this situation sprang from the use of land and its subdivision as the primary means of development control—at least land use and concrete was amenable to some control. In part it lay with the use of local authorities as the unit of planning. But it throws into relief the failure of provincial authorities to use the authority properly constituted in the provincial government by the BNA Act, to achieve the orderly development so popularly subscribed to at all levels of provincial urban affairs.

The provincial government was aware of a dilemma. In the 1950 Budget Speech, Premier Ernest Manning commented:

> As legislators, we are confronted with two extremes in public attitude as a result of the improved economic and financial position of the Province. On the one hand there is a tendency to regard increased revenue from the development of our resources as licence for reckless spending and irresponsible commitments to satisfy the demands of minority pressure groups without due regard to future consequences or the best interests of our people as a whole.
>
> On the part of others, there is a tendency to overcaution, which would unduly retard the bold and vigorous action necessary to continued progress and development. The Government does not subscribe to either of these extremes.[24]

The budget was to be aimed at facilitating the government's "pursuing at all times a vigorous program for the continued progressing development of our Province under a system of individual enterprise, assuring to each citizen a maximum degree of individual opportunity and personal freedom."[25] Income from natural resources had by 1950 replaced taxation as the province's major source of income. It accounted for 31.75 percent of estimated revenue.[26] The Department of Municipal Affairs' appropriation was to be increased in 1950 by $65,000, to a total sum of $347,000.[27] Public Works, on the other hand, was to receive $5.8 million more than the previous year, to a total of $23.7 million.[28] It was already clear that capital construction, rather than thought, planning, and appropriate direction of expansion — the very essence of "orderly development" — was to be the hallmark of the provincial policy.

The McNally Commission Report contains reference to the "unholy mess" of general urban form in which the city of Edmonton's new Town Planning Department started its work in 1949.[29] The report also observed that "In the short period of five years, planning in the two cities has produced lasting beneficial results, and has demonstrated the need for continued application of sound planning principles."[30] Within the jurisdiction of the cities planning was achieving results. It was in the wider area, within the jurisdiction of more than one local authority, and where the public interest was divided among competing local councils, that the intractable aspects of orderly development emerged. The McNally Commission observed that "When the needs of a metropolitan area have become obvious and pressing, they have traditionally been met by the creation of *ad hoc* authorities."[31] It cites examples across Canada in support of this generalization.

Why, however, should there be resource to *ad hoc* instruments when responsibility for provincial affairs rested with its government? Toronto, in establishing a federal type of Metropolitan Council, had by the 1950s moved towards neither purely *ad hoc* instruments nor provincial direction, but its Metropolitan mechanism still left the relation of its jurisdictional area to its hinterland and the relation of itself to the broader urban network of the province and of the nation as a whole unresolved. The identification of the reasons why the generally acknowledged intensification of relations in business, industry, and commerce across urban centres should occur concurrently with the favouring of *ad hoc* local governmental instruments — the very opposite of the trend in private business — remains one of the unexplained features of recent industrial society. Some explanation may be found in the entrenched nature of the BNA Act and provincial-federal relations, but there is none of a legal nature in municipal-provincial relations.

One explanation lies in the same principles as led to the separation of boroughs in the Poor Law Administration of 19th century Britain. By separating themselves off by means of borough boundaries, the rich were able to pay lower taxes for a higher standard of public services and receive fewer calls on their welfare account than if their taxes were spread over meeting the greater needs of impoverished areas. In Alberta, so long as provincial policy was aimed at recognizing the autonomy of each local authority and of distributing provincial grants through per capita and assessment criteria, it was, in effect though not in theory, maintaining the boundaries between human settlements that faciliated the same differential between rich and poor as applied under the Poor Law. In its analysis of per capita expenditures of the fringe areas around Calgary and Edmonton, as compared with these cities, the McNally Commission found "that the fringes are spending considerably less than half as much per capita as the cities in the Calgary area, and somewhat more than half as much in the Edmonton area."[32] In Calgary, in 1955, per capita expenditures were $91.21 as against $27.73 in Bowness and $42.72 in Forest Lawn. In Edmonton they were $94.34 as against $51.53 in Jasper Place and $56.68 in Beverly.

Ever since the early 1950s, and continuing through to 1971, local councils have not been above withdrawing from district planning commission membership if the latter came down in favour of another local council affected by the first council's proposals on expansion of boundaries, or for other reasons. The McNally Report records the behaviour of the Council of Sturgeon MD in 1950-51 involving a dispute with that of Beverly. When the District Planning Commission agreed to favour Beverly's application on the ground that Beverly needed some of Sturgeon's land for industrial development, and the Board of Public Utilities Commissioners upheld the commission in the main, Sturgeon withdrew its membership from the commission. Though still obliged to remain legally a member, it no longer participated, and in consequence compromised the effectiveness of the District General Plan.[33] Other examples of withdrawal are also provided in the report. The enforcement of any district plan therefore depended upon the voluntary membership of local authorities. An important part of a plan could fail because of obstructive tactics by a local authority who saw in it a cost to its ratepayers or a thwarting of its own ambitions.

The metropolitan centres, with land inside their boundaries becoming used up, felt obliged to expand into the periphery. Not only had their councils ambition, but they were also pushed by necessity. Up to the mid-1950s Calgary and Edmonton had had surplus land within their jurisdiction, but by this time the location preferences of private enterprise had pushed their development to the boundary in selected places. Their councils felt "hemmed in" despite having agricultural land within the boundary. This situation inevitably compounded their difficulties over expansion because peripheral local authorities had only to point to the unused acreage of the city to refute a claim for expansion. The city councils, however, were faced with the managers of private enterprise claiming that favourable sites for location contributed to, if they did not determine, the fate of their investments. The managers were faced with the stigma of failure if they could not acquire what to them was essential, and had to consider an alternative city for their enterprises. The report remarks: "Within each metropolitan area as a whole, there is a 'trend of development', both residential and industrial, which goes on regardless of municipal boundaries."[34] The case the cities first made to the Royal Commission was to annex large areas to themselves, but on second thoughts "suggested rather less ambitious extensions into rural lands, but both cities believe firmly in the planned control of land uses outside the city limits, as greenbelts."[35]

The "greenbelt" as proposed by Edmonton, was a form of zoning for land use whereby the city acquired rural land for agricultural, recreational, institutional, and even industrial purposes. But it was subdivision for residential purposes which constituted the point at which the line would be drawn.[36] Needless to say, organized real estate interests, as represented in city real estate boards, were opposed. In their view enough land should be incorporated to accommodate expansion for a generation ahead — considered to be 30 years.[37] The greenbelt concept to them constituted an unnecessary limitation in the early 1950s when the NHA and the federal government were wedded to single-family dwellings and before the interest of lending insititutions in downtown high-rises had matured.

The hesitancy on the part of the cities to urge incorporation of too extensive adjacent lands was based on financial and planning considerations. Calgary planners were willing to assume "that the district planning authority could and would exercise satisfactory control of land use outside the city limits" if a smaller area was incorporated.[38] As early as the mid-1950s, the metropolitan centres had become aware that as cities grow, "the per capita costs tend to rise, and not in a straight line but by a series of steps or jumps at certain critical population figures."[39] The incorporation of existing fringe areas would devolve the responsibility for their adequate servicing onto the metropolitan council — in effect, the Poor Law's boundary would be removed. Thus, adequate district planning became critical to the finances of metropolitan growth, just as city growth itself inevitably involved higher per capita costs. The cities' interests in their regions was double-edged.

The approach taken by Calgary and Edmonton towards this problem varied importantly. At the time the McNally Royal Commission was sitting, Edmonton's District Planning Commission had already developed a policy involving the dispersion of industry to established satellite centres around it — Fort Saskatchewan, Leduc, Stony Plain, — and a greenbelt in its immediate periphery. The policy was only partly successful, but it is interesting that it was formulated as early as the 1950s in view of the 1970 situation in Edmonton. The report commented on it favourably and saw in it the possibility of pioneering a new type of Canadian region.[40] This was at a time when satellite theory was still maturing, especially in Britain. Calgary, on the other hand, with few already established urban centres with a self-sustaining industrial or commercial base, was faced with the added difficulty of having to sponsor *de novo* satellite centres. For this it had no jusisdiction unless the province was prepared to act or one of the regional towns or villages effectively acted. Calgary's traditional policy was to concentrate development as far as it was possible within its own boundaries, and its choice of policy over satellite centre development, greenbelts, etc., favoured the continuation of its tradition.

It should not be assumed from this difference in policy, however, that Edmonton was relieved of the problems arising from its selective intrusion onto land controlled by adjacent local councils. This intrusion has occurred in both Calgary and Edmonton, for the location preferences of private investment remained highly selective and led to corresponding situations in the respective cities. But such processes inevitably involve the district planning commissions and their authority vis-a-vis the voluntary participation of local authorities. The McNally Commission was of the opinion that "the time has come to amend the legislation so as to authorize enforcement of a district general plan."[41] The method of enforcement discussed by the Commission was similar to that of Metro-Toronto, where the city was awarded extra-territorial planning powers through the Metropolitan Council. Affected local councils within the area were consulted by the minister before approving the greater plan, but the city retained the initiative. The Commission identified several difficulties in its application to Alberta and recommended against it.[42] Its own recommendations were to strengthen by amendment the existing planning machinery, and to give Calgary and Edmonton three members rather than one on the district commissions. The planning areas were to be enlarged, and a clear separation of staff in the city planning department and the district commission were to be introduced — a recommendation which had reference to Calgary as this separation was already the case in Edmonton.

The recommendations did change the processes which the Commission had been set up to consider. By missing out the potential but essential role of the province in planning, leading, and deciding multi-authority issues, the commission had no effective answers to disorderly practices occurring at the scale of metropolitan areas. It defended its position by reference to a false analogy. It argued as follows:

> No new principle is now being asserted nor is any new concept being advanced. We must all recognize that the smooth working of our democratic system often requires that the sectional interest must give way to the larger public interest. For example, the absolute ownership of property by an individual no longer implies a right to use it for any purpose the owner sees fit. If the law so prescribes, the owner must make the use of his property conform to the public weal. Without its zoning by-laws there could be no orderly development within the cities; all would be hodge-podge.[43]

If the attributes of a democratic system were to be logically extended, the provincial government had the right to require that city sectional interests give way to the interests of the province; if the attributes of ownership in relation to the public weal were logically extended, the provincial government was given the right by the 1867 constitution to claim that the metropolitan centres has no exclusive right to determine the locale of the province's industries, and hence its major tax base. But the commission could not see a way through its difficulties. It had to accept the power inherent in the cities, relative to adjacent local authorities. It remarked:

> Thus, in fact, there is nothing startling or out of harmony with our system of government when it is now recommended that all municipalities, both rural and urban, should be called upon to sink their individual ambitions, when necessary to conform to the regional plan which has been moulded to direct the orderly development of the total region.[44]

This was hardly in accord with that aspect of Social Credit philosophy that promoted the autonomy of local authorities and respected their rights of decision. Such unanimity of public authorities would not necessarily be acceptable to the managers of private investment either, for their techniques included the manipulation of public authorities in the search for the best deal.

Metropolitan financial difficulties were seen as arising from the cost and scarcity of developmental capital. This was the case despite the ever increasing provincial direct capital assistance, the growing road maintenance subsidies, education grants (which totalled $29.4 million or almost 24 percent of total estimated provincial expenditures in 1955)[45], health and welfare grants (which in turn were together almost as large as education), and a variety of other provisions. Rapidly increasing population, the lag in construction during the depression and the war, inflation, higher standards such as four to five single family dwellings per acre instead of higher densities, were identified as contributory.[46] But population was increasing at a mere fraction of the rate of increase in capital expenditure during the first post-war decade. In Calgary, the population increased between 1946 and 1955 from about 100,000 to 169,000, or by 69 percent. The gross debt increase, however, was in the order of fivefold, from $9.5 million to $50.5 million. In Edmonton, the population rose from 115,000 to 209,000 in the corresponding period, or by 82 percent while gross debt increased almost fivefold, from $16.5 million to $71.9 million. Per capita gross debt (excluding education) rose from $95.22 in 1946 to $299.04 in 1955 in Calgary, and in Edmonton from $143.81 to $343.24.[47] Net debt per capita had moved from $56.78 to $165.91 in Calgary over the same period.[48] Edmonton had managed to capitalize its extensive utility services from revenue to a greater extent than had Calgary. Edmonton's net per capita debt had moved from $109.97 in 1946 (dropping to $96.75 in 1948) to $150.45 in 1955.[49] Edmonton in its overall debt position had experienced a less rapid rate of increase in city debt than Calgary. This was due to Edmonton's starting the process in 1946 under wartime developmental pressures, and Calgary only in 1948. By 1955 the gap between the cities was closing rapidly.

The provincial government, by way of the 1950 Self-Liquidating Projects Act and the 1953 Municipal Capital Expenditure Loans Act, had supposedly come to the rescue of the municipalities in their search for capital. But it was to be a rescue that was rather long enduring. Prior to this they had floated debentures on the open market. By 1955, 78.3 percent of Calgary's debt was held by the province and in Edmonton some 53.5 percent. In Edmonton much of the debt had been incurred before the provincial schemes were introduced. The provincial position was to provide the local authorities, in practice mainly Calgary and Edmonton, with developmental money without attaching to such money the condition that it be used in the interests of the province considered as a whole. The McNally Commission had the metropolitan area — the city and its immediate hinterland, especially peripheral urban centres — as its terms of reference. There was no concerted province-wide enquiry into the consequence and *modus operandi* of metropolitan rapid growth and the relative degradation of the rest of the province.

The conditions which provincial considerations could have imposed with the supply of capital to the metropolitan cities were the allocation of appropriate industry to other centres in need of an industrial tax base, with residential housing at less cost to the local authority and home owner than that of urban sprawl in the cities; the introduction of rapid transit facilities for city workers across undeveloped land to residential areas sited in economic and congenial areas beyond the cities; the examination of high-rise and concentrated residential provisions for city workers wishing or having to reside in the city itself; the provision of high quality retail outlets in newly established residential areas instead of permitting their concentration in the downtown area; and the provision of mortgages at low interest rates. There was no institution in Alberta, and no department of government, whose responsibility it was to examine, reasearch, and impose the introduction of the developmental techniques likely on the one hand, to mitigate the circumstances growing in Calgary and Edmonton, and on the other hand, to examine the alternative possibilities available elsewhere in Alberta or in the cities themselves. Money, from natural resource exploitation, was seen as in itself sufficient to solve all immediate and identifiable problems.

The provincial decision to grant capital to the metropolitan centres on the assumption that they knew their own problems and interests best, led to a disregard of the extant tendency towards degradation elsewhere in the province. Concurrently, the more public money that became tied up in the metropolitan centres the more difficult was it to break the process. As the city debt increased, incurred to provide public amenities large enough to supply predicted rates of growth, so the more urgent did it become that industry and commerce be attracted to them to provide urban employment opportunities. Alberta's small towns were competing against both metropolitan city councils and the immediate predilections of private business and the locational stranglehold on mortgages granted the lending institutions by the federal government through CMHC and the NHA. Private business, itself anxious to optimize its profit-making circumstances—such as the existence of a large local market, availability of a labour pool, an educated labour force, all public amenities provided to the door, plus extensive transport facilities, pressed for rapid and continuous growth. The difficulty of city councillors, coping desperately with growth, was to turn "growth" into "development."

Councillors saw their problems as deriving from population increases, high standards of "public demands," the lack of available capital "to do it all with," the inflexibility of adjacent local authorities, and the ever enduring dilemma of immediate expediency and long-term requirements. The more business they attracted to themselves the better their tax base to pay for what they had already built; the better the chances of relieving urban unemployment and of providing for the city's children, the city's recreational and health needs, the aged, and the handicapped. The early 1950s was a time when the scale of organization to cope with social welfare, health, and education had not shifted above the local authority level to the extent it was to do the following twenty years. By providing the money, but no solutions at a scale larger than the metropolitan area, the provincial government was both elaborating the scale of difficulty within the city and incarcerating city problems within their own adjacent boundaries. But these processes of elaboration and incarceration were to back-fire on the provincial government by requiring them to continue its rescue operation, and undermining its position politically in the debates on the review of the Canadian constitution. It back-fired also on the remainder of the province by inhibiting the development of a network of urban centres, towns and rural local authorities with potential for take-off and reciprocal support to each other and to the metropolitan centres. In response to their shortage of capital, the cities were finding means of assisting themselves by avoiding the need to borrow. By using surplus revenue and reserves, Calgary had been able to provide eight million dollars of its $39 million (some 21 percent) spent on capital works between 1948 and 1953. This money also had the advantage of being free of the voter's approval, and that of the Public Utilities Commissioner, and thereby left the council free in the decision over its expenditure. The sale of city-owned lands had contributed over a million dollars. In Edmonton, the situation was more favourable still. The McNally Report shows the sources of capital funds, 1947-1955, to have been as in Table 10.

Table 10. Sources of capital funds, Edmonton, 1947-1955 (in thousands of dollars)

Source	*Amount*
Debenture Issues	57,775
Reserve Funds	28,014
Current Revenue	7,852
Pending Capitalization	4,747
Total	98,388

Of the total $98,388,000 in capital funds, almost $38.47 million was spent on "utilities plant extension" and only $41.01 million on "Public Works and services." The McNally Commission commented on Edmonton's fortunate owning of "so many 'profitable' civic utilities," and on the substantial savings in annual debt charges and therefore on property taxation.[50]

By requiring pre-payment of certain local improvements on land sold by the city instead of collecting it later on time-payments, the city was saved the task of finding the capital itself. Where private developers could be required to install all the utilities and physical services in large developments, the city's capital needs would be substantially assisted. The 1954 NHA terminated the joint lending arrangement between CMHC and the lending institutions, and introduced one whereby CMHC insured mortgages of lending institutions on residential construction. The Act also introduced the inspection role of CMHC allegedly as the banks were in no position to do it and bank mortgage money was urgently needed. CMHC's interest was in large-scale development projects in order to cope with "urban expansion." The NHA already provided for the part financing of public services to residential development. The stage was set by 1954 for the large scale developer to take over the capitalization of public services to the new development areas. In Calgary, two such developments — Glendale and Thorncliffe — were financed in this way by 1955, but Edmonton had not moved towards it at that time. The Royal Commission recommended that it should do so.[51] One of the effects of this change was to remove the costs of initial capital financing of development services from local authorities to the developer, and then on to the homeowner via NHA assistance. Thus, through provincial assistance direct to the local authority, and by greater use of NHA mortages and federal assistance to the home-buyer, the city councils were to be relieved of the pressure to find developmental capital for their rising populations and rapidly increasing commercial and industrial enterprises.

In 1954, Calgary's taxpayers were accounting for about 75 percent of city revenue; of this 75 percent the property tax contributed 80 percent, business tax 8.4 percent, local improvement levies 9.1 percent, and sewer service charges 1.7 percent. But the percentage was expected to decline in 1955 "thanks to larger provincial and federal grants."[52] Calgary in its evidence to the Royal Commission saw the answer to its predicted growing deficit to 1959 — when it was expected to be $6.6 million on certain stated assumptions — in terms of the province coming increasingly to its aid. It recommended that the province take up 50 percent of the gross costs of education, 100 percent of the gross costs of hospitalization, and unconditional grants-in-aid on a per captia basis, with a bonusing system for rapid growth and "demonstrated fiscal need."[53] This plea has a familiar ring in 1971, and for reasons that have tended to persist over the years. Evidence before the Royal Commission had highlighted public concern over the heavy burden of local property tax. Some had argued that just because senior levels of government were taxing more, local government tax should be reduced. The Commission observed:

> But this is surely a perverse way of looking at it; and it is unreasonable for the taxpayer to direct so much of his fire at his local taxes. If there is a "villain" in the tax-pile at all, it is the international situation, which compels the federal government to maintain high taxes for defence of the realm.[54]

Had the Commission broadened its "international situation" from mere defence expenditure to oil trunk lines, northern development, etc., to cover the whole process of national development under conditions of transferability of private capital over national boundaries, it would have been nearer the mark.

Such techniques as avoiding the necessity to incur debenture debt, and the increasing provincial capital assistance, do not explain why the rate of borrowing was so markedly greater than the rate of population increase. Among its explanations, the McNally Commission found the public to be expecting "complete services" more quickly than previously. It remarked:

> When a new sub-division is open up, the house-owner does not expect a long waiting period before all his utilities are in, his sidewalks laid, his street paved and boulevarded, public transport laid on, and so forth. The only way these public works can be undertaken quickly is by city borrowing.[55]

The Commission concluded that "the debt has been accumulated in response to public demand. It found there was no evidence of city extravagance or irresponsibility.

But if one searches the available literature, there is very little evidence of the newly arrived city immigrant from Canada's farms and small towns, or of the immigrant from overseas, demanding in an organized way that such a standard of service be provided. It may be argued that they moved to the city because of the standard set there — that it was part of their motivation in assessing the relative advantage of the two situations. But this is not the same thing as debt being accumulated "in response to public demand." It is true that property owners had tended to support city borrowing when put to the vote, but non-property owning citizens were at that time disenfranchised. The dwellers in the degraded peripheral centres adjacent to the cities, about whom the Commission had a great deal to say, had decided, perhaps deliberately, that they preferred lower standards if it involved them in less expense or debt. They stated, however, that they would prefer the city situation and were in favour of amalgamation.

The standards of city amenity were in large measure set by CMHC and the private lending institutions operating through the NHA. The fear of city engineers, on handing over to large developers the construction of services on the development site, was that the cost of maintaining an inferior service would fall on the city once the services were handed to the city on the development being occupied. Thus, to some extent the standards of service were dictated by the subsequent cost of maintenance over a given estimated life, both in respect of dwellings and public services. With the rising level of income after the war — concurrent with the rapid industrialization of production — the public capacity to pay for the standards set was apparent. But this is not a matter of debt being accumulated "in response to public demand." Rather it is a question of standards being set by decisions external to the citizen and in part to the cities themselves namely, by CMHC, the NHA and the lending institutions to which the immigrant home-seeking public was obliged to conform. The public either had to pay for those standards or else move to the peripheral areas. The incidence of second mortages, and the persistent inability of senior government to provide the means of housing and ever-increasing proportion of the lower income segment of the urban community bears witness to this conclusion.

This conclusion, however, does not account for the limited incidence of public pressure which was exerted on city councils for what rapidly came to be recognized as an appropriate standard of service. The explanation of this lies, however, in the relativity associated with "my" situation as taxpayer and property owner to "his" situation as enjoyer of an amenity. "I" do not now have this amenity but I am also a taxpayer and property owner. It is a matter of relative deprivation in a common situation of high standard service overall, when both parties are owners of land and improvements capable of capital appreciation in a developing situation. It is the same attitude as is found in the claim for equal treatment made by the managers of privately organized business. Any "unfair" treatment in their case is viewed as jeopardizing the viability of the company in the so-called competitive market situation, though each company seeks ardently to maximize its own advantage in its negotiation with the city before setting up business and in subsequent changes. There is, in addition, the common attitude of the individual in trying to get for himself as much as can be got from the collective. In 1971 it was not unusual to hear the owners of rural residential parcels some miles outside Calgary's city limits expressing their conviction of entitlement to the same water and sewage facilities as the city-dweller — after all, they worked in the city!

In the past the problems of the Alberta government have in part been derived from the expectations of Albertans concerning this entitlement to public amenities. This attitude had something to do with the end of the Liberal administration in 1921 and of the UFA administration in 1935. Similarly, it could be argued that the defeat of the Social Credit administration in 1971 was associated with their refusal to accommodate the metropolitan and urban centres generally with additional capital grants. The McNally Commission, in a comparison of debt among several Canadian cities, noted the relatively low per capita assessment which Calgary and Edmonton had in order to support their debt.[56] Yet Edmonton had the highest gross per capita debt of all cities listed and only four other cities surpassed Calgary's. The municipal debt, including school debt, had increased much faster in Alberta's urban areas than in any other province of Canada, save British Columbia. By 1954 Edmonton and Calgary had 90 percent of Albertan cities' debt, and three-quarters of all urban debt in Alberta.[57] Viewed in historical perspective, the Commission pointed out that "The city debt has been *relatively* much larger in the past."[58] The cities were not, in 1954, pressing against the limits to borrowing imposed on them by law as they had been in the depression. The City Act limited the *general* debt to 20 percent of the taxable assessment, and Calgary was, in 1955, using only 63.8 percent, and Edmonton 67.8 percent, of their legal permissible limit.[59]

The policy of the provincial government assisting the cities at low rates of interest, and through municipal grants-in-aid, had in part accounted for the high incidence of capitalization in Calgary and Edmonton by 1955. Alberta's benefits were being passed on to local government; yet the cities were demanding more. Public expectations of amenity and standard could be interpreted by city councillors as "public demands," and they were conscious of their electoral victories in terms of what their programs might offer the elector. The policy of the provincial government in 1955 was to maintain an explicitly fair and equal treatment of local authorities, and to demonstrate to the provincial electorate the high standard of its administration and the wisdom of the pay-as-you-go policy of Social Credit public finance. It was convenient to maintain such a posture so long as local action remained at the metropolitan city level and national action was carried on at the federal level.

The manoeuvres in Ottawa over the NHA, over the funding of cities trying to cope with urban sprawl and its attendant development costs, over the incentives to encourage private lending institutions to lend on residential mortgages (which had culminated in 1954 in the banks being brought into the mortgage field), over the control of the economy in its oscillations between unemployment and inflation, and over the demands for housing following the urban migration, were problems that could largely pass the provincial government by. The federal government had determined that point in 1935 and again in 1944. The Canadian national elector determined the fate of parties in Ottawa. The elected federal member was held responsible for the public problems of the urban unemployed and the scarcity of housing. The NHA and its amendments were the expression of his predicament. Within Alberta, it was largely the problems of city planning, regional planning, city debt, and the scarity of developmental capital, that preoccupied the attention of the provincial government. But it was precisely in these limited areas that the province was unwilling to take on the responsibility of leadership and the introduction of guiding policy for the province as a whole. *Laissez-faire,* equalized assessments, per capita grants, and additional financial assistance in civic buildings, grants-in-lieu of taxes and other calculable contributions were the expression of Social Credit philosophy. In the 1955 Budget Speech, the Provincial Treasurer, Mr. C. E. Gerhart, did touch a note of truth by saying (p.29):

> . . . the revenues accruing from taxation and the development of our natural resources, however buoyant,

will never exceed the constant need for progressive capital development and the consistent public demands for more and better standards of social services.

In the meantime, the cities, and particularly Edmonton, were rapidly narrowing their assessment base. As the proportion of commercial and industrial assessment had declined, a larger share of the property tax load was shouldered by residential property. In Edmonton, between 1946 and 1955, residential assessment had moved from $22.8 million to $131.7 million, i.e., over fivefold, while commercial and industrial assessment moved from $54.5 million to $100.6 million, or not even double. The percentage of the total assessment contributed by commerce and industry had dropped from 70.5 percent in 1946 to 43.3 percent in 1955.[60] In Edmonton, however, a good deal of industry had located outside the city limits, as the struggle with Strathcona over annexation bears witness. The appeal to the provincial government for increasing financial assistance on capital account was therefore being made in the face of rising property taxation burdens on the citizenry rather than on industry and commerce. Private business, benefiting as if was from high defence expenditure, public works at all levels of government, and from the general increase in standards of living, was being assessed locally at proportions declining relative to residential property. Yet business was the measure of city growth and the population migration was in response to the employment opportunities it offered. Business tax was increasing over the decade — from $0.4 million revenue or 9.5 percent of valuation to 1.4 million or 11.0 percent of valuation in Edmonton and $0.3 million or 7.8 percent of valuation of $1.0 million or 7.9 percent of valuation in Calgary[61] — but this tax's contribution to revenue remained insignificant overall.

The competitive struggle of cities to accommodate industry and commerce was being played out increasingly at the expense of the residential homeowner, whether through local property tax or the passing on of capital development costs to the developer and home-buyer through the federal NHA. It may also be asked who was benefiting most from the fivefold increase in capital debt incurred by the province's metropolitan centres in the first post-war decade? "Public demand," identified by city councillors and by the McNally Commission, was straining the use of the word "public" to include not only persons as individuals but corporate persons in the form of companies and corporations — the *in situ* expression of privately organized capital. Both classes of "persons" were demanding high standards, but with very different levels of opportunity to exploit them and of obligation to pay for them. When business may treat its local property tax as an expense — both for income tax purposes and as a cost of production to be passed on to the comsumer, — it becomes very clear who is enjoying an improving "quality of life," as the recent fashion phrases it. In 1956 the Royal Commission observed that "If if cannot be shifted, firms will tend to move — e.g., out of high property tax areas to low tax areas in the city."[62]

To sum up, the financial situation by 1955 was one where industry and commerce were contributing to city revenue by local taxation to a decreasing extent in relation to residential taxpayers; city councils had incurred debt at a many times greater rate than the population had increased, but were seeing their financial difficulties in terms of population increase and the cost of suburban sprawl; city councils were faced with "public demand" for an ever increasing standard of service, variety of service, and speed of service that in turn contributed to the attraction of more business and employment opportunities. The government's own philosophy had resulted in expanding capital servicing of urban "needs" as expressed in population increases; and councils had reduced their own capital requirements by passing off to home owners the cost of local improvements, and to homeowners, developers and the federal government the initial capital outlay on large development projects.

Calgary and Edmonton were still some 30 percent below their statutory limit on borrowing powers, and were seeking means of obtaining at below market interest rates yet greater amounts of provincial money. City councils' relation to local authorities on city boundaries was in conflict over both finance and planning. The McNally Commission had sided unequivocally with the right of the metropolitan centres to expand by annexation as well as to have the last word in regulating the form of development occurring beyond their boundaries in the jurisdiction of neighbouring authorities. The difficulties in the practical situation, with the advantage of hindsight, were obvious; but the Social Credit administration wished to persist in its philosophy of local autonomy and to rely on the good judgement and co-operation of its local authorities.

Recent Political Policy and Practice

The decisions of 1948-1955 established the determinants of many local events over the next fifteen years. By refinement and some diversification of instruments the provincial government maintained intact its policy and its relation to local authorities until the federal government's initiatives in the late 1960s. The slums, ghettoes, and riots of other North American cities did not appear in Alberta. The process of degradation in the rural areas was confined largely to hamlets and to the retail and service businesses of towns and villages. The population shift from southern to central and northern Alberta occurred as natural resource development increased in the northern areas and agricultural difficulties increased in southern Alberta. Calgary and Edmonton continued their public and private attraction of industry and business to themselves and, in Edmonton's case, to the region.

"Per capita" and equalized assessment criteria became the typical ingredient of provincial formulae to determine the amount of provincial assistance to be awarded any municipality. The provincial government was, and gave the appearance of being, a steady, adequate, and reasonably predictable administration that sought to avoid intrusion into local affairs, that legislated to meet human needs both across the province and in particular local circumstances such as those reflected in the New Towns Acts, and that reacted to, rather than led, the dynamic of the urban process occurring within its jurisdiction.

The new institutions of the past fifteen years tend to be elaborations of earlier ideas. The Municipal Financing Corporation of 1956[63] was an elaboration of the revolving fund principle introduced initially under the Liquidating Projects Act of 1950 and the Municipal Capital Expenditure Loans Act of 1953. The Alberta Housing and Urban Renewal Corporation of 1967 grew out of a committee established in the Department of Municipal Affairs in the mid 1960s and out of the changes to the Alberta Housing Act that were necessitated by Ottawa's desperate attempts to cope at the end of the 1960s.

By 1955 some $90 million had been made available under the Liquidating Projects and Capital Expenditure Loans Acts. The government was anxious to return to the local authorities decisions as to the amount and purpose of debt incurment in a clearer way than had been the case hitherto. Application for capital made to a department of the provincial administration — usually the Treasury — was embarrassing. By 1956 an independent corporation funded from the province, but not directly controlled by it, was preferred. Decentralisation of decision as a principle had previously been well tried in Alberta.

The 1956 Municipal Financing Corporation (MFC) Act provided for a board of seven directors, and a non-profit institution intended "to assist in municipal financing at the Board's discretion by purchase and sale of municipal securities at lowest possible cost, and to provide a convenient and accessible means to the people of the Province of investing in the debentures and other securities of provincial municipalities." (Section 3(3)). Though the MFC was the epitome of Social Credit philosophy of government in almost all its aspects, it also constituted the example *par excellence* of the provincial abdication of leadership in the direction of Alberta's urban process. The provincial government relinquished the most direct form of administration control of urban affairs available to it — public capital provision well below market interest rates in a situation of urgent need experienced by municipal councils, especially in the rapid growth centres.

The provincial government retained an influence, and even control, both by the designation of four persons to the board of directors and by the designation of voting rights to particular classes of shares, but it forfeited deliberately the right to say to any local authority that the condition of receiving such and such capital assistance is your undertaking to do, or not to do, a given act that in the provincial plan of urban development requires that such and such be executed in this or that way. Public control was instead left to the Planning Act, approval of local authorities proposals by the Board of Public Utility Commissioners and later by the Local

Authorities Board, and certain other mechanisms of influence by approval and negotiation. Provincial responsibility and leadership was transferred to an *ad hoc* board responding to the requests of local authorities whose situation necessitated their adoption of an egocentric attitude, a narrow and parochial perspective, and whose peers in the case of metropolitan city councils were metropolitan centres elsewhere in North America, rather than the smaller centres of Alberta itself.

The board of directors was to consist of the four government-nominated persons and three elected members. No member of the Government of Alberta and not more than one member of public service of Alberta could be nominated or elected. The shares of the corporation were to be classified as:

> Class A common shares allotted only to the Crown in the right of Alberta,
> Class B common shares allotted only to improvement districts, municipal districts, special areas, counties, hospital districts, school divisions and other minor local authorities of Alberta,
> Class C common shares allotted only to cities within Alberta,
> Class D common shares allotted only to towns and villages of Alberta.

The corporation was empowered to allot shares to local authorities "upon the basis of the populations thereof" (Section 10), who in turn were authorized to purchase shares by resolution or by-law of their councils. The ratio of classes of shares was fixed as 6:2:1:1 over the above alphabetical list, and the provincial government could increase the capitalization of the corporation from time to time "but not so as to vary the ratio between the numbers of Class A common shares . . ." and other classes (Section 10). Each of the Class B, C and D shareholders elected one member to the board of directors.

In this way influence and control over the corporation remained with the provincial government in the last analysis. The local authorities could never "take over" the corporation. The inherent conflict among local authorities owning Class B, C, or D shares was unlikely to engender even a unanimity among the minority. Control by the province was over the money allotted to shareholders, not over the process of urbanization as it was being played out in the province. No local authority was obliged to take up shares that might be allocated to it. There was no coercion of local authorities, but a non-shareholding local authority had no right of access to provincial capital through the corporation, or to contribute to the election of a representative of the class of local authority of which it was itself a part. Shareholding local authorities had one vote in the election of a board member for each share they held. The approval of shareholders was not required for any borrowings the corporation undertook. The corporation was empowered to appoint a staff, a president, vice-president, a chairman, secretary-treasurer, and a general manager.

The principal and interest of any borrowings of the corporation was guaranteed by the province. Its ceiling of borrowing was fixed at $750 million. Local authorities could also leave money deposited with the corporation at interest, and any profit of the corporation was to be returned to its shareholders. It was empowered to borrow money from financial institutions and to act as a financial agent for a local authority. But local authorities, whether borrowing direct from the corporation or using its agency services, had to procure the approval and assent of the Board of Public Utilities Commissioners and the ratepayers in the usual way. The corporation was not the means of controlling local authority finance, but the advice of governmental agencies involved with the financial status of a local authority could be sought. The Lieutenant-Governor in Council made regulations prescribing the rates of interest for deposits and loans, the manner of making loans and "the purposes for which loans may be made and prescribe the terms and conditions of any such loans" (Section 39(1)(c)).

The corporation started business at a rather difficult time. The Provincial Treasurer, E.W. Hinman, in the Budget Speech of 1957, remarked:

> It is unfortunate that the corporation must compete with industrial firms for the investors' dollar at higher interest rates which must reflect in higher taxes. The budget will reveal that the Government is doing a great deal to reduce these added costs to a minimum and to provide increased financial assistance.[64]

Inflation throughout Canada had led to the introduction of tight money policies by governments. At the same time the federal government introduced an export permit for the sale of natural gas to the United States pending a report from the newly formed Energy Commission. The United States had also moved to import oil from the Middle East and South America. Albertan oil imports became subject to the same controls. Alberta, for the first time, experienced "a cutback in our oil production to a point considerably below Conservation Board allowables and below the production necessary to permit profitable production of many wells. This meant lower royalties for Alberta."[65] The Provincial Treasurer added

> It has become apparent that we cannot look forward to a continuation of the rapid increases which have been usual in the revenue which we have come to expect from our natural resources.[66]

Nevertheless the government continued to find the capital needed by the MFC. By 1963, some $196 million was to be provided the corporation.[67]

Table 11 shows in round figures the sums of money provided through debentures to Edmonton and Calgary from 1957-8 to 1970.

Table 11. Municipal Financing Corporation debentures to Edmonton and Calgary, 1957-1970 (in millions of dollars)

Years	*Edmonton*	*Calgary*
1957-8	18.5	13.0
1959	16.0	14.1
1960	14.0	9.4
1961	17.1	7.9
1962	17.2	8.7
1963	12.5	9.2
1964	11.8	3.7
1965	16.3	13.7
1966	19.5	19.1
1967	21.0	13.1
1968	21.7	15.9
1969	22.8	19.3
1970	21.0	20.0
Total	229.4	167.1

The table shows the amounts to have varied from year to year, reaching a low point in 1964 — a time when the federal government's Municipal Loan Fund was giving considerable assistance. Table 12 presents the approximate totals received by the

Table 12. Municipal Financing Corporation debentures to ten Alberta cities 1960-1970 and per capita distribution*

Cities	*Amounts received $'000*	*Population 1966*	*Per capita receipts $*
Edmonton	193,909	376,900	514
Calgary	135,031	330,600	408
Lethbridge	11,625	37,200	313
Red Deer	9,281	26,200	354
Medicine Hat	6,175	25,600	241
Grande Prairie	4,889	11,400	429
Camrose	2,376	8,400	283
Wetaskiwin	1,867	6,000	311
Lloydminster	1,788	3,800	471
Drumheller	1,138	3,600	316

*Data kindly supplied in outline form by the Secretary of the Corporation.

ten cities of the province over the years 1960-1970, and the population of the cities in the 1966 census year. The per capita receipts — based on the total amount over eleven years divided by the 1966 population — are also shown.

The table shows no clear preference for money to be provided towards the metropolitan centres alone, though they are towards the top of the per capita distribution. By inspection, it seems that the amount of money provided between 1966 and 1970 has gone to the faster growing cities as measured by population increase. Lethbridge, for example, received well over $1.5m. in each of the years 1967-69. Similarly, Red Deer received sums on the one million dollar mark in each year from 1965-69.

Because of the demand on the Corporation's funds a figure of $50 per capita of municipal population (raised to $60 per capita for the winter of 1971-72) has been placed on borrowing each year, though amounts not taken up in any one year could be taken up at a later time to accommodate the erratic nature of municipal capital spending. The enormous disparity in absolute size of funds granted — from almost $200 million in Edmonton to $1.138 million in Drumheller — reflects the relative population distribution, but also shows the implicit trend towards encouraging the growth of those that "have" vis a vis those that "have not." The allocation encourages the trend of growth despite the distribution per capita in any year being applied to the province generally with scrupulous fairness.

The distribution of expenditure over the type of service capitalized shows the smaller cities spending up to 47 percent (in the case of Drumheller and 46 percent in the case of Red Deer) of their allocation on water and sewer services, as against 21 percent in Edmonton and 17 percent in Calgary. Similarly roads and bridges take up a percentage varying from 39.8 percent in Calgary (25.3 percent in Edmonton) to 10 percent in Drumheller and 11 percent in Medicine Hat. Calgary and Edmonton have very much larger percentages (18.5 and 28.6 respectively) under the heading of Utilities Plant and Line than any of the smaller centres.

The provision of 1956 did not quell the continuous demands for more money from the local authorities. The jealousies within the province centred around two interconnected issues: first, how much of the natural resource royalties accruing to the province were being devolved to the people and local authorities and how much being kept by the provincial government?; and secondly, how much were Calgary and Edmonton getting relative to all other local authorities? It was a typical response in a long Albertan tradition; but it was equally a consequence of the provincial government's lack of leadership and direction to the urbanization process. Had this leadership been made explicit — a provincial plan and the direction it was to take, been publicized and effective administrative techniques employed to execute it — the pernicious jealousies and suspicions derived from the "grab-all," "me first" opportunities of largely autonomous local authorities would have been subsumed under the direction of provincial policy with clearly demonstrable provincial achievements towards its goals made available for all to see and and work within. Criticism would have been directed to the goals and the means; but it would not have centred around the egocentric and eventually costly perspective of avaricious, organized local communities.

As early as 1955 the Budget Speech contained tables showing the provincial municipal assistance to all local authorities and to the cities of Calgary and Edmonton. This was continued for several years, but the tables appear to have been arranged to prevent the comparative analysis of this topic by yearly amounts. The analyst is bound to deal with a variety of actual and estimated amounts, as well as a variety of yearly aggregates.[68] Table 13 shows the estimated direct provincial assistance for 1954-55 and for 1958-59 for all local authorities and for Calgary and Edmonton.

Table 13. Estimated direct provincial assistance to all local authorities and to Calgary and Edmonton, 1954-55 and 1958-59
(in thousands of dollars)

Year	*Edmonton*	*Calgary*	*Edmonton & Calgary combined*	*All local authorities*	*Edmonton & Calgary as percentage of all local authorities*
1954-55	6,430	4,749	11,179	43,560	25.66
1958-59	16,190	13,026	29,216	96,416	30.30

The table shows the increase in direct provincial assistance to Calgary and Edmonton. By 1951 the percentage of Albertan population in these cities had reached 34 percent and it attained 46 percent by 1961.[69] The provincial government was therefore remaining true to its per capita principle of assistance. Similarly, the Provincial Treasurer, in the 1962 Budget Speech, pointed out that "total assistance to tax payers from April 1st, 1950 to March 31st, 1963, will be $1,045,634,703. It might be of interest to note also that our total oil revenues for the same period will amount to some $1.3 billion."[70] In addition local authorities had obtained provincial loans in excess of $496 million. It was thus apparent, at least from this data, that provincial revenues were being returned to the people and their local authorities to a substantial degree, and in a reasonably fair distribution.

It was in this Budget Speech (1962) that the Treasurer commented:

> Our hearts are so set on personal wants for which we must pay ourselves that we resent the contributions required of us, as taxes, to assure that certain minimum standards can, through public administration, become the heritage of every resident. Under such circumstances

> prudence and common sense forbid us to spend our reserves or to go into debt for ordinary expenses of Government . . . And so the decision was made to balance the budget this year.[71]

Later in the same speech, he said:

> I find it almost beyond comprehension that so many of our school trustees, our municipal councillors and hospital board members should go on day after day crying publicly that senior governments should provide more and more of the municipal revenue, that if more taxes are required senior governments should do the taxing, that by their failure to do these things senior governments are robbing our children of their rights and are endangering the future of our nation, that taxation of real property is the most onerous, the most inequitable, the most abusive of all forms of taxation. It is equally disturbing that these same people should bewail the threats to local autonomy which the very policies they advocate must make inevitable. It is paradoxical that one day they are critical of the injustices of creating local administrative units and delegating to them certain responsibilities which the British North America Act assigned to the provinces and the next day cry foul because the Provincial Government chooses to exercise some control over the local expenditure of funds provided by the Province. It seems incredible that urban administrators and urban taxpayers should assume that costs to them would be less under a broader tax base collected by the Province; for anyone who makes a study of the facts will soon be persuaded that the reverse is true.[72]

The consequential whirlwind of Social Credit philosophy was turning on Provincial Treasurer E. W. Hinman with vengeance. The relative deprivation experienced in the minds of individuals party to some of the highest standards of public service in Canada, coupled to the idea of getting all one could from the collective pot, were jeopardising the successful application of Social Credit principles. The issues that were to bring down the Social Credit administration in August, 1971, were evident to the Treasurer in 1962.

A threat was also coming, however, from another source, namely, the urban policy of the federal government by way of the Winter Works program, the Sewage Works program with its 25 percent forgiveness clause, and in 1963 the Municipal Development and Loan Board Act.

The federal government initiated the Winter Works program in 1960 with the dual purpose of creating winter employment and offering particularly the urban municipalities of Canada a chance to do a variety of needed public works. Alberta's municipalities undertook 737 projects in the 1960-61 program and 822 in 1961-62. The federal government paid 50 percent of the payroll involved, the province 25 percent, and the local authority the remainder. The total cost of the projects in the respective years was $21.1 million and $23.0 million, with the total payroll in the respective years amounting to $5.1 million and $5.6 million. The municipalities had had to contribute, in all, some $17.7 million and $18.8 million to get the work done, but the Provincial Treasurer remarked in 1962 that "the Municipalities financed their cost largely from provincial loans and grants, and to some extent from their reserves."[73] The municipalities were coming to find the federal government a useful ally to the provincial government in their search for capital, and this time from federal sources outside the NHA. The federal government of 1960 was trying to find ways of assisting urban local authorities at the same time as it respected the rights of the provinces under the constitution to control their local authorities. Extended support for manpower training, the start of industrial incentives for the location of industry in the more extreme areas of degraded Canada, and the winter works projects were expressions of this attempt.

The cities continued to take advantage of winter works until 1969. Their annual projects involved sums approaching $20 million a year over these years. Some 10,000 men were employed. In an apparent attempt to establish a direct link between the federal government and the local councils of Canada's major cities, the federal government voted $400 million in 1963 to be administered over five years through the federal Municipal Development and Loan Board. It was to be a system of low interest loans. The federal government was thwarted in its attempt to establish direct links with municipal governments only by the actions of the Quebec provincial government and a federal — provincial conference.[74] The money remained available, but the jurisdiction of the provinces over their local governments remained intact also. After the federal-provincial conference, the federal government proposed that each province receive a share of the money based on its proportion of population (1961 Census) to that of other provinces. Unlike the federal Industrial Incentives Act of 1969, there was in 1963 to be no discretion left to a federal minister over the proportional distribution among the provinces. Alberta's share was $29.2 million. Unlike some other provinces of Canada, Alberta opted to have the money administered directly through the federal Municipal Development and Loan Board, the CMHC, the Provincial Treasurer, and the local authority. In all, some 105 Albertan local authorities benefited from the scheme, 41 of these receiving loans in excess of $100,000.[75]

Table 14 shows the distribution of money over Alberta's municipalities whose total loans exceeded $250,000 under the scheme.

The range per capita of distributions in the $100,000 to $250,000 was from $247 in the town of Smoky Lake to $13 in Vermillion River county. The mean per capita distribution over the

Table 14. 1963-68 Municipal Development and Loans Board distribution over Alberta's municipalities in receipt of $250,000 or more

	Amount $	*Number of loans made*	*Sub-totals*	*Population 1966**	*Ratios: $ per head of population*
Edmonton (city)	11,322,094	23		376,925	30.04
Calgary (city)	3,945,292	41		330,575	11.93
Lethbridge (city)	776,507	8		37,186	20.88
Red Deer (city)	736,715	5		26,171	28.15
Lloydminster (city)	680,513	2		3,767	180.65
Grande Prairie (city)	648,567	8		11,417	56.81
	Sub-total over $500,000		18,109,688	786,041	23.04
Fort McMurray (town)	492,973	4		2,614	188.59
High Prairie (town)	481,838	4		2,241	215.01
Peace River (town)	454,218	5		4,087	111.14
High Level (town)	385,618	4		708	544.66
Drayton Valley (town)	360,549	7		3,352	107.56
Slave Lake (town)	356,623	5		1,716	207.82
Edson (town)	314,621	4		3,788	83.06
Canmore (village)	293,000	2		1,445	202.77
Brooks (town)	271,279	4		3,354	80.88
Wetaskiwin (city)	259,742	3		6,008	43.23
Medicine Hat (city)	254,333	2		25,574	9.94
	Sub-total over $250,000		3,924,794	54,887	71.51

In addition:
24 other municipalities received sums between $100,000 and $250,000
64 other municipalities received sums between $1,000 and $100,000

*The population date of 1966 is arbitrarily selected as the midpoint between 1964 and 1968. The population of each local authority at the time the loan was requested has not been obtained. Loans were made up to March 31, 1966, but payments in respect of them continued on into 1968.

24 municipalities was $45.63, but if four rural counties are omitted from these, the figure rises to $62.51 per capita. The average loan made in the $10,000 to $100,000 category was $47,480.

Since the allotment among the provinces had been made on a per capita basis, the provincial government decided in the first instance to distribute the money in a similar way over the province. This would demonstrate clearly the "fair and equal" basis of its administration. Also, after being advised by the province of the availability of the money and of its terms, local authorities were expected to initiate requests and submit plans and estimates. As applications could not be considered after March 31, 1966, the response of municipalities was expected to be speedy.

Events proved otherwise.[76] The provincial government again circulated the municipalities, more than a year after the inception of the scheme, to say the per capita allotment was removed and that all applications would be considered, provided they were received before the deadline. More applications followed from this change, but the real rush of applications came in only up to six months away from the deadline.[77] Some were received too late and were declined, or came in right towards the end when the funds were used up. Though the government took no steps to allocate funds or specifically direct funds to local authorities, it made use of them under the New Towns legislation or other legislation which enabled it to recognize a special status in a community. Funds were also offered to Edmonton towards the closing stages of the arrangement to ensure that the province's allocation was used up.

Table 14 shows that the distribution on a per capita basis varied markedly, from $544.66 for the new town of High Level to $11.93 per capita in Calgary.[78] The sub-section totals show that of the loans in excess of $500,000 the six cities in this category received $23.04 per capita, while of the towns and cities receiving loans from one-quarter to one-half million dollars the per capita distribution was $71.51, or over three times per capita that of the cities with the larger loans. Similarly the loans between $250,000 and $100,000 averaged $45.63 per capita, and $62.51 per capita if the three rural counties and one municipal district were excluded.

The five major cities of the province, Calgary, Edmonton, Lethbridge, Medicine Hat, and Red Deer, received among the lowest per capita allocations. Their weighted mean per capita distribution was $21.39, but the total sum allocated to them was $17,034,941 or almost 60 percent of all loans made.

Table 14 also suggests that the provincial government made good use of this federal money to provide many of the services required in some of the new towns of the province. In 1956 the provincial government legislated under the New Towns Act to identify certain places in the province, where a natural resource was to be developed by a company or corporation, which required the construction of a township either *de novo* or by radical improvement over an existing urban concentration.[79] The Act provided for the planning of the township site to be undertaken by the planning branch of the Department of Municipal Affairs. Construction was also undertaken by government, usually by contract, and the completed township handed over to local citizens as a local authority as soon as it was settled and the machinery of administration set up. The planning of the project took into account the anticipated size of the work force in the main company plant, the anticipated size of ancillary and supportive activities and, in those new towns that involved a radical reconstruction of an existing facility, the population already resident in the area.[80] The Act was administered by the Department of Municipal Affairs rather than by the Municipal Finance Corporation because the latter was essentially a shareholding proposition of established local authorities. "New towns" imply the growth of something not yet extant. The limit of $50 per capita implicit in the MFC funding arrangement would also be inadequate for the cost of a totally new town. For such reasons, new towns were better dealt with through the Provincial Planning Board and the minister, with cabinet approval of the loans of required, and the money disbursed through the Treasury. The government could thus justify its identification of certain localities by their special nature. Assistance to companies willing to undertake natural resource development in remote areas was justifiable in terms of provincial development generally, and particularly when it concerned areas remote from already developed parts of the province. For these reasons the Act did not compromise the basic philosophy of administration in the province.

In addition to formal new town development, other areas of rapid growth in the province which benefited from federal money included Slave Lake, High Prairie, Canmore, and Peace River. If the loans provided to such areas are added to the new towns, something like $3,250,000 was expended on growth centres already identified by companies and corporations for resource development, or for special government programs of development such as Slave Lake. This represented about 11 percent of the total loan to the province.[81] As might be expected, with new town development based upon the exploitation of new natural resources, almost all new towns and the rapid growth centres received high per capita loans under the federal scheme. They were located in the areas west of Edmonton and in the north of the province. The developed, small urban centres south and east of Edmonton who requested loan funding under the scheme, received per capita allocations approaching the $50 per capita average normally provided for under the Municipal Finance Corporation provisions.

The relatively high per capita allocation, involving loans of from $100,000 to one-quarter million, was in part accounted for by the high cost of construction in smaller towns and by the relative paucity of population to the cost of providing the services required. Unlike the larger areas, where additions could be made to an existing facility, smaller areas were frequently involved in providing the whole facility rather than only an addition to it. Similarly, as the addendum to Table 14 shows, the allocation of small sums, below $100,000, averaged out at $47,480, and was spread over a wide range of local authorities, some 64 small loans being made. On the basis of geographic spread over the province this was clearly and demonstrably fair.

The initiative of the provincial government in allocating these federally available funds in the way it did was significant from many points of view. Although the five major cities of the province received almost 60 percent of the total spent in the province, their per capita allocations were among the lowest. New towns and growth areas were allocated some 11 percent. The use of this money to support growth areas and new towns, that in turn supported the exploitation of natural resources by companies and corporations by providing an amenity for their employees and themselves, was a departure from previously existing provincial policy. In this respect, the New Towns Act was a significant and major change in emphasis from previous provincial philosophy. It involved the provincial authorities in taking direct initiative rather than encouraging the local populace to develop itself without superior guidance.

The change in policy was partly related to the experience which had been gained from oil development since 1947. Oil companies in their exploratory and developmental work had selected sites and, on their own initiative, developed town sites with a full range of recreational and other amenities. These company towns had virtually unsurped the authority of the province over its local authorities and had involved the companies in considerable overhead expense. How to hand over these towns to the province, especially when the company had little further use for them, was an inherent problem. Devon, for example, was never granted New Town status. The Imperial Oil Company merely transferred the township to the Department of Municipal Affairs. A further input to the policy came from a Provincial-Municipal Advisory Committee of six members set up by Order-In-Council on January 27, 1959, under the Minister of Municipal Affairs. This advisory committee contained a member from each of the Union of Alberta Municipalities and the Association of Municipal Districts and Counties, and was therefore a forum for consultation and teamwork between the two levels of government.[82]

The province's use of the 1963 federal money was in marked contrast to the federal government's original thoughts. The value of the stand taken by the Premier of Quebec in 1963 concerning provincial rights had been cogently illustrated. The original federal proposal was for a national measure to deal with unemployment, but as the $400 million provided was divided among the provinces according to their population at the 1961 Census, this intent was largely invalidated in terms of need. The federal government was obliged to introduce concessions to provincial autonomy to provide the provinces with a greater say in how the money was to be allocated. There is no indication that the original federal intention to involve CMHC in the administrative execution of the plan, hindered the application of policy in Alberta. Though there is no evidence explicitly stated in the parliamentary debates on the bill, it would appear that the Municipal Development and Loan Act was intended to be used mainly by the large urban centres. There is little doubt that their political influence, as seen in the representations made by the Canadian Federation of Mayors and Municipalities to Mr. Diefenbaker in 1962, might have brought about this result had the federal Loans Board alone been responsible for its administration directly with CMHC and the local authorities, and requiring provincial agreement only in principle. As it happened in Alberta, the influence of the provincial government seems to have been applied to the use of the money and, to some extent, to its own judgement of the province's needs.

The provincial government's responsibility for highways has provided a further opportunity to direct the urban development of the province. However, highways usually tend to enhance the centralizing tendencies of the major cities. Highways need to be understood in both their capacity to meet the needs of existing demands for transport and their capacity to determine the growth or decline of the towns and cities which they connect or influence. Road transport must serve the existing centres of production, though it can afford to pass by lesser centres not eligible for the service offered by the type of road under consideration. Thus, provincial policy had to favour Calgary and Edmonton if only for the reasons that their productive capacities had to be serviced and the public of the province expected to have easy access to them for a variety of its needs. Even if the policy of the Department of Highways is to construct roads to carry the maximum ton-mileage at the cheapest cost—and on this pretext to ignore the smaller towns and cities which lie just off its ideal route—its policy cannot ignore the centres from and to which its routes are planned. Calgary and Edmonton, therefore, are bound to receive the benefit derived from highway policy, though many lesser urban centres can be ignored along the route.

Accessibility to markets has always been one of Alberta's difficulties, as is shown in the thousands of miles of railway constructed in the province between 1882 and 1914. Accessibility to raw materials and their eventual export has recently come to dominate transport planning, particularly in northern Alberta. Many of the villages and hamlets scattered every seven to 10 miles along the lines of rail throughout settled Alberta bear witness to the former dependency on the railways to clear farm products out of the province. The demise of many of these small settlements and stations is not a consequence of railway policy, but is due to the widespread use of motor vehicles.

A glance at the road map of Alberta shows that the grid of major road intersections has shifted from one of about seven to 10 miles in an east-west direction and 20 to 25 miles in a north-south direction to one of about 80 to 100 miles in an east-west direction and 40 to 50 miles in a north-south direction. This change in the scale of the grid and in the axis of its directions reflects both the use of the motor vehicle and the creation of a central corridor of transport and development that moves from Edmonton through Red Deer, Calgary, and Claresholm to Lethbridge. The growth of an intersectory system, on an east-west axis, is discernable at widely distant points of the province. The route of the Canadian Pacific Railway in 1882 from Medicine Hat to Calgary and Banff provided the initial intersection with the north-south tendency of development. The Crowsnest Pass, Lethbridge, Medicine Hat rail and road intersection followed soon after the main line was built through Calgary. In 1970, with the opening of the Yellowhead Pass to road traffic, the road and rail route across north-central Alberta, from Grand Prairie through Edmonton to Lloydminister, the third of the east-west intersectory routes, was completed. Concurrently, the Grand Prairie - Peace River area, some 350 miles north west of Edmonton had been extending its links up the Mackenzie Highway and along the Peace River, as well as those that tie it to the Edmonton region.

These developments suggest the operation within the province of a trend towards the identification of particular towns whose position fortuitously places them in an advantage over others. If transport alone was the criterion of potential town growth the identification of such centres would be relatively easy. In addition to transport, however, a number of other considerations affecting growth become operative when growth is dependent on a laissez-fair policy.

Mention has already been made of the influence of lending institutions through the National Housing Act to centralize new house construction and the repair of existing dwellings. The tendency of industry and commerce to locate at centres of population which in turn influence their marketing opportunities, access to a variety of suppliers, and their ease of administration of loans and capital assets, has contributed very substantially to the process in the absence of provincial policy to the contary. In addition a number of less economically motivated influences exist. Edmonton in particular has benefited from these by being the capital city, the centre of government and administration, and by acquiring early a university and other cultural services.

Edmonton has used more public capital for municipal services than has Calgary. Table 15 attempts to show the per capita revenue, expressed in constant dollars, from "contributions, grants and subsidies" received by the three major cities of the province, Edmonton, Calgary, and Lethbridge, over the period 1951-1968 from provincial and local authority sources.[83] The data are derived from the annual reports for each year of the Department of Municipal Affairs, under the table "Cities — contributions, grants and subsidies." In the reports this table is broken down under the following sub-headings:

"Provincial grants," which includes the Municipal Assistance Act, the Public Welfare Assistance Act, Homes for the Aged and Infirm, Hospitalization Grants, and Other.

"Governmental enterprises," which includes the Provincial Crown Property Grants Act, the Municipal Public Utilities Surpluses, Contributions to Municipalities in Lieu of Taxes, and Other.

"Other contributions," which includes Sinking Fund, Excess Earnings and Other.

"Capital grants" of a provincial and other nature, but excluding federal government grants.

The population figures are derived from the first table of the same reports.

The data on receipts are presented in constant dollars to enable the additional observation to be made of the extent of real increase of these revenues over this period. The conversion factor, or deflator, used to obtain the constant dollar values, is as follows, based on 1949 = 100.

1949 = 100	1955 = 116.4	1960 = 128.0	1965 = 138.8
1951 = 113.7	1956 = 118.1	1961 = 129.2	1966 = 143.9
1952 = 116.5	1957 = 121.9	1962 = 130.7	1967 = 149.1
1953 = 115.5	1958 = 125.1	1963 = 133.1	1968 = 155.2
1954 = 116.2	1959 = 126.5	1964 = 134.4	1969 = 162.1

Table 15 suggests that by 1968 the constant dollar per capita revenue from sources contained in the Table was in the ratio of 55.60: 31.20.27.25 respectively over the three cities. The divergence between Edmonton and Calgary has emerged since 1957 and has expanded steadily since that time. In 1968 Edmonton obtained something over twice the per capita revenue from these sources than Lethbridge received, though this was the first year in which the differential has reached this extent and was in part due to a sudden increase in Edmonton's figure since 1967 and a decline in Lethbridge's since 1966. However, looked at over the 18 years involved, the differential between Edmonton on the one side and Calgary and Lethbridge on the other has been increasing, particularly in recent years. The mean per capita revenue over the 18 years is 27.67, 21.35, and 19.95.

The real value of revenue from sources identified in Table 16 has increased about five times in Edmonton, almost three times in Calgary, and over two-and-a-half times in Lethbridge over the 18 years from 1951 to 1968. Expressed as a percentage increase over the previous year's receipts, the rate of annual increase in the three cities is as shown in Table 16.

Table 16 shows that the rate of percentage increase or decrease, in constant dollar values, as reflected in provincial and local sources of revenue under the heading of contributions, grants, and subsidies, has been falling off in all three cities over the five years 1963/4 to 1967/8. The average annual percentage increase over this period was 13.98 percent in Edmonton, 16.8 percent in

Table 15. Per capita receipts in constant dollars from contributions, grants, and subsidies from provincial and local authority sources Edmonton, Calgary, and Lethbridge, 1951-1968

	Edmonton			*Calgary*			*Lethbridge*		
Year	*Population*	*Receipts*	*Per capita*	*Population*	*Total receipts*	*Per capita*	*Population*	*Total receipts*	*Per capita*
1951	159,631	1,880,750	11.15	129,060	1,423,480	11.40	22,947	271,783	11.20
1952	169,196	1,418,970	8.65	129,060	1,710,880	13.35	22,947	323,410	14.20
1953	197,836	2,829,570	14.60	156,748	2,074,510	13.35	26,986	331,192	12.75
1954	209,353	3,591,820	17.35	168,840	2,613,340	15.80	28,300	368,971	13.10
1955	223,549	3,927,290	17.10	179,711	3,646,620	20.50	28,300	385,700	13.20
1956	226,002	4,317,760	19.25	181,780	4,493,200	24.15	29,462	455,570	13.20
1957	238,353	5,214,930	21.20	192,577	3,688,750	19.30	30,323	459,656	15.50
1958	252,131	5,936,090	23.15	206,831	3,296,480	15.20	31,568	560,927	17.25
1959	269,314	6,190,880	22.25	218,418	3,721,660	17.85	32,782	606,300	18.15
1960	269,314	7,090,070	26.90	235,428	3,930,490	16.15	33,706	609,850	18.30
1961	276,018	9,005,410	32.20	241,625	7,002,660	28.25	34,911	654,390	18.30
1962	296,967	9.507,080	32.70	269,068	5,782,441	21.15	35,722	1,044,300	29.85
1963	303,756	11,478,950	37.25	294,924	6,480,090	21.30	36,257	1,023,280	28.80
1964	349,233	11,591,130	33.65	304,040	6,968,070	22.30	36,722	954,090	25.35
1965	357,696	12,722,480	35.20	311,116	7,988,890	25.20	36,805	914,600	24.30
1966	371,265	14,668,510	39.20	323,289	9,920,270	30.20	36,837	1,137,840	30.35
1967	381,230	19,129,740	50.70	335,806	12,494,680	37.70	37,022	1,009,350	28.00
1968	393,503	21,704,140	55.60	354,856	11,017,490	31.20	37,760	1,043,060	27.25
Mean per capita 1951-1968			27.67			21.35			19.95

Table 16. Annual percentage increase or decrease of contributions, grants, and subsidies in constant dollars from provincial and local sources—Edmonton, Calgary, and Lethbridge, 1951-1968

Year	*Edmonton*	*Mean rate of increase over 5 yearly intervals*	*Calgary*	*Mean rate of increase over 5 yearly intervals*	*Lethbridge*	*Mean rate of increase over 5 yearly intervals*
	percent	*percent*	*percent*	*percent*	*percent*	*percent*
1951/2	-24.55		-20.19		-19.00	
1952/3	99.41		-21.25		-2.41	
1953/4	26.87		25.97		11.41	
1954/5	9.34		39.54		4.53	
1955/6	9.94	16.15	23.22	23.45	18.12	11.40
1956/7	20.78		17.90		0.90	
1957/8	13.83		10.63		22.03	
1958/9	4.29		12.90		8.09	
1959/60	14.52		5.61		0.59	
1960/1	27.01	16.43	78.16	25.23	71.24	27.50
1961/2	15.57		17.43		59.58	
1962/3	20.74		12.06		-2.01	
1963/4	0.98		7.53		-6.76	
1964/5	9.76		14.65		-4.14	
1965/6	15.30	13.98	24.18	16.83	24.41	1.11
1966/7	30.41		25.95		-11.29	
1967/8	13.46		11.82		3.34	

Table 17. Total amounts received, in constant dollars, by Edmonton, Calgary, and Lethbridge from provincial grants, governmental enterprises, and other contributions and provincial capital grants, 1951-1968

City	*Total provincial grants*	*Per capita revenue '68 pop.*	*Total revenues government enterprises*	*Per capita revenue '68 pop.*	*Total other contri. & capital grants*	*Per capita revenue '68 pop.*	*Per capita revenue all sources '68 pop.*
Edmonton	57,334,930	145.70	80,320,040	204.12	14,550,600	36.98	386.80
Calgary	50,000,770	140.90	37,230,020	104.92	11,023,211	31.06	276.88
Lethbridge	5,655,746	149.78	5,616,216	148.73	882,307	23.37	321.88

Calgary, and 1.11 percent in Lethbridge. The falling-off began about 1960/61. Before that time the percentage increase had been rising, but was erratic. This erratic feature is most pronounced in Lethbridge.[84] Though falling off and erratic, the annual average percentage increase is still very considerable, about 13 percent to 16 percent per annum. This is considerably more than the annual increase of population as the increasing per capita value in Table 15 shows.

The breakdown by source of revenue suggests some reasons for Edmonton's position. The total amounts of money received under each of the sub-headings mentioned above, again in constant dollars, are compared for the three cities in Table 17.

Table 17 shows that Edmonton's relative position is largely accounted for by revenues from governmental enterprises. The constant dollar total for 1951 to 1968, divided by the 1968 population, was 204.12 in Edmonton as against 104.92 and 148.73 for Calgary and Lethbridge respectively. Edmonton's revenue from public utilities surplus has grown steadily and rapidly from 1957, reaching a constant dollar per capita amount of 16.69 in 1968.[85] In contrast, Calgary's public utility surplus, although having grown steadily from 1959, amounted to only 5.92 per capita in 1968. The corresponding per capita figure in 1968 in Lethbridge was 9.33.

The Table also shows that the total for 1951 to 1968 from provincial grants, divided by the 1968 population, was remarkably even over the three cities. The distribution was 145.90, 140.90, and 149.78 respectively. Similarly, the total from "Other contributions and capital grants," though favouring Edmonton over Calgary and Lethbridge, was not markedly out of proportion on a per capita basis.

Revenues from local governmental enterprises, therefore, have contributed more than any other single factor to Edmonton's advantageous per capita revenue over the items considered in this Table. The provision of low interest capital has been important to the city's business account, as also have reserves.

If attention is now directed to revenues from the federal government, the following situation emerges. Table 18 shows the revenue and per capita revenue, in constant dollars, from "contributions, grants and subsidies" received from the federal government by Edmonton, Calgary and Lethbridge.

The Table shows that an increase in the real value of revenues from federal sources has occurred in all three cities, but the amount received each year since about 1958 is only two to three dollars per capita in Calgary and Edmonton and three to four in Lethbridge. Relative to provincial and local sources the direct federal contribution under this heading is negligible. Over the 18 years, however, the real value has tended to increase by something in the order of six times, but this is an increase of from about 50 cents per capita to $3 per capita. On a per capita basis Lethbridge, since 1960, has benefited most from the federal government. The mean per capital revenue over 18 years from Edmonton and

Table 18. Per capita receipts, in constant dollars, from contributions, grants, and subsidies from the federal government—Edmonton, Calgary, and Lethbridge, 1951-1968

	Edmonton			*Calgary*			*Lethbridge*		
Year	*Population*	*Total federal receipts*	*Per capita*	*Population*	*Total federal receipts*	*Per capita*	*Population*	*Total federal receipts*	*Per capita*
1951	159,631	90,176	.56	129,060	42,874	.33	22,947		
1952	169,196	65,216	.40	129,060	85,599	.66	22,947		
1953	197,836	74,812	.38	156,748	79,860	.51	26,986		
1954	209,353	82,738	.40	168,840	36,999	.22	28,300		
1955	223,549	96,787	.43	179,711	161,525	.92	28,300		
1956	226,002	148,056	.66	181,780	160,885	.89	29,462		
1957	238,353	344,399	1.44	192,577	328,138	1.70	30.323		
1958	252,131	355,833	1.41	206,831	482,919	2.33	31,568	6,161	.20
1959	269,314	667,412	2.48	218,418	530,583	2.43	32,782	65,132	1.99
1960	269,314	359,593	1.34	235,428	473,101	2.01	33,706	80,193	2.38
1961	276,018	1,711,858	6.20	241,625	775,728	3.21	34,911	69,762	2.00
1962	296,967	1,110,639	3.74	267,068	720,162	2.70	35,722	131,565	3.68
1963	303,756	1,020,744	3.36	294,924	804,909	2.73	36,257	295,894	8.16
1964	349,233	900,301	2.58	304,040	884,843	2.91	36,722	159,387	4.34
1965	357,696	1,391,607	3.89	311,116	601,210	1.93	36,805	94,832	2.58
1966	371,265	2,028,110	5.46	323,289	596,059	1.84	36,837	245,251	6.66
1967	381,230	1,206,460	3.16	335,806	809,615	2.41	37,022	146,381	3.95
1968	393,503	803,333	2.04	354,856	890,260	2.51	37,760	180,680	4.78
Mean over 18 yrs.		692,115	2.22		470,292	1.79		81,958	2.26
Mean over the years 1958-1968		1,050,535	3.24		688,126	2.46		134,113	3.70

Calgary is 2.22 and 1.79 respectively and for Lethbridge for the 11 years since 1958, when Lethbridge first received revenue from the federal government, is 3.70. Over the 11 years 1958-68, the respective annual mean for the three cities is 3.24, 2.46 and 3.70.

The erratic nature of federal revenues is clearly shown in Lethbridge's receipts from year to year. This is particularly important in a small city because its total receipts from all sources is smaller and the effect of fluctuating amounts of federally derived revenues has a greater impact. Table 19 shows the results of a corresponding analysis made for Red Deer, Camrose, and Wetaskiwin in order to indicate the erratic nature of federal and other receipts in these smaller cities. The analysis also provides insight into any contrasts between the metropolitan areas and the small cities. Red Deer, Camrose, and Wetaskiwin were selected on no particular criteria except that Red Deer with a population of 26,730 in 1968 was some way between Lethbridge and the two small cities of Camrose and Wetaskiwin. Growth of population and size itself may have something to do with contributions, grants, and subsidies.

Table 19. Revenues, in constant dollars, from contributions, grants, and subsidies—Red Deer, Camrose, Wetaskiwin, 1951-1968

Red Deer

Year	*Total revenues*	*Per capita*	*Annual percent increase*
1951	55,505	7.35	
1952	123,235	16.27	122.03
1953	194,515	21.23	57.84
1954	113,985	9.75	-41.40
1955	187,230	16.02	64.26
1956	209,590	16.99	11.94
1957	244,970	18.04	16.88
1958	436,345	24.80	78.12
1959	475,825	28.84	9.05
1960	455,875	24.30	- 4.19
1961	835,145	42.58	83.20
1962	860,235	40.76	3.00
1963	780,380	33.77	- 9.28
1964	750,720	30.71	- 3.80
1965	1,013,900	40.24	35.06
1966	1,209,080	47.28	19.25
1967	1,276,705	48.78	5.59
1968	1,403,860	52.52	9.96

Camrose

1951	28,500	6.90	
1952	30,140	7.30	5.75
1953	34,110	6.80	13.17

Camrose *Year*	*Total revenues*	*Per capita*	*Annual percentage increase*
1954	36,110	6.40	5.86
1955	59,585	10.40	65.01
1956	66,810	11.50	12.13
1957	89,365	15.46	33.76
1958	70,960	11.74	-20.60
1959	65,970	11.07	- 7.03
1960	69,760	10.87	5.75
1961	139,975	20.22	100.65
1962	94,430	13.39	-32.54
1963	94,820	12.89	.41
1964	119,710	15.53	26.25
1965	259,510	33.67	116.78
1966	424,840	53.34	63.71
1967	247,980	29.66	-41.63
1968	174,310	20.56	-29.71
Wetaskiwin			
1951	15,920	4.20	
1952	16,960	4.40	6.53
1953	25,050	6.30	47.70
1954	36,680	9.20	46.43
1955	37,610	9.50	2.54
1956	44,010	9.80	17.02
1957	52,200	11.70	18.61
1958	61,270	12.67	17.38
1959	53,820	11.04	-12.16
1960	51,310	10.61	- 4.75
1961	79,470	15.00	54.88
1962	101,300	19.11	27.47
1963	66,800	12.06	-34.06
1964	84,260	15.21	26.14
1965	84,980	14.18	.85
1966	100,840	16.83	18.66
1967	156,660	26.08	55.36
1968	134,440	21.85	-14.18

The last column for each of the towns in Table 20 shows the annual percentage increase or decrease of "contributions, grants, and subsidies." The five yearly mean and range for each of the cities is shown in Table 20.

The very erratic situation shown in Tables 19 and 20 must lead to difficulties in the planning and use of these monies by the smaller cities. Limited as their professional services are, in both administrative and capital construction activities, these smaller cities are expected to cope with revenue fluctuations from sources largely beyond their control as high as +116 percent to -41 percent over three

Table 20. Means and ranges of percentage increases in contributions, grants, and subsidies for Red Deer, Camrose, Wetaskiwin, 1954-1968

	Red Deer		*Camrose*		*Wetaskiwin*	
Years	*Mean*	*Range*	*Mean*	*Range*	*Mean*	*Range*
1954-58	25.96	-41.4-+78.12	19.23	-20.6-+65.01	20.396	2.54-+46.43
1959-63	16.356	- 9.28-+83.20	13.448	-32.54-+100.65	6.276	-34.06-+55.36
1964-68	14.73	- 3.08-+35.06	27.08	-41.63-+116.78	17.366	-14.18-+55.36

years (Camrose 1965-67). What influence this situation may have on the settling of local mill rates and on the general administration of city finances we have not determined, but we suspect that the apparent unwillingness of Alberta's local authorities to make maximum possible use of *ad hoc* programs, such as the 1963 federal Municipal Development and Loan Fund, is related to this situation. There must also be consequences for five year capital planning.

The more general comparative analysis of the smaller cities relative to the metropolitan areas, in respect of contributions, grants, and subsidies, suggests a considerable variation in per capita receipts. Since 1961, Red Deer, for example, appears to have done better than even Edmonton, while Camrose and Wetaskiwin have done much less well. Red Deer has managed to obtain as regular a source of contribution as the three largest cities but the irregularity of contribution that appears to be common in the smaller towns and cities is apparent in the record for Camrose and Wetaskiwin. By inspection of further data it appears that Medicine Hat's receipts have a constancy greater than Grand Prairie's, though the latter's is steadier than the smallest cities. It would thus appear that after a given population point, perhaps 10,000-15,000 persons, there is a tendency for senior government contributions to steady off. Population size in this sense is only a surrogate of measurement for factors existing in both the urban centre and the senior government offices. We did not attempt to identify what these were in specific terms.

While these financial contributions were coming increasingly to assume a routine nature, the provincial government had initiated a new policy aimed once again at assisting the individual citizen of the province. It arose in part from the emphasis given a "minimum acceptable" standard of living by a Study Committee set up by Premier Manning in 1962 on Public Expenditure and Revenue.[86]

This new emphasis was to take several forms in the mid- and late-1960s, but its epitome might be recognized in the Human Rights legislation of 1966[87], Premier Manning's *A White Paper on Human Resources Development* of March, 1967, and the establishment of the Human Resources Research Council, and the Human Resources Development Authority the same year.[88] As early as 1962 steps were taken to greatly increase provincial aid to education. The $68.7 million appropriated to the Department of Education amounted that year to 27.9 percent of the total estimated expenditures of the government on income account. By 1970, this percentage had risen to 35 percent of the total budget, and was in excess of $405 million.[89] This educational policy coincided with Ottawa's Conservative administration's emphasis on technical education as its answer to urban unemployment. The Northern Alberta Institute of Technology was opened in 1961 and together with the Southern Alberta Institute in Calgary was being supported in capital and running costs by both provincial and federal governments. By 1962 some 15 centres in Alberta had instituted technical education services through this senior government support. University enrolments were increasing — to an estimated 9,000 in Edmonton and 2,200 in Calgary in 1962. The University of Lethbridge was then not even under consideration, but the extension of Community Colleges across the province was underway.

Similarly, in 1963, health was taken up as a further means of aiding the individual through provincial expenditure.

Department of Public Health estimates in 1963 were raised by $11.8 million to $87 million, and were then involving some 23.35 percent of the total revenue on income and capital accounts.[90] In sympathy with federal initiative, Alberta was turning to the introduction of "a program of medical care to help those residents in need of financial assistance in obtaining prepaid medical insurance."[91] The Alberta Hospital Plan, supported by the federal government to up to 40 percent of operating costs, was also increased by $8.9 million to a total of $63 million.

Later, in 1965, Premier Manning announced the details of government proposals for a "new program for a new generation of progressive people."[92] The 1966 budget was aimed at implementing this program in six areas:

— educational expansion and the creation of a Department of Youth,
— increased subsidies under the Alberta Health Care Program to enable all income groups voluntarily to participate,
— increased financial assistance to municipalities and tax discounts to reduce the burden of property tax on home owners,
— massive increases in highway and bridge construction and in public buildings,
— increased funding of cultural activities, parks and recreation, preservation of historical sites, etc.,
— Northern Albertan development by way of roads, airstrips, etc., and community services to people in the remote areas.

No new taxes were to be introduced and no direct borrowing was required to accomplish this. By 1966, Health was consuming over 21 percent of the budget.

Concurrently, the provincial administration had made a fundamental change in its own organizational policy. The Provincial Treasurer, A.O. Aalborg, announced in the 1966 Budget Speech that:

> . . . as the government attempts to meet the needs and desires of the citizens for increased services and new

> programs, every effort is made to accomplish this with the least possible increase in operational and administrative costs. Wherever possible new programs and services are integrated into appropriate departmental systems before new and separate entities are created. As the government grows in size and complexity it becomes increasingly important to avoid unnecessary duplication of functions or services. In recognition of this need to maintain a high level of operational and administrative efficiency the government will establish an Organization and Methods Unit under the direction of the Public Service Commissioner which will be available to assist all Departments to operate in the most efficient and economical manner.[93]

The Study Committee on Public Expenditure and Revenue had recommended the move.[94] By 1966, the government was beginning to face the implications of its own direct involvement and that of new and increasingly elaborate federal programs in the development of Alberta. Its long established policy of decentralization to *ad hoc* boards and commissions and to local authorities through the disbursement of funds was gradually coming into question. So was the government's convenient posture as guardian of the public's assets but patron by largesse of activities of its local authorities.

To some extent, and possibly to a major extent, though we have not examined the matter in sufficient detail, this change was necessitated by federal programs of health care, shared cost programs, fiscal agreements, the NHA, etc. The Hellyer Task Force was appointed in August, 1968 and the federal legislature was becoming engaged in its conflict over the Canadian constitution.[95] Dr. Harvey Lithwick was requested in 1969 by federal minister Robert Andras to commence his studies aimed at educating "us at the federal level, and other levels of government, and the people of our country and bring us to a common basis for understanding urban problems and the basic alternatives for dealing with them."[96] We suspect that the provincial government was repsonding to both external and internal pressures. Alberta was being introduced, willy nilly, into the national program of individual welfare, urban renewal, and industrial incentives. The critical point by the mid-1960s was the way in which the provincial administration was to respond to the federal initiative, and simultaneously to the persistent demands for money and services from within the province. The 1966 Organization and Methods Unit under the Public Service Commissioner was a start, but it had the appearance of being more a time-and-motion study approach than one involving a thorough reorganization of the civil service to fulfil a much more positive role in the leadership and direction of provincial, and especially urban affairs.[97] It would seem that the provincial government sensed the need for change, but that it did not know what to do in the rapidly changing situation with which it was confronted.

The federal urban renewal policy, arranged through the NHA, and which typified this period, was taken up in Alberta by way of a new Alberta Housing Act.[98] It was the first of many housing Acts and Amendments between 1965 and 1970. The 1965 Act created the machinery of co-operation with the federal government "for the provision of Housing and Urban Renewal."[99] It was two years ahead of the establishment of the Alberta Housing and Urban Renewal Corporation. This 1965 legislation carried forward the old tradition of enabling a local authority, with provincial approval, to enter into agreement with a federal authority over public housing in terms of the NHA. It also provided for the Lieutenant-Governor in Council to incorporate housing authorities consisting of such numbers of persons as he may determine to execute the agreements (Section 4). Local authorities were obliged to bear up to 10 percent of the costs of such public housing, but could borrow the money needed by debenture in the usual way. The original housing legislation had provided machinery for municipal involvement in public housing but the cities had made little use of it. In its evidence before the Hellyer Task Force in 1968, the City of Calgary indicated its intention to embark on a public housing program, and added:

> Enabling legislation was not available in Alberta for this purpose prior to 1965. Only recently was legislation changed to enable municipalities to undertake public housing projects using the loan-subsidy technique without an excessive contribution.[100]

The problem, however, had not been legislation, but cost and priorities.

Urban renewal was to be handled by the provincial government entering into an agreement with its municipalities and with federal authorities, or by a municipality entering an agreement, after obtaining provincial approval, direct with federal authorities. The Act outlined the powers of municipalities to buy, service, and develop land under urban renewal, and applied the provisions of the Planning Act as to local authority rights to stipulate by by-law the standards of building to be erected or maintained. Municipal planning commissions or development control officers of the municipalities could, by resolution of council, become the authorizing officer to act on behalf of the council under urban renewal (Section 10(3)). The provincial contribution to costs was also stipulated. The 1966 budget speech provided only $500,000 for subsidized housing and urban renewal, but in 1967 some $1.5 million on subsidized housing and $3.5 million "towards the acquisition and clearing of land for urban renewal" appeared in the estimates. The Provincial Treasurer added: "This latter sum may be wholly or partially recoverable if the new development proves to be profitable. Several areas are under study for both of these projects." [101]

This attitude was in marked contrast to the

recommendations of the Study Committee whose report was submitted in 1966. Although many of the committee's recommendations covered trivia, it was outspoken in respect of the need to co-ordinate and plan the province's highway program. The relation of highways to urban development seems never to have been co-ordinated in any planning mechanism of the province. The committee commented:

> Historically roads were probably built according to the adage "the squeaking wheel gets the grease." Hence, governments tended to use highway development as an instrument of political policy. Today economic need, rather than a political climate, must be considered the primary factor in determining priorities.[102]

In addition to recommendations on an improved secondary road system and the setting up of a district planning body, the committee made several recommendations on urban areas. The Department of Highways was advised to consult and co-operate with urban municipalities over "the need for building roads and structures through and around urban areas, and the financial problem of meeting the cost of such construction."[103] After considering the greater flexibility of funding road construction versus the fixed cost nature of education and health services, the committee observed:

> Apart from expenditures for education, outlays on roads and streets have been the largest single source of municipal expenditure. The larger cities are becoming increasingly concerned with the necessity of providing intra urban road systems capable of moving the thousands of vehicles which clog the present system twice a day. The Province has undertaken to provide 75% of the costs of actual construction; the acquisition of right-of-way remains the responsibility of the local government.
>
> Since the construction of these freeway systems will eventually entail an outlay of several hundred million dollars there is reason for concern as to whether local government can finance and carry even its limited share of construction costs and, at the same time, acquire the necessary right-of-way. There is some urgency in right-of-way acquisition as urban land values are increasing and, since it is impossible to avoid publicizing proposed routes, speculators are acquiring an interest in this real estate with a view of selling to government at an inflated price.[104]

A solution envisaged by the committee was the province providing "some sort of advance purchase fund which the cities can draw upon."[105] In addition, substantial additional grants to those already provided would have to be made. The possibility of the province assuming 75 percent of the right-of-way purchases was suggested.[106]

Thus, concurrent with the provincial government's policy of additional services to the individual citizen, the metropolitan centres were establishing their claim to the next round of additional municipal expenditure. The provincial government did not see this as calling for a co-ordinatory mechanism to connect highway and transit planning with other aspects of capital expenditure of the metropolitan centres — much of which was supported by the senior levels of government. The cities were being assisted in their claim by the rapidly evolving policy of the federal government — a policy whose intent was directed more to the older cities of eastern Canada and to the degradation of persons and city equipment of the east, than to the newer cities of Alberta. In urban renewal programs, housing for the poor, educational construction of all kinds, and in toying with the idea of capital assistance to urban transport, the federal government was setting the pattern of demand that Alberta's metropolitan centres could make on the province.

The provincial government's response, at least at the organizational level, was quite inappropriate to the situation. In addition to the Provincial-Municipal Advisory Committee set up in 1959, but which had suffered from a high turn-over of membership, a Housing and Urban Renewal Committee had been set up within the Department of Municipal Affairs, "to promote and co-ordinate interest in, and development of, housing and urban renewal projects."[107] It had six members, two drawn from each of the federal, provincial, and local levels of government. The Study Committee had particularly little to say about it. A local authorities board had been set up in 1961 to relieve the Public Utilities Board of some of its increasing responsibility. The former concentrated on debenture borrowing by local authorities, municipal finances, especially those of municipalities in default, and with the annexation of land by municipalities. After reviewing the sections and branches of the Department of Municipal Affairs, the Study Committee made no clear-cut recommendations as to its reorganization.

The absence of co-ordinatory initiative within Municipal Affairs and among provincial government departments already concerned with urban affairs and the absence of a provincial mechanism to relate the dynamic of federal urban initiatives to the needs of Alberta's urban centres, were to cost the provincial government dear in both political and financial capital. In part, the steps taken by the province from 1965 to 1970, reveal both its difficulties and its inability to cope.

In 1966 the Homeowners Tax Discount Act was passed.[108] It provided for the owners of any residence to claim a discount from the province on his municipal taxes. No owner could claim more than one discount in any year. Where an owner was paying municipal taxes of $51 a year or more, he could claim a $50 discount. On taxes less than $51, he had to pay only $1 in municipal tax. The amount of discount has been increased to $75 since. One intention of the Act was to relieve the owner of lower-valued property of municipal tax, leaving the owner of higher-valued property to pay his full contribution to municipal revenue less the $50 which applied to all owners.

The amendments to or re-enactments of the Alberta Housing Act each year from 1967 to 1970 illustrate the provincial response to the federal NHA and to federal initiative generally. Ottawa had had increasingly to find a solution to its dilemma of new housing in the metropolitan centres — costing more than even the upper range of the average Canadian home seekers could afford — and of the persistence of urban unemployment, urban physical degradation, traffic congestion, and potential urban riotous discontent. Mortgage interest rates were approaching 10 percent. The 1967 Alberta amendment defined a "family of low income" as one whose total family income was "in the opinion of the Province . . . insufficient to permit it to rent housing accommodation adequate for its needs at the current rental market in the area in which the family lives."[109] The province was clearly to maintain its own definition of the circumstances of its citizens warranting such special help. At the same time the province raised its own contribution to annual housing operating losses from 10 percent to 15 percent.

The 1965 Housing Act and all changes up to 1969 were explicit that the Minister of Municipal Affairs was the administering authority. Within the department the six-man Committee on Housing and Urban Renewal had been advising for some time. Under Section II of the 1967 amendment provision was made for the Lieutenant-Governor in Council to establish a corporation entitled The Alberta Housing and Urban Renewal Corporation "to carry out any of the duties and functions provided for by this Act and in addition such other duties and functions related to any Provincial program of housing or housing accommodation as may be assigned to it by the Lieutenant-Governor in Council." It was to be controlled by a board of directors nominated by the government. Its funding was to be via the Provincial Treasurer from the General Revenue Fund. Though this was a return to the traditional Social Credit principle of *ad hoc* administration rather than departmental administration, the practice conformed to that of other provinces of Canada and to the CMHC in Ottawa. As the Alberta Corporation was empowered to acquire real property, borrow money, issue debentures or mortgages, and liaise with CMHC over the provisions of the NHA, the principle had recognizable merit.

The issue of the corporation's influence over provincial housing policy was to some extent academic in 1967. The local authorities were empowered, with the approval of the province, to undertake land assembly projects, public housing projects, and provide rental accommodation. The corporation tended to be the provincial check on municipal proposals rather than the initiator of its own proposals.

The 1968 Housing Act, which repealed the previous

legislation, formulated housing procedures and the relations among governments more clearly.[110] A "land assembly project" was defined as one "for the acquisition, servicing and developing of raw land for housing purposes and aimed at providing serviced land for sale or lease" (Section 2(e)). Edmonton private real estate interests were shortly to learn the significance of the term, as the next Chapter shows. A "land development project" was concerned with land acquisition of any kind on which housing could be developed for disposal by lease or sale either with or without the land. Similarly, a "public housing project" concerned the land and housing units "in the form of detached, semi-detached, row housing, apartments, or of the hostel or dormitory type, or any combination . . . thereof undertaken to provide decent, safe and sanitary housing accommodation in compliance with the standards provided by the Province for lease or sale to families or individuals of low income" (Section 2(i)). The Act then proceeded to delineate the relation of the province to the federal authorities and to the municipalities, and of the municipalities to the federal authorities under each of the projects. These relations provided the opportunity for either or both the provincial and municipal governments to contract with federal authorities, save that the approval of the provincial government was required when a municipality undertook to do so alone. This may have been designed with deliberate flexibility to cope with Ottawa's changes in policy, but it was typical in that the status of the two levels of government within Alberta in their relation to Ottawa were to be almost equal. The province retained a final approving authority but the initiative could lie with either type of government. In its submission to the Hellyer Task Force in 1968, the City of Calgary recommended "an examiniation of the present administrative procedures regarding partnership action (federal - municipal) in matters of urban renewal and public housing with a view to streamlining such procedures so that decisions can be made more readily at the local level."[111] It would be difficult for the Alberta Housing and Urban Renewal Corporation (AHURC) to play much more than a co-ordinating role, unless there was a change in provincial government policy on *laissez-faire* and local autonomy.

The 1968 legislation empowered the AHURC to appoint "one or more experts or persons having special technical or other knowledge to inquire into an report in respect of any matter . . ." cogent to its duties (Section 27(2)). A number of studies were initiated at this time.[112] The corporation was also given explicit authority to acquire land "before it is actually needed for and in anticipation of any project or scheme mentioned in this Act" (Section 30). Such powers suggest, at least implicitly, that the provincial government had in mind the possibility of a much greater initiative in housing and urban affairs than had been the case at least for thirty years.

The 1969 amendment prescribed the ritual to be followed when urban renewal projects were undertaken by a municipality.[113] A notice in a local newspaper describing the proposed agreement and the area affected, where the agreement might be inspected and the time and place of public hearings, became mandatory as were the provisions covering by-laws under the Planning Act. The 1970 Alberta Housing Act, which in turn repealed the 1968 Act, changed the name of the AHURC to The Alberta Housing Corporation (AHC), and gave it a fully fledged constitution and explicit responsibilities.[114] The corporation was now "an agent of the Crown in right of Alberta and its powers may only be exercised as an agent of the Crown" (Section 3(2)). The minister, as chairman of the board of directors, was not necessarily the Minister of Municipal Affairs, but a member of the Executive Council charged with the administration of the Act. The Deputy Minister of Municipal Affairs and the executive director of the corporation were statutory members. The corporation was given wide powers over almost all aspects of housing and particularly over those concerned with the poor, the aged, and other special categories of persons. It was to have the major liaison role between the province and the CMHC. It made explicit the authority to which municipalities should refer in those aspects of their negotiations with federal authorities over which they had to consult, seek approval, or work co-operatively with the province.

The budget and staff of the corporation have increased considerably since 1967.[115] The corporation began at a difficult time in Alberta. Inflation, high interest rates (10 percent), unemployment, and a start to cutting back the long-established trend for provincial expenditures to exceed income were apparent. The appropriation of the Department of Municipal Affairs was reduced slightly in the 1968 budget. New forms of taxation were under consideration. The corporation made a modest start by way of studies into the urban process of the province and the taking over of NHA provisions in the province. It became the instrument whereby the minister and Edmonton City Council acquired 4,836 acres of land (known as Mill Woods) to the south-east of the city for residental and low-income accommodation. But by assuming its 1970 legislative role, the corporation became in Alberta not unlike the CMHC at the national level, save that the AHC does not have constitutional entanglements with provincial rights. The AHC is in a position to give provincial diraction to the urban process in Alberta in so far as housing and accommodation are an integral part of that process. But, at least until August, 1971 when the Progressive Conservative administration came to power, there was no clear policy direction from the political arm of government about the provincial process of urbanization.[116]

Though the corporation's relation to the initiative of local authorities is, as a consequence of recent housing legislation, inherently limited to recommending or approving, it could readily become the object of complaint from and dislike by the local authorities of the province. Whereas CMHC has been able to pass off much of the criticism directly towards it to the federal government, and the federal government has been able to explain its alleged indifference to the needs of the metropolitan centres as being caused by provincial constitutional rights and obduracy, the AHC and the provincial government have no such defence with regard to Albertan local authorities. The AHC is not quite in the same happy position as is CMHC to generate change or initiate direction in the urban process by subtle, administrative means at the official level. The effectiveness of the AHC is much more dependent on a political determination and direction of policy. Similarly, as so much of AHC funding is derived from CMHC, it is inevitably subject to the general and administrative directions of the federal authorities.

Provincial finances have come under increasing duress since 1967. Though the Provincial Treasurer, A.O. Aalborg, put on a resounding show of financial record in the Budget Speech of 1969, when Premier Harry Strom had assumed office, he was obliged to enumerate the increasing incidence of annual deficits.[117]

> He commented: "These comparisons clearly and conclusively indicate the urgent need to exercise a growing measure of firm and responsible restraint on expenditures during the 1970s."[118]

The accelerating rate of expenditure had to be curbed. The province sold $30 million Province of Alberta 71/2 percent debentures in the United States to cover the estimated deficit in 1969. His solutions were the usual ones—keeping expenditures below revenue (but with the policy of developing human resources continuing to have a high priority), improving the efficiency of government operations, finding new and additional revenue from taxation, and borrowing to finance highways and public buildings. The perplexity of Premier Harry Strom at the apparent failure of almost a decade of public policy devoted to improving personal services and amenities in the province may be illustrated by his frequent reference in 1969-71 to "the quality of life," and particularly in its urban aspect,[119] The Task Force on Urbanization and the Future, which eventually got off the ground in 1971, is an expression of this. Premier Strom was not alone in his perplexity, for similar feelings and expressions of concern were being uttered in Ottawa, and particularly by Messrs Paul Hellyer and Robert Andras, successive ministers responsible for housing.

The federal government by its shared cost agreements and other devices had virtually revolutionized the personal services available to the individual Canadian from health and welfare to unemployment insurance and technical training. The provinces were being asked to assume an increasing share of the costs. The anticipated deficits of the provinces were rising sharply. In Alberta the provincial emphasis on human services has since 1962 cost the government increasing sums of money. Education alone was taking up 35 percent of the total budget by 1970. Yet in the conclusion to the 1970 Budget Speech, the Provincial Treasurer commented: "As we enter the 1970s Premier Strom's Social Credit Government is deeply concerned over the plight and financial needs of many citizens in Alberta and in all parts of Canada which have resulted from inflation, high interest rates and sharp increases in the cost of living."[120]

Municipal councils were increasingly pressing the province for additional money. An Alberta municipal finance study published in January, 1968, under the title *Urban Crisis,* was intended to prove "the need for a complete realignment of fiscal policies vis a vis Provincial-Municipal relationships.[121] It was a plea, beautifully substantiated in its simplicity and presentation, for further aid to the municipalities and suggested the presence of an obligation on the part of the province "because of the broader tax base available to the provincial government."[122] It was said to be the lack of financial resources available to municipalities that constituted the 'crisis' component of the situation. The Education Foundation Fund was not proving adequate; the contribution of property tax to hospital costs was over-burdensome; greater provincial help in financing urban transportation facilities was required, and so on. The case made in *Urban Crisis* is the old familiar one of "given the present financing situation, property taxation will reach an unprecedented level in Alberta urban centres."[123] The McNally Commission had had to deal with the same case fifteen years before, as had the government in the depression. In their discussion of property tax as a revenue source, the authors treat at length the justice of moral attributes of the tax and find it to be regressive — "Those families in low income brackets pay out of their total income a larger portion for property tax than do those families in higher income brackets."[124] After further argument the case concludes that "Property taxation certainly is not the most desirable method."[125] The broader tax base of the province, it was argued, had to be used to support municipal services and expenditure.

The provincial government responded in part by setting up The Special Committee to Study Assessment and Taxation.[126] The committee's report indicated that "the two principal areas of complaint were exemptions and property taxes being used for social services."[127] Over the first complaint the traditional urban-rural comparisons were prominent, as were the tax-exempt status of governmental land and improvements, public utilities, etc. With regard to the latter complaint the committee's analysis revealed that:

> in the aggregate for all Alberta, the municipalities have been left with roughly the amount of revenue they received from their property taxes. In 1968, for example, the municipal tax levy, including property, business and frontage taxes amounted to some $217 million, and though municipal local government of all kinds received and spent $327 million, the amount left to municipalities after paying school and hospital requisitions was almost $194 million or 89% of local taxation. Not all of this was available for services to property, but it was available for expenditures exclusive of school and hospital needs.[128]

This observation referred to the aggregate for all Alberta, and the individual situation of any one municipality might be quite different. The range of circumstance of municipalities across the province was wide. The report continued: "Some municipalities may find themselves paying out on requisitions virtually all their revenue including the proceeds of the property tax. The smaller urban places suffer this complaint."[129]

In other cases non-tax revenues from commercial and utility operations of the municipality were substantial.

The committee recommended that the municipalities should continue to use the real property base, and other extant forms of taxation; that the province should continue its Education Foundation Fund and its equalization of local tax base, etc. But in addition: "The Province should announce . . . an intention to administer its requisition and grant system in such a way as to protect the municipalities' own finance responsibilities by assuring municipalities in the aggregate a fund for municipal needs equal to the aggregate proceeds of local property and business taxes."[130]

The principle would be extended after proper study "to assure that the aggregate of rural municipal levies is protected for rural municipal needs and that the aggregate for urban levies is protected for urban municipal needs."[131] This measure was intended "to regain the confidence of all Albertans in the grants and transfer systems, foundation fund and equalized assessments."[132]

By retaining the aggregate concept between urban and rural, and by recognizing that any extensions of this type of assurance to an individual municipality would, in effect, "destroy entirely the fundamental sharing between areas that is the essential purpose of equalization and foundation schemes,"[133] the committee was solving by way of further provincial funding the inequity that had developed among municipalities. It was also raising implicitly the question of the dominance of the metropolitan centres over the rest of the province. The committee was greatly concerned over the need "to protect and preserve local vitality." Local discretionary expenditure had to be provided to local authorities to preserve their capacity for responsibility. The committee, partly because of its terms of reference, failed to identify the issues which had led to the inequity its recommendation was designed to solve at further expense to the province.[134]

In its analysis "of the conceptual basis of our property tax system" the committee recognized it as being "a levy based on the capital values of certain items of property. The capital value is taken as the measure of tax liability and the tax is proportionate to that measure."[135] The phrase "capital value" is particularly difficult to define. When land was the means of production it had a much clearer meaning because of the relative uniformity of the commodity known as "property" among its possessors; but with the diversification of the means of production and the industrialization of the productive process the determination of "capital value" has become virtually impossible to define in ways likely to facilitate a comparison of the property of different persons. Yet assessors are expected to place values that fairly and equitably reflect the differential in value as between one unit of property and another, and thereby differentiate the tax each owner is obliged to pay. In Alberta, under the Municipal Taxation Act, 1967, land values and land improvement values form the basis of determining the rate of tax. The assessors of property value are obliged to consider:

> (a) any advantages or disadvantages of location,
> (b) the quality of the soil,
> (c) any profitable use that may reasonably be made of the lands,
> (d) the benefit to the land of an irrigation or drainage project,
> (e) such other considerations as the Assessment Commissioner may, from time to time specify.[136]

The committee recognized in its discussion of these considerations that assessors are placed in a very difficult situation. They cannot, for example, impute a nil meaning to the effect of location on property value. The committee observed:

> Location, as it affects the land as collateral, as a speculative investment, as a reservoir of wealth, a medium of exchange, a depository of value or a hedge against inflation, or simply as an historical or cultural or aesthetic preserve, may effect the determination of value. Any such aspect might be considered in the search for the value figure.[137]

Similarly, with regard to consideration (c) above, the word "use" has been interpreted to mean "highest and best use," but the wording of consideration (c) clearly introduces a judgement about hypothetical but real possible uses to which the land may be put. By providing an interpretation of use which involves maximizing value in use, the assessor is able to reduce some of the choices, but it still involves him in very difficult decisions.[138]

To illustrate the matter by extremes: in the case of a declining hamlet — and there are such hamlets, especially in southern Alberta — whose property is run down and whose house owners are renting accommodation to large families on welfare because their houses have no resale value and they have moved to city employment, is the assessor to decide on a "negative" property assessment? In law, of course, he has no such option. He is obliged to limit his thoughts to the point of recognizing in each piece of property a house of so many square feet, in use, in run-down condition, in a location suffering from disabilities relative to other locations. It is on the facts of physical materials and use that his judgement must lie. He cannot define the term "property" in its true social meaning — namely, the exclusion of the rights of others over particular physical objects of the world with a view to enhancing the returns made from its use or exchange to other people which would benefit its present rightful owner. In themselves, the physical objects of the world have no value. Only when related by one man to another man is "capital value" accrued. "Capital value" is a social phenomenon, not a physical one, but the assessor is bound to apply a physical approach — the structure is standing there, within the jurisdiction of a municipality — as the basis of his assessment rather than to use indicators of the social and economic forces impinging upon that structure. The inherent difficulty for the "objectivity" of the assessor is removed by the law and regulation stipulating the basis on which the assessment is to be done.

Similarly, with regard to location, the decline of the hamlet and the run-down nature of its physical plant are sure indicators that its property owner had failed to compete with those in other centres experiencing increasing values. Location is universally recognized as a contributor in such situations. Though the law obliges the assessor to consider this (consideration (a) above), whatever positive value he places on locationally declining property can have no measurable relation, in terms of the owner's losses, to a property of similar size and quality located in the profitable circumstances of a dynamic city area. The very demand by private productive capital to locate in the city, to encourage concentration, to benefit from "use" of its amenities, is the practical expression of this comparison. Property assessment, therefore, can be only the judgement of men obliged to put some value on a physical object — as this is the basis on which a tax contribution is made — but who are obliged to construe the value placed on it only in the most formal and narrow terms. As assessments are open to challenge and appeal, only the safest and most objective grounds should be admitted in the decision.[139]

The special committee had this to say about the assessor's role in the affairs of one person to another within a municipality:

> The assessor's list is an internal measure of taxability for the municipality. Its quality is determined within itself. The common basis rule and the fair and equitable rule apply to the various parts and regions of the base contained in the one municipality. The assessor is the responsible authority, in the first instance, to achieve common basis and fairness and equity.[140]

Within the confines of one municipality, and subject to the difficulties that are inevitably inherent in the assessor's judgement, it is perhaps possible to relate "capital value" equitably in its differences among people. As each local authority may decide its own mill rate the burden of taxation assumedly falls fairly on all parties subject to it. This is a philosophy pertinent to and practicable in the small, isolated town with a common basis of production. When the authors of *Urban Crisis* recognize property tax to be regressive, and when the province legislates the Homeowners Tax Discount Act, these authorities are only identifying the unanticipated practical consequence of assessors being legally obliged to assess value in only positive terms and in the narrowest sense discussed above.

But property tax as an issue of public concern does not stop at the level of the individual or of each municipality. Deliberate provincial policy has used assessment as a means of "equalizing" its grants to municipalities over a number of services. It thereby becomes an integral component of the jealousies existing amoung municipalities.

The Alberta Assessment Equalization Board has the duty to "equalize assessments." The board receives data in the form of "returns" from municipalities and in summary and recapitulation forms from assessors. In the words of the special committee, the board proceeds in this fashion:

> In its operation of equalizing, the board deals with the assessments of the municipalities as they are prepared and recorded by assessors. By increases and decreases of the assessments of municipalities, working with total property or with particular kinds of property within the total, the board attempts to attain assessments and valuations upon a common basis and fair and equitable as between one another. Such factors as the bard may deem necessary and that in the opinion of the board should be considered for any purpose of equalization, are considered in determining the equalized assessment of each municipality.[141]

The board must in practice juggle the values which the assessors have equitably determined for each municipality in order to make inter-municipal assessments equate "upon a common basis and fair and equitable as between one another." The values of all municipalities — irrespective of their potential for growth or demise, of their past record of growth or demise, of the inherent productive potential of their artifacts and resources, and of the publicly expressed locational advantages for business and industry of the way they can use their capital value — must be equated to a common dollar value. In the practical, down-to-earth reality of Alberta's urban centres, there could be no more explicit attempt at a magical rite than this! If "property" is given its social meaning, if "capital value" is the expression of a commodity's potential to return its owner a profit, then the rapid and expanding rate of growth of the metropolitan centres should be equated to the decline of other areas of the province not in terms of a comparable common base at zero, but in terms of some plus and minus scale that reflects at zero the increasing productiveness of the province as a whole. Then the relative contribution through property taxation of the "capital value" of commodities to the collective might be fairly and equitably measured. As the special committee itself observed, it was the smaller urban places that find themselves paying out on requisitions "virtually all their revenue including the proceeds of the property tax."[142] This does not apply to the metropolitan centres.

The seemingly impossible duty thus set the Assessment Board is resolved by the administrative necessity to make good a variety of inconsistent, often locally-decided concepts of value at the municipal level. In Alberta there is land now being assessed generally at 100 percent of fair actual value, buildings at 60 percent and 50 percent and certain other properties at 30 percent and 20 percent. [143] Municipalities have assessments which variously are expressed in the dollar values of 1942, of 1950, of 1968, etc. The board has to put such variety "upon a common basis" and "fair and equitable as between one another." To overcome some of the difficulties, and in consequence of its observation that "Property tax administrators are suffering at this time from a credibility gap,"[144] the special committee suggested:

> Though the statutes and regulations may expand upon the methods of determining value by means of market analysis, productive utility analysis, or cost of replacement investigation, it is exchangeable worth of all types of property that must be declared as the intended base. In order to establish this value, clearly and uniformly, *it is implied that all property subject to assessment should be valued and recorded at full one hundred percent, of fair actual value.* If proportional differentials of tax are to be applied to different classes of property, let that be done in the tax rate, not in the assessment base [145] (emphasis original).

But there appears to be an additional problem. The rule of thumb used to measure what constitutes a satisfactory ratio of residential to commercial and industrial assessment is 60:40. In Edmonton, Lethbridge, and Red Deer, the percentage distribution is as shown in Table 21 which suggests that the rule of thumb does apply in these cities.

Table 21. Ratio of residential to commercial and industrial assessments, Edmonton, Lethbridge, Red Deer

	Residential	*Commercial*	*Industrial*	*Other*
Edmonton	68.4%	24.5%	4.9%	2.2%
Lethbridge	63.5%	26.7%	9.8%	
Red Deer	61.0%	33.0%	6.0%	

Data obtained by interview.

If the mill rate is applied evenly across these assessments—at 60 percent for land and 60 percent for improvements—the individual homeowner is paying in total in the ratio of 3:2 as against business.

It would be difficult to argue that the capital value of productive artifacts, and especially their potential to produce wealth, as against their physical state, was in this ratio at all. There appears to be a thoroughly artificial value placed on business and industrial capital. When the use made of publicly supplied urban facilities is considered, then it also appears that business gets more than fair consideration. Bearing in mind that cities compete for the attraction of business, the possibility of their under-taxng business but collecting their underpayment from the homeowner cannot be ruled out. From the information made available to use it is very difficult to judge this matter with fairness.

The response by the Alberta Urban Municipalities Association (AUMA) to the special committee's report was a significant document from many points of view.[146] After recognizing the work done and, in general, concurring with the recommendations made, the position paper states, "we do, however, wish to reiterate that this piecemeal approach to resolving these problems, though helpful, is not a satisfactory or proper course."[147] Significantly enough, the AUMA had at its 1969 Convention called for the setting up of a commission "to review all aspects of this field, and that the commission be structured similar to that of 'The Ontario Committee on Taxation — 1967,' " with its terms of reference similar to those of the Ontario Commission. [148] These terms of reference had referred to the whole question of municipal expenditures and revenue, debts and other financial obligations:

> with a view to determining whether, within the constitutional limitations existing and having regard to present and potential financial requirements, such tax and revenue system is as simple, clear, equitable, efficient, adequate and as conductive to the sound growth of the Province as can be devised.[149]

The clear political challenge to the financing policies of the provincial government contained in the AUMA Position Paper, can be seen in the last page. Premier Harry Strom in his Position Paper to the September, 1970, Federal-Provincial Constitutional Conference, under a section headed, "The Problems of Urban Government", had outlined the arguments of municipalities in terms of inadequate revenue, inadequate control, inadequate management, and inadequate knowledge.[150] The municipalities were asking for radical solutions. He continued:

> The increasing assumption of traditional municipal responsibilities by provincial governments and even the federal government may seem to partly solve the financial problems, but this "solution" leads to a worsening of the problem of inadequate municipal control and reduces the advantages of local government. Understandably, the municipalities are not keen on any solution which reduces their autonomy.

> The municipalities tend to see the proper solution to their problems lying in a redrafted Constitution which, presumably, would on the one hand, guarantee their existence and responsibilities, and on the other, guarantee them adequate sources of income. The Alberta Government has given this suggestion careful consideration and recognizes its merit. However, we have concluded that municipal participation in redrafting the constitution is not the best meanr to solve municipal problems.[151]

The AUMA threw down the gauntlet at the conclusion of its own Position Paper in these terms:

> . . . but (Premier Strom) did not indicate how his government plans to resolve the problem.
> Let us then ask the provincial government:
> 1. Do you propose a comprehensive study on municipal-provincial fiscal problems?
> 2. Do you intend to continue this piecemeal approach?
> 3. Will you discuss with us your proposed plan of action?
> 4. May we participate and assist you in preparing terms of reference for a long range fiscal plan?[152]

These contrasting positions epitomize the political state of urban affairs in Alberta. Paradoxically, the AUMA was asking for "a long range fiscal plan," and the Premier understood their position as being "inadequate municipal control" with no solution to be found in measures that reduced their autonomy. In emphasizing fiscal planning, the AUMA had in mind the following:

> 1. There must be further integration of the provincial and municipal tax systems. All provincial and municipal programs and services should be carefully co-ordinated and the fiscal responsibilities of each clearly defined.
> 2. The provincial and municipal governments should prepare a joint or integrated long range financial plan. Planning of future services and programs is meaningless unless they are economically feasible and financial resources known.[153]

The intent of AUMA proposals — after reference to the Ontario Commission's terms of reference and constitutional partnership — was to set up the urban centres through a long range fiscal plan as entities with far more fiscal autonomy than hitherto. Property tax revenue to be available for services to property — rather than diluted somewhat by partial support for services to people which the province was not prepared to come up with in full — was the first step in that direction. The province since 1962 had undertaken the relief of city finances in part through direct support of personal services. The AUMA was seeking unencumbered control of property — the very instrument of city growth, attraction of business, and the epitome of wealth and its creation. It was precisely the autonomy of decision over the attraction of private investment to itself which had in the past led to metropolitan dominance over the remainder of the province. The process in turn had contributed, along with federal policies, to threatening the political status of the provincial government itself. Put crudely, if the cities got their way, local authorities would be administering people and property, and the provincial government the flora and fauna of the prairies.

Premier Strom was aware of the issues involved. In a speech to the AUMA conference in October, 1970, he pointed out that 17 percent of villages and towns had declined in population between 1951 and 1961, but 47 percent had declined in population over the five year period 1961-66.[154] Rural municipalities and all counties but one (Strathcona, on the outskirts of Edmonton) were in a similar position. In the same speech, after reviewing the choices of action available — including letting the present trends continue, reversing the present trend by strong policies, or working with or modifying the present trends but making them more efficient — the Premier remarked:

> These three latter approaches involve the setting of goals and priorities, and the development of policies, which in a co-ordinated way lead to the achievement of these goals. The problem with this approach is that the goals may not be realistic given the way people are prepared to act.
> But there is a fifth possibility — to develop policies with the people who must in the end co-operate in carrying them out — in this case, the public of all Alberta.
> One of the most effective means to co-operative development of policy is to recognize that people are most effective when working through groups which serve certain interests . . .[155]

He then illustrated the point by reference to the AUMA itself, and a host of other organizations from chambers of commerce and service clubs to government departments. Such organizations became effective because of the opportunities offered to promote their interests through promoting the interests of the whole, the social collective. He then added:

> It is for this reason, that the Government of Alberta has designed a "Task Force of Urbanization and the Future" to involve over a period of three years, all interest groups in Alberta willing to participate in the development of proposals for plans and policies; and of long-range solutions to present problems facing urbanizing Alberta; and perhaps more importantly, to anticipate future problems so as to plan for them or even prevent them before they occur.[156]

Thus, to the Premier, the setting up of goals and priorities, the development of policies, and the necessary co-ordination to implement them posed the problem of unrealistic goals "given the way people are prepared to act." This was, in effect, adopting the first of his rejected choices, namely, to let the present trends continue, for the trends are not the outcome of natural forces of the physical universe, but of the power of organization in financial, private and governmental terms, as structured and related together in the urban affairs of Alberta. By hoping "to develop policies with the people who must in the end co-operate in carrying them out," the Premier was hoping, by working through the new Task Force, to generate policies other than those envisaged as necessary by the formal organizations party to urban affairs; and, possibly, to get sufficient public pressure to bear on these formal organizations to oblige them to amend their position. In this sense, the Task Force was "a cop out," to use the current idiom, for something the provincial government was itself unwilling to undertake despite its knowledge of the necessity for it.[157]

The Task Force was itself more limited in its sponsorship than the AUMA itself. While the latter association had membership in the cities, towns, and villages of Alberta, the Task Force was sponsored by the ten cities of Alberta. The reason for this is unknown to us,[158] but there is a possible connection in the inherent conflict of interest among members of the AUMA. When Calgary and Edmonton are so pre-eminent in the province at large, and when their links of dependence are to the metropolitan centres beyond the province rather than to any small city within Alberta, the threat of disunity within the AUMA over its political relation to the provincial government is apparent. At the present time it appears likely — we were unable to get more than a hint of evidence on the point — that the smaller urban centres go along with Calgary and Edmonton's demands on the province, because of the "fair and equal treatment for all local authorities" policy of the province. Expressed crudely, the principle, "If Calgary is to get a million dollars out of some demand, I am likely to get five hundred," still gives the small urban centre something.

The question the Premier should ask is whether fiscal long-range planning alone is sufficient to give direction to the urban affairs of the province as a whole. If growth is a measure of vitality, the metropolitan centres have done particularly well under previous provincial policies. Urban physical planning (because of its effects on the long range implications for the siting of facilities and their use and therefore on the cities themselves) and provincial planning in its physical, regional, and general economic aspects, are fundamental matters the province alone must decide. The consequences for the lives of people adversely affected by excessive immigration to metropolitan centres and the rate of growth that such centres experience must be taken into consideration by some overall authority. That urban physical planning is as much a provincial concern as that of the cities themselves was demonstrated by the

McNally Commission. The critical, but as yet un-co-ordinated, role of highways and industrial locational incentives must be the responsibility of a senior government.[159] Financial planning must go hand-in-glove with physical and economic planning both in the cities and the province if the provincial policy of generating a viable and humanly satisfying urban culture in Alberta is to have meaning.

Premier Strom appears to have been aware of this also. In his AUMA speech he referred to the decision to place industrial development officers in each of five newly formed industrial development regions of the province. Co-ordinators were to be placed in Peace River, St. Paul and Lacombe; in Calgary to serve the south-west; and in Medicine Hat to serve the south-east. They were there not to compete for industry, but "to help municipalities in their respective regions analyze and develop to the municipality's fullest potential, resources and market possibilities."[160] They would also "vigorously attempt to convince industries of the attractions of locations outside the two major centres, but not as to lure from these centres industries which should properly, or by choice, locate there. In any event, we are confident that Edmonton and Calgary can present their own cases quite effectively."[161]

When Premier Peter Lougheed took over the provincial administration in September, 1971, his political support lay primarily in Calgary and Edmonton. The paradox of his position was precisely that his political support lay in the area where direction of affairs was needed most urgently in terms of the interests of the province as a whole — as the following Chapters on Edmonton and Calgary will show — but where it would be most difficult to institute the direction required. The power and influence of these cities have already been demonstrated. Premier Lougheed proceeded early to set up a further Task Force, on Municipal Finance, under the Chairmanship of Mr. Roy Farran, MLA, who had been alderman of the City of Calgary for several years and who was in 1972 Chairman of the city's Citizens' Budget Advisory Committee on the capital budget.[162] The fundamental problem of provincial vis a vis metropolitan centre direction of Alberta's urban affairs remains unresolved.

In the next section of this Chapter, we examine the way the Social Credit administration dealt with the question of municipal and regional planning during the era of rapid metropolitian expansion.

Recent Planning Policy and Practice

The Alberta government's contribution to planning legislation since 1953 has been limited to almost annual ammendments to the Planning Act. These amendments have been largely clarification of an increasingly complex and uncertain process. They concern the dual features of manipulation of influence or interest of particular groups affected by planning and the ritual associated with public notifications, proper procedures, and rights of appeal. The metropolitan city councils by 1953 had resolved to have prepared a "general plan," and had initiated interim development control as a stand-by measure until the "plan" and the zoning by-laws implementing it could be introduced. The 1960 amendment for the first time spelled out the mandatory and optional content of the "plan." The private developer had to be provided with essential outline information for his own programs of work. Similarly the council could publish by by-law its own Development Scheme (known in earlier legislation as an Official Scheme) whereby its own proposals for the public development of the area, and the steps to acquire the necessary land, would be announced. The amendment also made explicit the right of a council to adopt a general plan by parts. The legislation whereby only part of a plan could be adopted by a council, had been enacted as early as 1913, but the 1960 provisions facilitated the adoption of a part while the remainder was still under determination. The "objective" data and trend determinations required of plans since 1953 were taking time to produce and determine. Where a part of a city was already fairly well established it could apparently be readily brought under the aegis of a general plan, but even this was shortly to prove illusory.

The 1953 Planning Act had envisaged a relationship among three planning mechanisms: the general plan, interim development control, and zoning. The 1960 amendment made interim development control mandatory upon a council's resolution to prepare a general plan. The council, on the issuing of an Order by the minister, had to appoint an interim development board or officer to assist in the administration of interim development control. While this mechanism was in force a council could adopt zoning by-laws covering any specific part of its jurisdiction leaving the reaminder under interim development control. A zoning by-law established the standards and uses to be applied in the area and gave the public and developers a clear picture — before any development proposal was initiated — of council's intent for that area. Interim development control left considerably more flexibility to both council and developer through negotiation as to what could be introduced. Correspondingly, it heightened the uncertainty of residents and businesses in the area under development control over what might happen to their locality. Calgary, which has used development control extensively, has become, both as a citizenry and a council, increasingly sensitive over the participation of citizens in the developmental process.

The ritual associated with the passing of by-laws was changed frequently between 1953 and 1962. It was an expression of the manoeuvering for influence over detailed decision — e.g. lot size decisions — which represent the final expression of private investment's right to locate on the maximally rewarding site in conjunction with the right of citizens to protest the invasion of their property and neighbourhood by alien influences. In 1953, before giving second reading to a zoning, interim development control, development scheme or general plan by-law, the council was obliged to advertise the intent of the by-law and the place where it might be inspected, to hold public hearings on it, and to consider objections. All changes arising from this procedure were to be incorporated prior to final reading and adoption. The council then applied to the minister for approval. Similarly, any amendment to an existing by-law was subject to the same procedure. All interested parties had, by this ritual, to be seen to be given the right to influence the final outcome. In 1957 the council itself became the final approval body for zoning by-laws and the by-law was only required to be deposited with the provincial director. In 1959 the approval of by-laws by the Provincial Planning Advisory Board was introduced — apparently as a consequence of problems experienced in Calgary and Edmonton. This was where the final approval lay in 1960.

The provincial board from 1957 to 1962 was also the final appeal body on matters of development control, though, after 1958, where a council had set up a local appeal board, the appeal lay not to the provincial board directly, but to the local city council. Zoning by-laws, however, were treated rather specially on appeal. If the zoning by-law provided for a local zoning appeal board, then appeals went to it, but where this was not established the provincial board heard the appeal. A 1953 amendment obliged a council which was a member of a district planning commission or which employed a professional staff, to set up a zoning appeal board. The 1960 amendment made the local zoning appeal board's decision final. This, in effect, placed zoning decisions fairly on the shoulders of the local authority and its local instruments.

The interim development control mechanism, with its flexibility for both developer and council, required the protection of the provincial board. The greater discretion of councils under development control could permit abuse and misuse. Similiarly, as officials, rather than elected representatives, were to administer development control, the rigidity of official decision under development control (i.e. their very lack of discretion) required a more elaborate system of appeal. This system went from the Development Officer, to the Development Appeal Board, to the city council, to the provincial board. As a final matter of appeal one 1960 amendment permitted that "upon a question of jurisdiction or upon a question of law, an appeal lies from the Board to a judge of the Supreme Court of Alberta." (Section(7)(2)). The Act specified that only evidence presented to the board was to be admitted, as it was the intent that the appeal to the courts was only to assess the legality of procedures followed, not planning questions. This was the first time that specific reference had been made for opportunities to appeal to the courts. It was to be an opportunity increasingly used.

The amendments between 1953 and 1962 covering district planning processes were rather more substantial. The McNally Commission had concluded that "In the District Planning Commissions there exist adequate legal powers:

(a) to render technical planning services to member municipalities; and
(b) to draft the District General Plan."[163]

Accepting this, the commission questioned the possibility of district planning when the adoption and implementation of the district general enforcement of local planning controls all depended upon the voluntary action of the municipalities concerned. The commission also suggested that the decisions of the Provincial Planning Advisory Board were being taken on the criteria somewhat inconsistent with those of the District Planning Commissions, and in consequence were not supporting district planning controls:

> The Provincial Planning Advisory Board, in its regulatory and approval functions, does not in practice offer a method by which a district general plan for an area may be put into effect. In its administration of Subidivision Regulations . . . it is concerned for the most part with the internal aspects of subdivision, and not with the general location, or its conformity with a district general plan, and even some of its subdivision rules may be waived at the Board's discretion. In its appeal function, the policy of the Board is to pass upon existing municipal by-laws, not upon their conformity to a district plan.[164]

The McNally Commission illustrated their criticism of existing planning procedures with the decision of the Municipal District of Strathcona to withdraw from the Edmonton District Planning Commission (EDPC) in August, 1954. The Municipal District withdrew because EDPC opposed the development of Campbelltown (now Sherwood Park) on the grounds that it was too close to Edmonton, that it was too small to be a viable community, and that it did not conform to subdivision regulations.

The Campbelltown project was approved even though it was inconsistent with EDPC policies and was claimed to be undesirable in terms of Edmonton's future growth. The decision of the board was final and binding; therefore, there were no avenues of appeal. The Provincial Planning Advisory Board's decision involved a number of political actions which would require a case study in itself to reveal the entire picture. It was possibly this decision which led to the recommendation that no Minister of the Crown should sit on the Provincial Planning Advisory Board, but the McNally Report did not explicitly state the reasons behind its recommendation.

The McNally Commission's recommendations on planning in general and on the planning issues of Calgary and Edmonton are spelled out in Chapter 17 of the report. In sum, the recommendations attempted to provide the framework within which development decisions could be co-ordinated throughout the region. The commission concluded that the adoption of planning controls had to be made mandatory in order to achieve the desired co-ordination between regional and municipal development. Correspondingly, the region had to adopt the basic instruments of planning control already used by the cities: namely, interim development control was to be employed during the preparation of permanent planning controls, avenues of appeal and opportunities to amend the plans were to be provided, and the provincial board was to be the final level of appeal.

Although the above control instruments were not explicitly spelled out in the recommendations, the recommendations were premised upon the concept of interdependence between the city and its region, and particularly on the impact an urban centre has upon its immediate rural area. The terms of reference of the commission were such that it could only consider how to accommodate projected growth in the metropolitan regions; i.e., how to cope with the results of urbanization. The broader forces contributing to urbanization and the concomitant need for broader planning powers than land-use controls were legitimately left untouched by the commission. The emphasis of the recommendations was, therefore, on "district planning" and not on "regional planning" and all the broader connotations that that term implies.

In 1957 most of the recommendations were enacted.[165] The provincial board was permitted "in its own motion, or upon receiving an application of a district planning commission or a council" to recommend to the Lieutenant-Governor to establish a district planning commission (Section 10). The order establishing the commission was to specify the funds to be contributed by the member councils and the province. The district planning commissions were required to prepare and adopt a district general plan "to secure the orderly and economical development of the district planning area as a whole." (Section 101). However, membership was not mandatory (which conformed with Social Credit philosophy), nor were member local authorities necessarily contiguous. The spotty nature of volunteer membership was to prove a barrier to the realization producing the district plan. The district general plan was to describe land uses, the staging of the sequence of development, and to outline the necessary infrastructure. Other than the omission of the required financing program for public development projects, the district general plan was to be the municipal general plan writ large. In addition to being required to prepare the district general plan, the district planning commission was granted a wide array of optional responsibilities ranging from studies of boundary adjustment for municipalities within the commission's jurisdiction, to studies and recommendations on the attraction and location of industry (Section 102).

To control development during the preparation of a District General Plan, Section 113 required that a Preliminary District Plan was to be prepared and adopted by the commission as soon as possible. When a preliminary district plan came into effect, every council (the Act was not clear if this applied only to councils which were members of the commission) which had in effect interim development control was required to use the plan as a guide for decisions. If a zoning by-law was in effect, it was to be amended to comply with the plan. If neither had been adopted, the local authority was to adopt one of the controls to ensure that the provisions of the plan were implemented or at least not contravened. When a district plan came into effect, all councils were to adopt a zoning by-law to ensure that development occurred in accordance with it. As with the municipal general plans, the district general plan prevented local authorities from undertaking actions inconsistent with the plan. The preparation of other planning controls by the local authority was optional.

The district planning commissions were required by Section 105, a 1957 amendment, to hold public hearings and consider all objections before the confirmation of the district general plan. The plan came into effect upon being confirmed by the commission (Section 109). Public hearings were not required before the adoption of a preliminary district plan. As amended in 1959, Section 117 specified that the preliminary district plan was to come into effect when confirmed by the council and approved by the board. It was not clear whether board approval was also required for a district general plan when that stage was finally reached.

Section 120, added in 1957, permitted a local authority to refer to the district planning commission actions taken by another council having detrimental effects on itself. Section 121, as defined in 1957, permitted a council to appeal to the board a district planning commission decision on required conformance to a district general plan, on adopting a preliminary district plan, on questions of amendments, and on disputes with member councils. Similarly, Section 122 provided the commission the opportunity to appeal to the board the inaction or action of a council with respect to the council-adopted planning controls. The board was to become the arbiter between the principle of local autonomy and the conditions necessary for district planning. Section 123 allowed individuals to appeal to the board on proposed changes to district planning controls where conflict existed between the council and the commission. In all cases except those of law, the board decision was to be final.

The legislation as adopted provided controls intended to ameliorate the effects of development in those locations in which it occurred, but the legislation did not provide the means of controlling development decisions at a scale larger than the district planning commission area; therefore, there were no means available to direct growth to alternative locations or regions. Similarly, the amendments did not explicate the relationship of provincial board decisions to the practice of regional or local planning controls.

The quandary facing the provincial government by the early 1960s was the degree of autonomy to be granted local authorities when it became increasingly clear that the orderly development of the metropolitan region required decisions to be taken at a level beyond any one constituent member. Mr. Noel Dant, currently the Provincial Planning Director and co-author of the 1963 Planning Act, has recorded that

> At the end of 1961 the Minister responsible gave instructions for the complete Act to be reviewed, overhauled, simplified and rewritten in its entirety, stating as a general term of reference for the authors that all decision-making powers in the new Act should wherever possible be delegated to the elected representatives rather than to officials and other appointed agencies having power delegated to them.[166]

It was clear that the people's interest could best be safeguarded, in the minister's view, by enhancing the influence of elected councils. The two other categories of personnel — the council's official with bureaucratic rights to apply the regulations as prescribed to his office, and the professional city planner — were to be subordinated to the elected representatives. It was clearly a difficult decision, for all three parties to the administrative process were involved in the application of the legislation.

The explanation for the minister's preference, apart from his political philosophy, may lie in the concept of planning implicit in the legislation since its beginnings in 1913. Physical land-use planning has remained the mode of its expression. This comes out clearly in the 1963 Act's statement of purpose, namely:

> . . . to provide means whereby plans and related measures may be prepared and adopted *to achieve the orderly and economical development of land within the Province without infringing on the rights of individuals except to the extent that it is necessary for the greater public interest* (emphasis added).[167]

The public planning agencies as well as the private land owners were expected to guide and regulate the use of their land in an orderly and economic fashion to their respective best advantage. Provincial interests would be best served if the details on the ground were arranged in this manner. The private landowners were to be given the opportunity to co-ordinate their activities with public projects, and the indeterminacy of future decision was to be reduced by way of the general plan and zoning by-laws with public hearings and other ritual modes of reconciling conflict. It was inevitable under this concept that plans and amendments would conform closely to market forces. Also inevitable was the likelihood of the manipulation of public policy because of the flexibility inherent in the legislation and the continuation of expedient, *ad hoc* decisions rather than the pursuit of long terms and enduring conceptual proposals. The absence of any level of provincial leadership virtually guaranteed the continuation of "district planning" rather than "regional" or "provincial" planning.

At the municipal level, the 1963 Act permitted a local authority to establish a Municipal Planning Commission (MPC) which was to replace both the Town Planning Board and the Planning Advisory Committee as set out in the previous Act. Membership of the MPC was to be an area of uncertainty for several years. Membership could include lay as well as municipal officials, (but as amended in 1969, not less than one-half the members of the MPC of a city were to be appointed municipal officials).[168] This permitted municipalities which did not have technical personnel to form planning commissions. The commission was to advise the council on planning matters and "co-ordinate the activities of the various departments and agencies of the municipality with regard to the planning of orderly and economical development within the municipality" (Section 15(2)(a)). The MPC could perform such functions as were assigned to it by the local council with respect to a development control by-law or a zoning by-law. As amended in 1969, if the MPC was to function as an appeal body, no member of council was to be appointed to it. This amendment was recommended by the Attorney-General when it was discovered that a by-law prepared by a regional planning commission for a member municipality had councillors on the MPC, and whose decisions could be appealed to the council. In the 1963 Act, the MPC could serve as a subdivision-approving authority, and in the cases of Calgary and Edmonton the Act specified that the MPC of each city was to act in this capacity.[169] In 1969, Section 15 of the Act was amended, making it mandatory that the MPC was to serve as the subdivision-approving authority.

Similarly, the relation of public intent to private developers' interest has continued as another area of uncertainty. The 1963 Act had specified that the general plan was to contain proposals for the content of zoning by-laws. In 1967 this was extended to cover development control, though the amendment remained unclear as to whether the general plan had to include proposals covering both zoning and development control by-laws. A 1971 amendment required that financing and programming proposals written into general plans were to be "for a period of not less than five years after the adoption of the plan." (Section 96). This amendment was suggested by the City of Calgary which argued that proposals for a shorter period were meaningless. Private developers had to be assured of some consistency in public decision.

The relations among local authorities continued to be an area of difficulty. The 1963 Act permitted the council of a city, town, or village to include in the general plan such areas outside the municipality as were considered necessary for orderly and economical growth. In 1967 this was amended to permit any municipality, not just urban centres, to initiate action. This amendment was introduced to cope with a particular situation in which a village refused to prepare a plan, but the surrounding county wanted to prepare a plan for its own territory and for that within the village. In 1963, the Act did not specify the procedures to be followed should there be disagreement among the municipalities affected. In 1967, in response to a resolution adopted by the Alberta Urban Municipalities Association (AUMA), this was rectified by an amendment which required that the councils must agree by resolution, and should disagreement exist, the matter could be referred to the Provincial Board (the successor of the Provincial Planning Advisory Board).

The issues over which confusion and uncertainty existed were not limited to those affecting the relations of persons, authorities, and local governments. In addition the amendments passed between 1963 and 1971 show similar confusion over the mechanisms or instruments of control themselves. The following six paragraphs describe some of the more serious points of confusion in this area.

The 1963 Act permitted a council to adopt all or parts of general plans at any time during the operation of development control; however, this section was struck out in 1968.[170] The adoption of the general plan in bits and pieces was though contradictory to the concept of a general plan itself, and tended to inhibit co-ordination of development.

Although the 1963 Act dropped the term "interim" from the phrase "interim development control," the Act contained provisions for development control which in effect were a continuation of previous legislation. There has been some confusion since the 1963 Act was written as to whether development control was viewed as "interim" control or an alternative to zoning.[171] In 1967, Section 100(1) as amended, contained no reference to the zoning by-law, which could be interpreted as indicating that development control was seen as an alternative to zoning. Although Section 99 of the 1963 Act required that a zoning by-law be enacted upon the adoption of a general plan, a 1967 amendment allowed areas to be excluded from the zoning by-law and to be controlled by development control. This amendment had been requested by Calgary to permit that city to implement its downtown development plan. Interestingly, Calgary had proposed such a resolution to the AUMA but that body had defeated the proposal. In 1968 Section 99 was rewritten to permit a local authority exercising development control, after adopting a general plan, to enact a zoning by-law for those areas not covered. This would suggest that development control and zoning were intended as alternatives, although a court case, discussed by F.A. Laux,[171] concluded that development control was still to be interpreted as an interim measure.

The 1963 Act introduced provisions for the Land Use Classification Guide[172] which could be adopted by resolution of a local authority. Although not part of the development control by-law, the land use classification guide was to provide guidelines for decisions of officials and elected members made under development control. Laux, in "The Zoning Game: Alberta Style, Part II—Development Control," devotes considerable attention to the problems of interpreting the intent and application of this provision, which in practice in both Edmonton and Calgary, has tended to negate the difference between a zoning by-law and a development control by-law. Section 119(1) in the 1963 Act, which permitted a local authority to adopt a zoning by-law "to regulate use and development of land," made no reference to the intended relationship it may have a general plan. The zoning by-law was to be based upon a survey of existing development and was to designate the types and methods of use of land and buildings. Section 120 as amended in 1970 required that the zoning by-law "should be based upon a general plan or upon a survey of the existing land uses and conditions of land and buildings in the municipality."

In 1963, no land could be zoned for public use unless publicly owned. (Section 120). In 1965 an additional clause was added to this section by which privately-owned land zoned for public use must be acquired by the municipality or a public authority within six months from the date of the establishment of the zone. Otherwise the by-law ceased to be effective in controlling the use of the land. As amended in 1970, the Act did not indicate what the status of the by-law became if the land was not acquired in the specified time. This constraint raised an interesting point with respect to the interaction of planning controls. In Edmonton, the General Plan and the Master Plan for Parks have designated the North Saskatchewan River Valley as parkland. At the same time, privately owned lands were largely zoned for classes of land-use other than public. Because of the intent of the long range plans, lending institutions were hesitant to make money available either for mortgages or home improvements. Practically, the long range plans negated the zoning by-law which complied with the planning status. This situation may work to an advantage of the city, in that the property values tend to be adversely affected by physical deterioration, and by the fact that uncertainty as to the future of the area reduces the market value, in that it discourages potential homeowners from considering the area. The interaction of policy and planning controls warrants a research project in its own right.

In the 1963 Act, under a development control order, it was optional for a council to delegate to a development control officer, or a municipal planning commission, the authority to review or decide on applications for development permits (Section 105). A 1968 amendment made mandatory that the development control order authorize this delegation of authority. Similarly, in 1963, the zoning by-law could specify that the municipal planning commission or a municipal official was to act on behalf of the council with respect to administering the by-law.[173] In 1968, as under development control, it was made mandatory that the zoning by-law provided for the appointment of a development officer and the authority to consider applications was to be delegated to the MPC or the development control officer. The 1968 amendments would appear to contradict the intent of the 1963 Act, using development control, with respect to discretion because in 1968 either a local commission or an appointed official were assigned responsibility for discretionary decisions even under zoning by-laws.

As set out in the 1963 legislation, to adopt a zoning by-law, a development control by-law, or a by-law to adopt a general plan or a development scheme, a local authority was to have the Provincial Planning Director advise the council if the proposed by-law conformed to the Act.[174] In 1968 the responsibility was delegated to either the municipal planning commission or the development control officer in Calgary and Edmonton, to the director of the regional planning commission if the municipality was situated in a commission area, and to the director in all other cases. After making any necessary changes, the local authoritiy was to advertise the proposed by-law, hold a public hearing, hear all objections, make revisions and then submit the by-law to the Provincial Planning Board. After making changes requrested by the board, the local authority could adopt the by-law. In 1965 the Act as amended required that the by-law be submitted to the board after the third reading.[175] The by-law came into effect upon the board's approval.[176] In 1968 the requirements that the by-law be submitted to the board for approval were repealed. Final approval was to lie with the local authority.

This listing of confusion, of amendment upon amendment, could be considerably extended. A similar series of changes could be documented for the ritual of public advisement of proposals to adopt by-laws or amend them. Enough has been said to conclude that the arrangement of authority over planning at the urban centre and the district level within the province was in urgent need of clarification and direction. It is very difficult to determine the presence of any trend in the legislation of the past two decades.

The principle of local autonomy is compromised inherently in the relation of the metropolitan centres to their adjacent local authorities. Thus conflict and compromise are inevitable in the relation of city to district planning commissions. The value of professional planners, particularly for long-term advantages at both city and district levels, is mitigated by the provincial and city council preference for elected member rights of final decision, particularly over and issue of expedient, monentary advantage. The stipulation that general plans must be empirically based, and must reflect the organic dynamic of the city and its business interests, delays their speedy preparation and emphasizes the flexibility, but also the uncertainty, inherent in development control mechanisms. The conflict between the stability of use of an area, which its residents, lending institutions, and others with money invested in it wish to preserve, and the inherent instability generated by development initiated by large-scale, organized private investment seeking to locate to best advantage, encourages ambivalence on the part of the city councils towards the use of zoning versus development control mechanisms. The necessity to devolve the administration of day-to-day decisions on development applications to officials and local commissions, whether under zoning or development control by-laws, carries with it inherent uncertainty whereby officials under how far their discretion may extend and raises for elected councilors the worry that perhaps mistakes are being made.

Superimposed upon quandaries of this kind, however, is the persistent uncertainty of the rulings of the courts on the one hand and the decisions of the Provincial Planning Board on the other. Both metropolitan centres have been involved in litigation, the results of which gave them considerable inconvenience and uncertainty. In Chapter 5, the effects of some such decisions are discussed more fully in the case studies of Calgary.

Metropolitan councils are persistently faced with pressure to contain the applications of developers both within their own jurisdictions and beyond it. They must continue the growth process in the hope that it will facilitate the paying off of their own capital commitments and those of private investment in their midst. There is pressure upon them to recognize the savings inherent in orderly and economic development of the city and its hinterland, but they must also achieve the best advantage from clear cases of expediency. Overall there is the pressure to keep down the costs of city development and the consequent tax burden on the electorate. While the provincial government declines to adopt the role of leader in the province's urban affairs and declines to provide a clear picture of the type of urban culture the province is to have, and upon which provincial assets may be used; while it declines to provide constitutional powers and administrative instruments to implement it, with due regard to the consequences on the metropolitan centres as well as smaller centres, uncertainties surrounding the affairs of both types of centre are bound to continue.

There have been recent attempts to put greater order into district on regional affairs. The trend is discernable from about 1957, following the recommendations of the McNally Commission. As in the 1957 legislation, the 1963 Act contained provisions which permitted the Provincial Planning Board on its own motion or upon application by local authorities or a regional planning commission to advise the Lieutenant-Governor to issue an order to establish a regional planning commission.[177] The order was to specify municipal and provincial representation and the financial contributions of member municipalities and the province. In 1969 representation was specified in the Act. In 1971 representation on the regional planning commission was to be specified by the minister. A senior civil servant has suggested, however, that this discretion on the part of the minister was partly a consequence of the rush to prepare the legislation for the newly proposed Provincial Planning Fund. This is discussed below. It was not necessarily a deliberate change in the role to be undertaken by the province. A formula had not been established for representation by the time the legislation was presented to the House.

In 1963 the regional planning commission was required to

study resources and the development of the "region with a view to preparing a regional plan" for its area of jurisdiction, and was required to prepare as soon as possible a preliminary regional plan (largely a designation of permitted land uses) for control of development during the preparation of the regional plan.[178] The commission was to advise and, when requested, to prepare municipal planning controls for member municipalities. In 1968 this was expanded to cover all municipalities within the commission's jurisdiction, although as mentioned above, non-members were not required to contribute financial resources until 1969. The regional planning commission was to act as subdivision approving authority when authorized by the Provincial Planning Board. As with their predecessors (the district planning commissions) the regional commissions were granted a wide array of optional powers ranging from questions of municipal boundary adjustments to preparation of industrial development programs. A 1968 amendment made it mandatory that a preliminary regional plan be prepared, regardless of a resolution to prepare a regional plan, by January 1, 1972, or such further time as set by the board.[179]

It would appear from discussions with some of the directors of the regional planning commissions, however, that there is no agreed-upon, common base on which the respective commissions are preparing their general plans. Apparently the provincial administration has not indicated uniform content or standards of preparation in the regional plans. This was apparently an attempt to preserve the autonomy both of the elected local authority membership of the commissions and the professional integrity of the planners they employed. While the plans of each region will necessarily reflect the region's uniqueness and characteristics, the effect of this lack of co-ordination is to forestall the preparation of regional plans which could together be fitted into a overall provincial planning document. Thus at an administrative level the province is poorly equipped from a technical perspective to use the aggregate of general plans as a province-wide document. The 1972 amendment was introduced on the recommendation of the Provincial Planning Branch as an attempt to force the planning commissions to complete the preliminary regional plans. As the January 1, 1972 deadline was met, in part, by only two planning commissions, the deadline was extended by one year. The 1968 amendment, making mandatory the preparation of a preliminary plan, was an abrupt break with the philosophy of previous legislation which had left open to the local authority both the option of membership in a regional planning commission and the decision to adopt planning controls. The 1968 amendment indirectly committed all local authorities within regional planning commission areas to adopt planning controls by, first, making the preparation of a preliminary regional plan compulsory and, secondly, by requiring all municipalities within commission jurisdictions to adopt either development control or a zoning by-law upon the commission's adoption of the preliminary regional plan.

By 1970 the expansion of regional planning commissions had moved to the point where some 1,374,255 persons were estimated to live within the jurisdiction of the seven regional commission areas then established.[180] Only 194,590 lived elsewhere and were subject to the direct planning influence of the Provincial Planning Board. The jurisdictions of the seven commission areas varied considerably, in size and composition of population. They were known as the Medicine Hat, Oldman River, Calgary, Red Deer, Battle River, Edmonton, and Peace River Regional Planning Commissions and were numbered from 1 to 7 in the above order.[181] The obligation to include in a regional plan all the contents required under the 1957 legislation and in addition the proposals for the financing of public development projects, were enacted in the 1963 legislation.

Thus the mandatory requirements remained congruent with those of a municipal general plan. The 1963 Act obliged each council with jurisdiction over any part of the regional planning area to control development through a development control by-law as soon as the regional commission resolved to prepare a general plan. Similarly, where a decision of one council was considered by another to be detrimental to its interests it could refer its complaint to the commission whose decision was binding. Reference to the commission on matters under the Planning Act could be had whether or not the action was one coming within the purview of the regional plan or the preliminary version of the general plan. There was in this legislation, therefore, an implicit mechanism for the resolution of local authority conflict by the commissions. As their membership was made up by representation of member local authorities, the mechanism constituted a form of collective responsibility in so far as planning was involved.

With regard to regional plans, Section 82 of the 1963 Act specified that refusals of local council requests to a regional planning commission for amendments could be referred to the board; however, a 1970 amendment makes no reference to appeals to the board on amendment requests. Section 82 was amended in 1965 to permit a regional planning commission on its own volition to amend regional planning controls. This is covered by the provisions of Sections 85 and 86 which permit councils and the regional planning commissions to appeal to the board actions or inactions on the part of the other. The opportunity for appeal for individual citizens is not set out; however, avenues of appeal are open under municipal planning controls.

The newly conceived Provincial Planning Board, as of 1963, had membership denied only to Ministers of the Crown. The Provincial Planning Director was a statutory member. Thus the previous stipulation, that the board consist of representatives of government departments concerned with regional and urban development, was dropped. It was envisaged as functioning largely as an advisory board with co-ordinatory responsibilities towards regional planning commissions and appeal functions. A special condition was introducted in 1965, whereby development control appeals could not be heard by members of the board who were employees under the Public Services Act. This requirement, which had the effect of generating virtually a second board known as the development wing of the board, was eliminated in 1968.

The Alberta Planning Fund of 1972, by which greater provincial recognition was more explicitly given to regional planning, was one major change in the legislation of the past twenty years.[182] The amendment required that all municipalities, irrespective of membership, contribute to the fund according to a mill rate to be established for different classes of municipalities by the Lieutenant-Governor in Council. Thus though membership of regional commissions was still voluntary, financing them was not. The fund replaced the previous means of support for regional planning commissions by which the province contributed 60 percent and member municipalities the remaining 40 percent, distributed on a formula adopted by the local commission. The Act did not specify the contribution to be made by the province but it was to be in the order of 60 percent plus.

The Department of Municipal Affairs presented the arguments for the fund in these terms:[183]

> To date little has been accomplished in the preparation and implementation of regional plans due to a variety of reasons: Shortage of trained planners, concentration on day-to-day problems, the inability of the commissions and The Province to have complete representation of municipalities on the commissions, and the problems of financing regional planning commissions. If the Province intends to achieve proper and viable regional plans a new approach must be taken to the task.
>
> Financing of regional planning commissions is without doubt the most pressing problem confronting the commissions, associated with non-member municipalities who see very little being accomplished for the requisition imposed.
>
> The province has recognized the importance of regional planning commissions and has supported them to the extent of 60 percent of their operating expenses. However, the non-member municipalities still require service and at present are receiving this at the expense of the members.
>
> If the province is convinced of the merits of regional and municipal planning, then it would appear necessary that a uniform levy be applied by the province to all municipalities in order that all municipalities pay their rightful share of the cost of planning.

> In order to meet the growing concern of the municipalities in regional planning commissions of the cost of planning, attributable in part to increased responsibilities imposed on them by the province, it is recommended that the municipalities pay their share through a mill rate requisition on their equalized assessment to a planning fund. The province would then remit to the planning commissions their cost of operation, with the Provincial Board having the responsibility, as it now has, of scrutinizing each budget before approval . . .
>
> Planning costs will rise, partly due to increasing costs associated with the growth of the province, as well as the cost of preparation of regional plans. Municipalities now receiving planning services at little or no cost may, once they are paying for the services, request more assistance.

A comparison of the legislation as recommended in the report, and that which was eventually adopted, reveals one significant difference. Section 11(b) (7) of the report states:

> There shall be paid from the Fund provided under Section 11b to each Regional Planning Commission such sums as may be authorized by Order of the Minister, these to be applied to the operating costs of the Regional Planning Commission and of the planning departments of the Cities of Calgary and Edmonton.

As adopted by the Legislature, the corresponding section contained no reference to the City Planning Departments of Calgary and Edmonton. Although the legislation did not make membership of regional planning commissions compulsory, increased membership was expected and demands for services would increase as municipalities were required to contribute to the fund regardless of membership.

The introduction of the fund concept has generated opposition. Edmonton City Council went on record as opposing the fund in that, as interpreted by them, the fund provided evidence of increasing centralization of the planning authority at the provincial government level. The council moved:

> That we vigorously oppose further centralization of power in the hands of the Province as well as the financial threat to the City of Edmonton inherent in the amendment relating to the Regional Planning Commission, whereby the Province appoint the members and levy taxes against the municipalities to pay for the operation of the commission.[184]

The three Edmonton councillors on the Edmonton Regional Planning Commission elaborated their objections in an undated letter to the Executive Secretary of the Alberta Urban Municipalities Association.[185] Though recognizing the provincial government's intent adequately to finance planning in all local jurisdictions, they recognized several disadvantages: rapidly growing municipalities may require greater planning services than others, but their revenue would not recognize this need; urban centres, and especially Calgary and Edmonton, would continue to subsidize the planning activities of rural authorities thus making fund revenues in effect transfer payments to other authorities; and the elected representatives of the people would be losing their traditional right to determine monetary expenditures. In general terms they commented:

> We are in general disagreement with a total equalization approach to planning in this Province. Some jurisdictions may wish to maintain a high level of support for planning activities, while others may feel that money, in the short or long term, might be put to better use in other programs.

Calgary and Edmonton were unique in having municipal planning departments, and were therefore maintaining "a high level of support."[186] As the fund legislation stood they were supporting planning on a regional scale as well as their own municipal planning departments, but since even before the McNally Report of 1956 they had claimed the right to influence the planning of adjacent local authorities. On the other hand, had the legislation made provision for even part payment of the operating costs of Calgary and Edmonton's municipal planning departments — as the proposal of the Department of Municipal Affairs suggested — the charge of much more serious potential interference by the province in metropolitan affairs than already existed could well have been made. The provincial government was in a difficult dilemma, for it had no intention of assuming the role of planning leader in the province — despite it's paying 60 percent of approved costs of the regional commissions — and was anxious to involve every local authority in a fair measure of contribution to planning costs and in an adequate level of planning assistance.

The planning fund "proposal" argued in terms of facilitating regional planning in the province as intended by the legislation, but little progress has been made on regional planning controls. As of January 1, 1972 only the Calgary and Edmonton Regional Planning Commissions had completed the preliminary regional plans and no regional plans had been completed. The Edmonton planners had completed only the metropolitan part of the commission's area. The "proposal" suggested that the lack of progress was largely attributable to lack of funds. Similarly, the Task Force on Urbanization and the Future in its report, *The Role of Regional Planning,*[187] suggests the planning commissions must carry out some of their responsibilities at the expense of others because of budget limitations.

Although the fund was intended to facilitate regional

planning, there remained considerable ambiguity as to what the functions of regional planning were and what a regional plan was.[188] As mentioned above, one could interpret from the legislation that a regional plan was a municipal general plan writ large — establishing general categories of land-use somewhat like a sketch zoning map. Until more adequate means of determining the purpose of planning and of identifying its contribution to the development process are introduced, the existence of the planning fund is no guarantee that regional planning will be facilitated. The planning commissions will still be confronted with an array of responsibilities and insufficient funds to carry out all necessary activities. They will continue to set priorities in terms of the exigencies of the situation as it unfolds from day to day. No reference has been made to the make-up of the commissions and to the possible effect upon their activities of the political environment in which they operate. It could be said that much of a regional planning commission's efforts are devoted to municipal planning controls, i.e., matters of local concern, to keep the regional planning commission away from the more political issues which of necessity must be confronted where planning involves multiple jurisdictions.

It can be argued that much of the ambiguity and ambivalence is a consequence of the lack of firm regional planning policies, e.g., the legislation does not indicate how regional plans for all regional commissions are to be integrated or related to each other. On the other hand, it can be argued that there are implicit provincial regional planning policies which can be identified through actions taken by the province in such areas as highway and rail development, or local industrial incentives and subsidies. Further, the regional planning legislation, in part because it originated with attempts to cope with the problems of Calgary and Edmonton, is premised on the concept of an urban-centred region. The legislation is intended to cope with the product of urbanization and is not intended to intervene in the process of urbanization itself. Edmonton's hostility to the fund legislation suggests that Edmonton's councillors were sensitive to the advantages of provincial policies which have been operative for many decades. Their argument implied that growth rates will be determined by the broad and abstract process of urbanization, not by public intervention in that process. In consequence planning is seen as an activity intended to cope with, or be largely a remedy for, problems, rather than a deliberate activity intent upon turning "growth" into "development." Local autonomy was the fundamental attribute of provincial policy which ensured the continuation of Edmonton's regional dominance. City aldermen argued against basing the distribution of revenues upon population and assessment. This would appear to be in contradiction to the past provincial commitment to "fair and equal" treatment and the principle by which the province has traditionally based the distribution of revenues to municipalities and on which Edmonton, relative to other centres, had done so well.

Viewed in terms of the adequacy of the province's planning legislation to meet a highly dynamic urban situation, the mechanisms of control are oriented negatively towards intervening in the major contributor to this dynamic, namely, private investment. The legislation stops at specifying, rather ambiguously in some instances, the intended relationship among local, regional, and provincial levels of authority; it also facilitates the management of land by specifying a variety of relationships between municipal and regional controls and the intended relation of types of municipal controls to each other. By taking a physical object—land—as the root of men's relations with one another expressed through their property and political influence, and by controlling only the use to which owners may put their land and the standard of the improvement to be erected on it, the legislation has exaggerated opportunities for manipulation and manoeuvring, without proper regard for others who may be affected or for the long term interests of the city and its development. The uncertainty which surrounds the present situation; the hostility, envy, and suspicion which can readily be discerned in the attitude of one public authority towards another, and the patchwork nature of planning act amendments for two decades, bear witness to this state of affairs.

The legislation is appropriate to the largely equalitarian relation of persons to persons and local authorities to local authorities; to the overall struggle which men and their organizations were having with the soil, primary produce markets, uncertain transportation, and speculation and influence by companies based in eastern Canada, which typified Alberta before the First World War. It is not appropriate to the thoroughly differentiated power and influence that typifies Alberta in the 1970s nor to the highly organized nature and diverse character of private capital in today's world. The differentiation of local governments in the province has increased manyfold since 1913, when the assumptions upon which Albertan planning legislation is based were introduced. The influence of metropolitan city governments over senior governments, and their influence on organized private capital have increased beyond recognition in even twenty years. The wealth available through natural resources, manufacturing, and human skills are of quite a different order today, as also are the technical and engineering capacities of our time. The solution to this area of urban affairs can only be found in creating clear lines of decision which can control because they correspond to the real distribution of power. The concept of incentives, both positive and negative, is well developed in national and provincial policy in its relation to private enterprise, but it is apparently anathema in the relations among the public authorities.

The legislation at present is centred on the structure of relationships rather than on the processes of interaction that occur inevitably under the dynamic of urbanization. The present controls can only prevent a particular development decision, they cannot compel an event to occur. Zoning, for example, can be seen as a policing power after having established the conditions for development in advance. Zoning increases the predictability of possible outcomes, but the dynamic of the development itself is dependent upon the decisions of persons other than those involved in the control of growth. As zoning decisions are subject to appeal, and zoning by-laws to amendment, zoning as a mechanism does not ensure a predetermined outcome even if that was desirable. It is little wonder that the preference of metropolitan councils, and many of their officials, is for the flexibility and negotiation inherent in development control rather than zoning. Similarly, the general plan provides only an indication of a desired future and thereby mitigates only in part the risks experienced by private developers. In turn its "desired future" exaggerates the anguish of elected officials in their decision over proposals which intrinsically compromise the plan.

Flexibility and negotiation are inherently in conflict with the general tone of the legislation. Yet, coupled to the contract as the expression of their practical reality, flexibility and negotiation are of the essence of the modern urban dynamic. Discretionary power tends to lie as much with administrators as elected members under development control, though council guidelines and the like tend to be honestly adhered to by responsible officers. As Professor W. Alonso has remarked:

> . . . what is needed is not so much a plan but a planning process. That is to say, the Master Plan, reflecting its architectural ancestry, presented a picture of an ideal final stage . . . and the only question was how to carry it out. Today it is clear that in the nature of things every plan is tentative, both because information is imperfect and because there is no final stage: there is always a future beyond the stage projected. What is needed is continuous planning . . .[189]

That is precisely what no government has yet provided in the history of Alberta. Its absence has contributed substantially to the uncertainty, ambivalence, and political nature of the valiant but inadequate attempts of local authorities to cope with events in their own and in neighbouring jurisdictions. Incremental, *ad hoc* amendments by the provincial government to its planning legislation have tended to be reactions to particular situations and problems confronting one or other of the metropolitan centres. The province, by the grace of its constitutional powers, legislated to assist in the amelioration of its protege's problem, but conveniently stood clear of direct responsibility for the solution of the overall situation. The amendments were not directed towards the elaboration and implementation of an explicit and comprehensive provincial policy.

The principal means of urban development, namely, privately organized capital, knows no municipal or even regional boundary, nor is it constrained by considerations of equitable distribution of public resources. In consequence the ability of local authorities to influence and regulate its location is inherently limited. The possibility of major mistakes, long regretted decisions, are never too far from the minds of local leaders who take their responsibilities to the public and the province commendably seriously. The one irremovable attribute of the present social structure is the recognition by all responsible local leaders of the dire necessity "to remain on top of the situation." Any intrusion by the province into the "on top of the situation" position of the metropolitan centres is countered speedily and vehemently. Yet, paradoxically, this very defensiveness leads to the subordination of the metropolitan centres to the situation. Suspicion of the intent of others, a constant search for the means of getting one up on one's peers, care to ensure there is room to manoeuvre, and similar behaviour, typify the motives of local governmental leadership in the current structural arrangement. Within the context of this situation, and within the context of these motives, the provincial policy of local autonomy is in practice brought to nought. There can be very little autonomy, and very little choice within only a narrow range of possibilities when fear and suspicion govern the thought of responsible people. In this sense local authority leaders in the province live in hope, but not in faith; they live in fear of failure and mistakes, not in the joyful awareness of being an integral part of a great ambition subscribed to by virtually all levels of government and all sections of the people. Instead of fostering creativity and individual freedom, "local autonomy," as applied in the context of Alberta, at least since Leduc, has tended to "promote local apathy" among the "have not" towns and cities of the countryside, and the demoralization of the metropolitan centres.

Notes
Chapter 3

1. *Report of the Royal Commission on the Metropolitan Development of Calgary and Edmonton,* Edmonton: 1956, Queen's Printer, p.5. Difficulty was experienced in obtaining a copy of this report and an early draft was used for this analysis. For this reason, footnotes will refer to Chapter number and page, rather than to page alone. For short it will be referred to as the *McNally Commission Report.*
2. *McNally Commission Report,* Chapter 3, p.19.
3. Ibid., Chapter 4, p.15. Though not investigated fully, it is reasonable to suggest that the current mode of trailer park accommodation inside and out of the city is the same phenomenon in different guise.
4. Ibid., Chapter 4, p.12. The studies referred to were *Report of the Fringe Committee and Supplement, Fringe Committee Report,* Community Planning Association of Canada, Edmonton Branch, 1952.
5. *McNally Commission Report,* Chapter 4, p.10.
6. Ibid., Chapter 17, p.1.
7. Ibid., Chapter 4, p.17.
8. Ibid., pp.24-25.
9. Ibid., p.26.
10. Ibid., Chapter 11.
11. Ibid., p.3.
12. The McNally Commission dealt with this matter in Chapter 5, but in Chapter 11, p.39, an outline is given of the difficulties in working relationship between the two local authorities.
13. *McNally Commission Report,* Chapter 11, p.10.
14. Ibid., Chapter 12, p.35.
15. Ibid., Chapter 11. p.11.
16. Ibid., p.16.
17. Ibid., Chapter 12, p.33.
18. See Ibid., Chapter 12, p.31-33.
19. In the introduction to Calgary and Edmonton's General Plans, there are references to the influences over vast regions of Western Canada of these cities. At that point they are very willing to demonstrate their dominance. On the other hand, the Commission's recommendation on the annexing of Strathcona's industry would oblige the MD to revert "substantially to the position it was in some five years ago before the industrial assessment was of any consequence. It would be in no worse position than the other two rural municipalities which adjoin Edmonton." Chapter 12, p.32.
20. *McNally Commission Report,* Chapter 12, p.33.
21. Ibid., Chapter 5, p.13.
22. Ibid., p.11.
23. The *McNally Commission Report,* Chapter 5, pp.14-16 describes the process of expansion and increasing complexity of Calgary and Edmonton's planning instruments that developed between 1950 and 1956.
24. Speech delivered in the Legislature March 3, 1950. Queen's Printer, Edmonton, p.3.
25. Ibid.,

26. Ibid., p.13.
27. Ibid., p.15.
28. Ibid., p.16.
29. *McNally Commission Report,* Chapter 5, p.17. E.H. Dale, in his " Successive town and city councils in the evolution of Edmonton, Alberta, 1892 to 1966," Unpublished PhD thesis, Department of Geography, The University of Alberta, 1969, p.34, gives credit to this department for the relative orderliness achieved within the city by 1961.
30. *McNally Commission Report,* Chapter 5, p.19.
31. Ibid., p.20.
32. Ibid., Chapter 4, p.3.
33. Ibid., Chapter 5, p.29.
34. Ibid., p.36.
35. Ibid. See also Chapter 14, p.5. et. seq.
36. Ibid., Chapter 5, p.41.
37. Ibid., Chapter 14, p.5.
38. Ibid.
39. Ibid., Chapter 5, p.38.
40. Ibid., p.44.
41. Ibid., p.46.
42. Ibid., p.48.
43. Ibid., p.54-55. The contrast between the commission's position on private property rights in this quotation and its position on the Strathcona annexation argument discussed in the previous section, is notable.
44. *McNally Commission Report,* Chapter 5, p.55.
45. Budget Speech to the Legislature, March 4, 1955 by the Honourable C.E. Gerhart. Queen's Printer, Edmonton, p.17.
46. See the McNally Commission's explanations: *Report,* Chapter 6, pp.41-52.
47 Figures derived from the *Report,* Chapter 6. If the school board debt was added to gross debt in Calgary, the per capita figure rose to $356.98.
48. Gross and net debt is differentiated by means of self-supporting utility debt, the owner's share of local improvement debt and similar items.
49. Figures derived from the *Report,* Chapter 6, pp.8 and 28.
50. *McNally Commission Report,* Chapter 6, p.32.
51. Ibid., p.54.
52. Ibid., p.14.
53. Ibid., p.21.
54. Ibid., p.65. Direct defence expenditure in 1954 was $122.18 per capita or more than 40 percent of the federal budget. Later in the *Report,* the commission mentions the unique Alberta situation — "the contrast of full provincial coffers and declining debt, with low provincial taxation, and rising municipal taxes and even more rapidly rising debt" — but considers it of little practical consequence, p.73.
55. *McNally Commission Report,* Chapter 6, p.41.
56. Ibid., p.49.
57. Ibid., p.51.
58. Ibid., p.43.
59. Ibid., p.44. The general debt excludes debt incurred on local improvement account and on self-liquidating utilities account.
60. *McNally Commission Report,* Chapter 6, p.66. The commission was unable to indicate Calgary's position over time but considered the contribution of industry and commerce to city assessment in 1955 to be about 40 percent. *Report,* Chapter 6, p.66.
61. *McNally Commission Report,* Chapter 6, pp.27 and 6.
62. Ibid., p.71.
63. Originally enacted as Chapter 3, *Statutes of Alberta,* 1956.
64. Budget Speech to the Legislature, 1957, pp.3-4.
65. Budget Speech to the Legislature, 1958. p.3.
66. Ibid., p.4.
67. Budget Speech to the Legislature, 1962, p.26.

68. We have not attempted the task of unscrambling the figures by reference to Alberta's Public Accounts, or even to test if it is possible.
69. See Table in Chapter 1 of this volume.
70. Budget Speech to the Legislature, 1962, p.26.
71. Ibid., p.27.
72. Ibid., p.28.
73. Figures derived from the 1962 and 1963 Budget Speeches pages 9 and 7 respectively. The quotation is from the 1962 Speech, p.9.
74. See *The Politics of Canadian Urbanization,* vol.1 of this work, Chapter 4.
75. Alberta used 54.7 percent of its total loan on roads, bridges, sidewalks, and parking facilities, and a further 29.4 percent on water and sewer facilities. *Annual Report* of the Municipal Development and Loan Board, March 31, 1968, p.9.
76. It should be remembered that the local authorities had to provide one-third of the estimated cost, with a 25 percent forgiveness provision on timely completion, so that only those with available money or access to money could make use of the schemes; or the extent of its use was limited to the money available to them to meet their share of the cost.
77. We are grateful to the Deputy Provincial Treasurer for information on the details of the administration of this scheme.
78. Calgary went in for a large number of small loans, 41 in all. The reason for this has not been ascertained.
79. The Act was rescinded and a new one introduced in 1969.
80. The formula found most generally applicable was in the case of a *de novo* town three employees of the major source employment to one service personnel during the construction phase and settling to 2.8:1 after construction was completed. In towns involving radical improvements the formula was reduced to about 2.5:1. The size of families is usually greater in *de novo* new towns than the average, due to the age specific character of employees, and a figure of 4.2 persons per family is used as against 3.8 for the Alberta average. Information supplied by Mr. Noel Dant, Provincial Planning Director.
81. Not all the money required by new towns or growth centres came from this federal fund. The advances made to Fort McMurray for example, almost reached one and three-quarter million dollars, while less than half a million dollars was provided for by the federal scheme. Conversely, it was a condition of the federal loan, that it would be applied to municipal works that were additional to those already scheduled, had the scheme not been introduced. Money received by a municipality for winter works or by provincial grant was first applied to its loan request, and two-thirds of that request was then funded federally by loan with the 25 percent forgiveness applying to the latter only. The minister expected the money to come out at about 2 percent interest overall. (*House of Commons Debates,* 1963, 3:2930.)
82. One of the difficulties of the advisory committee had been its frequent change of membership and hence difficulty with continuity.
83. We acknowledge gratefully the assistance of the Lethbridge Economic Development Office for use of tables generated by them. We would particularly thank Mr. J. Dods for his calculations and advice.
84. To check the erratic feature of Lethbridge as a possible characteristic of small cities, a comparable study of Red Deer, Camrose, and Wetaskiwin was made. In general it was found to be the case, though the topic is discussed more fully a few pages on.
85. The figures for public utility surpluses are deducted from the original data source and not from the above tables. They are also expressed in constant dollars.
86. *Report of the Public Expenditure and Revenue Study Committee,* Edmonton, March, 1966, p.3.
87. *Statutes of Alberta,* 1966, Chapter 39.
88. The Study Committee concluded its report by a general recommendation on the development of human resources, op cit. p.128. The Human Resources Development Authority (HRDA) and the Human Resources Research Council

(HRRC) were set up by statute in 1967. *Statutes of Alberta,* 1967, Chapters 35 and 36 respectively.
89. Budget Speeches for the respective years.
90. Budget Speech, 1963, p.19.
91. Ibid.
92. Budget Speech, 1966, p.3.
93. Ibid., pp.13-14.
94. *Report of the Study Committee on Public Expenditure,* p.124.
95. See *The Politics of Canadian Urban Development,* vol. 1 of this work. Chapter 5.
96. Quoted from a CMHC press release, May 26, 1971, p.5.
97. *The Report of the Study Committee on Public Expenditure,* p.124, envisaged a nucleus of four to six specialists for organizational and work studies, advice on office mechanization, and assistance in implementation of improved systems.
98. *Statutes of Alberta,* 1965, Chapter 38.
99. Ibid., long title of the Act.
100. City of Calgary, November, 1968, Introduction.
101. Budget Speech, 1967, p.23.
102. *Report of the Study Committee on Public Expenditure,* p.23.
103. Ibid.
104. Ibid., p.105.
105. Ibid.
106. Ibid. The 75 percent formula for highways is often referred to by city hall officials as the "25 cent dollar."
107. *Report of the Study Committee on Public Expenditure,* p.87.
108. *Statutes of Alberta,* 1966, Chapter 37. The 1966 Report of the Study Committee recommended a change in the mode of applying the principle contained in this Act.
109. *Statutes of Alberta,* 1967, Chapter 34, Section 2(c).
110. *Statutes of Alberta,* 1968, Chapter 44.
111. City of Calgary, November, 1968.
112. For example, *A Satellite Community Study for the Edmonton and Calgary Areas,* October 1969, and *Alberta Housing Profile,* September 10, 1968.
113. *Statutes of Alberta,* 1969, Chapter 50, Section 5.
114. *Statutes of Alberta,* 1960, Chapter 57.
115. By 1970, the corporation had plans for an extensive capital program to cost nearly $40 million, including $21 million for land assembly and most of the remainder for low income housing, the aged, northern development etc. Central Mortgage and Housing Corporation was to be the major source of borrowed funds. Budget Speech, 1970, p.10. By 1971 some $7.2 million of provincial funds were appropriated for public housing, interest on debt, and general administration. Budget speech, 1971, p.10. In 1971 the Alberta Housing Corporation obtained $41 million from CMHC but this grant was reduced to $34.5 million in 1972.
116. In a speech to the Town Planning Institute of Canada, 1970 Conference, Edmonton, on July 21, 1970, Premier Harry Strom said, "In general, we are concerned that all planning in this province start with the goal of encouraging 'the individual to grow as a responsible, free, and creative human being.' In expressing this goal we recognize that we must be prepared to encourage people to participate in the process of planning itself." Press release, Office of the Premier, July 21, 1970, p.10.
117. These are summarized conveniently on p.3. of the 1969 Budget Speech.
118. Budget Speech, 1969, p.4.
119. See, for example, *An Address to the Alberta Urban Municipalities Association* by the Honourable Harry E. Strom, October 30, 1970, p.1.
120. Budget Speech, 1970, p.19.
121. *Urban Crisis,* Alberta Municipal Finance Study, January, 1968, letter of submission to the Premier and others.

122. Ibid.,
123. Ibid., p.10.
124. Ibid., p.11.
125. Ibid., p.15.
126. *Report of the Special Committee Appointed by the Government of Alberta to Study Assessment and Taxation,* Edmonton, March, 1970.
127. Ibid., p.7.
128. Ibid., p.32.
129. Ibid., p.33.
130. Ibid., p.34.
131. Ibid.
132. Ibid.,
133. Ibid.
134. The committee stated in the Introduction to its report: "Rather we see our contribution to be one of restating the fundamental agreements in the arguments and formulating positive recommendations to best accommodate the varying interests involved." Ibid. p.11.
135. Ibid., p.14.
136. The Municipal Taxation Act, Section 8(3)
137. *Report on Assessment and Taxation,* p.15.
138. For the recommendations of some city assessors, see *The City Assessors* . . .On: Report of the Special Committee Appointed by the Government of Alberta to Study Assessment and Taxation, September 15, 1970.
139. The committee found even among assessors some confusion about the intent of legislation where it prescribes values for assessment purposes. Op. cit. p.26.
140. *Report on Assessment and Taxation,* p.21.
141. Ibid., p.20.
142. Ibid., p.33.
143. Ibid., p.20.
144. Ibid., p.22.
145. Ibid., p.26.
146. *The Urban Fiscal Problem — Piecemeal or Aggregate Solutions?* Position Paper, The Alberta Urban Municipalities Association, 64th Annual Convention, 1970.
147. Ibid., p.1.
148. Ibid.
149. Cited in ibid., p.1.
150. *A Position Paper* by the Honourable Harry E. Strom, Premier of Alberta, September, 1970., pp.87-90.
151. Ibid., pp.91-92.
152. *The Urban Fiscal Problem,* p.5.
153. Ibid., p.3.
154. *An Address to the Alberta Urban Municipalities Association,* by Premier Harry E. Strom, October 30, 1970, pp.3-4.
155. Ibid., p.9.
156. Ibid., p.10.
157. The Premier was conscious of some difficulties in this area. In the AUMA speech he remarked, "In the meantime, the Government of Alberta is not using the Task Force as an excuse to 'wait and see!' " Op. cit., p.19.
158. In his address to the AUMA, p.16, the Premier referred to federal interest in Canada's cities and the need for federal-provincial-municipal co-ordination. As the task force was expected to form committees with representatives of rural interests, it is difficult to discern the Premier's reasoning. Some financial support from Ottawa was also expected during this stage of planning the task force. The task force was closed down by Premier Lougheed June, 1972.
159. We should add perhaps that the Department of Highways had initiated legislation (The City Transportation Act, 1970) enabling cities to designate transportation corridors and to have effective control over the land in those

corridors. The cities in consequence have been left a little freer to engage in long term transportation planning.

160. Address to the Alberta Urban Municipalities Association, p.20.

161. Ibid.

162. Premier Lougheed also closed down the Task Force on Urbanization and the Future in 1972.

163. *McNally Commission Report,* Chapter 5, p.34.

164. Ibid.

165. An Act to Amend the Town and Rural Planning Act, 1957.

166. Dant, N., "Brief History of Planning Statutes of Alberta" unpublished manuscript, p.6.

167. The Provincial Planning Act, 1963, Section 3.

168. The Planning Act, 1963, Section 15.3.

169. Ibid., Section 19(2).

170. Ibid., Section 108.

171. The reader is referred to F.A. Laux's "The zoning game: Alberta style," *Alberta Law Review.* vol.ix, No.2., 1971, pp.268-308 for a detailed discussion of ambiguities in the planning legislation with respect to the relationship of development control to zoning, and with respect to appeal procedures under both controls.

172. The Planning Act, 1963, Section 107.

173. Ibid., Section 1.22.

174. Ibid., Section 130.1.

175. An Act to Amend the Planning Act, Section 131.

176. Ibid., Section 132.

177. Ibid., Section 9.

178. The Planning Act, 1963, Section 14.1.

179. An Act to Amend the Planning Act, 1968, Section 71.

180. *A Proposal to Provide Equitable Financing: City Planning, Regional Planning, Provincial Planning,* prepared by the Department of Municipal Affairs, Edmonton, August, 1970. The title was changed in a later draft. See below.

181. The Task Force on Urbanization and the Future in a publication, *The Role of Regional Planning,* November, 1971, has compiled useful statistical and descriptive material on the Commissions, their boundaries, staffing population, and other details.

182. An Act to Amend the Planning Act, 1971, Section 11.

183. *The Alberta Planning Fund: To Provide Equitable Financing For: Regional Planning, Provincial Planning,* March, 1971. It is interesting to note that in an earlier draft of the "Proposal" (August, 1970) the title contained "City Planning." Also deleted from the August, 1970 report was the statement "At the present time the cities of Calgary and Edmonton receive no financial recognition from the Province, either for municipal planning or the support the cities give to the regional planning concept. This plan would compensate in part the cost of planning services in our two largest cities."

184. Edmonton City Council minutes, April 26, 1971, motion as approved.

185. Written sometime before January 29, 1971.

186. In the Department of Municipal Affairs "Proposal," the contributions of Calgary and Edmonton were to be reduced both absolutely and as a percentage of the total Regional Planning Commission area contribution. Changes in contribution of other local authority areas were also proposed, as were the revenues of several of the commissions.

187. Edmonton, November, 1971.

188. The task force report raises many of these questions.

189. Alonso, W. "Planning as a profession" in *Taming Megalopolis,* H. Wentworth Eldridge (editor), Autumn Books, 1967, p.582.

Chapter 4
Edmonton and Environs, 1960 to 1972

This Chapter describes in some detail the relation of the City of Edmonton to its immediate hinterland, offers an explanation for this relationship, and finally discusses the relation of municipal finance to city growth.

Existing Regional Policies and Plans

The General Plan adopted by the Edmonton City Council in May, 1971 devoted a chapter to the Edmonton Region, District, and Municipal Area. This set out the objectives for the city, and the principles on which its relationship to the region would be based. The centripetal nature of the city's approach is clear from this document.

The General Plan distinguishes between a region and a sub-region, which differ in their relationship to the city and in the nature of the public policies and decisions which influence development:

> Edmonton is the dominant centre of a vast region extending south to the Red Deer River, north to the Arctic Islands, east to Lake Athabasca and west to the Western Cordillera. This region is a spatial entity overlapping municipal, provincial and territorial boundaries.
> The Edmonton region is essentially that area in which the City of Edmonton plays a dominant role as a supplier of goods, as a centre of services, as an administrative centre, as a base of operations and as a financial and government centre. The demand for these services from outlying communities influence the provision and location of transportation and communication facilities and services. At the same time, the size of the region is dependent on the quality of the existing communications network and the extent to which this network is utilized and improved . . .
> Development within this region affects Edmonton profoundly by generally increasing business activity, tourism, and population, and consequently creates demands for new offices, homes, warehouses, transport facilities and industrial, government and cultural

> buildings.[1] Regional development can also be influenced by the many activities and services which exist in Edmonton. Edmonton and its region are, therefore, mutually interdependent and equally important to one another . . . Population growth in the region is, in part, dependent on the extent of new resource development. The exact nature of the future population pattern, therefore, cannot be established as vast areas of the region have yet to be explored to determine its full potential as a supplier of minerals and other products.[2]

Edmonton's sensitivity to natural resource development in the remoter region, most recently to oil discoveries in Alberta's north and in the Arctic, but of long standing in the history of the city, receives full emphasis in the General Plan. These resource developments have historically been dependent upon private enterprise decisions. No local, regional, provincial, or national authority exists to integrate these developments with Edmonton's own capacity to further them. The city is obliged, therefore, largely to depend on retaining flexibility and advantage over its rivals in order to cope with the dynamic of events in its remoter hinterland.

The General Plan also identifies a sub-region where the relationship is somewhat different:

> Within this broad economic region a much smaller 'urban centered' region exists which is delineated on the basis of the relationship established by the City's retail rather than its wholesale trade. Much greater personal contact is evident between the urban area and the surrounding rural municipalities, towns and villages. Many problems are common to all areas within this region, for example, water supply, and, in addition, the activity in one area could affect activity in another, for instance, air pollution.[3]

It was particularly in this sub-region that the city's influence could be positive and direct. The General Plan, however, observes that this influence is not entirely monopolistic, and is dependent on the capacity of local firms to meet the needs for services in the sub-region. The plan comments:

> Competition from other cities in Western Canada for providing services to the region is keen and the extent to which Edmonton will benefit from the growth in the region is dependent on how effectively local firms will be able to satisfy regional needs.[4]

It therefore behoves the city to establish the conditions necessary to retain and enhance its current advantages. The purpose of this section is to explore some of the recent attempts to cope with urban development in the sub-region loosely defined as the City of

Edmonton and its surrounding communities—Fort Saskatchewan, Leduc, St. Albert, Sherwood Park, Spruce Grove and Stony Plain. Within this region there exist local and regional authorities with mandates to ensure "economical and orderly" growth and development.[5]

Edmonton City Council's General Plan contains objectives and principles closely in accord with the intent of regional planning as defined in the Planning Act. There is reference to devising a strategy of growth, its direction, sequence and extent of development, "within and around the major urban centre of the region without the impediment of political boundaries"; to regulating land use in the interests of orderliness; to facilitating inter-area planning of common physical amenities such as watersheds and natural resources; and to co-ordinating objectives of provincial and national planning proposals.[6] With regard to the steps to be undertaken, there is provision for a Preliminary Regional Plan, and eventually a Regional Plan, to govern the regional aspects of land use and physical resource exploitation, with particular reference to the outlining of the general urban zone, agricultural areas, the generators of urban growth such as major industry and highway development with proposals on road services, public buildings, schools, parks, etc.[7]

With regard to the duties of the Regional Planning Commission, The General Plan envisaged the following:

> Although not primarily concerned with political boundaries and the form of local government the Commission should be concerned that effective control continues to be exercised over metropolitan and regional aspects of planning.[8]

Similarly, as pollution respects no political boundaries, it was a problem requiring close co-operation of local, regional, and provincial agencies. The Edmonton General Plan, in the interests of the city as a sufferer from pollution caused by others and as a local authority likely to suffer if its neighbours encouraged potentially polluting industry to settle in their jurisdiction under lower standards than the city demanded, moralizes over the need to ensure that "various authorities should be complementary and mutually supporting. . ." The plan then argues that certain principles should be supported: that the public come to see a good "quality of living" as a right, as is education or recreation, that each polluter should be held responsible for his damage, and that all concerned should recognize the rights of other living things.

The Edmonton Regional Planning Commission (ERPC) was intended to facilitate the co-ordination of development in the region by preparing a regional plan , and regional studies of land use and road services, and advising and assisting municipalities in the preparation of local planning controls. Co-ordination could also be facilitated by the provisions of The Planning Act which required that upon a preliminary regional plan being adopted, all local planning controls had to be made consistent with it.[9]

To realize these objectives, and as required by The Planning Act, ERPC has prepared a Preliminary Regional Plan, but to date only the metropolitan part has been completed:[10]

> The Metropolitan Part of the Preliminary Regional Plan defines permitted land use classes for the City of Edmonton, St. Albert, and portions of the Counties of Leduc, Strathcona (and Parkland). This area consists of nearly continuous built-up urban development whose parts are highly interdependent. The satellite communities function primarily as dormitory suburbs, depending on Edmonton to provide many cultural, institutional, educational, commercial, industrial and recreational facilities (parenthesis added).[11]

The Preliminary Regional Plan was originally adopted on January 8, 1958, and was amended and consolidated in 1961, and again in 1962. As of January, 1972, additional revisions were pending. Not surprisingly, the proposed revisions to the plan, which may be loosely defined as a generalized zoning plan, were required largely to permit urban development in areas previously designated as "Agricultural-General Urban Reserve," and to adopt amendments sought by local authorities to incorporate unanticipated urban developments. The pending revisions did not include any portion of the Municipal District of Sturgeon which, as permitted under the Planning Act, independently had a consultant prepare a general plan for its jurisdiction. In order for the proposed independent plan to be incorporated into the Preliminary Regional Plan, ERPC referred the proposed independent plan for comment to all municipalities affected. ERPC collated the responses and submitted these to the Municipal District (MD). The MD, after holding a public meeting before its council and giving the General Plan third and final reading for adoption, submitted a request to ERPC to have the MD's General Plan incorporated into the Preliminary Regional Plan.[12] The request was granted early in 1972. Had ERPC failed to comply with the MD's request, the MD could have appealed to the Provincial Planning Board.[13]

In addition to the omission of the territories of the MD of Sturgeon, the area defined by the Preliminary Regional Plan does not include the communities of Fort Saskatchewan, Leduc, Spruce Grove, or Stony Plain, all of which have experienced recent residential growth which in large part is a consequence of their proximity to Edmonton.

Despite these difficulties of procedure, and the omission of relevant territory of the region, the ERPC has managed to establish several planning and development policies affecting particularly the area immediately adjacent to the city's boundaries. These were enunciated in a report filed with the Local Authorities Board on the occasion of the Mill Woods annexation hearings on October 27, 1970. The report comments:

> In the past, this Commission has made recommendations on boundaries and annexations based upon broad planning policies on which there is substantial agreement between member municipalities.
> These policies relate to the following:
> (1) *Zoning*— The Metropolitan Part of the Preliminary Regional Plan has proved to be an effective method of coordinating the zoning and development in this area. Therefore, zoning matters need not be a main consideration in boundary extension.
> (2) *Decentralization* [14]—There is agreement that decentralization to regional towns and new urban areas where feasible shall be encouraged in every way possible. This policy has economic and other advantages for both the City and the outlying communities. This matter is relevant to the question of the boundaries of Edmonton since it will depend upon the amount of land needed on the periphery of the City.
> (3) *Urban Expansion* — To the degree that urban expansion occurs on the periphery of the built-up area, there is agreement that this should be within urban boundaries. This would apply specifically to residential development; however, if the urban area is to maintain a reasonable balance between residential and non-residential assessment the urban area should have within its boundaries an adequate supply of industrial land.

Though there is some evidence of "substantial agreement between member municipalities" over broad planning policies, there is no necessary agreement — as the MD Sturgeon case shows — over the desired form of regional development, and especially over the city's expansion. As the McNally Commission demonstrated in 1956, taxation rights and financial implications lie at the heart of most of these matters. Though Edmonton city, by adopting its General Plan by-law, implicitly accepted a commitment to support regional planning and development, the city's internal policy decisions suggest an ambivalence and a "convenience" perspective.

In the late 1950s Edmonton had engaged on a concerted policy to attract industry to itself. In 1958 an Industrial Development Board with its own director was established, and also an Industrial Commissioner. Mayor Hawrelak and the Director of Industrial Development made promotional tours to eastern Canada and elsewhere, as well as making representation to the railway companies. In 1961 the city broadened its promotional intent to the Edmonton region generally and set up the Edmonton Area Industrial Development Association (EAIDA). This was to encourage industrial and commercial development in Edmonton city, Jasper

Place, Beverly, St. Albert, Calmar, Devon, Fort Saskatchewan, Leduc, Stony Plain, and the municipal districts included in the then Edmonton District Planning Commission.[15] E. H. Dale observed:

> Whereas the Mayor and members of the public regarded this action of the Council as a retrograde step, the City Commissioners defended it in the belief that the Association would be effective in encouraging new industrial locations in greater Edmonton because of the fragmented jurisdiction of the municipalities over different parts of the metropolitan area; that any industrial advertising program, even if sponsored by the City alone, would have the effect of promoting the whole Edmonton area; and that it would be unlikely, because of the text of any particular advertisement, that interested industrialists would differentiate between the City and the surrounding area. (Commissioner's Report to Council, No. 39, July 22, 1963).[16]

In part the Commissioners' policy was a consequence of the city's lack of large tracts of land for large-scale industry. The city was duty bound to recommend in suitable areas adjacent to the city. It soon became obvious that it was the City of Edmonton which attracted industrialists, who having decided upon Edmonton, were free to locate anywhere in the region. Therefore, the Commissioners reported in December, 1964:

> . . . it is this magnet that should be more vigorously and clearly brought to the attention of industrialists and financiers wherever they may be.[17]

In consequence the constitution of the EAIDA was amended to give Edmonton city greater control over the association.[18] Later, in February, 1966, the Commissioners advised a return to promotion of industry by each civic authority after potential investors had been attracted to the Edmonton region in general. The city thereupon established an Industrial Development Department with the following purposes:

> The primary purpose of the Department is to develop and carry into execution a comprehensive program to attract and facilitate all aspects of economic and industrial growth in and around Edmonton. It being understood that this activity would include tourist promotion.
> In developing these objectives the Department would involve itself in all aspects of resource development, trade, industry, commerce and tourism insofar as these subjects affect the economic well-being of the Edmonton community.[19]

Edmonton subsequently resigned from EAIDA and has never rejoined the organization. Although the city returned "to purely civic promotion," the Industrial Development Office (IDO) was still to be concerned with industrial development "in and around Edmonton." In a recent interview a representative of the Industrial Development Office claimed in order to show that the IDO is not just a city-oriented operation, that of industries locating here because of IDO operations, 25 percent locate in the region outside of Edmonton city.[20] It was also stressed that the IDO recognizes the right of industry to locate where it desires, not where a municipality desires. The EAIDA has continued in existence despite the withdrawal of Edmonton city. The changing position of the city with respect to industrial development demonstrates that while the city recognized the benefits of regional development, it had, at the same time, to be aware that the location of the industry was critical to tax revenues. A municipality may support in theory the concept of regional development, but the reality of its financial implications, when in competition with all other municipalities in the region, jeopardizes the full application of the policy. In turn, regional municipalities are in a relatively powerless position to influence the city's policies, and though they may continue support for *ad hoc* promotional associations, they are in a relatively impotent position to affect the overall regional distribution of private investment in the interests of regional planning policy.

Subdivision Servicing and Residential Land Use Staging:

On February 12, 1968, the city adopted a new policy with respect to the servicing of residential subdivisions, a policy which would appear at first glance to be only a matter of local concern:

> The Committee recommends to Council starting in 1968 the developers be required to repay the servicing costs of all developments as determined by City Council, and that any departure from this policy must be approved by City Council.[21]

The issue had first been introduced on March 13, 1967, when Alderman Purves asked for a report of the city's policy with regard to the servicing of land in new subdivisions. On April 26, 1967, Alderman Leger moved "that a policy be developed so that developers can install the utilities in their own development."

Prior to the adoption of the new policy, the city had put in all subdivision services, the costs of which were to be amortized against the property over 25 years. The "commuted" value, which was paid to the city when the building permit was taken out, provided the city with a revolving fund of approximately $3,000,000 to install future subdivision services. Subsequent to the policy change, the developer was required to put up the property share of servicing costs. The city usually installed the subdivision services and was responsible for trunks and mains.[22] Although the policy change was explained as being necessary because the city was no longer able to afford the service, a representative of the housing industry has suggested that the city was, in fact, attempting to keep its mill rate down by making the $3,000,000 revolving services fund available for other purposes.

The adoption of the policy was not without opposition. In the December 7, 1967 issue of the *Edmonton Journal* developers were quoted as warning that the adoption of the policy would result in fewer housing starts and concomitantly higher prices.
In 1965, when the city had considered a similar policy, the Edmonton Home Builders' Association (EHBA) had opposed the change on the grounds that lots would not be available at the lowest possible prices because private developers would be faced with higher interest rates than was the city. EHBA also argued that the uncertainty as to the availability of serviced land would create inefficiencies in the house building industry, as the house builder would not be able to plan his activities one year in advance.[23] In a December, 1967 submission to council, the EHBA stressed the importance of the jobs and money which the house building industry contributed to the city, and argued that in consequence the city should ensure that sufficient serviced land was available.[24] Their arguments were based on the exigencies of the general situation of the times. They stated that the quality of servicing had been excellent in the past; and recommended that if the city was to withdraw from the servicing of land, this should occur over a three to five year period.[25]

Also at the end of 1967 the City Council was considering a report from its Planning Department on Residential Land Use Staging 1967-1971, wherein the projected five year population increase would be hypothetically distributed over the known growth areas of the city's suburbs. It was a mode of foretelling private developers what the city planners were anticipating, and concurrently allowing the city to co-ordinate its engineering of roads, sewers, and other needed services to the expansion areas. City Council refused the suggestion following a report from its Organization Committee that the program not be adopted because the installation of subdivision utilities by developers made staging unnecessary because the city would put in utilities where the developer put up the money. An alderman was quoted as arguing against the staging proposal because not only would the developer be responsible for servicing but development could be co-ordinated with the General Plan (which was not officially adopted until May, 1971). As reported in the *Edmonton Journal,* March 26, 1968, the staging program was not approved because it was argued that the proposal would kill competition and tend to create speculative increases in land markets. Developers opposed the program because it would give an unfair advantage to those permitted to develop. A developer argued that:

The report included certain specific areas for development

> in rigid sequence and excluded other specific areas where services are immediately available. He said the . . . area being excluded meant a delay of five years, and an increase in the price of the lots would result, which must be charged for the lots. He stated that those developers included in the Staging Report will have a ready market for their lots with no incentive to lower prices. (He) said that competition amongst the land owners must be increased instead of being eliminated if lower land prices are to be obtained.[26]

The private developer's difficulties were that staging would arbitrarily favour some holders of land rights for development over others. By their values all developers should have a fair and equal chance and thereby ensure the control of land prices by competition. A representative of the Public School Board argued in support of the Staging Report:

> That the Public School Board fully concurs with staging as such from their point of view . . . they could not rationally agree that land developers should have wide scope and latitude to develop where it suits them on the basis of free enterprise. He said it is Council's responsibility to guide development in stages to allow the School Board sufficient time for year to year planning.[27]

EHBA also strongly supported the proposal on the grounds that it would facilitate the house builders vis-a-vis the developers in their future planning; however, they did recommend a change in the distribution of expansion areas from those proposed in the report.[28]

The refusal of council to adopt the staging recommendation of its Planning Department, supported in turn by the Edmonton School Board and the Home Builders' Association, and possessing advantages in terms of orderly administrative practices for the City Engineer, could be interpreted as the city councillors' fear of the right of developers to determine where and when a subdivision was to proceed. As privately organized investors, developers had the right to develop both inside and outside the city's boundaries. By upsetting the supposed fair and equal chance which each developer possessed in his right to develop his land when and where he chose as the market opportunities dictated, the council appeared to be recognizing the relative advantage its staging policy would offer to municipalities beyond its boundaries. If this interpretation is correct, it appears that more orderly development of subdivision within the city, and the enhancing of orderly planning by the school board and others, was subservient in its importance to the threat posed by adjacent municipalities.

The Outline Plan Process and its Aftermath

In 1967-68, the city adopted a new suburban residential planning technique — the Outline Plan process. The Outline Plan, which was initiated with the West Jasper Place Outline Plan, usually takes into account an area which may be considered as a unit of growth for 60,000 to 100,000 persons. It establishes in general form the amount and location of major land uses and infrastructure. As explained by a member of the City Planning Department, the change from neighbourhood or block planning to outline plans was in part attributable to fragmented ownership, and to subdivisions which were a legacy of the land boom of the early part of the century. However, in the latter part of the 1960s city growth began to occur on virgin agricultural land under the control of large land owners. The City Planning Department was obliged to adopt a new approach to subdivision planning. The outline plan established guidelines for development and set the requirements for major facilities. Detailed subdivision planning became the responsibility of the developer and could be evaluated by city officials in terms of the outline plan guidelines.

Available housing statistics indicate that coinciding with the above policy changes, a number of problems emerged in the residential land market.

Table 22 shows the supply of serviced lots in developing residential areas of Edmonton covering one- and two-family development.

Table 22. Supply of serviced lots in developing residential areas of Edmonton

	Lots serviced since last count	*Vacant and serviced lots*	*Permits issued since last count*	*Column (1) minus column (3)*
May, 1965		2,796		
Jan., 1966		2,810		
Nov., 1966		2,575		
Nov. 9, 1967		2,627		
Oct. 15, 1968	976(A)	1,503	591(B)	385
Jan. 3, 1969	390	1,407	571	-181
Dec. 31, 1969	1,143	1,440	1,049	94
Dec. 31, 1970	886	1,636	646	240
Oct. 31, 1971	1,012	1,209	1,444	-432
	4,407		4,301	106

(A) The original source gave no indication of when the last count was taken, although data was provided for vacant and serviced lots for July 3, 1969, which may be the time period covered for lots serviced.
(B) For purposes of determining the availability of lots, the City Planning Department assumed that if a building permit was issued, the lot was developed. On the subsequent survey any cancellations were noted.
Source. Records of supply of vacant serviced lots in developing residential areas, City Planning Department, Research Branch, City of Edmonton.

Table 22 shows in column (2) an abrupt drop in the numbers of serviced and vacant lots in 1968. Unfortunately, data were not available on the number of lots serviced in each time interval prior to October 15, 1968; therefore, it has not been possible to compare the rate of servicing before and after the servicing policy change. The data presented in Table 22 also indicate that for the time period for which data were available, the number of lots serviced approximately equalled the number of permits issued.[29] However, it is important to note that in the first ten months of 1971, the number of permits issued exceeded the number of lots serviced by almost 50 percent. As will be seen later, the market price of lots in the city increased anywhere from 10.6 percent to 15 percent in 1971.

Table 23 indicates the wide discrepancy between both the actual number of lots serviced and the serviced reserve lots compared to the projections in the Residential Land Use Staging 1967-1971 study. It must be noted that the data for 1971 only cover the first 10 months and therefore understate the actual number of lots serviced. Subsequent to 1968, the number of available serviced and vacant lots has always been less than one half of the projected need. Similarly, the rate of servicing has been less than 50 percent of the projected need since 1969.

Table 23. Required suburban serviced lots, City of Edmonton, 1966-67[1]

	Projected lots to be serviced	*Ratio of lots serviced to projected need*	*Projected service reserve*	*Ratio of vacant and serviced lots to projected need*
1966			3,840	67.1%
1967	1,610		3,200	82.1%
1968	2,450	55.8%	3,300	42.6%
1969	2,550	44.8%	3,400	42.4%
1970	2,650	33.4%	3,500	46.7%
1971*	2,750	36.8%	3,600	33.6%

*First 10 months only

1. The source for columns 1 and 3 is the residential land use study, 1967-1971, City Planning Department, City of Edmonton, June, 1967; the source for columns 2 and 4 is the record of the supply of vacant serviced lots in developing residential areas, City Planning Department, City of Edmonton. It is not clear whether the two sources refer to the identical suburban areas, but the data indicate the discrepancy between estimated and actual servicing.

In a submission to City Council, the Edmonton Home Builders' Association expressed concern as to the effect the growing shortage of land was having on land prices:

We realize that our Civic Government has no more control over the cost of labor, materials, and financing than we have; but the one item of cost that the city can do something about is the one that has risen the most rapidly; that of course is land. Two years ago we could purchase land for $40 per front foot excluding improvements, now, assuming you can find a lot to purchase, you will pay from $80 to $85 a front foot for similar property; an increase of approximately 100%. For example: In 1966 the Petrolia area opened and there was a good supply of lots in the south section of the city. Lots were purchased from $2,100 to $2,500. However, in 1967 when the supply was diminishing, lots sold from $3,500 to $4,000. In fact the city had six lots in Petrolia that they put out to tender in April of 1968; they received approximately 300 bids from about 175 bidders; and the lots were sold from $4,050 to $4,260 plus local improvement charges.

The reason for the exorbitant increases in land prices is due to the shortage of serviced lots. The Residential Land Use Staging Report as published by the City indicated that as of December 31, 1967 there were approximately 3,200 serviced lots not built on and therefore constituted a serviced reserve. The report further stated that during 1968 our City would require an additional 2,450 lots be serviced and that only 2,350 would be built on thus increasing the reserve to 3,300.

The projection for 1969 was 2,550 to be serviced, 2,450 to be built, with the reserve rising to 3,400.

In fact there were only some 1,130 lots serviced during 1968 and there were 2,367 single family dwellings started reducing the reserve to 1,963. Based on existing registered subdivision plans we may expect that a mere 900 lots will be serviced during 1969 and if we again build 2,300 to 2,400 units the reserve will be completely exhausted.

One result of the shortage of serviced lots has been to place an increased demand on apartment sites. We find that apartment sites now cost in the order of $3,000 per suite which in turn has resulted in increased rents and placed an additional burden on those people in low and medium income brackets. The extent to which the artificial demand for apartment units has become (sic) is best illustrated by again referring to the Land Use Staging Report which indicated that during 1968 multiple housing accounted for over 73 percent.

Another result of the shortage of serviced land has been to expedite the extinction of the small builder. In 1967 the top twenty builders in volume in Edmonton accounted for only 42 percent of the single family dwelling constructed; during 1968 the top fifteen builders in volume accounted for 63 percent . . .

> In view of the obvious time lapse which would occur prior to lots being marketable (by private developers) . . . and in view of the current critical shortage of serviced lots we further suggest that the City service all existing land which can readily be serviced including the land recently purchased by the City as expediently as possible and if necessary under the former Land Servicing Policy thus placing serviced lots on the market until such time as private developers are able to meet the demands and provide a realistic reserve of serviced lots.[30]

The EHBA was particularly explicit over the relation of rising prices to serviced lot shortages, and emphasized that the situation was worsening. The assumed relation among lot shortages, an increased demand for apartment sites and rising apartment site costs is, however, less clear. The Land Use Staging Report had estimated a 53 percent ratio to single-family construction, but the actual rate in 1968 was 73 percent. The influence of the private lending institutions and the then current fashion for highrise development could account for the change, rather than the shortage and rising cost of residential lots — though the latter was tending to support the general trend of change.

A comparison between housing permits issued and the projections of the staging report indicates the shift to multiple family housing that the EHBA letter suggested.[31] Table 24 shows the comparative distribution of estimated and actual housing types for the years 1967 to 1970.

The Table shows, however, that during the four years combined the number of single family permits issued actually exceeded the estimated or projected need despite the marked falling off in 1969. The number of multiple family permits, on the other hand, exceeded the projected requirements in every year except 1970, and in total was up by 64.7 percent over the projected four year total. In 1968 and 1969 the permits issued were more than double the projections. As a similar phenomenon occurred in Calgary, and in the metropolitan centres of other provinces, the Edmonton situation was probably caused as much by the influence of fashion and the private lending institutions as by the shortage of residential lots.

Thus, as events turned out, the apparent fears behind the refusal of the council to adopt the staging recommendation of its Planning Department had little substance in the actual course of events. Because of the federal policy, and its support for the ambitions of private lenders with multiple family dwellings, both the council and the residential developers appear to have miscalculated, though the latter certainly stood to gain from the rising land prices encouraged by the shortage of lots. For the same reasons, the municipalities beyond the city boundaries stood to benefit in theory from neither the policies of city council nor the change in development emphasis from residential to multiple family

Table 24. Comparative distribution of projected and actual housing types, City of Edmonton, 1967-1970

	Estimated required dwelling units[1]					*Building permits issued*[2]				
	Total units	*Single and*[3] *two family*	*Percent of total units*	*Apartment*[3] *and row*	*Percent of total units*	*Total units*	*Single*[3] *family*	*Percent of total units*	*Multiple*[3] *family*	*Percent of total units*
1967	4,910	2,350	47.9	2,560	52.1	6,350	2,494	39.3	3,856	60.7
1968	5,250	2,450	46.7	2,800	53.3	9,335	3,612	38.9	5,723	61.1
1969	5,920	2,550	43.0	3,370	57.0	8,919	1,982	22.2	6,937	77.8
1970	6,180	2,650	42.9	3,530	57.1	4,714	2,291	48.6	2,423	51.8
Totals	22,260	10,000	44.9	12,260	55.1	29,318	10,379	35.4	18,939	64.6

1. *Source:* Residential land use staging 1967-1981, City Planning Department, City of Edmonton, June 1967.
2. *Source:* Edmonton Regional Planning Commission annual reports. *Note:* The data are for permits issued only, not housing starts or completions. The discrepancy between data on the number of permits issued in Table 22 and that presented here is that Table 24 data are for the entire city and Table 22 data are for only newly developing areas of the city.
3. The data for the projections and permits issued are not exactly comparable, in that data for two family units is apparently aggregated with other multiple family housing units in the ERPC data.

accommodation. As events turned out, however, the actual situation was the reverse.

The population changes occurring within selected centres in the Edmonton region during the period just prior to 1967 and to the present are given in Table 25.

The Table shows that coincident with the city's new servicing policy and failure to adopt the Residential Land Use Staging Report (which at no time made reference to residential development outside the city boundary), growth boomed in the satellite urban centres particularly Sherwood Park and Spruce Grove where population increases were in the order of 188 percent and 419 percent respectively over the seven years. Although the city's growth fluctuated between 2.7 percent (1966) and 4.1 percent (1968), the satellite communities in general experienced much higher growth; e.g., Spruce Grove reached 66.7 percent in 1970, Sherwood Park 33.3 percent in 1969, St. Albert 12.3 percent in 1971, Fort Saskatchewan 12 percent in 1968 and Leduc 13.4 percent in 1969.

A comparison of the actual population and the projected population of the City of Edmonton reveals that the Residential Land Use Staging Report consistently underestimated the actual population. If to this is added the population growth of the satellites, it can be seen that the staging report projections were significantly underestimated.

Interviews with representatives of the surrounding communities reveal that much of the recent growth has been "spill over" from Edmonton. These centres are developing into satellite residential dormitories. St. Albert and Sherwood Park have served this function for a considerably longer time. It was not so much the city's policy on industrial location which brought about the residential boom in the adjacent municipalities. The phenomenon in the Edmonton region since 1968 was more of a diversification of residential amenities involving multiple-storey apartment facilities, multiple-family dwellings, the city suburban home, and the outlying municipal home.

Despite the boom in adjacent municipalities since 1968, Edmonton city remains by far the most favoured location for new housing in the region. Table 26 shows the housing permits issued in selected centres of the region from 1961 to 1970 by type of dwelling.

Beginning in 1968 there has been an apparent shift to other urban centres as Edmonton's share of the total housing permits declined from 96.3 percent in 1967 to 70.9 percent in 1970 and of all single family housing in the region from 91.5 percent in 1967 to 60.3 percent in 1970. The number of permits issued in the city peaked in 1968, whereas in the surrounding communities, the number of permits has been increasing rapidly each year during the period 1968-70, 52.9 percent of the single-family permits, 89.4 percent of multiple-family permits, and 58.7 percent of the total housing permits issued in the satellites over the decade were issued in these

Table 25. The population of selected centres, Edmonton region, 1965-1971

	Population								
	1965	1966	1967	1968	1969	1970	1971	1966	1967
City of Edmonton									
actual	371,265	381,230	393,563	410,105	422,418	435,530	450,641	2.7	5.2
projected[1]			393,000	405,000	417,500	430,500	444,000		
Sherwood Park	5,900*	6,200*	7,000*	7,500	10,000*	13,000*	17,000*	5.1	12.9
St. Albert	9,426	9,828	10,243	10,191	10,530	11,249	12,637	4.3	4.2
Fort Saskatchewan	3,820	4,190*	4,430	4,961	5,302	5,734	6,328	9.7	5.7
Leduc	2,916	3,028	3,132	3,331	3,779	4,200	4,476	3.8	3.4
Stony Plain	1,480	1,370*	1,500*	1,600*	1,628	1,685	1,772	-7.4	9.5
Spruce Grove	580	590	667	723	1,110	1,850	3,012	1.7	13.1
Total growth by year								11,049	14,099
City growth as a percentage of total								90.2	87.5

Table 25. *(Continued)*

	Percentage change				*Percentage population growth, 6 satellites*	*Actual growth*
	1968	1969	1970	1971		
City of Edmonton						
actual	4.2	3.0	3.1	3.5		79,376
projected[1]						
Sherwood Park	7.4	33.3	30.0	30.7	52.6	11,100
St. Albert	-0.5	3.3	6.8	12.3	15.2	3,211
Fort Saskatchewan	12.0	6.9	8.1	10.4	11.9	2,508
Leduc	6.4	13.4	11.1	6.6	7.4	1,560
Stony Plain	6.7	1.7	3.5	5.0	1.4	292
Spruce Grove	8.4	53.5	66.7	62.8	11.5	2,432
Total growth by year	17,876	16,356	18,481	22,618		100,479
City growth as a percentage of total	92.5	75.3	70.9	66.8		

1. Residential land use staging, 1967-1971, City Planning Department, City of Edmonton, June, 1967.
*Figures, unless otherwise indicated, are from the local census. Estimated figures are asterisked.
Source: Edmonton Regional Planning Commission annual reports.

Table 26. Housing permits issued in selected urban centres, Edmonton region, 1961-1970 by type of dwelling

Urban centre	*Housing type*	*1961*	*1962*	*1963*	*1964*	*1965*	*1966*	*1967*	*1968*	*1969*	*1970*	*Totals*
St. Albert	SF[1]	276	577	352	80	70	43	51	39	159	213	1,860
	MF[2]			20		10				110	118	258
Sherwood Park	SF	154	118	154	89	127	100	97	278	624	866	2,607
	MF	16								360	185	561
Leduc	SF	32	35	34	18	13	16	16	70	75	125	434
	MF			12						26		38
Fort Saskatchewan	SF	28	20	22	48	27	39	51	179	67	58	539
	MF	12	19	6	6	44		12	84	81	128	392
Spruce Grove	SF	12	18	15	4	8	2	6	35	130	198	428
	MF									10		10
Stony Plain	SF	23	17	9	11	16	15	8	14	21	27	161
	MF					6			12			18
Devon	SF	11		4	1	3		4	2	22	21	68
	MF				12							12
Satellite totals	SF	536	785	590	251	264	230	233	617	1,098	1,508	6,097
	MF	28	19	38	18	60		12	96	587	431	1,289
	Total	564	804	628	269	324	215	245	713	1,685	1,939	7,386
Edmonton City	SF	3,516	3,213	3,113	2,372	2,768	2,059	2,494	3,612	1,982	2,291	27,420
	MF	1,322	1,677	1,835	1,740	1,684	1,641	3,856	5,723	6,937	2,423	28,838
	Total	4,838	4,890	4,948	4,112	4,452	3,700	6,350	9,335	8,919	4,714	56,258
Totals	SF	4,052	3,998	3,703	2,623	3,032	2,289	2,727	4,229	3,098	3,799	33,517
	MF	1,350	1,686	1,873	1,758	1,744	1,641	3,868	5,819	7,524	2,854	30,127
	Total	5,402	5,694	5,576	4,381	4,776	3,915	6,595	10,048	10,604	6,653	63,644
Percentage of Total	SF	75	70.2	66.4	59.9	63.5	58.5	41.3	42.1	29.2	57.1	56.7
Units by Type	MF	25	29.8	33.6	40.1	36.5	41.5	58.7	57.9	70.8	42.9	43.3
Edmonton	SF as % of Total SF	86.8	80.3	84.6	90.4	91.3	90.0	91.5	85.4	64.0	60.3	81.8
	MF as % of Total MF	97.6	98.9	98.0	99.0	96.3	100.0	99.7	98.4	92.9	84.9	95.7
	Edmonton Total as % of Region Total	89.6	85.9	88.7	93.9	93.2	94.5	96.3	92.9	84.1	70.9	88.4

1 SF = single family detached and semi-detached units
2 MF = apartments, row housing, etc., units
Source: Edmonton Regional Planning Commission annual reports

years.[31] Of particular significance was the shift of single-family permits to the satellites. Twenty-nine percent of all single-family permits issued in the period 1968 to 1970 were issued for satellites, as compared to 12.9 percent for the period 1961 to 1967, and 18.2 percent for the decade.

Table 26 also illustrates the shifts in housing types and growing importance of the satellites in the Edmonton housing market, but the data do not provide an explanation of the changes. It was shown above that just preceding the boom of residential growth in the satellite communities the city adopted a new servicing policy and a new planning process for suburban residential growth areas. A senior city administrator and a representative of the house building industry have suggested in a private communication that the rate of subdivision servicing within the city slowed down in 1968 because developers, faced with uncertain sales and desiring to minimize their outstanding investments, were hesitant to undertake the risk formerly shouldered by the city. He also suggested that this period coincided with a period of "tight" money and rising interest rates; therefore, developers, who tended to face higher interest rates than the city, could provide less money for servicing. However, as the newly adopted servicing policy was similar to the policies of surrounding communities, the developers in these centres were confronted with the same constraints. Therefore, the city's policy cannot be said to explain the residential growth of the satellite communities, but may have been a contributing factor.

Several other contributing factors have been suggested. In interviews with a representative of the Public School Board and a representative of the City Planning Department, it was suggested that the change in planning procedures contributed to delays in getting suburban residential land ready for development. The magnitude of the planning area ensures that plan preparation takes a considerable time. The outline plan establishes the intended pattern of development for the entire development area which usually includes areas outside the city's boundaries. Section 96(2) of the Planning Act provides that if a general plan includes land in more than one municipality, each municipality may adopt the general plan by by-law. In practice, this has not been done with the outline plans as the plans tend to be prepared independently of the plan of surrounding municipalities and there is also some ambiguity as to how the outline plan conforms to the planning controls defined by the Planning Act.

The outline plan appears to fall somewhere between the controls in the Planning Act and the Subdivision and Transfer Regulations in which the term is to be found. Regardless of these questions, as the outline plans are not adopted by the municipalities concerned, existing municipal boundaries influence the location of facilities. Procedures for adjusting such boundaries can be time-consuming; thus school boards, for example, desire to locate within known boundaries. Reaching consensus can delay the preparation of the entire plan.

It has also been suggested that as many of the developers in the surrounding communities are not active within the city, the oligopolistic characteristics of land ownership within the city has been influential both in the manipulation of land prices within the city and in forcing developers, not able "to get in on the action" within the city, to seek alternatives elsewhere. A representative of a major developer in one of the surrounding communities explained that because of their knowledge of the housing market, they were aware of the demand for single-family housing but at prices lower than were possible within the city.

Table 27 provides an illustration of the attraction of the surrounding communities to the potential home buyers.

Table 27. Subdivision land values—Edmonton and region, December 31, 1971

Municipalities	*Subdivision*	*Average front footage*	*Total*	*Percentage change from last year*	*Value/ front foot*
Edmonton	Rundle Heights	52	$ 7,500	15	$144
	Steele Heights	52	$ 7,500	15	$144
	Dickensfield	53	$ 8,500	13.3	$160
	Thorncliff	60	$ 8,200	13.5	$137
	Duggan	53	$ 9,200	10.6	$174
	Riverbend	60	$11,300	10.7	$188
	Millwoods (Richfield)	52	$ 5,500	N/A	$106
Sherwood Park	Mills Haven	55	$ 6,000	21.2	$109
	Maplewood	55	$ 6,000	27.6	$109
	Glen Allen	55	$ 6,000	N/A	$109
St. Albert	Braeside	60	$ 6,600	10.0	$110
	Lacombe Park	58	$ 6,100	10.9	$105
	Forest Lawn	60	$ 6,600	N/A	$110
	Grandin Park	60	$ 7,000	11.1	$117
Spruce Grove	Brookwood	54	$ 5,000	23.4	$ 93
Leduc	Willow Park	54	$ 4,700	16.0	$ 87
	Corinthian Park	54	$ 5,000	23.4	$ 93
Fort Saskatchewan	Pine View	54	$ 3,800	8.5	$ 70
Stony Plain	Meridian Heights	55	$ 3,200	N/A	$ 58

Source: CMHC Report—Land Values

As of December 3, 1971, of all the city subdivisions, only Mill Woods at $106 per front foot was cheaper than land in the surrounding communities — and Mill Woods was a special public land assembly project specifically intended to make lower priced lots available in the city. The averages in Grandin Park, in St. Albert, the most expensive lots outside the city, were $500 a lot and $20 per front foot cheaper than the cheapest lot in the city, excluding Mill Woods. In Spruce Grove, which experienced the most rapid growth of any regional community between 1968 and 1971, the land cost was only $93 per front foot and the average lot was $500 less than Mill Woods. Of the subdivisions listed, 70 percent of all lots were $7,000 or less and all of these were outside of the city.[32] The rate of price increase in Spruce Grove and Sherwood Park, the two fastest growing satellites, and in Leduc, exceeded the rate of increase of any city subdivision. (See Table 27.)

The major developer, referred to above, assumed that people would be willing to trade off the inconvenience and extra costs of commuting in order to obtain the desired housing. He also emphasized that some of the market was directly attributable to persons seeking a small town environment.

A matter of importance, but about which we were able to obtain only indirect data, is the influence of lending institutions on the trends discussed above. As a high proportion of mortgages taken out on single-family dwellings involve NHA finance, the influence of CMHC valuation policies is potentially great. CMHC bases its land valuation on the cost of raw land, plus servicing costs, plus a "reasonable profit." Thus, when large discrepancies occur between CMHC valuation and the current selling price of land, the difference tends to reflect market pricing on the basis of "what the market will bear" rather than the "reasonable profit" inherent in the CMHC valuation. Similarly, in its observations of land development as it is occurring on the ground, the valuations of CMHC from year to year and place to place tend to reflect the changing actual cost of developed land. But it is also possible for CMHC to bring an influence to bear on buyers' decisions in so far as by raising the valuation in selected places CMHC can bring the ratio of valuation to selling price closer to unity. Such near parity of valuation to selling price would facilitate purchases by reducing the amount of cash to be contributed by the buyer on seeking an NHA mortgage. The potential influence of lending instituations and of CMHC on residential locational decisions can therefore be considerable.

By 1971 demand for city lots had caused the market price to outstrip CMHC land valuations in Edmonton, thereby requiring a larger cash down-payment from the buyer. In the satellite centres, market price, though rising, was closer to parity with valuation, a circumstance favouring a lower down-payment for the buyer. Faced with the dilemma of relative size of down-payment for approximately the same standard of developed land, many buyers preferred the satellite communities despite the additional cost of the journey to work.

Thus in large measure, the decisions which have contributed to the growth of surrounding centres have been taken independently of one another, and not always on accurate predictive judgements. The effect of policy decisions taken elsewhere, particularly in Ottawa, has tended to be ignored or discounted in the judgements of the local decision makers. Although the city adopted a number of regional planning objectives and ERPC prepared a preliminary regional plan for part of its jurisdiction, actual development decisions were *ad hoc*. The city's subdivision servicing policy and the Residential Land Use Staging proposal were made without considering the regional implications. Development decisions were taken by private developers when they identified a situation to their advantage. ERPC encouraged "concentrated decentralization" but, as will be evident in the discussion of individual communities, there existed no co-ordinated policy of regional development by which the viability of a particular centre experiencing rapid development was ensured. The ERPC policy of concentrated decentralization may be said to be effective in limiting where development occurs, but ERPC had no means of directing developers to a particular location or to determine when development would occur. That ERPC has been successful in limiting residential development to existing centres may in part be explained by the fact that this coincides with the policies of private investors. A major developer in one of the communities told us that private investors only considered existing communities because of the perceived economies and advantages to themselves of connecting to existing services. A major exception was Sherwood Park which, in spite of ERPC objections, proceeded after approval from the provincial planning authorities.

Many parallels may be drawn to the situation identified by the McNally Royal Commission in 1956. The growth of the surrounding communities reflects both the impact of Edmonton's employment opportunities and Edmonton's inability fully to supply the demand for housing. The housing situation has prompted developers to exploit the opportunities in the surrounding communities. The satellites have relieved the city of the need to supply housing of certain prices and types, and in turn the city provides the residents of these communities with employment and services.

Though there is complementarity in this process, and the regional planning legislation following 1956 was designed to enhance and regulate its complementary nature, the problem of services vis-a-vis tax revenue remains. As pointed out by the McNally Commission in its discussion of fringe communities, the affairs of local municipalities are a regional and not a local problem. Their interdependence is weighted heavily by decisions taken within the city, but growth itself is regional in extent.

Without a co-ordinated regional development policy, co-ordination occurs, but only at the local level to facilitate the development of a particular subdivision or municipality. Each municipality attempts to cope with development within its jurisdiction independently of other municipalities. In the selected centres being considered, there are as many "attempts to cope" as there are municipalities. The particular policies adopted by a community are dependent upon the unique situation of that particular community — its economic base, its rate of growth, its expertise with rapid development, its long range development goals.

Local Municipal Attempts to Cope

In this section we describe the responses of Fort Saskatchewan, Leduc, St. Albert, Sherwood Park, Spruce Grove and Stony Plain, to their situation. Their location with respect to Edmonton is shown on the accompanying map (Figure 1). The

Figure 1

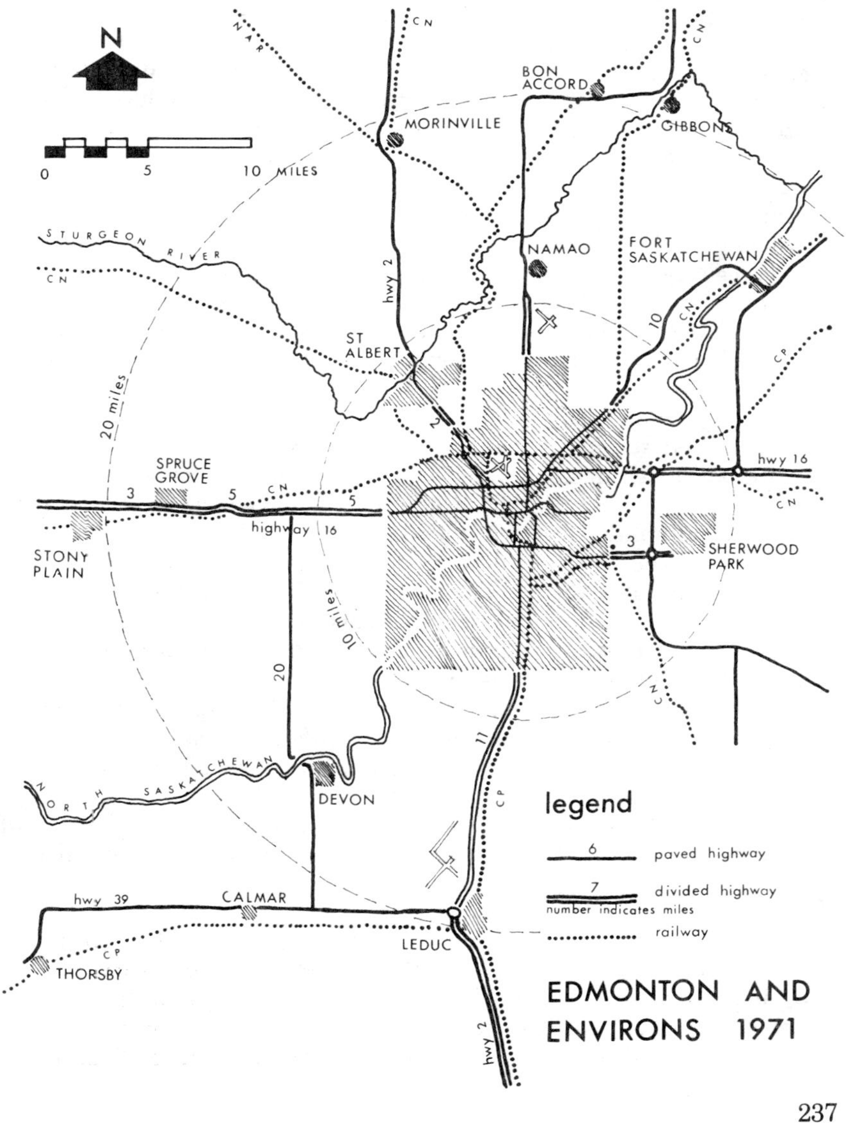

industrial and commercial building permits issued in these centres for the period 1965-70, are shown by number and value in Table 28 below. This Table will be referred to in the seriatim discussion of each centre's affairs. The Table shows an erratic incidence and value in the permits issued, though a considerable increase in 1969 and 1970 is apparent.

Fort Saskatchewan

Fort Saskatchewan's population increased by 65.7 percent during 1956 to 1971. (See Table 25.) A representative of the town attributed this to local industrial development and to the development of Fort Saskatchewan as a residential dormitory. In 1970 estimates indicate that more than 10 percent of the employed residents commuted elsewhere—to Edmonton, Namao, and various industries located in the region. This percentage of commuters may increase in the future, especially when Highway 15 to Edmonton is upgraded. Fort Saskatchewan is not a dormitory centre like the other centres being considered. It is in the enviable position of having a high industrial assessment .6 percent industrial, 38.4 percent residential, and 8.0 percent commercial. Of industrial and commercial building permits issued in the six satellite centres during the period 1965 to 1970,
46.8 percent of their value was in Fort Saskatchewan. Residential land prices in Fort Saskatchewan were the cheapest in the region, except for Stony Plain, and the price increase for 1971 over 1970 was the lowest for any centre for which data were available. (Table 27.)

Development Policies:

1. *Subdivision servicing.* The developer is responsible for financing and installing all necessary services within the subdivision.
2. *Acreage assessment* is levied against the developer for necessary oversizing of trunks and arterial roads.
3. *Offsite charges* are levied against the developer to cover costs of sewage lagoon and outfall. This policy has just been implemented; therefore, the town has had no experience with it.

Note: Park reserves are exempt from local improvement and acreage assessments, but school sites are not.

4. *Water.* Fort Saskatchewan, Redwater, the Municipal Districts of Sturgeon and Thorhild, and the County of Strathcona formed a joint company to build a water pipe line from Edmonton. The line was oversized by about 20 percent in anticipation of industrial development along its route. The province has deferred repayment of this portion, which is to be repaid as this excess capacity is utilized.

Leduc

Leduc experienced a population increase of 53.5 percent between 1965 and 1971, but from 1965 to 1968 the population had only increased by 415. Between 1968 and 1971 the population increased by 1,145 or 73.4 percent of the total increase. From 1951, just four years after the discovery of oil in the region, to 1968, the

Table 28. Industrial and commercial building permits issued in selected urban areas, Edmonton region, 1965-1970

		1965	*1966*	*1967*	*1968*	*1969*	*1970*	*Total*	*Total value expressed as percentage of value of all permits issued*	*Percentage population growth*
Fort Saskatchewan	No.:	3	7	8	6	17	8	49		
	Value:	$272,000	133,000	202,250	242,500	935,750	484,800	$2,270,300	46.8	14.1
Leduc	No.:	3	2	12	4	3	8	32		
	Value:	$170,850	8,000	115,300	57,500	59,000	32,135	442,785	9.1	9.4
St. Albert	No.:	7	3	3	4	3	2	22		
	Value:	$109,000	45,400	38,525	94,200	73,000	87,000	447,125	9.2	13.4
Sherwood Park	No.:	2	1	4	3	5	3	18		
	Value:	$307,000	2,000	267,700	15,700	34,375	268,000	894,775	18.5	52.2
Spruce Grove	No.:	1	3	3	3	5	4	19		
	Value:	$ 1,000	26,600	33,500	46,000	90,450	119,500	317,550	6.5	9.3
Stony Plain	No.:	4	2	5	7	2	2	22		
	Value:	$ 25,000	40,000	127,500	205,000	65,000	11,000	473,500	9.8	1.5
Total	No.:	20	18	35	27	35	27	162		
	Value:	$884,850	$255,000	$784,775	$660,900	$1,258,075	$1,002,435	$4,846,035		

Source: Edmonton Regional Planning Commission annual report.

population of Leduc had increased from 1,342 to 3,331, an increase of 1,489 or only 344 more than the increase from 1968 to 1971. A representative of the town attributed the growth, in part, to the International Airport but more directly to the increasing role of Leduc as a dormitory of Edmonton.

Two major Edmonton-based developers are active in Leduc. A representative of one of the firms indicated that the decision "to go into Leduc" was, in part, based upon the Alberta Housing Corporation's *Satellite Community Study* of Calgary and Edmonton in October, 1969.[33] Leduc received the highest rating of any centre in either the Calgary or Edmonton areas on the Community Evaluation scale.

Table 27 indicates that Leduc lot prices are nonetheless among the lowest priced in the region, only those in Fort Saskatchewan and Stony Plain being lower. The Leduc lots are from $500 to $800 less than Mill Woods and from $2,500 to $2,800 less than the next lowest priced city lots. However, it can also be seen that market price increase in 1971 exceeded that in the city.

Development policies:
1. *Suburban servicing.* The developer is responsible for all services within a subdivision.
2. *Offsite charges and acreage assessment.* The town does not charge either at this time. One of the developers has volunteered $50 per lot for recreation facilities within his subdivision and $35 per stall within the trailer park. Because of the inadequacies of the present development agreements, it is anticipated that future development agreements will require offsite payments.

To date, the rate of growth has not created severe financial problems; however, the proposed offsite charges suggest that the town anticipates a new order of costs in future developments, particularly to meet recreation needs.

To prevent future municipal financial problems, Leduc has opted for "balanced development," i.e., industrial as well as residential growth. The town is now in the process of establishing and promoting an industrial park. Industrial development will be dependent upon the comparative advantage of Leduc, with respect to the region in general, and similar centres in particular. (Table 28 indicates that 9.1 percent of the value of industrial and building permits issued in the six selected centres from 1965 to 1970 were issued in Leduc but no permit for a very large amount was issued in this period.) Leduc has been obliged to adopt its "balance development" policy if it is to continue to accept residential development and not to adopt significantly different development policies. The town is speculating that it will succeed and is proceeding to invest in the industrial park.

St. Albert

St. Albert experienced a population increase of 34.1 percent between 1965 to 1971, and as is evident in Table 27, 78 percent of this increase was in the period 1968 to 1971. St. Albert is a classic example of a residential dormitory in that there is almost no local employment — approximately 95 percent of the working population are employed elsewhere. It is also the site of the proposed Athabasca University, which is being held in abeyance at present pending more certain knowledge of University enrolment trends in the province at large.

Table 27 indicates that lot prices in St. Albert are the highest priced of all the selected centres. Lots are $500 to $1,400 less than any in the city with the exception of Mill Woods, and have experienced among the smallest price increases in the region.

Development policies:
1. *Subdivision servicing.* The developer is responsible for installing all services within a subdivision to town standards. The services are guaranteed by performance bonding for one year after being turned over to the town. The developer is responsible for oversizing of services within the subdivision to provide for future subdivisions beyond. The development agreement establishes how he is to be reimbursed.
2. *Offsite charges.* A $500 per unit offsite cost is charged to cover the costs of major municipal services, such as water and sewage services.
3. *Assessment.* Each single family house that is built must be assessed at a minimum of $6,000 to cover the costs of various municipal services such as hospital, eduction, administration and recreation services.

The development policies employed by St. Albert have been arrived at through a history of experience as a residential dormitory centre. In the late 1950s and early 1960s, St. Albert experienced a rapid population growth.

Year	*Population*	*Population Change*
1951	1129	
1956	1320	201
1961	4059	2739
1966	9426	5367
1971	12637	3211

In order that the necessary services might be provided, the town was placed under New Town status on January 1, 1957. Upon creating a New Town, a board of administrators is appointed by the provincial government to manage local affairs and is responsible to the Provincial Planning Board (at that time the Provincial Planning Advisory Board) for planning affairs and the Local Authorities Board (at that time the Board of Public Utilities Commissioners) on matters of municipal finance. New town status allows the issuing of debentures and the expenditure of monies without reference to existing assessment, tax levy, or population. Public funds primarily cover capital expenditures — sewer, water, streets, etc. When a new town is considered to be financially solvent, it is reclassified and a local elected council takes over. Before a new town may be converted to another status, all special loans and advances must be repaid to the province but are usually converted to provincial debentures. St. Albert has been the only application of the Act to date for a satellite community of a metropolitan centre. St Albert was converted to normal town status on July 3, 1962, at which time the total loans of $1,000,000 were converted to debentures. The council, faced with this debt, found itself in serious financial trouble. Its administration was placed again imder the control of the Local Authorities Board (LAB) at a loss of considerable local autonomy, as viewed by the community, in that the LAB made the final budget decisions. In 1969 the town was released from LAB control.

In approximately 1967 new budgetary and management practices were adopted to stabilize the municipal mill rate. Local improvement servicing was made a responsibility of the developer, thereby relieving the town of any expenditures on this account. To preserve the existing character of the town, policies were adopted by which future development was to comply with existing densities and distributions of housing types. To generate the necessary property tax to pay for the services required by the average sized family of 4.6 persons the town established a minimum permissable assessment for new single family housing at $6,000. The offsite charges were set by determining the major infrastructure costs related to anticipated populations and densities. These were originally established at $198 per new single family house, but this was subsequently increased to $500 per unit, effective January 1, 1972. Sewer and water systems were usually expanded to accommodate population units of about 10,000, but since the unit charge was based on the assumption that the funds collected would pay off the debt immediately following the facility's construction, the town was obliged to promote rapid development. Though lot prices were the highest of any satellite centre, its proximity to the city, its lot price advantage over city lots and the standard of its housing and amenities have in recent years enabled it to achieve the expansion required under its mode of development financing.

Sherwood Park

Sherwood Park has experienced the second fastest population growth rate during 1967 to 1971 of all surrounding communities under consideration, as well as the largest absolute growth of any centre. Some 52.6 percent of the total growth in these communities occurred in Sherwood Park. Between 1965 and 1968 the population increased by 1,600, but from 1968 to 1971 the increase was 9,500 or 85.6 percent of the growth for the total period. Sherwood Park, like St. Albert, is close to Edmonton city's boundary. Table 27 reveals that land prices averaged $1,500 per lot less than the lowest priced city lot, exclusive of Mill Woods. At a market price of $109 per front foot, land is $28 per front foot cheaper than any city land, again excluding Mill Woods. Some 32.3 percent of the available lots in the subdivisions studied in the Edmonton region were in Sherwood Park, but as indicated in Table 27, Sherwood Park experienced some of the highest price increases in 1971 over 1970 — some 27.6 percent in Maplewood.

Development policies:
1. *Subdivision servicing.* Most of Sherwood Park has been developed by only one developer. The county has required that the developer be responsible for financing and installing all services within the subdivision. As there has been only one developer, he has also been responsible for trunk services.
2. *Offsite charges.* In new subdivisions, the offsite charge is $100 per lot to upgrade services. If a new sewage outfall is required, the county will assess a charge per lot to help cover the offsite costs.

The developer dedicates the land necessary for public activities such as parks, schools etc., but as explained by a representative of the county, the original development agreement was very ambiguous on the question of who was responsible for the development of recreation areas.

None of the costs of offsite arterial roads were included in the original development agreement. These costs have been borne entirely by the county.
3. *Water.* The City of Edmonton supplies water and sewage treatment, but the lines from the city boundary to the hamlet are the responsibility of the hamlet. A representative of the county suggested that these services are not examples of the city demonstrating its responsibility for metropolitan growth, but rather that both services are profitable to the city.

Sherwood Park has a larger population than any town in the province and greater than five of ten cities, but it remains unincorporated. By remaining unincorporated, it has access to the tax revenues generated by the industry in the County of Strathcona, of which the equalized assessment is exceeded only by Calgary, Edmonton, and Lethbridge. However, the degree to which Strathcona industry has subsidized Sherwood Park was not researched.

Spruce Grove

Spruce Grove, a village of 667 persons in 1967, and a town of 3,012 persons in 1971, has experienced the fastest growth of all centres in the region — 419.3 percent from 1965 to 1971, but has only accounted for 11.5 percent of the population growth of the six centres combined. Land prices are comparable to Leduc and are $500 less than those in Mill Woods and $2,500 less than the next lowest priced city lots.[34]

Much of the recent growth is directly attributable to "overspill" from Edmonton. An Edmonton developer has purchased or has option on six quarter sections. One quarter section has been developed as a residential subdivision and a second one is now being developed. The developer's decision to invest in Spruce Grove was influenced by the fact that Edmonton did not have sufficient serviced land for middle and lower priced single-family homes. A previous developer had attempted to start a high priced 'large lot' residential development, but because of an insufficient market ran into financial difficulties. The present company speculated that because of Edmonton's situation, Spruce Grove "would go" as a more standard subdivision.

Development policies:
1. *Subdivision servicing.* The developer finances and installs all services in the new subdivision, carries the legal fees, and finances oversize requirements.
2. *Acreage assessment.* A $600 per acre assessment is levied against the land as it is developed to cover the costs of sanitary sewer, sewage outfall, and the sewage lagoon.
3. *Offsite costs.* Under the present development agreement the developer is not responsible for any offsite costs (i.e., for the costs of municipal services and recreation costs associated with development) other than the $600 acreage assessment. The town must rely upon other revenue sources to cover these costs.

In the present development agreement, only park reserves are exempt from acreage assessment and local improvement assessment. Schools, for example, being land intensive land uses, are faced with high local assessments. A representative of the town has suggested that future development agreements may include offsite charges for recreation facilities, trunk services, and will perhaps remove local improvement assessments against schools.
4. *Water.* A joint board was established by the towns of Stony Plain and Spruce Grove and the County of Parkland to construct a water line from the city boundary. The line is being built and paid for by the Department of Public Works as agents for the board. Debentures are being raised by the board. Twenty percent will be deferred until the board is in a position to repay; this was explained by a representative of one of the towns as a concession granted to the board as "fair and equal" treatment in view of the province's special repayment arrangement on the line to Fort Saskatchewan.

Spruce Grove, a community with little experience of development, has attempted to cope independently with very rapid residential growth stimulated by changes elsewhere in the region. To facilitate development, and to meet new Department of Health regulations, the town found it necessary to undertake a new sewage lagoon. In anticipation of future growth of the lagoon, sized to service 15,000 persons, the town became involved in a $425,000 debt, which, combined with other expenditures since the beginning of 1971, has raised the town's outstanding borrowings from $97,715 as of November 31, 1970, to $605,755.[35] The $600 acreage assessment, mentioned above, was adopted to recover the costs connected with the sewage system. In order to reduce the debt consequent upon the

Department of Health's requirement, the town must encourage growth. But development involves the town in providing not only new services but higher quality services. Since the present development agreement does not provide for the costs of other municipal services, the town must rely on other revenue sources.

As pointed out by a representative of Spruce Grove, the town's ability to meet its financial obligations through the property tax is limited to the point where taxes would deter potential residents. Likewise, the town is limited in the offsite charges it can demand from the developer as the developer in turn would pass these on through the land price. This in turn would dissipate the comparative advantage of Spruce Grove with respect to other satellite centres, particularly as it is among the more distant centres. As mentioned above, Spruce Grove must encourage growth because of the existing debts; but the town has no control over the rate of growth which lies at the discretion of the developer and his ability to attract buyers.

In a brief to the Department of Municipal Affairs, the financial implications of recent and anticipated growth were articulated.

> The . . . residential development over a two-year period has produced a community that is falling behind in its ability to supply services needed to maintain orderly expansion. The enormous expansion has also created a town with recreation facilities, designed for a population of 3,200 in 1972. In conjunction with other needs, the expansion has created the need for additional Institutional Buildings and public works equipment required to maintain and service the increased population and attendant facilities . . . The rapid growth of the community has created a higher than normal requirement for financing.[36]

The brief set out a development program for six major areas. It will involve substantial borrowing over the next five years to provide the facilities and services for the anticipated population:

> 1. To upgrade and relocate certain portions of the Town's Storm Drainage and Sanitary Sewage disposal system . . .
> 2. In order to improve the quantity of water required by the increased population, the Town of Spruce Grove became a member of the Parkland Water Board . . . To finance their share of the pipe line the Town of Spruce Grove will have to borrow an estimated $405,000.00 during 1972. In addition, and in support of an adequate supply during summer months and fire fighting requirements, the Town will also have to borrow an estimated $200,000.00 for the construction of a water reservoir and pump house due to the limited amount of water available from the

proposed pipe line during peak demand periods. The Town's water rates will be established at a level such that Town's storage and pumping facilities will be self liquidating. The wholesale rates established by the Parkland Water Board are to be sufficient to retire the $405,000.00 borrowed for construction of the water supply pipe line. However, the pipeline project will ultimately be self liquidating.

3. To encourage development of commercial and industrial areas Council feels that it would be highly desirable to provide Trunk Water Mains, Sanitary and Storm Sewer Trunks to these areas and hereby promote commercial and industrial growth to assist in maintaining a balanced basis of assessment.

4. With the standard of services being provided in new residential areas, Council proposes to improve the standard of services in the original Village Site . . . Phasing of these improvements will depend to some extent on the demand of the rate payers for such local improvements . . .

5. There is an additional need to improve the operation of the Town to a standard appropriate with the size of the Community.

(a) With an aim to improve the policing of a growing Community, the Town Council has contracted the services of the R.C.M.P. The said contract requires that the Town provide an adequate Police Station. A By-law was passed to provide financing for an estimated cost of $107,000.00 for the construction, engineering services and furnishings. $40,000.00 will be provided by a grant through the Provincial Government's Attorney General's Department, leaving an estimated $67,000.00 to be borrowed.

(b) The Fire Department facilities are well below standards required for a Community of approximately 3,200 people, and would involve the construction of a new Fire Hall, additional fire fighting equipment and employment of a permanent Fire Chief . . . There would also be a need to make provisions for Emergency Measures Organization and attendant training facilities, Town Administration Building, Town Library, Public Works Garage, etc.

6. The need for recreational facilities grows greater with each new home constructed in the Town of Spruce Grove. The Council of the Town of Spruce Grove anticipates the need to construct a Community Arena, Swimming Pool, an Athletic grounds providing a running track, football field, baseball fields and such outdoor sport areas as required to service the Community.[37]

The total estimated borrowings[38] were projected at:

Estimated local improvements	$ 777,040.00
Estimated general benefits	3,160,800.00
Total estimated costs	3,937,840.00
Financing	
required from Alberta Municipal Financing Corporation	3,548,850.00
other sources	389,000.00

> Town Council is very conscious of the fact that the proposed estimated borrowing requirements are far in excess of the amounts normally available to municipalities from the Alberta Municipal Financing Corporation . . . Town Council therefore respectfully requests the Department of Municipal Affairs' assistance in obtaining the necessary approvals for the additional financing required to expedite the proposed projects and prepare the Town for orderly and future development.[39]

The town is seeking special attention from the provincial government. Its rapid residential growth to date has primed a more diverse array of needs. It is seeking, in effect, some of the borrowing freedom normally associated with new town status, but does not want this formal status because of the loss to its autonomy and because of its knowledge of the problems which new town status created for St. Albert. Although local authorities such as Spruce Grove place emphasis upon local autonomy, the facts of its situation suggest that local autonomy is largely a myth. First, decisions made by the City of Edmonton, developers, and the Department of Health have created the financial situation the town faces. Secondly, to cope with these financial demands, the town must rely on the assistance of senior levels of government. The local autonomy being protected cannot be said, therefore, to imply self-determination beyond that of its right to negotiate development contracts with private developers. There is also the matter of status. "Local autonomy" continues to mean, however, local affairs within the constraints imposed by outside decisions.

In addition to seeking special provincial assistance, the town intends to promote industrial development and is hoping to service itself accordingly. The Edmonton Regional Planning Commission also encouraged the town to attempt to complement residential development with industrial development:

> The Edmonton Regional Planning Commission encourages and maintains a policy of concentrated decentralization of development into regional communities wherever feasible. Spruce Grove must be a contemporary town, planned, built and operated to serve present day needs and conditions . . .

2. Spruce Grove should be planned as a self-contained, self-reliant community. Industries, schools, churches and recreational and cultural facilities must be part of this community. Initially, however, the community will be heavily dependent on Edmonton for specialized services and employment.
3. In order for Spruce Grove to perform at a minimum level as an urban-industrial centre, sufficient jobs must be provided in the Village for a certain proportion of the projected 10,000 population. The goal for employment opportunity should be for a minimum one third of the labour force residing in Spruce Grove to work there. While the target of jobs is beyond the present employment trends, there nevertheless is a need to achieve this goal. The underlying intent would be to maintain Spruce Grove as a viable metropolitan centre by greatly strengthening the opportunity for employment.[40]

The ERPC submission, which encouraged industrial development and addressed itself to questions of physical design (relationship of roadways to land uses, neighbourhood units and their relationship to roadways, the role of the existing town centre, the location of recreation facilities . . .) did not discuss the financial implications of residential growth, but it did mention the need to undertake a capital improvement program. Although ERPC is in a position to be aware of the consequences of rapid residential growth and to have knowledge of the various development agreements of other centres in the Edmonton region, ERPC did not participate in the development agreement negotiations or advise the town. In fact, a representative of the town was insistent that the development agreement was not a planning matter and, therefore, not of concern to ERPC. In his definition of planning, ERPC was only to be involved in questions relating to the physical layout — issues to which the above mentioned ERPC submission limited itself.

The developer has recognized the need for a sound municipal economy if the residental market is to be maintained. He has options on industrial property and is promoting its development. As explained by a representative of the firm, he is confronted with the problem of determining the market for industry in this location — type of industry, space and service requirements. Because of the location of the industrial land with respect to the town's utilities, any industrial development faces enormous "front end" costs. Services must be brought from the town across Highway 16 and the CNR tracks. The costs have been estimated to be as high as $1,000,000, which may create land prices non-competitive with industrial land elsewhere in the region. Some thought has been given to providing reduced service standards (gravel roads, open ditch storm sewers . . .) to keep the service costs down. As can be seen from Table 28, Spruce Grove's record of attracting industrial and commercial investment is the lowest of all the centres studied. However, the population growth has stimulated interest in commercial development within the town, but as yet no indication of significant industrial development.

Spruce Grove is an example of the "concentrated decentralization" which ERPC encourages, but it is evident that ERPC has no means of ensuring the financial viability of the community. The situation of Spruce Grove is attributable to the unprepared state of local facilities to meet the rate and nature of growth with which it has been involved. Other than supplying water, the City of Edmonton has assumed no responsibility for the problems which growth has created. The developer, in one sense directly responsible for the dilemma facing the town, is promoting industrial development to ensure that the residential market is not jeopardized by municipal financial problems.[41] Apart from the facilities of new town status, the town council has little resource to senior government special facilities. The case of Spruce Grove is clearly one where the benefits of provincial direction of planning and the creation of facilities to meet its consequences, would relieve embarrassment in many quarters and ensure the success of regional, planned development.

Stony Plain

Stony Plain has experienced the smallest population growth of any of the centres during the period 1965 to 1971, experiencing a population growth of 292 persons, only 1.4 percent of the growth of the six centres. Stony Plain has not become a residential satellite of the order of the others. Table 27 indicates that Stony Plain has the lowest land prices in the region, but the prices are not comparable because the services provided are not of the same standard as those of other centres.

Development policies:

The development of the subdivision, Meridian Heights, for which only limited data are available, was an Alberta Housing Corporation (AHC) land assembly project. AHC undertook the thirty-acre land assembly project at the request of the town and functioned in the capacity of developer. AHC acquired the land, installed the subdivision services, and undertook to resell the land.[42] When the project was undertaken it was expected that it would provide land for five years. At the current rate of development, however, it will be much less. Much of the land has been sold although few building permits have been issued. Most of the lots were purchased by Edmonton builders and it is anticipated that most of the residents will be from outside the local community.

Stony Plain is at present a major agricultural service centre. The project just described was in part undertaken to accommodate the estimated natural growth of the town. However, as indicated by a representative of the town and with reference to the interest of Edmonton builders, the potential residents of the project will be predominantly from elsewhere. Stony Plain may begin to experience more pressures from outside to become a dormitory satellite. The town, if it experiences only residential growth, appears to be heading for the same servicing problems as Spruce Grove, but the town has no land feasible for industrial development.

The town used the services of AHC to ensure that land prices were controlled, and to relate the phasing of development to demand. To control the rate of development, the town has an agreement with AHC covering the rate at which lots will be sold. Stony Plain is now negotiating with AHC to undertake a second stage, but in this case Stony Plain is asking AHC to purchase land owned by the town and then to develop it. The town does not want to develop its own land and thereby become involved in the servicing costs. It employs AHC to control prices and the rate of development which it claims would not be possible were the land developed by private developers.

To facilitate the development and to meet Department of Health regulations, a new sewage lagoon has been constructed. To recover the costs of the lagoon, furture development will be assessed $200 per dwelling unit.

Collective Attempts to Cope

Of the six communities discussed above, the City of Edmonton supplies water to all but Spruce Grove and Stony Plain, to which service is expected in July, 1972.[43] A representative of the City of Edmonton explained that water is not viewed by the city as a means of controlling or directing metropolitan development. As explained to us, the City Council and the Commission Board have not refused service to the region and city processing is based on projections of demand for the metropolitan region, i.e., the city system is premised on the assumption that the city will be supplying the entire region, and to date no regional municipality has developed its own system after local well or water systems were proven inadequate.

The supply of water, as is also the consequences of water pollution, are topics of envy and concern among the local authorities. The benefits Edmonton receives from its utilities are well known in the region. The reconstruction of the Parkland-Stony Plain-Spruce Grove water line confirms the statement that the city can sell water cheaper than the user could process it. The local authorities investigated a number of alternatives and concluded that the city supply was the most economical. However, what effect the province's decision to defer repayment of 20 percent of the costs had on this matter was not determined.

As explained by a representative of the city, pricing is established to achieve equity for users both within and outside the city. The regional users have the right to appeal to the Public Utilities Board if rates are not considered to be equitable, but to date this has not been done. The water is supplied at the city's boundary to consumer-owned lines. Agreements have projections for five years with revised projections prepared in three years for the subsequent five years. The onus is on the peripheral community to provide storage, which is supplied in off-peak hours, to ensure local supply in peak hours and for fire fighting.

As early as 1960 the consequences of the dependency of regional centres on city services was raised by the then Edmonton District Planning Commission.[44] It remarked:

> contracts allow either party to terminate the agreement, the question is raised as to the position of the buyer if for some reason of necessity the City had to cease supply. Large investments have been made by these municipalities on the basis of this supply and the retirement of debentures is dependent upon the continuing supply of water. Despite the terms of the agreements, however, it is questionable whether the termination clause of the agreements would be exercised by the City Council because of those incurred costs.[45]

In an interview, the representative of the city stressed that once the city begins to provide service to a regional user, the city tends to have the same commitment as it does to clients within the city. He cited the St. Albert situation as evidence of the city's commitment — the city has continued to supply the town, although the agreement expired in 1967. The uncertainty as to the future of the Athabasca University was mentioned as contributing to the delay in reaching a new agreement.

In the past the city has been willing to supply the surrounding communities, but even though ERPC undertook the preliminary study on district water supply twelve years ago with a view to the development of regional policy, no policy has yet been formulated. Therefore, some of the questions raised at that time remain unanswered and are of importance today.

> It is probably true that the sale of water to outside users, at City rates plus a 35 percent surcharge, is a profitable arrangement, but questions may arise as to the relative claims on supply, and distribution of costs when the demand reaches plant capacity, and substantial investment is required for expansion.[46]

The city is now considering a west-end water treatment plant which the Water and Sanitation Department has stated must be completed by 1975. The department has suggested that 1974 could be "touch and go" should it be a dry year. Although it will take three years to complete the project, the council's Economic Affairs Committee has recommended a delay of one year because of uncertainties of location and land acquisition. The commission board recommended that a start be made this year because of the anticipated shortage. The city is clearly committed to this large capital investment in order to avoid taking the alternative of curtailing supplies to the region, but at the same time local financial problems may well affect the regional service as a whole.

In the absence of a regional water distribution policy, the question of pipe-line financing, identified also in the EDPC study, remains a critical issue. The pipe-lines discussed in that study were the result of unique circumstances. In the St. Albert line there was special financing under the New Towns Act, and in the Leduc line there were two intervening municipalities and the new international airport, both of which helped to finance the line. Provincial assistance was necessary for both the Fort Saskatchewan-Redwater line and the Parkland-Stony Plain-Spruce Grove line. In each case, the municipalities in question have negotiated special agreements with the province. The Municipal Finance Corporation has a particularly sensitive ear to water needs. The province has responded to the unique set of problems and granted certain concessions, but not within the context of regional development strategy.

In view of the concessions granted concerning the Fort Saskatchewan-Redwater line, by which the province has deferred repayment of a portion of the costs in anticipation of future industrial growth, the city is providing water which may well result in industrial development outside its boundaries. For years it has been trying to annex the existing industrial area to the east, a point raised in the ERPC study:

> An industry locating just beyond city boundaries for slightly lower land costs may be made possible because the city extends water supply, but this may have the dual effect of depriving the city of an added assessment while raising municipal expenditures to accommodate those of its workers who live in the city. Although this has not arisen as a problem it may conceivably affect the long range supplier of water in the area.[47]

A city representative acknowledged the problem but explained that to date it had not deterred the city from supplying the region.[48]

Regional water distribution illustrates the nature of provincial government intervention and assistance in regional development. The province has responded to particular problems or situations but the *ad hoc* interventions have not been within the context of a co-ordinated regional development strategy. On the other hand, the provincial actions, undertaken to resolve a unique situation or to facilitate a development, may be construed as examples of co-ordination at that level. For example, the province, through its agent, the Alberta Housing Corporation, participated directly in the development process in Stony Plain. Upgrading of regional highways, which increases the potential commuting distance, was suggested by representatives of many surrounding communities as leading to their growth as residential satellite communities. Private developers take advantage of the situation created. The provincial involvement is in part explainable in terms of the province's perception of its responsibility in an environment of municipal competition but with vicarious consequences for any one municipality within the regional context of growth. The province has not given direction, but facilitates development by responding to particular local demands — the Spruce Grove request for special attention is an example of the municipalities' perception of the province's role in this capacity.

The process of regional planning and development as set out in the objectives and principles quoted from the City's General Plan at the beginning of this chapter is dependent upon co-ordination and integration of development decisions, and the recognition of the interdependence of the municipalities within the region. However, the above description of the Edmonton region shows development in both its municipal detail and region servicing to be *ad hoc* and unco-ordinated. Although ERPC has prepared a preliminary regional plan for part of its jurisdiction, and has a policy with respect to decentralization, there exists no co-ordinated program for regional development. The policy of decentralization is without reference to any explicit or desired purpose, size, or location of these communities. There are no regional policies with respect to transportation, utilities, the role of public land ownership, economic development, pollution, and recreation. *Ad hoc* decisions to provide a particular service to meet a particular problem — for example, the freeway to the city from Sherwood Park (required to relieve the traffic congestion caused by commuters), or the upgrading of Highway 15 — may in turn exert pressure on the city's internal transportation system. This may influence the city's priorities both in terms of projects and transportation modes.

A senior planner with the city, when questioned on how future city expansion was co-ordinated with the region, claimed that the city was forced to plan in a "vacuum." The Preliminary Regional Plan was viewed as a "holding" action which prevented development until sufficient pressures were exerted to implement that form of development upon which consensus had been reached. The plan provided no effective guide for city growth. The search for consensus is a political process that is eased when situations become urgent and pressing. The decision reached by consensus may or may not conform with the purposes of the Preliminary General Plan. The contribution of the plan, as will be clearer in the following section on recent city annexations of land, has been largely to prevent certain types of low-density development, and thereby to forestall "leap-frogging." It has also facilitated annexations for suburban development contiguous to existing city development. The present situation tends to make the Preliminary General Plan continuously preliminary, rather than an outline of the future within which all developmental decisions, regional, city, and those particular to any municipality, would be co-ordinated.

Earlier it was suggested that parallels could be drawn

between development in the surrounding communities and development in the "fringe communities" described by the McNally Royal Commission in 1956. Some distinctions should be remembered. The fringe communities, as described by McNally, were largely developed by individuals and lending institutions who constructed housing often below standards permissible in the city. Similarly, municipal services were described as not being equivalent to those provided by the city. Development in today's surrounding communities is usually undertaken by large developers. This regional development has been stimulated by private developers exploiting a particular situation, who have been able to effect co-ordination of public and private resources to facilitate their particular development. The housing and municipal services within the subdivision are usually comparable to those in the city. The municipality has generally been required to provide the necessary major utilities, roadways, and recreation facilities. As described above, each community's ability or solution to meet the demand for these services has been dependent upon past experience and the local situation. Their attempts to cope show a wide variety of techniques and procedures.

Fort Saskatchewan, Spruce Grove, Leduc, and Stony Plain, though their internal situation — particularly their financial situation — varies markedly, have adopted a policy of "balanced" growth. They have attempted to compensate for the costs of residential development by facilitating industrial and commercial development. This policy places the municipality in direct competition with the city and other municipalities, as well as raising its debt for an increased variety and volume of services. The outcome of the policy is dependent largely on the locational decisions of private investors and industrialists, whose decision, in turn, is influenced by the desirability of the location or the costs of services and land. Should the municipalities be unsuccessful in their attempt, they remain with debt burdens and used land and facilities. Those just in the process of implementing their decision tend to turn to the provincial government for initial financing support which, in turn, tends to seek special criteria for its assistance in order to avoid a sequence of embarrassments resulting from the precedent such assistance may offer to other municipalities contemplating similar policies or in a particular unique difficulty.

St. Albert and Sherwood Park, both near the city, have policies encouraging a "dormitory" growth rather than a more balanced variety. Sherwood Park, by remaining an unincorporated hamlet, has retained access to industrial tax revenues collected by the county. Though it suffers from limited representation in local government, the arrangement obviates the financial problem inherent in dormitory situations generally — a problem of long standing, as the McNally Report indicated. St. Albert, on the other hand, has attempted to compensate for its lack of industry by requiring residential development to pay its way by establishing high assessments and/or mill rates, special charges for the privilege of a noise-free and pollution-free environment, low social service costs, and similar benefits. Its policy has been selective — a minimum assessment tends to set house prices that exclude low-income families, and may exclude young people anxious to stay near their parents but unable to qualify for a mortgage. Current tax policies effectively prohibit mobile homes in St. Albert. The policy has implications for other centres which become obliged to support a disproportionate share of low-income housing. If Athabasca University is finally established, it may have diverse consequences for St. Albert as the establishment of educational institutions does not have the same consequence for industrial tax revenue as other types of industry, but imposes peculiar demands on local authorities in terms of services to people. That St. Albert may have found a solution to its long term financial problems (which resulted in its New Town status and later administration by the LAB until 1969) is apparent from the increase in single and multiple family housing permits issued in 1969 and 1970 (Table 26), the attitude of CMHC and the lending institutions toward its development, and the lower cost of its land relative to that of Edmonton (Table 27).

Common to all of the satellite communities is the need to promote growth. This need is caused by the financing arrangements made to recover the cost of those services in turn needed to make the initial and subsequent changes. Each development generates a demand for additional services which local policy or situation may be ill-equipped to handle. Regional organizations, such as ERPC, recommend to municipalities that they undertake capital programming to determine the financial implications of a proposed development. But, as an ERPC representative remarked, small towns lack the technical ability to prepare these programs or to relate realistically the sequence of costs implied in any given development policy. Also, because such towns prefer to contract with a private developer — to save themselves raising the initial capital with which to develop land — they tend to lose control of the rate of growth and thereby to lose control over the program of public capital requirements. Looked at from the converse perspective, so long as the province can continue to come up with *ad hoc* or special provisions — such as a 20 percent deferment or loan repayment or provide special assistance to Spruce Grove — there is no real need for long range, effective programming at the local level. Each local crisis is met by the largess of the senior government.

Once the necessity to grow is appreciated, the local council in turn becomes involved in a competitive struggle with its peers. It tends to view jealously the manipulative advantages enjoyed by wealthier and better capitalized communities. The frequency with which low interest loans are provided by senior government — of the type afforded by the federal, 1963, Municipal Development Loan Fund, or the sewage legislation that preceeded it — is too low to allow many municipalities to take advantage of them at critical times in the growth process. The new towns, between 1963 and 1968, did particularly well under provincial administration from the

Municipal Development Loan Fund. In this sense the growing municipalities of 1962-68 were less subject to the rigour of "fair and equal" treatment for all than those starting the growth process in 1968. Recently the cities, but especially the metropolitan centres, by acting politically vis-a-vis the senior levels of government have been seeking constitutional entrenchment of a special and privileged position. The concept of local autonomy, when viewed within the competitive relation of municipal peers and the "fair and equal" treatment policy of the provincial administration, boils down to little more than the right to contract with privately organized capital. As the metropolitan centres have the edge over almost all peripheral centres — with the exception of petro-chemical plants in Strathcona (Sherwood Park) and similar enterprise in Fort Saskatchewan — in their contracts with and encouragement of private investment, the satellite communities remain relatively handicapped also in this expression of their autonomy.

The present independence of municipal decisions on development will probably continue to prevail. Two large subdivisions in the City of Edmonton, undertaken without reference to regional consequences, may have direct impact upon surrounding communities — Mill Woods and the development proposed by British American Construction Materials Ltd. (BACM).[49] Both are intended to put residential land on the market at prices competitive with the regional communities. The surrounding communities could continue to undertake debenture debts to install major services in anticipation of a continuation of the growth rates of the recent past. But the new city subdivisions will escalate the competitive process and could threaten the financial viability of marginal growth centres. On the other hand, newly adopted city policies of requiring developers to finance storm trunks and the "front end" costs of water and sanitary trunks may put even greater pressure on the regional centres. BACM and Mill Woods may have a more pronounced effect on the multiple family housing market than on the type of dwelling common in the surrounding communities, but the home buyer's preference in the market place is a slippery phenomenon and the policies of lending institutions are of considerable effect. Unless there is an abrupt change from the past, the situation of local authorities and their communities will continue to be dependent upon the private developer's perception of the development potential of the community vis-a-vis other opportunities within the region, be those in BACM, Mill Woods, or other competitive centres.

The surrounding communities have been meeting to exchange information on current development policies and to investigate the opportunities for greater co-ordination. Representatives of the communities stress that any such effort must take into account the unique situations of the different communities. It might well be asked if co-ordination is possible in an environment in which all are competing for growth.

Edmonton City's Boundary Adjustments

The post war development boom was centred predominantly within the city's boundaries, but "fringe communities" developed and major petro-chemical industries chose sites to the east of the city in the Municipal District (now County) of Strathcona. Through tax delinquency and land acquisition, replotting schemes and land exchanges, Edmonton city had managed to establish, by the end of the war, a reasonably co-ordinated pattern of subdivision, zoning control, and the public ownership of school, park, roadway and other public sites. Associated with this policy was one of "programmed development" based on the neighbourhood unit principle and a sequence of service installations. But the pressures of rapid growth and the shortcomings of its planning organization soon led it into difficulties. By 1951 most of the available developed land had been sold and shortages were raising lot prices. New residential and industrial land had to be purchased.

The city retained its first professional planner and organized a Town Planning Department in 1949. Interim development control measures were instituted by the provincial government and the separation of lay and professional aspects of planning were instituted in statutory organizational form. A Technical Planning Board of powerful administrative members was appointed in 1950, and the Community Planning Association provided the public voice in the planning process. The Edmonton District Planning Commission, set up in 1950, prepared an Outline General Plan — adopted in principle in August, 1951, and in substance in April, 1953 — which was purely advisory to, and not binding on, the city or any municipality.[50]

The McNally Royal Commission Report of 1956, after discussing the concept of local authority autonomy with respect to the Planning Act, concluded that to cope with the problems of development within the metropolitan region:

> — membership on the district planning commission should be mandatory, and that the commission should prepare a district general plan;
> — upon the district general plan being adopted, each municipality should enact the necessary planning controls or amend existing control to give effect to the municipalities share of the plan;
> — during the preparation of the district plan, interim development control should be exercised at both the district and local levels; and
> — individuals, local authorities, and the district planning authority must be provided the opportunity to appeal and to amend district and local planning decisions.

The conclusions reflect the McNally Commission's basic assumption that the metropolitan region was in fact one economic, social, and physical unit. There is a considerable literature evaluating the effect of the organization and size of municipal government according to a variety of criteria (e.g. efficiency, participation, quantity and quality of municipal services, accessibility, responsiveness). Had the commission stressed criteria other than administrative efficiency and access to metropolitan revenue sources, the recommendations might have been very different.

To resolve the planning and financial problems, the commission concluded that the scope of decision-making should be expanded to encompass the metropolitan region, and provide the city with practical influence over many of the existing externalities as possible. Amalgamation of local authorities and the annexation of land by the city from adjacent local authorities, were obvious techniques to accomplish this policy. However, the old problem of local autonomy was implicit in it. Although the provincial government implemented many of the McNally Commission recommendations on planning, similar action was not taken on the recommended boundary changes for the Edmonton area. Our enquiries could identify no explicit statement of reasons, but it may be speculated that the provincial commitment to the concept of local autonomy played a significant part in the outcome.

Without an explicit provincial policy covering the mode of growth of the city, the city's dilemma of how to cope with the growth at the periphery remained unresolved. Edmonton faced polar policy options.

> 1. The City could delay pending proposed annexation applications and await a provincial decision.
> 2. The City could annex properties as the need was perceived or in response to outside pressures. The decision would be appraised or dependent upon the situation of the case (need for land for proposed types of development, availability of utilities, etc.) or pressures from developers or pressures from surrounding municipalities, i.e., the decision to support a particular annexation application would be dependent upon the merits of the application rather than an overall regional growth strategy.[51]

The apparent inconsistencies of subsequent city decisions may in part be attributed to the consequences of following both options.

The city moved to annex a number of land parcels between 1956 and 1960. Table 29 shows the date, extent, and the reason for some of them, as revealed by City Council minutes or by reports to the council. The accompanying map indicates the area of the annexations. (See Figure 2.)

Table 29 shows the tendency for annexation requests to originate from private land owners in the area seeking to be annexed. The city was careful to indicate its terms with respect to the provision of services to the new areas. The property owners seeking annexation

Table 29. Partial inventory of land annexations, Edmonton City, 1956-1960.

Name	*Date*	*Extent in acres*	*Requested by*	*Comments*
Goldbar	1956	640	property owners	Done because of "the recent decision of the Government postponing direct action on the McNally Report for one year."[1]
Sections 7 & 18 Township 52 Range 24	1959	640	property owners	Done "pending a decision of the Provincial Legislature on the McNally Report . . ."[2]
Davies Industrial Annexation	1958	440	property owners	For largely industrial uses. Council agreed to annexation ". . . upon the express understanding that the City will not be obligated to provide services, facilities, or amenities . . . until it can conveniently do so."[3]
Ottewell	1959	560	property owners	Action on annexation delayed until the completion of a trunk sewer through part of the area.
Southwest Annexation	1959	6950	In part by property owners	". . . a sequence of development had been determined, based on engineering and other costs, and 'having regard to considerations or orderliness, economy and convenience'."[4]

[1]Board Report #9, February 2, 1956.
[2]City Council Minutes, September 13, 1956.
[3]City Council Minutes, August 20, 1957.
[4]City Council Minutes, May 24, 1960.

were private developers who were capable of controlling peripheral development and thereby influencing land prices by determining the quantity and timing of lot development.[52] The provincial government's inaction on the McNally recommendations tended to put the city at a disadvantage with respect to private developers. It was obliged to accommodate unanticipated developments in many instances.

The conflict which ensued over the southwest annexation illustrates the process. The pressure from the developers in the annexed area, whose proposals were not in accord with the city's "program," was strongly opposed by city departments and the Technical Planning Board. The opposition was based on the grounds of the proposal's contradiction with the metropolitan part of the Preliminary District Plan and the "evolving" General Plan, both of which were intended to prevent the premature subdivision of land.[53] Though the council recognized the merit of the case put up

Figure 2

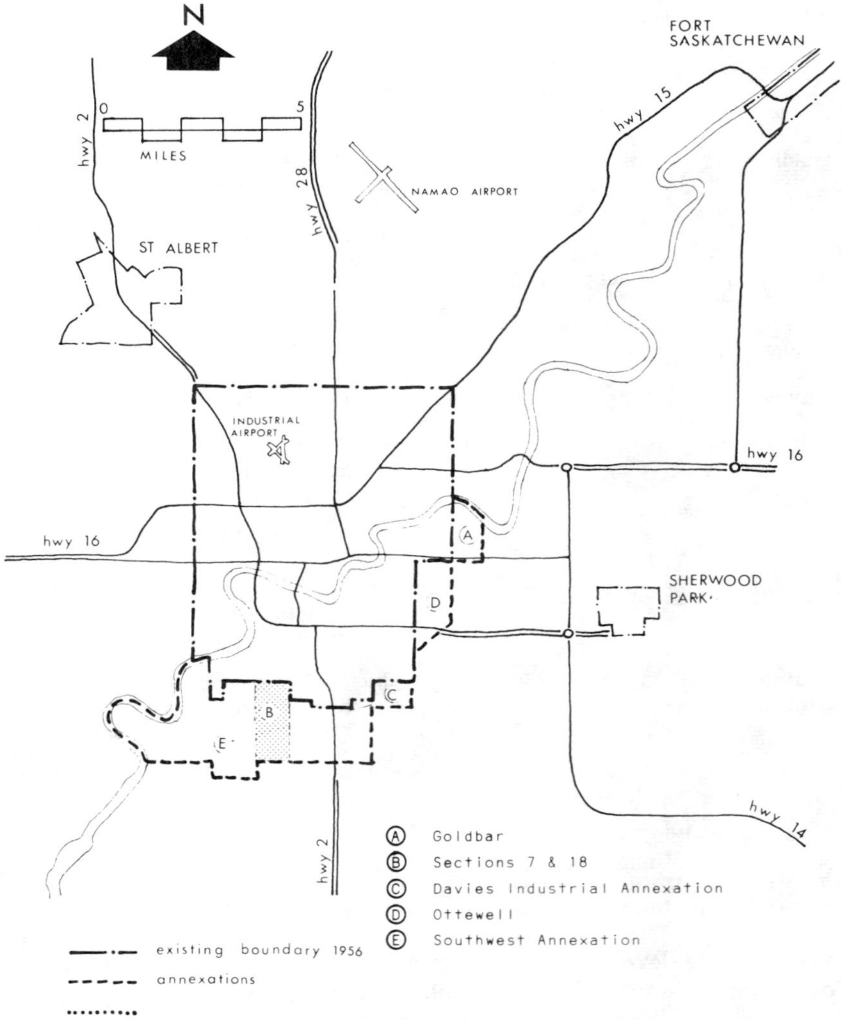

EDMONTON ANNEXATIONS, 1956:1960

by its own departments, the Technical Planning Board and the Planning Advisory Committee, it resolved on October 24, 1960:

> That we accede to the request of Westbrook Estates Ltd. provided it is without prejudice to our previous decisions of the pattern of orderly development and that Council requests the Edmonton District Planning Commission to rezone the property from 'High Density Agricultural' to 'General Urban.'[54]

Chan observed that "The Provincial Planning Advisory Board was shocked at the city's sudden alteration of decision." In a letter (October 27, 1960) to Commissioner Menzies, it remarked:

> The decision appears to indicate a reversal of what we have understood to be City policy with reference to the sequence of development in the lands recently annexed to the City . . . Our information to date has led us to believe that the development of the Westbrook land was rather a long way off in the City's schedule of development.[55]

The Edmonton District Planning Commission refused the city's request because it did not want to set a precedent. However, the Provincial Planning Advisory Board concurred with the city's request thereupon requiring the District Planning Commission to change the zoning.[56] The board, in spite of its concern that the council's decision contravened previously-agreed planning criteria, required the Edmonton District Planning Commission to comply with the council's decision. This would indicate that the board's decision was consistent with its position on Sherwood Park, in which it had hesitated to interfere with the freedom of a local authority.

The McNally recommendations were also used as a basis, although somewhat inconsistently, for supporting or opposing applications for annexation. In some cases, the fact that the parcels were within the area recommended by the commission for annexation was given as grounds, and, in other cases, although the parcel may have been within the recommended area, the city opposed the application on the basis that it represented piecemeal, *ad hoc* growth. The city was attempting to stay on top of its difficult situation. In response to the many pressures for annexation, the city established the Amalgamation Committee in 1957, to draw up a city policy or position with respect to city boundaries.

On June 26,1958, at a special meeting of council to hear the committee's report, council agreed to the committee's recommendation to annex

> the Towns of Beverly, Jasper Place and the Industrial Area of Strathcona with the City of Edmonton under one municipal authority along the lines recommended by the McNally Commission 'report'.[57]

Subsequently, on November 10, 1958, the council moved to annex all the area recommended by the McNally Commission.

However, in late 1959, the province intervened as the city proceeded with its annexation application to the Board of Public Utilities Commissioners:

> Following public statements made by the Minister of Municipal Affairs on matters affecting the question of

> annexation by Edmonton of the territory recommended for inclusion in the city's boundaries by the McNally Report, your Commissioners thought it advisable to interview Premier Manning and Mr. Hooke to ascertain the Government's intentions in respect to the City's applications to the Public Utility Board.
>
> After a full discussion, Premier Manning told your Commissioners that the whole question of amalgamation and the possible effect on it of government legislation which might be passed at the coming session of the Legislature would be discussed at a Cabinet meeting today (November 3, 1959) and the decision of the meeting conveyed to us immediately.
>
> Accordingly, this special meeting of City Council was called to receive this report.
>
> Premier Manning telephoned the Mayor this afternoon to say that after a full discussion, the Executive Council was of the opinion that it would be advisable for Edmonton to postpone its application to the Board of Public Utilities until after the 1960 session of the Legislature because of the possibility of legislation being passed which could affect the City's position.
>
> Premier Manning assured us that this postponement would not mean indefinite delay because it is the intention of the Government to finalize its decisions on the matters affecting amalgamation at the coming session.[58]

The City Council agreed to adjourn their application to the Board of Public Utilities Commissioners as suggested by the cabinet. The legislation to which the Premier referred was the proposed Industrial Tax Bill introduced in 1960.[59]

Although acknowledging that such issues were beyond its terms of reference, the McNally Commission had recommended that an inquiry be undertaken into industrial taxation in order to establish uniformity of assessment and the proportion of the assessment on which the mill rate was to be levied. Enabling legislation, called "The Primary Industries Assessment and Taxation Act," had been prepared in late 1957 but apparently had not been introduced to the Legislature. In the 1958 and 1959 annual conventions of the Alberta Association of Municipal Districts, resolutions were passed to the effect that the province should "take over" the full scope of industrial taxation. The legislation ultimately presented to the Legislature was largely developed by the Provincial Municipal Advisory Committee, established in December, 1959.

Two Bills were introduced in the 1960 Legislature:

> Bill 95 — A Bill to Provide for the Taxation of Certain Industries and the Distribution to Municipalities of the Proceeds thereof.
>
> Bill 129 — A Bill to Provide Authority for an Assessment of Certain Property Owned by Industries and Utilities.

Apparently the Bills were not conceived as means for directing development to desired locations, but purely as means of redistributing revenues. It was the intent of the legislation that taxes generated by certain industries would be collected by the province. The revenues would then be distributed by formula: (i) to the municipality in which the industry was located in order to compensate for the services provided, (ii) to those municipalities providing social services to the employees of industry, and (iii) to all municipalities in the province, as the resource being developed was a provincial resource which only "by accident" was located *or processed in* a particular municipality. The legislation was intended to provide for a more equitable distribution of school and hospital requisitions, but it had the potential to reduce the pressures for annexations of industrial development in rural areas but adjacent to urban centres, and also to reduce municipal competition to attract industry. However, the Bills, when introduced into the House, foundered on questions of distribution:

> In answer to requests for 'more time to study' the implications of Bills 95 and 126, it was decided (that the bills) should be withdrawn (parenthesis added).[60]

Alternative legislation, the School Foundation Program, developed in the interim between the 1960 and 1961 sessions, was adopted in the 1961 session. The School Foundation Program, which can be seen as a compromise for the Industrial Tax Bill, was intended to reduce the prevalent disparity of education revenues and expenditures resulting from the location of industry.[61]

That the School Foundation Program did not resolve the metropolitan area's predicament with respect to coping with its growth, as had been intimated by Premier Manning in November, 1959, is evidenced by subsequent actions taken by the city and surrounding municipalities.

Two decisions taken in 1960 reflect the recurring problem as the city continued its attempt to cope with individual annexation applications and at the same time be concerned with resolving the overall question of annexation. In May, 1960 it would appear that the city was considering reapplying for the McNally boundaries when the council agreed to the Amalgamation Committee recommendations:

> that the City Solicitor begin procedures to have the City's amalgamation application heard by the Board of Public Utility Commissioners. That your Committee be authorized to take the necessary steps to bring up to date the City's analysis of probable costs and other economic factors involved in amalgamation. (The Council also agreed) to begin negotiations with the Province and surrounding municipalities to arrange terms for equitable amalgamation (parenthesis added).[62]

Also, in November, 1960, the city was considering the annexation of a further 2,400 acres in Ottewell. The Commissioners' Reports 6 and 7 recommended no action be taken on these, but that if council decided to proceed, they should not proceed with any others until the picture had been clarified. Although the council did move to annex the area, it resolved:

> that no further annexation be considered until the amalgamation picture is cleared.[63]

But, in spite of the Premier's assurances when the city agreed to postpone its application for the incorporation of the McNally boundaries, the province had not effectively resolved the issues, nor had it committed itself to a policy with respect to the growth of Metropolitan Edmonton.

The Beverly Annexation, 1961

As early as May 27, 1957 the Town of Beverly requested that the City of Edmonton appoint a committee to study the matter of amalgamation. The council referred this request to a committee to be appointed by the Mayor to deal with overall amalgamation matters.[64] These negotiations were temporarily delayed by the province's request to postpone proceedings until the Legislature had resolved the questions of industrial assessment and taxation. The annexation was requested by the Town of Beverly and the owners of the land north-east, beyond Beverly, who had convinced both the city and the town that they should be included.

The pressure to reach a decision was illustrated in a council meeting at which:

> Mr. Baxter appeared in support of the letter from the Edmonton House Builders' Association, dated February 8, regarding amalgamation. He stated that in the last eighteen months the House Builders have experienced a marked increase in the land costs of the provision of single family dwellings. There is not sufficient land within the city limits to supply a normal one year's demand for housing for the citizens of Edmonton. They, therefore, ask that the boundaries be enlarged. During the last two years we have experienced construction in the areas outside the periphery of the City of Edmonton. If a sufficiency of building lots is not available within the city over the next few years, it will increase the purchase price per lot.[65]

The joint application by the city and the Town of Beverly was opposed by neither the County of Sturgeon (now a Municipal District) nor the Municipal District of Strathcona (now a County). The Public Utilities Board order made no reference as to how planning considerations influenced their decision. The order specified the conditions to prevail following annexation, with respect to taxation of specified classes of land, and did not abrogate the various utility agreements for the area involved.

In March, 1961, the council adopted the Amalgamation Committee's Report No. 1 namely:

> At the meeting of your committee held on March 10, Mayor Dr. Roper reported that an official delegation from the Council of Beverly had interviewed the Commissioners to ask us to proceed with the amalgamation. They stated they wished to become a part of the City of Edmonton without any conditions attached.
> The following was passed by the Committee, 'Whereas the Town of Beverly has made a request for unconditional amalgamation this committee reports to Council that we presently favor unconditional amalgamation of the whole area described by the McNally Report, subject to financial study and clarification of the recent Provincial legislation, and that the Committee submit a recommendation to Council at a later date on the basis of the financial study.[66]

However, in May the council moved:

> That the City support the application of Beverly for annexation to the City and that at the same time we apply for annexation of the sections East and North of the City as approved by the District Planning Commission.[67]

On December 30, 1961, 7,000 acres in the north-east, including the Town of Beverly, were annexed to the city.

The Jasper Place Annexation, 1964.

The annexation of Jasper Place in 1964 was the culmination of another series of debates. Some 10,800 acres were annexed including Jasper Place and properties to the west and south east of the city. (See Figure 4, p. 277). A petition from Jasper Place ratepayers was presented to Edmonton City Council as early as 1946. This was opposed by Edmonton's Taxpayers Protective Association on the grounds that the suggestion was a liability rather than an asset.[68] Almost ten years later, City Council was informed that:

> The Town of Jasper Place has notified us that the Town Council has appointed a fact-finding committee on all aspects of amalgamation with Edmonton and that this committee is prepared to meet with a similar committee from this Council. (The Council agreed to establish a committee to represent the City of Edmonton in these discussions with the Jasper Place committee.) (Parenthesis added.)[69]

Subsequent to the Premier's request in 1959 that the city postpone annexation considerations, the Jasper Place issue was not revived again until 1962, when the council agreed to the Amalgamation Committee's recommendation:

> Your Committee recommends that if the Town of Jasper Places applies for amalgamation with Edmonton this Council should take the position that such amalgamation should be dealt with only as a part of a comprehensive adjustment of boundaries to facilitate sound and effective development of the whole metropolitan area, and to make available a more equitable sharing of industrial tax revenues to assist in paying the costs of services to residential areas, and for those purposes your Committee recommends that if Jasper Place applies for amalgamation and application should be filed which would seek amalgamation with Jasper Place and a substantial adjoining area of the Municipal District of Stony Plain plus the section of the County of Strathcona containing the East Edmonton industrial area, and the Sherwood Park residential area using boundaries substantially as proposed by the McNally Commission . . .[70]

In addition, the city suggested that the province should pay the town's existing sewer and arterial street debts as well as certain costs of extending sewer and arterial streets in the enlarged city.

The concern as to the consequences of any future growth, even though the city had articulated the conditions under which it could accept annexation, was illustrated by a notice of motion presented by Alderman Prudham.

> In view of the uncertainty of the financial situations and as our Financial Commissioner has told us on various occasions that we are faced with an increasing mill rate for many years ahead, and also because the City is considering the rebuilding of the Civic Centre which will require large capital commitments; be it resolved that the City of Edmonton notify Jasper Place that although we look favorably on the proposed amalgamation as an end for which we should plan; nevertheless, because of the additional tax burden involved, we wish to suspend negotiations until such time as the financial requirements of the City are more clearly delineated.[71]

At the next meeting Alderman Prudham withdrew his motion and gave notice of motion that at the next meeting he would move:

> In view of the financial situation and as our Commissioner Tweddle has told us on numerous occasions that we are faced with new bridges and highway

programmes all of which will require large capital commitments; be it resolved that the City notify the Provincial Government that although we look favorably on the proposed amalgamation with Jasper Place, because of the additional tax burden involved, we do not wish to be bound to do so by Board order unless the Industrial Areas asked for in our application are also included.[72]

At the July 23, 1962 council meeting Prudham withdrew this motion. His motions, while both concerned with the consequences of annexation, had very different emphases. In the first motion directed to Jasper Place, he stressed the need for the resolution of internal problems before tackling external problems. In the replacement motion, he re-emphasized the council's conditions under which amalgamation was acceptable, and at the same time directed the motion to the province.

The application for annexation submitted in August, 1962, stressed the financial plight of the town and also suggested that amalgamation was necessary for the general benefit of the citizens of the metropolitan area. Although the city was in agreement, it took the position that annexation was acceptable only under specified conditions because of perceived costs of servicing and upgrading the existing services of the Town of Jasper Place.

At the Local Authorities Board hearings, Mayor Roper presented the city's argument after reviewing the history of events since the McNally Report, and the annexation of Beverly in 1962. He then added:

> With room for residential expansion in the south-west and north-east, the City had no intention of taking the initiative in any further extension of its borders in the then forseen future. On behalf of the City Council, I announced this publicly.
>
> Meanwhile, apparently, the financial situation and future prospects of the Town of Jasper Place continue to become less favourable. The Town Council appointed an amalgamation committee to meet with a similar committee from the Edmonton Council. After many meetings . . . the City Council adopted a recommendation of its Amalgamation Committee to the effect that if the Town of Jasper Place made application to be annexed to the city, then the city would contend that the solution to the plight of the Town should not consist in merely passing the burden to Edmonton. Our Council concluded that if Edmonton is forced to expand west it should also expand east . . .
>
> We do not seek to see our city grow because we desire growth for its own sake. Rather, we accept the fact that growth is inevitable and that one government of the enlarged area is the only effective way to administer it.[73]

The Mayor reiterated the history of decisions which had contributed to the plight of the city and surrounding municipalities — the outcome of provincial interventions in 1959, and the pressures from surrounding municipalities both to join and to remain independent of Edmonton. The city was apparently willing to cope with the situation following the Beverly and north-east annexation, but because of the plight of Jasper Place found it necessary to reassess its policy of expansion. It also gave the city another opportunity to argue for annexation of the Strathcona industries. The Mayor's statement was consistent with the conclusions of the McNally Report that, to administer and to plan the metropolitan area effectively, it should be under one administration. This was also re-emphasized in the city's submission. This brief also stressed that "as the water and sewage facilities of the area depend upon a single river and because the city requires land for industrial growth to ensure orderly growth, some early decision should be reached as to the responsibility for planning, financing, and servicing of fast growing suburban areas."[74]

The city's case raised questions as to the feasibility of administration and planning in an environment in which the city was subject to pressures from developers and other municipalities; in which critical decisions were in the hands of such agencies as the Local Authorities Board; and in which the city was responsible for providing services but did not have access to revenues which it defined as rightfully available to the region. On the other hand, the city did not address itself to the consequences of continued metropolitan growth on either the local region or the province, nor to the impact the annexation would have on those municipalities losing industrial assessment.

The County of Strathcona strongly opposed the annexation of its industrial areas. Strathcona's objections pointed out that although the city was advocating one administration for the region, the omission of urban residential centres, such as St. Albert, was inconsistent with the city's objectives. The county also emphasized that the city already had large, undeveloped, industrial areas; that for the county the annexation would lead to a reduction of revenues exceeding the reduction of expenses; that the Edmonton Regional Planning Commission was providing satisfactory planning services; and that for the continued viability of the region as an industrial centre, industry needed to be free from encroachment by noncompatible uses.

Direct and indirect submissions by industry to the Local Authorities Board hearings expanded on this latter point. Imperial Oil argued that it had purposely located outside the urban area because it was not an urban function, that its activity created certain obnoxious side effects, and that it provided its own services. The company also indicated that "it would be inadvisable from a corporate public relations point of view to openly oppose the City's application to annex Strathcona." A representative of the company emphasized that the industry did in fact contribute considerably to Edmonton as a supplier of goods and services.[75]

The Canadian Chemcell Company Ltd. was particularly concerned with the effect which annexation would have on its competitive position because of the potential taxes on fuels, etc. and the monopoly situation of city services:

> It must not be overlooked that when the Company decided to locate in Alberta, the laws then in existence, and indeed the historic pattern of municipal assessment and taxation, were such that Canadian Chemcell was entitled to assume that by locating in a rural area at a considerable distance from Edmonton, its taxes would be substantially lower than if it were to locate in an urban area. This was due to the fact that the Company would not be deriving the benefit of many services otherwise available to the general taxpayer, and also because it could assume that if other large industries locate in the same general area, the combined effect of their assessment would be to lower property taxes.[76]

The brief expressed particular concern as to the discretion which the City Act permits the City Council in setting business tax; they were thus concerned with the uncertainty to which annexation could contribute. The brief admitted that many industries, including themselves, were not desirable neighbours for residential and some other forms of development. They were concerned with which form of administration would be least likely to succumb to pressures for unfavourable development, and, as the county had proven itself on this, they favoured it:

> The Company does not wish to express any preference for one or another form of government. We have always endeavored to see that our raw material position was protected. The Company's decision to build its plant in a rural area and to develop its own utilities and services was based on a definite opinion that a petro-chemical plant for a variety of reasons should not be located in an urban area. Our opinion has not changed.[77]

The brief thus opposed annexation and explicitly stated that the company was looking out for "its own best interests."

Many of the arguments of Canadian Industries Ltd. corresponded to those presented in the previous submission. The company was concerned that:

> the fundamental legal position of the City makes it impossible to give commitments on policy which will bind future councils . . . The Company is thus placed in the unenviable position of having to consider whether, in the

> light of the various factors involved in annexation, that are of particular concern to the Company such as fuel and raw materials, land use, taxes and services, it is more probable that the existing situation in regard to these matters will be adversely affected if the industrial area remains in the County or is brought into the City. In the Company's view, there is no question but what its position will be immediately adversely affected by annexation unless suitable conditions are included in the Annexation Order, and possibly amendments made to certain legislation. Even assuming that in this matter the situation now obtaining in Strathcona could be carried forward into the City, the Company has come to the conclusion that it is more probable that pressures for adverse changes in the future would arise if the Company's plants were in the city rather than if they were in the country.[78]

The Local Authorities Board ordered the following annexations to the City of Edmonton to be made effective Monday, August 17, 1964:

> 1. The Town of Jasper Place;
> 2. Eight and one-quarter sections of land in Strathcona County, east and south of the city;
> 3. Three-quarters of a section of land in Stony Plain, M.D., lying north of Jasper Place;
> 4. Two sections of land lying south of Jasper Place.[79]

The annexations did not include the industrial areas of the County of Strathcona and Municipal District of Stony Plain.

The Local Authorities Board cited planning and administrative criteria in the decision to annex Jasper Place:

> The Town is situated upstream and upwind from the City, creating a situation when development of the Town directly affects city planning, whether for land use or for utility development, including the use of the North Saskatchewan River.[80]

Jasper Place was viewed as an integral part of the city, and should be annexed to the city to facilitate effective planning and administration, and to achieve a more equitable distribution of municipal costs and responsibilities. The board established that annexation would be of considerable financial benefit to the residents of Jasper Place, but challenged the city's estimates of costs of annexation. To do this, the board introduced information over and above that presented at the hearings by drawing on the skills and knowledge of the board members to assess the cost estimates presented by the city.[81]

The Local Authorities Board's assessment of the costs was

critical to the city's application to annex the industrial areas. The board has no obligation to accept any conditions, such as those specified by the city under which it would find annexation to be acceptable. Having concluded that the city had overestimated the costs of annexation, the board accepted the arguments of the County of Strathcona and the industries, that annexation was unnecessary and would adversely affect the county's mill rate. The board also expressed concern as to the consequences of annexation on the viability of the existing industries and industrial development:

> Urbanization of these major industrial developments could seriously affect industrial development.[82]

In making this statement, the board did not address itself to other questions which could be raised about the industries' briefs. Why should the industries be entitled to lower taxes by locating in a "rural" area even though the industries may be imposing housing, education, recreation, and other costs on surrounding urban centres? Their briefs advocated that they be allowed to remain under the county administration because they would then be more certain of more favourable future municipal decisions. The Local Authorities Board did not question why the county was more responsive to the industries nor if this situation was in the best interests of the county and the region. Their statement seemed to imply that the industrial area would experience further urban development if incorporated into the city, but that this could be countered if the city were to control development with zoning or development control by-laws. The statement did not acknowledge that, in fact, residential development in Sherwood Park was occurring in the vicinity of the industrial plants.

The Local Authorities Board recognized that the city required land for residential and industrial expansion. Therefore, eight and one-quarter sections were annexed to the city from the County of Strathcona. The Order did not specify the criteria for selecting this area. Planning criteria were recognized as being critical to the cases of the city and of the Town of Jasper Place. The decision of the LAB with respect to Jasper Place was specified in terms of increasing the possibility of urban planning; however, the LAB decision did not mention the effect of the timing and the extent of the annexation on regional planning. In fact, no reference was made to the existing Preliminary Regional Plan and the Edmonton Regional Planning Commission made no presentation to the hearing. Although the LAB refuted the city's cost estimates for the annexation of Jasper Place, the LAB's decision did not identify the future long-range consequences on the region if the tax base of Strathcona remained unavailable to the entire region. Observation of the LAB decision suggests that planning does not provide a context for the annexation, but rather planning considerations were received and treated as being equivalent to other information presented to the board. The decision inevitably had to be the outcome of trade-offs made among the various factors presented and represented.

As neither the province nor the Regional Planning Commission provide an urban development policy, the LAB must frame its decisions in terms of the merits of the particular annexation application. Therefore, the whole problem of urbanization contributing to the growth of the metropolitan region and to the concomitant problems, goes unaddressed in such annexation decisions.

Immediately following the Local Authorities Board's decision, the council unanimously resolved:

> That the City Legal Department move quickly to study the possibility of an appeal to the Courts under the Section 61 of the Local Authorities Board Act, with authority to the Legal Department to retain the services of a competent legal firm if deemed necessary. Also, that the Mayor and Commissioners on behalf of this Council move immediately to place the whole matter of amalgamation and the Board Order before the Cabinet and the assembled legislation of this Province by way of appeal and review.[83]

Other evidence of concern over the board's decision was illustrated by Alderman Julia Kiniski's notice of motion given on April 27, 1964:

> That a plebiscite be held to determine the wishes of the Citizens of Edmonton in regard to the amalgamation of Jasper Place.[84]

However, at the same meeting council struck a committee of three persons each from the city and Jasper Place to act as an administrative committee in connection with amalgamation. In spite of these potential protests there is no evidence that any formal action was taken by the city either by the Legal Department or by an approach to the province.

The Hanson Report, 1965-68

The city continued its attempt to resolve the issues following the adverse Local Authority Board decision over industrial developments and Jasper Place. But since 1959, following the Premier's request to postpone annexation applications in terms of the McNally Report's boundary recommendations, the city has never applied to the LAB to annex territory on such a large scale. In 1965, on a motion by Alderman Weinloss, the council sought from its internal financial advisors a study of recent experience, present activities, and projected ten year expansion with particular consideration being given to "the feasibility of re-applying for amalgamation of the industrial area . . . with particular attention to the degree in which the provincial government could participate with the city in relation to roads and bridge systems, hospital operations, and cost of education."[85] The issue came up again in 1967 in the

Commissioners' Reports 20 and 21 in reply to an alderman's motion to extend the city boundaries by ten miles. The council agreed with the Commissioners' recommendation that no application be made to the Local Authorities Board until an economic study had been completed.[86] In May the council agreed to the Organizational Committee's recommendation that a consultant be appointed to report on the advisability or otherwise of the City of Edmonton enlarging its boundaries.[87]

Pressure was being brought from interests in West Jasper Place in early 1967 for a further annexation in that area, but the Commissioners advised against it pending further study. By this time studies were regularly undertaken, and outline plans prepared, for areas of potential development on annexation to determine their developmental capacity and relation to servicing connections. In August, 1967, the Organizational Committee of Council recommended that:

> a study be commenced in regard to extending the City's boundaries in all directions and also recommends that Dr. E. J. Hanson be engaged to do the study so that an application can be made to the Local Authorities Board on March 1, 1968, to extend the City's boundaries.[88]

Dr. Hanson's report, completed in March of 1968, was primarily a fiscal study of amalgamation and annexation possibilities in the Edmonton metropolitan area within the terms of reference established by the city. He was:

> to search for the best and most appropriate form and area of local government in Edmonton area.[89]

In establishing the principles of urban government, Dr. Hanson identified three issues facilitating the development of metropolitan communities:

> The first is a matter of functions, involving the provision of various public services. The second is one of finance, involving the achievement of an adequate and equitable tax base, the raising of capital funds, and orderly budgeting. The third is one of the proper structure and organization of government.[90]

In arriving at his recommendations as to the form of local government and the area of jurisdiction, he relied heavily on the basic principles on which the conclusions of the McNally Report were based:

> The McNally Report provided a systematic, impartial, and thorough study of metropolitan governmental problems. The principles and recommendations of the Commission

cannot be ignored in dealing with the problems of municipal government in the Edmonton area.[91]

Although Hanson relied on the McNally study, the differences between the purposes of the McNally Royal Commission and the Hanson study must be clearly noted. The McNally Commission was initiated by the province to provide for provincial policy with respect to the metropolitan development of Calgary and Edmonton. On the other hand, Dr. Hanson was, in effect, commissioned by the city to consider its case for expanding its boundaries to accommodate future growth and to make available to the city the industrial tax revenues in the metropolitan region.

Working from the McNally principles of municipal government, Hanson established the requirements for a strong system of urban government:

> . . . the unit of urban government should correspond as closely as possible with the economic and social base of the area. Second, it should be organized on such a way that public services can be provided on a uniform basis throughout the whole area. Third, there should be co-ordinated administration to permit the provision of services and planning for the whole area. Fourth, urban government should be organized in such a way that it can make the best and fullest use possible of the metropolitan tax base. Fifth, it should be organized as to minimize complications in the provincial grants structure.[92]

He concluded that in order to realize these objectives, the area should include:

> (1) the industrial area immediately east of the present city; (2) the dormitory centres of St. Albert and Sherwood Park; and (3) enough additional land to permit the planning and provision of a continuous supply of residential housing, to provide room for industrial expansion, and to create a pleasant physical environment.[93]
>
> The main conclusion of this study is that the City of Edmonton should be be expanded to include a metropolitan area of nearly 300 square miles . . . Such an area would have social and economic unity. It would be politically integrated, and it would provide scope for administrative efficiency, and secure fiscal integration and equity. Finally, it would simplify provincial-municipal relations in the Edmonton area.[94]

The proposed boundary is shown on the accompanying map. (See Figure 3).

The report presented five primary recommendations:

Figure 3

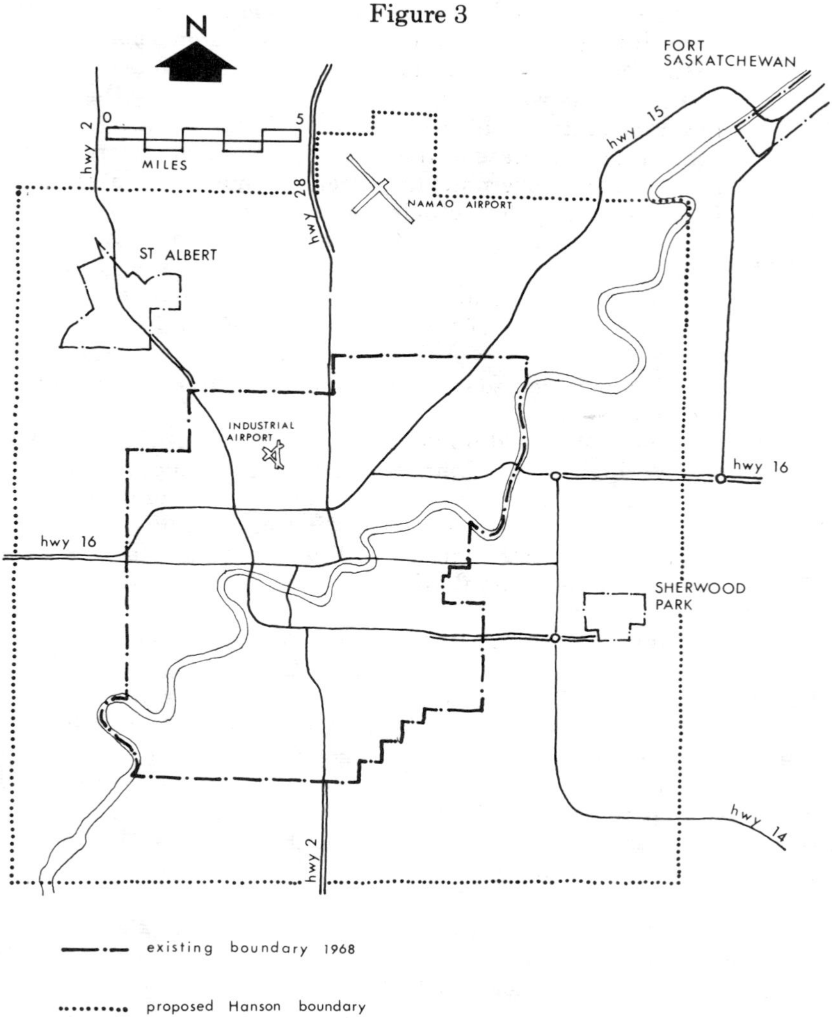

EDMONTON : Proposed Boundary

(1) The City of Edmonton should approve in principle the expansion of the city in all directions to include the metropolitan area (defined above).
(2) The City should apply for the annexation of the Review Area of 51/2 square miles west of 170 Street, as presented in the Report of the Planning Department in February, 1968, subject to the proviso that the timing should be left at the discretion of the Commission Board, pending the availability of capital funds, and the availability of land in the area concerned at reasonable prices for both public and private uses.

> (3) The City should approve in principle the appointment of an Intergovernmental Committee or Commission on Amalgamation in the Edmonton area which would discuss and negotiate ways and means for implementing the first recommendation. This Committee or Commission, consisting of representatives of the provincial government and the local governments concerned should try to arrive at an acceptable and efficient solution for the promotion of good government of the Edmonton area as soon as possible.
> (4) The City should undertake comprehensive and continuous studies of the present and potential system of revenues in the City of Edmonton in order to widen the revenue base and to enhance its yield in an equitable and efficient way.
> (5) The City should appoint an Intergovernmental Officer whose chief responsibilities would be to conduct the studies recommended under No. 4, and who would maintain contacts and negotiations regarding matters of intergovernmental concern, with all governments — local, provincial and federal, affecting the city.[95]

In May, 1968 the council agreed that Dr. Hanson's recommendations Nos. 1, 2, 3, 4, 5 on pages 220 to 222 be adopted, and that a committee be struck consisting of the Mayor and a number of aldermen to meet with the Premier and members of his cabinet to discuss the setting up of this committee and to the setting up of time limits to get these reports back and acted upon.[96] Council also agreed that the city would proceed to apply annexation of the two sections west of the city, which were within the area Hanson suggested under point two above.

Hanson's recommendations included both long range and short range policies for annexation and strategies for implementing the boundary changes. He concluded that because of the issues involved, implementation was beyond the terms of reference of the Local Authorities Board and, therefore, properly lay directly with the provincial government and not with a government agency such as the Local Authorities Board:

> as the question of appropriate structure of municipal government in the metropolitan area is a problem of such large standing, it should be referred directly to the Provincial Government.
> A Local Authorities Board . . . was set up to deal with many of the jurisdictions of the Public Utilities Board in Alberta. Included in the responsibilities of this Board wre matters of annexations and alterations in the boundaries of municipal governments, including potential changes in the Edmontn Metropolitan area.
> In the end, however, it is the political responsibility of the

provincial government to shape the structure of local governments and to delegate its authoritiy to them.[97]

The province was unreceptive to the recommendation. The province recommended that the Local Authorities Board should conduct preliminary hearings to allow all municipalities to present the issues. It was intended that such a procedure would provide the cabinet with the information necessary to make a decision. The province contended that this was an issue which involved all the municipalities concerned rather than itself and the City of Edmonton. The city refused to apply to the LAB for a hearing. In

Figure 4

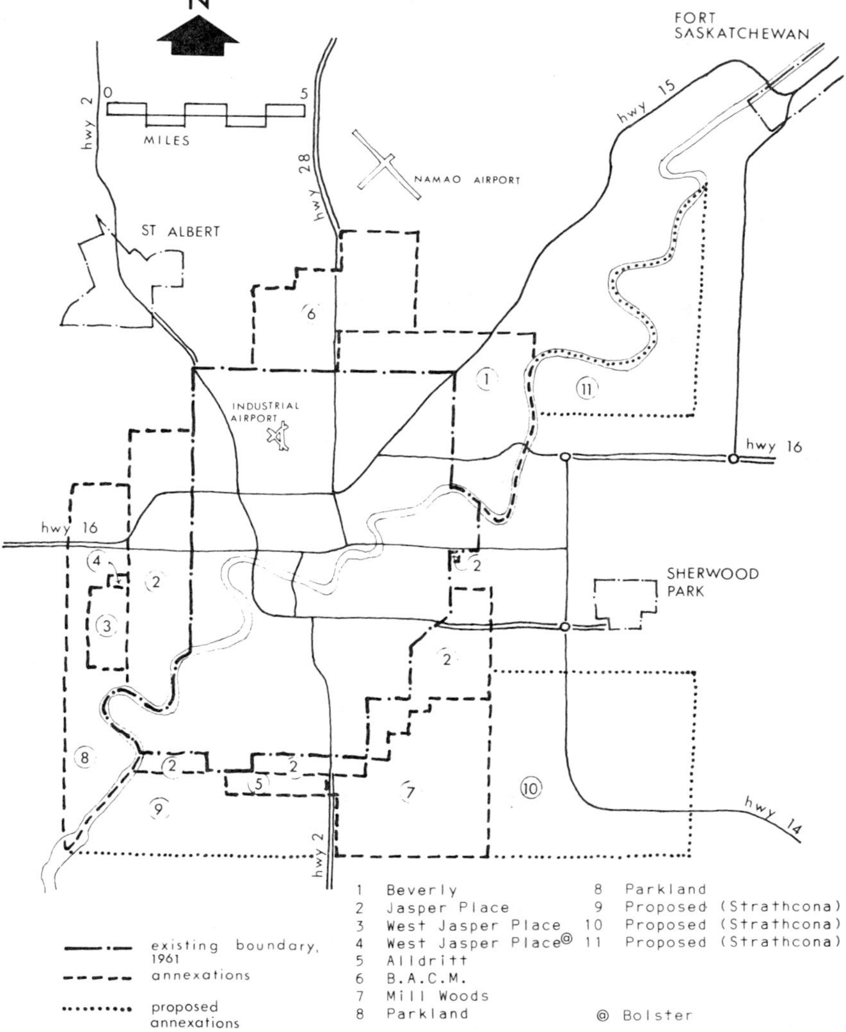

EDMONTON ANNEXATIONS, 1961 : 1971

its view, the matter was a provincial concern; the city did not believe that the issues could be resolved in the LAB's legal context, and to prepare the city's case an estimated $100,000 would be involved.

The City Council's dilemma has hardly changed since the 1956 McNally Report — it could attempt either to implement the boundaries as recommended by the Hanson Report, or to continue to add to its jurisdiction with *ad hoc* annexations. Consistent with its previous actions, the city has adopted both alternatives. On February 28, 1972 the City Council decided to approach the provincial cabinet for support to adopt the "Hanson Line." In recommending that the city should proceed with the West Jasper Place annexation, Hanson pointed out the relationship to historical precedents:

> West Jasper Place is in the nature of the various annexations which were made before 1961 to provide additional space for residential development in the north, east and south.[98]

This was to prove critical because not only did the city apply for the recommended West Jasper Place area, but it has subsequently applied for, and been granted, the Mill Woods area, and nine and three-quarter square miles in Parkland. It has also supported the BACM annexations;[99] two further developments involving annexation have been granted to private interests (both of which were opposed by the city); and the city has now approved the annexation of three more peripheral areas. (See Figure 4).

Recent Annexations, 1968-1971

The annexations of these four years will be treated in rather more detail. They illustrate both the expansion process *per se* and the administrative and political process occurring within the larger process.

1. *West Jasper Place*

The council applied, in terms of the Hanson recommendations, to the LAB for the annexation of West Jasper Place. [100] In a brief submitted by Lamb Holdings to the LAB at the time of the subsequent hearings, Lamb Holdings indicated that its initiative, in a brief submitted to council, had led to the council's decision to have its Planning Department look into the potential for annexing the area. Interviews revealed that the city administration opposed the annexation, but that council resolved to move in spite of this opposition.[101] The city administration had prepared the West Jasper Place Review Area Outline Plan, on which work had commenced about a year before the hearings and covered an area much larger than that contained in the application. The city made its case for annexation on two main grounds. First, the city needed more residential land. By July, 1968, one month before the application, there were 1,349 vacant and serviced lots available as against 2,037 a year before.[102] Secondly, the sites for public services such as those required by schools and water reservoirs in that area of the city could be provided in the annexation area.

At the hearing, the city informed the LAB that a majority of the landowners had agreed to sell land required for public highways to the city for $4,500 per acre. The city also requested that this agreed-upon price be made a condition of the LAB order. The LAB refused this request, stating that such a condition was beyond its jurisdiction; and that even were it within it, there existed alternative legislation by which the city could obtain land for public highways. The city apparently had no agreement with landowners for other public uses, and by 1971 was negotiating for school sites — for which the annexation was intended to provide — with landowning developers demanding six or seven times the above price.

The Edmonton Regional Planning Commission supported the annexation on the grounds that the proposed annexation was part of a larger area for which an outline plan had been prepared.

The Municipal District of Stony Plain, in which the land in question lay, opposed the application — although it was not opposed to annexation *per se,* but rather to the nature of *this* annexation. It argued that it was "piecemeal" and would create inefficiencies in providing municipal services, particularly road maintenance and school busing, in the area immediately to the south of the application area.

> The Municipal District of Stony Plain, No. 84, opposed the City's application because it would cause administrative problems, waste, and duplication. The Municipal District submitted that the City's proposal . . . was objectionable since it was a piecemeal annexation which would produce confusion, uncertainty, inefficiency and would not produce orderly development.[103]

The municipal district claimed that it had no desire to prevent the city from obtaining land necessary for orderly growth; therefore, the municipal district suggested that the city should be taking in four sections, as the other two were slated for development in the near future and were included in the West Jasper Place Outline Plan.

> The annexation of the four sections would serve to eliminate the main problems respecting general planning and development, road maintenance and school bussing.

The Local Authorities Board concurred with the city arguments that land was needed for residential development and that services could be economically extended to the area. In granting the application, the board also acknowledged the validity of the arguments made by the MD of Stony Plain, but was not prepared on its own volition to annex these areas, even though the board was "convinced that servicing of these areas will logically follow." The reason given for not so acting was largely procedural:

> The property owners (of the sections concerned) have not received notice of the proposal nor been given an opportunity to be heard on the matter. (Parenthesis added.)

The board explicitly stated that it had no jurisdiction over the provision of utilities and that its decision was in no way to abrogate existing agreements.[104]

2. *West Jasper Place (Bolster)*[105]

At the Local Authorities Board public hearings, March 3, 1969 to consider the application for annexation by the owner of two forty-acre parcels immediately to the north of the area annexed by Board Order 3981, the applicant submitted that the rate of development in the area made development of the parcels involved "amenable to orderly and necessary urban development."

It was also submitted that the proposed development would conform to that proposed in the West Jasper Place Outline Plan. The applicant proposed that annexation would not mean premature extension of sewer and water facilities just because the area was part of the city, but that it would facilitate planning for orderly development; i.e., the developer argued that although the proposed use was in compliance with the city's intent, planning could not be started until the status of the area was settled. He wanted to be in the city in order to work with the Planning Department to determine the future of the area.

In the case of the second forty-acre parcel, the applicant argued that annexation was in the public interest as CMHC had approved the area as suitable for badly needed low-rental housing under the Limited Dividend Program. Apparently, CMHC had indicated interest in considering 200 units of such housing once it was annexed, although as revealed in an interview with a senior official of CMHC, the corporation in principle tries not to become involved until there has been some local authority response to a proposal. The corporation tries to avoid giving moral support to a project which can be used as ammunition in negotiations with other levels of government. At the LAB hearing, the applicant's representative conceded to the City Solicitor that, although the housing project was used as an argument for annexation in no way would either the developer or CMHC be obliged to implement the project.

> The City opposed the application as: premature to city requirements for development lands in the area. The city submitted that sewer and water facilities were not likely to reach (the area) . . . until 1972 at the earliest . . . granting of the application would lead to further piecemeal annexation applications which should not be considered until the City decides on a longer range annexation plan. (Parenthesis added.)[106]

The city based its opposition upon the recommendations contained in the Commission Board Report of February, 1969, with which the council concurred:

> Should they be annexed the stage would be set for additional requests all around the city's periphery for similar annexations, all of which in your Commissioners' thinking should be delayed pending overall application to be made as suggested in the Hanson Report. The owners of the land will no doubt be contending that their property is urgently needed for housing, public and private, but to open the area up for early development would entail major expenditures which the Commissioners think could be better used in undeveloped areas already inside the City's boundaries.[107]

The city may thus be seen as opposing "piecemeal" annexation until the larger boundary issues could be resolved.

At the LAB annexation hearing, the Edmonton City Planning Director, after elaborating on the above position, argued an additional point:

> . . . It's been our view in the Planning Department . . . that it's most essential to look further down the road to consider those major components of city expansion and growth, which should be assured as a first priority . . . the area should be taken into account which can be looked at as a unit of growth and as I've indicated we're looking to areas of 60 to 80,000 in that kind of an order. This kind of area allows for the establishment of . . . what we call for want of a better term a Town Centre . . . Secondly, that the great difficulty in the past has been to establish what major public land use requirements there will be . . . in areas of expansion, freeway locations . . . and these take enormous amounts of land . . .[108]

The position of the Commission Board and the arguments presented by the City Planner, although both were opposed to the proposed annexation, reveal a further dilemma for the city. The Commission Board was suggesting that annexation be delayed until the boundary situation had been resolved in principle. The planner was accepting that annexations of a lesser order than the "Hanson Line" would occur, but that any annexation undertaken should comprise a "planning unit," i.e., a unit in accord with current planning administrative policy. Up to that time the policy of the city on annexation was the "Hanson Line," adopted in May, 1968, and the decision to annex West Jasper Place was in terms of it. Any annexations of the scale described by the City Planner, however, could be said to be contradictory to the official city policy. Though the planner was presenting a professional planner's view rather than city policy, such statements by the city's own departments could jeopardize the city's case before a public authority. Yet for the city to fail to bring forward the arguments of responsible professionals might render its case unconvincing. To avoid such a dilemma, therefore, the city may base its case on political or situationally advantageous grounds, rather than on planning grounds.

The County of Parkland (formerly the Municipal District of Stony Plain) opposed this new annexation proposal on the same grounds as it had opposed the earlier West Jasper Place annexations, i.e., it opposed "piecemeal" annexations, and proposed larger scale annexations.

In spite of the arguments that the annexation should be delayed until an overall policy had been formulated, and the inherent dangers of setting a precedent for future *d hoc* applications, the LAB approved the application. The decision was based on the grounds that the proposed uses were consistent with those planned and likely to occur in the near future; "that the city had already sufficient planning studies" to indicate that lands would be used "and useful for comparatively short-range urban-type development"; and that annexation would facilitate the planning of the area by the owners and give the city direct planning control. The LAB decision made no reference to long-term planning or to concern which had been expressed by the city and the Edmonton Regional Planning Commission that the annexation could contribute to pressures for future small-scale annexations. The LAB based its decision on the merits of the case before it, viewed in its narrower context.

3. *Alldritt Annexation*[109]

The Alldritt annexation illustrated the consequence for the city of its inconsistency with respect to the West Jasper Place and the Bolster annexations, which played an important role in the applicants' arguments. The application was made "by a majority of the registered owners." The applicants' solicitor argued that the lands were within the area and conformed to the uses defined by the General Plan (not adopted at that time) and by an outline plan being prepared by the City Planning Department; and that the lands were also within the boundaries recommended by the Hanson Report which had been adopted by the city. The solicitor suggested that a shortage of medium-priced residential lots would occur in the area in less than five years unless the area was annexed.[110] Because of the time element required to plan and to develop the area the applicants stressed that lead-time was required to ensure a continuous supply of medium-priced homes. The city did oppose inclusion of the lands but did oppose the timing and its piecemeal nature. The applicants, pointing out that the city had supported the West Jasper Place annexation, and that it had agreed to support the proposed BACM annexation[111] even though no plans had as yet been prepared, suggested that these were evidence that the city supported piecemeal annexation even although the city's formal policy opposed it. The City Planner argued that although this might be true, the former annexation was made in the context of an outline plan, and the BACM area:

> constituted a unit for planning purposes or an outline plan area but although it constitutes piecemeal planning in the greater context, that we refer to it as something which can be handled in planning terms to ensure orderly 'economical development.'[112]

The city objected to the annexation on the grounds that it already faced demands on capital investment in several development areas, that it required time to work out expansion problems with adjacent municipalities, that a large scale boundary adjustment should not be prejudiced by piecemeal applications, and that premature annexation could prevent desirable overall planning.

At the LAB hearings, the Director of the City Planning Department presented the city's expansion policies and the perceived or desired role of planning in city annexation policy:

> . . . when City Council adopted the recommendations of the Hanson Report on annexation, in May of 1968, it in effect adopted a comprehensive policy favouring large scale approach to annexation . . . accordingly when the present application for annexation which is before you now was presented to City Council in November 1969, it was resolved that 'since the City of Edmonton is presently negotiating with the County of Strathcona for a larger portion of land in this area, the City requests that this proposed annexation be tabled until negotiations for the larger area have been completed and logical city boundaries established to the south'. On January 26, 1970 when learning that Alldritt was going to proceed . . . Council instructed its Administration to oppose the application at the Local Authorities Board hearings. It is my understanding that the City's intentions after negotiations with the County of Strathcona have been completed is to make application to annex all agreed expansion areas within the County at one time . . . possibly extending south to another mile down to the boundaries recommended under the Hanson boundary.[113]

With regard to planning matters, the Director of City Planning suggested that:

> before annexation procedures should be logically initiated . . . it seems to us that a definitive statement showing the capability of the subject area to be serviced and developed should be made. This principle is reflected in the City of Edmonton's proposed general plan which includes the following basic objectives: To develop lands within the

metropolitan area in accordance with priorities established on the basis of need and cost of servicing, to provide a plan whereby development can be efficiently programmed in order to coordinate the provision of all public services and utilities in the most orderly and economic manner to ensure that suburban expansion takes place in the most orderly and economic manner . . . In order to meet these objectives detailed planning studies must first be undertaken. The City Planning Department is currently preparing a development policy and guidelines report . . . intended to determine any constraint in the development of the area south of Duggan.[114]

The City Planner also explained that General Plan studies indicated that land within the city in this area could contain growth for the next five years. This would allow time for annexation proceedings for the overall development.

The application was also opposed by the Edmonton Regional Planning Commission on the grounds that it was "piecemeal," that the city was currently negotiating with surrounding municipalities, and that the City Planning Department was preparing an outline plan for a much larger area. The County of Strathcona, in which the land was sited, did not oppose the application.

The following reasons were given by the Local Authorities Board for granting the application:

— the applicant established to the Board's satisfaction that there will be a demand and need for additional medium-priced residential lots in this south side area well within a period of twenty (20) years, a period deemed by the Board to be a desirable planning period,
— the lands are within the area defined by the proposed general plan and conform to the proposed use,
— the lands are within the proposed Hanson boundaries,
— the supply of land could modify prices,
— The City's and the Edmonton Regional Planning Commission's principal reasons for opposing the granting of the annexation application are not compelling reasons for the Board to refuse the petition.

The board suggested that actual development would be dependent upon construction of a storm sewer, to serve Mill Woods, which would pass through the site. The LAB refused to comment upon the matter of "prematureness" with respect to the negotiations with the County of Strathcona because it was not party to the discussions:

— The matter of opposition because of the 'piecemeal' nature of an annexation application is not of any real consequence in light of the seven (7) applications for annexation of lands to the City, which have been heard or are to be heard as a result of formal applications before the Board, in the past seven (7) years. It appears that similar annexation applications may continue to be made under present circumstances.

— In respect to the matter of the generation of new and additional 'pressures' on the city for utility extensions, which translates into 'pressures' for capital funds, the Board feels that such demands are normal requests and are answered when the City Council adopts its annual capital program and budget.

The LAB stressed that its Order was not to affect any right of Calgary Power or other utility suppliers with existing agreements for utility services in the area, nor was the Order to determine who was entitled to provide services. Although neither Alberta Government Telephones (AGT) nor Edmonton Telephones made formal presentations to the public hearing, a letter to the LAB from AGT on August 10, 1970, reminded the board of the June 21, 1963 (but presently contested) City-AGT boundary agreement which fixed the service boundaries for both telephone companies. In reply, the LAB stressed that the explicit references to Calgary Power was adequate to cover the telephone situation.

The LAB explanation for granting the application is particularly interesting because it disregarded the City Planner's explanation of the planning process and the city annexation policy as incorporated in the Hanson Report. However, the LAB explanation relied on both the proposed city plans and the Hanson report, which has never been formally submitted to the LAB, as reasons for annexation. The LAB decision would suggest that plans do not provide the context for annexation decisions. The LAB disregarded the arguments of both city and regional planning authorities on the grounds that the application was consistent with proposed plans for the area; but the plans were only proposals and were subject to much change before adoption. The LAB position regarding "prematureness" may be said to prohibit a local authority from determining the timing and location of peripheral development. The LAB suggested that the city could still control timing of development by installation of services, but at the same time the LAB acknowledged that "pressures" for capital funds were part of the financing of development.

In early 1972 the city adopted a new servicing policy under which the developer is responsible for financing the "front-end" costs of trunk services. It may be concluded, therefore, that should the city be confronted with future annexations of this type, it will not have control over the timing of development, and will have in turn little opportunity to "rationalize" the development of peripheral suburbs. The LAB stressed that it was not party to the the negotiations between the city and Strathcona and that it therefore could not comment upon the timing with respect to the negotiations. The application was also approved because it could modify city land prices, but the annexation order in no way commits the developer to any specified land prices. The board does not evaluate the consequences of annexations on land prices, or housing prices subsequent to an annexation; thus this reason for granting the application may be seen to rest on a belief in the market situation as a determinant of price.

The LAB apparently recognized that the application was not only consistent with the history of annexations to the city, but also would likely be consistent with the anticipated future. But such an assumption may itself become a self-fulfilling prophecy in that by continuing to approve such annexations, the board may be ensuring that similar applications will continue to be made. In this sense the instrument of the province is party to the continued difficulties of the city to establish as fact its long-term annexation policy, and continues to facilitate the manoeuvres of private developers in their relation to the city.

4. *BACM*

The public hearings for the BACM annexation application were held in Edmonton, May 19-22, 1970.[115] The "applicants," consisting of BACM Ltd.[116] and other landowners comprising more than 80 percent of the landowners, submitted that the area, ten and a half sections, should be annexed to the city because:

> — The area forms a 'natural well-defined planning unit' to which city sewer and water and storm systems may be economically extended;
> — The territory is suitable for residential development and its use for this purpose is supported by City Council;
> — The area is not encumbered by extensive existing urban-type development;
> — There is a need for low priced residential land which can only be realized at prices of approximately $3,500 per acre or less for raw land. 'City Council's endorsement of annexation of this north territory, even though considerable additional lands are to be made available for low cost housing to the south-east of the city (Mill Woods), is evidence of need for additional lands in the city to combat the high lot prices.'[117]
> — Development of the BACM area in conjunction with development of the new Athabasca University site lying about one and one-half (11/2) miles to the north-west of the area proposed for annexation, will lead to efficient planning of traffic arteries running in both north-south and east-west directions.
> — . . . section 20 (6) of the Municipal Government Act provides the municipal district with an avenue to remove any financial hardship which it may suffer as a result of the granting of the annexation application.
> — Any financial and administrative problems that

> Sturgeon School Division No. 24 may have are due to loss of territory, function and enrollment over a period of years. — The annexation . . . is not the cause of the (school) division's impending demise, and should not deter the granting of the present annexation application (parenthesis added).[118]

At the LAB hearing the President of BACM Development Corporation expanded upon the reasons for annexation:

> There are, of course, very many advantages to this kind of long term coordinated development program. That is both to the public sector and to the private sector. It allows for proper and careful deliberate planning considerations, long-range plans for transportation systems, to meet education needs, and all these things. Edmonton's inventory of raw land is nearly depleted to the point of not being available at all, certainly not at a price that can be used, additional land must be made available. (Comparative land Prices: 55 foot lot with equal services — Edmonton $7,500, Sherwood Park $4,300, and Calgary $4,000 to $5,000). (Parenthesis added . . . the lot prices were included in the President's remarks.)[119]

BACM suggested that Mill Woods, as a means of controlling land prices, "will ease the situation for people that are prepared to live in that area," but that because there are demands for housing in many part of the city one area would be insufficient.

The president indicated that the BACM 50 percent dedication for public uses, which exceeded the normal 36 to 38 percent, would provide:

> 10 to 14 percent of the lands that we develop for the first five years for public purposes, but in particular for public housing sites. We also agreed that in the event . . . the rate of development is not to our expectations, that we would . . . guarantee 100 acres minimum. Our purpose again was to merely seek from the city their blessing, hopefully cooperation in going forward but not one dollar. We are not looking for any financial support in any way and this would mean that we would pay the full costs of extending the present trunks and so on to the development area. The extension of the storm sewer alone is an amount estimated as being in excess of one million dollars.[120]

On questioning by the counsel for both the MD of Sturgeon and the School Division (SD) of Sturgeon, the president acknowledged that BACM had proceeded with a program of land acquisition before consulting the city, the Edmonton Regional Planning Commission, the Planning Committee of the MD of Sturgeon, or the SD of

Sturgeon.[121] He suggested that there was nothing unusual in their not having contacted any level of government prior to acquiring interest in the land proposed for annexation where:

> there is a climate of speculation; and we feel that exists in the City of Edmonton, and so in this situation we had no alternative in our opinion but to do it the way we did.[122]

He suggested that the city and the province had done the same thing in Mill Woods.

The City of Edmonton supported the application even though the area under consideration had not been included in the General Plan because:

> — Addition of the territory will materially assist in meeting the cit's immediate and long-range needs for lower cost housing.
> — City growth should be in all directions and be under annexation rather than by development of fringe communities which cannot avoid heavy development and operational costs, and which in time must seek the city's water and some other utilities.
> — The city's General Plan (which was not adopted until May 1971), which is subject to review each five years, is flexible. The within (sic) residential plan as well as the south-east development area plan are radical but in no way an undesirable departure from the General Plan.
> . . . a municipal district should be able to adjust to losses of territory and diminution in revenue for the urban growth needs of a city.
> — It is the duty of the Provincial Government — and the Board — to provide boundaries and a tax base that will allow municipalities which are adverse in interest to co-exist.[123] (Parenthesis added.)

The application was opposed by the MD of the Sturgeon, No. 90, because:

> — The desire of land owners to realize a profit in converting agricultural land to urban land uses is 'not proper ground for granting the application';
> — There is no need for residential land in the city;
> — The area is not suitable for residential land because of the Namao Airport and Speedway Park;
> — The territory was not contemplated in the City's General Plan;
> — Neither the Edmonton Regional Planning Commission's Preliminary Plan (metro part), nor the METS Report projected the areas as being suitable for accommodating one hundred thousand (100,000) persons and it is not in

the general public interest to entertain such a drastic change in the General Plan.
— Development of the BACM territory will interfere with future residential growth patterns envisaged in the long-range metro plans.
— City support of the BACM annexation and development proposals has been influenced by the excess dedication of land by BACM Ltd. — a private business enterprise.
— This private enterprise development proposal should not be allowed to disrupt the organization and operation of member municipalities of the metropolitan area.
— Annexation of the territory to the city will result in serious financial hardship for the Municipal District of Sturgeon.[124]

Both the applicant and the MD of Sturgeon relied heavily on the arguments of planning consultants to support their respective cases. The planning consultants to BACM explained that the development was in the context of the metropolitan part of the Preliminary Regional Plan:

> My feeling is that the strength of the document (the Preliminary Regional Plan) . . . is in its capacity for rational change to meet emerging metropolitan needs. I feel that this proposal should be viewed in . . . this context, in change and need for adjustment. In this context we might examine what are the changes that in fact in the past few years have emerged. The fact that the city limits in the north are near completion and this has been an area which has absorbed a great deal of recent housing development. The area which had put certain (pressures) on utilities, now these problems have been resolved and the area can now be serviced. There is an added new factor of a new university being located in the north-west and this presents problems . . . So that this combination of factors together with other factors which we have considered in this brief shows us that there is a need for further revision and adjustment (to the) preliminary regional plan in this area . . . I do not believe that this is basically incompatible with the basic premises of the document (parenthesis added).[125]
>
> The project would proceed within the framework of an overall outline plan.[126]
>
> . . . the outline plan as envisaged by the City of Edmonton, is a series of communities which will not only have housing, but a core of shopping, apartments, service buildings of this kind. I think this will be in keeping of the City policy in all of their recent outline plans.[127]

The planning consultant for the MD of Sturgeon also used the

Edmonton Regional Planning Commission's Preliminary Regional Plan and the city's General Plan to support his arguments, but he opposed the annexation application. He suggested that:

> there is no crisis in terms of land supply in Metropolitan Edmonton (particularly when Mill Woods is taken into account) and accordingly, there should be no place for panic actions or major disruptions of the General Plan for Edmonton and the Preliminary Regional Plan.[128]
> The departure from The General Plan for the City of Edmonton, which was the product of 18 years of consistent and major planning effort and The Metropolitan Plan for the Edmonton Region, which evolved through the last 20 years, could only be condoned if it contributes to the overall pattern of regional development.[129]
> . . . the evolution of planning and development is proceeding in an exceptionally sound course and the Edmonton area achieved a degree of urban structure unparalleled in Canada. This is mainly reflected in the land use designation and provision of land for development, controls and principles of planning for region. The urban core and metropolitan areas are planned and organized. Alternative regional growth centers are not established as yet; however, the control of land use and land conservation is applied throughout the region.[130]
> . . . annexation could seriously affect the public interest . . . and in terms of financial hardship which could be imposed on the remainder of the M.D. of Sturgeon.[131]
> This is probably the strongest ground for objecting to the BACM proposal as in seeking their own interests the applicants are endangering the existence of an established municipality. This responsibility belongs to the provincial government and only after serious research of all the pertinent facts and by considering the entire region physically and the entire range of government-municipal relationship . . .[132]

He also presented as evidence positions taken by city departments to illustrate that the city was supporting the application contrary to all advice it had received from the administration. Thus, he asked, how can the annexation be reconciled in terms of municipal, metropolitan, regional, or public interests?[133]

The city's solicitor challenged some of the statements attributed to members of the city's administration, as material taken from newspaper articles which had not been verified. The solicitor went on to explain the relationship of City Council decisions to administration recommendations:

> as a matter of law, the position of the City is the position taken by the Council. And the City Council of the city is

> represented by the Mayor and the Aldermen, and in the strictest sense, and I think in a very practical sense, the advice that may have been given to them, either by the Commissioners or by the staff members is not relevant. (The solicitor explained that he had only filed with the LAB what the Council had decided, as that was all he considered to be relevant.) Because what the Council decides, as a legislation body, is something that we shouldn't guess at, we should take their decision on its face value (parenthesis added).[134]

The counsel for the MD of Sturgeon challenged the explanation presented by the city's solicitor:

> I agree with him that a decision is made by Council . . . But what I am saying is, is this an intelligent and sensible decision, based on the best available professional advice given to Council, or is it in point of fact a decision made in complete contradiction to advice?
> I suggest that the Council may very well have flown directly in the face of advice from the Planning Department, from the utility people, from school boards, I think this even is indicated to some extent by the discussion in regard to staging of development over the next 30 years, which apparently took place in Council. And which, apparently, was motivated by school board complaints.
> I am not prepared . . . to agree with (the City solicitor) . . . that the fact the Edmonton Council has said this is the thing to do, makes it right. And I'd say that this Board in making a decision in a matter of this importance, having the effect it does on the municipal district and the school division is entitled to have a clear picture of what was proposed by trained professional people, so that it can ascertain whether Edmonton's approval of this annexation is a piece of nonsense or a well considered municipal action (parenthesis added).[135]

Evidence of the differences over the BACM proposal between the City Council and the city administration may be revealed by comparing the administration's recommendations and the council's resolution to support the annexation. When the annexation proposal was originally presented to council, the council had referred it to the Commission Board for study. The City Planning Department, at the Commission Board's request, had prepared the study.

After receiving and reviewing the comments on the BACM proposal from various city departments, the Planning Department report stated:

> If the rate of development indicated by BACM was to be

> sustained, the transportation difficulties would be such as to render the general proposal unacceptable from the municipal point of view. This statement can be made because at no time was a growth area North of the City contemplated and allowed for in developing the transportation proposals for the City at large.
> The area is not served by good arterial roadways, proposed freeways or proposed rapid transit facilities . . . The major aterials leading to the downtown area are 97 Street and 127 Street, neither of which can be relied upon to provide any capacity for the scale of development contemplated. There will be substantial transportation costs to the City if the BACM proposal goes ahead. If the rate of development is fairly slow . . . this will not be too problematical, but if there is rapid development, the inability of the City to provide the necessary connections to the downtown area may cause or contribute towards the dilutation of the principle of a strong central area development. Strong and direct lines of communication are necessary if a strong downtown area is to be developed and maintained. In this context, public transportation facilities are most important. Edmonton Transit reports that presently congested arterial roadways will cause substantial inconvenience as far as bus operation is concerned. It would be an unattractive mode of travel. However, the area nearest 127 Street could hope for relief with the construction of the North West rapid transit line (to 118 Avenue and 122 Street). As far as public transportation is concerned, the area adjacent to and east of 97 Street is premature and costly, and would involve the development of a totally new system based on a rapid transit line along 97 Street, the economic justification for which will not exist for many years into the future.[136]

The report included a statement by the City Engineer that:

> the sewer data was inadequate in terms of rendering a specific opinion on the storm drainage system envisaged by BACM The sanitary sewer capacity *is not* adequate to handle the area controlled by BACM and lying east of 97 Street (emphasis original).[137]

As reported in the Planning Department Study:

> a major problem exists for Edmonton Water which can handle a growth of only 50-60,000 people. The capability for the whole area is approximately 120,000 people (BACM, plus other potentially developable land). Once the population threshold of 50-60,000 people is reached, no water supply can be provided, except by the construction of a new major line from an upstream water treatment

> plan. This kind of new facility, ringing the west and north end of the City, could not be expected for 30 to 40 years (parenthesis orginal).[138]

Neither of the school boards opposed the proposed annexation, and as suggested in the Planning Department Study, the annexation was expected to resolve a particular problem for the Separate School Board. The Public School Board, although not opposing the annexation, emphasized:

> School Board officials are most anxious to obtain a general commitment to City growth patterns . . . If development is to occur, it should occur on an orderly basis so that school facilities can be provided at minimum cost and maximum efficiency and should preferably be based on an overall plan . . . The general burden of uneconomic deployment of school funds falls to the taxpayers at large.[139]

The school board was explaining that if growth occurred simultaneously in many areas, the school board would be required to provide inefficiently used facilities and perhaps could not provide all the required facilities. The school board was also suggesting that although the responsibility of establishing a city growth policy was that of the council, if avoided, the school board could be held as the scapegoat for contributing to increased taxes.

After reviewing the comments on the proposal from various city departments, the Planning Department recommended:

> that the City consider annexation and development only for those lands lying West of 97 Street to the flight path restrictions from 137 Avenue to the Namao Air Force Base; but such annexation and development be only considered following the submission by the developer of sufficient data which will provide:
> (a) a proper examination of the engineering feasibility and cost involved;
> (b) a clear indication of the staging of development;
> (c) a complete review of the commitments which the City would be obliged to undertake;
> (d) a commitment with regard to the method of handling the very difficult fragmented subdivision areas;
> (e) for the proper integration of major regional roadway connections;
> (f) adequate buffering to any residential development in the vicinity of Speedway Park. (93 decibel recording — October 12, 1969).
> It is further recommended that the City oppose annexation of land for development in the area of 97 Street *as the City cannot* meet the obligation to supply water, public

transit, basic transportation facilities and sanitary sewage facilities to that area (emphasis original).[140]

The Commission Board recommended to council the initial paragraph and sections (a), (b), (d), (e) and (f) of the above. It amended section (c) to read:

> (c) a complete and accurate statement of commitments of the Company with regard to development of land and the commitments which the City will be obliged to undertake;

and added the following:

> (g) that this be contingent on the Company's dedication of 50 percent as indicated in their proposal with a guaranteed minimum of 100 acres whichever is greater, and in no case in any area annexed will the dedication be less than 40 percent;
> (h) that any additional land requirements by the City can be purchased at the Company's average cost per acre plus carrying charges.
> IT IS FURTHER RECOMMENDED that the land east of 97 Street await general annexation proceedings which are currently being studied by the municipalities involved, the City, and the Government of the Province.[141]

It will be noted that the Commission Board supplemented the conditions under which annexation should be considered by requiring a minimum dedication and by fixing a price for any additional land which the city may require. The Commission Board recommendation with respect to land east of 97 Street was considerably modified from that contained in the Planning Department recommendation. Whereas the Planning Department had recommended outright opposition, the Commission Board only suggested that annexation of the area be delayed until overall annexation proceedings were resolved.

At a special meeting of City Council on October 23, 1969, the council passed the following motion:

> That the City give its consent in the necessary statutory form to the annexation of the land involved in the BACM annexation proposal and in addition approve in principle the servicing and development of such lands commencing at an early date, the developer to negotiate a performance bond and development agreement in a form satisfactory to Council; that support of this annexation proposal means that there is a clear understanding that the City is not committed in any way to the installation of services or building of roadways until development agreements satisfactory to the City have been completed between the

> developers and the City along the lines of the recommendations (a) to (h) inclusive contained in the Commission Board Report dated October 23, 1969, and that the developer agree to utilize the services of all available City utilities in servicing the annexed area.[142]

The council decision varied considerably from that recommended by the Commission Board. The council decision supported the entire BACM annexation and made no reference to the recommendations of the administration that the area east of 97 Street be either opposed or delayed. The council apparently overlooked the technical problems of servicing the area which the Planning Department had outlined in support of its recommendations. Although the conditions (a) to (h) were retained, they were no longer conditions for support of the annexation but rather were to be conditions for commencement of development.

Although the council did act contrary to the administration's advice, representatives of the city administration, in interviews, have identified some of the city's difficulties at the time. The city was facing a residential land shortage "crisis."[143] The city did not have the financial resources to provide the necessary land; therefore they found the offer of BACM very attractive because it allowed the city to shift many of the initial development costs to the developer. However, as emphasized by representatives of the city, in view of the technical problems outlined above the costs to be shouldered by the developer may be only the "tip of the iceberg" relative to those likely to be faced by the city.

Calgary Power Ltd. submitted that the Board Order should establish the conditions for the supply of electric power and energy and that these conditions should conform to the existing agreement between the city and Calgary Power Ltd.[144] The counsel for Calgary Power questioned the president of BACM on one of the conditions required by the city, namely: that the developer agree to use the facilities of all available city utilities in servicing the land. The president suggested that BACM would abide by the Local Authorities Board decision; but he indicated that there was no completed agreement as to the use of city power, although negotiations were in process.

For this particular hearing the Edmonton Regional Planning Commission at Meeting No. 237, May 6, 1970, concluded that:

> participation in the hearing should be limited to providing pertinent planning information if the Local Authorities Board so desire it.

The LAB largely accepted the arguments favouring annexation. It granted the application in full:

> The land was needed within the city to control land prices and to provide low and medium income housing.

> The land was suitable for urban residential purposes, and the planning authorities will have time to consider the "noise pollution hazards" (Namao Airport, Speedway Park) that may relate to future residents in the area . . . Any financial or administrative problems that the Municipal District of Sturgeon No. 90 and Sturgeon School Division No. 24 may suffer as a result of the annexation being granted are solvable by the authorities themselves or with complementary action at the level of the Lieutenant Governor in Council (Section 20 (6) of the Municipal Government Act) in respect to school financial and administrative difficulties, and should not obstruct anticipated municipal and school development aimed at providing the greatest good to the greatest number.
> In view of the governing legislation recited, the Board is of the opinion that it does not have jurisdiction to take measures to remove any financial hardship that may come to exist as a result of the annexation (parenthesis original).[145]

The LAB cited the fact that the land was within the Hanson boundaries, although the Hanson Report had not been submitted to the LAB. The Order was not intended to affect any existing utility agreements and the LAB refused to order the applicants to use Edmonton Power in accordance with the City's "condition of support." Because the Order involved large areas of agricultural land, which would probably not be developed for 15 to 20 years, the LAB established "protective assessment" for *bona fide* farmers.

The BACM annexation illustrates many of the issues involved in metropolitan planning and development. Private interests were able to obtain City Council's conditional endorsement for the annexation although such urban development had not been anticipated in either the city's General Plan or in the Preliminary Regional Plan, Metropolitan Part, and was against the recommendation of much of the city's professional advice. The case, as presented for annexation, rested heavily on the need for low-priced residential land and the need for more choices of development areas. The city aldermen, in voting to support conditional annexation,were presumably acting in the interests of their electorate. Their interpretation of the needs of the city at that time made the annexation desirable. They proceeded to hedge this judgement with as many advantageous conditions as could reasonably be proposed; but they remained powerless to impose them in the face of a LAB decision. On the other hand, the LAB felt obliged to consider the case on its merits and on the basis of the applicant's objectives. Annexation orders, however, do not oblige the developer to fulfil the claims made at the hearings unless these are specifically mentioned in the Order. Similarly, according to the chairman of the LAB, the board does not monitor the development of annexed areas in order to determine whether the developer complies with his stated purposes. Nor does the board feel obliged to determine the *post hoc* consequences of its particular decisions — it has no staff capable of conducting the necessary research.

In consequence the people of Edmonton as local taxpayers, or the provincial government by providing financial assistance to the city, have no recourse to the longer-term implications for them of council decisions taken to meet a current situation but against the advice of professional personnel. Similarly, the citizen has no knowledge of alternative possibilities — such as satellite developmental proposals — which could achieve the same purpose as the application for annexation. Such matters suggest that the provincial government's search for an improved "quality of life" for the citizens of its cities is negated by its own unwillingness to provide the explicit direction required for the citizen to pass judgement on any particular application.

Although in the hearing the proposed annexation was justified as a desirable planning unit, and as consistent with the planning objectives of both the Municipal and the Regional Planning Commissions, the decision to develop was not made in the context of existing plans, but rather with knowledge of the flexibility of planning controls. The decision by the developer to assemble the land before informing the municipal authorities or public planning agencies suggests a certain confidence that the planning controls could be amended, that council endorsement could be gained, and that annexation would be granted. Developers appear to be astute observers of City Council predicaments. The developers justified their actions because of the "climate of speculation" said to exist in Edmonton, and by reference to similar actions taken by the city and the province in public land assembly in the South East Development Area.

In this application, planning arguments constituted a considerable portion of the hearing. Planners appeared to present both the merits and demerits of the annexation. The planners favouring the application stressed the necessity of the flexibility of planning controls in order to cope with the changing conditions which may result subsequent to any particular decision, development, or innovation — e.g., the resolution of the technical problems of providing utilities to the area, the willingness of the developer to install the necessary trunk facilities, and the proposed Athabasca University were all advanced as examples of change with which existing plans should be sufficiently flexible to cope.[146] They also argued that although the area was not anticipated to receive intensive urban development, the proposal was to be consistent with established city planning principles, i.e., the area was of sufficient scale that it could be considered a planning unit and could support the range of services deemed necessary in residential development. The Preliminary Regional Plan was said to have served the function of preventing undesired low-density development, thereby permitting the more desired proposed development.

The planning consultant to the municipal district argued that the development was not consistent with the directions of urban growth established by the city's General Plan, and that to break from these would cause diseconomies both to the city and in particular to the municipal district. Although he acknowledged that the regional plan functioned as a holding device, he argued that because no alternative metropolitan growth patterns had as yet been established, it would be premature to undertake developments of the scale of the BACM proposal. He emphasized the fact that urban development had been unanticipated in the area because of its marginal character for residential development — because of its proximity to the Namao Airport and Speedway Park and because of the problems of providing public services and access to the city. As made evident in the City Planning Department study, the proposed development would require public investment, largely municipal, to provide the necessary public services. These could be prohibitively expensive because the development had not been predicted. Therefore, even if the flexibility of existing land-use plans was stressed, no account was taken of the inflexibility of other plans such as those for transportation or utilities currently planned to service other areas of growth.

A representative of the city administration, in interview, cited the administration's recommendations as illustrations of the "politics of planning." On the basis of "professional considerations" of such problems as transportation, water supply, etc., the conclusion was to oppose the BACM proposal. However, because of the "housing crisis" and the "bonuses" promised by BACM, such a recommendation may have been poorly based in its practical context. The council's subsequent decision was suggested as illustrative of why planners present "diplomatic" arguments; but the whole issue raises many questions about the nature of the information presented to the council and about the proper status of direction and planning in public matters.

If information is conditioned by what is envisaged as being "politically acceptable," and the assumptions kept implicit, the user for whom the information is supplied becomes "deceived" if he in turn makes his decisions on the assumption that the information is strictly professional and impartial. The point at which purely technical considerations must be given the weight necessary to overrule a favourable disposition towards a project by elected councillors is determined by a variety of temporal, financial, and situational conditions. If metropolitan councils can expect almost always to be aided by one or the other senior government when in difficulties, the point tends to move increasingly towards favouring the odds of the private developer. The latter, ever sensitive to opportunities in business, and with a keen ear to the ground on the problems facing city hall, prepares his case in such a manner as to indicate the likely solutions to a variety of remotely connected matters he knows to be troubling the city. Under the ritual of the public hearing, and by the use of cross examination by professional lawyers and planners, the city's formal, institutional means of developmental control are both upheld and brought to nought in the interests of the respective parties. The work of the professionals who prepare these formal instruments and whose duty it is to calculate the technical and financial implications is overthrown and the faith of both councillors and public in the institutions of local government to generate genuinely developmental advantages for the city is paralysed.

The BACM annexation resulted in changes in city development procedures when for the first time the city required a development agreement to complete the outline plan. It should be noted that in the City Council's resolution supporting the BACM annexations it required:

> the developer to negotiate a performance bond and development agreement in a form satisfactory to Council.[147]

A development agreement is a legal agreement setting out the details of development and the financial obligations and responsibilities of each of the parties involved. The outline plan procedure, as described in earlier annexation hearings, had first been used in the West Jasper Place development area, and, as explained by city representatives, the city was encountering problems because the outline plan had not committed the developer to formal development procedures, e.g., how, and at what cost, school sites were to be obtained by the public authority. Because the initial subdivisions had considerably deviated from the outline plan in West Jasper Place, the city became confronted with a shortage of land for public facilities and was left negotiating over inflated prices.

Now that the city has transferred responsibility for the financing of all services to the developer as stipulated in the development agreement, this instrument may provide the city with a means to control the timing and location of development. However, because of the greater financial implications for capitalizing the development and because CMHC, the NHA, and lending institutions become increasingly identified with and involved in the success of the development, the local authority may in fact become subject to increasing pressure over timing, become increasingly threatened in its statutory right to control local affairs, and become increasingly obliged to make adjustments to other developmental priorities it has in hand in order to swing its resources over to the larger developments supported by superior political and financial weight. While such possibilities are inherent in the situation, the provincial government and its *ad hoc* boards may continue to sit idly by. In the case of BACM, council did not approve the development agreement until January 1972, over one year after the annexation became effective. The decision was delayed by problems in determining how the school boards were to obtain sites, and by council's reluctance to decide the point prior to the civic elections in October, 1971. The new council was to decide on the agreement.

The BACM hearing also demonstrated an ERPC position on annexations. In previous hearings once the major muncipality had prepared or had supported an annexation, the Regional Planning Commission usually supported the annexation. However, as explained by a representative of Edmonton Regional Planning Commission, the commission only undertakes an analysis, or the preparation of a position statement on an annexation question if so requested by a member municipality. In the BACM case neither the city nor the MD of Sturgeon did so; thus the commission representative appeared at the hearing only as a planning resource. The ERPC, by not volunteering an analysis of the annexation, avoided becoming involved in the conflict between its member municipalities, but as set out in the Planning Act, one of the optional functions of the Regional Planning Commission is to determine desirable municipal boundaries.

The LAB decision raises the question as to where responsibility lies for the financial implications of city growth resulting from pressures exerted by privately organized capital. In the Jasper Place decision of 1964 wherein the city had requested annexation of the industrial areas of the County of Strathcona in order to compensate the city for the costs of amalgamation with the Town of Jasper Place, annexation of the industrial areas was in part rejected by the LAB because of the potential financial impact which a separation could impose on the County and the Metropolitan Region, and because of its possible potential threat to industrial development. The 1964 application arose from mutual discussions between the local authorities. In the BACM application the financial impact of annexation on the MD-of Sturgeon was established by the LAB to be the responsibility of the province. On this position, the LAB was consistent with the 1964 Strathcona decision in that it suggested that it was not a sound principle to annex for the purpose of redistributing "net portions of tax revenues. A provincial variation of a grant structure may well accomplish the same end, if need is shown to do so."[148] The BACM application, however, was motivated by perceived profits attributable in part to public investment in the Athabasca University and in part to public planning decisions which had zoned the land for agricultural purposes thereby establishing a land price much lower than if it had been zoned "general urban." Re-zoning increased the potential price upon conversion to urban uses but at the same time could involve provincial assistance to compensate the municipal district for any financial hardship created. Similarly, in the Alldritt Annexation case, the LAB decision in favour of the private developer was said to compromise the city's capital investments in other areas, and would involve the city in the construction of a storm sewer which would, however, be required to service Mill Woods. The city, therefore, can be involved not only in administrative inconvenience but in costs of capital construction and potential wastage of resources through inefficient administrative preparedness.

In 1970 the Municipal District of Sturgeon applied to the

Lieutenant-Governor in Council to be compensated for the financial consequences of the BACM annexation. This application was referred to the Minister of Municipal Affairs for a recommendation. The Minister of Municipal Affairs notified the municipal district that he had reported to the cabinet that his department had determined that the municipality had not suffered financially and was, therefore, not eligible for compensation. Following the election of the new government in August, 1971, the municipal district has reapplied for compensation. The municipal assistance grant for 1971 was based on the pre-annexation population, as the grants were awarded prior to completion of the census. However, the 1972 grants will be based on the reduced population, unless the provincial government reassesses the situation. We did not find whether or not other revenues were made available to the MD of Sturgeon by the province.

If the municipal district does suffer financial hardship, one might ask whether these costs should be charged to the private development of the area, or at least to the city which supported the change. Any provincial assistance can be interpreted as being a subsidy from the province to the city or to the developer, and therefore as a hidden cost of metropolitan development.

5. *Mill Woods*

On September 18, 1970 the City of Edmonton applied for annexation of the South East Development Area, now called Mill Woods. It was a public land assembly project involving the city, the province, and the federal agency CMHC. Mill Woods was anticipated to provide the city government with a means of controlling residential land prices within its boundaries.[149] As explained in the City Planning Department memo of May, 1969, because of the particular situation at the periphery of the city:

> development opportunity (had been) limited . . . It has been under these circumstances that a number of development companies have been able to maintain development programs to such an extent that the cost of land has become a serious impediment to the basic growth philosophies of the City. It should be stressed that the cost of land in one part of the city for one generalized land use will affect the value of land in all other parts of the city. It is plain that a city undergoing rapid growth, such as Edmonton, is going to have high land requirements in both the developed areas and the suburban areas to facilitate that growth (parenthesis added).[150]

Mill Woods was conceived as a program which could reduce land prices which in turn could benefit both the city and future home buyers.

Assuming that the program is carried out, the effect on

> land prices in the city will be spectacular, not only in the expansion areas, but also in the redevelopment areas. The City has very major land acquisition programs within all parts of the city and it is, therefore, in the very great interest of the City to dramatically reduce land values in terms of the acquisition of land for public purposes.[151]
> In order to overcome, and to somewhat reduce, the incidence of inflationary prices on land it is necessary that the City find a means of acquiring land at a reasonable price so that the saving may be passed on to ultimate purchaser.[152]

It should be noted that Edmonton had traditionally used city-owned land in order to control development and land prices. As discussed earlier, in the late 1940s and early 50s the city had had considerable public land which had reverted because of tax defaults during the depression. In 1951 and 1954 the city had purchased land in part to control land prices. The Commission Board Report No. 8, quoted above, referred to the Legislative Committee studies which expressed the need for a land acquisition policy and also quoted the council policy adopted January 20, 1969:

> That the City continue the policy started in 1968 of acquiring land for future subdivision at locations that can be serviced in the not too distant future, and that funds for such purpose be included in the Capital Budget.[153]

In selecting the new area for residential growth, the administration stressed several reasons for breaking from the normal directions of development. The General Plan, even though not formally adopted by council until May 18, 1971, stressed the desirability of the existing pattern of growth, and as a proposed public policy provided information about the likely future form and direction of city growth. Similarly, in order to minimize the costs of storm sewers, city development was generally proposed along the river. The residential growth alternatives were also said to be constrained by industrial zoning in the city's periphery and the Namao airbase to the north. Development companies, anticipating a continuation of the present direction of residential development, were said to control much of the land in the path of projected residential growth. Therefore, the south-east was selected for the land assembly program because it was thought that the property would be cheap relative to the normal growth areas because it was zoned "agricultural" by the Preliminary Regional Plan and, therefore, private investors had not anticipated intense urban development. The administration also stressed the need to change the pattern of industrial zoning. It was suggested that excessive perimeter areas had been zoned for industry and would not be required for industrial purposes for twenty or thirty years. A break in the industrial zoning was seen as a necessary form of intervention if the city was to be in a position to influence residential land prices.

The city administration envisaged selling land in the program area at a price sufficient to pay for all the municipal costs of development and still be sufficiently below existing prices to reduce residential land prices elsewhere in the city. The council subsequently required the development to meet the same conditions as apply to private developers, namely: the project must finance all necessary trunk services required to service the site.[154] The project could also be compared with city utilities policy in that it is expected to show a profit, and profits realized are to be turned over to general revenues and not to be retained within the project. The first lots were put on the market in late 1971 (approximately one year later than anticipated when the project was first proposed) at $106 per front foot including local improvements. This was $38 per front foot less than land in any other developing city subdivision. It is currently impossible to evaluate whether or not Mill Woods will have a significant impact upon city residential land prices because the storm sewer to the site, to be completed in 1974, will delay until 1973 the opening up of any major additional subdivisions.

By charging against the project the capital costs for which a private developer would be responsible, the project now must not only be self-sufficient but must encourage further growth to pay off those debts incurred on it which are capable of being spread over subsequent developments. Thus, the mode of financing may have changed the criteria determining the rate of growth. Originally, the project was intended to provide the city with a means of influencing residential land prices by providing the city the means to manipulate the number of lots on the market. As subsequently arranged, the rate of development will be determined largely by the need to realize a certain "cash flow," in turn set by the financing of the project.

The south-east area was also selected because of the council's commitment to develop a "strong downtown core." The General Plan emphasized the importance of a strong downtown core, which in turn requires an efficient transportation system to provide the access necessary. The Metropolitan Edmonton Transportation Study, completed in 1963 for the Edmonton Regional Planning Commission, has provided the framework for the development of an arterial roadway and freeway system:

> However, the staging program for roadways is related more closely to the capability of the City to pay for rights-of-way and construction, rather than the relationship of need for facilities to the expansion areas. Therefore, we have the situation whereby the North East parts of the City and the South West parts of the City, the two largest expansion areas, are not programmed for substantial roadway development because of the costs and difficulties involved. The South West part of the City is expected to rely for many years on the South East Freeway (Millcreek) and this particular facility could be utilized immediately to

facilitate development in the South East area itself. In other words, a new direction of growth can be justified for transportation reasons, where the transportation plan being implemented is part of an overall plan but its method of staging does not best serve the areas of substantial growth as presently proposed (parenthesis original).[155]

The estimated cost of the South-east Freeway was anticipated to be much less than the South-west Freeway, partly because the route could use undeveloped city-owned land — the Mill Creek Ravine — which had been computed at no cost in determining the costs of alternative routes. However, because The General Plan, adopted by City Council in May 1971, following the computation of the costs of the South-east Freeway, requires that parkland taken for roadways must be replaced, the cost of the South-east Freeway would now be required to include the replacement value of the amenities provided originally by the natural environment of the ravine.

The proposed South-east Freeway, which was presented as a major advantage of the location of the Mill Woods project, illustrates the relationship of peripheral development to inner city areas. To provide access from the periphery and thereby to facilitate the development of the "downtown," a natural ravine in an older inner city area — itself poorly served by parks — was to be used for roadways. In May, 1971, after considerable action and protest by citizen groups both from the inner city area and the city at large, the City Council resolved that no freeway was to run through the Mill Creek Ravine. This created an interesting dilemma in which an administration project (subsequently endorsed by council), based upon the council's enabling policies, had proceeded upon the assumption that access would be provided by the ravine. The council has now denied this access. To date no alternative has been established. Thus, the pressures are building to rescind the council's decision and counter pressures are building to develop the recreation potential of the ravine. In April, 1972, the City Council voted to delay final decision on another project — McKinnon Ravine Freeway — intended to serve the west end of the city, until a comprehensive transportation study has been completed, even though the city had already spent considerable money clearing the trees and preparing the roadbed. This decision came after a concerted protest by citizen groups protesting the destruction of the natural amenities, the provincial grant system by which the city is only required to pay 25 cents for every dollar spent on freeways, the futility of trying to resolve transportation problems by means of more facilities for private automobiles, and the future costs to which the city would be committing itself if it continued to build freeways. The city now faces a situation in which, on one hand, it supports a "strong downtown core" and which, as outlined in the City Planning Department report on the BACM proposal, is dependent upon "strong and direct lines of communication"; and on the other hand, is confronted with providing prohibitively expensive freeways to the South-west, the North-east, and the BACM development areas, and has decided to eliminate and delay freeways to Mill Woods and West Jasper Place respectively. If it is true that a "strong downtown core" is dependent upon a good transportation system, and that, as many would argue, a freeway system is incompatible with that objective, then the city must develop an alternative transportation plan.

The Mill Woods project was largely conceived and developed within the city administration. Council authorization was sought and obtained for the Commission Board to exercise options for land assembly when the council adopted the recommendation:

> That the City Commissioners be authorized to serve as agents of the City to effect options for land purchase; subject to Council approval through normal channels of the actual purchase arrangements; and subject to controls established by a budget appropriation.[156]

Subsequently, the council concurred in the commission board's recommendation that:

> The Municipal Council of the City of Edmonton hereby resolves that the City Commissioners are authorized to approach the Alberta Housing and Urban Renewal Corporation with a view to identifying land assembly projects eligible for government support under the National Housing Act and the Alberta Housing Act.[157]

To support the recommendation, the Commission Board stressed that the Hellyer Task Force had strongly recommended that municipal governments participate in land assembly.

However, neither of these recommendations made explicit to the council the nature, location, or scale of the proposed land assembly project. This situation was reflected in a recommendation of the Public Works Committee:

> That they (the Commissioners) shall have the authority to take options of such lands as they in their discretion shall deem in the best interests of the City, provided that they shall not be authorized to expend for option money in any one year more than ten percent of the alloted budget for land purchases in that year (parenthesis added).[158]

However, to ensure that the council would be informed of the Commission Board's land assembly activities at some point, council concurred in the Public Works recommendation:

> That options must be reported within one year to the Public Works Committee.[159]

To prevent land speculation from inflating prices in the project area, the administration stressed that pre-planning and research activities must be necessarily restricted to maintain the desired secrecy.

It is apparent that the administration had originally intended to proceed on its own, without direct provincial involvement other than Alberta Housing Corporation support. However, Section 127 of the Municipal Government Act requires that if a municipality wishes to purchase land (the Commission Board was authorized only to take out options) in another municipality, that municipality must be notified. Such notification could well have jeopardized the secrecy sought. The problem is a long standing one.[160]

However, action taken by the provincial government in July, 1969, eliminated the need for the city to proceed with the land assembly on its own. Shortly after The Honourable F. Colborne became Minister of Municipal Affairs, the province approached the city with an offer to participate in the resolution of the city's land problems:

> In recognition of the increasing demands being placed on our major municipalities and the rising costs of services and land which are ultimately being reflected in the high cost of housing, the Province, through its Alberta Housing and Urban Renewal Corporation, is prepared to offer assistance to your municipality in the area of assembling and/or servicing and selling land for housing purposes primarily directed at providing land for low cost housing purposes.
>
> The proposal which we are offering is one where our Provincial Corporation will undertake to incur all costs related to the borrowing and financing of such projects with partial cost sharing for trunk services and will be prepared to negotiate the administrative arrangements for effecting such a program.
>
> If the City is interested in the proposal, we would welcome the opportunity to discuss the matter at an early date.[161]

The city responded quickly to the province's offer of assistance:

> Thank you very much for your letter of July 11th, describing the Province's offer, through the Alberta Housing and Urban Renewal Corporation, to help Edmonton assemble and/or service and sell land for low cost housing. It is coincidental that your letter arrived just as I was about to send out a letter to you suggesting that we get together to discuss this matter.[162]

The council participated in a meeting on July 24, 1969 with the minister "to discuss the province's offer to participate in a land assembly program for the City of Edmonton. At this meeting it was agreed that Mr. Bob Orysiuk meet with the Chief Commissioner to discuss the possibility of provincial involvement through the

Alberta Housing and Urban Renewal Corporation in a land assembly program in the south-east section of the city."[163] The notes of the meeting to the aldermen for October 17, 1969, stated that it was imperative that the aldermen become acquainted with the land assembly program in Mill Woods prior to deciding upon the BACM proposal which they were to hear on October 23, 1969.

The immediate response was in part possible because the city had already adopted a policy (March 10, 1969) to use the services of the Alberta Housing Corporation. The province had been invited into the issue. Later in July agreement between the Alberta Housing Corporation and the city was reached that:

> the Province was to option and purchase the land in the total development area including the land lying within the city's corporate boundaries. It was felt that it would be, in the long run interest to have only one level of government involved in optioning and acquisition of property.[164]

In view of the province's unwillingness to act on the McNally and Hanson recommendations or to adopt a formal policy with respect to the city's growth, this marked a major shift in the province's position. It was, however, consistent with previous provincial intervention in a local authority's affairs at the point where particular situations and problems could be resolved only by its doing so, and where a precedent was not likely to be set. Also consistent with the "fair and equal" philosophy of the provincial government, was its making the Alberta Housing Corporation's land-assembly facilities available to all municipalities. In fact, an identical offer was made to the City of Calgary by The Honourable F. Colborne, but that city declined to accept the offer.

Until a special meeting of the Commission Board on October 17, 1969 was held to announce the project publicly, the council was not informed of the details of the land assembly project. Some aldermen, by the time it was made public, were becoming concerned over the increasing inflexibility of the city's position in the face of the Mill Woods negotiation plus the BACM agreement. On June 28, 1971 Alderman Leger asked, "What commitment of assurance was given the Government that Council would approve the purchase from the Government"? The city administration in its written reply remarked:

> No commitment was ever given by the (City) Administration to the Government that Council would approve the purchase. It was always understood that the Commission Board could only recommend to Council that the Mill Woods land be purchased from the government; and that this recommendation to purchase would only be made when an agreement satisfactory to the Commission Board and the Government could be placed before Council. After the Government made known the Land Assembly

project on October 17, 1969 the administration worked with the Alberta Housing Corporation on an agreement for purchase by the City. This agreement was recommended to Council by the Commission Board on April 13, 1970. In closed session that date Council amended the terms of the agreement; then in open session, Council passed the following resolution: 'That the Commission Board be authorized on behalf of the City of Edmonton to enter into a memorandum of agreement with the Alberta Housing Corporation respecting the purchase of land in the South-East Development Area, and amendment thereto.' Thereupon the Mayor publicly signed the agreement. Then, and then only, was the City 'committed' to this purchase (parenthesis added).[165]

The nature of the agreement between the city and AHC was briefly described by the City Solicitor at the LAB annexation hearings, November 24, 1970.

> The Alberta Housing Corporation has entered into an agreement with the City which calls for the gradual acquisition of those lands by the City so that they may be made available for housing and related purposes in accordance with an organized scientific developmental plan and it is further provided in that agreement . . . that if for any reason the City is unable or unwilling to acquire any part of the lands then the Crown Corporation reserves to itself the right to market it . . . elsewhere so that there will be that development throughout the whole of this large area that was anticipated by the Provincial Government and by the City when this unique enterprise was entered into . . .
> . . . that under the date of 29th of June, 1970, the City did enter into binding agreement with the Alberta Housing Corporation under which over a term of fifteen years the City must acquire the land or alternatively make it possible for the Corporation when the City fails to acquire to dispose of them otherwise.[166]

The discussions between AHC and city representatives were premised on the assumption that the city would annex the area and acquire the land when needed. As suggested by a representative of the city at an August 26, 1969, meeting:

> The city should take title at the purchase price plus a certain percentage, that the Province would act as an agent of the city, and that the city would buy the provincial holdings.[167]

AHC intended to use the profits earned on the sale of the land to the city to fund land assembly projects elsewhere.

At a Special Commission Board meeting, October 17, 1969, to announce the project publicly, the minister explained that a meeting was to be held with all concerned municipalities to resolve the question of annexation, at which time he would explain that piecemeal annexation was not a good solution. There can be little doubt, therefore, that though the administration had not committed the city to the project, no alternative to city ownership had been seriously considered.

At the Local Authorities Board hearings, the city advanced the case for annexation; in fact, there apparently was no representative of the Alberta Housing Corporation present.[168] First, the city argued that the province, through the Alberta Housing Corporation, had "acquired title to a majority of the lands in the territory . . . to allow the city or other designated bodies to successively develop the lands."

The city brief to the LAB repeated the reasons for the land assembly project, and mentioned *inter alia:*

> The City at present, has no way of guaranteeing the maintenance of an adequate supply of and reasonable price for lots. Land in the declared expansion areas is under private ownership and servicing and prices depend upon private sector decision. The decision to establish a new direction of residential growth involving annexation in the south-east is considered essential if land for housing is to be available at an uninflated value and with adequate supply. Such a decision will ensure a constant and sufficient amount of land for all forms of housing and hopefully land prices will be stabilized in the city generally.[169]

The city representative also explained that, as with the BACM application, the area had not been designated for urban use in either the city's General Plan or in the Preliminary Regional Plan, Metropolitan Part.

Thus, the city was attempting to take advantage of the opportunity created by low land prices, as had private interests in the BACM annexation. As the Preliminary Regional Plan had designated the area as low density agricultural land use, and for small-holdings, the underdeveloped nature was an advantage and would "provide for maximum flexibility in overall planning" and development of the area. If a function of planning is assumed to be to increase the predictability of development decisions, the BACM and Mill Woods annexation applications would hardly support the assumption. On the contrary, to the extent that predictability was achieved by existing plans, the decisions taken by private interests had virtually forced the city itself to take unpredictable actions — namely, the support of development not anticipated in its own official plans. The secrecy which surrounded the negotiations of the BACM acquisition of land rights and which typified the handling of events by the City Commissioners and the AHC over Mill Woods bears witness to the nature of the difficulties.

The Edmonton Regional Planning Commission filed written approval of the annexation proposal and an explanation of their policies with respect to annexation with the LAB on October 22, 1970. In justification of its past policies it added:

> It should be pointed out that this Commission's Land Use Policies and the cooperation between the member municipalities over almost twenty years, made the assembly of this area of land reasonably possible. The past policies preventing the premature fragmentation of agricultural land were effective in keeping the land units as large as possible.[170]

The County of Strathcona did not oppose the application. Although it had originally requested that the land to the west of Mill Woods to the river should be included in the annexation, the county consented to withdraw this condition to expedite the application.[171] Similarly, the ERPC had agreed that:

> the County's suggestion that the boundaries should go to the river is a logical one. However, because of the urgency in getting the south-east assembly area annexed and the complications involved in obtaining all the information for such an added area, it is the recommendation of staff that this additional area should be handled separately.[172]

The Director of City Planning, in response to the counsel for the County of Strathcona on questions as to why the city had refused to annex the area to the west, stated:

> . . . the Edmonton Regional Planning Commission does an excellent job in (preventing undesirable urbanization of scattered subdivision of land), so it would not be my personal fear that through lack of annexation of the land to the west that there is inadequate control (parenthesis added).[173]

The City Planner also suggested, in explaining the city's objections to annexation of the area to the west,

> I think that perhaps the major reason is that (in) the south-east area, there is the opportunity through the substantial public ownership characteristic of the land to develop the area with some reasonable price and have some kind of control effect on development elsewhere . . . this would not apply in the case of the strip of land that you referred to extending west to the River which is in its entirety under private ownership and where the cost in assembling land

for public purposes is part of a land bank system, could be . . . excessive compared to the south-east area.[174]

At the LAB hearings the city planner was able to state that the southern boundary would remain for twenty or thirty years; therefore, the county's counsel, concerned about the future expansion of the eastern boundary, asked if it is the "ultimate extension of this area to the east for an equal period of time." The city planner was unable to give any assurance, but he knew of no plans for residential expansion at that time.[175] Although private landowners did not in general object to the annexation they were concerned about the impact of annexation on their taxes and rights to develop. The city, in its applications, had included privately held lands in addition to land assembled by AHC. At the hearing, the city guaranteed the level of services presently provided by the County of Strathcona. The utility companies did not make an appearance at the hearings; however, Calgary Power Ltd. filed written representation requesting protection of existing rights of way and protection of its exclusive service rights in the area. This application differed from the BACM annexation in that it did not involve the Fringe Area Exchange Agreement between the city and Calgary Power Ltd.

The LAB, in annexing Mill Woods to the city, effective January 1, 1971, in large accepted the reasons advanced for the application: the need for residential land; the need to control land prices; the suitability of the area for flexible development plans; the possibility of economical development of utilities and transportation facilities. The Order also provided "bona fide" farmers protection from "urban-type" assessment and taxation, and it included the usual caveat that the Order in no way abrogated existing utility agreements.

One can speculate on the outcome had the Local Authorities Board refused the application: this was unlikely in view of the provincial involvement, but had it done so the city would then have been faced with the provincial agency, the Alberta Housing Corporation, developing a satellite on its immediate boundary. The situation was possible within the agreement between the city and the corporation. Such a situation emphasizes the danger inherent in decisions made in the context of the present land market and the administrative difficulties inherent in the current legislation. What role the province played in the decision is not fully known, but the province held a meeting with the concerned municipalities to stress the need for annexation. Also, both the County of Strathcona and the ERPC, although recognizing the logic of a larger annexation, willingly compromised to "expedite" the annexation of Mill Woods. It would appear that support for "piecemeal" annexation, in the tradition of Edmonton's boundary changes, is attainable when sufficient weight is thrown behind the measure to get the concurrence of the affected authorities. The arguments presented at the hearing by the city against the larger annexation were consistent with Edmonton's "piecemeal" tradition, although inconsistent with the city's position on adopting the Hanson Report.

Mill Woods has provided the city with some room to manoeuvre in its various relations with developers and adjacent local authorities and over city residential land prices, etc. To date there has been no decline in residential city lot prices, but the council's actions may have prevented prices rising higher. In seeking to gain a profit from its Mill Woods lots, the city was applying to land its current utility policy and continuing its post-depression policy on land assembly in the public interest. With the pressures temporarily abated the council turned again to the policy implications of the Hanson Report; but, yet once more, it did so in the practical context of yet additional "piecemeal" annexation proposals.

6 *Some Further Proposals*

In mid-July, 1971 the council's Legislative Committee recommended applying to the LAB to annex a portion of the County of Parkland. Certain other proposals, largely "filling in" the annexations of previous years, were made subsequently. The aldermen were by no means unanimous in their support of these because annexation in terms of the "Hanson Line," or a modification of it, held planning and administrative advantages. The council was on record as opposing "piecemeal" annexation.

At the February 29, 1972 council meeting, the council decided to propose to the province the desirability of establishing the Hanson boundaries. To this end, an approach was to be made to the Metropolitan Affairs Committee of the provincial cabinet. In a preliminary brief to the committee, the city wished rather than raising annexation,

> to more specifically discuss our city's boundaries and the future form of urban government in our metropolitan area.[176]

The brief reaffirmed the conclusions of the Hanson Report concerning the need for a unitary form of government for the region in order to facilitate planning, administration, and a more equitable distribution of tax revenues. The brief also stressed Hanson's conclusion that the resolution of the situation should be a responsibility of the provincial government and not of the Local Authorities Board, an agency of the government. The brief went on to explain that as a consequence of the province refusing to respond to the Hanson's recommendations and encouraging the city to negotiate the boundary issues with surrounding municipalities, only "limited success" had been realized. Therefore, at the February 29, 1972 City Council meeting, the council recommended that:

> 1. In discussions with the Metropolitan Affairs Committee, emphasis should be on the fact that unitary government

for the Edmonton socio-economic region is the underlying reason for extending our boundaries. The City is not merely engaged in a search for more living space.
2. That the area sought for annexation lies within the so-called Hanson Line, or an approximation of it, with particular reference to the County of Strathcona and the Municipal District of Sturgeon. The Western boundary has been close to satisfactorily settled.
3. That the City recommend to the Provincial Cabinet that an independent boundaries commission, perhaps comprising one commissioner, be set up to consider and recommend on the effects of Edmonton's proposed annexation on the County and the MD, and to set the boundaries. Membership on the Commission should be chosen from outside the Province. Included in the commission's terms of reference would be a study on the economic impact of expansion on the city and surrounding municipalities.
4. That the City request the Province to prohibit piecemeal annexations unless they are acceptable to the City; that is, that those initiating them agree beforehand to meet conditions desired by the City, including land dedication and price of land sold to the City for municipal purposes.
5. That the City recommend to the Provincial Government that a green belt be established outward from the City limits a distance of 10-15 miles in which further urban development be forbidden and further development of any kind be limited to parcels of not less than 40 acres.
6. That the City request the Province to pay for the proposed ring road around the City, regardless of its location inside or outside Edmonton's boundaries now or in the future. [177]

Immediately upon the city's announcing its intentions, the surrounding municipalities announced their opposition to the proposed annexation and, as had the city, made their opposition known to the province. Thus until the province makes its position known, the Edmonton boundary situation remains as it has in the 16 years since the completion of the McNally Report — the city maintaining the need for a major realignment of boundaries but faced with the prospect of small-scale annexations. It is, however, turning increasingly to the province for assistance.

Summary and Discussion

Professor E.J. Hanson was fully aware of the political and administrative complexity involved in implementing his recommendations. He envisaged the expansion of the city boundaries from 85.6 square miles to a 117-mile square plus the Namao Air Base. In 1966 the population of the toal area was 377,000 within the city and 30,000 in the outer 200-odd square miles.

He envisaged that the initial annual cost to the city would be two to three mills, but that provincial adjustment grants could readily cope with this.[178] The McNally Report of 1956 had come to roughly the same conclusion. In addition to suggesting a Commission or Committee on Government in the Edmonton Area, Hanson proposed that "comprehensive and continuous studies of the present and potential system of revenues of the City of Edmonton be undertaken, in order to widen the revenue base, and to enhance its yield in an equitable and efficient way."[179] To this end, an Intergovernmental Officer should be appointed, whose duties would also include contact with the provincial and federal governments and neighbouring municipalities.

The discussion and study involved in negotiations with provincial and affected local governments — which was to be particularly a city concern unless the other governments involved developed comparable expertise — was in part a recognition of the limitations of the LAB. Hanson observed:

> The Board is essentially an administrative one, consisting of three provincial civil servants in the Department of Municipal Affairs . . . Like any administrative board, it is expected to make decisions within the limits of public policies determined by the provincial government. It is not intended to be a policy-making, political body. The Local Authorities Board is very competent in dealing with the administrative aspects of its jurisdiction . . . The proper governmental structure of the Edmonton Metropolitan Area is a major problem, calling for decisions by the Government of the Province of Alberta, the policy-making body in this province on municipal government. We do not think it would be fair and reasonable to ask the Local Authorities Board to make what is essentially a political decision. Regardless of the decision it made, it would be accused of being partial.[180]

The city was exposing itself when entering litigation before the LAB in matters of "provincial importance and which affects the general welfare of Northern Alberta in a comprehensive way."[181] The need for negotiation with the province over the sharing of initial and transition costs of annexation was essential, but the LAB had no authority to decide what grants or payments the province should make either to the city or any other local authority. Hanson identified other reasons for the provincial government to become involved politically, administratively, and financially on these matters of crucial concern to urban affairs. The Committee or Commission on Government in the Edmonton Metropolitan Area, rather than a Royal Commission or other instrument, seemed to him most appropriate.

The difficulty with Professor Hanson's suggestion is that it remains a partial answer to a partial problem. While negotiation with the province over compensation grants to adjacent municipalities adversely affected by city annexation would assist them momentarily, the city boundary still exists in a context that will perpetuate its use in the current urban process. New transportation techniques may readily facilitate the "leapfrogging" of residential and industrial settlement in the new peripheral centres. Greater leisure resulting from a four-day work week may readily change homeowners' preferences for rural living. The responses of adjacent urban centres will remain competitive rather than constructively and mutually symbiotic and co-operative.

A study of Fort Saskatchewan conducted in June, 1970, just over two years after the Hanson report was published, outlined potential consequences for outlying communities which the Hanson Report had not considered:

> The annexation proposed in the Hanson Report includes 90 square miles of the County of Strathcona encompassing the industrial area east of Edmonton and the unincorporated residential area of Sherwood Park. It is this portion that would have the greatest effect on the Town of Fort Saskatchewan since the education for the town is provided by a shared cost system common to the County of Strathcona and Fort Saskatchewan.[182]

Comparing three alternatives: the existing school system, the residual as a consequence of annexation, and Fort Saskatchewan should it form an independent school system, the study found the costs per pupil would be $635 for the existing, $655 for the residual, and $661 for the Fort Saskatchewan system. The study also estimated the supplementary requisitions required for each system.

The consultants concluded that because of the financial consequences and the potential quality of services under either the residual or independent system that:

> If Edmonton is successful in its annexation bid for the total area suggested by the Hanson Report, Fort Saskatchewan should actively exert all the political influence it can toward the reorganization of county boundaries in the Edmonton Region with particular regard to the creation of larger joint school administrations.[183]

Although we have not verified the accuracy of this Fort Saskatchewan study, it nevertheless illustrates an issue not discussed by Hanson.

It also illustrates the likely continuation of political pressure to seek partisan advantages of short and long term consequence. Hanson's proposals, even if implemented, are not likely to change the process which has existed for so long and which in turn has generated the difficulties illustrated by the annexations.

The problems of satellite communities may in turn be

exacerbated if the city's boundaries are extended as recommended. Readily available and cheap city residential lots would threaten their developmental plans and financial commitments. Conversely, rapid transit systems, if extended to satellite communities, may in turn exacerbate the city's problems and leave it in a position of unused and vacant residential development of the type it experienced through the depression and the war years. Such contrarieties in the possible future are endemic in the current process of decision making. The irony of the situation is to be found in the fact that the provincial government and its instrumentalities are already deeply involved in the rapid transit proposals of the city and in the land assembly operations of at least one of the satellite communities (Stony Plain). Similarly, the provincial investment in the University of Athabasca has already stimulated private developers (BACM) to seek annexation of land for residential purposes outside the area taken into account in the General Plan. The city, in turn, was obliged to move with the provincial government in annexing Mill Woods, also in an area outside the General Plan. The predictability for which the Planning Act has its rationale at the general planning level, and for which the Edmonton Regional Planning Commission has in large measure a justification for existence, has been brought into question.

In several of the annexation hearings it was suggested that the Preliminary Regional Plan, Metropolitan Part, has provided a control by which low density urban development was forestalled to facilitate future comprehensive and intensive urban development. The "plan," a holding device, consists of zoning designations viewed as interim rather than final land uses. The Regional Planning Commission has complemented the Preliminary Regional Plan with a policy of concentrated decentralization particularly in existing regional urban centres. These policies are considered means of preventing "sprawl." However, the commission does not direct nor does it have the authority to promote development in these locations; it must wait for developers to approach a particular urban centre with a proposal. Its role in shaping the form of development is dependent upon decisions beyond the control of the commission. To be comprehensive, the policy of concentrated decentralization must be complemented with a plan for transportation, public utilities, and other required public services. To be effective, it will require changes in municipal finance practices.

Municipal planning controls, such as the General Plan, may provide a basis for decisions even if not formally approved. At the annexation hearings, many witnesses and submissions, and many LAB decisions, made reference to the General Plan even before it was officially adopted. However, the desirability of present municipal planning comes into question when one considers the Mill Woods and BACM decisions. In both cases, as a consequence of speculators anticipating development as recommended by the General Plan, the city was forced to support or to undertake projects not predicted by the plans. In fact, the city itself assumed that it was necessary to undertake a clandestine operation, before undertaking research or planning, to effect the land assembly. This fact suggests that the information made available in plans may contribute to excessive public "costs" through inflated land prices. Does this imply that planning information should not be revealed? This drastic measure could perhaps be obviated by a policy of integrating the taxing policies with planning policies. In many of the annexations special property tax concessions were made to classes of landholders until the property was developed for urban purposes. However, where urban development is anticipated, land prices tend to be inflated. Perhaps the appreciated value of land attributable to public actions, such as plans, should be considered a public and not a private benefit. Perhaps re-investigation should be undertaken to make operational the 1913 Planning Act provision for "betterment" by which such benefits would accrue to the municipality.

The review of the McNally and Hanson metropolitan studies and the history of annexations reveals that the sequence, timing, location, and scale of peripheral development and boundary changes may be initiated and resolved by institutions other than the city. Many of the annexation applications were initiated by private developers and the city has been obliged, often unwillingly, to evaluate the particular application to determine whether or not to support it. The decision to support a particular annexation, in turn, was determined by a particular set of issues confronting the city at that time, rather than being based upon the comprehensive and generally understood plan.

A senior official of the Regional Planning Commission has suggested that annexation procedures be revised. The Local Authorities Board, upon receiving an application for annexation, should refer the question to the planning authorities affected to permit them to analyze the application from a planning point of view prior to the LAB proceeding further. This would establish a checkpoint in the process and would considerably alter the planner's role. Rather than merely providing evidence at the public hearing that is received and reviewed on an equal basis with evidence presented by other witnesses, planning policies could provide a framework or a context within which other evidence would be considered. The suggestion appears to have considerable merit only under conditions where a larger-scale plan than presently available has been announced by a governmental authority with power sufficient to make it stick. If implemented under existing arrangements, the suggestion would only compromise further the relationship of professional planners to the elected representatives of government.

At the 1970 Alberta Urban Municipalities Association (AUMA) annual conference, the association supported a City of Edmonton resolution that the Municipal Government Act be amended to require that requests for annexation must have the approval of either the municipality in which the application area is situated, or the municipality to which the area is to be annexed. The government replied:

> The Government is not prepared to implement this request as it would in effect be a denial of individual rights and would also make ineffectual the Local Authorities Board's decision making powers.

The reply was consistent with the province's commitment to individual autonomy but it avoided acknowledging the consequences such a position has on the affairs of a particular local authority or region. The comment with respect to the role of the Local Authorities Board is difficult to interpret. Possibly the provincial government was unaware of the reality of the urban situation and the inherent difficulties of the LAB as presently constituted, which Professor Hanson so clearly identified.

The AUMA resolution concerning the question of who may initiate an annexation application is of particular concern only under the present structure of affairs. When, as has occurred frequently in the past, individuals or developers are successful in convincing the LAB to annex regardless of the plans, priorities, or budgets of the municipality, the municipality is put into the position of responding to these decisions rather than predetermining its own development. The province failed to adopt the metropolitan boundaries recommended by the McNally Report or those of the Hanson Report. The failure to establish a metropolitan, regional, or provincial development policy is consistent with the province's commitment to the concept of local autonomy, in that to adopt the boundary recommended in either report, the province would have had to impose its will *post hoc* against the protests of the surrounding municipalities. Likewise, the Local Authorities Board's decision in 1964 in response to the County of Strathcona's objections to annexation of the industrial areas, in part reflects a concern of the county's autonomy.

Yet the case studies of annexations suggest that the provincial principle has not been consistently applied. Annexations have been granted or refused without compensation for the inequities which may be attributable to the changed or existing municipal boundaries. A commitment to the concept of local autonomy must acknowledge that it entails costs and benefits to different parties. The lack of regional or provincial development guidelines, in part, forces local authorities to plan and to adopt policies as if they were independent of the region. Annexation applications were usually advanced or opposed in terms of particular internal situations. The net result of such a perspective is to foster a competitive relationship between local authorities—a competitive relationship which in turn ironically places urban affairs under the *de facto* determination by federal policies and the decisions of national and international lending institutions.

Municipal Finance and City Growth

In this section we sketch the state of city finances and then proceed to discuss the mode of handling Edmonton's finances as they relate to the predictions of city growth. The two themes recurrent over many decades — that increasing assistance will be required from senior governments, and that property tax is inadequate to meet the increasingly diversifying services which the city is obliged to provide and operate — remain as pronounced today as ever they have been. Our emphasis is not on any particular solution to these themes; but rather on the mode of administration, the design of action and interaction, adopted by the city either in response to or as initiator of the recurrent situation with which it is faced. The cities of Alberta documented their dilemma in 1968.[184]

The federal and provincial governments sought answers to the same metropolitan financing problem particularly in the 1960s. Inherent in it is a more general, national problem which concerns the relation of urban physical expansion, in the form of public and private investment to ensure "growth," and the human problems of unemployment, "alienation," and behavioural aberrations of many kinds. Related also is the degradation of vast areas of Canada, and to a lesser extent of Alberta, which the federal government's industrial incentives legislation and other programs have been aimed at mitigating. We do not intend to raise these matters in this section, though the fundamental question of the nature and rate of metropolitan growth vis-a-vis the remainder of the province and the nation are implicit in our discussion.

Capital Expenditures

Although considerable attention is currently being focussed on the ability of municipal governments to cope with financial requirements, no long-range development guidelines with their financial implications have been adopted by the City of Edmonton. The Public School Board, in its report 'Accommodation Report and Building Program 1971,' states emphatically that until the city adopts a program of urban growth, it cannot prepare a long-range capital budget.[185] In spite of the Public School Board's position that capital estimates cannot be prepared until development guidelines have been established, the Commission Board has prepared the *Estimates of Capital Expenditures for the Years 1971-1980,* and the *1971 Current Budget* which includes a five-year projection of general expenditures and revenues. These projections include only municipal government finances and are exclusive to the financial requirements of school facilities. The *Estimates,* which were prepared prior to the adoption of the General Plan, were not prepared in the context of an officially adopted plan or a specific program of development. Appendices Nos. 1 and 2 of the General Plan contain various outline plans which appear to have formed, at least in part, the basis for predicting future capital requirements.[186] The General Plan, as adopted, does not provide a fixed program of development, but rather indicates the probable location and timing

Table 30. Capital Estimates, 1971-1980 (*in thousands of dollars*)

		1970 $	*% of Total*	*1971* $	*% of Total*	*1972* $	*% of Total*	*1973* $	*% of Total*	*1974* $
Transportation	Transit	636		1,074		14,957		19,547		20,902
	Engineer's Dept.									
	Public Works[1]	12,600		11,429		11,390		11,390		11,390
	Miscellaneous	1,470		2,493		2,545		1,435		1,125
	Airport	805		426		530		552		570
	Sub-Total	15,511	20.9	15,422	18.2	29,422	27.9	32,924	33.5	33,987
	Annual % Change			-0.6		90.8		11.9		32.2
Utilities & General	Water & Sanitation	12,292		15,811		16,864		12,886		9,923
	Street Lighting[2]	995		755		615		637		611
	Water Mains[2]	585		720		755		790		825
	Lateral Sewers[2]	3,800		3,572		3,314		3,340		3,560
	Walks & Paving[2]	6,010		6,532		6,150		6,455		6,565
	Boulevards[2]	10		10		10		10		10
	Edmonton Power	10,776		9,913		11,172		11,673		12,030
	Edmonton Telephones	12,698		12,917		13,723		13,318		11,794
	Garage	580		854		975		725		775
	Property & Building Management	1,085		8,200		11,228		3,662		3,663
	Sub-Total	48,831	65.9	59,284	69.9	64,806	61.5	53,496	54.5	49,756
	Annual % Change			21.4		9.3		-17.5		-7.0
Protection of Persons & Property	Fire	446		856		826		650		618
	Police			799						
	Sub-Total	446	0.6	1,655	2.0	826	0.8	650	0.7	618
	Annual % Change			271.1		-50.1		-21.3		-4.9
Community Services	Health	185		185				185		
	Land	4,422		5,000		5,000		5,000		5,000
	Library	130		30		30		430		16
	Parks & Recreation	4,078		5,171		5,171		5,532		4,900
	Social Service	50		75		75				75
	Royal Alexandra Hospital	472								
	Sub-Total	9,337	12.6	8,433	10.0	10,276	9.8	11,147	11.4	9,991
	Annual % Change			-9.7		21.9		8.5		-10.4
	TOTAL	74,125		84,794		105,330		98,217		94,352
	Annual % Change			14.4		24.2		-6.8		-3.9

[1]Contains only that portion of public works for which the city must borrow debentures.
[2]Local Improvements (property share)
Source: Estimates of Capital Expenditures for the Years 1971-1980 Summary, City of Edmonton

of future developments. The BACM and Mill Woods annexations, neither of which were anticipated in the 1967 draft General Plan, illustrate that the General Plan can be drastically altered within a very short period. Similarly, the capital costs of telephone services in newly annexed areas and the costs of participating in co-axial television, were not included in the *Estimates*. The *Estimates* did provide a base line to which could be added additional identified projects whose starting dates were flexible. It also gave some order to the arrangement of priorities.

The omission of the capital costs of the telephone system must be taken in the context of the current dispute between the city and the Alberta Government Telephones over the right to provide services to areas outside the 1963 city boundaries, but which have been or will be annexed since that date. As these are not included in the *Estimates,* both the costs and revenues of future growth are understated. Similarly, the *Estimates* were prepared without detailed

% of Total	1975 $	% of Total	Total $	1971-75 % of Total	Total $	1976-80 % of Total	Total $	1971-80 % of Total	% Change 1971-75	Ratio of % Change of Expend. to % Change of Pop. 1971-1975
	24,422		*80,902*		*19,745*		100,647			
	11,390		56,989		56,825		113,814			
	1,385		8,983		6,775		15,758			
	582		2,660		3,051		5,711			
33.0	37,779	37.2	149,524	30.9	86,396	18.7	235,930	25.0	145.0	10.43
	11.2									
	10,301		65,785		52,823		118,608			
	637		3,255		3,370		6,625			
	870		3,960		5,030		8,990			
	3,790		17,576		21,125		38,701			
	6,565		32,267		30,450		62,717			
	10		50		50		100			
	14,477		59,265		100,896		160,161			
	11,446		63,198		58,930		122,128			
	1,100		4,429		4,950		9,379			
	3,660		30,413		43,785		74,198			
52.7	52,856	52.1	280,198	57.9	321,409	69.7	601,607	63.6	-10.8	-0.78
	6.2									
	590		3,540		2,735		6,275			
	374		1,173				1,173			
0.7	964	0.9	4,713	1.0	2,735	0.6	7,448	0.8	-41.8	-3.01
	56.0									
			370		185		555			
	5,000		25,050		25,000		50,050			
	16		586		1,152		1,738			
	4,897		23,554		23,448		47,502			
			200		225		425			
10.6	9,913	9.8	49,760	10.3	50,510	11.0	100,270	10.6	17.6	1.27
	-0.1									
	101,512		484,205		461,050		945,255		19.7	1.42
	7.6									

reference to the effect of the location or form of city growth resulting from recent annexations. The capital estimates appear to be based on extrapolations of present trends, and demonstrate a continued commitment to both the rate and form of growth that has taken place in the city, i.e., contiguous growth at the periphery and increasing densities in the existing, older, built-up areas. Keeping in mind these limitations, the *Estimates* may be taken only as statistically indicative of the order of the city's future capital demands during the budget period.

Table 30 indicates that for the period 1971 to 1975, yearly capital demands, which are shown to be at a maximum in 1972, are projected to be 19.7 percent greater in 1975 than in 1971, i.e., to increase from $84,794,000 in 1971 to $101,512,000 in 1975. The requirements are projected to fluctuate considerably from year to year. Over the five year period 1971-75, a total of $484,205,000 is estimated. The total requirements for the subsequent five year period, 1976-1980, are projected to decline to $461,050,000.

For the period 1971-75, transportation facilities are estimated to require ever increasing amounts — from 18.2 percent ($15,422,000) of the total capital requirements in 1971 to 37.2 percent ($32,779,000) in 1975, or an increase of 145 percent. This increase is attributed to transport which is projected to increase from $1,074,000 in 1971 to $24,422,000 in 1975. In the detailed accounts [187] (not presented here) rapid transit is projected at $430,000 in 1971, $13,455,000 in 1972, $17,500,000 in 1973, $18,800,000 in 1974, and $22,700,000 in 1975. In the 1976-1980 period, transit capital requirements are estimated to be only about one-quarter of the previous period, thus making transport costs in general decline from about 31 percent ($149,534,000) for 1971-75 to about 19 percent ($86,396,000) for 1976-80 of the total capital requirements.[188]

During both the 1971-75 and 1976-80 periods major public works (freeways, bridges, etc.) were projected at $8,430,000 in 1971, and $8,800,000 for all years 1972 to 1980 (the details are not shown separately in Table 30, but are included in Public Works expenditures). This could prove to be very inaccurate should the city undertake the proposed freeway system outlined in the Metropolitan Edmonton Transportation Study (METS). This was a study of the roadway transportation requirements of Edmonton and its region, completed in 1963 for the Edmonton Regional Planning Commission. An independent study made subsequently of the projected freeway system concluded that the predicted costs of the original study were grossly underestimated.[189] Experience in other cities, e.g., the Spadina Expressway in Toronto, tends to confirm that original estimated costs are often underestimated by an order of magnitude of two or more.[190]

Of the $8.8 million to be allocated to major Public Works each year, $3.8 million is projected to be a provincial grant. The estimates appear to have been based upon the assumption that the provincial government will continue to provide roadway grants at approximately the same level as it has since 1966. This level was described by W. E. Gillespie, Roadway Design Engineer, City of Edmonton, as follows:

> In 1966, the Province passed legislation providing $50 million over a five year period for assistance to Alberta Urban Centers in developing new Transportation Facilities. Edmonton's share of these funds amounted to some $22.5 million, averaging out at $4.5 million per year. With these funds being matched by the City, some $9.0 million per year has been spent on Edmonton's major projects. A further expenditure of around $4.0 million per year by the City on the normal street paving program brings the total to around $13.0 million per year.
> The province shared in costs as follows: Freeways — 75% of construction; Approved Arterials — 50%.[191]

In April 1970, the provincial government adopted a new "Act Respecting Transportation Systems in Cities." According to this Act, in order to qualify for provincial transportation grants, a city must:

1. Undertake and/or complete a comprehensive area-wide Transportation Study.
2. The City Council shall by by-law establish a transportation system in accordance with the Transportation Report, and the by-law shall designate the transportation system.
3. After second reading of the by-law, City Council shall hear and consider representations of any interested party.
4. After the by-law is passed, the City may enter into a Cost Sharing Agreement with the Province covering any approved facility within the system.[192]

The City Council passed the required by-law on December 23, 1971, after a considerable delay following the second reading given in April, 1971. The proposed by-law was tabled at that time because of public opposition and disagreement with the Council over the contents of the by-law. The by-law was eventually adopted to qualify for provincial grants, but the city does not have a comprehensive transportation system plan, only a number of uncoordinated sections of roadway to which council had consented at some time in the past.[193] The by-law has already been amended by City Council on March 27, 1972, to include rapid transit.

Provincial transportation grants have been available only for roadway development—design, engineering, and construction,—but not for studies or land acquisition,—and not for public transportation in general. This may in part explain the emphasis which the city has placed on roadway construction. Also, in order that the city might both take advantage of the provincial money and at the same time minimize land acquisition costs, the city adopted a plan of developing transportation facilities largely on city-owned land—primarily the ravines and the river valley.[194] Much concern has been expressed by citizen groups and individuals about the destruction of the city's natural amenities by such roadways—a destruction which the city finds convenient to attribute to the influence of provincial policy on city priorities.

General Municipal and Utilities expenditures, for the period 1971-75, are projected to decline from almost 70 percent in 1971 to 52 percent of the total capital requirements in 1975, i.e., an absolute decline of $6,428,000. However, as noted for transportation, within the time interval there is considerable fluctuation from year to year. For the interval 1976-1980, a large, predicted investment in Edmonton Power and Generation contributes to an increase of almost 15 percent over the 1971-75 total, i.e., and increase from $280,192,000 to $321,409,000. This will increase the proportional share of the total capital requirements for this category from about 58 percent for 1971-75 to about 70 percent for 1976-1980.

Over the period 1971-1980, the share of total capital costs required under the heading "Community Services," is predicted to remain almost constant at around 10 percent. "Protection of Persons and Property" is estimated at about 2.0 percent ($1,655,000) for 1971, but in subsequent years this is predicted to require between 0.6 percent and 1.0 percent of the total capital requirements. The item is estimated to decline by about 42 percent for the period 1976-1980 ($2,735,000) from 1971-75 period ($4,713,000).

A comparison of the estimated annual capital expenditures with the estimated annual increase of population is complicated by the large fluctuation or "lumpiness" of capital expenditures from year to year. In Table 31 below the estimated capital expenditures are expressed as a three-year running average and are then related to the estimated city population.

Table 31. Estimated capital expenditures and population, City of Edmonton, 1970-75

Year	*Averaged capital expenditure $'000*	*Estimated population**	*Ratio $ per capita*
1970	74,125	435,000	170.40
1971	88,061	450,800	195.34
1972	96,258	465,600	206.74
1973	99,466	481,000	206.79
1974	98,194	496,900	197,61
1975	97,932	513,000	190.90

*Population estimates are derived from "1971 Current Budget, Summary Schedule," City of Edmonton, p. 63.

The Table suggests that the per capita expenditures are estimated to increase from 1970 to a peak in 1972-73 and then to decline below the averaged figure for 1971. Over the period 1971-75 capital expenditures are estimated to increase from $84,729,000 to $101,512,000 (Table 30) or an increase of 19.7 percent. The estimated increase in population is from 450,000 to 513,000 (Table 31) or an increase of 13.9 percent. Thus capital expenditures are estimated to increase faster than population by a ratio of 1.42:1 over the five years, with the ratio between 1971 and 1973 being very much greater. Disaggregated by the sub-headings in Table 30, the same ratio for transportation is 4.26 to 1, -0.88 to 1 for general municipal and utilities expenditures, -5.16 to 1 for protection of persons and property, and 1.08 to 1 for community services. These ratios are very much influenced by the particular years selected because of the great fluctuations estimated to occur from year to year. The ratios, even when more reliably determined, only become meaningful when compared to the costs of providing services in urban areas of different sizes — a topic where much research is needed.

Capital Revenues

The City of Edmonton will be increasingly dependent for the financing of its capital programs upon "to be arranged" debenture borrowing, i.e., from sources other than those currently available from various public agencies both provincial and federal.[195] Utility reserves, which have traditionally played a significant role in City finances, are projected throughout the period 1971-75 to be approximately 2.5 percent below the estimated 1970 contribution of $6,334,000.

The "to be arranged" debentures for the period 1971 to 1975 increase 94.7 percent from $23.3 million to $45.4 million. The "to be arranged" debentures constitute 38.0 percent of all debenture needs in 1971 ($60.5 million), and increase to 58.8 percent in 1975 ($77.3 million). The city is likely, therefore, to become increasingly dependent on other sources of capital than the Municipal Finance Corporation (estimated to provide $21.750 million in 1971 and $24.476 million in 1975). For the total period 1971 to 1975, debentures make up 75.5 percent (and fluctuate between 71.4 percent and 78.1 percent of total capital revenue) as compared with 65.2 percent in 1970. These comparisons illustrate the urgency of the city's demand for access to greatly increased capital revenue if its anticipated programs are to be fulfilled. A similar picture emerges with regard to running expenditures and revenues.

Running Expenditures and Revenues

No projections of current expenditures by specific categories are available. The total expenditure requirements, 1971-75, as estimated in the 1971 budget estimates, are given in Table 32. This Table suggests that there will be an anticipated increase of expenditure of 45.6 percent (from $78.3 million in 1971 to $114.1 million in 1975) over the five year period, as against a 36.4 percent increase in revenues. There is to be an anticipated increase of 70.2 percent in receipts from municipal taxes. The mill rate is predicted to move from 24.50 in 1971 to 32.13 in 1975 (a 31.1 percent increase), and the assessment base from $872.0 million to $1,131.6 million (a 30 percent increase). The percentage of the total revenue which local taxes are anticipated to provide increases from 27.3 percent to 31.9 percent over the five years. The actual situation does not appear to be working out quite as predicted even at this early stage.

In the 1972 Current Budget Overview, the changes in general expenditures and revenues for the period 1968-1972 were analyzed by the Commissioner of Economic Affairs.[196] As illustrated in Figure 5, "the potential impact on property tax is dramatically increased by a combined fall-off in government grants and utility contributions."[197]

As the provincial grants level off and the contributions of utilities play a lesser role, the burden is transferred onto property as a major alternative municipal revenue source. As explained by a representative of the city, the potential increases in utility rates are

Table 32. City of Edmonton general revenue and expenditures (excluding schools) five year projections, 1971-1975
(in thousands of dollars)

	1971	*1972*	*Percentage difference 1971-72*	*1973*
Expenditures	78,326	86,404	10.3	95,207
Revenues	56,961	62,282	9.3	66,571
Municipal taxes	21,365	24,122	12.9	28,636
Assessment base	872,047	979,549	12.3	1,026,858
Mills	24.50	24.62	0.5	27.89
Taxes as percentage of total revenues	27.3	27.9		30.1

Assumptions:
1. That 1971 estimates as submitted to City Council will be approved.
2. That population will increase as estimated.
3. That existing intergovernmental fiscal relationships will not change.
4. That the proposed new method of financing hospitals not be considered; effect on deficit of Royal Alexandra Hospital cannot yet be determined.

dependent upon comparative rates of services elsewhere: e.g., Edmonton Telephones' rates are largely determined by AGT rates. The city administration believes that until utility rates are increased elsewhere, the city cannot increase rates for city-owned utilities.

Other city representatives suggest that utility reserves have been used in the past as general revenue to keep the mill rate at an artificially low level, but that this may have been at the expense of maintaining adequate reserves to finance future expansion of city-owned utilities. The administration and the council are now beginning to recognize the need to maintain sufficient reserves to ensure that the utilities are able to finance their own expansion, but this requires that property tax makes up more of the city's general revenues. The city representative also suggested that the projected property tax increase will be serious relative only to the historical situation in the city.[198] If the projected property tax increase is approved for 1972, the percentage increase of 27.9 shown in Table 32 for the year 1972 will be increased to 38.4 percent of total general revenues — as is illustrated in Figure 1. The increase in capital expenditure under the heading "General Municipal Utilities" for 1972 (Table 30) suggests that the city is moving to upgrade these revenue-producing services. Increases are estimated for water and sanitation, Edmonton power, Edmonton Telephones, garage, and local property improvements.

The rapid increase in running expenditures (45.6 percent) compares with the 19.7 percent increase estimated for capital expenditures over the same period. In contrast with the fluctuating nature of capital expenditures, annual running expenditure is predicted to increase at a relatively constant rate of about 10 percent per annum. When related to the estimated population increase of the

Percentage difference 1972-73	1974	Percentage difference 1973-74	1975	Percentage difference 1974-75	Percentage difference 1971-75
10.2	104,866	10.2	114,052	8.8	45.6
6.9	71,574	7.5	77,699	8.6	36.4
18.7	33,292	16.3	36,353	9.2	70.2
4.8	1,077,525	4.9	1,131,592	5.0	29.8
13.3	30.89	10.8	32.13	4.0	31.1
	31.8		31.9		

5. That the contribution from city owned utilities will not change substantially from the 1971 amount.

Source: The City of Edmonton 1971 Current Budget, Summary Schedules, p. 64.

city, the increase in general running expenditure is in the ratio of 3.28:1.

Discussion

The foregoing data suggest that the city is faced with the dilemma that the rate of increase of capital and current expenditures will exceed that of income from traditional revenue sources. In consequence, the city must increasingly rely on "to be arranged" debentures and increased property taxes, or else face a reduction in the quantity and/or quality of services. In 1972 the city was considering the adoption of a 'no growth' current budget, by which was meant no increase in services or staff in spite of population increase. However, even a 'no growth' budget would mean between a 5 and 6 mill property tax increase, a representative of the city explained, in order to cover increases in wages and salaries, inflation, and similar attritions.

Should monies not be available for the projected debenture borrowing, will it be possible to transfer more of the financial responsibility onto property taxes? As was pointed out by the Canadian Federation of Mayors and Municipalities:

> These taxes notoriously lag in their response to economic growth. Being regressive, they are subject to increasing taxpayer resistance as they are pushed toward the limits of political acceptability. As a result, municipalities are increasingly dependent on provincial government grants which are often of the conditional nature so regularly criticized as stultifying to provincial authority when applied in a federal-provincial context.[199]

Figure 5

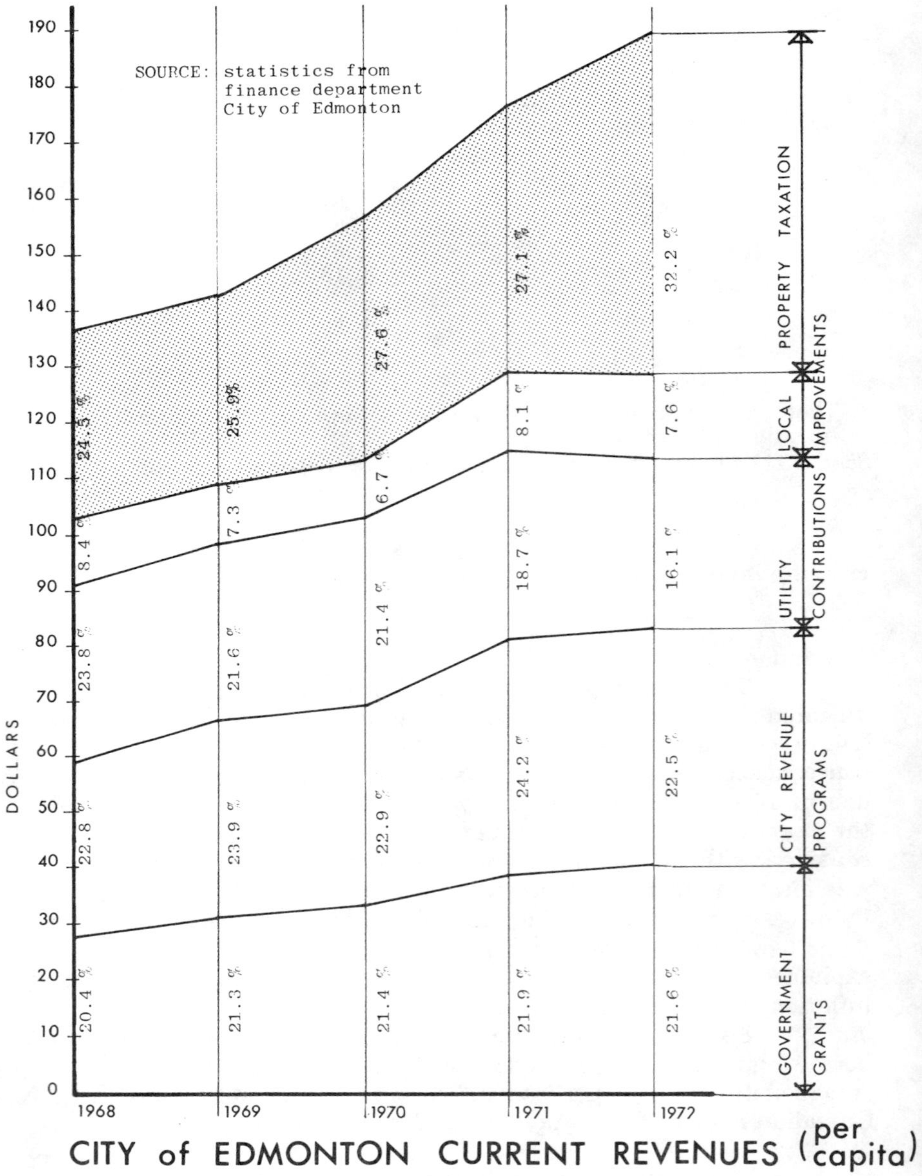

As transferring an increasing share of future municipal cost to property taxes may not be politically feasible, the city can realize the quality of services upon which the budget estimates are based, by either greatly increasing its debenture debt (and, in turn, increasing property taxes because of debt charges) or by establishing new financial and decision-making relationships with the higher levels of government. Like other metropolitan centres of Canada it is urgently pressing for the latter, but on terms that do not compromise "local autonomy."

The reliance on "to be arranged" debentures raises a number of concerns: the availability of funds in outside money markets, the possibility of high interest rates, and the impact of debt service charges on current expenditures. It also warrants an examination of the way in which the city plans its own affairs. The draft General Plan, prepared in 1967, states:

> Future expenditure policies will require a very careful evaluation of the City's financial position in relation to its outstanding debenture debt and the existing foreseeable revenue sources.[200]
>
> In 1966, approximately one out of every five revenue dollars was spent in retiring debt charges, more than any other category, excluding education costs. This is approximately five percent higher than the rate recommended by municipal finance experts. Edmonton was burdened with the third highest per capita debenture debt (excluding school debt, net self-supporting public utility debt and sinking fund) of the twelve largest cities in Canada in 1964 (parenthesis original).[201]

This is the case despite the very favourable terms on which local authorities were able to borrow from the Alberta Municipal Finance Corporation. The Commission Board pointed out in 1970 that:

> Over the past few years, the City has embarked on a major capital expansion program. Borrowings for general purposes have been substantial. Moreover, during the same period, interest rates reached record high levels, repayment of these borrowings is now reflected in current operations. Debt charges now represent 25.7 percent of City Expenditures.[202]

At the City Council meeting, concern was expressed over the level of debt service charges and the council recommended:

> A review must be made as to the desirable level of debt service charges in relation to total current expenditures and a program established to aim for the relationship shown to be desirable.
>
> It is recommended that such a study be undertaken for a separate report to Council for consideration and discussion.[203]

Table 33 provides a comparison of the city's 1969 debenture debt with those in other Alberta cities.

Table 33. Comparative debenture debt over nine Alberta cities, 1969.

Debt charges	*Total ($)*	*$/Capita*	*Percentage of total current expenditures*[1]
Edmonton	16,704,848	40.70	26.3
Calgary	13,826,120	37.50	25.9
Lethbridge	1,339,100	34.60	22.8
Red Deer	982,793	36.50	25.0
Medicine Hat	477,875	18.60	13.8
Grande Prairie	441,375	37.20	30.8
Camrose	225,266	25.40	19.6
Wetaskiwin	196,206	30.50	27.8
Drumheller	77,559	14.80	12.9

[1]Only certain categories of current expenditures are included in the Table. Those excluded are recreation, provision for revenues, contributions to general capital and loan fund, and joint and special expenditures which are included in the Department of Municipal Affairs' data.
Source: Municipal Statistics Including Improvement Districts in Special Areas for the Year Ended December 31, 1969, Department of Municipal Affairs, Edmonton.

Edmonton has the highest per capita debt charges, but when taken as a percentage of total current expenditures, Grande Prairie and Wetaskiwin have higher rates, and Calgary and Red Deer expend comparable portions of their general revenues on debt charges. Also, from data available in the same Municipal Affairs report, it is noted that approximately one-third of the Edmonton debt charges are attributable to public utilities, which are revenue producing. Only Medicine Hat, with 42 percent of its debt charges attributable to public utilities, exceeded the City of Edmonton; the provincial average for all Alberta cities was 26.9 percent.

A variety of reports to City Council have expressed concern over the financial implications of future city growth. The arguments and suggestions of three of these — the City Planning Department, the school boards, and the City Commission Board — are now briefly reviewed.

The City Planning Department

The City Planning Department, in the draft General Plan, argued that the city would not be able to meet all future capital demands:

> The City of Edmonton is currently on the verge of the largest capital expenditure in its history. Roadway and bridge proposals, Civic Centre Development, servicing of new areas, school expenditures, urban renewal and the maintenance of adequate utility service that will require financing. It is clear that present sources of revenue are inadequate to meet

> all the City's needs and it is essential that the public receive the best value for every dollar spent. Since all demands for new public facilities cannot be satisfied, good financial planning is necessary to ensure the optimum allocation of resources within the financial capacity of the City. Good financial planning will only be achieved through the implementation of a sophisticated *Capital improvement program* (emphasis added).[204]

The plan then pointed to one of the administrative lacunae involved:

> . . . In general, the capital estimates listed capital items projected by individual departments. While such listing is valuable in providing an indication of the general level of future capital expenditures, the presently established procedure does not allow for the preparation of priority listings or a careful review of the City's proposed capital expenditures in light of community goals or General Plan objectives.[205]

The plan suggested capital improvement programming as a technique by which the city could establish prorities and long-range capital programming:

> A capital improvement program is a long-range plan of capital expenditures extending over a period ranging from fifteen to twenty years. The program provides a picture of work to be performed and financial estimates. The program also consists of a capital improvement budget which covers the first five years of the program and an annual operating budget.[206]
>
> The capital budgeting process or the implementation of the capital improvement program originates with the preparation of a long-range physical improvements program.
>
> . . . On the basis of information received as to rate and direction of growth and objectives of City development, each Department will prepare cost estimates of the desired public improvements. Concurrently, the Finance Department must prepare a long-range financial analysis of the City's future revenue patterns. Following completion of the departmental estimates and a financial plan, the Department Heads will transmit their requests to the Planning Department which will then assemble and coordinate the estimates submitted. The responsibility of coordinating the long-range estimates lies with the Planning Department in view of the close relationship between a capital improvement program and the General Plan.[207]
>
> While coordinating the long-range estimates, the Planning Department must also prepare a tentative schedule of

> priorities keeping in mind such major considerations as the City's financial position, the objectives of the General Plan and the relationship between the design and timing of projects and Provincial plans.[208]
> Capital programming emphasizes planning and is a valuable technique for centering attention on classes of expenditures which are difficult to evaluate and finance. A capital budgeting program for the City of Edmonton will provide a means of assuring that projects will be executed in accordance with predetermined priorities of need as well as the ability of the City to pay.[209]

The emphasis of the Planning Department's proposal was on the rationalization of the planning and decision-making processes. The department was not suggesting a program for urban development nor commenting upon the uncalculated effects of annexations on the costs of growth. Rather, it was suggested a means for optimizing the use of available revenues through improved planning techniques.

The question of how to implement the institutional change required within the city administration — and thereby to establish the Planning Department in such a crucial role — was not asked. Resistance to such a change in part explains the actions taken on the proposal to date. At the City Council meeting November 16, 1970, to review the General Plan clause by clause, the proposal on the department's Capital Improvement Program was referred:

> City Council directed that the Chapter dealing with Financing and Programming be referred back to the Planning Department for consultation with the Finance Department for further enunciation of the principles and objectives.[210]

At the May 18, 1971, meeting of City Council, the original principle that: "The capital improvement program should be prepared by the Planning Department and reviewed and revised concurrently with the General Plan five year revisions,"was amended to:

> The Commission Board should be responsible for the preparation of a capital improvement program, with the establishment of an effective procedure within the administration to accomplish this, through the establishment of appropriate administrative procedures incorporating advanced budgetary techniques.[211]

Thus, the function was assigned to the Commission Board, to supplement the co-ordinatory responsibilities for which this level of administration is concerned. Capital improvement planning and co-ordination was to lie with an executive office rather than with a functional department. As set out in the draft General Plan, the preparation of the five year capital improvement budget was to be the responsibility of the Finance Department.

As amended at the May 18, 1971 council meeting, the one-year capital improvement budgets were to be presented in sufficient detail to permit evaluation of "the implications such expenditures may have on the annual operating budget of the City" and "its effect on subsequent operating budgets." Present procedures do not make explicit the implications of present programs on the future financial situation of the city. As explained by a senior city administrator, capital expenditures provide the foundation for development and once development occurs the city is confronted with the operating costs. It is essential when considering capital expenditures that the concomitant operating costs not be ignored — "The surprise that tends to be expressed at each annual budget is unnecessary. With more effective planning perhaps the surprise element could be eliminated or at least reduced."[212]

Although the principle of capital improvement programming has been adopted, a planner with the city suggested that it is still a very grey area. Its transfer to the commission board may lead to difficulties. Since the Planning Department does not report to the board through the Commissioner of Economic Affairs, but rather through the Commissioner of Public Affairs, the Planning Department would appear to be effectively removed from the budgeting process. Other criteria than the rationality and co-ordination of planning would appear to have been applied. For example, the discussion of annexation decisions showed the questionable feasibility of capital improvement programming within the existing structural arrangements. Many decisions influencing the cities capital improvements are made outside the jurisdiction of local government— not the least of which are the Local Authorities Board decisions on annexation applications and the "understandings" reached with the management of large scale private companies and the City Commissioners. The city is virtually obliged to establish its priorities within constraints imposed upon it from outside rather than within the framework of an "optimum" plan for development for either the city or the metropolitan region. The resistance to the proposal made by the Planning Department appears to be due not to an unwillingness on the part of the city to plan and develop concertedly, but to the unfeasibility of such planning in the context of uncertainty within which the city is placed.[213]

In 1967 the City Planning Department prepared a report, *Presidential Land Use Staging 1967-1971,* which recommended a five-year program of residential development at the periphery of the city. Though a valiant first attempt, the report suffers from some omissions. The report did not indicate why growth would occur in specific locations, nor did it estimate the costs of the recommended staging plan — although the utilities expansion and roadways were considered in determining the feasibility of development, actual costs were not projected. The scheduling of services and their costs, such as school facilities, were not mentioned. Similarly, the significance of the process by which land was to be annexed to the city, and the impact of land ownership on staging, were not investigated. No mention was made of the proposed change in subdivision servicing policy, by which the developer was to be responsible for financing of all subdivision services. City Council declined to adopt the proposed plan, largely on account of the last two factors. Council was concerned that by committing itself to a specific program, land speculators would be provided with information with which to ensure maximum profits through the diminution of speculative risk, and thereby be afforded the potential to create a land monopoly. Council decided that because of the new subdivision policy, which was adopted on February 12, 1968, a staging plan was not required.[214]

Both the Planning Department's proposals apparently failed to acknowledge the politics in which policy changes were made. We conclude therefore, that any proposal for improving the budgetary process must make explicit not only the planning, management, and control functions of the budget, but also the various interdependencies of power relations involved. This operational component of the budget, in addition to the quantities of money involved, appears to be critical in the process of putting order into the financing of city development.

The School Boards. The Public School Board pointed out that it is impractical and unwise to prepare a long-range capital budget in the present context of uncertainties:

> The uncertainties related to the three major factors which will affect development in all Outline Plan areas [(a) the availability and the cost of borrowing money for land development and housing construction; (b) City Council's approval or rejection of individual Outline Plans and conclusion of development agreements between land owners and the City; (c) Council's attitude toward the adoption of a plan of development] result in a development picture so obscure that any attempt at long-range capital budget projection would be inappropriate and makes even short-term decisions increasingly difficult (parenthesis added).[215]

The Public and Separate School Boards in their joint brief to council were primarily concerned with residential development at the fringe of the city. These growth areas generate the greatest demand for capital investment in school facilities. The brief emphasized the need for the rationalization of the planning process *per se*.

> The timing of development of new areas is almost as critical as the total number. If not carefully programmed, we will certainly be unable to comply with demands for new schools as our capital expenditure is funded on an annual basis by the Provincial Government and this capital allotment is relatively fixed. It is, therefore, distinctly to our advantage from the point of view of levelling capital expenditure if the demand for new schools is a steady demand, which can only be brought about by careful programming by the City. Failure to level our capital expenditure will give rise to

severe accommodation and trasportation problems in peak expenditure years, and a permanent siphoning off of capital funds to other areas of the Province in non-peak years. Surges in capital expenditure which are beyond our control will, undoubtedly, be followed by equally uncontrollable surges in operating costs. Such increases are particularly significant in view of the Provincial Government's proposal for a 6% annual escalation in School Board operating costs, and would result in an increase in the amounts that we would be forced to request by plebiscite.[216]

We would suggest that sufficient variety of areas to satisfy public taste and the provision of serviced land at reasonable cost could be accommodated by the development of fewer than 11 new areas, especially as the 2,500 acre City-owned development in the south-east (Mill Woods) should give Council effective control of the residential land market . . . In our considered view, the development of the south-east area and the City's control of the land market in land, makes staging of residential development practical.[217]

If we are to maintain the present standard of education presently offered in this city, and if we are to be in a position to both improve facilities and programs in the older schools, the City Council's cooperation in keeping expenditure on new schools at a reasonable level is essential.[218]

Both the Planning Department and the school boards were expressing concern with the financial implications of the present and future growth of the city, but their conclusions were significantly different. The Planning Department suggested that all future capital demands cannot be met from available resources, but if new decision tools were adopted, the payoff from expenditures could be optimized. The message stressed in the school boards' brief was that they were unable to provide necessary future accommodation if the present dispersed and unplanned growth was allowed to continue. This situation threatened a reduction in the quality of service. However, the condition of their meeting the demands upon them was a development program that utilized facilities to a maximum. A continuation of the cyclical pattern of both capital and operating costs could significantly affect the quality of their service and contribute to an increase in debt charges.

The Planning Department's advocacy of staging residential growth was consistent with the position the Public School Board wished to have. In 1967, when the Report was first discussed, the school board had stated that it was the responsibility of City Council to facilitate planning and co-ordination.[219] But without a policy commitment to a program of development, and with developers responsible for the financing of subdivision servicing and trunk services, the planners can only but speculate as to the rate at which the various plan areas will be developed. If development remains unco-ordinated, all areas could develop at an equal rate resulting in pressing demand for school facilities. The problem confronting the school boards is said to be a lack of co-ordination, not one of the rate of or amount of development within the city. From their point of view, the council must establish priorities and a program for development no matter how undesirable this may be from the city's political point of view.

As no program of development has been established, the school boards have been forced to employ several alternatives: the use of portable schools (proposed in the 1972 Public School Accommodation Report), small starter schools (currently used by the Separate School Board), or over-building in anticipation of future enrolment. To be eligible for provincial contributions for ancilliary facilities, the Public School Board has adopted a relatively large, minimum-size school which, in the early phases of residential development, is not fully used.

The joint brief also pointed out that the fluctuation in school board expenditures results in reduced provincial grants and consequent direct costs to taxpayers because of increased supplementary requisitions in peak periods. The need to co-ordinate development, stressing the opportunity which development provides the city to maximize its share of provincial funds, leaves unasked the question of the influence on costs of speculative private investment in land for which the city has had to give highest priority in its policy decision. The city's failure to adopt a staging plan contributes to fluctuations in school board operating expenditures. The province currently requires that if a school board wants to exceed an annual budget increase of 6 percent, the board must seek approval by plebiscite. The board is thus faced with the alternatives of either cutting back staff (an option taken by the Public School Board in 1971) or having a plebiscite. Should either school board be required to take such action, it may be argued that it is a consequence of the city's unwillingness to take the unpopular step of committing itself to a formal program of development.

Commission Board. The Commission Board in Report No. 4, January 22, 1971, stressed that:

> Salary and wage settlements have been running at very high levels in recent years. If municipal services are to be maintained at an acceptable level, the burden of such settlements must be reflected either in increased property taxes or increased user fees.[220]
> . . . City revenues and assessment values are not increasing at the same rate as increases in the demand for services, with the result that an increase in property taxation cannot be avoided. It is fully recognized that additional sources of revenue must be provided, or, alternatively, that the City must be relieved of the expense to which it is now subjected, but the legislation under which we operate does not permit either of these remedies.[221]

Wages and salaries are a component of current expenditures over which the city can exercise little control unless policies are adopted by which labour is replaced by technology or the service is transferred to others, or curtailed. Professor Hanson emphasized the labour-intensive nature of local government, and found that "Wages and salaries currently account for more than 55 percent of the total general expenditure of the City of Edmonton, including the school systems." He then argued that "Since the remuneration per worker in the economy rises almost twice as fast as the price level, on the average, municipal and other governments face rising expenditures continuously."[222] The point has been taken up by other economists.[223] If city services cannot take equal advantage of technical efficiencies as productive or manufacturing industry, the urban centres are bound to experience additional costs in proportion to the rise in the relative wages paid in other sectors of the economy. Cities, like other forms of government and labour-intensive organizations, may become locked into a situation of unavoidably spiralling costs determined by the rate of pay fixed under increasingly automated production processes elsewhere.

The Commission Board report saw the maintenance of municipal services as involving either increased costs to the residents of Edmonton or additional revenue sources to be obtained, or that services must be transferred. T.E. Adams, Commissioner of Economic Affairs for the City of Edmonton, in his 1972 Current Budget Overview, January 17,1972, repeated the City's position, described in 1971.

> The heart of the city's fiscal problem is the multiplication of service responsibilities against a jurisdictional deficiency to develop new revenues. Restricted revenue sources versus growing expenditure yield increasing pressures on the property tax. With understandable resistance to tax increases that could inequitably affect property owners, the results may be seen in:
> a) restrictions on legitimate service increases with concurrent frustrations and decline in civic morale:
> b) tendencies to undertake cost-shared projects or services which may well disrupt local decision priorities and authority:
> c) consideration of local service responsibility priorities when faced with a growing inability to be effective on all fronts, and
> d) consideration of alternative local revenue sources to support expenditure demands.[224]

Adams expressed concern about the effects of the alternatives on both "civic morale" and "local autonomy" unless fundamental municipal-provincial relationships are changed. This point was taken up in the Commission Board Report No. 4. Changes in provincial-municipal financial relationships were necessary to implement possible remedies to the city's financial plight. Adams emphasized the urgency of a "fundamental" examination of fiscal policy. With respect to the setting up of the provincial government's Urban-Provincial Task Force he noted that ". . . 1972 must be viewed as a transition year as both municipal and Provincial levels strive for sounder fiscal policy bases for the sharing of service responsibilities."[225]

Thus, at the Commission Board level, city finance problems come to be seen largely in terms of inter-governmental relations. There is reference in their reports to the political problems associated with city-directed development, and to the benefit that may be derived from program examination "on a cost-benefit basis which requires understanding of the real services demanded and provided."[226] The Commissioners have also been considering long-range economic planning techniques which could identify and predict the costs of feasible alternatives. A representative of the Commission Board suggested that present planning techniques were too inflexible and unresponsive to changing conditions. Present planning, he said, cannot evaluate the consequences of alternative courses of action. This may be even more critical with the new servicing policy because the courses of action will tend to be determined by developers, rather than by public policy. The city will require a mechanism to evaluate the capital and current expenditures that alternative private decisions impose upon it, and as development will not be determined by a public program, the city must be able to react to each proposal or situation as it arises.

Thus, despite the recommendations of three affected parties on rearranging the relation of finance to city growth, the actual course of affairs appears to be moving in a direction favourable to the influence of private developers on city expansionary policy. A combination of at least three influences is bringing this about, namely: (1) the recurrent financial difficulties of the city and consequent inability to retain control of the servicing of development land under the ownership of private developers, (2) the recurrent uncertainties surrounding the implementation of the city's formal planning instruments, such as the General Plan, with the consequent ineffectiveness of budgetary predictions covering the expansion of development both within and beyond the city boundaries, and (3) the recurrent ambiguity over the "market forces" and individual's choice of residence which at one moment encourages regional urban centres to plan for residential and business expansion and, at the next, threatens either the city or the regional centre with diminution of growth and consequent financial embarrassment. Several other influences may readily be identified, but these are sufficient to demonstrate the urgency of some form of direct provincial intervention to provide the leadership necessary in the developmental affairs of the Edmonton region. Under existing structural arrangements local authorities in every form are in difficulties financially: in their planning, in their prediction of the future, in the morale of their officials, and in the consequences of their activities on their citizenry.

As a measure to rationalize its own internal affairs, the City Council established in May, 1970, a Public Facilities Priorities Planning Committee. This was to be responsible to the Municipal Planning Commission, and to prepare a plan of priorities for public facilities — after reviewing the feasible alternatives for future long term growth.

> It is intended that when these studies are completed, feasible alternatives with attendant costs will be presented to City Council for a decision as to the most desirable pattern of growth which has some flexibility and is consistent with forecast budget limitations.[227]

The Public School Board's 1971 accommodation report mentions that "the progress on the preparation of this plan has been slower than anticipated." In fact, the terms of reference do not specify a date as to when the "feasible alternatives" were to be presented to council. Thus, "it is uncertain whether a plan for programming of public facilities will be presented to or adopted by City Council in 1971,"[228] even though the council may be making decisions on the 10 to 12 outline plans which are of direct concern to the school boards.

The Public Facilitities Priorities Planning Committee did not prepare a plan in 1971, and in fact was largely inoperative. Interviews have suggested that the committee was too large and that, as it was not made up of senior persons, the representatives could not make decisions for their departments. A representative of the city also suggested that the committee was not provided adequate resources. Its task was conceived of as being largely technical. The committee chairman was recently made responsible for the staging of development (primarily utility extensions) in outline plan areas. Whether or not the establishment of the Public Facilities Priorities Planning Committee was but a ploy to appease the school boards is not known. But at a more general level, one might ask if the terms of reference of the committee were feasible in view of the city's subdivision servicing policy, and, more particularly, the new storm water and sanitary trunk financing policy. On the one hand, the city set up the committee to establish the costs of alternative development programs, but on the other, has largely made decisions as to timing, location, and phasing of suburban development the responsibility of the developer. As the costs to be carried by the developer exclude city-wide transportation facilities, major utility plant costs, and the like, the possibility remains for the city to establish a co-ordinatory mechanism of these with the developer's actions. However, with policies for development whereby the developers are required to put up all front end money, development will largely be dependent upon financing possibilities rather than planning considerations, and will almost certainly be undertaken without considering the regional consequences. An amendment to the NHA that provided yet further assistance to developers in meeting their costs would be a great advantage! The city, which has before it a number of alternatives for program planning, is in desperate need, to quote a city planner, of a "master strategy."

Notes
Chapter 4

1. Per capita personal incomes in Alberta and Canada moved as follows from 1935 to 1955:

Year	*Alberta*	*Canada*
1935	$ 244	$ 309
1940	392	432
1945	692	755
1950	1,007	979
1955	1,292	1,257

Cited in *Alberta Industry and Resources,* Alberta Bureau of Statistics, 1970, Table 62.
2. The City of Edmonton, *The General Plan,* By-law 3279, adopted May 18, 1971, p.19.
3. Ibid., p.24.
4. Ibid., p.22.
5. This section will look only at urban development within the urban centres, although considerable acreage of quasi-urban development is occurring within the surrounding rural municipalities.
6. *The General Plan,* p.26.
7. Ibid., p.26, Principles of Regional Planning, Section (1).
8. Ibid., Principles...Section 6.
9. The Planning Act, 1963, Section 91.
10. Section 71 of *The Planning Act,* as amended in 1968, required the Regional Planning Commissions to complete the Preliminary Regional Plan by January 1, 1972, or such further time as set by the Provincial Planning Board. The Edmonton Regional Planning Commission (ERPC) has requested an extension to complete the plan for the entire region.
11. The City of Edmonton, op cit., p.26.
12. The Planning Act, 1963, Section 82.
13. Ibid., Section 85. Preliminary evidence suggested that the General Plan of the MD of Sturgeon was a very contentious issue. The MD bitterly opposed the annexation by British American Construction Materials Limited (BACM). Initially, Edmonton similarly opposed the adoption of the MD's General Plan. Both the city's Commission Board and the Edmonton Municipal Planning Commission (MPC) opposed the proposed plan. The Commission Board recommended to council that the city's representatives on the ERPC oppose the proposal. The MPC suggested that adoption should be delayed until ERPC had completed a study of regional growth alternatives in that the MD proposal may hinder "orderly and economic" growth. Although several of the urban communities within the MD of Sturgeon initially expressed their opposition to the proposed plan, little opposition was evident when the ERPC adopted the plan. We have not analyzed the decision in order to determine what compromises were made to facilitate the adoption of the Plan.

14. In other ERPC documents, the policy on decentralization has been described as a policy of concentrated decentralization, by which it is intended that urban development not occurring within the city be encouraged to locate in the existing regional communities, rather than in a dispersed fashion.
15. Dale, E.H. "The role of successive town and city councils in the evolution of Edmonton, Alberta, 1892 to 1966." Unpublished PhD thesis, Department of Geography, The University of Alberta, 1969, p.521.
16. Ibid., pp.521-22.
17. Cited in Dale, op cit., p.522.
18. The argument used to achieve this was that Edmonton's share of the association's budget was $30,375 of a total of $39,748. Ibid., p.522.
19. City Council minutes, February 28, 1966.
20. This figure has not been verified in this research project.
21. City Council minutes, February 12, 1968, Organization Committee Report, No.5.
22. On January 24, 1972, City Council adopted a policy which requires 100 percent of the cost of storm trunks systems to be charged "directly to residential development areas in proportion to the benefits received." Oversizing costs are to be carried by the developer on an interim basis; these costs are to be refunded to the developer upon the development of adjacent areas benefiting from it, but the first developer will not be able to transfer the interest costs to the city. Developers will also be required to provide initial funding for water and sanitary trunk extensions. These costs will be recovered from the city which will raise the funds through the sale of services, but the developer will be required to absorb the interest charges. Prior to 1971 approximately 20 percent of the storm trunks were charged to the properties as a local improvement. In 1971 this was increased to about 60 percent and in both cases the remainder was raised through debenture borrowings. The new policy is intended to charge to residential areas those costs associated with it and to relieve the city of financing trunk extensions to the many peripheral growth areas. As explained by a city planner, the developer is now required to shoulder the risks — it is the developer's responsibility to ensure the viability of a project. He also suggested that the policy is to the advantage of large firms able to raise the necessary capital.
23. Letter, December 16, 1965, to the Mayor and Council, City of Edmonton, submitted by Charles H. Frigon, President of the Edmonton Home Builders' Association.
24. Letter, December 13, 1967, to the Mayor and Council, City of Edmonton, submitted by the Edmonton Home Builders' Association.
25. Ibid.
26. City Council minutes, November 14, 1967, Committee of the Whole Report No.24.
27. Ibid.
28. Letter, October 31, 1967, to the Mayor and City Council, City of Edmonton, from the Edmonton Home Builders' Association.
29. Data were not available on the relationship of the number of housing units completed to the number of permits issued. The relationship could be very much influenced by the housing type and location.
30. Letter, January 20, 1969, to Edmonton City Council, submitted by the President, Edmonton Home Builders' Association.
31. Comparative data for the City of Edmonton were 28.8 percent of the single family permits, 52.3 of the multiple family permits and 40.8 percent of all permits.
32. No data were available on Mill Woods.
33. *A Satellite Community Study for the Edmonton and Calgary Areas,* The Alberta Housing and Urban Renewal Corporation, October, 1969, pp.87-90. The study pointed out that "The demand for land in the Town of Leduc has increased during the past years" and the price has risen in sympathy, p.89.
34. The Alberta Housing Corporation Satellite Study 34. Ibid., p.92 mentions that lots in Spruce Grove were listed at $3,300 to $3,500. By December 31,

1971 lots had increased in price by 42.9 percent. A similar increase occurred in Leduc.
35. Town of Spruce Grove, Brief to the Department of Municipal Affairs: regarding finance borrowing requirements, prepared during 1971, p.2.
36. Ibid., pp.2 and 3.
37. Ibid., pp.3, 4, 5, 6.
38. Ibid., tables 2 to 6 inclusive.
39. Ibid., p.6.
40. Submission by the Edmonton Regional Planning Commission staff, re: *Spruce Grove Development Plan,* August 24, 1970, p.1.
41. The social conflicts which may develop between residents of the old village and those of the new suburb have not been researched.
42. The basis of its selling price was raw land costs plus servicing costs plus interest.
43. The city supplies many other users in the region in addition to these municipalities.
44. *The Edmonton District Water Supply: A Preliminary Study,* Edmonton District (now Regional) Planning Commission, 1960.
45. Ibid., p.13.
46. Ibid., p.14.
47. Ibid., p.48.
48. Data are not currently available as to the revenues the city receives from regional water uses; however, the City Water and Sanitation Department intends in May, 1972 to compile data for 1970 and 1971.
49. See page 286 and following, and page 301 and following.
50. Chan, Wah May Winnie, "The impact of the Technical Planning Board on the morphology of Edmonton." Unpublished MA thesis, Department of Geography, The University of Alberta, 1969, p.91.
51. Dale, "Successive town and city councils," p.302.
52. Further research is required into the respective roles of annexation and land ownership with regard to timing, location, rate, function, costs etc. Of development. The contrasting policies of Edmonton and Calgary with respect to the expansion of city boundaries following the *McNally Report* appears to provide opportunities for comparative analysis.
53. Dale, "Successive town and city councils," p.343.
54. Cited in Chan "Impact of the Technical Planning Board," p.102.
55. Ibid., p.102.
56. Ibid., p.104.
57. City Council minutes, June 26, 1958.
58. The City Commissioners' *Report to City Council,* November 3, 1959.
59. "The story of the Industrial Tax proposal." Unpublished brief, Department of Municipal Affairs, *circa* 1961. This brief documents the history of the 1960 Industrial Tax proposals.
60. Ibid., p.20.
61. Local school board needs, over and above those met by the fund, were to be raised by the local school board submitting a supplementary requisition to the local municipality. It has been argued that the supplementary requisitions are tending to place municipalities in a position similar to that predating the School Foundation Programs. Investigation is required to determine if this is attributable to excessive spending by the local school boards, by under-contributions by the province, or the refusal of local authorities to co-ordinate development policies with the school boards.
62. City Council minutes, May 6, 1960.
63. City Council minutes, November 28, 1960.
64. City Council minutes, May 27, 1957.
65. City Council minutes, February 13, 1961.
66. City Council minutes, March 13, 1961. Amalgamation Committee Report No.1.
67. City Council minutes, May 5, 1961. Amalgamation Committee Report No.2.
68. Dale, "Successive town and city councils," p.315.

69. City Council minutes, May 27, 1957.
70. City Council minutes, February 19, 1962.
71. City Council minutes, June 25, 1962.
72. City Council minutes, July 3, 1962.
73. Local Authorities Board hearings re: Annexation of Jasper Place and other lands to the City of Edmonton, Exhibit 9, Opening Address by His Worship the Mayor, Dr. Elmer E. Roper, City of Edmonton, pp.1-4.
74. Ibid., Exhibit II, City of Edmonton.
75. Letter from J.W. Hamilton, Imperial Oil Ltd., to Mr. Anthony Adamson, April 26, 1963. (Adamson prepared a report for Strathcona against the annexation.)
76. Submission by Canadian Chemcell Company Ltd., to the Local Authorities Board, May 30, 1963, p.22.
77. Ibid., p.30.
78. Submission by Canadian Industries Ltd., to the Local Authorities Board, May, 1963.
79. Hanson, E.J. *The Potential Unification of the Edmonton Metropolitan Area,* 1968, p.22.
80. Local Authorities Board Order no.1234, March 31, 1964, p.4.
81. Although the Local Authorities Board hearings can be likened to a court, decisions need not rely wholly on the information presented. As set out in Section 32 of the Local Authorities Board Act: "All hearings and investigations before the Board shall be governed by rules which may be adopted by the Board, and in the conduct of hearings and investigations before it the Board is not bound by the technical rules of legal evidence."
82. Local Authorities Board Order no. 1234, p.20.
83. City Council minutes, April 6, 1964.
84. The motion was lost on May 11, 1964.
85. City Council minutes, April 26, 1965.
86. Ibid., March 13, 1967.
87. Ibid., May 8, 1967.
88. City Council minutes, August 8, 1967. Organizational Committee Report No.1.
89. Hanson, *Potential Unification,* p.2.
90. Ibid., p.s 3.
91. Ibid., p.48.
92. Ibid., p.s 3.
93. Ibid,. p.s 17.
94. Ibid.
95. Ibid., pp. S 17 and s 18.
96. City Council minutes, May 27, 1968. The recommendations referred to are those quoted above.
97. Hanson, *Potential Unification,* p.19.
98. Ibid., p.27.
99. To be discussed later in this chapter.
100. City Council minutes, May 27, 1968, and application made on August 28, 1968.
101. Our enquiries were unable to document the conflict or the reasons for council's decision.
102. Data from the Planning Department, City of Edmonton.
103. All unannotated quotes are taken from the appropriate Local Authorities Board Order no. 3981, *The Alberta Gazette,* January 15, 1969, pp.114-120.
104. An indication of the expectations of the press over municipal competition was revealed by an *Edmonton Journal* headline following the board's decision. This described the decision as a victory for the city over the MD., *The Edmonton Journal,* December 30, 1968.
105. For a complete summary of the arguments and an explanation of the Local Authorities Board decision, see: Local Authorities Board Order no. 4192, *The Alberta Gazette,* May 31, 1969, pp. 1227-1233.
106. Local Authorities Board Order no. 4192, *The Alberta Gazette,* May 15, 1969, p.1227.

107. City Council minutes, February 2, 1969.
108. Local Authorities Board, Transcript of Annexation Hearings re: R. Bolster Property (Lot A) March 3, 1969, p.40.
109. For a complete summary of the arguments and an explanation of the decision see: Local Authorities Board Order no. 4804, *The Alberta Gazette,* August 15, 1970, pp.1582-1589.
110. In March, 1970, there were 1,469 vacant and serviced lots in the developing subdivisions (data from City Planning Department, City of Edmonton).
111. To be discussed later.
112. Transcription of Proceedings. Annexation No. C-20-A, City of Edmonton, re: Alldritt Construction Ltd., held in Edmonton Court House, room 9, March 4, 1970, pp.65-69.
113. Ibid., p.50.
114. Ibid., p.56.
115. For a complete summary of the arguments and an explanation of the decision see: Local Authorities Board Order no.5008, *The Alberta Gazette,* January 15, 1971, pp.207-222.
116. British American Construction Materials Limited.
117. See Note 110 regarding numbers of vacant lots in Edmonton.
118. LAB Order no.5008, pp.209,210.
119. Transcript of proceedings of hearing before the Local Authorities Board in regard to the proposed BACM Annexation of Land...Remarks made by Mr. V.S.G. Lewis, President of BACM Development Corporation and the Vice-President of BACM Ltd., May 19, 1970, p.32.
120. Ibid., p.35.
121. Ibid., p.97.
122. Ibid., May 20, p.53.
123. LAB Order no.5008, pp.211-212.
124. Ibid., pp.210-211. The MD of Sturgeon was opposed because the loss of territory and revenue would further reduce its ability to provide a full educational program and would create administrative difficulties.
125. Transcript of proceedings, May 19, p.47.
126. Ibid., p.62.
127. Ibid., p.109.
128. Ibid., May 21, p.92. However, as pointed out above, in March, 1970, there were only 1,469 vacant and serviced lots available in the developing subdivisions in the city.
129. Ibid., p.113.
130. Ibid., p.119.
131. Ibid., p.93.
132. Ibid., p.112.
133. Ibid., p.118.
134. Ibid., May 22, p.126.
135. Ibid., p.127.
136. *BACM Proposal,* The City Planning Department, The City of Edmonton, October 1969, p.7.
137. Ibid., p.8.
138. Ibid., p.9.
139. Ibid.,
140. Ibid., p.11.
141. Ibid., p.1.
142. City Council minutes, October 23, 1969.
143. In January, 1969, there were 1,394 vacant and serviced lots in the developing subdivisions; in March, 1969 this had declined to 1,300 and by December, 1969 the number had increased to 1,440. (Data from the City Planning Department, City of Edmonton.)
144. The Fringe Area Exchange Agreement of January 1, 1961. Both authorities were capable of providing power.
145. LAB Order no. 5008, pp.214-217.
146. It should be noted that the City's General Plan, although referred to

throughout the hearing, was not officially adopted by the City Council until May, 1971.
147. City Council minutes, October 23, 1969.
148. Local Authorities Board Order no. 1234, March 31, 1964, p.18.
149. In March 1969 there were 1,300 vacant and serviced lots available in the developing subdivisions. (Data from the City Planning Department, City of Edmonton.)
150. City Planning Department memorandum, May, 1969, p.1. Although in this memo the onus for high land prices was put largely on the private developer, city servicing policy and planning procedures, as discussed earlier in this chapter, may also be seen to have contributed to land problems.
151. *A New Area for Residential Growth for the City,* City Planning Department, January 30, 1969, p.1.
152. Commission Board Report no.8, February, 17, 1969, p.1.
153. Ibid., p.4.
154. The costs of an estimated $6 million storm sewer, to be completed in 1974, are to be charged to the project. As with private developers, the Mill Woods project will be able to recover from any future subdivisions which benefit from this expenditure, payment in proportion to the benefits received, but interest charges incurred cannot be recovered. Therefore, it will be to the advantage of Mill Woods to encourage developments which will benefit from the storm sewer.
155. *New Area for Residential Growth,* p.2.
156. Commission Report no. 8, February 17, 1969, p.1.
157. Ibid., March 10, 1969, p.1.
158. Financing and Budgeting Committee Report no.7, April 1, 1969.
159. City Council minutes, April 29, 1969.
160. E.H. Dale, in discussing the purchases of land by the city in 1951 and 1954, has described the contrasts in the freedom of the city and private developers to buy land beyond the city boundaries, and has suggested that changes in the legislation were introduced to ensure that private developers could "speculate on land with greater ardor." "Successive town and city councils," pp.297-299.
161. Letter from the Honourable F. Colborne, Minister of Municipal Affairs, to His Worship Dr. I.G. Dent, Mayor, City of Edmonton, July 11, 1969.
162. Letter from Mayor I.G. Dent, City of Edmonton to the Honourable F. Colborne, Minister of Municipal Affairs, July 16, 1969.
163. Bargen, Peter (Chief Commissioner, City of Edmonton) *A Review of Provincial Involvement in the Land Assembly Program,* September 8, 1969, p.1.
164. Minutes of a meeting with Mr. R. Orysiuk of the Alberta Housing Corporation with Mr. P. Ellwood, City Planning Department, and Chief Commissioner Peter Bargen, City of Edmonton, July 28, 1969.
165. Annotated agenda, Edmonton City Council, July 19, 1971, pp.59,60. Reply to Alderman E. Leger's question, June 28, 1971.
166. Transcript of public hearings, Annexation C-20-A4, City of Edmonton, South-east Development Area, held at Edmonton Court House, room 9, November 24, 1970, pp.9 and 72.
167. Meeting of the Alberta Housing Corporation and city representatives re land assembly, August 26, 1969.
168. For a complete summary of the arguments and an explanation of the decision see: Local Authorities Board Order no. 5010, *The Alberta Gazette,* January 15, 1971, pp.226-230.
169. Submission by the City of Edmonton, prepared by the City of Edmonton Planning Department, November, 1970, p.3.
170. Item XIV, October 7, 1970 meeting of the Edmonton Regional Planning Commission: consideration given to the city request for annexation.
171. Letter from representative of the County of Strathcona to the City Solicitor, October 19, 1970.
172. Item IXV, October 1970 meeting ...(see Note 170).

173. Transcription of Local Authorities Board hearings on South-east Development Area, November 24, 1970, p.31.
174. Ibid., p.30.
175. Ibid., p.28. The Counsel's misgivings were subsequently realized when despite the planner's position that no plans for the area under question were in process, the City Council on July 19, 1971 authorized the Commission Board to begin annexation application proceedings for it (see Map 4).
176. The City of Edmonton, *City Boundaries and a Unitary Form of Government, A Proposal,* brief submitted to the Metropolitan Affairs Committee of the provincial government, March, 1972, p.1.
177. Ibid., p.4.
178. Hanson, *Potential Unification,* pp.218-219.
179. Ibid., pp.221-222.
180. Ibid., p.223.
181. Ibid., p.224.
182. *Economic Study: Town of Fort Saskatchewan,* Hickling-Johnston Ltd., Management Consultants, June, 1970, p.2.
183. Ibid., p.39.
184. *Urban Crisis: Alberta Municipal Finance Study,* prepared by the Cities of Alberta, the Alberta Urban Municipalities Association, and the Public and Separate School Boards in each city, January 8, 1968.
185. It should be noted that the provincial Department of Education requires the school boards to prepare three-year estimates of enrolments and facility needs.
186. The General Plan and the appendices were adopted as By-Law 3274 by City Council on May 17, 1971.
187. Ibid., Table 5 - 1.
188. That the data can be viewed only as illustrative may be demonstrated by comparing the Commission Board's proposed 1972 estimates with the estimates in Table 30.

	Commission Board 1972 estimates	*Table 30 1972 estimates*	*Approved 1972*
Total capital estimates	$102,000,000	$105,330,000	Approximately $88,000,000
Rapid transit	$ 230,000	$ 13,455,000	

189. *The Immorality of the Motor Car.* An information project of the University Practicuum in Community Analysis, Community Resources Division, The Department of Extension, The University of Alberta, Winter Session, 1970-71.
190. Nowland, D. and N. Nowland, *The Bad Trip,* Toronto: 1970, House of Anansi. Also "Transportation: Who Plans? Who Pays?" Bureau of Municipal Research, Civil By-laws, 1970.
191. Gillespie, W.E. (Roadway Design Engineer, City of Edmonton), "Progress report on Edmonton's roadway program," presented to the Edmonton Chamber of Commerce Council meeting, September 16, 1970, p.2.
192. Ibid., p.3. See also *Statutes of Alberta,* 1970, Chapter 19. "An Act respecting Transportation Systems in Cities," assented to April 15, 1970.
193. When The General Plan was adopted in May, 1971, the chapter on transportation was omitted because of the uncertainty of transportation planning in the city. It is to be incorporated into the General Plan when the city has a transportation plan.
194. It will be recalled that one of the major arguments for the Mill Woods land assembly project was the use of Mill Woods Ravine as a freeway connecting the project to downtown.
195. The data are available from the City of Edmonton, "Capital Estimates — Source of Funds Summary," 1970.
196. Adams, T.E. (Commissioner of Economic Affairs, City of Edmonton) *1972 Current Budget Overview,* January 17, 1972.

197. Ibid., p.2.
198. These arguments have not been empirically verified in this research.
199. Joint Municipal Committee on Intergovernmental Relations of the Canadian Federation of Mayors and Municipalities. "The Municipality in Canadian Federation," p.6. It is pointed out that even the unconditional grant is a "mechanism of control for the senior government in the matter of their size, the method of their distribution and, of course, their continuing existence," p.13.
200. The General Plan, The City of Edmonton Planning Department, p.151.
201. Ibid., p.155.
202. Commissioners' Report no.4., "1971 Current Budget," p.2.
203. *Revisions to the General Plan Suggested at the Council Meeting held November 16, 1970,* City of Edmonton Planning Department, February 1, 1971.
204. General Plan, City of Edmonton, p.155.
205. Ibid.
206. Ibid.
207. Ibid., p.156.
208. Ibid., p.157.
209. Ibid.
210. *Revisions to the General Plan,* p.4.
211. Appendix II, *Amendments to The City of Edmonton General Plan,* City of Edmonton Planning Department, May, 1971, p.18.
212. Personal interview.
213. We are aware of the possibility of internal administrative conflict over the re-allocation of power and decision which the capital improvement program under the Planning Department would have involved. We did not pursue the matter in sufficient detail and the information was not formally offered to us, so we cannot comment further on this point.
214. City Council minutes, March 25, 1968.
215. "Accommodation report and building program," Edmonton Public School Board, p.6.
216. Joint brief by the Public and Separate School Boards presented to City Council April 16, 1970 re: *Staging of Residential Development,* p.1.
217. Ibid., p.2.
218. Ibid., p.4.
219. City Council minutes, November 14, 1967.
220. Commissioners' Report no. 4 to the Aldermen of the City of Edmonton, January 22, 1971, p.ii.
221. Ibid., p.xi.
222. Hanson, *Potential Unification,* p.151.
223. See, for example, W. Baumol's "Macroeconomics of unbalanced growth: the anatomy of urban crisis," *American Economic Review,* vol.LVIII:3, June, 1967, pp.415-426.
224. Adams, *Budget Overview,* p.1.
225. Ibid., p.3.
226. Ibid., p.2.
227. City of Edmonton Planning Department Report, February 1, 1971 to City Council, p.3.
228. Edmonton Public School Board, "Accommodation Report," p.6.

Chapter 5
Calgary and Urban Politics, 1970 to 1972

City Politics

Calgary is very proud of its industrial expansion and of being the oil and gas centre of Canada. The city's 1970 *Annual Report* is eloquent about the variety of industries located in the city — it "is still maintaining its rate of two new or expanded plants per month, plus a large number of warehouses where light industry often locates."[1] Some 700 firms are engaged in manufacturing in Calgary, and 74 percent of the 631 Canadian oil and gas exploration, development, and producing companies have their head offices in Calgary.

Conspicuously lacking in this annual report is reference to, or even acknowledgement of, the contributions of public investment from senior governments to the city's capital and running services. The Commissioner of Economic and Community Services concludes his own statement in the report with the comment "Calgary should be looking to the senior governments to provide new and diverse sources of revenue, particularly revenues which reflect the changing levels of the economy."[2]

Concurrent with this perspective, the City Planning Department in the Calgary Plan, first released in March, 1970, but having a substantial Addendum added in April, 1971, has made a penetrating analysis of ways in which the city's future growth may be more rationally implemented with consequent saving to the city.[3] The Plan observes:

> If the existing level of service and mobility is to be maintained and if existing programs are fully implemented the City would be faced with capital expenditures of great magnitude. This plan suggests that present programs are unrealistic in terms of the City's ability to pay, given present revenue sources.
> Thus the increased size of the City and the complexity and scale of problems associated with this growth generates a need for a planned framework within which individual developments can proceed . . .[4]

The authors recognize explicitly that fiscal and land planning are dependent for their effectiveness as a community service on being related "to a series of overall objectives aimed at providing politicians with a meaningful framework of reference for decision-making."[5] Similarly, a realistic approach is adopted towards the identification of commitments inherent in the current situation that are not readily amenable to amendment. The Plan observes:

> A review of the form that growth has taken in the past suggests that there are implicit in present civic development policies the following commitments:
> 1. A commitment to, and deliberate encouragement of, growth of the City at the maximum obtainable rate.
> 2. A commitment to private transport and the motor vehicle as the means of movement throughout the city.
> 3. A commitment to the present form of growth of continuous outward expansion.[6]

The authors then conclude that "It is clear from the analysis that follows that no policies should be accepted without examination of long-term financial implications and without detailed considerations of alternative courses of action."[7]

The Calgary planners, therefore, are asking questions about the means of coping with the costs of rapid expansion. Among their various suggestions, they enunciate the first step as being "the formulation of a clearly defined long-range policy framework, based explicitly upon the desires of the community at large, and established through sound technical advice. The problems to be realized and the deficiences to be corrected in this area are formidable."[8] As was the case in Edmonton, the rational of the planner is expressed in a "long-range policy framework," though the way of getting to this goal is different in the two cities. The planners of both cities are conscious of the benefits to be derived for the metropolitan regions from direction of some kind. In Edmonton the Planning Department was expected to undertake the co-ordination of financial and planning programs for growth, and submitting proposals to council. This principle was accepted, even though the Commission Board eventually received the job. In Calgary, the fundamental issues raised in the plan have not yet led to administrative action,[9] but the Plan suggests:

> 1. As an interim measure, the immediate review of all existing programs and expenditure proposals in the light of a projected possible cumulative revenue deficiency of $460,000,000 by 1986;
> 2. Subsequently, review of the costs and implications of other forms of urban and regional growth; and
> 3. The introduction of methods of evaluating objectives and priorities, and utilizing limited municipal financial

> resources in the best interests of the taxpayer. These techniques are available now and can be readily adopted for use in the City.
>
> While the measures in themselves are not solutions to any one problem, they will provide a systematic means of dealing with the difficult problems of allocation of limited financial resources which could, on the basis of present forecasts, arise in the future.[10]

Despite the planners of both cities emphasizing the urgency of setting objectives and determining priorities, Calgary, no less than Edmonton, is pressing for more financial assistance from senior governments, particularly from the province. The cities' affairs, viewed in a more general context, are such that even when their councils move decisively towards setting the instruments to determine these policies, they become caught willy nilly in *ad hoc* decisions which lead only to the undermining or compromising of their attempts. These *ad hoc* decisions are taken in terms of the exigencies of issues such as unemployment, housing, and land shortage, the proposals of private investors, or programs offering some temporary amenity from a senior government. The decisions do not always, by any means, result from untidy or untimely internal administration, but largely from the encapsulated position of the cities in the provincial and national policies of the senior governments. In addition, our observations suggest that many city aldermen are not adequately serviced by supporting information nor prepared by training or experience to cope with the immensely complex implications of a major task such as the approval of the annual budget estimates. In consequence, the elected representatives tend to spend long hours in budget debates not on the critical issues of policy and direction that the city and its administration desperately require, but on relative trivia and detal that in practice can get smoothed out in the monthly running of the city's finances and administration.

In this chapter we emphasize this aspect of city affairs. Calgary is the example *par excellence* for this purpose, and we wish to emphasize that the city is not unique in this respect. For research purposes, however, the issues are revealed most clearly in Calgary's affairs.

The City's Budgets, 1971 and 1972.

The city council receives advice from a variety of sources in the preparation of its annual estimates. Each city department submits estimates on capital and running account covering the program of work proposed for the year, including items carried forward from previous years and those predicted to continue into the future beyond the financial year in question. These are collated eventually by the City Commissioners, and are coupled to a five-year capital expenditure program and to even longer-term spending predictions.[11] To obtain greater citizen participation, council approved in January, 1971, the setting up of the Citizens' Budget Commission, chaired that year by Alderman Ross Alger, to review the city's budget proposals and the public's business. The commission was also charged with obtaining the best advice and assistance available from the general community and "to make recommendations to elected representatives on priorities of expenditure."[12]

The commission quickly recognized that its range of choice over proposals for the capital budget was very narrow. It commented:

> Many of the expenditures submitted for approval do not require decisions to be taken so much as prior decisions to be endorsed and quantified in terms of money. Policies adopted and decisions taken prior to budget time, in some instances many years ago, must now be honored and the necessary funds raised . . . some budget items do not specifically reflect specific policy decisions of council so much as a mere continuation of our way of life. For example, an enormous annual expenditure is required to provide the streets and roads on which to operate the automobile."[13]

So long as this practice continued the annual expenditure on this last item alone was predicted to be some $20 million "whether council writes such a policy into its records or not."[14]

The larger estimated capital budget items in 1971 were listed as:

1.	Street Construction:	$17,092,700
2.	Public Housing:	16,500,000
3.	Waterworks:	14,715,000
4.	Electric System:	5,695,000
5.	Urban Renewal:	3,712,964
6.	Storm Sewers:	2,590,000
7.	Parks and Recreation:	2,953,000
8.	Public Library:	2,100,000
9.	Sanitary Sewers:	2,050,000
10.	Transit System:	1,794,700

The commission recognized that the city's growth was the main reason for the overall increase in capital expenditure but reconciled its dilemma in these words:

> . . . So long as the City grows unchecked, larger and larger facilities will be needed to serve the growing population. If there is an optimum size for a city (said by some to be 500,000), the decision to halt growth at this level should be taken well in advance of its attainment, and all planning geared to that end. Alternately, (sic) if

> unfettered growth is wished for, this too should be decided upon and so stated. In either case a conscious premeditated judgement is preferable to a situation where events are left to decide our future for us.[15]

The two transportation items — street construction and the transit system, together involving almost $19 million — were taken up by the commission at some length. Expansion and upgrading of existing streets had been influenced by traffic congestion and existing traffic patterns. The commission recommended, as a matter of high priority, that:

> All facets of transportation within the city should be co-ordinated. Decisions should be made for the long-term development of transportation in Calgary, considering:
> 1. the most desirable system of moving people within the city;
> 2. whether or not to discourage the use of the automobile in the downtown core area;
> 3. what alternative methods of transportation are available to us;
> 4. restrictions of freeways to the perimeter areas of the City.[16]

Having stated that the "objective of the transit system's estimated budget" was "to develop an efficient publicly-owned system of moving people within the City, primarily in and out of the central core area," the commission recommended that "there should be an investigation by experiment of the rapid transit approach to transportation in the downtown area. . .[and that]. . .the whole area of transportation should be treated as a priority item."[17] Under a section headed "Rapid transit vs. freeways" the commission recognized the interrelated complexity and significance of transport policy for the future of the city. It commented:

> No meaningful look into the future can be made without encountering the vexatious problem of surface transportation. Because of the magnitude of the expenditures involved for either an extension of the present highway system or for the introduction of a rapid transit system, and because of the impact on future urban living of these two concepts, one is compelled to the conclusion that important long-range decisions must be made in this area in the near future. So many budget items hinge on transportation that if orderly and efficient progress is to be made by the City, the future direction of transportation must soon be decided upon. The decision will be affected greatly by the policy adopted on the growth and ultimate size of the City, referred to above.[18]

To what extent the commission accurately reflected the city's thoughts on the use of transit within the built-up area and freeways outside it, was not ascertained. But the commission was clearly aware of the prospect of the council proceeding to decisions in the absence of adequate overall conceptual planning. This matter has particular relevance to the 1972 decision of council on Calgary's Transportation By-Law, to be considered later in this section.

The Waterworks vote was recognized as necessary to provide the city with a second water system — the Bearspaw project. The project was needed only to cope with anticipated growth. It was to be financed largely from Waterworks Department Reserves ($5.3 million) — only $2.6 million was to come from city borrowing — plus a proposed increase in water and sewer rates.

Similarly, urban renewal was to be assisted largely by senior government funds and the city would benefit by the removal of "antiquated buildings and attracting new industries, activities, building and increased employment." Public housing was recognized as innovative and with important implications socially and economically. It had involved almost no expenditure in 1969, but an estimated $16.5 million was proposed for 1971. In this respect the commission commented:

> The City's involvement here is undoubtedly the outgrowth of the availability of senior government funds plus operating subsidies.
> Because the City has only recently entered this area, there would appear to be a lot of catching up to do . . .
> What is the City's long range policy in this area—how large—how costly, etc.? Are the current budgeted per unit prices ($16,500) too high? There seems to be a lack of financial information on Public Housing; 1970 data should be at hand for review when considering the 1971 budget.[19]

The commission was concerned over the high vacancy rate in the city's privately owned apartment blocks. Some 2,800 units were vacant, or 7.2 percent of the city's 40,000 apartments, and the commission asked if the city had investigated "the placement of some of the low income families (older folks or small families) in existing units, and the subsidization of rent, as an alternative to the steady enlargement of the civic investment in public housing."[20]

The commission recognized, however, that the matter was not quite so simple. Public housing, urban renewal, and other programs were heavily supported by the federal government in order to cope with urban unemployment. The city's capital budget had to provide for the city's minority financial interest in a total program that would stimulate the city's economy manyfold. Thus even if the mill rate and services rates had to rise to cope with the scale of capital investment, the city would still be operating to the general advantage of the citizens. The commission argued:

> . . . if the mill rate had been reduced as instructed by the Budget and Finance Committee through a reduction in expenditure, it would undoubtedly have been achieved at the expense of employment. In other words, a reduction in expenditures would have reduced the number of employees which the City would normally have hired. This would be inconsistent with the action of Council when the capital budget was being considered; at that time certain projects were brought forward in point of time so as to provide more jobs and more employment in 1971 than might otherwise have been the case.[21]

The procedures whereby the budget was prepared caused the commission some concern. The commission understood the budget to be "a financial plan for the future designed to implement policy decisions reached currently and in the past." Thus, it commented, "the 1971 estimates must surely be a summation for 1971 of the fiscal prediction of the outcome of policy decisions arrived at on a day-to-day basis in the past, and the correlation of those decisions with the resources of the city in order to achieve a practical matching of civic expenditures and revnues."[22] The policy implications of the council's decisions, however, are far from being explicitly worked out in any detail. Major decisions, such as to proceed with a transit program, are given attention, but the administrative consequences of a practical issue, such as to annex a given parcel of land, are less well prepared. The commission identified the problem in rather less clear terms, but referred to the necessity of establishing "a clear distinction between policy and administration," and considered that the task should be done by the Budget Finance Committee of council when reviewing budget estimates. The commission remarked:

> Presumably policy is a matter for Council to determine; the execution and administration of that policy is the duty of the civic administrative personnel. The budget review then becomes an overall appraisal of the financial effect of policy decisions on the upcoming year, and ought not to concern itself with a great mass of detail. The budget reviews which we attended concerned themselves with great masses of detail which were inefficient guides to the kinds of decisions which had to be made.[23]

The commission's concern over procedures was taken up again later in the report when it observed:

> During the debate on the current budget 1971 estimates, the Commissioners were requested to review the budget as submitted, with a view to reducing the mill rate to 64 or 65 mills. No instruction was give to the Commissioners as to how to effect this reduction. The reasons advanced on

behalf of the request were that many taxpayers could not afford an increase in taxes, and that on a budget the size of the City of Calgary's a certain amount of corporate fat could be found.[24]

The concept of reducing the budget without guidance from the policy instrument of government was, in the commission's view, "not a good one." The council had tended to become lost in a mass of detail over the amount of specific budget terms. If the mill rate was considered too high, for whatever reasons, the City Commissioners were instructed to search for areas where cuts could least painfully be made; but they were obliged to do so without policy direction concerning the service to be affected. It could be argued that this procedure amounted to ensuring efficiency in the administration (the removal of fat in the public budget) and was therefore analogous to the adjustment of private companies to difficult market conditions; but elected representatives responsible for decisions concerning public money cannot behave in such a manner at a time of financial stringency without thorough debate of the issues involved.

As events turned out in 1971, the commission was of the opinion "that a mill rate of 66.7 mills as recommended by the (City) Commissioners represented a fair level of taxation for Calgary taxpayers in 1971, having regard to all of the circumstances of which we are aware."[25] In fact, the mill rate for 1971 was fixed by council at 64.5 mills.[26] On the capital budget, the commission had observed that it was only possible to implement its proposals because the city had previously set aside revenue funds as reserves to the amount of $10 million (including depreciation reserves). The city's system of cash reserves thus "helps to smooth out the irregularities of municipal spending, it stabilizes the mill rate and thus, in our view, it is a desirable feature of a good taxation system."[27]

The problems of procedure were to re-emerge with yet greater clarity in the determination of the 1972 budget. This budget was fixed at a time of greater financial stringency than in 1971, and therefore offers an opportunity to identify more clearly the process of city decision-making, the conflicts inherent in it, and the mode of compromise. Briefly stated, the process over four months was one of proposal and counter-proposal, "buck passing," with an eventual decision made by the authorities technically in a position to make it but not formally elected to do so. The explanation of the process revealed in the analysis is, once again, the nature of the city relative to senior governments and their instruments, the influence of the public on the elected members, and the absence of clear-cut direction and leadership in both the provincial government and the council itself.

A Citizens' Budget Advisory Commission was again struck by council, in December, 1971, to review the proposed capital works budget.[28] The city's Chief Commissioner made his position clear to both the Advisory Commission and the council's Finance Committee on the question of possible budget cuts:

> The chief commissioner told the city finance committee and the citizens' budget commission that they weren't going to saddle the commissioners with having to decide where cuts should be made.
> 'We're going to bounce the ball back to you', he said. 'Where do you want us to make the cuts?'[29]

The city's finances were in some difficulty. The City Commissioners had recommended the municipal part of the mill rate be increased by 3.9 mills, from 22.4 in 1971 to 26.34 in 1972. The city's assessment and revenue growth had not kept pace with financial requirements. The city's capital budget had increased by $81 million between 1970 and 1972 as compared with an increase in gross city debt of $54 million between 1960 and 1969. Civic employees had been awarded salary increases involving an additional expenditure of $7.3 million. Revenue producing utilities were expected to provide about 9.6 mills worth of revenue, but the revenues accumulated over previous years could not be used up indefinitely without threatening the capital needs of the utilities themselves. The Citizens' Advisory Commission, in its majority report noted that the city's gross debt, including school board, was estimated at $335,603,880 in 1972, but that such a debt "is well within prudent borrowing limits . . ."[30] The limit it estimated as safe was $500 million or about 50 percent of the current assessment. Its debt was part of the provincial overall debt, and the commission argued for an increase of borrowing from the Alberta Municipal Finance Corporation (AMFC). The AMFC's quota of $50 per capita had been increased as part of the winter works program to $60 in 1972 — to yield Calgary some $24 million — but in the commission's view:

> There is a good case for the City to ask for the guaranteed borrowing limit to be raised to $70 per capita for a yield of some $28 million. Certainly, the City should make it quite clear to AMFC that it does not buy the argument that the extra $4m (or $10 per capita) for 1972, if borrowed before May 1972, is only an extraordinary, one-shot extension of the quota.[31]

In consequence, the commission could not recommend recourse to the open market for some $8.5 million as the City Commissioners had suggested.

Had the estimated capital budget for 1972 been approved without cuts, it would have raised the city's debt service charges by 2.5 mills. The council's Finance and Budget Committee had cut back the estimates after the line item review, with which the commission concurred. This had been done against the advice of the City Commissioners who "were concerned with anti-employment policies and believed council wished to proceed with some $3 million of winter works where a contribution of 75 percent of labour costs could be expected," from senior governments.[32] Programs not otherwise recommended had been included for this reason. The commission, however, "had some doubts about the wisdom of many of these make work programs so long as Calgary's unemployment figures remained tolerable as compared with other parts of Canada."[33] The $86 million capital budget was so large as to raise doubts as to whether Calgary was physically capable of carrying out its works at a competitive price.

At a joint meeting of the Finance Committee and the commission, on December 22, a severe pruning of some $10 million had been made to the capital budget by line item consideration. This was achieved by deletions and deferrals — particularly $2 million on Lincoln Park and Mount Royal College — "pending a report from the Land department on the proper allocation of costs and responsibilities."[34] A $3.3 million public housing budget was approved, of which $100,000 was to enable the city to consider projects not fitting the existing public housing programs.

The Public School Board budget, amounting to almost $80.1 million, represented a projected mill rate increase for the city of 2.9 mills over the 1971 figure. The province's School Foundation Program was expected to provide $61.2 million of the total amount, but the city seemed to be heading for an additional expenditure of $6.9 million over 1971. In the school board estimates was a sum of $45.6 million for teachers' salaries — or 75 percent of the estimates — and a further 12 percent of the estimates was for debt-servicing charges. Some 87 percent of the budget was thus "fixed." The Mayor was reported as saying that "the city has no intention of trimming its spending program to affect that increase." He reportedly described the budget at "staggering" and added, "it looks as if the school board is trying to squeeze every last dollar out of the taxpayer without having to go to a plebiscite."[35] The city, by being vicariously responsible for school board expenditure over and above the provincial provision, was having to carry an unexpectedly large amount. The Minister of Education had earlier warned school boards that the fixed 6 percent annual increase in expenditures covered by the province would not be increased.

Following the press reporting of remarks about the school board's estimates by various community leaders, some school trustees decided to respond. The press coverage of the local row was considerable. The trustees charged that they were the subject of "a vigorous attack against education by innuendo," and objected to a suggestion that the city should cut the school budget "without compunction." The community leaders who had made criticisms were seen by trustees as "fellow travellers on the road to deliberately undermining the confidence of the public in the schools of this province." They recalled that when in 1967 the city had decided to cut the school board's budget, they were denied permission to do so by the Local Authorities Board "which completely supported the program and spending estimates of this board." There was a danger of "a complete breakdown of any meaningful relationship at all between the school board and the City Council."[36]

Meanwhile, press reporters and commentators had become increasingly embroiled in the row. There were references to a Tammany Hall atmosphere pervading city hall, and allegations were made that the Mayor and the city administration had bowed to organized labour in granting civic employees large salary increases at the taxpayers' expense.[37] Concurrently, the provincial Minister of Municipal Affairs had stated publicly that 1972 was to be a belt-tightening year and the $38 million provided by the province in 1971 to the municipalities from oil royalty revenue would not be increased.[38] The municipalities should not expect any increases from the royalty fund. Press editorials commented on the provincial government's review-of-the-situation policy for 1972, but argued that the "reform" in municipal-provincial financial relations was long overdue.[39]

The Public School Board, after unsuccessfully enquiring from the Separate School Board as to the possiblility of sharing buildings, approved the expenditure of $12.8 million for the construction of 10 new Calgary schools over the period 1972-74. This was additional to an earlier approval of $15 million for additions to existing facilities and for four additional schools.[40] The retiring Superintendent of Schools, Dr. Robert Warren, in a press interview warned that the real financial impact of education costs was to come in 1973. At that time a plebiscite to approve expenditures in excess of the authorized provisions might become necessary.[41] The outcome of a plebiscite is a grave uncertainty. City residents have come to expect that each new suburban development should be serviced by schools as a way of life. In comparison with the province's policy of regionally centralized schools in the rural areas and small towns of the province, the city school system is immensely convenient. On one occasion, when school trustees were considering closing Manchester Elementary School on the grounds that the expense was out of all proposition to the low teacher-pupil ratio and the industrial invasion of the neighbourhood, a protest meeting of parents argued that it would "undermine community foundations by cutting residential property values." The chairman of the local Parent-Teachers' Association reportedly argued: "take the school out and you have shattered the community's reason for existence. A school is the nucleus of any neighbourhood."[42] To get to a nearby school, the children would have to cross Macleod Trail, which was a traffic hazard and unpleasant in winter. An alternative was busing them elsewhere. Attendance had dropped from 100 pupils in 1962 to 54 in 1971-72. Thus, though residents of small towns in the rest of Alberta(at least at present) are constantly faced with incoveniences concerning their children's schooling, city residents react very strongly to the application of economy measures in their community. If city residents are faced with the prospect of having to pay for their convenience or going without and are asked to vote on it by plebiscite, the outcome could be very uncertain.

By February, 1972 the city administration was tackling the task of cutting down still further its estimated capital budget. Parks and recreation services, library services, and street construction were to receive special scrutiny on this occasion. Some three to four million dollars were involved. The council had empowered the Mayor and City Commissioners to cut or defer the required amount if it became impossible to secure extra funds.[43] A capital budget of $74 million was finally approved by council, which was $6 million in excess of revenue sources known to the city at that time. The Mayor reportedly congratulated the Citizens' Advisory Commission for its cost-conscious efforts and remarked, "Higher taxes will appear to be inevitable unless we get a fairer share of provincial revenue."[44] Significantly, the press report on this topic concluded:

> Council accepted the committee's decision to table consideration of a $1.5 million police headquarters expansion program, *since apparent conflicts between siting and staging of the new provincially-built remand centre have left expansion plans up in the air* (emphasis added).[45]

Thus, in the cases of the Lincoln Park and Mount Royal College, and in that of the police headquarters' expansion program, lack of administrative co-ordination over developmental planning between the two levels of government permitted large capital expenditures to be deferred.

In early February, 1972, Mayor Rod Sykes was turning his attention to ways of increasing city revenue. Premier Peter Lougheed was being approached to implement a "selective sales tax." Cars, boats, recreation equipment, and other luxuries were suggested as the basis of selection. The city was also overhauling its fees for business licences — reputedly the first overhaul since 1913.[46] The Mayor saw the current fee schedule as meeting only the cost of administering the services associated with the licences, and ignoring the revenue-producing abilities of licensed businesses. Feed manufacturers, fish retailers, coin laundries, poultry farms, and trailer courts, were of particular concern. The basis of equitable taxation, Mayor Sykes argued, was that those who could pay more should do so. Press editorial comment was to the effect that the principle would constitute a form of corporate income tax, and the city may be constitutionally debarred from instigating it.[47] The editorial commented:

> One can conceive all sorts of abuses creeping in were the secrecy which has been built for good reason around income information at the federal level to be risked at the level of local politics. Business licences might very well be granted or refused on the basis of how much money certain firms or individuals were making or were likely to make, for example.[48]

The Mayor had also discussed with the Premier the possibility of imposing a supplementary assessment on buildings under construction and those completed since the property assessment in October. People currently payed mortgages on buildings from the time construction started, but taxes on the buildings began only on completion of the building. This was predicted to save the taxpayer 2 mills.

These efforts were being made before council's debate on setting the 1972 mill rate. The press had forewarned the public of the likelihood of a substantial increase based on the assumption of an additional 2.5 mills in debt charges, 2 mills for the school boards' increases, and pay increases for civic employees amounting to about 1.5 mills. Thus, a 6 mill increase over the 64.5 mills of 1971 seemed likely. Other predictions had indicated an 8 mill increase. The Mayor's response to these warnings was reported that they were "totally unfounded" and "fabrications."[49] Some aldermen were said to have commented that the 1971 rate was fixed at "an artifically low level," and that the city should have taken its mill rate increases in gradual steps.[50] The Minister of Municipal Affairs, despite his early January statement about freezing oil royalty disbursements to local authorities, had agreed by mid-February to increase municipal assistance from $38 million to $42 million. Mayor Sykes returned to the theme of the property tax having "outlived its usefulness as a source of revenue." Raising property taxes was only deferring the evil day — the answer lay in the province's ability to create an additional revenue source which was both guaranteed and substantial. The minister reportedly replied that the Mayor knew better than to foist a sales tax on the province, to which, in an case, the Conservative administration was opposed. He commented: "We're aware of the city's problems — I hope he's aware of ours. Certainly, the province can't invent another source of revenue."[51]

Meanwhile in council meetings, a split was developing over the level of proposed expenditure on parks and recreation. They were scheduled to involved $8.3 million, and were threatened with cuts. There was still a jump of a million dollars over 1971. The swimming pool program was earmarked for $560,000, and arenas and athletic parks for a further $212,000. Mayor Sykes, who reportedly blamed aldermen for demanding more recreation facilities than could be afforded, was immediately rebuked and accused of talking "nonsense" and being "naive."[52] The argument was that council merely reflected the wishes of citizens in the matter of bathing pools and arenas. The Mayor noted that parks and recreation expenditure over the past 10 years had increased 700 percent against a population increase of 50 percent. He said that the situation was totally out of control and could rebound on the city if it made an appeal for greater provincial assistance to the province.[53] Now that the capital investment in pools and arenas had been made, "There is no way past expenditures can be undone," and water had to be put in the pools. Two aldermen in debate criticized the absence of "a clear set of priorities of recreation spending."[54] The original amount was eventually approved.

An attempt to cut a further $400,000 from the budget led a City Commissioner to suggest that perhaps the advice of a consulting firm hired to streamline city hall management procedures would make the expenditure unnecessary. But this sum was not reduced either. The Mayor was at this point suggesting that "a short trip to the open market" might temporarily save the imposition of an additional 2 mills to the property tax. The province had pumped an additional $19 million into the School Foundation Fund which would give Calgary an additional $4 million.[55] The Mayor now believed the mill increase could be held at 3.9 mills, and that a possibility existed of preventing any increase. One mill could be saved the homeowner by changing the assessment formula to transfer additional taxes to the industrial and commercial sector, and the province might yet agree to his proposal on a supplementary levy on incompleted buildings.[56] Lastly, council was turning its eye to the school board vote. Questions were asked why the city had to pay for school health services which should be met by the school boards and the province. The Finance Committee was considering setting the municipal portion of the mill rate there and then, leaving the school and hospital requisitions to be dealt with later. The Mayor conceded that such a move would "put the school boards in a rather awkward position." The move would, in effect, show the public how adequately the city had dealt with the financial stringency and measure very explicitly the amount of tax increase due to education. The prospect of the 1973 budget requiring a plebiscite on school expenditure would be a future sanction on school board over-expenditure.

By the end of February, a 16-page minority report from Mr. Joseph Yanchula of the Citizens' Advisory Commission had reached the public.[57] It was originally hastily prepared in time for council's January 31 meeting, but an addendum to it added his observations of that particular meeting — "it was essentially a rubber stamp affair lasting about three hours. Half of the time was spent on discussing the restoration of the Public Health Centre in the Huntington Hills area to the budget . . . a matter of some $167,000. It was interesting to see a majority of the Aldermen squirm, turn tail and vote in favour of the measure, instead of standing on principle, and insisting that the Province take over its rightful responsibility."[58] As can be seen, this document was not the most impartial of accounts.

The minority report starts with a criticism of the form of presentation of the budget and of the absence of notes — "280 pages of numbers with much blank space on almost every page."[59] There was no explanatory material on which to base intelligent conclusions. Mr. Yanchula remarked:

> The general impression was the City Administration people were competent but almost without exception, each

> department was attempting to enlarge its empire at the taxpayers' expense. Again and again the mayor had to repeat what eventually, even to me, became rather tiresome homilies about treating the taxpayer's money with respect instead of thinking of it as 'playmoney.' There appeared to be a cat and mouse game going on during the budget hearings — the Administration presenting as non-informative a budget as possible and then hoping the council would not inspect individual items too closely.[60]

His observation of the City Council was in these words:

> It became painfully obvious that the Mayor was the only council member on the budget sub-committee who really knew what was going on. Only when he was present did I get the impression that the budget was actually scrutinized. When he was absent we were merely turning pages.[61]

From his observation of council's performance he concluded that "the present Mayor appears to be single handedly responsible for saving the tax payers about $10 million per year."[62] An enlarged council — to 40 or 50 members — could ameliorate, in his view, the consequences of the apparent lack of expertise on the council.

His criticism of individual budget items was radical in its thought. For example, he observed that in what was labelled as the "1972 program," over $33 million, or 38.4 percent of the $86 million "program" was for street construction. This was about 19 times the $1,753,400 allocation for the transit system, but "Fortunately the Provincial Government will save the city from part of its folly and contribute only about half of the $8,428,825 the administration hoped would be forthcoming from provincial coffers."[63] The road estimates had had to be cut. The city, in his view, was being cut by freeways, expressways, major arteries, "and many sorts of more obscure labels." A system of one-way streets might equally serve the purpose, especially if exclusive bus lanes were provided — "such streets would not divide communities and still carry as much traffic as freeways."[64] The Mayor's Pollution Committee and other bodies had recommended several drastic changes in the city's transit system, including express bus lines, and heated waiting shelters, but on enquiry, Mr. Yanchula had found them still to be "under consideration" and not made part of the 1972 budget debate. No city with fewer than a million people, he argued, had a rapid transit system, but Calgary in its General Plan and elsewhere was already involved in the planning for one. It was not in the library, parks and recreation, and similar minor estimates that cuts should be made but "in the still-bloated street construction program. The City is reluctant to slow down in this sector for fear of losing the Provincial contribution."[65] The minority report was a fundamental attack on the highest capital cost items in the city and on the "way of life" which people were obliged to lead because of the continually expanding investment in transport facilities, parking meters, and related items.

By mid-March, the Public School Board had found its surplus from 1971 to be in fact $2.26 million, rather than $1.7 million. There was also a chance of collecting additional money from the province and some saving had been made on a teachers' strike. The board approved an $80.64 million school budget, revised upward from its original $80.08 million figure. It was up $7.4 million, or 10 percent over 1971, and represented a 2.9 mill increase for the taxpayer.[66] The school administration with the trustees' agreement, had recommended "that the excess surplus be used to restore previous deletions in the maintenance area."[67] Mayor Sykes replied by suggesting that the provincial government investigate the Public School Board's budgetary procedures. It was "overtaxing the citizens of Calgary."[68] Shortly afterwards, the school board planner warned the City Planning Commission that failure to set aside specific land for school sites would lead to a direct charge on the taxpayer. Apparently a developer in a new subdivision had not set aside land for a school site. Private developers should be warned that schools might not be built in new subdivisions for several years, and homeowners should also take heed of this possibility. School board officials admitted that busing may have to replace the erection of new schools in every suburban subdivision, though this could be avoided if developers added several hundred dollars to the lot price, and the proceeds were paid into a special fund. In mid-April the school board reportedly refused to supply a copy of its 1972 budget to the city. There was apparently no legal requirement for this to be done.

On April 18, *The Calgary Herald* reported the Mayor as having had a thirty-minute telephone conversation with the Minister of Municipal Affairs. The Mayor was still expecting some measure to relieve the taxpayers of 2 mills of the threatened increase — "The prospect of holding the mill rate at its present level for the next two years is very good."[69] The following day the Mayor reportedly suggested that provincial changes in municipal finance in 1973 would permit the city the next year to reduce its mill rate to 49 mills.[70] This prospect arose from the possibility of the province taking over the costs of education, hospitals, health, welfare, and social services from the city. The property tax would then cover only strictly municipal matters.[71]

Meanwhile, however, the Mayor continued his criticism of the school board, and at one point suggested that the city might refuse to collect the school tax on behalf of the board. This remark led to a threat of legal action to oblige the city to do so, if necessary. The school board chairman reportedly charged that the Mayor had political reasons for causing "a furore" over the school board's budget.[72] Both the public and separate school board chairmen emphasized in press interviews that they were in no way subservient to City Council or to the Mayor — school trustees receive their mandate direct from the electorate, as do city councillors. But the press comment a few days later indicated the existence of about 240 empty classrooms in city public schools, and argued that it would make "good sense to try to fill at least some of them before building new ones."[73] Similarly, the new enrolment figures were declining from about 3,000 in 1967 to 1,000 in 1971. Busing seemed to be the only alternative if the city and the developers could not be more rationally co-ordinated.

In council's Finance and Budget Committee, the Mayor moved that the city strike a mill rate of 64.5 mills, the same as 1971, despite the City Commissioners' intimation that to pay for the programs approved a mill rate of 70.3 would be necessary. The Mayor had expressed his hopes of new provincial legislation providing new revenue for the city. The City Solicitor, however, indicated that he was unsure that the city could deliberately set a mill rate to bring in less than the estimates required. The term "bona fide" was used in legislation concerning the efforts of the city to predict its expenditures. The Mayor indicated that there was precedent for it, and he outlined the various measures that he expected would increase city revenues. Some aldermen objected to setting a mill rate on the assumption of promises.[74] Press editorials were describing Calgary's "on-again, off-again" mill rate as "a bit ridiculous." Politicians like to spread good news quickly — ". . . and that is the trouble with Mayor Sykes' good news. It all seems to depend upon someone else in some other part of government to do the talking."[75] Eventually, City Council introduced a compromise by way of a two-stage bill, and voted it in unanimously. An initial tax instalment based on the 1971 rate of 64.5 mills would be made, and in the event of anticipated relief not forthcoming a rate of 68.6 mills would be levied effective December 1, 1972. The mill rate was formally fixed at the higher figure, with the lower to apply if possible at the later date. The final 4.1 mill instalment might, therefore, never be collected. *The Calgary Herald* in an editorial of April 26, remarked: "Politics has rarely stood out so clearly in a civic tax-setting exercise. If all the ifs eventually become realities, the proponents of the instalment scheme will no doubt lay claim to glory. They may well try to do the same thing should the ifs become impossibilities, by trying to lay the blame at the door of the provincial government."[76] The same day the Minister of Municipal Affairs said in Edmonton that "The only assistance I can think of that will be coming is the increase in the municipal grants which has been approved and any help they may get from a supplementary assessment roll."[77] The Mayor had had a breakfast meeting with the Premier and the minister that morning.

The consultant's report on the management of city hall was released to the press on the same day. *The Calgary Herald* staff writer, Gary Parks, predicted City Hall staff to be heading for a "top-to-bottom staff overhaul in the next 12 months," with several "early retirements" and a number of demotions of senior personnel. Some senior staff will get salary increases "and will also be part of a new incentive bonus scheme, the final details of which have still to be worked out."[78] The Mayor indicated that council was determined "to treat everyone fairly and even generously in these difficult circumstances."[79]

In Early May, 1972, a public school trustee called for a freeze on all new school construction until existing vacant classrooms were filled. If the school construction program continued as predicted as many as 1,000 classrooms could be empty within four years. The public and separate schools have to share facilities, or face bankruptcy "trying to preserve separate identities . . ."[80] The provincial Minister of Education announced that a freeze on the building of new schools, unless absolutely necessary in a new facility, would be announced. This was to apply to all except those for which a contract had been let.[81]

These Gilbert-and-Sullivan or Micawber-like incidents epitomize the city's difficulties. The Planning Department's General Plan, realistic within the confines of the commitments identified by the planners as inherent in the community's values, relates costs and revenues to its projected execution. The City Commissioners faithfully pull together the various departments' estimates of expenditure for their particular fields of interest, cut back certain items at that point, and prepare a draft budget. The council, largely ignorant of the implications for policy of the line-item, detailed proposals, identifies certain matters of a trivial nature to consider in terms of one or other ethic or responsibility of government, while relying on its committees to handle both the detail and principle implicit in the draft budget. To encourage public participation in public business, council appoints citizen advisory commissions with varying views and diverse levels of approach to the city's finances. When proposed expenditures exceed anticipated revenue, a series of cuts are requested which City Commissioners are expected, without guidance, to achieve partly as a procedure to shrink any possible fat left on departmental estimates and partly to gauge the least sensitive political areas where cuts might be made. Concurrently, the Mayor and some aldermen engage in public debate with related local authorities — the hospital and school boards — and with the provincial government. The debate with related local authorities is intended to achieve either cuts in their proposed expenditure, or an increase in revenues from the provincial government under service areas for which these authorities are uniquely responsible. The city's discussions with the provincial government are kept at a more general level to squeeze either an advantageous change in municipal-provincial relations generally or added funding from existing provisions. Blame for publicly known difficulties tends to be passed to the provincial government's allegedly niggardly policies or onto the city's civic staff, as was the case in 1972.

At no point in the decision-making process is a public airing given to the relation of the mode of city development — whether of concrete fixtures or of human services, or of capital items and consequent recurring expenditure — to its current and future costs. The City Commissioners come nearest to the task, but the delegation of duties to specialist departments and the inherent necessity to cope with daily decisions make its effective execution difficult. From time to time, council debates critical policy matters, such as a rapid transit system or an antipollution policy, and money becomes earmarked for its future consideration, but the city's annual estimates are not geared explicitly to policy application in a concerted and directed fashion. Both the 1971 and 1972 Citizens' Advisory Commissions commented on the relation of administration to policy, and Mr. Joseph Yanchula's minority report of 1972 specified the relation of policy to money, to planning, and to the citizens' mode of living. City policy on major matters exists, but it is evident less at the council table in explicit debate than in the routine activities and in departmental reports which get dealt with as routine. Everyone associated with city hall seems conscious of the need to review, to plan and direct affairs with wisdom, and to show responsibility; yet all are aware that its affairs bristle with "problems" of community-wide significance.

For large measure, however, the near stalemate is a consequence both of financial and policy dependence on the senior levels of government and of inability to cope with pressures from individual citizens. The citizenry is vocal in the defence of its own particular property and in the standard of service it enjoys. For example, school busing, though entirely sensible in terms of the capital cost of school construction in partially developed subdivisions and industrially invaded communities, is vigorously opposed. Major issues concerned with the dependence on senior governments will be discussed in the sections that follow; but it is convenient to point out here that there is a conflict between the City Commissioners and the Chairman of the 1972 Citizens' Commission over the size of the capital budget and the need to generate work for the unemployed through federal and provincial grants while threatening competitive prices when tendering for public works. Such *ad hoc* expenditures can play havoc with city planning as well as leading to unanticipated running costs in later years to keep intact the services provided by the initial capital injection. A similar argument applies on a much larger scale to housing developments supported by various NHA programs, as well as to road construction on the basis of the 25 cents dollar, and to other senior government programs.

Similar complications readily emerge from the level of assistance provided public institutions in Calgary by provincial grants. While the pressure on the government to increase municipal assistance was exerted, the province decided to provide an $8 million grant towards a museum in Calgary's downtown core — to be built to the east of a proposed civic convention centre. The University of Calgary was preparing its capital requests. A $5.5 million grant was provided for the construction of the new judges' court and remand centre. The $1.9 million federal winter works program was approved, and the federal "Local Initiatives Program" provided funds for additional specific projects. There were other boosts to public investment in the city. During discussion of the grant for the judges' court and remand centre, the Mayor reportedly indicated that the grant illustrated "the government bending over backwards to show a co-operative spirit," and that he was now optimistic "that the Lougheed government will co-operate with the city and it will try to carry out its promise of respecting local autonomy."[82] On completion, the building was to be handed back to the province for $1 as token of its ownership.

Thus, during the discussion with the province, considerable sums were entering the city under other public votes and were in turn stimulating employment. These sums, however, did not mitigate the pressure on the city to finance its operating budget. Senior government programs in turn involve additional running costs for the city which, in the years ahead, will influence the city's operating budget. This point was raised explicitly by Alderman Peter Petrasuk, President of the Alberta Urban Municipalities Association, who suggested in Quebec City during the 35th Annual Convention of the Canadian Federation of Mayors and Municipalities that the CFMM should become "a political force if it meant allowing municipalities to 'have a say' in policies and programs affecting them." He commented: "The senior governments implement programs without even considering the effect. We (the municipalities) end up paying the shot, but we are never consulted."[83] Mayor Sykes, while agreeing that lines of communication should be established, said, "There is a great danger at the federal level," and he feared that a tightly controlled lobby was trying to turn municipalities into a third political force.[84]

Concurrently, Mayor Sykes shows a thorough acquaintance with the politics of urban development at the federal level. It would appear that he is quite aware of the consequence of joining the Eastern Canadian establishment in a "power play" to strengthen the position of municipalities with regard to the federal government. At the 34th conference of CFMM, held in Saskatoon during June, 1971, the Mayor opposed a resolution ". . . asking the federal government to increase substantially financial assistance for municipal sewage treatment . . ."[85] The Mayor:

> . . . argued that Calgary had constructed a separate sewage system itself over the last 15 years without additional funds from the federal government, and saw no reason why Western Canadians should help pay for what is essentially a problem in the older eastern cities.

It is politically expedient for the Mayor to argue the desirability of maintaining close consultation with the federal government and, at the same time, to continue to exert pressure on the provincial government for more financial assistance. However, it should be made clear that the City of Calgary, despite the cries from city politicians concerning the need for more funds, is already receiving considerable provincial government assistance through the auspices of the Municipal Assistance Act and Municipal Finance Corporation and also through a variety of other programs.

Thus, the 1970 annual report of the city states as follows:[86]

> In accordance with the Provincial School Foundation Program the City was required to remit to the Foundation the equivalent of 28 mills on the equalized assessment for a total of $22,757,846.
>
> Supplementary Requisition for the Calgary Public School Board in the amount of $9,844,950 and the Calgary Separate School Board in the amount of $1,543,770 were assumed by the City.
>
> Total expenditure of the Calgary Public School Board was $63,521,636 financed as follows:

School Foundation Program	$52,053,313
Misc. Revenue and other Government Grants	$ 3,722,847
City of Calgary Supplementary Requisition	$ 9,844,950

> Total expenditure of the Calgary Separate School Board was $15,429,572 financed as follows:

School Foundation Program	$13,369,687
Misc. Revenue and other Government Grants	$ 516,115
City of Calgary Supplementary Requisition	$ 1,543,770

Through contributions to the School Foundation Program and supplementary requisitions, the City of Calgary experienced an overall cost of $34,146,566, made up of $22,757,846 to the fund and $11,388,720 in supplementary requisitions. In other words, of the total expenditure (Calgary Public School Board and Calgary Separate School Board) of $78,951,208, the foundation program and miscellaneous revenues contributed $44,804,642; or 56.75 percent of the city's overall expenditure on education. This contribution becomes more significant if considered in terms of what small towns and villages receive in the way of assistance from the School Foundation Program. While small municipalities are being encouraged to endorse, or to accept regional educational facilities, the cities of Edmonton and Calgary remain in the fortunate position of being able to provide school facilities for practically every subdivision and neighbourhood. The evidence indicates that the expenditures associated with this standard of provision are being born by Alberta as a whole. In these terms, it is difficult to comprehend the city's claim that it needs additional help.

The Mayor is in the difficult position of being unwilling to place further tax burdens on Calgary homeowners, and recognizing that it would be unrealistic to support a "power play" for increased constitutional status, he has chosen to exert pressure on the new provincial government by reminding it of its campaign promise to lift the costs of certain services from the shoulders of property owners.[87] He anticipated a 1973 mill rate of 49. Presumably, if the government's negotiations over oil and gas revenues prove to be fruitful, the Calgary Mayor can expect to receive greater financial assistance in the future. However, this additional assistance, if it is forthcoming, will not resolve those problems derived from explicit policy nor ameliorate the disparate conditions which exist between this urban centre, its region, and the province as a whole

The Planners' Search for "Rationality" and its Constraints

Citizen participation in the city's planning process is a firmly established arrangement. In an article published in the Town Planning Institute of Canada's *News,* August, 1971, the then (Calgary) Director of Planning noted: "Unfortunately, our first primitive efforts at community participation that we believe most worthwhile did tend to frustrate ambitious schedules. However, participation in the government process is now accepted and is proving to be the keynote of our programme."[88]

This citizen participation, apart from involvement in city committees, is sporadic. Some professionals and "advocate planners" who provide assistance at the neighbourhood level often oppose the city and its Planning Department's proposals. Their values express the wish to build up neighbourhoods according to the views of their residents. Communities such as Inglewood have received federal financial assistance through the Local Initiatives Program for this purpose. Participation frequently expresses an individual's or community's concern about property values, neighbourhood disturbance, and pressure on community services. For example, during March, 1972 considerable public protest followed a proposal that a youth hostel be located in the Hillhurst area of Calgary. The complaints ranged from fear that the hostel would bring into the district what one man called "hippie-types," to concern that the hostel would intrude into a quiet neighbourhood and that the facilities would be inadequate to serve the estimated 70 persons using the hostel daily.[89]

Calgary residents in general are not encouraged either to take an active interest in the city's affairs beyond those which affect their immediate neighbourhood, or to view the implications of their neighbourhood involvement for the city as a whole. Council meetings are public and announced in the mass media, but no regular institutions exist to contact the citizenry over city-wide issues. From time to time a "store front" technique in a neighbourhood is instituted particularly when locally, politically sensitive issues are at stake. Furthermore, because planning and development decisions involving the developed areas of Calgary are fraught with political consideration, the council accedes more readily to the development applications proposed for the outlying areas or the periphery of the city. This readiness has been further encouraged by the speculative activities of so-called "land squires" who own land in the developed areas. However, this makes still more difficult the task of making policy for the form and direction of city growth in general. The council insists that its major responsibility is not so much to formulate goals and objectives for the city's growth as to provide housing and employment for Calgarians. The fulfilment of this latter responsibility leads council to accommodate private interests.

Furthermore, each alderman represents a specific city ward and sometimes feels obliged to yield to the demands of particular citizen groups, even though their demands may be contrary to the interests of the city as a whole, or be in conflict with current planning and fiscal policies.

In addition, there are over 75 reasonably well-organized "community associations" in Calgary. The City Council frequently receives requests from them. Since these often involve matters requiring financial assistance, and pertain to specific community projects, the question of setting precedents arises. The city administration's posture is not unlike that of the provincial government with regard to assistance to municipalities. For example, on March 27, 1972, the City Council dealt with a request from the Southview Community Hall for a loan of $16,753. During the discussion that took place over this matter, the Chief Commissioner warned the council of the consequence of setting a precedent. He noted that grants to assist certain projects would ensure the inevitability of increased operating costs for the city, particularly in recreation. The Mayor pointed out that if the council approved this request it could allow every other community association the right to expect similar assistance.

Interestingly enough, the Southview project, an addition to the community hall, was initiated in response to the federal Local Initiatives Program. However, since the community had been unable in the time allotted to obtain enough public vouchers to secure a loan of $9,000, the community had decided to approach the council. The council was able to arrange matters to the satisfaction of the community eventually.

When a "special case" arises, the council usually responds positively to community appeals for financial assistance. Also, when senior government funding is at stake, the council tends to arrange financial assistance. For example, on February 29, 1972 *The Albertan* reported that following a fire which had destroyed the community's recreational facilities, the Bridgeland-Riverside community would be receiving assistance from the City Council. In addition, the report noted, "Council also came to the rescue of a North Hill community group in danger of losing a $24,000 local initiatives grant from Ottawa." It is not unusual in fact for council to decide contrary to established policy in order to accommodate senior government programs. These *ad hoc* decisions further make more difficult establishing firm planning and financial policy.

Senior members of the city's administration support, and

have taken action to promote, the formulation of long-range planning policy. In May, 1972 it was decided to separate a research section from the Planning Department, and give it departmental status. Titled, "Management Systems Development," this new department has been described an an "in-house consulting service for the city" and was initiated as a response to a clear lack of long-range city policy. Because of this lack, the City Council has been "making decisions in a vacuum, based on gut feelings." Relying on sophisticated systems analysis and extensive use of a computer the department will attempt to develop forecasting techniques, to determine methods for evaluating policies and policy alternatives in terms of their long-range implications, and to provide the City Council with consistent advice. It is also envisaged that the department will become involved in short-range policy matters.[90]

While the new department will not be directly responsible for policy formulation it will attempt to facilitate the preparation of plans and projects through inter-departmental co-ordination. It is imperative, one individual has observed, that it be understood that rational planning depends upon the integration of those departmental decisions regarding sewers, waterworks, the electric system, and so forth. Furthermore, it was observed that such decisions have an influence on city growth and can be used as "tools for city design." For example, the Transportation By-Law was prepared on the basis of the Planning Department's land-use predictions and assumed the continued extensive use of the automobile. Similarly, with regard to sewer pipes, there has been a tendency, because of the uncertainty emanating from the lack of development policy, to provide "over-capacity." This has had cost implications for the city and is also considered to have contributed to urban sprawl. Matters of the kind mentioned, it is hoped, can be more sensibly dealt with by systems analysis based on inter-departmental co-ordination and integration.

The assumption behind the change, as one interviewee expressed it, is: "If the City Council is provided with better information and facts it will be in a better position to make better decisions." Up to this point in time, it is argued, council has been unwilling to commit itself to policy decision and has simply been "fighting brush fires from day to day." With proper advice and more information some persons feel that council will acquire a better understanding of the long-term implications of their decisions and take action to "avert disasters." Indeed, there is explicit intention to place the responsibility for decision directly on the shoulders of decision-makers, and to make it more difficult for them to pass the blame for mistakes.

Some evidence suggests that a concerted campaign is being waged by administrators and planners to introduce more efficiency into the city's operations and thereby obliging council to make "rational" decisions. Though it is felt this campaign will be a lengthy one, the assumption on which its success is predicated is a greatly enhanced ability of council to remain "on top of the city's situation" in the face of a variety of frustrating uncertainties. There is also a certain irony in this approach in the face of council's decision to appoint management consultants to advise on the management of city business and to forestall the $40,000 budget cut proposed in the Finance and Budget Committee with consequent superannuation of staff.

In the meantime, the council continues to rely on its planners to accommodate its reluctance to establish firm developmental policy. When local political difficulties arise, the Planning Department may be requested to intervene in a local situation of conflict between citizens and the city over a development proposal or other planning matters. Such intervention, the evidence suggests, is a consequence of council's search for a compromise solution. For instance, the department was requested to consult with the residents of the Victoria Park area concerning plans for the expansion of the Calgary Exhibition and Stampede site. The department mounted a "store front operation" and managed to obtain a variety of views concerning the proposed expansion. The complexities of the situation will not be dealt with here, but it became clear that in order to ". . . realistically comply with the Planning Advisory Committee's requirements, it would be essential to work with the Calgary Exhibition and Stampede Board to develop a plan which would achieve the dual purpose of meeting their legitimate long-range expansion and use-diversification needs, and preserve Victoria Park as a viable residential area."[91] During the following months several compromise solutions were suggested, including ". . . a gradual integration of Victoria Park and the Stampede."[92] By May, however, it was reported that ". . . local residents are really getting tired of the uncertainty."[93] An alderman and city representative on the Stampede board were quoted as saying: "I think that if we don't soon get something done, the people will take the law into their own hands." This statement was in response to ". . . a rash of recent complaints from area residents concerning fighting, vandalism and deteriorating housing . . ."[94] Apparently the City Planning Department had been unable to formulate a compromise which would satisfy both the residents of the area and the Stampede board. The City Council's refusal to act according to the proposals and documents submitted by the department led to a very difficult situation for the residents.[95] Instead of dealing with the matter in a straightforward manner, the council tried to divert responsibility for direction to the Planning Advisory Committee, thus managing to avoid the burden of making a clear-cut decision.[96]

An incident where citizen involvement in planning was related to issues wider than neighbourhood protection and survival was the Windsor Park affair. Public concern, to a large degree, emanated from an interest in the possibility of being able to sell property to developers. In this situation as well, the Planning Department was requested to consult with residents of the area. A letter from the Assistant Deputy Director of Planning to the

Commissioner of Operations and Development, dated December 28, 1971, notes:

> City Council at its meeting of May 11, 1970, considered By-law 7871, reclassification from R-2 Two Family Residential to R-4 General Residential District and gave the by-law first reading, with second and third readings being deferred to allow the Planning Department time to prepare a plan for the whole of the Windsor Park Area. Many meetings were held with the residents over the ensuing months as part of the process of preparing the Windsor Park Plan. These meetings culminated in the presentation of the Plan to the Operations and Development Committee on May 3rd, 1971, at its meeting held in St. Anthony's Elementary School near the Windsor Park Area.

The letter continues:

> The Windsor Park Plan itself recommended that the area immediately south of 56th Avenue be rezoned from R-2 Two Family Residential District to accommodate a maximum of 90 persons per net acre . . .[97]

Having delineated the various development guidelines that the department felt should apply following rezoning, the letter explains: "The Operations and Development Committee however, felt that R-4 densities (150 people per net acre) should be allowed south of 56 Avenue . . ." A city official involved with the plan has attributed the committee's position as being a consequence of pressures applied by city politicians, residents of the area, and other interested parties. He explained that the density recommended by the committee would allow residents to sell their land to developers for the construction of apartment buildings. During the course of the public meetings and consultations, it was argued that since many of the residents were retired and owned older homes of little re-sale value they should be permitted to sell their property to interested developers. Apparently interested developers gave support to this "cause under the guise of citizen participation" by providing "moral and social" arguments for the residents' use.

The Deputy Director's letter observes that: "City Council at its meeting of May 10, 1971, considered the recommendation of the Operations and Development Committee along with a report by the Director of Planning . . . The report from the Director of Planning, in essence, set out the same concern and conditions that the administration felt should be applied to development south of 56th Avenue as outlined in the Windsor Park Plan . . ." The council decided to approve the recommendation that the maximum density should be 150 persons per net acre and passed By-law 7871 accordingly. However, the letter observes that the residents of the area, apparently to protect their potential interests, were not satisfied, viewing the "conditions of development which were endorsed by City Council" as "onerous" and requiring review. Concerned about the residents' comments pertaining to off-street parking, community facilities, and open space, the Planning Department took the position that the conditions endorsed by council ". . . are conducive to good development in the southern portion of the Windsor Park area . . . Consequently, the Planning Department would recommend that these conditions remain unchanged for future development in Windsor Park." Earlier in his letter, the Deputy Director also observed:

> The Planning Department's main concern, in view of the fact that 56th Avenue appeared to be an acceptable zoning boundary to all parties in the community, was to ensure that redevelopment which might occur south of 56th Avenue would not have a detrimental effect on existing R-3 land north of 56th Avenue and on the community as a whole.

Thus, though density conditions were changed, the development conditions were reaffirmed as they protected the interests of others. The department viewed the incident as a victory even though the council had agreed to the 150 density guideline rather than to that originally recommended by the department. Thus, not all decisions to accommodate developer interests result from pressures applied by large companies, but may result from pressures applied indirectly through individual homeowners interested in substantial benefits to be gained from the interests of such companies.

Among other difficulties, the City Planning Department has had to suffer prolonged criticism from the Mayor's office. Shortly after being elected for the first time, the present Mayor made his opinions of planners known to Calgarians and Albertans generally. *The Lethbridge Herald,* on April 3, 1970, reported:

> Mayor Rod Sykes of Calgary rapped town planners in Alberta Thursday as he spoke to members of the Alberta Assessors' Association at its 10th annual convention being held in Lethbridge.
> He said planners' failures were not in technology but in the management and judgement of the priorities of people. Social problems are being ignored and town planners are only interested in the physical aspects of planning.

The report noted that the Mayor explained, "Alberta has planned economic social segregation," and:

> Town planners are only concerned about maximum stability at a minimum economic risk. Financial toll gates are set up and the people who can't afford the price are weeded out.

A few days after the Mayor's speech, on April 6, 1970, *The Lethbridge Herald* reported:

> City Development Commissioner . . . has accused Mayor Rod Sykes of deliberately attempting to destroy the city planning department.
> Replying in a prepared statement to persistent attacks including one at Lethbridge recently by Mayor Sykes on town planners, (the Commissioner) said the mayor is trying to humiliate, degrade and intimidate, thereby damaging staff morale to the point where the department is incapable of fulfilling council's instructions and driving some senior civic officers to the breaking point.
> He said numerous resignations of key people are real and imminent.

The report noted:

> In an interview, Mayor Sykes said the commissioner's statement is 'extremely intemperate and an emotional outburst.'
> 'I think it can be explained on the grounds that (the Commissioner) was under pressure from a number of people,' the mayor said. 'There is no question that a number of aldermen are looking for personal political advantage in any trouble they can find.'
> Mr Sykes said (the Commissioner's) statement is based on a misinterpretation of views he has expressed on several occasions and added that public statements by city administrators are totally destructive.
> 'I can't condone this behavior and I don't think it will continue. I look on this incident as regrettable, but there may be a positive side. I hope it will lead to a positive resolution of the planning department's problems.'
> Mr. Sykes said he does not plan to moderate his criticisms of the planning department and in future will seek to have internal city hall problems aired outside the public arena.

The Mayor's comments led to a public confrontation between his office and the Planning Department. By August, 1970 certain aldermen took up the fight with the Mayor. On August 6, 1970, *The Lethbridge Herald* reported, "Anti-Sykes Campaign Launched":

> Ald. . . . says he will start a campaign at city hall to correct statement by Mayor Rod Sykes which could be damaging to the city's image or employee morale.
> 'From now on I will go out of my way to set the record straight and keep the public informed.
> 'I want to take a calm and sensible approach to this thing,

> but I think it's important that this man (Mayor Sykes) doesn't stay in office after the next election.'
> Ald. . . ., in his first year on council, said in an interview he was concerned senior aldermen had not taken a stand. It was time city council told the mayor his leadership was damaging.
> 'Everyone was a little in awe of the mayor in the light of his big election majority and we have let him do almost anything.'
> Morale was particularly low in the city engineering, planning, and police departments, Ald. . . said.

While the public row has subsided, city planners remain very conscious of the city's political atmosphere. One planner has offered the opinion that for "survival" and career reasons it has become necessary for his colleagues to submit to demands from city politicians, even though these demands may run contrary to sound planning principles. From time to time, Planning Department recommendations have been not so much an expression of the views of the department, but an attempt to accommodate short-term political interests. The evidence indicates, however, that the department does make every attempt to maintain some order in the city's planning process.

Planning Department recommendations on a variety of developmental matters are decided at departmental pre-planning meetings, normally chaired by the Deputy Planning Director. Members of the department, including the Development Officer and a representative from CMHC, attend the meetings to review development applications and other planning matters. Frequently the members analyze the contents of circulation lists containing the comments of other city departments interested in particular proposals.

Generally speaking, city planners feel that the Planning Department should be involved in the preparation of a detailed city plan based on explicit policy and planning techniques that would include a clear delineation of districts, their relationship to one another, and the policy to be followed regarding their rates of growth and the nature of their development. This rational perspective, however, conflicts with the immediate concerns of city politicians, the broader range of public problems — housing shortages, unemployment, city slum potential, etc.

In a report published November 27, 1971 in *The Calgary Herald* about the Director of Planning, who had just resigned, it was stated that:

> (The Director) experienced six turbulent years with the department. He had one bitter public clash with Mayor Sykes, but more often had to sit silently through a barrage of criticism aimed at his department. Despite all that (the Director) points to many positive developments — in

downtown Calgary, in the closer liaison between City Hall and communities, in the preparation of sector plans to remove the uncertainties and disappointments that have plagued homebuyers. He also takes pride in the efficiency of the planning department.
'This year the entire staff has processed building and site plans worth more than one million dollars per working day,' he says.

Some of the criticism of the Planning Department by city politicians is a result of the department's inability to restrict development activities in the city. The administration has sometimes attempted to establish policy for certain areas of Calgary before permitting development to occur. A particularly good example is provided by the Nose Hill area. Encompassing over 3,000 acres, the hill has been of interest to developers for a long time; however, the City Council decided that the Planning Department should review the various development alternatives for the area and prepare policy for the council's consideration. Decisions on development applications involving the area had been postponed until policy was approved. Reporting on a Calgary Planning Commission meeting during which the Nose Hill Development was brought forward, *The Calgary Herald* of April 27, 1972 observed:

> Operations and Development Commissioner . . . explained why the city administration is reluctant to commit itself at this stage . . .
> He said development must wait until all the implications are placed before council on the future shape of Calgary.
> In the next two years, the city planners will continue a study to assess the future alternatives available, if the city is to secure the most economical and desirable form of internal growth.
> (He) said the study will seek to integrate transportation and utility costs and social and environmental factors so that the administration will know the implications of whatever form of growth the city favors.
> 'But when the facts for a decision (on Nose Hill) are not yet available, we should not make a decision', he said.

However, the report noted that ". . . two citizen members of the commission weren't prepared to accept without question a two-year 'freeze' on Nose Hill development." They:

> argued that the planners were contradicting their policy of a year ago when they supported a population of 20,000 on top of Nose Hill.
> Along with (another citizen member) he sought more detailed information on the amount of land Calgary has within its present boundaries that is suitable for residential development.

> 'The more land we have available in this city the cheaper it will be', (he) said, in arguing his case for opening up Nose Hill for development. (Parentheses added.)

According to the *Herald* report:

> . . . co-ordinator of current planning operations, said planners opposed immediate development of Nose Hill five years ago: 'But it is only now that we are making in-depth studies that we are able to prove that point.'
> He cautioned that if the city allows 20,000 people on Nose Hill, it won't be able to stop another 20,000 north of Nose Hill and that could in turn lead to a 14th St. West freeway.
> In their report to the commission, the planners said Calgary has within its existing limits 18,500 acres of land suitable for suburban residential expansion.
> All these areas could absorb more than 400,000 persons if developed to current density standards.
> (Commissioner of Operations and Development) estimated that even without Nose Hill the city has a 15-year supply of land for the market to play with.
> He said that opening up Nose Hill and adding to the land supply would not necessarily mean healthy land competition.

Despite the arguments of the planners and commissioners, an alderman and citizen member expressed the opinion ". . . that withholding Nose Hill would in fact artificially increase land prices." The commission decided to ". . . recommend that City Council allow development of two areas on the lower slopes of Nose Hill." A decision on a development application involving one of these areas had been postponed by the Planning Commission on March 15, 1972, and on that occasion the Commissioner of Operations and Development had repeated his view.[98]

Even in those instances where the City Council has taken a firm policy position on development, formal attempts have been made to persuade the council to take a more relaxed posture. This pressure is not a direct challenge by private interests, such as might occur at law, but the use of arguments asserting the prevailing concerns of the community or the hypothetical consequences of the council's policy. The council was opposed to land assembly on the supposition that an artificial scarcity of development land would raise lot prices. Council cannot readily take an initiative. Indeed, implicit in Calgary's situation is the fear of displeasing private interests, even though these interests necessarily compromise the long-term development interests of the city as a whole.

Those developers who are in the fortunate position of having the full weight of such federal programs as CMHC behind them may, if the city holds out on policy against their interests, decide to invest their capital elsewhere. Since such developers carry out large-scale operations, such a threat could cause grave political and social repercussions in a metropolitan centre experiencing a housing shortage and population and industrial settlement, and having a large portion of its work force employed by the construction industry. In Calgary, rightly or wrongly, there is frequent reference to an alleged pull-out of developers from Edmonton when Edmonton assembled the Mill Woods area. The council's decisions are influenced by the arguments of private management and by such notions as treating all companies "fairly." Also influential are the aldermen's preconceptions of the contributions of companies to the city's development and daily affairs.

The situation is complicated by still other factors. What are locally referred to as "small land squires," i.e. people and small companies who engage in speculative land acquisition in the path of anticipated city development, are said to preclude in large measure the possibility of the city's easily developing through contracts with large-scale developers. For council to interfere in the rights of persons and small companies on land acquisition would result in charges of interference in the rights of the individual to speculate and charges of favouring the large concern. The prerogatives of private landowners have been traditionally well respected in Alberta. Large concerns, in turn, may readily side with small companies and individuals in order to safeguard the rights of private interests in land. The city and large concerns could get together quite explicitly to work in concert to attain the city's targets, but this would imply a monopoly arrangement on development. The evidence obtained to date suggests that the practice of *ad hoc* city decision making, though recognized as cumbersome and inconvenient, is a *sine qua non* of the practical situation. Private companies have learned to live with it, to use and manipulate it, and therefore tend to safeguard it. The activities of "land squires" are but a part of the situation with which large developers have learned to cope, and are used by them in their arguments to manipulate council and its administration.

During a discussion in 1970 of an unaccepted provincial offer to make $6.3 million available to establish a land bank in Calgary — *a quid pro quo* for provincial assistance to Edmonton over the Mill Woods land assembly project — *The Calgary Herald* reported a council debate in these words:

> . . . north division manager of Carma Developers Ltd., told council that large land areas suitable for residential development in Calgary are being held back by speculators and 'land squires.'
> Clusters of small holdings exist, but to develop them would mean bypassing large chunks of suitable residential land, he said.[99]

The City Commissioners are continuously concerned with "the most economical and desirable form of internal growth." All city operating departments are willingly and actively formulating plans to guide their own activities and ostensibly to seek to co-ordinate their own activities with those of other departments. This rational[100] administrative emphasis, however, continues to conflict with the politician's concern about more immediate problems and his relation to the power of private capital and the citizen vote. The "Downtown Development Guidelines" serve as an example of the Planning Department's attempts at introducing a rational perspective. In November, 1969, *Architecture Canada* published an article concerning Calgary's "Plus-15" program. In part it stated:

> The fast growing city of 336,000 is now well launched on a controlled development program for its downtown core which, in concept and scale, is one of the most advanced of its kind.
>
> The program seems to have come about without too much fuss and fanfare, and it is being carried out within a planning and development philosophy based on the premise that what is good for the citizen and the city is also good for business, commerce and the developer.
>
> The solutions to the problems of the city centre are expressed in the planning department's "Downtown Development Guidelines."
>
> The approach is to separate pedestrian, private and public vehicular traffic, develop a traffic circulation system to increase accessibility and avoid congestion; and adopt for the 180-acre downtown core a technique of development control, in place of control by zoning, which not only encourages but makes possible maximum economic development of building sites while, at the same time, improving the public amenities and the quality of civic design.

Significantly, the City Council has never officially adopted the "Plus-15" program; instead "Plus-15" works on a bonus system ". . . whereby density and height restrictions (are) removed in return for additional open space and pedestrian connections."[101] Generally speaking developers have accommodated the guidelines and made use of the bonus system. Many feel that council should make the guidelines firm policy for downtown development, and continue the practice of bonuses. The city's former Planning Director stated:

> In spite of initial skepticism it is now accepted that the system will be largely operational within the next 5 years, and even the strongest critics have accepted that the flexibility and benefits of such a system could not have been achieved if each development had been conceived individually.[102]

However, the City Council maintains its position. This is attributable to its desire to maintain a flexible situation with which to negotiate with developers. So long as guidelines are not too firm council and large concerns can negotiate, and the amounts of money involved are so large that the "land squires" and small concerns are not involved. Council may impose sanctions to get its way — to direct the process of downtown development, for there is at least one example of a developer who chose to ignore the guidelines and thereby forefeited the bonus. Apparently this caused little concern among council, its posture being one of accommodating development proposals with or without the sanction of its bonus system. Recently, however, there is evidence to suggest that the council is becoming more inclined to favour a firm application of its guidelines so long as it appears that they will not discourage development in the downtown core. We did not determine what was leading to this apparent change in attitude.

The Calgary Plan proposed an approach to resolving problems presently associated with the city's rapid growth (see p.00). At a meeting of the Planning Advisory Committee on November 24, 1971, the Mayor:

> . . . addressed the Committee and advised as to its role and responsibility for the formulating and development of policies which would establish the future of the City and the growth and character of the Community within the general plan. If, in the opinion of the Committee, the Calgary Plan, in its present form, would not achieve the best results then the Committee had the opportunity to apply itself to updating the plan as a continuing process. Further, the Committee should not only concentrate on the 'physical' planning of the City but should also consider the sociological aspects of the City's future form. This must be done if the City was to achieve the best land utilization possible while considering all the problems of future urban growth. Imagination and initiative would assist the Committee in its coming to grips with the problems of urban development.

At a later point the Mayor . . . advised members that matters for discussion would arise from many sources:

> (a) Members of the Planning Advisory Committee
> (b) Items referred to the Committee from other Committees or from Councils
> (c) Citizens making personal or group submissions before the Committees
> and, as an example, suggested that he himself would be requesting the Committee to review and report on the matter of the Calgary Stampede expansion and the Victoria Park Sector Plan.[103]

The Assistant Deputy Director of Planning outlined to the committee his concerns, namely:

> (a) The ability of the City to maintain present services of the City should (it) continue to expand.
> (b) Growth, private transport and movement of vehicles within the City, outward expansion of the City, forms of urban growth and alternatives, satellite cities and concentration of density.
> (c) Finances available and how best used.
> (d) Form of Government.

Significantly, the minutes refer to remarks made by an alderman:

> Alderman . . . expressed his concern as to the quality of life available to citizens of the future should present urban sprawl continue in its rate of growth. He requested the Committee to give serious consideration to the implementation of a plan of study which would lead to the City making a decision on the nature and form of future City growth.

In response:

> The Assistant Deputy City Planner advised that concern in these matters was already being expressed at the Provincial, Regional and Urban level and the City is formulating an Urban Studies Group for continued review of the matter and that the terms of reference for the Urban Form Study will be available in the next three (3) months.[104]

The Mayor's remarks had reference to both general city form as expressed in the General Plan and the need to update it "as a continuing process." Concurrently, he gave an example of the type of "matters for discussion" likely to be referred to the committee and included the Stampede Grounds expansion/Victoria Park Sector Plan. Thus, the Mayor envisaged it as having an immediate administrative and advisory role. It would appear that the committee's attention could readily be directed away from the longer term policy issues. The Deputy Directory's remarks concerned the initiation of an "Urban Studies Group," whose terms of reference had still to be formulated. From the minutes, little attempt appears to have been made to encourage interest in the alderman's comments. In turn the alderman merely . . . "thanked the committee for their attention to this matter and requested that the chairman and the committee attempt to ensure that the 1972 Planning Department Budget contained funds for these Urban Studies."[105] Since the committee is composed of a number of citizens, not all of whom are properly informed of the city's complex planning problem, it will be relatively easy for the committee to become bogged down with insular concerns, despite its wider responsibilities.

A number of city planners are rather dubious about the urban study proposal. They argue that council still remains reluctant to establish goals and objectives for the city's development. It is therefore improbable that a "continued review" by either the Planning Advisory Committee or the proposed Urban Studies Group will occur. Some planners have suggested that the "Urban Studies Group" will simply be another addition to the proliferation of City Hall committees which, in turn, provide council with the opportunity to avoid issues and responsibilities of a particularly sensitive nature. Similarly, they fear that council will use the Planning Advisory Committee as another instrument for rationalizing its inability to make critical decisions, or use it as a means for excusing unfavourable decisions to particular lobbies. Furthermore, the committee is seen as offering an opportunity to the city administration to manipulate the city's affairs in its particular interests. It is apparent that the committee will have difficulty in formulating development policies without explicit guidance from City Council. Despite their doubts about the Urban Studies Group and the Planning Advisory Committee, however, city planners remain satisfied that citizen participation on these bodies and others, such as the Planning Commission, Citizens' Advisory Budget Committee, and Development Appeal Board, prevents the planning process from falling totally into the hands of city politicians and the professional staff. In the planners' perspective of the situation, citizen involvement is an essential component of the process of checks and balances in the local distribution of power.

Housing and Developers

The increase of interest in Calgary's low-cost housing arose in 1968 from public concern over the inadequacy and cost of housing for the lower-income groups. In January, 1968, a report[106] was submitted to City Council from the Social Planning Council of Calgary — a volunteer organization of concerned individuals — emphasizing the critical nature of the housing shortage and particularly the plight of low-income families and unattached individuals. The report stated:

> Even low-middle-income groups in the Calgary population are no longer financially able to rent decent housing of their choice. Calgary's standards of housing cannot be enforced because decent dwellings are just not available for families and individuals removed from substandard housing.[107]

The city had not taken advantage, it was argued, of CMHC and other provisions to handle the matter. City Council had, in 1966, resolved to set up a Housing Authority, but it had not been implemented. In 1968 the city was awaiting senior government approval of a city-wide urban renewal study, but the plight of individual Calgarians had been largely ignored.

On the usefulness of private enterprise in the low-cost housing field, the Social Planning Council's report stated:

> The Social Planning Council supports the role of private enterprise in meeting housing needs through building activities. Pending a change in federal legislation to broaden the role of private enterprise in building homes for low-income families, the Social Planning Council believes that public intervention is necessary. Assistance in some form is required for families and individuals in the low-income groups and for families whose annual income falls in the low-middle range, below $6,000.00.

The City Council had, up to that time, been reluctant to take action which might be interpreted as "public intervention" in an area construed as belonging to the private sector. The Planning Council, recognizing the sensitivity of its analysis and recommendations on public intervention, apparently decided to emphasize the principle of private-sector responsibility, and therefore justified the exception on the grounds of delay in federal legislature amendment — "Pending a change in federal legislation to broaden the role of private enterprise in building homes for low income families . . . "

In the City of Calgary's submission to the Hellyer Task Force in November, 1968 the case for additional support to meet the housing shortage was based on the rate of interest and higher construction and land costs. The city's submission argued in these terms:

> A combination of these factors has led to a change in development trends which has resulted in a change in demand by those in the $4,000 - $8,000 a year income bracket who must now seek rental accommodation of which only a limited supply is available. The greatest single problem must thus be attributed to the lack of investment funds to cater to accommodation for this income group.
> To provide accommodation for people displaced by urban renewal and because of the shortage of low-cost housing, the City is embarking on a public housing program . . . While the City has already taken active steps to enter the public housing field, it is our belief that the greatest emphasis in the housing field on the part of government, should be directed toward stimulating housing construction by private enterprise. This, we believe, can be best accomplished by insuring adequate provision of mortgage funds for lower cost housing units, and limited dividend housing projects, prior to accommodating the general housing market.

Against this background of rapid growth and change, the Council of the City of Calgary welcomes the opportunity afforded it to comment on the role that the Federal Government can play in achieving orderly urban growth and in ways in which the National Housing Act could be altered to better achieve community goals.

The submission contained detailed comments on the provisions of the National Housing Act, federal policy, and on the city's recent steps to acquire land and erect accommodation.

The city responded rapidly to Ottawa's "experimental housing program" in 1969. On February 20, 1971 *The Calgary Herald* published a report entitled, "House-hunting has become 1971 sport for all Calgarians." Written by Ken Hill, a staff writer, the report explained:

> House-hunting two years ago in Calgary was a pleasure reserved for the well-to-do while the masses looked on in envy.
>
> It's different in 1971.
>
> The stands have emptied. Former spectators are now active participants in choosing from the widest and most attractive selection of houses available to Canadians.
>
> Under an assortment of federal, provincial and municipal government aid programs the low-wage earner in this city now has an excellent crack at home ownership.
>
> This compares with his Eastern Canadian counterpart whose housing aspirations have been narrowed to 800 square feet of living space tunneled degradingly into a low-rental apartment structure.
>
> It would be grossly misleading to even suggest there is a house available to every family unit in Calgary. But this is a Utopian dream that is closer to realization here than in any other comparable Canadian centre.
>
> Calgary, therefore, is not making an idle boast when it claims more detached housing units per capita than any other Canadian city. It is a title to be proud of.

Within two years, Calgary's acute housing problem had been relieved to a substantial degree. The staff writer attributed this to the federal experimental housing program which:

> slices through red tape to allow rapid development of projects. Government officials have closed portions of their restrictive regulation books to allow a cheaper form of subdivision development.

The program referred to was CMHC's amortization of a loan over 50 years at 7⅞ percent plus the provincial interest subsidy of 2 percent to produce a net interest of 5⅞ percent.

The cost of the units averaged $11,750, and down-payments required 5 percent or about $600. The owners had to have incomes sufficient to meet the monthly carrying charge of about $80 involving them in no more than 25 percent of salary. In a report to council's Special Co-ordinating Committee on Housing, August 13, 1971 the city's Planning Director observed:

> It is of interest to note that the experimental housing programme has relied on houses which could have been built conventionally as far as compliance with the building code is concerned. Waivers have been almost entirely confined to subdivision and city servicing standards. In other words, experimentation has been on land development rather than building forms.

The experimental nature of the CMHC project was therefore not so much in house design as in the city's services and development arrangements for housing.

Besides this "experimental housing," council has been involved in the construction of public housing. According to an Alberta Housing Corporation pamphlet, the cost to the municipality works out in the following way:

> Financial assistance is available for public housing through the following two ways:
> (a) Through the Federal-Provincial-Municipal partnership arrangement in which the Federal Government contributes 75% of the capital cost, subsidy and operating losses, and the Provincial Government contributes 15% of the capital cost, subsidy and operating losses, leaving 10% to be borne by the Municipality. These contributions are usually amortized over a period of fifty years for administration purposes.
> (b) By the Provincial government obtaining a 90% loan of the cost of construction and land from the Federal government with the Provincial government contributing 10% of the capital cost. The Federal participation in the subsidy is 50% with a 40% provincial contribution leaving a 10% subsidy to be borne by the municipality.[108]

The council's Housing and Urban Renewal Department uses the above arrangements through a "proposal call" system. The department advertises for bids from private developers. Having received the bids, the department negotiates with the developers who respond, in turn, by taking into account the city's needs in terms of such factors as location, aesthetics, price, CMHC requirements, and similar considerations.

Perhaps not surprisingly criticism has developed regarding the City Council's practice of subsidizing public housing. On November 16, 1971 the Special Co-ordinating Committee on

Housing received a copy of a letter which questioned the continuation of this practice. The letter, from the Calgary Property Taxpayers' Association, explained:

> For some time there has been a growing concern among property taxpayers of Calgary with regard to the subsidized policy of City Council. From 1966 to 1970 housing was scarce, but since 1970 there has been an excess of housing as illustrated in the Herald advertisements. Each day there are 14 columns of unfurnished suites and three or four columns of furnished suites with plenty of houses available. This in effect has been the period of excessive subsidized house building.
> In other words, the property owners, who have borne the burden of paying taxes to the city, are in a position now of having to pay even higher taxes to subsidize competition for scarce tenants from property only partially occupied because of subsidized housing.
> We would therefore request — until such time as the housing surplus is absorbed — that City Council desist from building any more subsidized housing.
> If City Council insists on its present policy, private building — which employs many men — will diminish and taxes on empty buildings will not be paid.
> The example in Europe is that when there is subsidized housing private enterprise gets out of the business of providing accommodation and the result is a devastating permanent shortage of rental accommodation . . .
> If a certain percentage of the population has to be subsidized in housing, the most sensible way is to distribute these tenants in private enterprise suites, thus preventing a queer looking subsidized area that will ultimately degenerate into a ghetto, be an eye-sore and lower the beauty of our city.

On March 10, 1972 *The Calgary Herald* published a report of a meeting held by the Taxpayers' Association.

In part, it noted:

> During the meeting, the city and provincial governments were accused of indifference toward the plight of property owners, being uncommunicative when approached by the association for facts about the public housing situation, and empire-building at the expense of private enterprise. Apartment owners said the demand for commercially developed housing drops as public housing becomes available. Building contractors switch to public housing, and private accommodation will be more expensive as it becomes scarcer.

As public housing grows, they said, higher taxes will have to be paid by the shrinking proportion of the population owning their homes and paying property taxes directly, and paying indirectly through renting in commercial apartments.

The Taxpayers' Association has continued to argue that Calgary has a surplus of housing accommodation of various kinds. Despite this, however, others argue that there remains a shortage of housing for persons in the lower-income bracket. The suggestion that the council subsidize the low-income person to occupy a commercial apartment has been made by local apartment owners and others on several occasions. This particular idea is presently being examined by the provincial government and was considered by the Citizens' Advisory Budget Committee on Calgary's capital budget. In response to the latter, the minutes of the November 16 meeting record that the members of the Special Committee:

> . . . noted that numerous proposals have been received from the same firms who have rental accommodation on the market. As such, the Committee felt that the public housing program was catering to a different income bracket and no unfair competition was being created.

The problem was one of the ups and downs of business, rather than unfairness to any particular company. The minutes also recorded that "no public housing has been constructed in 1971 and that a real shortage exists of two-bedroom and bachelor units."

The "real shortage" referred to above, which still exists, was for two-bedroom and bachelor units suitable for senior citizens. Generally speaking, however, public housing shortages continue to be a problem for Calgary.[109] *The Calgary Herald* reported on March 1, 1972 a discussion which took place at a council Finance Committee meeting:

> Under cross-examination by the Mayor, city social service director . . . was adamant that Calgary does not have enough social housing at present.
> 'There is a waiting list to get into Shaganappi Village and the people who live there now say it's the best housing they've had for the money they pay,' he said.

Regarding "subsidized private accommodation," the press report noted that the city Social Service Director preferred social housing to subsidized private accommodation "because we know how much we pay in rent for public assistance recipients who live in private accommodation." The Mayor also commented on how well known it was that landlords had no hesitation in charging the maximum if the public purse was paying the rents. On the other hand, the consequences for the commercial house builder could not be ignored.

The Mayor knew that "social housing creates more problems and less profit for private investors and developers, when it should produce a reasonable profit and fewer problems."[110] He also predicted that social housing would be the most serious of problems faced by governments in the next few years.

City aldermen continue to question the city's involvement in social housing and to question the appearance of some of the projects. *The Calgary Herald* reported on a later meeting of the Finance Committee in these words:

> Alderman . . . Tuesday called for a halt on public housing projects until a total review can be made of city policy. 'I'm tired of seeing big blocks of housing erected near major arteries instead of being blended into residential communities' . . . [111]

Public criticism of such projects has also been pronounced. Taking the "Eau Claire project" as an example, *The Calgary Herald,* January 5, 1972 reported that at a public meeting petitioners against the project:

> . . . charged public housing will bring down property values and deter private developers from locating in the area.
> They also claimed the development will overtax school facilities in Eau Claire.
> 'Besides, it isn't a good place for anyone to live,' said . . . 'The city is building accommodation for growing families right downtown, where there are a lot of accidents and pollution, and right near the river where small children can drown.'

Facilities for the poor, therefore, become the subject of criticism from the better-to-do, no less than from city aldermen and commercial building interests. By requiring special consideration which results in lower than commercial rates of rental and particular kinds of building in particular places, facilities for the poor disturb the balance of otherwise profitable or capital-engendering arrangements. The fact that it was the local city council who moved to take up senior government incentive capital in this area of public policy has led the council into being the object of broadly based criticism.

Public criticism of public housing projects is usually based on such narrow concerns as the extent to which such projects may affect neighbourhood property values. However, certain public objections to specific projects, and particular aspects of the criticism expressed by a few city aldermen, have had the support of city planners. Planners have observed that developers frequently take advantage of the "proposed call" system to get rid of property which is not considered suitable for more expensive accommodation; or property for which it would be difficult to negotiate conventional lending arrangements. Developers, as will be illustrated in the MacEwan Glens case study at the end of this chapter, are not opposed to public and low-income housing. Planners often argue that under present federal government policies public housing projects are secure "money makers," but are sometimes impossible to support from a planning point of view. In fact, quite recently, the Municipal Planning Commission was preparing to support city planners by itself opposing the construction of a public housing project, at 10th Street and 3rd Avenue N.W., which had been approved by City Council. The city planners viewed the location as being particularly inappropriate for the kind of project being proposed; however, apparently the Mayor was able to dissuade the Commission from opposing the project and he made a strong verbal attack on the Planning Department. The press has observed that "No plan for a public housing project can be regarded as complete, it seems, until it has been opposed by residents or property owners of the area concerned."[112]

Though Calgary has tackled the low-income housing needs with vigour under federal and provincial incentives, the current problem is seen to be the difficulties middle-income people are experiencing in purchasing homes. A press staff writer, under the title, "Homeowning — the middle class is feeling the pinch," identified the $9,000-$12,000 income group as the one affected.[113] While the rich could afford large enough down-payments to mitigate the effects of mortgage interest rates and the poor were recipients of government subsidies, the middle range had no recourse. They were referred to as "the silent majority." The average cost of a single family dwelling was reportedly $23,354, in Calgary exclusive of land, against a Canadian average of $22,912.[114] Yet Calgary was experiencing a building boom in 1971. The Planning Department processed a record $193.8 million building permits. Some 4,166 new single family residences were approved, or 1,120 permits more than in 1970. Government-subsidized housing in 1971 had fallen off, as also had duplex construction.[115] Despite the incidence of apartment vacancies, the value of apartment buildings under construction in the first four months of 1972 was greater than the corresponding period in 1971. Thus despite all the problems and difficulties raised in public, from the General Plan to low-cost publicly subsidized housing and apartment vacancy rates, the relentless growth process was continuing.[116]

Whatever may be the average cost, or the cost of different house types, the city has received considerable publicity over its large-scale housing projects. The widely read *Canadian Homes*[117] ran a survey of housing across Canada. It described Calgary as "one of the few cities in Canada that's making a serious effort to provide houses that the majority of its citizens can afford to buy. With the backing of a concerned house building industry, the support of labor and of church and other citizens' groups, Calgary's mayor and city council have managed to cut through the bureaucratic and public resistance that holds up the construction of low cost housing in other cities." It mentioned that its own survey, in July, 1971, showed that 21 percent of all houses for sale were priced under $15,000, and 84 percent were priced under $25,000. It identified in particular the development of Engineered Homes Ltd. and Nu-West Homes Ltd., with attractive dwellings in the $16-$18,000 range. This publicity was important because in 1970 the city had declined a provincial government offer of $6.3 million to commence a city-owned land bank. As in Mill Woods, Edmonton, the cost of lots might be brought down by public ownership of a land bank. The idea was revived by a Calgary alderman in 1972 in the face of the city's recent building boom.[118]

One fear which had led council to the 1970 refusal was apparently that the services of the Alberta Housing Corporation would involve provincial influence over land within the city's boundaries, particularly if the province considered that the land was not being developed sufficiently speedily within the city's boundaries. It also had fears about what a city land assembly project might do to lot prices even if it removed the speculator's influence. City officials argued in 1972 that the "rampant speculation" in Edmonton's city lots which followed that city's Mill Woods annexation and land assembly scheme would recur in Calgary.[119] Calgary, in 1970 and 1972, was said to be benefiting from a highly competitive situation among developers which ensured the availability of housing at low prices. Accompanying this argument, however, were expressions of concern over large developers acquiring control over a considerable amount of land within the city. The City Commissioners were asked to identify how much useful land remained undeveloped within the city and how much of it was held under the control of private firms.[120]

City records, in a partial inventory of six major land developers, showed the following holdings, scattered in most cases from parcels of a few acres to a parcel of 1,200 acres:

Kelwood Corporation 1,200 acres,
Quality Construction 1,275 acres,
BACM 1,600 acres,
Carma Developers 3,750 acres, including two joint ventures with Nu-West Ltd., and a 640 acre block outside the city boundary (then the subject of the MacEwan Glens annexation discussion).
Nu-West Ltd. 1,225 acres, including 225 acres outside the city boundary. (The company also had options on additional land in south-west Calgary.)
Western Realty 1,450 acres (some of which was industrial).

The total was 10,500 acres, and other smaller developers had assembled parcels under 1,000 acres. The council, intending to ensure the continuation of "healthy competition," considered that steps should be taken to encourage outside developers to take an interest in Calgary. *The Calgary Herald* believed the Mayor "still intends setting up a committee to investigate dealings of city land developers."[121] A similar report appeared on March 2, 1972, when the Mayor had reportedly told the Calgary Planning Commission: "I am concerned that industrial land which we service and make available to industry at cost or above cost is being bought and then resold at a much higher profit."[122] The city was not to be in the business of providing land to speculators at the taxpayers' expense.

The Mayor moved in April, 1972 to put the city's own house in order by public disclosure of a real estate register of names of persons associated with City Hall who had land interests and, secondly, to place the names of all landowners from whom the city buys land on the council agenda. The mayor observed that the latter practice used to be common, but that recently only the legal description of the land had been made public. While such measures are commendable in the competitive situation which Calgary appears to have, the above partial inventory of land developers' holdings gives no guarantee of the availability of developed lots to the public home buyer. The mode of land servicing — which must involve contractual agreements between the city and its public utilities on the one hand, and the developer on the other — tends to determine the speed, scale, and direction of lot availability unless the developer is capable of servicing on his own account. Each year the city negotiates a "Residential Development Agreement" with the Urban Development Institute (UDI), an organization which is comprised of, and represents, development companies and financial lending institutions engaged in development activities in Calgary. The objects of the society are:

> (a) to promote well-planned communities by encouraging the reasonable and unselfish use of land for residential, public, commercial and industrial purposes;
> (b) to promote efficiency and a high standard of ethics among persons, firms and corporations engaged in the business of land assembly and development;
> (c) to promote pleasant and efficient relationships between such persons, firms and corporations and Municipal Planning and other Governmental authorities and agencies;
> (d) to promote economies in the planning and installation of utilities and other services with a view of making building lots and sites available to the public and the building industry at the lowest possible cost.[123]

The UDI, Alberta Division, considers itself recognized in both Edmonton and Calgary as representative of the development industry in Alberta and, therefore, the instrument to negotiate with cities over industrial and residential servicing, development agreements, zoning by-laws and revisions, general plans, site planning standard, apartment development and so forth.

The "Residential Development Agreement" applies in cases of large developments such as subdivisions, as distinct from individual development applications where the development permit pertains.

In 1972 the Commissioner's Report to the City Council's Operations and Development Committee, advised that the UDI had approved a revised agreement between the city and themselves. The report stated:

> During the negotiations for the 1971 Agreement, the Commissioners advised the Urban Development Institute that the road cost-sharing policy would be the subject of a major review for the 1972 Agreement. To this end, the developers share of roads has been increased and the following policies will apply:
> (1) All streets up to and including the 40/72 foot residential collector should be at the developer's full cost. These collector roads are designed to serve the developments only and therefore are felt to be a legitimate charge to the developments. This change will require revisions to Clause 51 of the Standard Agreement.
> (2) Major thoroughfares, whether divided or undivided would be cost shared by the developer with the City paying for only extra width and depth over the collector standard. This type of facility serves the development and other areas and normally provides designed intersections at 1/8 and 1/4 mile spacing with direct single family residential frontage not allowed. This would eliminate Clause 9(a) and 9(b) and will increase the contribution of the developer to this category of road.[124]

The report also noted that: "Higher categories of roads such as expressways and freeways will continue as a City responsibility for the time being." Included in the "Recommendation" was the observation: "It is imperative from UDI's point of view: that this document be approved by April 10 in order that adequately serviced land is available for the housebuilding industry."

Although the members of the Operations and Development Committee agreed with the Commissioners' recommendation after short debate, the Mayor took issue with the revised agreement at the council meeting. He questioned the refusal of developers to pay a portion of the costs of freeways and expressways, and pointed out that it was unfair for the average citizen to have to bear the total financial burden for such expenditures. A Commissioner observed that the developer would simply recover additional expenses from the homeowner and that the City Council must determine whether or not it wished to add substantial costs to the developer in 1972. It was also noted that the total amount spent each year for freeways and expressways was fixed by the provincial government's share of the overall costs. Further debate involved points covering the financial responsibilities of car owners, whether or not industry and business use freeways more than the average citizen, and whether the fact that developers provide a service in supplying housing should be taken into consideration during cost-sharing negotiations. The Mayor stated that, taking into consideration federal housing policies, he had no sympathy for developers experiencing cost increases. Further, he explained that he was becoming increasingly tired of hearing from developers that they cannot pay for those services which enable them to reap substantial profits. In addition, he observed that "there is no limit to their increases but there is to ours" and "I work for people who have trouble paying taxes, not developers."

A Commissioner explained that the question of "who should pay for what" received heated discussion during the negotiations with UDI over the agreement. The council was informed that during the course of the negotiations, there had been agreement that to place further costs on the developer, other than those agreed upon, would be "going too far in one jump," and that such additional costs would be reflected in property values. However, it was observed that the new agreement was of a standard nature and in no way precluded special costs resulting from "leap frogging," i.e., development occurring in areas beyond the current limit of city services. Continuing to question the developers' agreement to pay a portion of the cost of "bread and butter services," and their refusal to accept a fair share of the cost of providing "luxury services," the Mayor recommended that the question of cost-sharing arrangements for freeways and expressways be referred back for consideration. The council approved this motion with the understanding that the agreement, as negotiated by the Commissioners would come into immediate effect (April 10, 1972). Concern was expressed that if the agreement was held up a number of developers would be unable to get certain projects underway.

While the Mayor's position was in defence of the city's obligation to meet as little of road (and expressway and freeway) construction as could be arranged, the UDI's position was to avoid having to oblige the lot purchaser to pay for more of the services than were necessary. Both parties appeared to have in mind that senior governments were party through their subsidization mechanisms — NHA, CMHC, AHC and provincial road subsidies — to the defraying of the costs on transfer to the lot homeowner. The agreement of 1972 was apparently so easily dealt with by the Operations and Development Committee and by the council in its ratification — after further negotiation by the Commissioners with UDI over expressway and freeway costs — because of the ability to pass off the costs to other costs to other levels of government or to the lot buyer. The costs of development — including freeways — had apparently to be incurred inevitably. The city's concern was only to see that as much was taken off the city as could be arranged.

The 1972 agreement is a long and detailed document. It provides, however, for the developer to develop "only that portion of the sub-division outlined in red on the attached plan",[125] and no construction or development was to take place without prior application to the City Engineer and his written permission obtained. Similarly, the developer was bound to meet city specifications and designs in force on 15 February of the construction year to which the agreement refers.

Thus, the city has formal control over the developments occurring within its boundaries. The decision to develop a particular parcel of land rests, however, with the developer as landowner, but it is feasible only if arrangements can be made with the city over the servicing required. This applies to raw land commercial development as well as low-cost housing arranged through the "proposal call" system, though the details of land ownership may vary. The detail of the agreement is a consequence of the mode of arranging for and financing these services. The developer is thus able to estimate with accuracy the costs, and therefore the lot selling price, of his proposal and thereby to assess the chances of his sales in terms of the market. The city, however, is not able explicitly to direct the area of development next required unless it can do so by vicarious incentives such as predetermined freeway and transportation corridors, trunk line service provisions and similar critical factors entering the administrative convenience and cost component of the developer's proposed activities. In practice, however, Calgary submits proposals on location, staging, and estimated costs of trunk services to UDI for comment. Upon agreement on location and staging the city undertakes the necessary installation, thereby permitting the developer to proceed as landowner and subdivider within the annually arranged agreement. It is a neat, mutually workable arrangement; but the more the city transfers to developers by way of their paying the cost of services and covering a greater range of services, the less the influence of the city will be.

The Alberta Division of the UDI has existed for about 15 years, and is organized into two chapters, one in each of the metropolitan centres. Its relation to the City of Calgary was said by one of its officials to have been very positive over a period of 10 to 15 years and had, in his view, been responsible for creating the favourable development climate for Calgary in recent years. Relations with the City of Edmonton had been difficult, but were improving. The differences in the development policies of the two cities had made it easier for UDI to work in Calgary than in Edmonton. In Calgary, as was noted previously, proposed amendments to city planning control by-laws were referred to UDI for comment before enactment, but this had not been the practice in Edmonton. Edmonton's decision to plan and service subdivisions themselves had left little room for UDI contribution, while Calgary's policy had been explicit and co-operative. A UDI official ascribed the difference in the two cities' land prices to their differing approaches to UDI.

The nexus of relationships associated with UDI, city

departments and policies, senior governments and lot buyers in the two metropolitan centres is extremely complex. We have been unable to gain little more than a passing picture. It is clearly an important research area not only in Alberta, but in Canada generally. We observe that UDI's move to ratify a Canada-wide constitution — started three or four years ago — coincided with the federal move towards a national urban policy for Canada. Within Alberta, the UDI is said to hold frequent discussions with the Provincial Planning Branch, and we were told that it has contact with CMHC and the Ministry of State for Urban Affairs in Ottawa. There is little doubt, therefore, that in so far as UDI is an organized institution directly associated with one of the critical aspects of urban form and planning, its affairs and relations with governments at all levels will be important in the urban developmental process whatever the direction to be given that process by the differing levels of government in Canada.

At the provincial level, it is important that further research is speedily conducted into the alleged relationship of UDI to City Hall in Edmonton and Calgary on the one hand, and lot prices and city development on the other. This raises for empirical examination an array of issues: Is competition among developers responsible for keeping land prices down, or is this merely the benefit of co-ordinated activity expected of any large scale organization in interaction? What is the possibility of city form being determined by developers rather than city council, and what is the consequence which such determination by either party would have on any provincial direction of urban affairs? Is it necessary or not, for government to move towards facilitating the public assembly of development land? How easily might population and industrial concentration be enhanced or reduced as a matter of provincial government policy?

Transportation and the By-Law Charade

Transportation corridors and transit systems perhaps more than any other single influence shape the form and character of a city. The Calgary General Plan treats the subject in these terms:

> It is fundamental to relate transportation needs, routings and thoroughfare design to the type of city that we wish to create. The danger, on the basis of past experience is that the transportation system will decide, at great expense to the environment, the type of life the majority of our citizens are going to lead. To avoid unnecessary public expenditure, decisions on the type of overall transportation network must be made sufficiently far ahead and related to land use and other environmental factors.[126]

The case study that follows, of the handling of Calgary Transportation By-law No. 8500, is an example of council's inability, or unwillingness, to establish the type of policy required to control and implement this critical factor in the developmental process.

In 1970 the provincial government passed the City Transportation Act.[127] This Act was the outcome of discussion between the cities and the provincial Department of Highways and Transport, and dealt with provincial government involvement in the planning, financing, and development of urban transport systems. Premier Strom in 1970 said that this Act enabled:

> . . . cities to designate transportation corridors and to have effective control over the land in those corridors. This will allow long-range planning by cities, without the necessity of spending large sums of money immediately in order to ensure available space some twenty or thirty years in the future . . . the province is interested in seeing the cities develop balanced transportation systems and that it will provide funds toward the construction of urban transportation facilities . . . whether these be highways, rapid transit, moving sidewalks, or whatever . . . provided that they are part of an integrated transportation system.[128]

The legislation provided for all land titles in designated areas to be endorsed with a notice to the effect that "The city must acquire land which has been in a protection area for three years or longer if the owner so requests, by purchase, or, if necessary, by expropriation."[129] The compensation payable, however, was not to take into account any development carried out subsequent to the establishment of a transportation protection area unless such development was covered by a permit. Also, the compensation payable would not reflect the enhancement or depreciation in the value of property which was attributable to its inclusion in a transportation protection area. There was also provision for appeal boards. The Premier saw in legislation such as land assembly and the City Transportation Act a means of giving the cities the "breathing room they need to grow healthy over the next few decades." He considered these steps as "examples of the general means by which this province contributes to municipal planning: the provision of loans and enabling legislation."[130]

The Lethbridge Herald, on April 2, 1970 reported that the Minister of Highways had just introduced amendments to the City Transportation Act. Among these amendments was one that would ". . . allow a property owner who feels unfairly treated by the city to take the question to the Alberta Supreme Court." The report also observed that a Progressive Conservative MLA referring to the general nature of the legislation, said . . . the legislation went too far in protecting the needs of the community at the expense of the individual rights.

> (The MLA) said the bill was 'offensive' in part to Calgary and Edmonton councils because of provisions that any

> proposed transportation plan must be approved by the government.[131]

In response, the minister:

> . . . said it was 'logical' the province should have some say if it was going to help pay for such systems. He said the legislation was drafted in consultation with the two cities.

Among the documentation given to Calgary City Council at the public hearing on By-Law No. 8500 on February 22, 1972 was an outline of the provisions of the Act and the way the city had worked within them. Under Part I of the Act, which deals with the establishment of transportation systems, the city government is given the responsibility of covering the costs of construction and maintenance of all transportation facilities within the city's boundaries. The Act also provides for the possibility of financial assistance by the province towards these costs on condition the city complies with two stipulations. These were outlined at the public hearing in these words:

> (a) Must have prepared a comprehensive study report for the development of a transportation system designed to service the needs of the entire City. Discussions with Provincial authorities have clarified that this requirement has been met through the production of the Calgary Transportation Study, the several reports on rapid transit under the general name of Transit for Calgary's Future and, as well, the various more detailed functional study reports that have been produced dealing with specific aspects of the highway transit system. These are listed in detail in Bylaw No. 8500.
> (b) Must have passed a bylaw which establishes and designates a transportation system for the City in accordance with the transportation study report. Bylaw No. 8500 has been drafted in order to meet this particular requirement. However, whereas the Act states that the transportation system must be in accordance with the transportation study report, the Provincial Government has recognized that all technical transportation recommendations do not necessarily meet with total municipal endorsation, and consequently, the defined urban transportation system need not comply in all respects with previously prepared transportation reports. For this reason, the roadway system shown and described in Bylaw No. 8500 covers only those roadways which are in existence or are under construction, those proposed for construction in the next five to seven year period and future alignments which have been approved in principle

> by City Council. The rapid transit routes shown consist only of the northwest, downtown and south lines, since they are the only ones which have received any in-depth alignment study.[132]

The legislation also set a deadline date of October 31, 1970 for the passage of a city by-law, unless that date was extended by the minister.[133] Though the date was extended, Calgary was required to pass the by-law, and have it forwarded to the minister, by February 29, 1972 if the city was to expect financial assistance towards transportation system construction in 1972. As the council arranged the public hearing only on February 22, it was clearly not anticipating any substantial changes to its proposals from the hearing. The documentation provided at the hearing partly covered this point by noting that by-laws were amendable at a later date with the approval of the Lieutenant-Governor. The documentation noted:

> This is seen as being an extremely important clause in the Act, since it does not tie the city irrevocably to the transportation system shown in Bylaw No. 8500. It is to be expected that changing needs and circumstances in the future will dictate the necessity of adding or deleting portions of the system and changing the category of others.[134]

The third reading before council was expected to occur either at the same meeting of council as the public hearing or at a special meeting.

Part 2 of the Act deals with the Protection and Acquisition of Land. Under this point, the hearing documentation read as follows:

> *Part 2 — Protection and Acquisition of Land:*
> It should be clearly understood that passing of Bylaw No. 8500 does not mean that land required for right-of-way for the transportation facilities is automatically "frozen" or restricted in any way. This part of the Act, however, recognizes that the City may consider it necessary to impose some measure of control on land required for transportation purposes. It provides, therefore, for the passage of further bylaws which will designate the right-of-way for any or all of the facilities covered by Bylaw No. 8500 to be a *'transportation protection area'*
> As with Bylaw No. 8500, those bylaws which designate transportation protection areas must be advertised at least once a week for two consecutive weeks at least 14 days prior to passage of the bylaws, and that representations from any persons having an interest in the lands covered by the bylaws must be heard.

> Furthermore, this part of the Act also makes it possible for the City to pass later bylaws abandoning all or any part of a transportation protection area established by previous bylaw. (Emphasis original.)

The public hearing lasted several hours, during which time various community groups expressed their concern about the contents of the by-law. It was pointed out that the rapid transit routes outlined on the by-law map, if implemented, would have a devastating effect on a number of communities and parkland areas. Furthermore, it was observed that the council was responsible for providing direction of a kind that would place the interests of people rather than "automobile worshipers" in the forefront. Moreover, it was remarked that not enough attention had been paid to the points raised in the Calgary Plan. In this regard, it was suggested that established transit routes could be used to re-direct growth and check urban sprawl. Responding to an argument that the map meant very little, one individual observed that developers were taking a particular interest in it. A brief, prepared by the "Society for Pollution and Environmental Control" had noted:

> This proposed bylaw is considered by some to be a mere formality, required by the province in order to qualify for road construction funds for this year. Yet what is often considered provisional, flexible, and not binding by planners, is, once it is put into the form of a bylaw, considered by the elected officials to be the last word, and a commitment to construction. All the more so when the bylaw contains a map of route alignments.
>
> The proposed bylaw carefully states that the City may later amend the bylaw from time to time by the addition or deletion of transportation facilities (sic) or by changing the category of others. Yet we contend that it will not be enough to add or delete, if the *system proposed* itself is inadequate. It is very hard to make alterations to a system once the basic grid, the *structural pattern,* has been laid down. (Emphasis original.)[135]

This brief also questioned whether or not the "proposed system" had been prepared in terms of the region as a whole.

> How does the proposed system tie into existing or future road networks *outside the city limits?* It will certainly affect development in outlying towns — have these regional relationships been taken into account? (Emphasis original.)

This challenging brief later referred to the City Planning Department, under council direction, having been set the task of studying the alternative growth forms possible in the city. Very different land use models had been prepared. Thus, "For the first time, the transportation implications of alternative growth forms will be available on a comparative basis," but it would be only in the late fall of 1972, that this would be finally available. As matters stood, the proposed by-law merely projected the existing condition, and the on-going round of daily decisions taken in the city would tend to entrench these conditions into rigid patterns. The "breathing room" the cities needed, as the Premier had seen it in 1970, was hardly materializing.

> The society's brief concluded its point in these words: The transportation system proposed, with major freeways and expressways at northern, southern, eastern, and western edges of the city will reinforce this existing outward extension of low density areas, in all directions. In order to serve this pattern, *many* miles of parallel feeder roads will be necessary. In fact this 'sheet' form or 'sprawl' requires more miles of road construction than any other form of city growth.
> Thus while for the period 1970-1986, $154 million is projected for rapid transit construction, $482 million is projected for "Freeways, Expressways, and major Streets." *General Plan (14.2)*

This is in light of the Plan's call for:

> 1. As an interim measure, the immediate review of all existing programs and expenditure proposals *in the light of a projected possible cumulative review deficiency of $460,000,000 by 1986 . . .*
> 2. Subsequently review of the costs and implications of other forms of urban growth and regional growth.
> *General Plan (14.9)* It is stated by some that failure to pass this bylaw by a specified date will mean losing some $15 million in provincial funds for road construction from 1971-1972.
> There are certainly some essential road constructions which have been approved and should go ahead soon, especially the new bridge couplets at both ends of the city downtown core. This amount to be lost is negligible compared to the almost $500 million proposed road budget for the next 15 years, *if* passing this by-law commits the City into the system as drawn on this map. Committed to an intolerably expensive transportation system servicing an uneconomic and dehumanizing form of future growth.[136]

Another written submission, from the Bowness Community Association's Planning and Development Committee, commended the city "for the comprehensiveness of the proposed

Transportation System By-law No. 8500; for the fact that it properly incorporates both roadway and rapid transit systems, and for the obvious concern about long-range transportation needs which this proposal represents."[137] This brief continued by presenting recommendations on detailed aspects of the road planning proposed in the Bowness area, including places where off-street parking might be provided, safety features, future roadway alignments and by-passes of the community, etc. Other issues arose during the discussion such as the possibility of making car owners pay the major portion of road expansion costs through a user tax formula, and the possibility of reducing air pollution by discouraging use of private cars.

The most critical part of the debate, however, centred on the by-law itself and the supporting documentation. No clear policy had emerged, it was argued, from the more than 30 documents provided on the by-law. What information was provided lacked consistency and explicit statement, the by-law map was incomplete, e.g., with freeways ending on river banks, and was inconsistent with the written information provided.[138] Much of the data contained in the documents, it was alleged, was out of date.

Throughout the hearing, the Mayor held to his position that the passage of the by-law was a "charade we are going through to please certain people in Edmonton." He observed that there was a mechanism for subsequent amendments to the by-law and that the by-law did not commit the city to certain corridors, to control access, to build, to protect rights-of-way or, in general, to any definite policies. The by-law would, in effect, simply enable the city to qualify for provincial government road construction grants. Pointing out that the city had already borrowed nine million dollars of the expected 15 million dollars for 1971 road development, the Mayor suggested that failure to pass the by-law would have grave implications for the 1972 capital budget and mill rate.

Despite the Mayor's arguments, certain aldermen felt that the council should request further time from the provincial government "to do our job properly" and to re-evaluate the by-law. The Chief Commissioner observed that the current provincial legislation required the council to pass the by-law before grants would be made available to the city. Moreover, it was pointed out that the Chief Commissioner and City Engineer had had lengthy discussions with the provincial administration and that although the Department of Highways was aware of the deficiencies of the by-law, it would not authorize grants until the by-law had been passed. The Mayor observed that all the proper channels had been used and that he refused to participate in any action that would make the by-law a public spectacle. He also noted that the city was proceeding with a number of studies and that up to that point in time the council had been doing its best to make decisions as information became available. While he agreed that it was a "piecemeal approach," the city had no practical alternative if it wished to obtain provincial grants. He blamed the senior government for not meeting their responsibilities with regard to transportation problems being experienced by large urban centres.

An attempt was made to have the by-law tabled in order to enable the city to make one last attempt at negotiation with the provincial government; this failed. The by-law passed with a vote of 8-4. The press comment on the incident was restrained but pertinent. An editorial in *The Calgary Herald* remarked:

> City Council appears to have climbed on a freeway to nowhere by passing the transportation by-law contained in a fuzzy presentation which purports to outline the future transportation needs.
>
> The mayor accurately described the transportation by-law as a charade, and council acknowledged that it was passed only to protect the city's eligibility for $15 million in road construction grants.
>
> The long-suffering taxpayers of Calgary should expect the elected guardians of the public trust to stand on their heads in front of City Hall for $15 million, but acquisition of the money doesn't absolve them from their seeming determination to evade the transportation issue.
>
> Calgary is at the crossroads of rapid transit versus the automobile. The half-baked transportation by-law is a credit to no one, and an analysis of the accompanying map shows freeways starting and ending nowhere, and expressways and other arteries with gaps and bizarre junctions.
>
> After a decade of fencing with the transportation problem the city still isn't in possession of a workable long-range transportation plan. Calgary is one of the few cities of its size in the world which has mastery over the entire planning area.
>
> For years, City Hall has promised to produce a comprehensive total transportation plan. It has asked the provincial government for help, only to be told a plan is needed first.
>
> In 1968, the Calgary Transportation Study indicated how rapid transit and highway networks could be integrated. Since then there have been a series of fragmented reports, and studies.
>
> The by-law passed by council apparently formalizes the city's right to begin land acquisition for future transportation needs. Can it be serious about setting aside land for transportation routes that do not exist?
>
> Downtown and regional shopping interests obviously have opinions on the course of future transportation, and their wishes will have to be considered. A workable transportation system cannot be evolved without facing the problem squarely.

Politicians and planners continue to hedge with watery excuses about the complexity of the issues. The city cannot afford to continue its concentration on the automobile. The view must be expanded.[139]

Though the council was engaged, as the Mayor termed it, in a charade, it had no alternative given the time it had taken to do the job required in 1970, the provincial legislation, and the grant conditions imposed by the provincial Highways Department. The province had been generous in its postponements, but was now seeking a clear planning proposal. Interviews with city planners revealed their opinion that the difficulties the city had experienced in drafting its plans resulted in part from lack of advice, clear information, and explicit policy on the part of the provincial Highways Department and other provincial departments inevitably involved. To illustrate their point, they referred to changes in provincial policy as stated by ministers since the 1970 City Transportation Act. On checking this topic, we noted the following statements:

On October 30, 1970 *The Albertan* reported the Minister of Highways, in an address to the Alberta Urban Municipalities Association, as saying that transportation experts must do their utmost to plan rather than buy a way out of traffic congestion. By 1980, it was said, an estimated 80 percent of the population would be urban-oriented and appropriate money had to be transferred from rural to urban transport systems. The minister reportedly remarked: "It is desirable to transport high volumes of people quickly and cheaply but it will be necessary to advise Alberta's two major cities that rapid transit is too rich for the blood of the provincial government right now." At that time, in Ottawa, the federal government was considering the question of assistance to metropolitan transport systems on the basis of previous federal interest in Canada-wide highways and the case for servicing the national population now that so much of it was urban centred. In the end, the federal government declined to act, partly because of the constitutional difficulties with the lower levels of government involved.

In January, 1972, some five months after the Conservative administration took office in Alberta, the Minister of Highways and Transport was reported as saying, "At this time, rapid transit systems are premature. The cost that would be involved at this time would be far greater than the benefits you could give to a small part of the population."[140] In the opinion of the press reporter, the Conservative minister adopted the same position as his Social Credit predecessor in saying that cities could go ahead with planning future transportation systems "but the province is not prepared to finance them yet."[141] However, both Calgary and Edmonton have rapid transit systems on the drawing boards and budgetary provision to continue with their examination. Experimental pilot projects using existing equipment are under consideration. One of the difficulties currently identified is changing the public's attitude to the use of the automobile — a universal phenomenon in all industrialized countries.

It would appear, therefore, that the City Planning Department has a case concerning the uncertainty on the part of the province. From a research point of view, the critical issue is rather to determine the extent to which the symbiotic relation between city and provincial transport planning permits the city sensibly to proceed prior to explicit policy formulation on the part of the province concerning (a) the region in which the city exists and its linkages to other regions and cities of the province, and (b) how the province envisages the city transportation system to be evolved because of the high rate of subsidy afforded the city by the provincial government. The city's encapsulation geographically and financially would appear to make the city planners more dependent on provincial policy decisions than *vice versa,* but research would reveal the nature and extent of factors having relative dependence and independence which at least would facilitate the administrative aspects of getting the two jobs done in a reasonable time. If the provincial government moves to assert its constitutional authority over urban planning in Alberta, the delineation of policy decision between the two authorities would become much clearer, and responsibilities explicitly allocated accordingly.

If provincial policy is not made explicit, but grant money to Calgary remains contingent upon provincial receipt of a transportation plan, Calgary will continue with its "charade." This may continue until popular pressures within the city build up to demand action, or a change in federal policy on the financing of urban transport occurs — very probably quite suddenly. In the meantime, Calgary continues to put road widening and construction as the major single expenditure item in its annual capital budget and has indicated it will do so for several more years. This action draws subsidies from the provincial government, ensures work for the unemployed, and also assists in ensuring adequate business is done in Calgary to keep the city growing and visibly attractive to further private investment. Persistence in this policy will increasingly entrench the present mode of city growth. Concurrently, the provincial government is unable to see its way clear, "at this time," to move ahead with a concerted program on rapid transit.

While this administrative and policy stalemate continues, the degree of difference between the metropolitan centres and the small urban centres of the province continues to expand. The costs of providing urban metropolitan services appear to be rising disproportionately to the population increase in these centres — as it has for several decades. Since the city's long-range planning and goals are dependent upon provincial policy on issues such as transportation corridors and other "design tools," provincial grant money cannot seriously be taken at present as being the means to either the city's or the province's eventual plan or goal. These should rather be seen as revenue to the city in response to a game of "charades" played at a much larger level than the Transportation By-law revealed. It is a game increasingly taking a political as well as fiscal form. The *ad hoc* nature of city decisions on developmental issues is not merely the expression of an inability on the council and city administration's part to do any better. It is a matter that reflects explicitly the inability or unwillingness of the provincial government to play a role in the developmental process which would permit local governments to play theirs with rationality and purpose. In passing the City Transportation Act, 1970, the Provincial Legislature had in mind that its grants would be related to formulated city transport plans. The coercive element in the legislation is explicit in the conditions laid out for the grant. While this form of politics has its place in public administration, it implies inevitably that both governments have their house in order.

An indication of the social chaos likely to follow from the existing situation is revealed by attitudes and predictions expressed to the press. On March 24, 1972, *The Calgary Herald* reported the following comments made by the city's Chief Commissioner on the new Transportation By-law. He was addressing a meeting of the Calgary Chapter of The Appraisers Institute of Canada. He remarked: "I suspect there will be a number of court cases to test the validity of the law." Though he was not implying the by-law was unsound legislation, the fact that it "impinges very basically on the traditional rights of property ownership" made it sensitive legislation. Property owners were affected in having reduced access to their property, limited compensation through expropriation of city negotiation, and a reduced ability to sell their property. The city in turn was obliged to buy all land within a protection area within three years of the passing of the by-law.

The implications of the legislation were endless in so far as land values in and adjacent to the protection areas would be affected, a new system of appeals would need to be worked out, and the consequences for developers within the city's built up area and beyond would be indeterminate. The press report on the Chief Commissioner's speech concluded in these terms:

> He maintained, however, that such a by-law is a necessary 'insurance policy' to protect downtown land values. 'We dare not let the centre of the city begin to strangle (or) hundreds of millions of dollars of real estate will suffer.'[142]

On the other side of the coin, however, is the real estate value of property in the suburban built up area of the city in and adjacent to the "transportation protection area." Council was appraised at the public hearing in February, 1972, of a threat to this area of the city, through a written brief submitted at the hearing by the Calgary Chapter of the Mortgage Loans Association. This association identified the necessity of the council moving expeditiously to determine explicitly the "transportation protection area" as provided for in Section 10 of the legislation. This step would be taken by a subsequent by-law specifying the particular areas of land. The brief said:

> Provided that both the first and second stages of this procedure are completed by the City within a reasonable time, the Act appears to provide equitable and adequate remedies to the owner of land affected by the by-laws.
> If however the City, having taken the first step, neglects or fails to proceed promptly with the second step, the remedies to the owner of land affected by the by-laws do not come into force and will not come into force unless and until the City proceeds with the second step. The act provides no time limit within which the City is compelled to take the second step.
> If the City, having taken the first step, fails or neglects to proceed promptly with the second step it is submitted that the mere publication of the first By-law and map showing the approximate location of the transportation facilities will have the effect of creating uncertainty and will adversely affect property values in the immediate vicinity of the proposed location of such facilities, and in particular the proposed location of the Rapid Transit System. No provision is made for compensation to the owners of any property so affected.

Thus, though compensation was implicit in the legislation and City Council was itself committed to the principle of compensation, the application of compensatory justice, in fact, required the city to act promptly in the second stage of area delineation. Only this measure could implement administratively the safeguards to the rights of property owners affected by the Transportation By-law.

The Mayor's attitude to the passage of the by-law in the first instance had been that it was a "charade we are going through to please certain people in Edmonton." Within the city iself, however, the by-law has the potential of engendering political consequences by way of setting off city-centre financial interests from the interests of concerned suburban property owners. If the city continues to present its plan to the province merely to become eligible for the annual road grant and delays the passage of a by-law identifying the "transportation protection areas," the province, to safeguard the property interests of suburban dwellers, may be obliged to impose an additional time restriction on the city. Such an action, however, would only reinforce the fear expressed in the brief by the Society for Pollution and Environmental Control, namely; that the rigid pattern of current growth forms would be entrenched. By having again to act more speedily than it wanted, the city would be given no chance to review the alternative long-range growth patterns being worked out by the Planning Department. It would tend, through administrative necessity, to opt for the growth patterns most in conformity with existing arrangements and politically non-disturbing to the most powerful of local interests.

Thus, under the present situation, the provincial government is bound to continue its annual grant arrangements to the city to enable it to continue in turn with its *ad hoc* decision making and road construction program. It would appear that the sanction used by the province in the passing of its legislation in 1970 was inappropriate under the conditions pertaining to the political, administrative, and planning situation within the City of Calgary. This does not mean, however, that the sanction is inapplicable under other conditions both within the city and in the region around it. The transportation system and its corridors will be required, and the necessary measures will hurt some property owners or other. It will not be a popular measure. But the present situation appears to be conflict-producing without any tangible returns in the physical aspects of development, in the rationality of administration, or in the financial and economic advantages transportation systems could provide. The present sanctions have only led to citizen concern, and to fear on the part of financial interests, and have brought the city's administration into ridicule.

Calgary and Its Region

The Calgary Plan states:

> What has become apparent . . . is the extent to which surrounding municipalities are now in economic terms, part of the City of Calgary. It is no longer valid to preclude the region from any consideration concerning the form of future growth.
>
> What is needed now, as a first priority, is a detailed economic review of the costs involved in the present form of growth prescribed by artificial administrative boundaries relative to other forms of growth including the possibility of satellite communities.[143]

And

> The facts should now be faced. Present legal boundaries do not necessarily signify the future shape and size of the city. In the not too distant future it will become increasingly clear that our "urban fringe" now covers a substantial portion of the region. It will become more apparent that interrelationships between the City of Calgary and such towns and villages as Cochrane, High River, Beiseker, Strathmore and perhaps some that do not exist today, will become new problems *competing or co-operating* with each other for their solution. Problems of urban expansion, transportation, education, recreational development, and resource development will require more detailed attention.[144] (Emphasis original.)

Many regional and municipal planners hold the view that a regional approach to growth and development is the most rational solution to the problems being experienced by both Calgary and its region. A number of city planners argue that steps should be taken to encourage the development of satellite communities in the Calgary region. This, they suggest, would both ameliorate many of the problems Calgary is experiencing as a result of continued rapid growth and revitalize the smaller communities located in the region. In addition, planners argue that the cost of promoting the development of satellite communities and the region as a whole should be a great deal less in the long run than the cost of financing Calgary's rapid growth. One senior city planner has observed: "There must be a point when it is cheaper to start a newer system." For example, while a rapid transit system for commuters travelling from satellite communities to Calgary would involve a high initial cost factor, the overall cost would not be great. Since in many cases railway tracks already exist between regional communities and the city, the operating subsidy seems to be the major financial consideration. On the other hand, for communities to be able to develop as viable satellites, they would require additional financial assistance from the provincial government. Moveover, the various local authorities, including the City of Calgary, would have to be willing to co-operate with one another on a regional basis.

The concept of planned regional growth and development in the Calgary context involves a number of factors, not the least of which is the consideration of developing independent, viable communities located at a distance from the city. In contradistinction to the Edmonton area where satellite communities are much closer to the city and more dependent upon the metropolitan centre for their economic viability, the development of Calgary's satellites would depend more on the recognition of regional interrelationships and the "mutual interdependence" of municipalities. The Calgary Plan states:

> It is urgent that we begin to acknowledge that Calgary is part of the region in the same context as Cochrane or Okatoks and other urban centres with each taking advantage of the other amenities. It is this mutual interdependence that creates the quality of and opportunity to take full advantage of the environment.
> It is the *extent* to which this interdependence is recognized which will determine the form of growth that Calgary, High River, or Drumheller will take: in other words whether the region will be developed for the long-term benefit of its inhabitants as a whole or merely for the short-term advantage of minority interests.[145] (Emphasis original.)

The prospect of introducing rational regional planning involves two main factors — the effect of provincial government policy on regional co-operation among municipalities and, the government's criteria for providing assistance to municipalities. The Calgary Plan is very adament about the provincial government's responsibility as the province's "planning authority." Referring to the "Calgary Regional Planning Commission," The Calgary Plan observes:

> The Regional Planning Commission a composite body of representative members of cities, towns, villages, rural municipalities, and improvement districts has been created by the Province to oversee the process of urbanization and growth of the area around the City of Calgary. *This body is not a government and does not possess political power.* In practice the Provincial Government through legislative power and the right of veto of planning proposals and control of tax policies, is the planning authority.
> The Provincial Government and the City of Calgary have been perhaps too passive with regard to regional planning, allowing these agencies to find their own way with only slight leadership or indication of the very important role they could or should play.[146] (Emphasis original.)

The solutions to many of Calgary's problems and those of the region, appear to lie in a co-operative approach to planned regional growth and development. Recognizing the importance of regional planning, The Calgary Plan draws attention to the responsibility of the provincial government to provide policy direction and the circumstances whereby such planning can be promoted. It observes that the Planning Commission, not having legislative authority, cannot be held responsible for doing much more than fulfilling its obligation "to oversee the process of urbanization and growth of the area around the City of Calgary."[147] Stating that *'There has been little apparent concern towards rectifying the inadequacies that exist in regional planning,"*[148] the Calgary Plan observes: "It is apparent that there is no easy prescription for the solution of these many questions." However, the Plan notes that ". . . there are some fairly well defined directions that bear consideration"[149] and comments on one piece of provincial government legislation:

> *A clarification of the Planning Act as it relates to regional planning is urgently required.* The Act should reflect the fact that sound urban development with the health and viability of our cities, towns and villages plus the rational development of natural resources and the preservation of the countryside for everyone's benefit and enjoyment is the prime consideration in the Province.[150] (Emphasis original.)

Thus, the Plan, having reviewed the provincial government's role as the province's "planning authority," goes on to clarify the province's obligations to establish policy for the entire province's rational growth and development.

The evidence indicates that present provincial government policy encourages competition among municipalities both large and small rather than the co-operation required to promote regional planning. That municipalities compete is reflected in the following statement taken from the minutes of Calgary's "Industrial Expansion Committee," February 15, 1971. The Industrial Development Officer

> . . . drew to the attention of the Committee some press releases from the City of Edmonton re: 1970 development. He suggested the figures quoted were very misleading and not representative of the City of Edmonton. He felt comparisons between the two major cities as had been used in the release could only be detrimental to the overall good.[151]

The Development Officer was probably less concerned about "the overall good" than about how the press release would affect or reflect Calgary's potential to attract private investment. The larger urban centres commonly promote themselves by publishing information which might be beneficial to them in their competition with one another.

These senior government programs which have the purpose of encouraging industry to locate in areas other than the metropolitan centres have been soundly criticized by certain Calgary officials. In addition to his reference to press releases, the Development Officer, referring to the Industrial Developers' Conference in Toronto, "advised Mayor Sykes's speech at this conference, during which he spoke against federal and provincial incentive programs, had attracted considerable interest." Later, on June 17, 1971, the Development Officer advised the committee:

> . . . that it was too early to assess any effects the new Provincial program might have on industrial development in Calgary. He indicated that one industry based in the City was opening a plant in Claresholm to take advantage of the Provincial incentive but was also retaining its plant in Calgary. He will be reporting further when more information is available.[152]

Evidently, the Development Officer had been attempting to determine whether or not the provincial incentive program was having a detrimental affect on the city's potential to attract private investment. The minutes suggest that there is no willingness on the part of certain city officials to co-operate with senior government action aimed at assisting outlying and regional areas located in the Calgary region.

Concerning the matter of competition, the Calgary Plan observes:

Until such time, then, that the government takes action to ameliorate the competition for property tax revenues, it will remain virtually impossible to persuade municipalities to develop a co-operative posture towards regional planning. The provincial government eventually distributes municipal assistance in accord with population size. Loans provided through the Municipal Finance Corporation are based on population size and a municipality's ability to repay. Under the circumstances, the large urban centres receive the lion's share of provincial assistance.[153]

For certain communities to develop into viable satellite communities they would require "special assistance," and this, in turn, would require the provincial government to review its present criteria for providing assistance to municipalities. It has been observed:

> When it perceives a possibility of rationalizing special assistance for a particular municipal project the provincial government is prepared to provide aid if it views the project as a worthwhile undertaking. But it must be emphasized that the possibility of receiving special assistance often depends on the government being able to direct attention to the unique circumstances of a project. Those projects which might be viewed as precedent-setting in terms of the province as a whole receive very little apparent attention. The government, in other words, is careful to ensure that any special assistance given to a centre does not commit the government to a precedent which might have province-wide application.[154]

A secure property tax base is directly related to private investment. Business and industrial expansion provides job opportunities and these, in turn, result in population growth. A more secure property tax base and increased opportunity to introduce other assessments are related to this population growth. Senior government assistance, as the two volumes of this present work document, also directly relates to population growth. Therefore the competition among municipalities for private investment is not only a consequence of the present property tax system but is also a consequence of the criteria currently used by the provincial government to provide assistance to municipalities. Thus, in addition to facilitating the development of selected growth centres, and satellite communities, a change of criteria would also ameliorate the competition among municipalities.

The Calgary Plan recommends:

> 1. In order to achieve even the most modest objectives in the development of the region it is self evident that the entire economic region must be included in the planning

> area. To this end it is recommended that financial assistance be requested from the Provincial Government to determine the extent of this economic region and the best means to:
> (a) preserve the quality of the regional environment;
> (b) provide such basic facilities as transportation, housing, education, health, and employment to the benefit of the total region.
> (c) provide a much greater freedom of choice with respect to modes of living, mobility of labour, location of industry, recreation facilities etc.
> (d) provide for a more economic form of growth than exists today.[155]

Municipal Competition and Regional Planning

Although the new Preliminary Regional Plan has been approved by the member municipalities of the Calgary Regional Planning Commission, it may not provide a mechanism for resolving the crucial planning problems that face the region as a whole. The initial Preliminary Plan, adopted by the Regional Planning Commission on July 29, 1963 offered a much greater opportunity for the Planning Commission to control the direction of resource development and land use planning.[156] The later, present version was prepared in accordance with the expressed desires of the commission's individual municipalities. The new plan could undermine the commission's authority to take the initiative in regional planning. While the new plan supposedly represents what the various municipalities want, it avoids the basic issues inherent in developing rational, comprehensive policy for the Calgary region.

In 1963, the Preliminary Regional Plan stated:

> The Commission is concerned with principles arising out of the essential differences between urban and rural purposes of municipal organization and development. In essence the urban municipalities are designed to provide and administer territories for the habitation, employment and recreation of high densities of population requiring highly sophisticated levels of service to both land and people. In contrast, the rural municipalities are designed to provide and administer to the needs of low densities of population mainly employed on the land in agricultural pursuits, and requiring a moderate level of service to people and a minimum level of land.[157]

The initial preliminary plan, having outlined the above "general premise," provided "the general framework for guiding regional development." However, during the ensuing years, this framework came under critical review by Planning Commission members, particularly the Municipal District of Rocky View.

Through the annexation decisions of the early sixties, the MD of Rocky View lost a large portion of its population and land area. The population within the boundaries of the MD dropped from approximately 10,900 to approximately 7,000. In 1965, however, the census results revealed that the population of Rocky View had risen to approximately 8,500 and, in 1971, the initial results of the dominion census showed that its population total had gone over the 10,000 mark. As its population grew again after annexation, Rocky View grew more concerned to seek amendments to the Preliminary Regional Plan. These amendments, by and large, were an attempt to remove those constraints contained in the preliminary plan which prevented certain forms of development from taking place in the rural areas. For example, in 1968 Rocky View applied to the Provincial Planning Board for an amendment to the Preliminary Regional Plan intended to rezone sections of land for a limited range of agriculturally oriented industry. This application was submitted to the Provincial Planning Board after the Regional Planning Commission had refused to support the request. The Calgary Regional Planning Commission Submission to the Provincial Planning Board in support of the commission's decision to refuse an application by the Municipal District of Rocky View noted that the Regional Planning Commission's formation "was a voluntary and spontaneous one by the participating municipalities," and drew "attention to the feelings of amity and understanding that have always characterized the co-operative efforts of the Members of this Commission, since its inception in 1950." Continuing on, the submission made the following observations concerning the MD's application:

> It might well be asked that, if this appeal does not represent a change in mutual understanding, what does it represent? The Commission submits, Mr. Chairman, with all other detailed issues being set aside for the moment, that this application by Rocky View is symptomatic of a much greater issue than the mere desire to begin another urban fringe, 1968 style. That greater issue involves the whole validity and practicability of the principles of regional planning and of urban and rural development control. It includes questions such as whether we should have some sort of an urban region as the basis for long-term development control. Inevitably, it also involves questions related to municipal economics, tax resources, and finances because, when regional development control measures commence to impinge upon, or are believed to impinge upon, the individual municipal financial scene, the reaction is bound to produce a result such as this hearing today.
>
> It is contended, Mr. Chairman, that the solution to this problem will not be found in the mere granting by this Board of Rocky View's appeal, because such a solution

> would have a negative effect. It would be negative to the very principles of the McNally Report, as well as to the existing, enunciated principles of both regional and urban development in this area. In fact, it would be the initial retrogressive step in acknowledging the inevitability of an urban fringe. How long would it be before annexation were again contemplated?

While stating the commission's reasons for opposing the Rocky View appeal, the submission also noted that:

> . . . it is also possible that the rejection by the Board of Rocky View's appeal might be no more than a short-term solution, because the overall problem claimed by Rocky View would then remain unsolved.

Referring to the policy statements contained in the Preliminary Regional Plan and noting "the inconsistency of the proposed industrialization in the view of the hitherto successful annexation and development control policies subscribed to by all (commission) members," the submission observed:

> Any deliberate industrializaiton amendment to the Plan would be a contradiction of the joint principle of those statements, and would first require that the principle, and the supporting statements, should be somehow conditioned or amended, or struck out.

And:

> If they are not struck out and the Board grants the appeal; or alternatively if the Board in its wisdom decides that the principles are no longer valid, and consequently instructs the Commission to review and modify them accordingly; the end would be the same and the principle of fringe industrialization would be accepted. What then?
> On the one hand, at this moment we are concerned with an application near the City of Calgary, but on the other hand in the future we will most assuredly be concerned with the rural towns and villages. What serves Peter must also serve Paul.

To illustrate what the possible financial implications of approval might be for other commission members, the submission noted:

> At least one of our rural towns is watching the outcome of this appeal with some interest, because of a situation wherein local farm implement supply and machinery dealers are allegedly contemplating a mass move to an

opportune location about one mile out of town, closer to the highway, but not on it. The direct loss of the town's dollar business volume would be about one quarter, while the indirect loss cannot be calculated. Neither can the direct and indirect loss in taxes. This town is relatively well off in that its commercial tax revenue comprises almost 28%. A reduction to 20% could be calamitous. These taxes help this town to provide the educational, hospital, administrative, retirement, cultural, social, recreational, and general services for its own convenience and that of the surrounding agricultural area. With such revenue losses would we then have on our hands another town on the downhill grade? — And then another?

With reference to the Rocky View presentation, the submission observed that:

> Rocky View has produced the information that about 27% of property tax revenue in 1967 came from industrial and commercial sources. These sources comprised mostly pipeline and power line rights-of-way and appurtenances, four large petro-chemical plants, and miscellaneous small industrial plants, highway commercial operations, and recreational developments such as Happy Valley. It will be readily seen that the employee-dollar assessment ratio is exceedingly low, and therefore extremely advantageous. However, the chief net advantage to Rocky View's industrial and commercial tax revenue position is that only relatively minor sums need be put back into servicing these particular tax resources. This is in contrast to the urban experience wherein proportionately large sums are expended in the construction of sewer and water plants, mains, trunk and service systems, streets and highways, and fire and police protection. In other words the urban commercial-industrial tax resource needs and gets a substantial capital, maintenance and service benefit. This substantially reduces the net tax dollar benefit to the urban areas, as opposed to the rural experience.

However:

> Notwithstanding the foregoing, it must be accepted that the rural municipality surrounding Calgary on three dynamic sides suffers a continuing barrage of urban-derived pressures and demands that promise it no apparent municipal profit. Many of these pressures are well known (sic): land speculators, ex-city country residents who have fled the City yet continually demand improved city-like services; vehicles of urban destination and origin battering down a first-class rural road system that just cannot be

> made to cope with the abuse because of lack of municipal financial resources; the cost of collecting garbage, junk, and abandoned car bodies on municipal roads.
> All these matters serve to feed the frustrations of the rural rate-payer and administration, and collectively help to form the basis for the 'tax balance' objectives of the Municipal rezoning application.

In conclusion, the submission noted that the commission wished to:

> impress on the Board that the Commission's refusal to accept the desired amendment, and its support of its negative position, should in no way be construed as the closing of a blind eye to the problems claimed by Rocky View. Rather, it is believed that this submission, and the record which you have on file of all of the Commission's dealings with the matter, are ample evidence to the contrary. Simply, the Commission does not feel that the way to deal with the problem is by abandoning presently established development control and planning policies so as to commence a fringe industrial area abutting the City limits and two provisional highways.
> If the problem is, in fact, one of economics and tax resources, and if it is going to be a recurring and worsening problem, then perhaps it is appropriate for this Commissions' Members and the Province to start thinking of a regional form of government, perhaps a regional city. Such a city might envelop all those areas experiencing the dynamic forces of urbanization, and assume administrative and financial responsibility for them. In this way it might be possible to rationalize the new fringe growth outside the present City limits. However, the prime objective of such a move should be to preserve the municipal economy and way of life of the bona fide farmer and his local government against the mounting economic and development pressures from the expanding City.

The submission yielded some major insights into the kinds of problems and questions which had developed concerning regional planning in the Calgary area. While the submission was primarily intended to support the commission's refusal, it did not reject the MD's arguments as being altogether irrelevant or trivial. Rocky View's application, in fact, brought to the forefront a "greater issue": ". . . the whole validity and practicability of the principles of regional planning and or urban and rural development control." Having pointed out that the possibility of "long-term development control" directly involved ". . . questions related to municipal economics, tax resources, and finances," the submission observed:

that if indeed the municipalities are going to be able to continue their joint support of the orderly, urban and regional development principles inherent in The Planning Act, the Province in turn is going to have to take a closer look at the practicabilities of municipal and educational organizations and boundaries, and the distribution of tax resources, particularly in the vicinity of large, dynamic urban centres such as Calgary.

On October 16, 1968 following a public hearing which had been held May 10, 1968, the Provincial Planning Board issued "Board Order 286-M.-68." Included in the board order was the following statement concerning the Rocky View appeal:

> In appealing the decision of the Calgary Regional Planning Commission not to amend the Preliminary Regional Plan so that agricultural-oriented industry may be established in the Municipal District, the submission is put forward as a method by which the Municipality can improve the tax revenue-expenditure imbalance caused by the increasing urbanization of rural areas.
>
> Urbanites are showing an increasing tendency to settle in the country, retiring there from urban occupations or living there while actually pursuing their urban employment.
>
> Agricultural land, some of it of the highest quality, has been sterilized and irretrievably lost as a result of the forceable intrusion of the urban flow into the rural area, commonly known as urban sprawl.
>
> This is borne out in Rocky View by the ever increasing demand for country residential parcels by ex-urbanites. The five and ten acre subdivisions created in the 1910-15 period are being developed and new parcels are being created at an ever increasing rate. The inherent problems of this intrusion, in the main, are the reason for increased costs for municipal education and services . . .

The order also recorded the essence of the submission presented by the City of Calgary:

> The City of Calgary representative in his submission stated that in the City's opinion, there are four main factors to be taken into consideration as regards the proposed amendment to the Preliminary Regional Plan. These are:
>
> (1) The direction of the City growth.
> (2) The nature of the space available.
> (3) The stabilization of residential neighbourhoods.
> (4) The need to control regional growth.
>
> Studies indicate that residential growth will

eventually be north and west with a corridor to the south. Due to the projected expansion of the airport, no further development is being allowed in the northeast. If narrow corridors such as those proposed are allowed, maintenance becomes more expensive and the need to maintain balance more acute. It is expected that the growth of the City will be more than double in the next twenty years. The industrial area now has considerable vacancies sufficient for the next 20 to 25 years. It is submitted that it is premature at this time to abandon the principles laid down and to allow this amendment would set a precedent leading to full scale industrial development in fringe areas.

The Provincial Planning Board's decision was worded in the following manner:

> Under authority vested in the Board pursuant to Section 89 of The Planning Act, Statutes of Alberta, 1963, as amended; the Board has decided that the decision of the Calgary Regional Planning Commission be upheld and the appeal denied.

For the moment, at least, it appeared that the MD would have to continue to labour under what it considered to be restrictive regional planning policy. Perhaps of greater importance, however, is the fact that the board decision gave no indication as to whether or not provincial authorities were prepared to bring the MD's position under close examination.

Although the Planning Commission continued to refer to the "co-operative efforts of the Members of this Commission," discord among the members became increasingly more apparent. Indeed, the commission planners began to find it more and more difficult to convince Rocky View that the Preliminary Plan, intended as a guide for development and planning, was not responsible for placing the MD in an incapacitated position. From the MD's point of view, the Plan tended to obscure the practical realities facing the rural areas and to support continued growth and expansion in the urban areas. The commission planners and certain member municipalities understood the concern expressed, but would not support amendments to the Preliminary Plan which would run contrary to those policies which secured the principles of regional planning. Other members were only interested in these principles insofar as they protected local economic interests.

The difficult position of the planners was exacerbated by the fact that it appeared that the provincial government had no intention of considering the legislative changes which would encourage the members to become more co-operative with one another. The planners were unable to acquire full support of the policies outlined in the Preliminary Plan, although they were able to draw out responses sympathetic to their own point of view as to the importance of regional planning. As time went by, certain members become more emphatic about the discrimination they perceived as being inherent in the Preliminary Plan, and more critical of both the commission's planners and the positions taken by member municipalties. A representative of Rocky View prepared a brief entitled, "Regional Planning as Designed and Practiced in the Southern Portion of the Province of Alberta with Particular Reference to the Region Surrounding the City of Calgary."[158] Of particular interest are the following statements:

> The question arises why the City of Calgary which has its own Planning Department and prepares its own General Plan and Zoning Bylaw, should have the right by virtue of three votes, to decide what the elected representatives of the adjacent rural municipalities should or should not do. Criticism of the foregoing statement is expected, that the statement is unjustified, that the writer does not know what he is talking about, but experience and history has shown that the statement is fact. The influence exerted by the representation of the large urban area upon the representation from the small urban centres, together with the representation from the provincial government which are usually urban-centred, far outweighs the effective voice of the rural representation, and this type of administrative board structure has been a detriment to proper regional planning.

Describing the Preliminary Regional Plan as ". . . a status quo document which did not project or suggest what the orderly and economic development of the municipalities affected by that plan would or should be," and ". . . a restrictive and negative piece of legislation protecting the environmental growth patterns of the large urban centre," the brief stated:

> Efforts have been made by the rural Councils of the municipalities in the Calgary Planning Region to have the above facts recognized and remedial action taken. They have been frustrated in their efforts by the neglect and 'don't give a damn attitude' of the representation on the Regional Commission Board. It is only when a proposal of the rural area immediately affects the urban member that he becomes activated and alive. This lassitude on the part of the urban representation encourages, allows the planning staff to make recommendations and invoke politics which are never questioned. It is an indirect delegation of policy making authority to the planner by the negative attitude of the public representatives. The planners themselves cannot be wholly criticized for the lack of good planning in the regional area, part of the responsibility must rest in the laps of the appointed

representatives of the municipalities in that they have not questioned or debated thoroughly the recommendations that are presented to them, nor have they demanded documentary evidence based on surveys and studies to validate these recommendations. Therefore how else can you expect to have good planning which is based on nothing?[159]

On April 30, 1969 the Council of the MD of Rocky View submitted a brief to the Calgary Regional Planning Commission on the policies and provisions of the Preliminary Regional Plan, 1969. The introductory statement, having noted that:

> . . . due to the vibrant changes that have taken place in our regional area since 1953 and since 1963, new thought and action is required in planning guide-lines, for not only the next five years but the next decade . . .

went on to say:

> In the period from 1953 to 1963 this Municipal District supported the premise that there should be a large metropolitan urban area and that sprawl of a residential, commercial, industrial nature should be discouraged. It was felt that if the City of Calgary had extensive large land holdings that our municipality could preserve its rural-agricultural characteristics and that was the reason for the 20 acre minimum subdivision policy. History has now shown that this 20 acre policy was not valid or practical in that it would not prevent residential sprawl which is the worst kind. By referring to 'worst kind,' this type of sprawl affects the economic base structure of a rural municipality in that the costs of providing educational and hospital services have now almost become prohibitive without the additional support of a commercial and industrial tax base. This same reason which we have just stated was the reason used for the large and extensive annexations by the city of Calgary. This municipal authority needed the commercial and industrial development in order to off-set the liability caused by residential expansion within their corporate boundaries.

The brief concluded its introductory statement, saying:

> We are now at the crossroads in planning the region surrounding this large urban centre and we submit that the present regional plan as proposed is not and shall not be acceptable to the Council of this Municipal District unless effort is made at this time to formulate a regional policy which will encourage a strong economic growth of

> this Municipal District. We further suggest that we are prepared to withdraw from the Calgary Regional Planning Commission and formulate our own general plan proposals should our recommendation not be acceptable as we feel that these recommendations are valid and logical.

Before proceeding with its suggested revisions, the Council's brief pointed out:

> The basis for our submission is that Part 4 of the Planning Act of the Province of Alberta authorizes and instructs that a Council of a municipality is responsible for the formulation of a general plan of its municipality.

And:

> It is felt by the Council of this Municipal District that a general plan should be undertaken for all rural members of this Commission on the basis of what is required by the Councils of these rural members and once these general plans are prepared and adopted, then the Commission shall incorporate the three rural general plans into one regional plan. We acknowledge and concur that there will be differences in policy between the three rural members but we would like to point out that the three rural municipalities are different economically and geographically and that our problems with respect to rural development are also different. The preceeding statements, gentlemen, are our first recommendation.

The Municipal District's recommended revisions of 1969 sought to place it in a more flexible position with regard to accommodating certain kinds of private investment. In addition, certain of the revisions, if endorsed by the Planning Commission, would have considerably reduced the authority of the commission. In conclusion, the Rocky View brief stated:

> This Council irrevocably states that it is opposed to the present form of the Preliminary Regional Plan. We do not deny that planning on a regional basis is a necessity but it must be of the positive attitude and be acceptable to the public at large. The members of the Council of the Municipal District of Rocky View No. 44 are aware of the public opinion in their municipality, not only from the farmers but the smallholders, and it therefore must lie with the Council to establish zoning regulations which will plan and guide the Municipal District but also must be accepted by the public. Unless this plan and guide are acceptable to the public it will not be worth the paper it is written on.

And:

> We respectfully submit that the Council using the assistance of the Commission, must establish the future zoning policies of this Municipal District and when they have been formulated they shall be presented in the way of a Municipal District general plan and Zoning Bylaw. It is at this time that the Commission can then incorporate the Municipal District general plan in conjunction with the general plans from other rural municipal units into a regional document which will be acceptable to the electors and ratepayers of those municipal units.
> If cooperation on this matter and compromise cannot be extended or reached, then this Council feels that it will have no alternative but to withdraw from the Planning Commission and proceed to prepare its own general plan in compliance with Part 4 of the Planning Act.

Having failed to obtain support from the Regional Planning Commission for adjustments to the Preliminary Plan which would permit it to promote a policy of urbanization, the Council of the Municipal District of Rocky View passed the following motion on August 11, 1970:

> Moved that the Council advise the Calgary Regional Planning Commission and the Provincial Planning Board that, pursuant to Provincial Planning Board Order No. 219-M-70, the Municipal District of Rocky View No. 44 will honor its 1970 requisition in the amount of Five Thousand, Sixty-seven Dollars ($5,067.00), with further notice being given that as of January 1, 1971, this Municipal District shall consider itself as a non-member of the Commission and only pay for those services requested by the Council of The Municipal District of Rocky View, pursuant to the terms and provisions of the Planning Act for non-member service; and further that the Minister of Municipal Affairs be requested to obtain an Order in Council from the Cabinet classifying this municipality as a non-member effective January 1, 1971.[160]

In a letter dated August 13, 1970, the MD informed the Minister of Municipal Affairs of the motion, and added:

> I have been further instructed to advise you that the Council have taken this action after three years of serious thought and negotiation and discussion. They regret their position, but feel they have no alternative and that since they have engaged their own municipal planner, it is felt that planning studies of our municipality can be formulated using our own resources.

As far as we know, the MD did not receive a direct response from the minister.

In order to obtain some control over urban/regional development, the Calgary Regional Planning Commission has directed itself almost entirely to the problem of subdivision and land development control. Through the use of its Preliminary Plan, the commission is attempting to encourage "good quality development" around the periphery of the City of Calgary, and "To formulate regional planning proposals that will give valid direction to the orderly and economical development of the region." The high cost of residential land units in this area ensures that there will not be a recurrence of the "shack development" which received so much attention by the Royal Commission in 1955. Although the plan is a "workable" document, it has been tempered to accommodate the views of politicans, civil servants, and private interests. For example, professional planners have expressed the view that only land of marginal value should be subdivided in the rural area which surrounds the City of Calgary. However, this has been objected to by members of the commission who feel that it would be unfair for certain property owners to realize a profit from poor land if those with better quality property were unable to do the same. This posture has created concern for planners who believe that agricultural land should be reserved for farming purposes. On the other hand, because the taxes on land adjacent to the city have increased significantly, and operating costs have risen rapidly, many farmers have been forced to sell their property. The old adage of being "land rich but money poor" appears to apply in this situation and for this reason certain recommendations of the professional planners have not been accepted by commission representatives from the rural areas.

The Preliminary Plan is aimed at controlling development so as to ensure that the land presently contained within the boundaries of urban areas will be developed and that there will be some control over expansion in rural areas. The planners think that without an overall policy with regard to the location of private investment, investors will attempt to avoid the high costs of urban property by locating their developments in rural areas. The planners are also concerned that an apparent economic location for industry will prove in the long run to be quite the opposite. There are examples of private companies which have found that the operating costs of road maintenance, fire protection, busing employees to work and so forth, make the outlying areas thoroughly uneconomic. For such reasons, the planners are interested in encouraging commercial ventures to locate within the boundaries of urban areas. Extractive industries on the other hand, are encouraged to locate in the rural areas.

With regard to the question of housing development, the planners have found it wise to discourage small-parcel subdivision on land immediately adjacent to the boundaries of the City of Calgary. As long as there is still a great deal of land within the metropolitan area available for subdivision, they consider it sensible to deter developers from attempting to subdivide property outside the city boundaries. This, they assume, enables the city to plan for the expansion of services in an economic manner. Presumably, as such expansion takes place it will become more economical to provide services to property on the periphery of the city limits. At the moment this property is protected from disorderly development, to some degree, by current zoning regulations and subdivision policy.

Although the Preliminary Regional Plan is a document which is supposed to offer direction to development and growth within the boundaries of the Calgary Regional Planning Commission, it is a holding document, designed to prevent the type of fringe chaos and urban sprawl that occurred during the early fifties. The plan, however, has not received complete endorsement from all the members of the Planning Commission. The Municipal Districts of Rocky View No. 44 and Kneehill No. 48, particularly, have expressed concern about some of the plan's main policy features. Although the Preliminary Plan focuses on controlled development, the MD of Rocky View considers its overall policy as one which constrains the development of a secure tax base outside the boundaries of urban areas.

Agreement from certain members of the Planning Commission for the policy statements of the Preliminary Plan is therefore linked to the present provincial government property tax formula and to the way in which this formula relates to municipal finances. As long as property tax remains the basis for financing education and other social services, the municipal districts will continue to hold their belief that the Plan restricts the possibility for them to develop a more secure tax base. In comparison, little concern is expressed for the likelihood that *ad hoc* development, which the present Preliminary Plan is trying to prevent, might result in the same problems which received attention from the McNally Royal Commission in 1955.[161] Since the Planning Commission is not empowered to deal with taxation questions and matters relating to municipal finance, it is unable to dissuade rural municipalities from attempting to urbanize. The provincial government, because of its control over various programs and politics which have direct implications for regional planning, retains power over planning in the province and is, therefore, the planning authority. Thus, because of circumstances beyond the control of the commission, the Calgary Preliminary Regional Plan is from a practical point of view a holding document. Whatever import this plan may have for regional planning depends very much on the persuasive powers of the professional planners, rather than on the implementation of firm regional planning policy.

The present provincial tax formula is the greatest inhibiting factor in achieving agreement among commission members on matters related to questions of regional development and planning. While this situation continues, planners will be unable to produce a preliminary plan which is anything more than a document of compromise, tempered to accommodate certain political and economic considerations. Apart from zoning and subdivision proposals, the present plan does not contain anything of lasting significance with regard to regional planning. More substantive policy proposals will only gain acceptance as a result of a provincial government decision to change and clarify the Planning Act, and, concomitantly, to revise certain other provincial and legislation policies. Of the latter policies, those which concern taxation, the distribution of provincial resources and revenues, the co-ordination of provincial government programs and services, are of particular importance. Until radical changes are brought about in these policy areas, the Planning Commission and its planners will be unable to fulfil, with any large degree of success, their responsibility for planning regional development and expansion.

Regional Planning: Conflict and Compromise:

The new Preliminary Regional Plan incorporates many of the amendments proposed by the Planning Commission's member municipalities. Each member municipality and local authority was sent a draft of the plan after it had been prepared by the commission's zoning committee. Part of the covering letter explained that:

> Section 74 of the Act provides that copies of the Plan should be sent to public authorities having jurisdiction in the area covered by the Plan and that those authorities should have a period of up to six weeks within which to submit any representations to the Commission. Your comments are invited accordingly.[162]

At a meeting of the Okatoks Town Council held on January 18, 1971, the Regional Planning Director:

> explained that the previous Regional Plan was effective as of 1963 and it was thus necessary to make revisions. These consisted of bringing the plan up to date clearing repetitions, obscurities and ambiguities. The Plan was on a regional outlook rather than being limited to one municipality. It required greater co-operation amongst the various members of the Regional Planning Board. This was particularly necessary because of the fact that factors in one area could have considerable influence in other parts of the region. As between the rural and urban areas it was considered that extractive or primary industries should be situated in rural areas. This would leave secondary industries to be located in urban centres. Even under such an arrangement provisions would have to be made for modifying such arrangements. Some suggestion had been made by other agencies that allocation of tax revenues would have to be made on a different basis than those presently obtaining.[163]

The director's comments, as interpreted from the minutes, emphasized that if the new Preliminary Regional Plan was to provide a basis for regional planning its policies would have to reflect a greater willingness for municipalities to co-operate with one another. Member municipalities would have to recognize their regional interdependence and to de-emphasize their own individual interests. These interests to a large degree were, and remain, a manifestation of particular provincial government policies as they relate to each municipality's financial position and potential is attract further private investment. There was, therefore, a distinct possibility, which the Planning Director recognized, that the nature of the specific policies to be contained in the Preliminary Plan would be determined by each municipality's commitment to improving its potential to accommodate and attract private investment rather than by any sincere commitment to regional planning. Because economic considerations had frequently impinged on the process and general advancement of regional planning, the director anticipated that certain arrangements would have to be modified from time to time in order to accommodate particular situations. The director however, attempted to seek a compromise which would be acceptable to the member municipalities but would not be inimical to the furtherance of regional planning.

In response to the director's remarks the Okotoks' Council:

> . . . expressed themselves that while a difference of opinion might be present as between municipal government and the Planning body yet municipal governments must be largely guided by experts.[164]

Thus, while the council admitted the importance of having professional advice, it also perceived a possibility that there would be a "difference of opinion." Presumably this difference would arise at the point at which professional advice ran contrary to the council's attempts to secure the municipality's financial position i.e. the point at which policy recommendation limited the municipality's capacity to attract private investment and/or to accommodate certain kinds of development.

Following the above remarks, the council expressed concern about proposed provisions regarding density and land use control. Accordingly, the council proposed that Part III, Section II, Subsection 10 should be amended to "expand the referral zone around urban municipalities free from one mile in the proposed Plan to two miles as in the existing 1963 Plan."[165]

Similarly feeling that "the Density and Land Use Control Provisions as outlined . . . are too generalized and that a stricter guideline for secondary industry should be introduced" the Town of High River, at its council meeting, suggested that "there might be strict controls throughout an area of perhaps five miles from an urban area and requests the Administration to draft an amendment to express these things."[166]

Also concerned about Subsection 10, the Village of Cochrane made this observation:

> As almost any industry can be directly related or oriented to agriculture it is felt that this portion of the plan as it now reads is so generalized it may be difficult to enforce and suggest that better or more detailed guidelines be set up as they are for other types of development. The generalization of this portion could have a strong detrimental effect on the urban areas that need additional industry to survive and prosper and unless the rural industry be compatible with the urban development there should be some policy to discourage it.[167]

This municipality's interest in having clearly stated policy regarding the location of industry included in the Preliminary Plan illustrates the way in which a municipality links its own economic interests to planning legislation. Apparently a Preliminary Plan, at least from the point of view of this village, not only acts as a guideline for development and growth, but also functions as a means of protecting municipal interests as they relate to economic growth. In other words, the village wanted some assurance that other local authorities, particularly the municipal districts, would not gain an advantage in terms of attracting private investment. The village saw the Preliminary Plan as a means of enforcing some control over the location of industry. It is noteworthy that while senior governments appear to be unwilling to directly intervene in the area of industrial location, authorities at the local level appear to be prepared to propose such intervention particularly if it will place them in a more favourable position in terms of their municipal competitors. In response to the village's observation, the "Administration" proposed for consideration that:

> In the selection of industrial uses . . . it is specifically intended that the determination of their direct relation or orientation to agriculture shall be based upon the direct nature of their industrial process or activity with agriculture and not merely upon the orientation of their custom or trade with the agricultural community.[168]

The concern expressed by the municipalities concerning the width of the referral zone suggests their unwillingness to lose control over their outward expansion to adjacent local authorities, particularly the municipal districts. The commission's "Administration" prepared the following comment as a response to the village's statement of concern:

> In connection with the Village's concern over compatibility of industries outside and near the urban area, it is suggested that the amendments drawn for the Town of

High River might provide for the desired cooperation. Otherwise it is noted that the proposed Preliminary Plan specifies a one-mile referral zone which the Town of Okotoks has suggested should be extended to two miles.[169]

Further comment outside that received from the member municipalities was provided by the Minister of Highways and Transport. The minister's submission noted that:

> It is not the intention of this Department to be unduly restrictive in the issuance of development permits adjacent to highways but we must at all times protect our Highway System. We do not feel that spot zoning is compatible with the requirements of today's highway system and we very much hope that the plan will convey this intent to the local taxing authorities and provide them with sound guidelines in establishing their development control By-Laws.[170]

These comments of the Minister of Highways and Transport and a related submission from the Municipal District of Foothills (dated January 27, 1971) well illustrate the position of the Regional Planning Commission vis-a-vis provincial government departments. The MD of Foothills submission stated that:

> At the meeting of the Council of the M.D. of Foothills No. 31 to discuss the preliminary regional plan, the Council decided that they wish to have the area between Highway NO. 2 and 2A on the south side of Highway No. 23 presently occupied as a Drive-In Theatre zoned Highway Commercial.
> They would like to have this proposal advanced as an amendment and they have also asked that this be referred to the Department of Highways.[171]

In addition, the "Council also discussed the matter of the Medium Density District being extended." As a result of this discussion the council requested that specific "sections" be added to the "Medium Density Zone." Referring to the first request, the commission's administration noted that:

> This site was not submitted to the Department of Highways and Transport in September, 1970 as one of the locations which the Commission proposed to designate High Density for Highway Commercial use in the Plan then under draft by the Zoning Committee. The location of each highway commercial subdivision and development has to be approved by the Department before either can proceed. Under this circumstance it is suggested that the matter should be referred to the Department and if a

favourable reply is received the location may be included in the Plan by amendment.[172]

Provincial legislation often gives authority to a department to make a decision with regard to development even though the area of concern may have import for planned regional growth and development. Another example of a department's authority is the following extract from the statement prepared by the Minister of Lands and Forests with regard to the Preliminary Plan (dated January 25, 1971):

> I wish to advise that the preliminary regional plan has been carefully examined by officials of my department and we are in agreement with the proposals with the following exceptions or reservations.
> (1) Part 2, Section 2, Paragraph 5(b) - is in direct conflict with Section 6 of the Public Lands Act and consequently should be deleted.
> (2) It is understood that in the low density areas in the green zone that there will be no conflictions with the management of public lands for timber, water shed protection, etc. pursuant to the Forests Act and Regulations.[173]

In addition to provincial government departments, certain federal departments are also interested in the contents of Preliminary Regional Plans. For example, a statement was received from the Director of the National and Historic Branch, Department of Indian Affairs and Northern Development.[174]

The Minister of Highways and Transport, in his submission, observed:

> Your proposed new plan has now been reviewed by this Department and I am somewhat concerned that it does not give more specific guidance to the taxing authorities from the point of view of the type of activities that will be allowed in the various areas under their control. The plan takes a very practical approach to the problem of subdivision density and we feel that this is definitely a step in the right direction. It does not, however, have any provision that would prevent the establishment of spot zoning at any location including the areas adjacent to our primary and secondary highways. We have found in the past from experience that the establishment of spot zoning along our highways is not compatible with the type of service our highway system must provide today. Spot zoning very definitely detracts from the safety and operational efficiency of our highways by encouraging undesirable ribbon development.[175]

And:

> I have no doubt that the current councils of the various taxing authorities are sincere about their policies and may well develop a comprehensive plan under their development By-Laws. I am however somewhat concerned that as the personnel on the councils change, their policies may also change in a manner that would be detrimental to the highway system. It would also seem that the councils should have some support from the plan to help them resist pressures from private developers for subdivisions or zoning that would be contrary to good planning practices.[176]

The minister's comments resulted in the preparation of additional amendments to Subsection 10 already amended as a result of the submission by the Village of Cochrane.

Compared to the problem of attracting private investment in a competitive situation, the question of "specific guidance" was given short shrift by municipalities. For certain municipalities such guidance in their view would have limited their potential to accommodating certain kinds of private investment. Certainly there was an unwillingness to agree to policies which might limit the freedom of a local authority to reach agreement with investors on such matters as location. This is not to say that the municipalities enjoyed having to succumb to "pressures from private developers" but to suggest that they had little choice so long as it was necessary to compete with other municipalities for private investment. Even though accommodating private developers might require decisions which would run "contrary to good planning practices," this was not so important, in the view of certain municipalities, as the need to secure the local tax base and to maintain a competitive position.

Although the Department of Highways and Transport has a flexible policy regarding the location of primary or extractive industries, it will not "relax its development control" for other "industrial uses" unless ". . . they are in an area covered by an outlined plan," and other provisions are made. In essence, the department's policy regarding industrial location can be considered a good indication of what the provincial government's views are on this matter. The department's policy was in line with the views of the regional planner and the larger urban centres. The municipal districts, particularly Rocky View, and smaller municipalities, were not so inclined to support a policy which restricted their efforts to establish a stronger industrial base and to promote "urbanization."

The proposed amendments while bringing the Preliminary Plan into concert with department policy, did not solve the other matters related to comprehensive planning policy or "specific guidance." Perhaps the Regional Planning Director hoped that the continuing discussion with the member municipalities would produce fruitful results in this regard. Certainly he and his colleagues did not have the authority to demand that the members agree to more specific policy. And even if he had had such authority, certain members — those more adversely affected by certain provincial government policies — would be placed in extremely unfair positions relative to their opportunity to improve their economic positions. In other words, giving additional authority to the Regional Planning Commission would not help to resolve the very practical problems facing certain member municipalities.

Of the amendments proposed by the Municipal District of Kneehill No. 48 the most significant was that which dealt with Part 2, Section 1, Subsection 1. It entailed changing the word "shall" to "should" so that the clause would read as follows:

> 1. (h) Commercial development should be located within the limits of urbanized areas but provision may be made for the location adjacent to the highways of appropriate commercial services to accommodate highway travellers.[177]

Significantly, the council minutes of January 18, 1971, record that the Planning Director was advised "that Council wishes authority to allow certain commercial developments in the rural area of this municipality. The main example quoted was an application which is now pending for an auto body shop."[178] In response to the proposed amendment the director "stated he would have no personal objection to changing the word "shall" to should." These amendments were aimed at improving the MD's position to accommodate new forms of private development, such as subdivision development, and reducing the authority of the Planning Commission over certain matters.

The MD of Rocky View suggested, among other amendments, that section 2 should read as follows:

> An area of land being proposed for the siting of a resort cottage subdivision *should* have the basic natural attributes of water frontage, ample vegetation, rolling topography, and relative isolation from highways and urban areas and in its discretion the Regional Planning Commission *should* decide as to the suitability of a proposed area or location with respect to the said attributes. (Emphasis original.)[179]

Rocky View also proposed to amend Part 3, Section 3, Subsection 7(d)(ii), which read:

> '7. (d)(ii) Parcels of less than 20 acres gross shall not be created within two miles of the Calgary City Limits or within one-half mile of a provincial highway.[180]

The amendment specified particular areas where "parcels of less than 20 acres" would be prohibited "but would allow all other areas within two miles of the Calgary City Limits to be rezoned for parcels less than 20 acres gross." The MD of Rocky View stated:

> If the two (2) mile limit zone is restricted to the above noted the Council of the Municipal District of Rocky View No. 44 is prepared to accept the condition that parcels of less than twenty (20) acres gross shall not be created in these areas on the basis that they are subject to a detailed development and land use study by the City of Calgary which should be completed within two (2) years. The Municipal District is reserving the right to review these areas within the two (2) year period for a possible amendment at the expiry of that period.[181]

The amendments proposed by Rocky View had the aim of making it possible for the MD to accommodate, with the commission's approval, the subdivision of property into smaller parcels than had previously been allowed. These amendments, also included specific areas of land within the two-mile zone around the periphery of the city. However, the overall impact of the amendment would be dependent upon the city agreeing to complete a land-use study within a two-year limit. If this was not done, the MD had the option to proceed with its own plans to subdivide, unrestricted by stringent planning policy and unhindered by the lack of city policy. It can be assumed that the MD did not wish to be restricted by planning policy which, in its view, only benefited the urban communities, particularly Calgary. The proposed amendments in effect placed the onus on the city to decide whether or not it was prepared to determine policy regarding growth corridors. Failure to produce such policy would place the city in the position of having to make development decisions in terms of decisions already taken by the Municipal District.

The City of Calgary submitted a number of proposed amendments. Included in the background material was a statement from the Mayor's Office dated January 26, 1971. Arguing "that the minimum parcel size of 20 acres must remain for at least a two mile greenbelt adjacent to its boundaries," the statement explained:

> We believe that the proposal to develop two acre small holdings on a cluster basis will be, in the long run, seriously detrimental to the environment, to orderly development, and to the economic servicing of these clusters of development at such time in the future as municipal services may be installed. We believe that the long run implications of this proposal should be thoroughly examined by the Provincial Government before it is implemented.[182]

The statement also observed:

> We consider it necessary to prevent continued high-density residential development from passing across our boundaries so that we may be able to direct future

> development in the directions most economic for the City — meaning that there is a logical infill of areas already adjacent to services that may not take place if developments are allowed to sprawl in directions which developers themselves desire for their own private interest. Consequently, in the overall public interest we would propose to encourage greater density within the City limits and such infill as City Council considers desirable.[183]

Touching upon the responsibility of the provincial government, the statement noted:

> We believe that a thorough study of all the factors affecting regional growth is desirable; we believe that this is a provincial responsibility and such study should be implemented by provincial authorities who have the regional responsibilities already and whose decisions are more likely to be impartial and objective than any municipality or municipal district. This means that our own planning department, that of Edmonton and that of any municipal district would not be the proper body to carry out the necessary regional studies. We recommend that a full study be undertaken before the recommendations of the McNally Commission and the policies based on that report are replaced by any new policies. The McNally Commission report has served the province well for fifteen years and it has yet to be demonstrated that is no longer viable.[184]

The Mayor's statement also supported the principle that noxious and extractive industries should be encouraged to locate in the municipal districts. These districts, on the other hand, should not be permitted to accommodate those developments which could be suitably located in the city. The statement further observed:

> We believe that there is a significant area for positive co-operation between municipal districts and the City of Calgary for the location or relocation of suitable industry within the municipal districts and we will encourage any positive program that can be of mutual advantage.[185]

The Director of Planning submitted a report entitled, *The Proposed Preliminary Regional Plan — 1970,* to the Regional Planning Commission.[186] Observing that the "prime concern of the City with this document lies in the proposals for residential subdivision adjoining the City's present boundaries, and for industrial uses in the rural areas and restrictions on subdivision within the City limits," the director noted that the city verbally endorsed the following statement:

> The remarkable expansion of Calgary's boundaries up to 1964 brought under the City's control extensive areas of land for future growth. The resulting great open spaces between active urban development and city boundaries served to remove from the City's immediate concern the realities of the new subdivision fringe building up outside its boundary. If this subdivision build-up continues at the present rate the next city generation will be confronted with an endless stumbling block to economical urban development.
>
> The resulting fragmentation of huge areas of land is distressing to the land conservationist, while the widespread dispersal of development is costly for municipal and educational services. To continue present methods of land fragmentation which occurs in the path of the next generation of city expansion is also contrary to accepted premises and purposes of regional planning.[187]

Pointing out that the above statement "serves to emphasize the primary concern of the City to protect from fragmentation those areas which currently lie beyond the City limits but in the path of future urban growth", the director went on to observe:

> At present subdivision beyond the City limits is largely restricted to Agricultural Use with a minimum parcel size of 20 acres. This has effectively prevented the undue fragmentation of agricultural land and has protected the enviable degree of urban compactness which characterizes the City of Calgary as opposed to the seemingly endless sprawl of unplanned semi-urban clutter which extends far into what used to be rural countryside on every side of so many other cities on this continent.
>
> Undoubtedly, a thorough study of all the factors of City growth and metropolitan development is urgently needed and it is hoped to undertake such a study as soon as possible but meanwhile the pressing problems of subdivision and development on the City fringe demand a solution in terms of the Preliminary Regional Plan.[188]

He also said:

> Most of the arguments against the location of residential development in rural areas are equally applicable to industrial use. However exceptions undoubtedly occur in relation to the extractive industries which are directly site-oriented (i.e. sand and gravel pits) or strategically located to serve the operational field (i.e. gas processing plants, pulpmills, and sawmills); in fact, such uses are often best located well away from urban settlements due to their unpleasant smell or overpowering visual contact.[189]

The director's report drew attention to the proposition that given the opportunity a number of city residents would move to the rural areas and the small outlying communities:

> It is recognized that the drastic movement of population to the City from the rural municipalities and the consequent impact upon their tax base could to some extent be alleviated by satisfying the desire of many citizens to live in the country. In this respect Calgary is by no means hungry for more population with all the related expense of additional services and any encouragement for people to live in commuter villages or satellite towns may be to the City's advantage.[190]

The 1970 Preliminary Regional Plan was adopted by the Calgary Regional Planning Commission on February 5, 1971. At the February 15, 1971 meeting of the City of Calgary's "Industrial Expansion Committee" the misgivings of the Village of Cochrane and the Town of High River were alluded to.
The minutes of the meeting record the following under the heading "Industries Bordering the City Limits":

> . . .(the) Director of Planning, advised the meeting that the Calgary Regional Planning Commission had adopted the Regional General Plan at a recent meeting and this must now receive the approval of the Provincial authorities. The City's concerns on this plan were that the areas of future growth of the City deserved some protection and that industrial development should not be allowed within two miles of the City limits. The Village of Cochrane had asked that more detail be included in the plan to explain "farm oriented industries". The Town of High River suggested that applications for development within five miles of a town should be referred to that town for consideration.
> (the Director) stated that he was recommending to the Board of Commissioners that
> (a) the City indicate to the Town of High River, the City's support of the principle made in its suggestion, and
> (b) the City initiate an appeal to have the plan amended to require that applications for industrial development within two miles of the City's borders be referred to the City, and should the decision of the Calgary Planning Commission be felt to be unfair, that the matter be resolved by the Regional Planning Commission.

No specific recommendation was made with regard to the Cochrane proposition.

The Municipal District of Rocky View continued to believe that the Preliminary Regional Plan placed the MD in an almost powerless position. On June 3, 1971 the MD submitted "A brief on appeal to the Provincial Planning Board regarding the Calgary Preliminary Regional Plan, 1971." The Reeve representing the Municipal District explained to the members of the Provincial Planning Board that:

> I am here representing the Council as well as 10,000 people. Our object in being here is that we have the strong belief that our municipality should be developed constructively, orderly, and economically. Our object is also to acquire a viable constructive and mutually acceptable Regional Plan not only to the Commission members but also to the public at large who will also be affected by this plan. In our endeavor to do so we are submitting this appeal on the new Regional Plan on purely a constructive basis.
> We sincerely believe that planning has come to play a very important role in our present and future growth structure. In order to give effect to good planning, we therefore must provide a constructive and unbiased plan, free of detailed, restrictive measures that are biased, selfish and prejudiced. We believe a Regional Plan must be general, flexible, and offer valid acceptable guideline policies. We believe a Regional Plan must be permissive as compared to that proposed and adopted by the City of Calgary, and not be mandatory in detail.
> The municipal District of Rocky View is a very large municipality and probably one of the fastest growing municipalities in Alberta. It is fortunate in a sense that planning is coming into the picture in our infancy and can achieve good results, not only now but in the future, provided we have sensible policies and agreements.
> The Municipal District of Rocky View plays a very large and important role in implementation of a good plan, as well as being the principal target.

The Reeve's opening remarks offered the opinion that the Preliminary Plan had been designed to protect the interests of the City of Calgary and, consequently, was aimed at restricting the Municipal District's opportunity to develop "constructively, orderly, and economically." It was argued that because the plan imposed constraints on the district's freedom to make responsible choices, the document must be considered "biased, selfish, and prejudiced." Throughout the statement it is implicit that the MD felt more a "target" of the plan than a participant in the formulation of regional planning policy.

The Reeve's remarks reflect the Municipal District's feeling that the Preliminary Plan was primarily oriented to accommodating the city's desires; in fact, the Reeve went so far as to suggest that much of the policy contained in the plan, if not all, had originated with the city. Comparing itself to the city, the MD felt itself to be in a position of relative impotence with regard to the possibility of bringing about changes in regional planning policy at the commission level. This feeling of impotence had presumably encouraged the district to initiate an Appeal to the Provincial Planning Board. The Reeve did not enlarge upon the role of the planning commission in the process of preparing the Preliminary Plan. The MD perhaps did not view the commission, since its membership was, in the opinion of the MD, weighted in favour of the urban centre, as the mechanism through which ". . . a viable, constructive and mutually acceptable Regional Plan . . ." could be developed.

Of the amendments contained in the Rocky View appeal a few are of particular interest. Referring to the "decision of the Commission to include in the Plan an amendment submitted by the Village of Cochrane," the appeal noted:

> The indecision of this section negates and confuses the provisions of subclause 10(c) (vii). It specifically states that the intention of this previous clause is to determine what industries are agriculturally oriented and based. This is a direct intrusion by the urban point of view into the economic development of the rural community upon which they heavily rely. It has become quite evident in the last two years that when the agricultural community is in economical difficulties, then it also affects the urban areas large and small, to a greater and longer degree. It is only with a healthy rural economy that the urban centres can survive.
> The Council also submits that it is of no concern to an urban Council what local economic procedures are taken by a rural Council, and industrial development on a limited scale is of local economic concern.
> We respectfully request the Board that this section be struck out as being superfluous.

With regard to subsection 10, subclause (b) (iv), of the Preliminary Regional Plan, the appeal stated that:

> The Council strongly objects to this provision, in that it will sterilize land after zoning has been granted for smallholding or country residential purposes. It is indicated in this section that twenty percent of the parent parcel shall be used for subdivision, leaving sixty percent under the same zoning classification, which is very restrictive as to land use. It becomes quite evident that there would be a tendency for the residual parcel to end up in a situation detrimental to the community at large, in that no agricultural activity, other than the growing of grass, could be carried out on it. Under the present

> provincial assessment and taxation laws, this becomes a liability not only to the land owner, but to the municipality.

Continuing on, the appeal observed:

> The Commission has submitted that the purpose of this section is to conserve land by this restriction. We submit the purpose is to make high price lots for high income families and not to conserve land. The first basic concept of land conservation is to use that land and not let it sit idle and stagnate. We feel that a relaxation of this provision is in order so that the land owner will have a multiplicity of choice in subdivision design which would allow a beneficial land use program in the regional area of Rocky View. By this we mean after zoning is established, a land use subdivision varying from two acres to four, ten, twenty, or forty.

Referring to the "designation of location of new Hamlets," the brief explained that "The authority for the designation and location of Hamlets and the authority for approval of subdivision must be isolated from each other." Having noted that:

> The designation and location authority for Hamlets is pursuant to the present provisions of the Municipal Government Act and is now vested in the municipality and the Minister of Municipal Affairs;

the appeal went on to state:

> However, in this section of the Plan the designation, location authority and subdivision authority is combined and vested in the Regional Planning Commission. We question the validity of this section as we can find no supporting provincial legislation empowering the Regional Planning Commission to enact its own legislation . . .

and:

> We therefore appeal this section on the basis of eliminating confusion, legal entanglements and contend that the designation of these authorities must be isolated and maintained as such.
> We therefore request that the wording "designation" and "location" be deleted from the Plan.

Presumably the MD's desire to limit the authority of the planning commission prompted the above amendment. The MD, this evidence suggests, expected that by having direct dealings with government departments the possibility of obtaining "fair" hearings was greater than that which would be expected at the commission level. Presumably the MD did not wish the commission to have an authority over "the selection and approval of locations for new hamlets," as it might prove to be an obstacle to the MD's goal of promoting certain kinds of development. Certain members of the planning commission were, and remain, very emphatic about not permitting the MD to attract development away from the urban centres, particularly Calgary. By ensuring that the commission did not acquire authority over the creation of new hamlets, the Municipal District could feel somewhat more secure about the possibility of being able to promote such development. For the Department of Municipal Affairs to hinder or overrule a district's decision in this area could bring about the accusation that the government was interfering in the affairs of a local authority. The Municipal District, therefore, was in effect using provincial government legislation to circumvent a regional organization which, in its opinion, was not able to make objective decisions or was unwilling to do so.

The final point of the Municipal District's appeal to the Provincial Planning Board dealt with the matter of industrialization. Drawing attention to Part III, Section III, Subsection (c), Subclause (vii), the brief stated:

> The words "and which" in the second last line on this page to be deleted and word "or" to be inserted. This section is self-explanatory and limiting and is clearly spelled out. In its original form when this section was introduced, it was intended to permit four types of industry in the rural municipality, namely: (a) farm oriented industry; (b) Industry requiring a minimum of municipal services (c) Industry requiring large areas of land; (d) Industry of a pollutant nature.
> However, we now find the wording to combine (b), (c), and (d) and limiting the permitted industry to two categories, which must comply with three qualifications before being permitted.

A "Board Order," dated October 27,1971 dealt with the appeal submitted by Rocky View, which had been discussed at the June 3, 1971 public hearing.[191] The Preliminary Regional Plan was later further amended, probably in accordance with the order of the Provincial Planning Board, to satisfy the objections of the Municipal District.

The MacEwan Glens Affair

Since the 1964 annexation decisions, planners employed by the Calgary Regional Planning Commission, have endeavoured to encourage commission members to endorse a rational regional planning approach to growth and development. However, throughout their discussions with member municipalities, the planners have encountered considerable opposition to certain of their policy recommendations. The perspective of the planners, as reflected in their recommendations, frequently conflicts with the immediate individual interests of the various municipalities. Since these interests are associated with factors which exist quite outside the jurisdiction of The Planning Act, regional planners have found it almost impossible to obtain endorsement for certain of their policy recommendations.

Municipal participation in the re-drafting of the Preliminary Regional Plan eventually yielded little more than a compromise document. At practically every stage of the discussions, the planners found it necessary to modify or abandon their principal policy recommendations in order to accommodate the desires expressed by each member municipality and the decisions of senior government authorities. The planners were left with a more permissive document than the one which had previously existed. While the policies contained in the new Preliminary Plan are in concert with the individual interests of the various member municipalities, the question of establishing sound planning guidelines for the entire region remains unresolved.

Until recently, the original Preliminary Regional Plan acted as a restraining influence on *ad hoc* development proposals of certain kinds. Before the re-drafting of this plan was concluded, however, a significant event occurred. On March 9, 1971 the registered owners of lands adjacent to the City of Calgary applied to the Local Authorities Board for annexation of their land to the city. In addition:

> The applicants were joined in the petition by Carma Developers Ltd., Calgary, purchaser of the South-East Quarter and the West Half of Section Seventeen (17), Township Twenty-Five (25), Range One (1), West of the Fifth Meridan under Agreement for Sale dated January 2, 1969.[192]

The development company submitted the following "Reasons For Petition" with their original application:

> REASONS FOR PETITION:
> The reasons advanced in support of the petition include the following:
> 1. The area sought to be annexed will fulfill the City's need of suitable additional lands for moderately priced residential development capable of attracting Federal mortgage funds primarily for single family housing ranging in retail price from $14,000.00 to $18,000.00 without subsidy. It should be noted that multiple family units are also included in the proposal.
> 2. The lands in the area form a part of the natural discrete

planning for further expansion of the City of Calgary. The larger planning unit of which the territory is a part is presently defined by natural land features and in the future will be further defined by man-made features including the future expansion of 14th Street North West and future expansion of Sarcee Trail.

3. The area sought to be annexed is eminently suitable for residential development by reason of such factors as:

(a) Natural features of the lands allow urban residential development with natural open space and an opportunity for an exciting view;

(b) The lands may be serviced economically through extensions to existing City water and sanitary sewer systems;

(c) Accessibility can be provided by the logical extension of the existing City street system in future transportation plans of the City;

(d) The lands lie outside the influence of present and proposed flight tests associated with the Calgary International Airport;

(e) The lands are not encumbered in any way by existing urban development as the present use of land is wholly agricultural.

4. The annexation of the lands will provide more than $50,000,000.00 of new construction which would not otherwise be available in the area due to the lack of such moderately priced residential development land and thus the said construction will provide many new jobs for Calgary and district residents while ensuring single family housing for moderate income groups.

Shortly after the submission of the annexation petition to the Local Authorities Board, the LAB requested the City of Calgary Planning Department to present "this matter . . . to the next council meeting in order that the Local Authorities Board may be advised of any comments of views they have regarding it."[193]

The Director of Planning therefore submitted a report to the City Planning Commission outlining the action required before annexation and the implications of the annexation. The action required before annexation included the building of storm sewer outfalls, the establishing of certain sewer easements, road-widening, and resolving the "question of electrical services to the area."[194] Concerning the implications of annexation, the director's report said:

> The objective of the annexation is to provide Carma Developers with suitable additional lands for moderately priced residential development capable of attracting federal mortgage funds primarily for single family housing ranging in retail price from $14,000 to $18,000 without subsidy, as well as some multiple family units. While the

advantages of the proposed annexation are detailed in the attached petition, there are considerable operational and cost implications of this proposal to the City of Calgary.[195]

These "operational and cost implications" included road-building costs, extensions to the water-delivery system, a deficit of up to $46,800 annually for transit services, a new fire station, high costs for busing school-children, and a variety of detailed planning considerations.

Seeking to get the annexation application endorsed, the development company presented a detailed analysis of the way in which the proposal, in its view, would coincide with expansion plans for the city. There is evidence to suggest that Carma disputed a number of the observations made by certain city departments. On February 1, 1971 the city's Director of Planning wrote to the City Engineer and observed:

> (Carma representative) appears to dispute your concern over the availability of utilities in this area and seems to believe that Section 17 can be drained satisfactorily with easements. Also I wonder whether the cost of water supply, both in this area and South East of the Airport, is a significant cost in relation to roadway costs when determining priorities. It would be appreciated if you could review these matters at your earliest convenience so that we can decide whether we pursue annexation as a practical alternative to a development of Nose Hill.[196]

Despite the questions that arose concerning the developer's analysis, however, the position of the company was enhanced by the availability of federal mortgage funds. These provided an additional attraction insofar as the City Council was concerned, particularly at a time of unemployment. In a letter to a City Commissioner, a representative of Carma Developers observed:

> Carma require the co-operation of all City departments to accomplish the annexation. I believe it will provide many jobs for Calgarians (with the mortgarge funds available for such projects) as well as providing excellent housing for moderate income families.[197]

Perhaps not surprisingly, the company made no reference to the Preliminary Regional Plan's policies regarding urban sprawl and the importance of retaining certain lands for agricultural purposes. The lack of interest in matters of this kind is well illustrated by the fourth statement of the proposal that the lands are "wholly agricultural." Too, there was no reference to the city plan's emphasis on the need to establish "growth corridors" and to prepare "sector plans." It can be suggested that the developer found it convenient to ignore these and other local planning concerns, or was unaware of them.

On April 14, 1971 the Calgary Planning Commission passed the following motions:

> 1. That the Commission recommend to City Council that a policy be established whereby an additional mile be annexed to the western eight miles of the City's northern boundary, in order to straighten out this boundary.
> 2. That the Commission recommend to City Council that this application for annexation be supported on the basis that it is the first stage in achieving the wider annexation detailed in the first motion.[198]

Taking into account the interest of senior city officials in proposals of the type presented by Carma, there is a reason to understand why the planning commission decided not to submit a negative recommendation to the City Council. Since the commission is responsible for securing "orderly and economic development," it would be logical to assume that this municipal body would be inclined to give priority to recommendations from the planning department. However, the actions of the commission in this case seem to question this assumption. Even though the department's submission did not include a forthright recommendation, the information provided in the report brought into question, among other things, the developer's statement that the proposal was in line with a logical extension of city services. The report makes it quite clear that in order for the city to provide services to the development, there would have to be a large expenditure of public revenues; this would mean public subsidizing of a low-cost housing development, initiated by a private company using a federal mortgage program.

The commission's quick response to the annexation proposal is partly explained by the minutes of the liaison committee for its meeting of April 8, 1971:

> In the interests of relieving the employment situation, the City was anxious to have the first application dealt with as expeditiously as possible, to enable the construction of homes in this area to proceed this summer.[199]

At the same meeting, the Reeve, representing the MD of Rocky View:

> stated that the Council of MD No. 44 would be considering this application at its meeting on April 13, 1971. He suggested that, to avoid irregular boundaries, consideration might be given to annexing the full eight square miles, i.e. moving the City's boundary from 80th Ave. to 96th Street West.

Following these remarks:

> The meeting expressed its favour to the annexation of the eight square miles but felt there might be some opposition to such action which would prolong a decision by the Public Utilities Board. It was therefore agreed that two applications should be submitted (a) one dealing with the three-quarter section, to which there were no known objectors, and
> (b) a second application dealing with the balance of the eight square miles, submitted jointly by the City and the Municipal District.

Interestingly enough, the committee found it necessary to move that an application concerning the three-quarter sections should be submitted, even though the developer had already submitted such an application. Perhaps this was done in order to obtain MD support for the developer's application. The liaison committee's motions clearly supported the annexation of the entire eight square mile area. The city and the MD should submit a joint application for annexation of that area not covered by the developer's application.

The liaison committee endorsed a Commissioner's request that "they bring these annexation applications to Council at the April 26th meeting, by which time the decision of the Municipal District of the Rocky View would be known." During the meeting, the representative of Rocky View pointed out that it was desirable that the boundaries of school divisions should be changed at the time of annexation to coincide with the boundaries of the municipalities. The committee minutes record that:

> while it was acknowledged that conditions could not be attached to an application for annexation, it was agreed that, if the annexation is approved, a request from the municipalities should be forwarded to the Minister of Education that a Ministerial Order be issued to adjust the school division boundaries.

It is important to note that the above refers to the municipalities making a request to the Minister of Education.

Following the meetings of the City Planning Commission and the liaison committee, a Commissioner's report regarding the proposed annexation of property north of the City of Calgary was presented to the City Council at its meeting of April 26, 1971.

> The Commissioners were requested by the 'Liaison Committee re problems involving the City and adjacent municipalities' at their meeting of April 8 to forward the annexation applications submitted to the City of Calgary from the solicitors of the registered owners of the three-quarter sections north of the City (Huntington Hills area) to this meeting of Council. It is intended that the decision from the council of the Municipal District of Rockyview

will be available for this meeting of Council. Accordingly we are reproducing a copy of the minutes from the Planning Commission meeting of April 14 which were approved at the April 21 meeting. *Recommendation:* The commissioners concur with the recommendation of the Planning Commission and also the suggestion by the Liaison Committee that we avoid any irregular boundaries by annexing the full eight square miles instead of just the three-quarter sections of property requested by the petitioners, by moving the City's boundary from 80th Avenue to 96th Avenue North, between 15 Street East to 85 Street West.

Action recommended: Approval of the recommendations contained in the Planning Commission minutes of April 14 and for the annexation of the three-quarter sections requested by the petitioners as well as the additional mile to the western eight miles of the City's northern boundary in order to straighten out the boundary.

One member of the City Council has explained that he had interpreted the Commissioners' report as having recommended that the Carma application should be part of a comprehensive application for annexation. It is significant that this report: (i) did not mention that the liaison committee had agreed that "a request from the municipalities should be forwarded to the Minister of Education", and (ii) did not refer to the liaison committee's decision that "a second application dealing with the balance of the eight square miles (be) submitted jointly by the City and the Municipal District." The planning commission recommended that the Carma Developer's "application for annexation be supported on the basis that it is the first stage in achieving the wider annexation . . .," while the Commissioners' report referred to "the annexation of the three-quarter sections requested by the petitioners as well as the additional mile to the western eight miles of the City's northern boundary in order to straighten out the boundary."

Taking the Commissioners' report under close scrutiny, it is understandable that certain councillors thought that the report dealt with the annexation question in its entirety. Furthermore, the Commissioners' report did not deal with the various observations made by the City Planning Department's report, although the two were submitted together. One city alderman has explained that he relies almost totally on the recommendations prepared by City Commissioners rather than assessing the significance of supporting detail. Compounding this situation was the council's willingness to support a recommendation pertinent to a development proposal that did not appear to set the stage for political problems. The contentious issue of piecemeal annexation, a question that did concern certain aldermen, appeared to be satisfactorily resolved in the Commissioners' report, even though the question of initiating the second application was not dealt with. Other matters, particularly ones related to the costs of extending municipal services, do not appear to have received the close attention of council. However, the evidence indicates that Carma Developers Ltd. took the opportunity to discuss the annexation proposal with city officials and aldermen. For example, a representative of the company wrote the following to a City Commissioner:

> Would it be possible to have the MacEwan Glens annexation petition outlined to the Committee on a confidential basis as the Municipality of Rocky View will hear our proposal Tuesday, March 9th, 1971, at 2:00 p.m. and I believe as many Aldermen as possible should be aware of the situation before it hits the press . . .

And further on:

> You might announce that if any detailed information is required by individual Aldermen that I am prepared to see them at their convenience to discuss the application more completely.

In addition to the Commissioners' report, copies of the developer's petition and the Planning Department's report were submitted to the City Council. Following discussion, the council passed the Commissioners' recommendations.

At the Regional Planning Commission meeting on May 7, the Director of the City Planning Department, who was in attendance, was requested to render an opinion on the specific issue of the proposed annexation. The commission minutes report that :

> Upon questioning, Mr. Rogers of the City Planning Department elaborated on the technical aspects of the proposed annexation. While it is true that growth-corridor studies have not been carried out, the City is growing north, south, and east directions at the same time. Vehicle travel time from the north is shorter than from the south and, consequently, the indicated desire line for growth is north of 80th Avenue (Huntingdon Hills), particularly in view of the effects of the new Blackfoot Trail. The four square miles encompassed by Nose Hill present servicing and access difficulties as the area is over 4,000 feet in elevation. The possible future density of this area has been reduced to approximately one-half of that expected in a normal subdivision owing to the large, open escarpment areas and limitations on the thoroughfare network. Fourteenth Street is not proposed to be upgraded to freeway standards to 80th Avenue. Consequently, all major access to the subject area is proposed to be in an east-west direction via 80th Avenue to either Shaganappi Trail or Blackfoot Trail. Because all utilities and access would be

> more related to an east/west pattern of growth, the City is supporting this annexation on the basis that it is the first stage of achieving the ultimate annexation of a strip of land one mile wide by eight miles long on the northern city boundary, all of which will contribute to either the western or northern sectors.[200]

That the City Planning Director's comments at the Regional Planning Commission meeting were not a genuine expression of the real sentiments of either himself or his department, can be illustrated by comparing the comments with an excerpt from the Calgary Plan:

> . . . the increased size of the City and the complexity and scale of problems associated with this growth generates a need for a planned framework within which individual developments can proceed. Long range transportation corridors must be reserved well ahead of time to allow immediate residential projects to proceed with confidence that the development will not be adversely affected by subsequent corridor requirements.
>
> The establishment of such corridors is not an easy matter, however, since conflicting demands for preservation of parks and viable business or residential communities will always pose a dilemma when trying to introduce a new transportation system.
>
> At this time certain questions need to be asked. How large should the city be? Should it be allowed to extend indefinitely? Is the present form of growth the most economic method? Is continuing growth and expansion up to, for example, the magical figure of one million a worthwhile objective?
>
> It is only in recent years that urban governments have come to realize that fiscal and land planning, to be of any real value to the community, must be related to a series of overall objectives aimed at providing politicians with a meaningful framework of reference for decision-making.

Although the director acknowledged that "growth-corridor studies have not been carried out," he did not point out that the city still lacked "a series of overall objectives" regarding growth and development. Since the City Council had decided to support the annexation application, it can be assumed that the Director of the City Planning Department was not in a position to give overt approval to the declared opposition of the Municipal District and the Regional Planning Director.

The report submitted to the Calgary Regional Planning Commission meeting of May 7 by the Regional Planning Director questioned the wisdom of the proposed annexation:

> . . . City Council is agreeing to the immediate annexation of the subject Section 17 lands, in the wider context of a policy to annex the eight square miles in total along its northern boundary. It is understood that the City intends to take early annexation action on the balance of the whole eight miles.
> The Planning Department Report to the Calgary Municipal Planning Commission indicates that certain access and servicing problems will result from early development of the Section 17 land. However, it is observed here that these represent matters of direct municipal concern which will be resolved internally. The Report also indicates that Sector Planning has not been extended to the area. As a consequence the precise relationship of the area, not only to existing development, but more importantly to long range development of surrounding sector lands, has not been determined.

After reviewing the features of the area under consideration, the Regional Planning Director raised four questions:

> 1. Whether there is a shortage of suitable developed or economically developable land in this City to the extent that the immediate piecemeal annexation of Section 17 land is necessary or desirable notwithstanding the claims of less expensive lots, and whether the development of the overall 'B' Sector will be affected.
> 2. Whether the annexation of lands should be contempleted until following the completion of substantial sector planning of the 'B' Beddington Area to establish the relationship of the subject Section 17 and other immediately adjacent lands to overall development and to a system of development phasing of the Area.
> 3. Whether the proposed annexation of the entire balance of the eight-mile strip of land into the City is reasonable at this time, or bears relationship to the Preliminary Regional Plan objectives of establishing corridors of orderly growth into the countryside.
> 4. Whether the annexation of any lands should be contemplated unless coterminous municipal and school boundaries and agreed educational services are co-ordinated in the action.

He observed, ". . . it seems that the objectives of the Preliminary Regional Plan are not being met."

The director went on to note that Rocky View was having second thoughts about the proposal:

> The commission has received advice that the Rocky View Council on April 27th reviewed the matter, coming to the

> conclusion that it is not at this time prepared to agree to the annexation of Section 17 lands or to an immediate application by the City for the annexation of any of the eight square miles in question. Its reason in essence are related to the problem of coterminous school boundaries and the absence of any intent by the Calgary School Boards to construct schools in the area; and to its reluctance to embark on an annexation programme at this time which is not directly related to the projected study of City growth corridors.

The director emphasized that the "essence" of the MD's concern was the matter of coterminous boundaries. To some extent, the MD was far more concerned about the question of coterminous boundaries than the need for establishing "city growth corridors." The significance attached to the latter need can be interpreted as simply a supporting argument for the MD's opposition to the application until such time that there had been a ruling on the question of coterminous boundaries. Earlier, at the liaison committee meeting, representatives from the MD had indicated their approval of the annexation of the eight mile strip.

The MD of Rocky View drew attention to the piecemeal nature of the annexation proposal, and to the proposition that it lacked proper planning "because of the absence of sector plan development showing future needs in the Beddington Creek growth corridor." These two points coincide with those expressed by the Director of the Regional Planning Commission. In addition, the MD also gave another reason for its opposition to the annexation:

> No agreement has been made on coterminous school and municipal boundaries. Annexation will not result in an automatic change in school division boundaries, which is a separate matter not under the Local Authorities Board, and the Municipality does not wish to find itself in the position of providing school facilities for a high density of population. It has already had a long-term and unfortunate experience arising out of lack of resolution of coterminous boundaries because of previous annexations.

In conclusion, the municipality contended "that these problems should be resolved before any annexation can be supported." The commission minutes explained that:

> The Commission was advised that the Local Authorities Board has acknowledged that the annexation of the three quarter sections of Section 17 would be in relation to the ultimate annexation of the eight-mile strip. There was concurrence that the school division boundaries should be coterminous and perhaps development should be withheld by the City until coterminous arrangements are made.

> Rocky View indicated that the timing of development is important and presents overriding considerations. Therefore, all problems should be resolved prior to any annexation since the future annexation of the eight-mile strip could be delayed indefinitely by objectors.

Although the LAB may have been informed that the city's decision had been to endorse total annexation of the eight-mile strip, the planning commission does not seem to have been advised that, up to that point, a second annexation application had not been submitted to the LAB. Rocky View re-emphasized the need to proceed with the total annexation, and to resolve the question of coterminous boundaries. After further discussion, a commission member "moved that the matter be tabled until the question of coterminous school boundaries is resolved." This motion was withdrawn, and the following proposed by representatives from the MD of Rocky View:

> . . . moved that the Commission recommend to the Local Authorities Board that it is opposed to the annexation of a portion of Section 17 for the following basic reasons:
> 1. Piecemeal annexation
> 2. Lack of coterminous boundaries
> 3. Lack of sector planning for the Beddington Creek area.

This motion was defeated.

Having defeated this motion, the commission passed one prepared by representatives from the City of Calgary:

> . . . moved that the Commission advise the Local Authorities Board that it recommends approval of the annexation of the W.1/2 and S.E.1/4 17-25-1-W/5th subject to the following conditions:
> 1. That the Local Authorities Board establish a definite time table for a hearing on the annexation of the eight-mile strip of land; and
> 2. That the question of the coterminous school boundaries be satisfactorily resolved.

This particular motion could be construed as a ruse designed to draw attention away from the directors's analysis. The director's report, it can be argued, was an attempt to keep alive the sentiments of regional planning, as outlined in the Preliminary Regional Plan and expressed in the city plan. For certain members, however, the major concern was a commission posture which could not create difficulties at the annexation hearing. Certainly, the two motions contained little real substance. The LAB is not in a position to set a date for a hearing until it has received an application, and coterminous boundary matters are usually resolved at the municipal level in discussion with provincial government authorities. Although the director warned commission members that the motion would prove to be ineffective, he was virtually ignored. Indeed, the final motion of the meeting dealt with the "filing" of the director's report. It appears that the report received very little comment. This has been attributed largely to a clash of opinion that exists between the MD of Rocky View and the director on such matters as the Preliminary Regional Plan.

During the Regional Planning Commission meeting, certain other matters were discussed and recorded in the minutes:

> It was observed that development of a residential subdivision does not commence immediately upon annexation, and the question of school boundaries could be resolved before construction begins. It was further questioned whether a definite need has been demonstrated for this annexation, having regard to the existence of large undeveloped areas of land still within the present limits of the City of Calgary, and it would therefore seem premature. In discussion, it was observed that a variety of housing types and choice of building areas should be available in all parts of the City in order to keep costs down; and having regard to the cost of development of Nose Hill with its resultant higher land costs, lower-priced land should be made available for residential development in the vicinity.

Although "it was observed" that "lower-priced land should be made available for residential development in the vicinity" of Nose Hill, no information was provided concerning land already available within the city boundaries for such development. There is no explanation in the minutes as to why the development of Nose Hill would suggest a need for a low-cost housing development in the vicinity other than from the point of view of providing "a variety of housing types." It should be remembered that the Director of the Regional Planning Commission felt it necessary to question the assumption that:

> there is a shortage of suitable developed or economically developable land in the City to the extent that the immediate piecemeal annexation of Section 17 land is necessary or desirable.

In point of fact, there does not appear to have been an investigation into the question of the availability of "lower-priced land" within the city boundaries for low-cost housing developments.

Then the Calgary School District No. 19 School Board prepared a "Submission to the Local Authorities Board."[201] The submission made a number of observations concerning the financial implications of annexation from the point of view of providing school services, and concluded by pointing out that for several years to come children would have to be bused to schools elsewhere in Calgary and that this would be expensive.

The Calgary School Board was concerned about the costs of providing school services to the land proposed for annexation. This cost, and those mentioned in the City Planning Department's report, suggest that to provide services to "low-priced" land, Calgarians would have to make a substantial financial contribution through the mill rate and supplementary requisition. However, the city administration attempted, as a matter of political expediency, to avoid being held responsible for additional education costs.

Even though certain council decisions require an expansion of school services or more facilities, the council is often reluctant to consider the amount of the local school board requisition as a matter for which it might be partially responsible. In other words, the council leaves the responsibility for coping with increasing education expenditure with the school board, although certain of these expenditures clearly result from council decisions. There is a tendency for certain city officials to become annoyed by the fact that the school board, in their opinion, attempts to interfere with city planning by demanding that City Council decisions be in accord with the board's views regarding growth.[202] The school board's responsibility is seen as being solely that of providing for the educatonal needs of Calgarians. Attempts by the board to intervene in matters of planning policy have been conveniently interpreted as unwillingness on the part of that body to handle its own responsibilities. It is argued that if the board is unable to accommodate a particular situation, "it should say so" and indicate "when it will be able to do so." The school board's submission however noted:

> We also wish to inform you it has come to our attention there are several other similar relatively small projects for urban development in the offing such as the Scenic Acres property north of Bowness which would presumably require annexation procedure. However, we are not aware that due consideration has yet been given to establishing a definite master plan policy for the form of expansion of the greater metropolitan Calgary urban area.[203]

In addition to the costs associated with school construction, the school board is held responsible for providing certain services for the land which it has acquired. The board is "treated the same as any other developer," and must make provision for sidewalks and so forth. If the board is unable to acquire land out of community reserve, it must be prepared to pay the purchase price of other property. For serviced land, this proves to be a costly endeavour. As is the case for all the board's expenditures, these expenses become a direct charge to "the taxpayer at the provincial government level" or "is paid for by the municipal taxpayer by means of the local school board requisition." Understandably, the City Council does not wish to be linked with expenditures that place additional burdens on Calgary ratepayers. It has been observed that the council, in order to escape financial responsibilities for certain of its decisions, "shoves the burden onto the school board or the developer." In the latter case, the home buyer ends up paying for the cost of land development. So, although the City Council may avoid being accused of creating additional financial burdens for the individual, the Calgarians as ratepayers and/or consumers still finally pay the price for services. In addition, because the city must extend services to the land which is to be developed, the ratepayer bears this cost as well. Insofar as the servicing and development of the actual property is concerned, responsibility is determined through negotiations among the interested parties, such as the developer, the school board, and the city. The final decision is prepared in the form of a "Development Agreement."

After reviewing the financial implications of the proposed annexation, the Calgary Public School Board requested the Local Authorities Board:

> that should you see fit to approve annexation at this time, you give consideration to imposing the following conditions:
> (a) The applicant or developer be required to provide to Calgary School Board and Provincial standards and regulations at his expense (as per other City services)
> 1. Fully serviced and landscaped elementary and junior high school sites.
> 2. A fully serviced public junior high school facility simultaniously and within the initial development.
> 3. Other elementary schools and landscaped sites as and when required.
>
> (b) The assessment and taxation of properties in the area be self-supporting as regards school service costs so that it does not become a disproportionate liability to the taxpayer of the City at large — for example, the applicant or developer to pay in full that portion of any school bus transportation costs which is in excess of provincial government grants.[204]

In Section 3 of its submission to the Local Authorities Board, the school board made the following significant observation:

> (a) It would be most undesirable in the urban setting, to plan school facilities and service for this 480 acres in isolation from the surrounding lands.
> (b) It is not possible to properly plan for *orderly and economic development* of schools without having reasonably firm parameters resulting from comprehensive study of general land uses proposed, transportation corridors, etc., for a larger geographic area.[205] (Emphasis original.)

To emphasize the need for proper planning, the school board quoted a section from the Calgary Plan.

> In future, the form of City growth must be more closely related to environmental and economic considerations with the preservation of natural amenities and a distribution pattern of residential densities which minimizes the cost of municipal services.[206]

Further on in the report, the board made further reference to economic planning and its relationship to environmental factors.

> The provision of educational facilities and service for an urban community have an enormous impact on the environment and lifestyle of that community for many generations. We consider that in the complex urban setting of our time, such service is unlikely to be provided in an orderly and economic manner if this is done on a piecemeal basis and without due consideration to the in depth planning process related to future City growth patterns.[207]

The preceding statement is very similar to one contained in the Calgary Plan's chapter entitled, "Financial Implications of the Present Form of Urban Growth," namely:

> It is self-evident that . . . expenditures, particularly those involving investment in long-lived capital items, cannot be made on an *ad hoc* or expedient basis, without incurring the very real danger of mis-allocating limited municipal financial resources. Involved here are the difficult problems of the establishment of policies, priorities, and implementation techniques aimed at a rational and systematic allocation process designed to obtain the maximum benefit from any given municipal expenditure.[208]

Of import is the fact that the school board used the Calgary plan to buttress its reasons for opposing the annexation proposal. The board attempted to show that sensible long-range planning policies are an integral part of the business of providing school services "in an orderly and economic manner." It used the Calgary Plan to argue certain propositions favourable to itself in terms prepared by the City Planning Department and accepted in principle by City Council. But, since the school board is primarily responsible to the Department of Education, it is in a better position than the City Planning Department and the regional planners to make firm recommendations at the local level.

The school board submission to the Local Authorities Board concluded by stating:

We request this Board to give special consideration to the concerns regarding orderly and economic management of suburban sprawl expressed by the Calgary School Board. After careful consideration of this matter, and in view of all the implications, the Calgary School Board finds it necessary in the interests of the local educational taxpayer to state its objection to annexation of the property for urban development at this time.[209]

The Chairman of the Board of Trustees wrote to the Minister of Education on April 23, 1971 concerning the annexation proposal:

At a recent meeting the Calgary Public School Board was informed of the MacEwan Glens residential subdivision proposed by the City of Calgary in an area which is presently outside the city.
The Board is concerned that development of this isolated area as a rush, low-cost, housing project at this time is not orderly and economic from the school service point of view and would almost certainly result in accommodation problems being experienced at the schools within the city. Development of the area would likely involve the Calgary Public School Board in substantial transportation costs wherever the school pupils were accommodated. It is our understanding that, due to servicing capacities, the 3/4 section involved might have to stand on its own for several years before adjacent lands could be developed.

The chairman received the following response, dated June 9, 1971:

The Honorable R.C. Clark and officials of this Department have discussed your letter of April 23 in which you expressed concern about the proposed MacEwan Glens residential subdivision, and this letter has been referred to my office for acknowledgement and response.
Since the boundaries of municipalities and school systems are co-terminates in all developed areas of Alberta, the Calgary Public School District will have no option but to have its boundaries adjusted to include this new area when it becomes a part of the City of Calgary. The municipal authority may proceed in this matter without consent or approval of the school authority, although consultation would certainly be desirable and probably useful to both parties.
It is acknowledged that this proposed move by the city could cause space and transportation problems for your Board, and when the exact nature of these problems is determined the Department of Education would be pleased to receive representation from your Board. No specific

> commitment can be made at this time except that this Department will look sympathetically at any special problems which your Board may encounter because of this development.

The deputy minister's letter implied, and certain individuals felt, that the Department of Education had concluded that the approval of the annexation application was inevitable. Some even suggested that the department's readiness to consider arrangements, whereby "special problems" could be resolved, indicated that the government was prepared to accommodate the developer and had not seriously measured the overall effects of annexation. From the school board's point of view, the department's response ignored a whole range of problems. The emphasis on "special problems" did little to ameliorate concern about the board's financial capacity to cope with the situation that would develop after annexation. It was this concern that encouraged the school board to prepare the detailed submission for the Local Authorities Board.

When the necessity arises, the provincial government does make it a practice to have close contact with private companies which are interested in initiating development projects within the province. On June 11, 1971 the Minister of Education responded to a request for information from the President of Carma Developers Limited.

> Attached hereto for your information is a copy of a letter which . . . Deputy Minister of Education, wrote to . . . Chairman of the Calgary School Board, regarding the proposed MacEwan Glens residential subdivision.
> I am hopeful the information contained in the letter to . . . will provide you with the information requested in your letter of June 1st.

The above suggests that, whenever possible, the provincial government does attempt to assist private companies in their negotiations with municipal authorities. From the deputy minister's letter, it can be concluded that the department was prepared to make arrangements, of a certain kind, with local authorities to overcome problems that might arise as a consequence of development. It is important to note that the deputy minister's letter emphasizes the "special" nature of problems. This can be partially interpreted as concern about setting a precedent, which might have long-term implications for discussions with local authorities.

During the early part of May, the city received a letter from the Local Authorities Board which stated, in part that:

> . . . it is noted that your Council would prefer the annexation of additional lands rather than the three quarter section of property as requested by the petitioners in order to avoid any irregular boundaries.

And, further on:

> Would you please advise this office if your City plans to make an annexation application within the next few weeks covering the lands referred to in the above mentioned Clause. Your early reply would assist this Board in considering hearing dates for these pending applications.[210]

At the end of May the Director of Planning wrote to the Commissioner of Operations and Development.

> . . . having reviewed with the staff the additional request from the LAB for a submission on the full eight square miles, which was suggested by City Council and confirmed by the Calgary Regional Planning Commission, I now wish to bring the following matters to your attention:
> (1) We have become aware in the last several days of a number of other proposed requests for annexation, north west of the City (one of which is the subject of a written submission by Nu-West), and one proposal by the City of Calgary south east of Calgary.
> (2) We are also aware that there will be determined opposition by the Municipal District.
> (3) We anticipate that there will be some delay in effecting coterminous school boundaries with the new boundary of the City, a condition of the Regional Planning Commission's support.
> (4) We are aware that Carma has bought 80 acres of land in the east half of Section 10 (Huntington Hills) confirmed by the attached letter to your office, dated May 25, 1971, which will effectively take the immediate "heat," and water supply from the development of lands in Section 17.
> (5) We have been informed by residents of Strathcona Heights, annexed in 1956, that they intend to oppose the annexation on the basis that the previous annexation of their property has brought them little but grief.
> On the basis of the above I believe that any hurried "deal" that will effect the immediate annexation of lands north of the city will inhibit other annexations that may be comtemplated. I also believe that the City should invite statements of interest on this and other annexations from interested parties before review by City Council of the whole question of annexation.[211]

The Planning Director's report for the City Council, rephrased and changed from that which had been sent to the Commissioners, noted, in part:

> . . . that a premature presentation to effect the annexation of eight square miles north of the City will inhibit other annexations that may be comtemplated. It is suggested that the City should invite statements of interest on all proposed and contemplated annexation from interested parties before review by City Council of the whole question of annexation.[212]

The Board of Commissioners, having taken into consideration the Planning Director's presentation, indicated to the City Council that they concurred with the director's recommendation for a deferment of the annexation hearing. Recommending ". . . that we invite submissions from parties interested in having their lands annexed to the City of Calgary," the board further suggested ". . . that these submissions be received by the City no later than July 30, 1971, in order that Council may consider the submissions at a Public Hearing to be held on October 4, 1971."[213] And,

> In view of this development we recommend that Council authorize the City Solicitor to apply to the LAB for an adjournment of all hearings relating to annexations until Council has had an opportuntiy to consider *all* proposed annexation and establish a policy thereon.[214] (Emphasis original.)

Despite the Commissioners' support for the Planning Director's recommendation, the City Council, following an address from a Carma representative, decided to file the Commissioners' report. Apparently the Planning Director had hoped that such factors as the threat of public criticism from the residents of Strathcona Heights, the problem of coterminous school boundaries, and the fact that Carma's purchase of 80 acres of land would both satisfy this company's immediate developmental needs and provide more housing accommodation for Calgarians, would encourage the council to support a request for the deferment of the annexation hearing. Presumably such deferment would have permitted the Planning Department to formulate policy, for the City Council's consideration, to cover the whole question of annexation applications. The evidence indicates that the forceful arguments of certain aldermen, coupled with a persuasive presentation from the Carma representative, led to the filing of the Commissioners' report. Moreover, the council apparently decided to ignore the question of "whether a submission is to be forthcoming on the full eight square miles."

The final petition submitted to the Local Authorities Board by Carma Developers Ltd. for the annexation hearing, was substantially different from the one that had been originally prepared. Part 3, subsection (c) was changed to read:

> access thereto may be provided as logical extensions of existing and future street plans of the City. It is planned to

develop 80th Avenue to 4th Street in the initial development stage.

Part 4 was divided into two parts:

(4) there are no alternate lands (in the City) which are suitable for such a development with such a favourable cost to the ultimate purchaser.
(5) the development will provide $50,000,000 worth of new construction.

Additional parts included:

(6) the area would provide some 1,500 forty-foot lots for single-family dwellings and 450 multiple-housing units, for a projected population of 8,000 persons.
(7) the MacEwan Glens site plan has adequate open space, park land space and provision for school sites.
(8) raw land prices in the City have been rising rapidly in the past few years. The MacEwan Glens project, due to its favourable initial land purchase price, can offer the eventual buyer of a home therein a saving of about $1,000 per forty-foot lot, strictly on the basis of raw land cost, as compared with a similar lot located in Section 10 in the city.
(9) persons with incomes of approximately $5,000 per annum may qualify for an NHA mortgage to pay for their single-family dwelling in the proposed MacEwan Glens Subdivision. (An example was cited: Estimated cost of a forty-foot serviced lot — $3,200; home 864 square feet — $10,835; total estimated price - $14,035. Down payment — $700; Mortgage $13,335, 71/2 percent over 40 years; estimated monthly payment — $87; monthly taxes — $25 (estimated); estimated total monthly payment — $112; qualifying annual income — $4997; estimated qualifying monthly income — $415).
(10) the subject three-quarter sections form part of the eight square miles which the City has indicated it proposes to annex on its northern boundary and which annexation is favoured by the Calgary Regional Planning Commission. The present application should be treated as the first phase of the larger impending application. (Parentheses added.)

Problems regarding the question of the 80th Avenue right-of-way, first outlined in the City Planning Director's report to the Municipal Planning Commission, appear to have been resolved, although there is no evidence to suggest that the City Council had decided "to allocate the necessary funds" for the purpose of widening 80th Avenue. The developer continued to argue that the lands involved "may be serviced from extensions to existing City water and sanitary sewer systems," even though the director's report pointed out that storm sewer outfall and sanitary sewer easements would be required. Problems associated with water capacity limitations were not touched upon by the developers. The information provided by the Regional Planning Director, concerning the "negative development factor" which existed because of the closeness of the Calgary Airport was dismissed, since "the lands lie outside the 'interfering' influence of present and foreseeable proposed 'noise cores' of Calgary's International Airport." Questions relating to the amount of "suitable developed or economically developable land" within the city boundaries received the developer's general verdict, which does not appear to have received outside analysis, that "raw land prices in the City have been rising rapidly in the past few years." Moreover it can be interpreted that the reference to "Section 10" was an attempt to counter the planning director's notion that the company's purchase of "80 acres of land in the east half of Section 10" would "take the 'heat' off" the city regarding the development of Section 17.

The points to be found in the City Planning Director's report and those outlined in the Regional Planning Director's presentation, were not given in evidence during the LAB hearing. Consequently, they could not be used to examine the developer's petition. During the course of the hearing, the City of Calgary was represented by counsel who:

> . . . filed with the hearing as Exhibit No. 10, a letter dated April 27, 1971, addressed by the Assistant City Clerk to Carma Developers Ltd., advising that City Council had on April 26, 1971, ordered adoption of Clause C.27 of the Commissioner's Report re: Proposed Annexation of Property North of the City of Calgary (Approval). The adopted clause reads: 'Approval of the recommendation as contained in the Planning Commission minutes of April 14 and for the annexation of the three-quarter sections requested by the petitioners as well as the additional mile to the western eight miles of the City's northern boundary in order to straighten out the boundary.'[215]

The Director of Regional Planning simply ". . . read into the record an extract from the Minutes of the Meeting of the said Commission held on May 7, 1971 . . ." Presented in the extract were the two conditions which had been approved by the commission at the May 7th meeting.

> 1. that the Local Authorities Board establish a definite timetable for a hearing on the annexation of the eight-mile strip of land.
> 2. that the question of the coterminous school boundaries be satisfactorily resolved.

In the "Board Order No. 5505," the Local Authorities Board adds the following "Board Note" in parenthesis beside the first condition:

> "No such application is before the Board at this time . . ."

And attached to the second condition, a "Note" which explains that:

> This matter is not within Board's jurisdiction but lies with the Minister of Education.

Further on in the Board Order, the LAB repeated that it regarded the matter of coterminous school district boundaries to be outside its jurisdiction:

> A copy of a letter filed as part of Exhibit No. 19 and addressed by the Deputy Minister of Education to the Calgary School Board Chairman on June 9, 1971, respecting the possible annexation of MacEwan Glens Subdivision, acknowledged the attendant school problems and invited representations thereon with the view to assisting the Calgary School Board in advising them, if the Minister of Education, in fact, includes the annexed lands in Calgary School District No. 19.

Significantly, while the deputy minister did acknowledge that the proposal "could cause space and transportation problems," he mentioned "special problems" rather than "attendant school problems." Dealing with the school board's submission, the LAB explained that:

> The Board is of the opinion that it has no jurisdiction to give direction in school matters, as is sought in the Calgary School Board brief.

and also observed that:

> The establishment and alteration of school district boundaries (to include the West Half and the South-East Quarter of Section Seventeen 17) is within the purview of the Minister of Education under the provisions of The School Act.

Having failed in its attempt to have the annexation proposal opposed at the Regional Planning Commission level, based on reasons related to its piecemeal nature, the "lack of coterminous boundaries," and the "lack of sector planning for the Beddington Creek area," the MD of Rocky View employed, independently of the planning commission, the services of a planning consultant. At the annexation hearing, the MD was represented by the Reeve and the planning consultant. They opposed the granting of the application on the following grounds:

1. the City's annexation application is piecemeal in nature and premature to the City's need for additional lands. The City should commit itself to growth within its present limits until 1978, the present target year for completion of the economic review under the City's General Plan By-law.
2. planning of the general area should be further advanced before the annexation application is considered, particularly in respect to:
(a) completion of desirable sector plans for the "B" Beddington area (of which Section Seventeen (17) is a part) which is not due for completion for some time yet.
(b) definition of 'corridors' for orderly growth from the City into the countryside which should be firmly established in relationship to the proposed eight-mile annexation strip on the City's north limits, prior to the granting of the present annexation application.
3. the present application leaves the Municipal District in a position where it is uncertain of long-range planning in the area respecting roads, schools, subdivisions, community development, etc., an undesirable situation."

The MD presentation closely resembled the report prepared by the Regional Planning Director for the commission. In fact, during an interview, it was explained that the planning consultant, along with MD representatives, decided to use the director's report and present it to the annexation hearing.
The LAB was not impressed, and explained that:

> The Municipal District of Rocky View, while opposing the granting of the application, did not produce evidence to support its own suggestion that there was no need for the additional lands and, further, the municipality did not produce evidence to refute that introduced by the applicant to establish such need.

and,

> The Municipal District's further concerns dealt primarily with long-range planning which are matters which the Board feels, transcend municipal boundaries and should not be compelling reason for granting or rejecting the present or any annexation application.

The last statement suggests that even if the Regional Planning Director had been able to argue his report as evidence, much of it would have been deemed as having no direct bearing on the annexation question. It is apparent that the LAB finds it efficacious to consider only that evidence which states the position of an individual local authority on an annexation application. Those presentations which can be interpreted as being directed to questions of long-range planning, involving more than one municipality, are considered by the LAB as being beyond its sphere of jurisdiction.

This policy of the LAB undermines the very principle on which regional planning policies are based, and on which planning decisions are supposed to be made. The situation is such that it would appear that the LAB, a provincial government agency, has the authority to establish policies which may conflict with stated provincial government objectives pertaining to regional planning and the development or formulation of long-range planning policies. Further, decisions which exclude consideration of long-range planning matters can exacerbate the conflict which exists among municipalities, which, in turn, makes it more unlikely that regional planners will be able to carry out their responsibilities as stated in the Planning Act.

The "Hanson Report" of 1963 is worthwhile considering at this point. On the role of the LAB, the report notes that:

> The Local Authorities Board has jurisdiction over many matters under the number of provincial statutes pertaining to municipalities. One of these matters is that of annexations and alterations of municipal boundaries. The Board is essentially an administrative one, consisting of three provincial civil servants in the Department of Municipal Affairs. This Board may conduct hearings when municipalities apply for boundary changes and annexation, and it renders decisions within the framework of relevent provincial statutes. Like any administrative board, it is expected to make decisions within the limits of public policies determined by the provincial government. It is not intended to be a policy-making, political body.[216]

With regard to its recommendation concerning amalgamation of the metropolitan area of Edmonton, the "Hanson Report" makes the following pertinent observations:

> . . . we do not advise the City of Edmonton to make an application for an annexation hearing to the Local Authorities Board. First, it is not sound and appropriate for the City to place itself in the position of litigant in a matter which is of provincial importance and which affects the general welfare of Northern Alberta in a comprehensive way.[217]

Despite the fact that the Hanson Report was directed to the question of amalgamating the Edmonton area, it has application, it would now appear, to the Calgary metropolitan area as well. The report observes that:

> The question of the appropriate structure and area of municipal government in the Edmonton Metropolitan Area is a problem of such long standing that it should be referred directly to the Government of the Province of Alberta.[218]

Until the Carma proposal, the question of annexation in the Calgary metropolitan area had not received much attention since the 1961 annexation hearings. With the Carma application, a whole set of factors related to municipal government and regional planning came to the fore. These factors were treated very summarily by the LAB. The observation that such matters "transcend municipal boundaries and should not be a compelling reason for granting or rejecting the present or any annexation application," appears to be an attempt to cope with a situation when there is an absence of provincial government policy or legislation which would provide direction on matters involving more than one municipality. That the LAB has decided not to allow specific matters related to long-range planning to interfere with a decision regarding an annexation application, is probably a consequence of the emphasis that the provincial government places on local autonomy. The result of this emphasis is reflected in the continuing conflict among local authorities and the undermining of planning policies, both regional and local.

> Board Order No. 5505 explains that:
> 1. The applicant established that the West Half and South-East Quarter of Section Seventeen (17), Township Twenty-Five (25), Range One (1), West of the Fifth Meridian should be annexed to the City of Calgary to provide needed additional relatively low-cost raw lands for development of a substantial number of moderately-priced single family homes, including multiple family units. Evidence indicated that raw land prices in the City were rising rapidly.
> No evidence was presented to establish the competitive availability of similar type lands within the present City limits.
> 2. The lands are economically serviceable with extensions from existing water, sewer and road systems in the City of Calgary and lie in a raw state with topographical features desirable for residential development.
> 3. The lands form part of the further residential development which is conceived for the northern area of Calgary on both sides of 80th Avenue.
> Both the City of Calgary and the Calgary Regional Planning Commission have approved the three quarter section annexation, the City of Calgary having approved annexation of additional lands both east and west of MacEwan Glens (the 'eight-mile strip' referred to in

evidence). The Municipal District of Rocky View, while opposing the granting of the application, did not produce evidence to support its own suggestion that there was no need for the additional lands and further the municipality did not produce evidence to refute that introduced by the applicant to establish such need.

The LAB evidently decided that the Carma proposal offered a means of ameliorating the shortage of "moderately-priced single family homes, including multiple family units," in the Calgary area. In the opinion of the LAB, the MD presentation did not bring into question the Carma argument that such a shortage existed. At the same time, however, no consideration appears to have been given to the effect that the annexation would have on land values around the periphery of the city. Time and again, it has been found that once development is permitted to occur on land adjacent to a metropolitan centre, property values will increase substantially on the periphery. This would suggest that future development will have to take into account land prices containing increasing speculative components. The Carma proposal, therefore, although presented as a way of dealing with an immediate low-cost housing shortage by utilizing moderately priced land, may have the consequence of encouraging speculative activity, but this time on the outskirts of the city. Related to this point, is the observation that the "artifical boundaries" of the city have been the major determining factor for the high cost of city land. Since land within the city boundaries becomes increasingly more expensive as development occurs, entrepreneurs have found it desirable to purchase land for certain projects at a distance from current development, leaving older areas to suffer through a period of decline and degeneration. Thus, while it may be conceded that by supporting the Carma proposal, the city did ensure the availability of land for low-cost housing to resolve an immediate and apparent shortage, the problem of land prices within the city boundary remained unresolved. Moreover, and of perhaps more importance, by supporting the Carma project, the city illustrated a willingness to encourage the kind of urban sprawl that is currently concerning planners at both the regional and local levels.

The land area of Calgary is more than sufficient to accommodate the city's present and much of the future population growth. Without doubt, therefore, the lack of certain types of housing accommodation results from the high cost of land, as has been the case elsewhere in Canadian cities. Certainly there is no shortage of raw land. Frequently, it has been suggested that the creating of "land banks" could help to put an end to the current housing problems facing Calgary. The provincial government has, on occasion, provided the city with the opportunity to take up this option. Recognizing the need for low-cost housing in the two largest metropolitan centres of the province, the Minister of Municipal

Affairs sent the following letter, dated July 11, 1969, to the mayors of Edmonton and Calgary:

> In recognition of the increasing demands being placed on our major municipalities and the rising costs of services and land which are ultimately being reflected in the high cost of housing, the Province, through its Alberta Housing and Urban Renewal Corporation, is prepared to offer assistance to your municipality in the area of assembling and/or servicing and selling land for housing purposes primarily directed at providing land for low cost housing purposes.
>
> The proposal which we are offering is one where our Provincial Corporation will undertake to incur all costs related to the borrowing and financing of such projects with partial cost sharing for trunk services and will be prepared to negotiate the administrative arrangements for effecting such a program.
>
> If the City is interested in the proposal, we would welcome the opportunity to discuss the matter at an early date.

The offer of assistance by the minister in 1969 was taken up by Edmonton, but Calgary ignored it. Similarly, even though the argument continues that Calgary suffers from a shortage of developed land for low-cost housing, the city has not made an attempt to avail itself fully of the services offered by the Alberta Housing Corporation. The Alberta Housing Corporation still provides a "land assembly" program.

With respect to points (2) and (3) of the Board Order, it is important to examine the LAB's willingness to accept the presentations to the effect that the developer's proposal was compatible with the predicted direction of the city's growth. Since the City Planning Director's report was not considered in full, questions pertinent both to this proposition and factors related to the extension of city services, did not have to be reviewed by the LAB. The MD presentation, which included observations regarding orderly planning and growth, was disposed of quite easily by the LAB's interpretation of matters "which transcend municipal boundaries." Of course, the LAB could only expect that if there were problems from the city's point of view, the Planning Director or some other representative of the city would have brought them forward at the hearing. Instead of this occurring, the LAB was informed that the city in general was not only in favour of this particular annexation but would also endorse, or had approved, annexation of additional lands. While the LAB gave a lot of weight to this additional approval, it should be remembered that with regard to the MD's "conditions," it had noted that application for further annexation had not been received. Of interest, even though an additional application had not been submitted, the LAB interpreteted the MD's position as being one of approval for the Carma application. The Board's summary did not refer to the MD's "conditions."

Out of frustration with the Regional Planning Commission, the MD of Rocky View had decided to employ its own independent planning consultant to present the MD case to the Local Authorities Board. The fact that the LAB decided to approve the annexation did nothing more than further exacerbate the MD's ill feelings towards agencies which seemed unprepared to treat its position with sympathy and understanding. On November 30, 1971, the *Rocky View News and Market Examiner* reported:

> The board bluntly rejected objections submitted by Rocky View rural district council, Calgary regional planning Commission and Calgary public school board. For good measure the board added a scolding for Rocky View.
> The main concern of all three local authorities was for long term planning particularly in school facilities. The board was asked to require that school boundaries should be coterminous with municipal boundaries.
> The local authorities board, while assuming authority over municipal planning, claimed it was not responsible for education. It rebuked Rocky View for appearing to be concerned with long term planning.
> Such an attitude, it implied in its loftiest tribunal tone, was not a concern for a mere local authority and should have no bearing on application for annexation . . .
> Appearing on behalf of Rocky View council, Reeve Sanford Sydness and planning consultant Frank Marlyn argued that the proposed annexation was piecemeal in nature and was also premature. Present target year for completion of the city's general plan was 1978 and all development should comply with the general plan.
> Sydness said corridors should be established for orderly growth out of the city prior to any application for annexation. The present application left Rocky View in a position of uncertainty on long-range planning.
> A similar argument was submitted by Calgary school board which also called for long term planning of school requirements . . .
> Calgary regional planning commission suggested the local authorities board should establish a definite timetable for hearing a city application for annexation of an eight-mile strip along the north city limits. The commission also suggested that any order for annexation should make school boundaries coterminous with municipal boundaries.
> The local authorities board replied that it had no formal application from the city for annexation of the eight-mile strip and it had no jurisdiction over school matters . . .
> The board also expressed some scorn for the Rocky View council stand by stating it had not produced evidence to support its claim that there was no need for additional land for housing.

The above report represented the feelings of a number of individuals associated with local authorities in the MD of Rocky View. While it has been suggested that Rocky View was basically concerned about coterminous school boundaries rather than long-range planning, the point was made that the LAB appeared to be "assuming authority over municipal planning" but refusing to take into consideration the effect of its decision on long-range planning. Moreover, the LAB seemed to be unaware of the lingering after-effects its decision would have on the possibility of bringing to fruition a regional plan based on inter-municipal co-operation. The following editorial comment was included in the November 30, 1971 edition of the *Rocky View News and Market Examiner,* and illustrates the general concern:

> For many years the Calgary area has been subject to town and country planning by three levels of government—local, regional and provincial. Throughout those years there has been heavy talk about long-term planning. When a private individual proposed some minor development of a residential or commercial nature he was told he must comply with the general plan.
>
> Now we find there is yet another level of government intervening in the field. It is the local authorities board which transcends and ignores those guidelines for long-term planning.
>
> As a result Rocky View rural district council, which thought it had some jurisdiction in municipal planning, found itself in an embarrassing situation when it opposed an application for piecemeal annexation of 480 acres of land by the City of Calgary . . .
>
> It should be noted that although the application was for annexation by the city, it was submitted by private land owners and a city development company. Although Calgary city council had endorsed the application, it went further and suggested that instead of piecemeal annexation there should be an eight-mile strip along the northern city limits "to straighten out the boundary." This was pointed out by Calgary regional planning commission director Rhys Smith who also asked the board to make an order that school boundaries should be coterminous with municipal boundaries.

He too was brushed off. The board said it had received no application from the city for annexation of an eight-mile strip. The local authorities board has established a precedent here which could open the door for further piecemeal annexations requested by developers. It has also seized powers over planning authorities. It is not a happy situation for municipalities struggling to do justice over planning controls with their limited staff.

Following the annexation decision, the matter of coterminous boundaries continued to be a contentious issue. A memorandum, dated December 10, 1971, from the Planning Director to a member of his staff stated the following:

> . . . I would appreciate your talking with the Legal Department regarding the question of the City's position and ability to change School Board boundaries to ensure that they are coterminous with City Administrative Boundaries.
>
> As you can appreciate if this is the prerogative of the School Board, the implication is that politically the School Board could force us into a situation where we could face Metropolitan Government and a greater urge on the part of Rocky View to urbanize in order to spread the load of increased school taxes to people who are not residents in the municipal district.
>
> This information should be made available prior to your proceeding with the circulation of the letter from the School Board.

With reference to a letter from the Calgary school board (December 6, 1971) the Assistant Deputy Director of Planning wrote to the city's Legal department. Part of the deputy director's letter, dated December 19, 1971, stated:

> It is . . . clear from this letter that the School Board is not anxious at this time to have the annexed area included within their school district. However, if it is not so included there are obvious problems relating to taxation and the provision of adequate educational services to the area.
>
> Before we circulate the subdivision plans of MacEwan Glens to the appropriate School District for their comment we would appreciate receiving from you advice as to whether the City can make representation to the Minister of Education to have the annexed land included in the School District #19 or whether such representation has to originate from the School Board itself. Should the City be able to initiate this action advice as to the form this should take and reference to appropriate legislation would be useful.

In early January, 1972 the Commissioner of Operations and Development wrote to the Assistant Deputy Director of the Planning Department and stated, in part, that:

> I shall be glad to receive a copy of the advice of our Legal Department on the question as to whether the City can initiate a request to the Minister of Education to have the annexed land included in School District No. 19.
>
> I think it is important that we should not take any such

action, except as a last resort, as I am sure it is the desire of City Council to work more closely with the School Board rather than move toward a confrontation.[219]

Continuing on, the Commissioner observed that the liaison committee, at its meeting of April 8, 1971, had agreed to request the Minister of Education to issue a Ministerial Order to adjust the school division boundaries should the annexation be approved. This fact led the Commissioner to suggest that:

> Perhaps we should discreetly approach Municipal District No. 44 to make a request to the Minister to adjust the boundaries. We could then support this request.
> As soon as we have more information regarding the legal situation and the anticipated time table for development, we will be in a better position to decide what course we should take to ensure a rational solution to schooling for the residents.

In a memorandum dated January 25, 1972 the City Solicitor advised that "Under the School Act the Minister of Education has the role and unfettered authority to establish a school district . . . Should you feel it desirous to have the subject land included in a particular Calgary School District the only official manner to do this would be to have the Council pass a resolution requesting same." And in a letter dated the same day an official of the Department of Education wrote:

> The general policy of this Department has been that unless there are compelling reasons submitted to the contrary, school jurisdiction and municipal boundaries should be coterminous. A recommendation has gone to the Minister that this policy be continued particularly with respect to the land mentioned in your letter of January 24. We have not as yet received confirmation from the Minister that this will indeed obtain but have no reason to expect that there will be a change in policy.
> As soon as we have clearance from the Minister to proceed, an order will be prepared which will transfer the land in question from the Calgary School Division No. 41 to the Boards of the Calgary School District and the Calgary Roman Catholic Separate School District as has been the case in every other annexation to the city to this date.[220]

Eventually the land was transferred. Confronted on the one hand by the possibility that the MD of Rocky View would use the lack of coterminous boundaries to further their arguments concerning urbanization and, on the other hand, by the lack of co-operation from the school board, the city officials sought an indirect method to obtain a Ministerial order. As well as providing a clear illustration of the considerations city officials have regarding the relationship of the city to its region, the strategy used also gives an indication of the way in which the Planning Department may be drawn into the political machinations of City Hall.

While the city was proceeding to resolve the coterminous boundary question, another concern, of greater significance, came to the fore. In a communication to the City Engineer, dated December 31, 1971, the Commissioner of Operations and Development observed, in part, that:

> I am finding it increasingly difficult to understand the justification for the annexation of the land at this time as its urbanization would seem to me to be premature.
> Now that the land has been annexed, however, with the support of the City of Calgary to permit housing "ranging in retail price from $14,000 to $18,000 without subsidy," the City has some obligation to encourage such development.
> It is my view that this new area should not be allowed, in any way, to prejudice the completion of development in West Thorncliffe and the East half of Section 10. It is also my view that this development should be totally self-supporting with all financial outlays met by the developer as long as this development does not conform to a logical extension of urbanization and the extension of roads and services. I presume that you are in consultation with Carma Developers regarding the development of these lands, and would be grateful if you would keep me advised as to progress.

A few days before, on December 8, 1971, the Commissioner had met with the Deputy Planning Director and the two aldermen who had recently been appointed as the city's new representatives on the Calgary Regional Planning Commission. Following the discussion about the MacEwan Glens proposal the director in a memorandum to a number of his staff, observed:

> Two days ago I met with Commissioner . . ., Alderman . . . and Alderman . . . concerning MacEwan Glens, at which time the two politicians raised the basic questions as to the long term impact of the MacEwan Glens proposal, with respect to the form (of) urban growth.
> It is my feeling that any studies on urban form which we will be undertaking in the near future will be largely ineffective, unless we can establish a firm policy with respect to annexation and the City's responsibilities concerning the approval of any large new areas for development.
> With this in mind, I would like you to prepare terms of reference on work required to be done, in order to establish

> an overall policy with respect to annexation, such that it can provide a stop gap and further reinforce the policies set out in the General Plan, namely the Planning Department should be proceeding with a review of urban growth forms.
> I regard this particular item, of establishing an annexation policy, to be of highest priority, if you are to be able to proceed with adequate insulation over the next two years. Please advise when you have this information available.[221]

One may surmise that encouragement from the Commissioner Of Operations And Development led the deputy director to take action to restore some order into a situation that had every possibility of producing chaotic planning problems for the city. The Commissioner had only recently been appointed.

The serious interest of the two aldermen was probably also an influential factor in persuading the deputy director to take the initiative. During the ensuing months, the aldermen took action to prevent the MacEwan Glens development, or proposal, from proceeding. One of them prepared a report, dated February 24, 1972, for the City Council's examination.

> Since my appointment as one of Council's representatives to the Calgary Regional Planning Commission, a number of matters concerning the annexation of MacEwan Glens have come to my attention which have resulted in a growing conviction that the City's decision to support the annexation of MacEwan Glens was approved in haste without full appreciation of the immediate economic implications, nor the longer term planning implications for the City of Calgary.[222]

Further on, he observed:

> In reviewing the history leading to Council's decision of April 26, 1971, to support the annexation, (and the subsequent decision of June 7 to not vary their decision despite the recommendation of the City Planner and the Board of Commissioners), it appears members of Council tended to place such weight upon the then current arguments and concerns for the development of housing at lower cost *to the buyer,* that the implications of increased costs *to the rest of the taxpayers* was overlooked. (Emphasis original.)[223]

Concerned about Carma's arguments regarding the shortage of undeveloped land the alderman observed:

> Recent City Planning figures indicate that there are approximately 30,000 acres of undeveloped land within the

> City boundaries suitable for urban development, over and above foreseeable acreage requirements for industrial use. Based on average densities of 22 persons per acre, this means there is sufficient land in Calgary to accommodate a population growth of 660,000. This does not include the increased densities that will occur due to redevelopment in existing built-up areas such as the city core, and along future rapid transit routes.
> Surely the addition of the 480 acres in MacEwan Glens is insignificant in view of the above figures. While detailed land and servicing costs in alternative locations have not been provided to Council, there must be other areas equally economic to develop, particularly if the share of the additional costs of municipal and school services are properly allocated to the costs of each lot in MacEwan Glens rather than as a tax charge against the City at large.[224]

Having observed that:

> I understand the Commissioners will be reparting to Council on the costs and timing of providing sewer, water and other services to MacEwan Glens and they feel that it would not be practical in any event to attempt to construct these services this year. Therefore, development would not proceed until 1973 at the earliest. Since this means the development will not be able to provide land on which to build moderately priced residences this year, the apparent urgency which may have motivated Council's decision last June to support annexation is now removed. If the urgency still exists to have such land available this year, it will have to be found elsewhere.

The alderman recommended that the City Council,

> Advise the Calgary Regional Planning Commission that the City wishes to withdraw its request for reclassification of MacEwan Glens to High Density District and direct the City's representatives to oppose any such application from any other source. If the Calgary Regional Planning Commission concurs, Council could anticipate that the developer may appeal the decision to the Provincial Planning Board.[225]

During the latter part of November, 1971, the City Council had decided to request the Regional Planning Commission "to initiate, pursuant to Section 82 of the Planning Act, the necessary action to designate"[226] the annexed land as a "high density district." According to the Preliminary Regional Plan, all the lands within the city boundaries were designated "high density district." This description enabled urban development and subdivision within the city to proceed without constantly changing the regional plan. However:

> The lands abutting, but outside, on the northerly portion of the City were designated "medium density district," which permits a maximum of sixteen parcels of land per quarter section.
> The above-mentioned Annexation Order changes the City boundary, but does not change the boundaries of districts designated in the Regional Plan. Thus, the subject lands, under provision of the Planning Act, cannot be re-zoned to urban uses, or subdivided into urban lots, unless the Regional Plan is first amended to designate them as "High Density."[227]

Such action should permit the City Council to deal with Carma Developers' proposals. The alderman's recommendation was, therefore, as he recognized, "a reversal in a major policy matter" which would have serious effects on the developers and others. On the other hand he observed: "However, our responsibility to the taxpayer is now clear."[228]

At this same council meeting in November, considerable concern had been expressed about the costs to the city of accommodating the MacEwan Glens proposal. While Carma representatives insisted that such matters as utilities and school facilities would not be a problem, city experts indicated their strong objection to some of the aspects of the development. One alderman argued that "extraneous costs" should be incorporated in the Development Agreement so that the city would not experience additional expense. Others argued the need for city annexation policy. Certain aldermen questioned whether or not the city had a commitment, at least an ethical one, to accommodate the Carma development. Several concerns were expressed that if Carma was forced to incur additional costs it would be unable to build low-cost housing. All in all, the council appeared to be unable to resolve the problem and left the Commissioners to continue cost-sharing negotiations with the company. Apparently there had already been three of four meetings and many questions remained unresolved as the City Council discovered.

On March 3, 1972 the Calgary Regional Planning Commission, with the encouragement of the two city representatives, refused the amendment to the preliminary plan. Thus the annexed land remained "medium density" "which, because of its location within the two mile corridor, restricts subdivision to mimimum 20 acre parcels."[229] Subsequently, following a tabling motion on April 12, 1972, the Municipal Planning Commission, having received advice from the City Solicitor and the applicant's solicitor, was left with the following legal opinion:

In reply to the Planning Commission's request for legal direction in the above noted matter, I must confirm that the Planning Department has been advised that before the Calgary Planning Commission considers any application for subdivision, the Development Control By-Law and the General Plan must be amended to include this new annexed area. In the interim any application, be it an application for a proposed outline plan or any application for subdivision, must comply with the preliminary regional plan.[230]

In his presentation the applicant's solicitor observed:

The City of Calgary was, of course, represented at the annexation hearing when MacEwan Glens was annexed to the City and as appears at page 5 of Order No. 5505 of the Local Authorites Board, The City of Calgary and the Calgary Planning Commission both approved the annexation. It is difficult to believe that the members of the Calgary Regional Planning Commission when they approved the annexation considered that the population density would be likely to remain at the same level as it would in the municipal district and therefore it is difficult to understand the Calgary Regional Planning Commission rejecting the City's application to amend the preliminary regional plan so as to change the density. The Planning Department has, however, reported to the City that the City's hands are tied because of the position taken by the Calgary Regional Planning Commission. If this were so, the Calgary Regional Planning Commission could effectively limit the boundaries and the development of the City of Calgary.[231]

Further on he pointed out:

The applicant seeks nothing more than an opportunity to present its proposals for development of the annexed area, and to show that its proposals for utilities and services are feasible. If no appeal is taken from the decision of the Calgary Regional Planning Commission, the City may find itself in the position that all future applications for development on annexed lands will be in jeopardy.[232]

In conclusion, having referred to Board Order No. 5505, the solicitor noted:

In light of the fact that the Municipal District of Rocky View did not at the Local Authorities Board hearing offer any evidence to counter the evidence accepted by the Board that lands should be annexed for the development

> of a substantial number of moderately priced dwellings, and in further light of the fact that the Calgary Regional Planning Commission approved the annexation at the hearing where this evidence was given, the present action of such Commission in rejecting the City's application for amendment is not only most inconsistent, but operates as a direct rebuff to The Local Authorities Board.[233]

At the time of writing questions relating to the MacEwan Glens proposal had not been resolved. Overall, the entire annexation endeavour provides an excellent example of the complex interrelationship of urban and regional growth, and the forces which encapsulate, and frequently inhibit, attempts to promote rational planning.

Notes
Chapter 5

1. City of Calgary *Annual Report,* 1970, p.5.
2. Ibid., p.23.
3. The Calgary Plan: A General Plan prepared on behalf of the civic administration by the City of Calgary Planning Department, March, 1970, and Addendum dated April, 1971.
4. Ibid., addendum, p.1.2.
5. Ibid.
6. Ibid., p.14.1.
7. Ibid.
8. Ibid., p.14.8.
9. As late as mid-May, 1972, when this chapter was being prepared for submission to the Human Resources Research Council, the city announced an administrative change. Some details are provided in the following section of this Chapter "The search for rationality and its constraints."
10. Ibid., p.149.
11. In 1972 the council received a *Long Range Capital Program 1972-76* and had in hand a Research Report no.9 entitled *Forcasts of Revenues and Expenditures to 1986,* prepared by the Planning Department, August, 1970, and other documentation additional to the General Plan and prepared estimates.
12. *Report on 1971 Capital Budget,* part 1. Citizens' Budget Commission, February 22, 1971.
13. Ibid., p.2.
14. Ibid.
15. Ibid., p.15.
16. Ibid., p.3.
17. Ibid., p.12.
18. Ibid., p.16.
19. Ibid., p.4.
20. Ibid. This matter reappeared for discussion in the 1972 budget review, when the Conservative provincial administration expressed an interest in it.
21. *Report on 1971 Capital Budget,* part II. Citizens' Budget Commission, February 22, 1971, p.10.
22. Ibid., p.1.
23. Ibid.
24. Ibid., p.7.
25. Ibid., p.11.
26. City of Calgary Current Budget, 1972 Estimates, p.14.
27. Citizens' Budget Commission Report, part II, p.6.
28. The commission was chaired by Mr. R.A. Farran, previously a city alderman, who was elected to the Alberta Legislature in 1971. He was later to chair the province's Task Force on Provincial-Municipal Fiscal Arrangements.
29. *The Calgary Herald,* December 17, 1971.
30. Summary of observations by the Citizens' Budget Advisory Committee regarding the City of Calgary's 1972 Capital Budget, p.1.

31. Ibid., p.2.
32. Ibid., p.4.
33. Ibid.
34. Minutes of the Standing Policy Committee on Finance and Budget, December 22, 1971.
35. *The Calgary Herald,* January 4, 1972. In fact the 1972 Public School Board budget was prepared within the following terms of reference set by the board in June, 1971: "Administration is directed to prepare a budget for 1972 in which the expenditures will balance revenue available from all sources other than a plebescite." These instructions were adhered to.
36. Ibid., January 12, 1972.
37. See, for example, *The Albertan,* January 5, 1972, Fred Kennedy's column, "I write as I please."
38. Statement by the minister, January 5, 1972.
39. See, for example, *The Albertan,* January 7, 1972.
40. *The Calgary Herald,* January 13, 1972.
41. Ibid., January 17, 1972.
42. Ibid., May 18, 1972.
43. Reported in *The Albertan,* February 1, 1972.
44. Ibid.
45. Ibid.
46. *The Calgary Herald,* February 9, 1972.
47. Ibid., February 10, 1972. In earlier decades municipalities received revenue from a local income tax. The right was transferred to the province in 1932.
48. Ibid.
49. Ibid., February 15, 1972.
50. Ibid., February 12, 1972.
51. Ibid., February 23, 1972.
52. Ibid.
53. Ibid.
54. Ibid.
55. Ibid., February 24, 1972.
56. Ibid., February 25, 1972.
57. "Separate comments of Joseph Yanchula as a member of the Citizens' Budget Advisory Committee regarding City of Calgary 1972 Capital Budget." January, 1972.
58. Ibid., pp 14-15.
59. Ibid., p.1.
60. Ibid., pp.1-2.
61. Ibid., p.2.
62. Ibid., p.3. This remark was underlined for emphasis in the report, the only underlined observation in the document.
63. Ibid., p.3.
64. Ibid., p.4.
65. Ibid., pp.15-16.
66. *The Calgary Herald,* March 16, 1972.
67. Ibid.
68. Ibid.
69. Ibid., April 18, 1972.
70. Ibid., April 19, 1972.
71. Though far from clear, the impression seems to have come from the Citizens' Advisory Committee's final report. Mr. Roy Farran was its chairman.
72. *The Calgary Herald,* April 20, 1972.
73. Ibid., April 24, 1972.
74. Ibid., April 21, 1972.
75. Ibid., April 22, 1972.
76. Ibid., April 26, 1972. See also Fred Kennedy's column "I write as I please," in *The Albertan,* April 26, 1972 and May 5, 1972.
77. The Calgary Herald, April 26, 1972.

78. Ibid., April 25, 1972.
79. Ibid.
80. Ibid., May 8, 1972.
81. Ibid., May 9, 1972.
82. Ibid., March 1, 1972.
83. Ibid., May 24, 1972.
84. Ibid.
85. Ibid., June 17, 1971.
86. City of Calgary *Annual Report,* 1970, p.17.
87. The Mayor has one additional source of revenue — private business in its many forms. The difficulty of coping with this area is discussed later in this volume.
88. "Regional potpourri," *Town Planning Institute of Canada News,* Town Planning Institute of Canada, August, 1971.
89. *The Calgary Herald,* March 27 and 28, 1972.
90. The Calgary General Plan, March 1970, p.12.2, refers to a management information committee, and to increasing use of a computer by Land, Engineering, Assessment, Tax, Planning, and other departments, for technical and statistical retrieval, and to developing techniques such as critical-path analysis to assist administrative procedures. Geo-coding and an information system would be an integral part of the new service.
91. Minutes of the Meeting of the Technical Co-ordinating Committee for Land Use and Transportation Planning, February 9, 1972. Previously, at the January 17, 1972 Planning Advisory Committee meeting, it was "Resolved that this Committee request the Calgary Exhibition and Stampede Board and the City Planners prepare and report back, within thirty days, alternative recommendations that will make possible both the retention of a viable residential community in Victoria Park and the necessary Calgary Exhibition and Stampede Expansion."
92. *The Calgary Herald,* May 9, 1972.
93. Ibid., May 19, 1972.
94. Ibid.
95. The Planning Department has prepared a report regarding the "Future of Victoria Park and proposed sector plan"; and the "Calgary Exhibition and Stampede Board future long-range development plan."
96. The Planning Advisory Committee will be discussed later.
97. This letter was contained in the material provided for the Operations and Development meeting of January 10, 1972.
98. *The Calgary Herald,* March 16, 1972.
99. Ibid., February 29, 1970.
100. "Rational," that is, the special sense of "bureaucratic rationality," i.e. implemented according to plans and rules set out beforehand to guide the implementers to a fore-stated goal or end.
101. "Regional potpourri."
102. Ibid.
103. Minutes of the committee.
104. Ibid.
105. Ibid.
106. *Housing in Calgary,* The Social Planning Council of Calgary, January, 1968.
107. Ibid.
108. "Public Housing," Alberta Housing Corporation, Public Relations Department.
109. *The Calgary Herald* of March 2, 1972 contains a reference to a waiting list of 700 persons needing low-rental accommodation.
110. *The Calgary Herald,* March 1, 1972.
111. Ibid.
112. *The Albertan,* January 5, 1972.
113. Peter Walls in *The Calgary Herald,* May 6, 1972.
114. Cited by Walls in *The Calgary Herald,* May 6, 1972 from Central Mortage and Housing Corporation's statistical report for 1971.

115. Reported in *The Calgary Herald,* January 3, 1972.
116. There appeared to be a lack of information on the detail of housing needs in Calgary both in respect of size and type of accommodation and the ability to pay for it. To some extent this was a consequence of officials waiting for the 1971 Census data to become available. We also noted that the Alberta Housing Corporation was involved, on the request of the municipality, with a "Need and Demand Study," likely to indicate Calgary's housing requirements.
117. Carried as a section in *The Canadian Magazine* and *The Canadian Magazine Star Weekly,* October, 1971.
118. *The Calgary Herald,* February 29, 1972, report on a meeting of City Council.
119. We have not verified the veracity of the relation assumed in this argument.
120. This discussion centred on the MacEwan Glens annexation which is described in detail later in this Chapter.
121. February 29, 1972.
122. *The Calgary Herald,* March 2, 1972. It might also be pointed out that although the city does not assemble residential land, it has assembled and serviced industrial land for many years. It was reported to us that, in general, private developers prefer residential to industrial development, as industrial lots may lie idle for a long time and the capital invested in them therefore proves costly. We have not verified this claim.
123. The Urban Development Institute Charter. The UDI has four provincial divisions, the Maritimes, Ontario, Manitoba, and Alberta, each of which is registered as a society. A Canadian-wide UDI has existed for three to four years and is about to ratify a constitution. The Alberta division has existed for about 15 years.
124. Report dated April 10, 1972.
125. *The Calgary Plan,* March, 1970, p.2.1.
127. *Statutes of Alberta,* 1970, Chapter 19.
128. Address to the Town Planning Institute of Canada, July 21, 1970 by the Honourable Harry E. Strom.
129. Ibid.
130. Ibid.
131. With the change in government in 1971, the MLA became the new Minister of Municipal Affairs.
132. City of Calgary Transportation System By-law no. 8500, Supplementary Information, pp.-12.
133. We have not determined the reason for the provincial government's haste in the content of this legislation.
134. Clause 4 of the Supplementary Information, p.2.
135. Brief by the Society for Pollution and Environmental Control to the public hearing, February 22, 1972.
136. Ibid.
137. Bowness Community Association, Planning and Development Committee. Report to the Mayor, February 18, 1972, p.1.
138. *The Calgary Herald,* February 4, 1972, p.21, contains a useful copy of the map referred to, but it is there stated explicity as being "a conceptual representation," and for all full details reference should be made to the City Engineering Department.
139. *The Calgary Herald,* February 23, 1972, editorial.
140. Reported in *The Calgary Herald,* January 26, 1972.
141. Ibid.
142. *The Calgary Herald,* March 24, 1972.
143. The Calgary General Plan, Chapter "Urban growth," April, 1971, p.1.2.
144. The Calgary General Plan, Chapter "The Calgary region," April, 1971, p.11.1.
145. Ibid., p.11.2.
146. Ibid., p.11.1.

147. Ibid.
148. Ibid.
149. Ibid.
150. Ibid.
151. Minutes of Calgary's Industrial Expansion Committee, February 15, 1971.
152. Minutes of Calgary's Industrial Expansion Committee, June 17, 1971.
153. The Calgary General Plan: Chapter "The Calgary region," April 1971, p.11.1.
154. Jankunis, F. (editor) "Contemporary administrative problems" in *Southern Alberta: a Regional Perspective* by John K. Kenward, Department of Geography, The University of Lethbridge, 1971, p.100.
155. The Calgary Plan: Chapter "The Calgary region," April, 1971, p.11.2.
156. The Preliminary Regional Plan was adopted by the Calgary Regional Planning Commission on July 29, 1963. It was amended May 1, 1964 and October 1, 1965. The Calgary Regional Planning Commission was formed in 1951.
157. The Preliminary Regional Plan as amended (1965) Part 1, Section 2, Subsection (1) (i); p.9.
158. Office files of the MD of Rocky View.
159. Ibid.
160. MD of Rocky View Council minutes, August 11, 1970.
161. See Chapter 3 of this volume.
162. A copy of the Preliminary Regional Plan prepared by the commission's zoning committee was submitted to the commission December 6, 1970. A Notice of Motion to adopt the plan was made on December 15, 1970.
163. Minutes of Okotoks Council meeting. The portion of the minutes dealing with Preliminary Regional Plan was submitted to the Regional Planning Commission.
164. Ibid.
165. Ibid.
166. Minutes of High River's Council meeting January 13, 1971. The portion dealing with the Preliminary Regional Plan was submitted to the Regional Planning Commission.
167. Minutes of Cochrane Council meeting (date of reply: January 20, 1971). Portion concerning the Preliminary Regional Plan was submitted to the Regional Planning Commission.
168. Schedule "6" of "Guide sheet as to replies and suggested action resulting from referral of the Preliminary Regional Plan," February 1, 1971.
169. Ibid.
170. Letter from Minister of Highways and Transport to Calgary Regional Planning Commission, January 27, 1971.
171. Minutes of MD of Foothill's Council meeting (date of reply: January 27, 1971). Portion concerning the Preliminary Regional Plan was submitted to the Regional Planning Commission.
172. Schedule "13" of the "Guide Sheet."
173. Letter from the Minister of Lands and Forests to the Calgary Regional Planning Commission, January 25, 1971.
174. Letter from Director of the National and Historic Branch to Calgary Regional Planning Commission, December 29, 1970.
175. Submitted with letter of January 20, 1971.
176. Ibid.
177. Submission from the MD of Kneehill no. 48, January 18, 1971.
178. MD of Kneehill Council minutes, January 18, 1971. Portion concerning Preliminary Regional Plan was submitted to the Regional Planning Commission.
179. Submitted by the MD of Rocky View no. 44. Reply to Regional Planning Commission January, 1971.
180. Submitted by the MD of Rocky View no.44. Date of reply to Regional Planning Commission: January 26, 1971.
181. Ibid.

182. Submitted by the City of Calgary's Board of Commissioners. Date of reply: January 26, 1971.
183. Ibid.
184. Ibid.
185. Ibid.
186. Submitted by the City of Calgary's Director of Planning. Date of reply: January 26, 1971.
187. Draft of Preliminary Regional Plan: "Statement of objectives," part I Section II, p.7.
188. Calgary Planning Director's submission, January 26, 1971.
189. Ibid.
190. Ibid.
191. Board Order: October 27, 1971.
192. Application for annexation; Local Authorities Board, March 9, 1971.
193. Planning Department Report, March 30, 1971.
194. Ibid.
195. Ibid.
196. Letter re MacEwan Glens, February 1, 1971.
197. Letter re MacEwan Glens, March 9, 1971.
198. Calgary Planning Commission minutes, April 14, 1971.
200. Calgary Regional Planning Commission minutes, May 7, 1971.
201. "Submission to the Local Authorities Board by the Calgary School District No.19," undated.
202. These views are quite frequently in accord with those expressed by the city's Planning Department.
203. "Submission by Calgary School District 19," p.2, (Section 3).
204. Ibid., p.3 (Section 8).
205. Ibid., p.1 (Section 3).
206. Ibid., p.2 (Section 3).
207. Ibid., p.3 (Section 6).
208. The Calgary Plan: Chapter "Financial implication of the present form of urban growth," April, 1971, p.14.1.
209. "Submission by Calgary School District 19," p.3 (Section 8).
210. Local Authorities Board to the City Council, May 5, 1971.
211. From Director of Planning to Commissioner of Operations and Development, May 31, 1971.
212. Planning Director's Report to City Council, June 1, 1971.
213. Commissioner's Report re: MacEwan Glens; June 2, 1971.
214. Ibid.
215. Local Authorities Board; Board Order no.5505.
216. Hanson, E.J. *The Potential Unification of the Edmonton Metropolitan Area,* Edmonton, March, 1968, p.223.
217. Ibid., pp.223-224.
218. Ibid., p.225.
219. Letter dated January 3, 1972.
220. On February 1, 1972, the assistant deputy director responded to the commissioner and attached a copy of a letter addressed to Mr. Cote of Underwood, McLelland and Associates Ltd., from Director of Field Services, Department of Education of the provincial government.
221. Dated December 10, 1971.
222. Re: MacEwan Glens Annexation and Development, February 24, 1972, p.1.
223. Ibid., p.2.
224. Ibid., p.3.
225. Ibid., p.5.
226. City Council documentation for November meeting.
227. Ibid.
228. MacEwan Glens Annexation and Development, February 24, 1972, p.5.

229. Documented at the Municipal Planning Commission meeting of April 12, 1972. It should be noted that Carma Developers Ltd., had submitted subdivision and land use amendment applications for proceeding to the appropriate authorities.
230. Documented at the Municipal Planning Commission meeting of April 19, 1972.
231. Dated April 17, 1972.
232. Ibid.
233. Ibid.

Conclusions

The Relative Inconsequence of Provincial Decisions

This inquiry began with the search for issues within Alberta which would contribute substantially to a future research program into urban affairs. But limiting the study to Albertan affairs would have made the study artificial. Not only was Alberta linked constitutionally to the federal government and to other provinces, but the metropolitan centres and the degraded rural areas of Alberta were themselves linked directly to national policy. In addition, through the decisions of major privately-organized investors, many urban centres and particularly Calgary and Edmonton, were linked to other metropolitan centres as part of a larger system. The public relations and advertising techniques of local centres directed explicitly at attracting private investment, and the swings of fashion from surburban single-family dwellings to high-rise blocks, spoke eloquently for the influence of private investors' decisions on Albertan urban affairs. Such extra-Albertan influences, and the clarity of their influence, threatened the veracity of any province-wide conclusions which might emerge from an enquiry limited to Alberta alone.

In consequence, Volume I, *The Politics of Canadian Urban Development,* was written while the field-work into Edmonton, Calgary and several Albertan towns was underway and while Albertan governmental policies in historical sequence were being analyzed. The work is thus much larger than originally intended, but it has made possible a perspective to both Albertan and Canadian urban affairs which is rarely found in the current literature.

Several themes run persistently through the evidence whether it is concerned with Albertan metropolitan affairs or with the federal national urban policy for Canada. Most important of these themes is what we have called "the relative inconsequence of provincial government decision." In the companion volume this theme was revealed in the relation of provinces to federal initiatives on such matters as the National Housing Act, The Central Mortgage and Housing Corporation, the private lending institutions, possible amendments to the British North American Act, federally sponsored research into urban affairs, and the evolution of the national urban policy. In this volume this same theme emerged in the relation of provincial government policy to the urban developmental process in Edmonton and Calgary, and to smaller local authorities. The Social Credit administration adopted explicitly, and applied in practice, a philosophy that deliberately encouraged local authorities to be responsible for their own affairs. Fair and equal treatment for all, and the defence of local autonomy were made to appear as the corner stones of provincial-municipal relations. While these principles ruled, Calgary and Edmonton, both before and after the major oil discoveries in 1947, had phenomenally high rates of population and investment growth. The Social Credit government's philosophy particularly favoured metropolitan concentration. Provincial revenues came to be distributed on a per capita basis over an ever-expanding range of personal services to the province's citizens and to the councils and local authorities of the growing metropolitan centres to meet their ever-rising expenditures on capital and operating budgets.

By permitting the metropolitan centres' councils and their administrations to set the pattern of their capital expenditure— in turn subsidized by an array of senior government grants, low interest provisions, subsidies, etc.,— the provincial government became vicariously committed both to the pattern itself and to subsidizing a considerable proportion of running costs which followed inevitably from the initial capital investment. The school boards' expenditures — both capital and operating — illustrate the vicarious nature of the province's commitment, but there are many others in addition.[1] City councils, on the other hand, were caught up in the necessity to budget for increasing expenditures on road construction and higher standards in order to protect the interests of downtown investors and allay the annoyance of city drivers held up at intersections en route to and from suburban areas. By remaining vicariously committed to the pattern implicit in city capital expenditures, and by providing no alternative direction to the province's urban development, the provincial government let itself be made the scapegoat for financial and political difficulties recurring persistently within the metropolitan centres. These difficulties were momentarily resolved from time to time by *ad hoc* or special provisions — such as by changes in the Planning Act, by the monetary services of the Alberta Municipal Finance Corporation, and by municipal assistance grants — but provincial action on each occasion was no more than a temporary palliative to an endemic process of conflict and compromise within the affairs of the metropolitan centres.

Concurrently, through its indecisive urban policy, the provincial government was caught up with the provincial process of rural degradation. This process has not matured in Alberta as severely as in other parts of Canada, nor is the Alberta government yet involved as deeply as some are elsewhere in Canada with the problem of coping with extensive urban physical and human degradation. Yet it has apparently taken no effective and timely measures to curb the trend incipient in the province — a trend about which comparative material is abundant in the rest of Canada and elsewhere in the industrialized world. The government's hesitancy in this area is in part itself the consequence of its indecisive urban policy, in part the consequence of its ambivalence over the necessity to implement effective measures which would result in the distribution of privately organized enterprise over the province in the interests of the province, and in part the consequence of failure to co-ordinate federal provisions theoretically aimed at the same end with those of the province.

The point at which this hesitancy over rural provincial degradation and the indecisive urban policy coincide, is the metropolitan capital budget. Associated very closely with this matter is that of metropolitan land annexation and development policies. These two critically important matters were discussed generally throughout this enquiry, but were emphasized in detail in the studies of Calgary's handling of the provincial City Transportation Act 1970, and of Edmonton's annexations. These two matters may be identified in the long-range General Plans of Calgary and Edmonton, where the emphasis on costs of transport, street construction, etc., is prominent; in the McNally Commission Report (1956); the Hanson Report (1968); and in the interest the daily press has in the issues of annexation and property tax. The property tax for municipal, school, and health purposes, becomes the topic of principal local concern because it is amenable to local political use, as well as conveniently forming the basis of the next round of argument to gain further finance from the province. But viewed in the wider perspective of the urban process, property tax is a symptom rather than a cause. The citizenry bears the brunt of taxation *per se;* property tax is but one of several calls upon its pocket. The significance of property tax is much more in terms of its political value, than a matter of substance in taxation policy. Property tax is also politically important in regulating the relation of one local authority to other local authorities whether within a common jurisdiction, e.g., city council and school board, or within separate land jurisdictions, such as Calgary and Edmonton.

The vicarious commitment of the province to the capital budget of the metropolitan centres, while permitting the city to determine its pattern of public investment, places the provincial government in the role of "second fiddle" in the provincial direction of urban affairs. As the "urban" has for at least the past two decades in Alberta, and for longer in other parts of Canada, been the dominant cultural expression of society and the determinant of its dynamic, the provincial second-fiddle role has encouraged an active political role by the cities. The cities have recently demanded partnership with the senior governments in any constitutional review or change. Within Alberta, municipal-provincial politics takes the form of a speedy ministerial reply to city mayors' claims for broadened municipal tax bases, new municipal-provincial relations generally, and a persistent claim by the cities to have greater freedom of decision over and a greater amount of "free" money with which to handle their particular problems. The cities demanded greater freedom of discretion over public expenditures, while the provincial government was genuinely espousing a policy of laissez-faire, local authority autonomy, and fair and equal treatment for all local authorities. The apparent paradox in this situation requires more detailed analysis.

Local Autonomy and Encapsulation

The theory of local autonomy as perceived in Alberta was to permit the locally elected council, school board, etc., to carry the responsibility for local decisions subject to specified approvals from the citizens over certain capital expenditures and the regulations prescribed by the provincial authority. The province was careful to prescribe regulations applicable in their execution to all local authorities, save in those cases where board classifications were made such as cities, towns, villages, counties, improvement districts, etc., and occasionally on the basis of "urban" and "rural" differences. By "universal" prescription, these gave equal opportunity, theoretically, at least, for local authority councils to take advantage of provincial amenities. A local citizenry, by its right of election, got the local government it deserved which, in turn, manipulated the "universality" of provincial amenity to its local needs and best advantage. The provincial government thereby left open to all local authorities the opportunity "to get ahead"; the responsibility for failure was left local, and the province could provide, as an extraordinary, non-precedent-setting incident, any particular help it might consider appropriate to afford a local council or its citizenry. From one point of view this arrangement was a "cop out" for the provincial government, allowing it the opportunity of convenient electoral gains from its largesse, if required. From another point of view, it was an arrangement whereby the "natural forces" of the economy and the energy and enterprise of the citizenry were free to play themselves out without artificial, and therefore "wasteful," stimulation from the province. Developmental decisions were essentially left local, though the province has legislated a variety of province-wide controls from beautification of highways in the 1920s to pollution control and recreational parks. Where regulative measures, even of a more serious character, such as provisions of the Planning Act, have been introduced they have not seriously interfered with the rights of local authorities to negotiate with private investors, save at the level of public utilities and transport.

The theory, therefore, contained much of the laissez-faire doctrine of classical capitalism but using special and extraordinary aid to the needy, preferably on a self-help basis rather than charity. The differential of opportunity in self-help between a small town and a metropolitan centre was never recognized as being subject to human choices. The laws of nature were viewed as determining the differential.

The application of this theory was warped, however, by the nexus of relationships: (a) with which the provincial government was enmeshed constitutionally, (b) by means of which large scale organized private capital could locate its plant or productive investment under terms negotiable with all levels of government and concurrently contract with employees equally flexibly placed in their place of residence and movement, regardless of administrative and political boundaries, and (c) by means of which the citizenry — both as individuals and as corporate citizens — could establish claims for services and conveniences from public authorities regardless of the claims and needs of others less influentially placed or in greater need than themselves. This nexus of relationships encapsulated, as it were, the provincial government.

The competitive nature of inter-provincial incentives for the attraction of private industrial investment is well known in Canada. Its expression has been exacerbated by the influence of federal government policy in the Department of Regional Economic Expansion (DREE), Maritime provinces incentives, the Industrial Incentives Act, the Prairie Farm Rehabilitation Act, and so forth. The consequence of federal initiative through the National Housing Act — to subsidize the cost of mortgages for domestic residential units through the services of private lending institutions rather than provincial governments — had been to deprive the provinces of any influence they might have had over the distribution of residential property. Only in the mid-1960s — and in 1967 in Alberta — were the provinces disposed to institute province-wide housing authorities of their own. The Alberta Housing Corporation has expanded its activities from urban renewal and low-cost housing projects to land assembly and housing in general but does not yet provide for that important aspect of The National Housing Act which encourages private institutions to lend to those in the middle and upper income brackets. This is still retained as a federal-CMHC-private lending institution-developer-homeowner prerogative.

With regard to private enterprise and its employees, the provincial government was ambivalently placed in several respects. In so far as private investment and population increase enhanced the dollar value of tax revenues within the province, as well as the returns from federal distributions using a per capita formula, they were an advantage; but they added significantly to provincial costs for personal services, such as education and health, and the capital requirements of roads and railways. When its principal economic resource was agriculture the province was particularly prone to booms and depressions. The sequence of establishing provincial departments in the 1920s and 1930s bears testimony to the provincial government's concern for manufacturing and natural resource exploitation to broaden the economic base. The surge of revenue from oil and gas exploitation from 1948 to 1958 was used in Alberta to develop the provincial infrastructure of roads, education, and health services, and to provide annual grants to local authorities. But uncommitted benifficence was the rule rather than conditional assistance to local authorities as a means to a province-wide scheme of urban development. Local autonomy had to be, and was, respected.

Provincial ambivalence was further enhanced by the "fair and equal" aspect of local autonomy theory. In attracting development, many small towns have become financially over-extended through capitalizing the public amenities thus required. Under the present circumstances, a community may have to modify its developmental standards and place its quality of life in jeopardy while accommodating private investment, but the provincial government is not necessarily considered responsible. If the provincial government assumed responsibility — decided whether or not a particular development should be allowed to proceed — this would be interpreted as an invasion of local autonomy and contrary to the government's policy of permitting local authorities to make their own decisions. As local authorities view themselves as autonomous entities, any provincial interference in the initiative of one could be construed as interference in the rights of all.

What pressures were brought to bear over the possible annexation of the Strathcona industries to Edmonton, as recommended by the McNally Commission, we do not know; but a decision to support such a recommendation would have considerable implication for provincial policy. While local authorities view themselves as autonomous entities, the competitive relation among them is encouraged. When one local authority succeeds in attracting private enterprise, it becomes correspondingly less inclined to co-operate with others. Only when a number of local authorities have become reduced to thoroughly degraded circumstances is it possible for provincial initiative to be readily acceptable, and even under these conditions, as at Crownest Pass[2], continuous jealousy and skirmishing for minor local advantages continue to thwart the co-operative spirit.

Coupled to this is the provincial theory of developmental co-ordination, which assumes that co-ordination of activity will occur at the local level. But funds are held available at the provincial level for local authorities to call upon, and the timing of their applications is entirely unco-ordinated except in so far as issues like local unemployment or slum clearance tend to set fashionable demands. The mode of using funds obtained by application is also left largely to local decision. The senior government, being relieved of the onus of having to co-ordinate province-wide demands, leaves the local authorities subject to the conflicting influence of their *private investors, developers and industrialists etc., on the one hand and the public requiring expensive amenities on the other.*

Private enterprise largely determines the developmental process in any given centre or region. The province is simply the benefactor of local authorities in desperate need of capital. The metropolitan centres, however, faced with high capital expenditures to cover city expansion both of developed acreage and of the style and standard of public services have had increasingly to rely on the open market or on provincial institutions by way of sinking funds, revolving funds, and more recently, the Alberta Municipal Finance Corporation, to obtain the capital. By pursuing a policy of decentralized bureaucratic administration, i.e., by devolving decision to *ad hoc,* specialist boards and commissions outside the formal departmental structure of the civil service, the provincial minister responsible can leave the detail of decision to the devolved authority and have the issue decided on the merits and fairness of the case. Matters of principle can always be referred to him and the Cabinet. This system permits the practice of fair and equitable treatment to all concerned to be publicly recognizable and at election time the government can claim to have run an impeccable and honest administration. Indeed it had, but the processes occurring with this "distant" and honest administration have a way of catching up with it and making it decreasingly tenable. Concurrently, the system of provincial administration virtually precludes the possibility of provincial direction to Alberta's increasingly urban situation even if the tenets of local autonomy were to be compromised.

The metropolitan centres, by incurring provincial debt through AMFC debentures or floating loans on the open market, have been entitled to assume both in theory and practice that they possessed the autonomy of action and decision that private companies have. The confusion of the McNally report, by arguing through false analogy on this very issue in relation to private property, bears witness to this assumption concerning the rights of decision and action enjoyed by a local authority. As the metropolitan centres have come to accommodate more than half the provincial population, and as the tax revenue these cities generate for the province increases, their interests have come to dominate provincial government decision. Amendments to the Planning Act were made largely to suit the convenience of the cities. They had little regard either to the relevance of the amendment or to the suitability of the principle implicit in the Act itself to the needs of lesser urban centres. The metropolitan-dominated region is the principle implicit in the Planning Act, despite the conflict of this principle with the theory of local autonomy in its application to the adjacent local authorities.

The autonomy of decision and action afforded the metropolitan centres in particular has enabled them to pursue policies aimed at attracting increasing quantitites, and increasingly diverse forms, of private investment. In this they met and continue to meet the requirements of private enterprise. These policies also helped to resolve several other problems: those of ensuring the adequate use of public investment already made in city plant (the utilities and property tax facilities), of coping with the pressing matters of urban unemployment, of benefiting from unused but developed land, and of benefiting from capital appreciation of buildings (particularly in downtown cores) which would assist the mill rate and add to the city's "free" revenues by way of property tax and municipal grants. But this very attractiveness of the metropolitan centres — an attractiveness deliberately engendered by advertising on the part of city councils and by advice at the provincial level given to industries contemplating locating plant in Alberta — have led concurrently to the degradation of rural areas and small centres in the remainder of the province. It has led also to local authorities adjacent to the cities — particularly to Edmonton — attracting large-scale industry (Strathcona) and threatening to establish sizable cities adjacent to the major city. The authority of regional planning commissions and their predecessors came into question as appeals to provincial levels of authority were compromised because of "local autonomy."

Increasingly as Calgary and Edmonton have grown over the past three decades, the provincial government has become "boxed in." It can neither direct the provincial urban growth process, nor limit it. While the federal government, through CMHC and the lending institutions, can be decisive in its direction of private residential and development investment, the province cannot afford to use its constitutional rights over local authorities to divert the process in directions other than into the metropolitan centres. It can neither intrude into metropolitan affairs at decisive points — and the Mayor of Calgary described the ritual of formal plan preparation and a public hearing on the city's Transportation By-Law as a charade carried through at the behest of people in Edmonton — nor openly move to assist by worthwhile discriminatory measures the development of urban centres other than Calgary and Edmonton. The myth of "natural forces" determining events has proved particularly convenient. The province has been left the opportunity, however, of increasing its financial support and underwriting the cities' capital and operating expenditures. As the power and influence of Calgary and Edmonton has increased in the province's affairs, so the more encapsulated has the provincial government become.

The cities, in turn, have been bound by ideologies serving their own legitimacy. Such valued beliefs as the rights of individual and corporate citizens to accrue capital gains and to benefit from land speculation as small "country squires"; the need for them to be shielded from the disturbing effects of expropriation in the public interest, and the right of citizens to be kept advised and forewarned of local authority intentions, have been vehemently upheld. The community's affairs have to be public, while those of private investers enjoy the privilege of secrecy.

The encapsulating condition of local authorities is identifiable in four dimensions — outward in their relations to each other, inwards in their relations to their own departments, professional cadres of staff, and the provincially-sponsored local commissions and boards, upwards in their relations to senior governments, and downwards in their relations to the local citizenry.[3] Much of this study has been concerned with the ways in which one or other or these relations come to compromise decisions. But the consequence of this interplay of forces is to make manipulation and manoeuvre the typical feature of local government administration. In this it contrasts with the possible role of local authorities as the means of servicing, on the one hand, a provincial direction of urban affairs, and on the other, the practical day-to-day needs of local citizens.[4]

The manipulation of relations typifies all four dimensions of the encapsulated condition. Our study has analyzed the outward dimension by way of annexation procedures, the McNally Commission's and Professor Hanson's reports, and the affairs of satellite communities. We have also shown that the inward dimension, to council's own administrative and professional staffs and local boards, has particular consequence for city planning and financial arrangements. The absence of co-ordination in this dimension permits city politicians to pass responsibility for mistakes and errors of judgement to professional personnel within their own administration. The professional personnel in turn respond with recommendations clothed in appropriate political garb; they instigate tactics of their own to limit or increase the range of the elected council's responsibility for decision. The process takes the form of a game. Lack of co-ordination at this level, in turn permits the council the flexibility to respond to senior government proposals and sanctions, or to the proposals by developers and private investors, without being restricted by firm policy for the future. Precedent is little respected, and each decision is supposed to be based on the unique features of the case.

In the upwards dimension to senior levels of government, we have seen that authorities may select those programs convenient to themselves. They may, by negotiation, manipulate both the provisions laid down for the program and the way the senior government envisages the intention of the program. The federal ministers responsible for housing came, by 1970-71, to be making *in situ* inspections of urban renewal and low-cost housing projects under the NHA. Many of these federal government programs have been ends specifically directed to easing unemployment, housing the poor, stimulating the economy, etc. Local authorities may as equally use them for their own purposes; there is no requirement that they should contribute explicitly to a plan of urban development. Such programs may be used finally to meet the needs of private developers, relieve lending institutions of surplus investable cash and thereby accumulatively prevent a fall in the rate of interest, and provide amenities to local citizens, such as swimming pools, transient accommodation, parks and recreation facilities, etc., for which the city's running budget is ill-prepared to cope.

The downwards dimension to the local citizenry whether individual or corporate, as has been illustrated in this study, is expressed through a variety of formal institutions prescribed both by the province and the local authorities — public hearings, and the rituals of notification, and appeals, etc. — which have come to form the content of many amendments to the Planning Act since 1963 and which are contained in many city by-laws. In addition to these, citizens may personally approach elected officials. Calgary in particular has encouraged citizen participation in public affairs, from an advisory committee on the annual capital budget, to committees of citizens to find solutions to local conflicts. Citizen participation of this kind, however, is involved largely with very local developmental detail — the lot-size issues of city administration. At a more general level, the formal hearings of city council, on planning and transportation by-laws, for example, are often the occasion for considered briefs by neighbourhood or interest groups where the services of volunteers with professional experience may be used to influence the direction of more general affairs.

Where we have examined the relation of council to *corporate* citizens in the downwards dimension, a different situational context for action emerges. Organized private investment is not averse to using the interest of private individuals to support its requests to a local authority. If it can show popular support for its case, its influence over council decision can be considerable.

The scale of proposal by private investment is influential, too. In large-scale negotiations, e.g., where the city core is at stake, where large acreage of raw land may be developed, or where a major industry may be attracted, matters tend to be dealt with by City Commissioners, the Mayor, or select committees. This mode of approach does not appear to be due so much to a policy of closed-door, secretive negotiation, but rather because the adjustments which the city will be obliged to make have widespread repercussions and because private enterprise, in order to make its case to City Hall, may have to reveal embarrassing amounts of information about itself and its plans in full awareness that its competitors would dearly love to have that knowledge. Private enterprise therefore demands confidentiality in its negotiation with City Hall. Then, within the city's administration, adjustments are required to be made to the annual programs of engineering services, of annexation procedures, of estimates of expenditure and revenue in various departments. Estimated tax assessments, and provincially available grants and subsidies, etc., must all be related to the outside proposal. In this sense it is not untrue to say that the public's institutions respond to the initiatives of privately owned capital, and do not require privately owned capital to accommodate itself to them. This does not mean that private initiative *rules* the affairs of the city, — it is far too symbiotic in nature, but it does suggest that the needs and requirements of private investment, rather than those of the public, set the pattern of city direction and development. Concurrently, in theory at least, one could argue that the lack of direction of the urban developmental process is the consequence of the city's relation to corporate citizens and the initiative they so frequently and expertly take.

And yet large-scale private enterprise is not averse to conforming conscientiously to the requirements of long-term plans and proposals in the public interest. Management is usually sensitive to the advantages of good relations with government and public institutions. For example, the management of Strathcona's industries was remarkably silent before the McNally Commission, and was capable of adjusting to the taxation implications of recommendations made in either direction, although they had their preferences, naturally. More recently, large-scale land developers have become competetive in their relations with metropolitan governments over the acquisition of land — either among developers as in Calgary, or between the local authority and developers as in Edmonton — to regulate lot prices to the homeowner. But in so far as development agreements are coming increasingly to pass the cost of a growing variety of services to developers, and via the NHA to the lot buyer, city councils may be able to negotiate with developers over the precise areas where land development may occur. This new level of co-operation may provide the means for cities to direct the area of development in the interests of their plans, rather than letting themselves and their plans be just the instrument for the speculator's realization of profit. This is an area of study which we did not pursue adequately, but we noted the evolution of the Urban Development Institute as a powerful force in Alberta and potentially in Canada as a whole.

Thus, the theory of local autonomy has the dual effect of emasculating the local authorities' potential for the direction and orderly development of urban areas and of affording private enterprise the opportunity of directing urban development towards its own needs and convenience. Yet there appears to be no inherent necessity for this. While the vested interests of land developers and lending institutions, or factory plants, offer potential points of resistence to provincial and municipal direction, such resistence usually occurs in defence of property already in existence. Private enterprise management can adjust internally to a public program faithfully implemented when future plans are being envisaged. Thus the possibility of governments assuming a deliberate directional role in urban affairs is not necessarily contrary to the interests of private enterprise. It is only when investment must be defended, when the manoeuvres and manipulations of public authorities might threaten past investments, that managers of privately organized capital must respond politically. The federal schemes of industrial incentives show that many private investment decisions can be extremely flexible.

Planning and the Political Process

The paucity of explicit direction of urban development, whether from the federal, provincial, or local governments, contributes to escalating urban costs. Without such direction, public investment, particularly in metropolitan centres, cannot sensibly be related to an enduring, long-term purpose. It tends to be made with an eye to resolving a current issue, or to meeting a popular or political fashion — unemployment, a sluggish economy, housing the poor, urban renewal, etc. It can also serve the interests of powerful companies ever anxious to be serviced to the last possible convenience. City and regional planning authorities struggle manfully to generate general plans of enduring significance only to find them compromised by developmental decisions, rapidly outdated by the empirical trend of events, ignored in the interests of an immediate short-term advantage, or nullified in their details by court decisions.

This inwardly stultifying situation is in turn exacerbated by the paucity of overall direction of province-wide planning. The Provincial Planning Branch and the Department of Municipal Affairs in general, coupled in turn to supra-departmental, *ad hoc* boards and commissions — the Provincial Planning Board, the Public Utility Commission, the Local Authorities Board, the Municipal Finance Corporation, etc., — appear to be either ill-equipped, unable, or unwilling to give to metropolitan affairs the direction which would remove the inward conflict which the cities experience. The cities' leaders are jealous of their own autonomy, jealous of any provincial favour to any other local authority, envious of the growth of others, and desperate for money to save themselves from having to raise the mill rate. It is a vicious combination of circumstances where politicians are given ample room to pass blame to others and where the benefits of rationality, technology, planning, and large-scale organization become diminished, as the level of taxation suffered by the citizen amply demonstrates.

Though we have not been able to study the role of supra-departmental boards and commissions at both provincial and regional levels to the extent necessary, the evidence which we have suggests that their concern is more to regulate the internal affairs of autonomous local authorities, and the affairs between such authorities, than to decide issues before them in terms of a provincial or regional urban policy.[5] We have also sensed, though not examined adequately, a lack of co-ordination among the departments of the provincial government. Co-ordination at this point is rapid and effective in the task of supplying information to each other in defence of outside criticism or if some detail of administration is going wrong. It is at the point of concerted endeavour to co-ordinate affairs of the present in the interests of a predictable future, that this level of public administration appears to have difficulties. The provincial Cabinet is said to be the point of co-ordination of policy intent on directing the present into a future. But we are not convinced that the term "policy" in this regard equates with the type of decision-making the empirical situation of the province appears to demand. "Policy," as used in the political institutions of the province, appears to mean either abstract issues such as "local autonomy," "private enterprise versus a planned economy," etc., or else a detailed decision coupled to a minor matter of administrative ambivalence. The lacuna is the critical area in between.

Again, emphasizing that we are dissatisfied with our work in this area, we mention that a relation appears to exist between the encapsulated position of the provincial government in the federal context and the variety of urban-influencing services emanating from Ottawa in one form or another. In Volume I, we identified the relative inconsequence of provincial decision in regard to the NHA and the decisions of private lending institutions over the locale of their mortgage investments. The McNally Commission, in 1956, described one consequence of this in its discussion of the fringe areas of the Albertan metropolitan centres. We noted that this position appears to have been modified in recent years as a consequence of new development policies and the scale of developmental operations. But there appear to exist other provincial-federal relations with corresponding repercussions for the province.

The urban renewal program, CMHC in its many activities, industrial locational incentives, technical education and job training programs, the Municipal Development and Loan Board, etc., are extant or past phenomena which illustrate this matter. The federal government has shown an increasing interest in urban transportation, while its support of airports, defence establishments, and other direct federal investment in the province constitute recurrent expenditures. Many decisions of the federal government over new urban programs are taken on the basis of assistance towards meeting popularly sensitive issues, a few are taken specifically with an explicit urban developmental policy in mind. Dr. Harvey Lithwick's studies in the federal national urban policy for Canada bear witness to a change in the trends of the past. That the federal government itself is caught in its own tangled circumstances, outward to other nations — defending the autonomy of Canada in the world at large — and inwards to the provinces and private corporations, is a point we cannot discuss. But the implication of this fact is to oblige the provinces to gear themselves within their own administrations to applying such federal resources with maximum effect. Yet this has not been achieved in Alberta. In the Maritimes the federal government itself appears to have had to assume to some degree this important co-ordinatory role. But the historical evidence suggests that the federal government is continuously engaged in a process of amending the NHA, and adding further millions of dollars to one or other aspect of urban affairs, industrial incentives, degraded rural area resuscitation, etc. Alberta should be ready not only to use these federal spin-offs to best advantage, but possibly identify where their effects could most readily be felt in the provincial plan of development, as has been done in Ontario, Quebec, and the Maritimes.

Alberta's handling of the 1963-68 federal Municipal Development and Loan Fund showed refreshing use of such money to build new towns and to support the rapidly growing centres which had been identified and supported by large, private, resource-exploiting corporations. Though the provincial initiative tended to be taken only towards the end of the program, after the established local authorities had had their chance, the events do illustrate the kind of benefits capable of coming from deliberate and co-ordinated provincial initiative. The question is one of expanding expertise and modes of co-ordinatory practice which would greatly enhance the potential for provincial initiative. As we have seen, there is an interstice between policymaking on a grand but vague scale and on a small and highly detailed one and it is in this area that the provincial government might usefully develop greater capacity. It presently appears to be ignored. Inevitably, expanding this area would mean creating a new series of para-departmental institutions — institutions different in purpose and status from the supra-departmental boards and commissions mentioned above. New research endeavours would also be required. It would also mean a deliberate reduction in the isolationary and "hands-off" attitude we identified in interviews with officials in some of the provincial departments. This problem has been addressed in the federal civil service, also over urban affairs, and we recommend that further enquiries be made into it.

The paucity of policymaking on a large but detailed level in the province excacerbates political manoeuvring in municipal-provincial relations. Through their encapsulated position within a theory of local autonomy, the metropolitan centres cannot effectively plan and mature their long-range intentions because the region in which they operate is not under their control or anyone else's either in an overall way. The examples of the City Transportation Act, 1970, and the regional plans of the Regional Planning Commission — the completion of which had been postponed from year to year — may be cited to show the impossible task set the professional engineers and planners in this respect.[6] It is not always the paucity of empirical data which delays these professional inputs to the planning process. As the case of Calgary's Transportation By-Law and the developmental difficulties of several small towns around Edmonton showed, the absence of explicit provincial direction on critical matters also complicates the professionals' task. Professionals become obliged to relate in practice to the political manipulations of elected interests rather than to the application of their skills to a rational developmental process. They are obliged to draft developmental plans on assumptions which prove eventually to be either false or impracticable. They are used as guides and mentors by elected representatives when it suits them, and are sloughed off as an embarrassment by these same representatives when the plans or policies are challenged.

Rational planning is confused at times with a straight-jacketing of decisions. People fear a technocracy taking the place of a democracy, and suspect that experts are undermining the power of the city council. Rational planning needs to be understood more thoroughly, more widely. Rational planning is not only carried out in the form of city general plans, regional plans, transportation plans, etc., but in the field of land developers' plans and city centre financial institutions' plans. In each case a set of rationally prepared courses of action have been set up by the various bodies involved. In the former instances, the plans are made public so that the plans of others may be related to them, but in the latter, the plans are kept a secret lest competitors get into the act with adverse consequences. These then have a better chance of being carried out because the public does not challenge them. The open plans of the city, however, are subject to challenge and debate and because the rational planning process comes before the public eye in this instance only (as it appears) it is suspect. The city must therefore do its work in the daily flux of the situational context.

It has to be said also that the city as such is not in the forefront of social change. It is a rather rigid institution, and individuals have made a lot more adaptations and changes in their lives than have institutions.

The 1867 BNA Act has only recently become questioned as suitable for an industrial-urban culture, and this questioning arose more from political issues than those from rational perspectives to developmental issues. The Alberta Planning Act has been based in principle on land use and subdivision control since 1913. City financial estimates and controls are prepared with roughly the same categories as when the Department of Municipal Affairs for several decades — up to 1971 — consisted of a mass of virtually incomprehensible statistics interpretable only by the initiated. The absence of descriptive comment or even elucidation in these reports makes them questionable research documents. The reports of many boards and commissions are so generalized as to reveal very little about policy issues or what is going on. The philosophy of local government, though apparently approaching changes at the end of the Liberal administration in 1921, has remained largely unchanged in Alberta. Even when provincial coffers were bulging with royalties, the resources thus provided were not used to implement different principles, but to entrench the old. Urban institutions in Alberta show a rigidity that becomes expressed both in daily gossip and in research assumptions in the form of the determinism of inevitability of city growth. Annexation problems in Edmonton in 1912 were not different in principle from those discussed in the McNally Report of 1956, or in Professor Hanson's Report of 1968.

People in Alberta's urban centres tend to think entirely in terms of the *ad hoc* day-to-day political aspects of local decisions. In this, the press is a useful ally, for neighbourhood communities in their objections to a city proposal or acquiescence in a developer's proposal, resort willingly to press coverage. Only at a later stage is there resort to legal mechanisms of conflict resolution, and in such cases the validity of the local authority's entire control mechanism becomes open to question. A similar legal situation can exist when developers come into conflict with the city, though they are much less inclined to use the press in support of their cause. The elaborate ritual of public announcement, procedures, etc., can be seen as being both a defence of the rights of people to be heard and a safeguard of the propriety of decision-makers. But the use of ritual in the adjudication of conflict is a sensitive index to the legitimacy of authority. Alberta's Planning Act since 1963 has been the subject of frequent amendment, largely on matters of procedure. In this it is symptomatic of a situation verging not on anarchy, but on a stalemate in the system of checks and balances which controls the arrangement of power and decision making. The mode of decision-making becomes, in consequence, increasingly *ad hoc,* becomes less and less directed by policy or formal planning (whether financial or physical), and must come to be perceived as no more than a contest of power and influence.

Mayor Rod Sykes has become known as a personality across Canada in the few short years of his term of office. He is very sensitive to the numerous forces impinging on Calgary, from federal dilemmas and decisions to the state of mind of Calgarians. He has a shrewd understanding of the contradiction between planning as a long-term public service and the demands of a populace immensely sensitive to the defence of its immediate proprietory interests. It is not coincidential that he has been in conflict with his city planners on the one hand, and with the alderman and selected citizenry on the other. Nor is it coincidental that Calgary openly claims to benefit from competition among large-scale land developers and its arrangements with the Urban Development Institute over comment on city by-law proposals and amendments. The Mayor legitimately, in terms of his own situation, sees the demands of the province over a city transportation plan as being an irksome necessity involving him in a local charade. As Mayor he has to have maximum room to manoeuvre and manipulate in order to forestall the consequences of stalemate in the system of checks and balances. He has to know where action is possible.

Mayor Ivor Dent of Edmonton, quieter and more systematic in his approach, has proven effective politically through the Canadian Federation of Mayors and Municipalities, for example, when he signed, as President of CFMM, its brief to the federal government on partnership and constitutional change. We did not, however, examine in detail the Edmonton City Council's internal political processes.

Municipal processes are typified by great sensitivity to political, legal, administrative, and social issues. This sensitivity is far more concerned with the relations among people in present circumstances than with planning for their futures enduring physical arrangements which would give form and substance to the city and provide the environmental structure and conveniences within which an urban mode of living is made meaningful to men. As a result the physical investment in the city which must be carried out on a here and now basis, is made without adequate consideration for its implications for the region, the province, or even for the city itself. Enormous attention is given to development control and to the confusion between zoning and development control as planning mechanisms. City planners come to "administer" planning rather than to relate the past to the present and the present to the future.

The rigidity of process and institution is associated with the encapsulated nature of both provincial and local governments. Technical innovations — the motor car, reinforced concrete, rapid transit technology, etc., — lead to changes more readily than do the institutions of government. The federal government began to see this in the early 1960s. Its policy of upgrading the degraded regions of Canada through private and public investment, and its hopes of decentralizing the cities, evolved into Dr. Lithwick's urban studies and Mr. Andras's national urban policy. Its purpose was to give direction to the nation's urban growth process. Ottawa's approach to date has been to obtain the concurrence of all levels of government across Canada to proposals on urban development and urban affairs emanating from research done and policy made in Ottawa. There has been a federal drive for national unity. The implementation of the policy appears to have been particularly slow and cumbersome, even unsuccessful, largely because the intention threatens the autonomy of decision and constitutional status of the province. The BNA Act is the province's last line of defence against their own metropolitan areas, on the one hand, and the federal government, on the other. Provincial freedom to manipulate and manoeuvre — the only approach left to an encapsulated authority — would be further jeopardized. Provincial governments are not prepared to suffer a demise on these terms. The stalemate at the three governmental levels threatens to continue, while private companies and corporations receive increasing quantities and more diversely arranged subsidies, grants, and concessions from all levels of government.

The Potential Roles of the Provincial Government

In the concluding remarks of Volume I, we argued that the municipalities, rather than the federal government, should be the level at which governmental planning and private enterprise relate together in the interests of a national urban policy.[7] This suggestion followed the argument that senior governments were coming increasingly to influence decisions on private investment prior to that investment being made. Many federal and some provincial programs are now designed to operate this way. Our reason for putting the municipality in this role was that it is the place where monetary capital is transposed to fixed assets, and where public investment relates directly to the productive process, and the public comes to share in this investment. We also suggested this role for the municipality because federal attempts in 1970-71 to implement a national policy through governmental unity, tri-level co-ordination, and so on, were meeting with little success.

Federal intrusion through the NHA, CMHC, DREE, and other instruments and programs has come increasingly to contribute to the encapsulated condition of provincial governments. But the condition of success of any new federal-provincial relation in a new national urban policy for Canada, is that provincial governments are made genuinely responsible for the application of urban policy within their geographic and legal jurisdictions — or within such other jurisdictions as are necessary for sound administration. The reason for the past failure of provincial governments to accept and implement a recognizable responsibility for urban policy has been their encapsulation between federal and local governments as against the flexibility afforded the management of organized private investment.

It has not been an unwillingness so much as an impotence.[8] The Alberta government should be responsible for determining the policy applicable to its jurisdiction. There is a variety of choice. If it should opt for a policy of concentrating the vast bulk of population and productive resource into two or three metropolitan centres, leaving the remainder of the province to agriculture, timber, fishing and recreation outlets for the cities, so be it. At least its policy would be explicit both nationally and to its local governments. A basis would exist for the planning of metropolitan areas and of the remainder of the province. If it should decide on policy that recognizes a limited, steady, co-ordinated expansion of the major cities with a network of regional and ancillary urban centres serving a variety of functions locally, regionally, and provincially, again the end is explicit. Other possibilities come readily to mind. Under existing circumstances, the encapsulation of both provincial and local governments permits urban expansion and decay to be treated as if these processes were natural phenomena. The "market," as if it were gravity, is supposed to determine the ups and downs of affairs. This is ideological nonsense and is merely an excuse for human impotence in what is a thoroughly human and cultural domain.

Provincial governments, however, are currently in no position to act as the situation requires of them because: (a) the flexibility inherent in private productive investment and its location could jeopardize their efforts, as the Social Credit administration came to learn in the late 1930s; (b) the federal government has chosen, as a matter of policy since 1935, and reiterated in the NHA of 1944, to provide private lending institutions with the right of decision over matters affecting the domicile of the working population — whether in suburban sprawl or in high-rises; (c) metropolitan local governments, because they are the place where monetary investment is transposed into fixed assets, can manipulate the provincial government into providing increasing quantities of public investment and operating revenue to cover their potential deficits, and into doing so without the explicit right to co-ordinate the metropolitan centres' development with provincial or regional affairs surrounding them. (These metropolitan governments are also absolved from the duty of contributing directly to the costs experienced by persons resident in areas they degrade and whose affairs they threaten. This duty is passed to senior levels of government and assumed to be taken care of through taxation differentials and "public policy" towards such areas. The "universalism" of senior governmental legislation and regulation, however, continues to assure that those who have, continue to get); and (d) popular beliefs about the nature of social and political relations, the nature of man himself, and the essentials of a "sound economy" get taken up at federal, provincial, and local government levels to be used for party political ends or to be turned to advantage by some powerful private organization vicariously involved in political affairs.

Federal policy has moved for some decades toward abandoning the "universal" attribute of its legislation, and particularly its financial policies. Considerable sums of federal money are distributed to places which it recognizes as in need. The swings of fashion largely determine the basis of identifying "need," from prairie farm rehabilitation, land and soil utilization, equal opportunity, guaranteed incomes, etc., to pollution, and marine fish stocking. New programs come to light annually to serve as answers to some or other identified "problem." Provincial governments look jealously at these contraventions of "fair and equal" treatment, but have for many years recognized the merits of a differentiated federal policy as a national necessity. Much of their jealousy, however, is derived from pressures within their own province which oblige them to find money for "pressing urban problems." Local city councils could, it seems, handle all the problems if only they were given the means. The federal government, it seems, just will not do the sensible thing of transferring public money to where the growth and productive resource of the nation are so clearly evident — to the provinces with troubled metropolitan areas. Yet historically, these areas have received ever-increasing sums of money, but are never satisfied, nor able to find lasting solutions. Solutions lie, however, not in the redistribution of money *per se;* but in the purposes and direction for which money is to be distributed and used.

With each of the provinces responsible for determining its urban policy, and with the federal government explicit about the extent and nature of its financial support towards provincial policies and plans, the ogre of central federal direction of urban affairs would be removed from Canadian urban politics. The national unity and almost dictatorial direction that lie implicit in Mr. Andras's policy and Dr. Harvey Lithwick's report would be dissipated to levels where political acceptance of a national urban policy for Canada is within the bounds of reality. The role of the federal government would remain as that of national co-ordinator. It would co-ordinate the impinging affairs of the world beyond Canada with the internal aspects of national urban affairs as administered in detail by provincial governments. The provincial-federal relation would then be less one of jealousy of each other and more one of reciprocally related partners in the decisions required to implement a deliberate policy on Canadian and provincial urban development. The difficulty of current federal-provincial relations over urban affairs is the assumption that there is one urban policy to which the provinces must adjust. This assumption is unreal in the face of diversity across Canada and the difficult relations existing in municipal-provincial affairs.

Provincial policies on urban form are likely to be diverse. For example, the geographic factors alone, not to mention such features as the port facilities, and so on, of British Columbia, provide for considerable difference in urban policy — city form, location, economic support, etc., — than in Alberta. Similarly, the industrial and metropolitan centres in Ontario provide differing possibilities and constraints from those of Alberta. This variety in provincial urban forms and policies would afford latitude to the federal government in its influence and direction of support. Currently this latitude is exercised as an aspect of a "special" program, leaving the expectation abroad that the orthodox process of a megalopolis construction is still a fair one to assume. The subtle modes of incentive and negotiable provision which typify federal policies on locational aspects of private investment could be replaced by explicit federal favour in support of a provincial policy of a given kind. The provincial policy in turn would have been explicitly related in its economic and demographic content to national policy. If all this were to happen, private investment would have to take notice.

Concurrently, the provinces would be afforded room to negotiate both upwards to the federal government over the matters relevant to it and downwards to their local authorities. But the relationship would tend toward negotiation over means and ends rather than to manipulation and manoeuvre of each other. The variety of federal forms of assistance would facilitate provincial efforts in furthering their unique policy by sequential timing arrangements and para-provincial co-ordination. The essence of our suggestion is thus its enhanced variety of decision and action at both levels of senior government. In this, our suggestion is antithetical to the straight-jacketed, almost changless nature of the current urban institutional arrangements.

Within Alberta, the consequence of a clear, well-worked-out statement by the provincial government on the form of urban expansion and the policies to be followed to achieve it would be dramatic. A whole host of encapsulating situations would disappear and local authorities would have immediately to turn their attention to the mode of adjusting to provincial policy, instead of the means of competing with the province and their peers in the absence of policy. If Edmonton intended to adopt policies whose consequence would be disastrous to the future of satellite regional centres in the face of provincial policy to support satellite development, then Edmonton would be expected to pay for the consequences of its damage. Similarly, if Calgary decided to continue spending over $20 million a year on street construction and widening to service its downtown core and expanding suburbia, without reference to provincial policy affecting the development of transit-linked centres in the region, then Calgary would be obliged to pay for it without a subsidized dollar. The province will have increasingly to consider the north of the province, for example, the Peace River region in relation to the McKenzie River, as both oil transportation and federal highway policy appear to be requiring it. Similarly, Southern Alberta's developmental difficulties require to be thought through and policy formulated. These are aspects of regional provincial affairs which an urban policy must serve.

At the present time the consequences of the cost of growth are not brought home by way of the mill rate to the metropolitan taxpayer. There is the assumption that all the hustle and bustle, bigger expenditure, larger turnovers, etc., must be generating wealth. They are, of course, for some. When mayors are threatened with a mill increase they expect provincial support in detail, as well as a review of municipal-provincial relations. But, as the metropolitan centres are almost the only places where significant growth is occurring, it stands to reason that they should be supported, so provincial grants are concentrated on the cities. The vicious circle is perpetuated with no genuine attempt to assess the costs of continued metropolitan modes of growth, nor of the absence of a clear provincial urban policy. Only when the costs of continued expenditure in support of unco-ordinated growth are brought home through the mill rate, will a clearer understanding be obtained of alternative growth possibilities within the city itself, and as a consequence of fruitful city-region-province interaction. The general plans are explicit about the costs of the current mode of growth.

Paradoxically, local authorities may be more prepared and would certainly be very much more able to proceed with decisions over priority and sequence of development if they knew the content of provincial urban policy. The "freedom" of local autonomy has for some time turned into fetters, and an explicit provincial policy would, though it appears paradoxical, free the cities to move concertedly and deliberately towards meeting their role within the wider context of the province. Calgary and Edmonton are clearly pre-eminent; but in a lesser way so are Lethbridge, Medicine Hat, and perhaps Red Deer, Grande Prairie, and Lloydminster. Such urban centres, (and there are others) have fought their way forward despite the metropolitan centres and the absence of provincial policy. There is little difficulty in recognizing the regionally centered cities and towns of the province. [9] The smaller towns in their relation to provincial urban policy will create decision difficulties. Many of these offer advantages, both as service centres and residential areas with large lots for families who like that way of life. But to cope with the demise of many of them, a system of removal incentives to families and small businesses faced with losses should be introduced to encourage their relocation.[10] The province has had experience with new towns for two decades, and the only change required in this respect is reliance not on the employment offered by a large exploiting enterprise, but on a more varied employment base supported by provincial incentives to people and industry over costs of relocation. The provincial government would have to rely on its own reputation to secure its investment rather than investing in a good security identified first by private management.

The second major decision required of the province is the mode of coping with the current flexibility of private investment. We suspect this currently to be an area of widespread misunderstanding, prejudice, and fear. It is therefore particularly urgent that research be carried out into it. This will be considered further in the next section, but at this point we mention that our observations suggest a greater readiness than is popularly supposed on the part of private enterprise management to go at least half way to meeting public policy demands.

Their flexibility extends to ingenuity when the circumstances require it. There is already a very varied array of supportive and incentive mechanisms — ranging from taxation, through transportation policy and training schemes, to locational grants — to smooth out many of the cost difficulties of private business. The only place we have identified where such formal schemes are nullified in their effect, is in the current policies of the metropolitan centres towards the attraction of private investment. So long as the provincial government continues to rush to the aid of these centres whenever their rates of unemployment are high, their estimates of expenditure threaten to raise the mill rate, and their urgent capital proposals are in need of yet additional subsidy, there remains little chance of private enterprise management coming to feel the threat of rising urban costs and to consider this in making decisions about location.

Private management's locational decisions would be better served if a well-prepared system of public services were already built into the urban centres identified for growth and industrial development in the provincial urban policy. Where volumes of water are crucial, where power and energy needs are pronounced, where transport is of particular concern, etc., provision must be spelled out in a provincial urban policy. At the present time, the process is almost reversed. While a satisfactory level of service for individuals has been provided over much of the province, the provision of special services for a particular industry has to be made after the locational decision has been made. This provision of service is how they ensure growth to themselves to the detriment of smaller centres which are possibly better located for some reason or other than the larger centres, but which are not capitalized appropriately to accommodate it. When the provincial government subsidizes much of the metropolitan over-supply, it cannot rightly claim to be impartial in its influence over metropolitan and small centre growth. Thus, negotiable provisions at all three levels of government have come to be important in the locational decisions of companies.

Lastly, the role of private lending institutions needs to be considered. Their influence partly concerns the downtown core of the cities, partly concerns the decision as to where family units — single-family dwellings or apartments — will be constructed, partly concerns the influence of land developers on city growth, and partly concerns lending to private persons and businesses for a varied array of activities. The overriding consideration of many of these lending institutions is the safety of their investment. In so far as they hold in trust the savings of citizens, this is obviously an area of concern both to them and to governments. But how far this trust has become blurred by the opportunities for monetary gain in a rapidly changing financial world we were unable to judge. While the evidence has led us to believe that private lending institutions have been largely responsible for decisions that have resulted in the present form of city concentration, there is no inherent reason why this situation need continue. It may be argued that their behaviour and their influence is as much a consequence of their own situational context as a matter of deliberate judgement on their part to influence city growth in the way they appear to have done.

We are conscious that we know too little about the influence of private investment decision on the form of city growth (and vice versa); but we are intrigued by the absence of explicit reference to it in federal urban policy deliberations. It may be that the role of lending institutions has become so entwined with federal political struggles as to be ignored in the world of its reality. It may be that the relation of lending institutions to the federal government and its banking system is so symbiotic as to be considered coexistent in its relation to urban policy. We do not know. But it is apparent that the matter must be raised and resolved if the provincial government is to have a genuine responsibility for urban policy within the province. We do not wish to pass judgement on the Social Credit policy of the 1930s, but the independence of policy that Alberta demonstrated at that time, just as Quebec has been doing in other areas more recently, and British Columbia is also prone to do when convenient, is akin in its attitude to the approach towards urban development suggested here.[11] There would be little purpose served if provincial leadership in urban policy came to be directed by the influence of private lending institutions over locational decisions — a matter which made federal government look rather foolish for over for two decades!

There is in these suggestions a possible conflict of organizational principle. The increasing scale of world organization, both governmental and financial, coupled to the increasing industrialization of the economy and increasing urban mode of living for world populations, will tend to encourage the federal government in its attempts to centralize within itself, urban decision making in Canada. Yet the suggestion made by this study is that provincial governments be made responsible for urban policy within their jurisdictions. This presupposes a decentralization of organizational decision. In so far as this is conflicting, a distribution of function is required. While the national economy, finance and fiscal policy are federal matters, planning of public services and leadership in facilitating the *in situ* distribution of productive services and human occupations may usefully fall to the provinces. Currently, there is a bewildering mixture in the distribution of the various services and responsibilities among the governments. There is very little trust in each other's instruments and machinery. From this perspective, the BNA Act does not appear to have given much guidance to the influences shaping urban policy, except that events and circumstances in the depression appear to have been used to determine the relative inconsequence of provincial decision over urban developmental matters. The federal and provincial governments should reconsider this whole area concurrently with their deliberations over possible urban policies.

The Implications for Research

Our concern in this concluding section is to suggest the areas of research most likely to be rewarding in Alberta's urban process. We are not concerned with the relevance of the Alberta situation for theoretical matters, though there are rich possibilities in this regard. It is also beyond our capacity to list seriatim the questions of importance. Rather we identify the broad areas within which the research of many disciplines may usefully be done to contribute to the knowledge required for governmental and other purposes. We do not advocate that any search for "perfect knowledge" or a absolute certainty over any trivial matter be undertaken. In the dynamic of events such knowledge is inclined to be out of date before it is used, and much unnecessary care can be devoted to levels of accuracy which are rarely needed in the applied situation.

What has struck us forcefully is the paucity of studies which aim to catch, within tolerable limits of accuracy, the bird's eye view of large-scale processes. We welcomed E. H. Dale's thesis on the contribution of municipal government to Edmonton's historical development, not alone because an immense amount of work had been put into it, but because it tried to deal with a large-scale topic bravely. Over recent decades, the social sciences have tended to study less and less in more and more detail. Such an approach is useful more in the natural sciences where the known constancies of relationship make it worth while and offer recognized applied uses. While there is certainly a place in the social sciences for such studies, fashionable emphasis can forestall the contribution of less accurate and more conjectural studies to the understanding of large-scale processes. (These more conjectural studies are also more risky for the researcher's reputation!) We acknowledge that not all researchers are given to the broader study, but greater encouragement appears necessary to those who are. Concurrently, we would recommend that the provincial government provide financial help to those masters' degree candidates intending to do a field-work enquiry into a topic of limited scale. The contribution of this scale of research has been overlooked in Canada generally from a financial support point of view. The larger-scale studies are dependent on the detailed work done at the base if they are not to become overly conjectural and speculative.

The topics of research concerned may be broadly divided into three. First are those of an enduring nature irrespective of the policies yet to be decided by the two senior levels of government. In this category fall topics such as inter-provincial relations[12], provincial-federal relations, the response of Alberta to particular federal programs, the consequence for Alberta of federal policy in the Canadian North, the ways in which other provinces of Canada have related to federal urban initiatives, etc. Second are research topics which become important if the current federal national urban policy for Canada comes to nought, or is amended in such a way as to continue the trends of the past thirty years under the guise of a new name or fashionable swing of emphasis. In such an event, the encapsulated situation of the provincial government and of Alberta's local governments would continue much as before. The urban process within the province would hardly change. This encapsulated situation throws up a set of research topics peculiarly its own. Third, in the event of fundamental changes in governmental urban policy being introduced, then a new emphasis to research immediately emerges.

Whatever direction governments may go after this series of conferences is passed, there is clearly an urgent need for the Alberta government greatly to increase its research capacity in urban affairs. If the federal government remains intent on managing national urban policy, it will still be in the interest of Alberta to match the federal research input. Alberta could readily be drawn unsuspectingly into the federal orbit of urban research and planning in ways detrimental to the province or to any chance the province may have of taking its own initiative. The metropolitan centres of Alberta, for example, have generated a research capacity for other reasons than status and pleasure. Their competitive relation *inter se* and to other Canadian centres, their manipulation of senior governments, and their difficulties with rapid growth have all contributed to this trend. The province might take heed of the conditions that encourage research. Research is fundamental to success in political processes. The relative inconsequence of provincial decision in the past may have obscured this point, but research should not be treated as a luxury in today's affairs.

Research topics of an enduring nature — irrespective of possible policy changes — should be additional to the array of data currently collected routinely by official agencies or done as special projects by such agencies. The federal monographs on the censuses, on Canadian urbanization, the reports of the Economic Council, etc., are good, standard fare and should be supported. But the research likely to aid the province most tends to be comparative in nature. For example, what alternative models are there to planning legislation than those based on land use and subdivision control? Where have they been tried, under what conditions and with what effects? Under what conditions would they aid the Albertan context? Similarly, how have other provinces dealt with federal urban programs, with what results? It is this comparative perspective that will assist in providing a variety of choices when decisions have to be taken. There is far too much convenient amendment to worn-out principles on the Alberta statute books to suggest long-term success in the handling of the province's affairs.

Within this type of research topic also fall those concerned with private companies in the province. Our enquiries revealed interest in the oil industry, and certain groups or types of industry; but we found nothing that revealed the conditions under which companies were, for good reason, bound to locate in metropolitan centres or were capable, with given public services supplied, of carrying on successfully in other centres. There are economic studies on this problem, but they are rarely based on field-work in the actual companies. They tend to rely on statistical evidence to the exclusion of *in situ* field analysis. Our field studies of certain industries in Southern Alberta suggested that internal company policy — particularly on labour, training and housing — was crucial to their success in the smaller and degraded centres.

We also found that public services were desperately slow to respond to the requirements of such companies. There was in these services a rigidity, brought about both by local government encapsulation and by the inability of provincial departments to make decisions that would "stick," which frustrated company management and made it look with favour on the flexible opportunism of the metropolitan centres.

More casual observation (the question urgently needs further research) suggested that private lending institutions have staked out regions of the province where their business is predominant. To some extent, this is due to the paucity of business in certain areas, which makes it pay to limit what there is to one company. But we noted a similar regional emphasis in certain other areas, e.g., the agricultural machinery industry, but to a lesser extent. If regionalism is the necessity for certain companies, it is as well to know it. Company use of government policy to invade the territory of another company is not unknown. Similarly, it is necessary to know what conditions govern the spread or distribution of large retail stores in the province. Some large retailers interviewed were explicit about their "catchment area" and could show the number of accounts opened by people at given distances from the store. Such information becomes vital in assessing the needs of smaller growth centres for good retail services, for considering the use of incentives to retailers offering a wide range of goods in centres intended for growth, and so forth.

There is an enormous area of research required into private enterprise. As previously mentioned, private enterprise is the subject of very fixed and often prejudiced conception. This fact has led to business management itself being hyper-sensitive and suspicious of enquiry; but we found no inherent difficulties in researching this area if the usual courtesies and respect for confidence were evinced. Many managers showed a keen sensitivity to the exploitation of governmental amenities and its possible consequences for them. While their expertise in handling governments is evident in many instances, their disposition to respect public authorities and to work within the terms of public policy was equally clear. We suggest that much more research be done and published into the conditions necessary for both parties — public and private — to work to mutual benefit. The old theory of a separation of activity in this hypothetically conflicting relationship is gone for good, and would be better forgotten. The facts of the current world suggest that an intimate, symbiotic relation exists between governments at all levels and privately organized capital at all levels. This fact should be faced squarely and made the subject of published analysis, particularly if a fundamental change in urban policy — nationally or provincially — is under serious consideration. Further, the dynamic of private organization should be studied continuously.

The second topic of research concern — that topic dependent upon little effective change being introduced in senior governmental urban policy — requires an identification of research problems likely to reveal the political nature of current urban affairs. We considered, and argued, that manipulation and manoeuvre were currently the typical feature of local government, and, to a lesser extent, of the provincial government in its relations inwards to the province. We also argued that because of the encapsulated situation and stalemated condition of public authorities in so far as the "direction" of urban growth was concerned, private enterprise in a variety of forms, but especially the land developers and lending institutions, were in fact setting the pattern of growth. Further, we argued that a great deal of public investment is being made for purposes oblique to a deliberate urban developmental policy — unemployment relief, housing the poor, road construction, etc. While assisting the urban condition, and the condition of urban dwellers, much public investment was devoted to coping with "growth," to the relief of "pressing problems," etc., rather than being explicitly directed to long-term planning and to rewarding means to ends relations.

The irony of the situation is shown in the fact that the metropolitan centres contain much of the expertise of the province which appears currently to be under-effective. Besides the local conflict of professionals with administrators and elected councils, is the difficulty experienced by locally responsible professionals from the paucity of provincial direction. Given the encapsulated situation of governments generally, one area of potential relief and benefit to local authorities in Alberta would be clearer and more explicit provincial policy on matters such as transport, energy supplies, water and pollution control, etc., as they affect the cities. If metropolitan regions only could be assisted — if a province-wide provincial policy proves too much — by being advised what the province expected on, say, rapid transit and regional rapid transit, the professional cadres of local government staffs would be able to plan with greater certainty and confidence. They could then relate more administratively, and less politically, to their elected authorities if this major unknown was resolved.

We suggest that the greatest benefits would arise from political analysis and studies of the economic, engineering, and planning aspects of, at least, regions. At present, the city-bound professional has limited rights beyond his own political jurisdiction, the regional professional is caught up in a politically difficult situation, and the provincial professional is inclined to think that "local autonomy" means that the others should decide. It is fundamentally a provincial responsibility to set the level of co-ordination and to see that provincial inputs of decision relieve the current tendency to stalemate at the subordinate levels, both municipal and regional.

Further, there is an urgent need for the re-examination of the costs of city growth under the existing encapsulated situation. There are strong indications that costs are rising substantially faster than population. This has been the case for some decades, but the extent of the differential should be watched. Though the argument was often put to us that it would be more expensive to provide similar public services in other urban centres than Calgary and Edmonton, we could find no empirical studies that demonstrated it. We only observe that present metropolitan capital expenditure is serving as a useful tool to obtain greater and greater quantities of senior government finance, without much evidence of long-term direction and identifiable economic return on its expenditure. We observe also that many smaller centres have unused capacity in many items of public services, are keen to expand, have useful potential in land and labour, and could complement the metropolitan centres in many useful ways.

Lastly, if a fundamental change is introduced by one or both senior governments, the need for research will be considerably greater. Every relationship among governments and between government and private enterprise will be affected. In such an event, the emphasis of provincial research should initially be given to provincial-federal relations as they affect urban development. The provincial administration may, because of research staff shortages, have to rely heavily on the advice of its municipal and regional planning commission staffs to prepare the evidence and serve the advice on internal provincial urban affairs while the provincial-federal relationship is worked out. The first step in such a situation is for the provincial government to declare clearly and unambiguously what its policy on the critical aspects of urban development will be.

The critical aspects include transportation (rapid transit as a metropolitan service, and as a regional service), the relation it proposes to take up concerning mortgage lending services in the cities and selected smaller centres, its policy on public or private land assembly and speculation on land values, the explicit identification of growth centres to serve the metropolitan, regional and provincial interests, the provision of selected public amenities in such centres ahead of the location of private industrial and commercial investment in those centres, and the role it expects Calgary and Edmonton to play in the provincial urban plan. That Calgary and Edmonton will be the most affected by such a drastic change in policy goes without saying, but these cities have much to gain from a more deliberate identification of their contribution to their regions and to the province. Their pre-eminence is beyond question. There will be the need to relieve them of much of their current capital debt if their rate of growth is to be slowed and made more rationally directed to their metropolitan role within the province. This debt already consumes a sizable percentage of the mill rate, and it cannot be allowed to make these cities high-cost places in which to work and live, nor to disqualify them from the additional public investment required of them to play a genuinely provincial role.

A second step is for the provincial government to distribute its professional and departmental senior staff throughout the province. We do not envisage a system of regional government, but a system of senior professional and administrative officers settled with some permanence in the identified growth centres of the province in order to relate local issues, both planning and administrative, to provincial and, where necessary, federal points of decision making. A provincial urban policy (and certainly a federal urban policy) cannot be administered from head office alone. The occasional visit of ministers and senior administrators is inadequate without a cadre of locally resident officers. Centralization was a feasible proposition under theories of "local autonomy," "provincial autonomy," and what have you. The facts of the matter are that urban inter-communication and symbiotic connectedness no longer permit this administrative mode to be effective. The point of final decision may lie far removed, but the context of the local situation tends to determine the enduring mode of eventual operation. It is therefore in the local situation that responsible and trusted officials must be placed. Their duties would be primarily co-ordinatory. This is undeniably a senior government responsibility the moment the senior governments assume a *de facto* responsibility for the direction of urban affairs.

We do not envisage that the *de facto* responsibilities of local governments will be reduced; though the *de jure* and ideological "freedoms" supposed to adhere presently to local government may well be. The evidence we have suggests that local authorities are unable currently to direct urban development in ways they themselves often seek and unsuccessfully aspire to. Provincial leadership and senior government support may well provide local leaders with a sense of achievement scarcely evident today. There is a clear area of research potential at every local level, both municipal and provincial. Many will be local studies with local relevance; but they are nonetheless important for their usefulness at this level.

In the final analysis, any urban policy will be measured on the ground, in the local scene, and in the minds of local people.

National accounts, grand political strategy, and recurring problems appear to be its measure currently. The error of federal urban policy in 1970 was precisely its ignoring of the local influence — it had to assume a non-existent and non-achievable local co-operation. No society, whether rural or urban, can be built on the basis of abstraction alone. The memory and accuracy of the computer can be an immensely useful asset, but it is the living of people that finally determines a cultural existence and its future. Science is but one of man's tools, and research is a critical attribute of the scientific mode of thought; but the conditions of men's lives, what they are able to put into it in ways that are meaningful to them, determine their final response to an urban cultural mode. The public participatory policies of all levels of government in recent years have been aimed in the right direction, but the condition of participation under present social arrangements has been heavily political and rather rarely advisory. In this area also, useful research contributions could be made.

Notes

1. Though it may be argued that a child's education or a citizen's health must be subsidized irrespective of where he lives, there is evidence of high convenience expectations coupled with empty classrooms and difficulties in the planning of new services because of developmental discontinuity in the urban administration of education.
2. Kenward, J.K. "Political manipulation and rewards in the Crowsnest Pass, Southern Alberta." Unpublished MA thesis, Department of Political Science, Sociology and Anthropology, Simon Fraser University, Burnaby, British Columbia, July, 1971.
3. We are conscious that the senior levels of government suffer encapsulation through elective institutions, but the case of local government differs in the directness of the relation of citizens to their representatives.
4. That the national urban policy for Canada of the federal government tacitly assumes a federal direction of urban affairs was mentioned in volume I of this work. But in the present argument we assume that the provincial governments could direct urban affairs.
5. Our inability to do the work necessary was a consequence of time limits rather than non-co-operation on their part. We would like to thank the officials of provincial and regional boards and commissions for their efforts at assisting us and for putting up with our questioning and concern over details.
6. We suspect a similarly difficult situation exists in the more specialized and narrow administrative concerns of health and education, but have not pursued it in detail.
7. *The Politics of Canadian Urbanization,* vol. 1 of this work, Chapter 7, p.318.
8. That the depression of the 1930s should have been the time when federal policy moved so explicity to encapsulate the provinces, at least in respect of housing, appears to have a significance for historians and sociologists greater than we have identified. Possibly this is linked to federal-provincial politics, possibly to monetary and fiscal politics of that time, and possibly of federal politics internationally over such matters as protectionism, free trade, etc.
9. Presently there is a mystery and uncertainty surrounding which of the smaller urban centres should be considered as having growth potential. This is a fanciful situation that should be cleared up speedily to remove the uncertainty surrounding both public and private investment decisions. There can be no meaningful planning in such centres and regions so long as this prevails. The work of Regional Planning Commissions is correspondingly thwarted so long as this uncertainty remains. Because of their membership, these commissions are unable to make public the identification of obvious growth areas. The provincial level of authority should do the job and thereby free the regional commissions from their encapsulated situation in this important respect. There would be no need for a planning fund and similarly laborious administrative trimmings were steps of this kind implemented.
10. There has been some experience of this in the Maritimes recently, and we understand the scheme was used in Alberta before, but we have not pursued it.

11. One critical factor in the future will be the role to be played by the provincial housing authorities — in Alberta by the Alberta Housing Corporation — relative to provincial urban policy, the NHA, CMHC, and the lending institutions.
12. Perhaps it is uncommon to have urban affairs understood through inter-provincial relations, but we refer to such matters as provincial industrial incentives policies, water policies and their consequences for Alberta; coal exploration and its effects on Albertan towns, etc.

Bibliography

The purpose of this bibliography is to list in one place the sources for the material quoted and the statements made in the text of both volumes in this study. The items in the bibliography are grouped according to kind of source and to status of publication. Generally, they move from published material fairly easily accessible to unpublished material not so easily accessible.

I. Non-Governmental Sources

A: Books

Alonso, W., "Planning as a Profession," in H. Wentworth Eldredge (ed.), *Taming Megalopolis,* New York, Praeger, 1967.

Bailey, F. G., *Strategems and Spoils,* Toronto, Copp Clark Co., 1969.

Berton, Pierre, *The National Dream: The Great Railway 1871-1881,* Toronto/Montreal, McClelland Stewart Ltd., 1970.

— *The Last Spike: The Great Railway 1881-1885,* Toronto/Montreal, McClelland and Stewart Ltd., 1971.

Blue, John, *Alberta: Past and Present,* Volume One, Chicago, Pioneer Historical Publishing House, 1924.

Blumenfeld, Hans, *The Modern Metropolis,* Cambridge, MIT Press, 1967.

Brewis, T. N., *Regional Economic Policies in Canada,* Toronto, Macmillan, 1967.

Gershaw, F. W., *Saamis: The Medicine Hat,* Medicine Hat, Val Marshall Printing Ltd., n.d.

Gerth, H. H., and Mills, C. W., (eds.), *From Max Weber,* London, Kegan Paul, Trench, Trubner and Company Ltd., 1947.

Gertler, Leonard, O., "Some Economic and Social Influences on Regional Planning in Alberta," in Gertler (ed.), *Planning the Canadian Environment,* Montreal, Harvest House, 1968.

Hanson, Eric J., *Local Government in Alberta,* Toronto, McClelland and Stewart Ltd., 1956.

Hellyer, Paul T., *Agenda: A Plan for Action,* Scarborough (Ont.), Prentice-Hall of Canada Ltd., 1971.

Irving, John A., *The Social Credit Movement in Alberta,* University of Toronto Press, 1959, paperback ed., 1968.

Johnson, L. P. V., and MacNutt, Ola J., *Aberhart of Alberta,* Edmonton, Co-op Press Ltd. for the Institute of Applied Art, 1970.
Kellough, W. R., and Beaton, W., "Anatomy of the Housing Shortage," in R. Matsushita (ed.), *Issues for the Seventies: Housing,* Toronto, McGraw-Hill, 1971.
Kenward, John K., "Contemporary Administrative Problems," in Dr. F. Jankunis (ed.), *Southern Alberta: A Regional Perspective,* Department of Geography, University of Lethbridge, Lethbridge, Alberta, 1971.
Kindleberger, Charles (ed.), *The International Corporation, Cambridge. MIT Press, 1970.*
MacGregor, J. G., *Edmonton: A History,* Edmonton, M. G. Hurtig Publishers, 1967.
MacPherson, C. B., *Democracy in Alberta: Social Credit and the Party System,* University of Toronto Press, second edition, 1962.
Moore, A. M., Perry, J. H. and Beach, D. I., *The Financing of Canadian Federation, the First Hundred Years,* Toronto, Canadian Tax Foundation, 1966.
Myrdal, Gunnar, *Rich Lands and Poor,* New York, Harpers, 1957
Nowland, D. and N., *The Bad Trip,* New Press/House of Anansi, 1970.
Thomas, L. G., *The Liberal Party in Alberta,* University of Toronto Press, 1959.
Turner, Louis, *Invisible Empires,* New York, Harcourt, 1971.

B: Journal Articles

Boumol, W., "Macroeconomics of Unbalanced Growth: The Anatomy of Urban Crisis," *American Economic Review,* 58 (1967), 415-426.
Gibson, John, "The Impact of the Railroad on Urban Patterns . . . An Alberta Example," *The Albertan Geographer* (Department of Geography, University of Alberta, Edmonton), 1 (1964-65), 41-6.
Hanson, E. J., "Provincial Grants in Alberta," *The Canadian Tax Journal,* (Sept.-Oct., 1953).
Laux, F. A., "The Zoning Game: Alberta Style," *Alberta Law Review,* 9 (1971), 268-308.
— "The Zoning Game — Alberta Style: Part II, Development Control," *Alberta Law Review,* 10 (1972), 1-37.
"Regional Potpurri," *TPIC News* (Town Planning Institute of Canada), August 1971 and August 1972.

C: Newspapers

The Albertan, October 30, 1970; January 5, January 7, February 1, April 26, May 5, 1972.
The Calgary Herald, February 29, 1970; February 20, August 14, November 27, December 17, 1971; January 3, 4, 5, 12, 13, 17, 26, February 4, 9, 10, 12, 15, 23, 24, 25, 29, March 1, 2, 10, 16, 24, 27, 28, April 18-22, 24-27, May 6, 8, 9, 13, 18, 24, June 17, 1972.
Canadian Homes section, *The Canadian Magazine and The Canadian Magazine Star Weekly.* October 1971.
Edmonton Journal, March 26, December 30, 1968; November 17, 1971.

The Financial Post, December 14, 1957; January 16, December 18, 1971.
Lethbridge Herald, April 2, 3, 6, August 6, 1970.
Rocky View News and Market Examiner, November 30, 1971.

D: Theses

Anderson, James, "Change in a Central Place System: Trade Centres and Rural Service in Central Alberta." Unpublished MA Thesis, Department of Geography, University of Alberta, 1967.
Bussard, Lawrence H., "Early History of Calgary." Unpublished MA Thesis, Department of History, University of Alberta, 1935.
Chan, Wah May Winnie, "The Impact of the Technical Planning Board on the Morphology of Edmonton." Unpublished MA Thesis, Department of Geography, University of Alberta, 1969.
Dale, Edmund H., "The Role of Successive Town and City Councils in the Evolution of Edmonton, Alberta, 1892 to 1966." Unpublished PhD Thesis, Department of Geography, University of Alberta, Edmonton, 1969.
Kenward, J. K., "Political Manipulation and Rewards in The Crowsnest Pass, Southern Alberta." Unpublished MA Thesis, Department of Political Science, Sociology and Anthropology, Simon Fraser University, Burbaby, B.C., 1971.

E: Reports, Briefs, Unpublished Manuscripts

Bowness Community Association, Planning and Development Committee, Report to the Mayor, February 18, 1972 (Calgary).
Canadian Chemcell Company Ltd., Submission to the Local Authorities Board, May 30, 1963 (Edmonton).
Canadian Industries Ltd., Submission to the Local Authorities Board, May, 1963 (Edmonton).
Dant, Noel, "A Brief History of the Planning Statutes in Alberta," unpublished paper.
Hickling-Johnson Ltd., Management Consultants, *Economic Study: Town of Fort Saskatchewan,* June 1970.
The Immorality of the Motor Car, An Information Project of The University Practicum in Community Analysis, Community Resources Division, The Department of Extension, The University of Alberta, Winter Session 1970-71.
Seymour, Horace L., "Town Planning Progress in Alberta up to December 31st, 1931," manuscript in Provincial Archives, Edmonton.
Social Planning Council of Calgary, *Housing in Calgary,* January 1968.
Society for Pollution and Environmental Control, Brief to the Public Hearing, February 22, 1972, Concerning City of Calgary Transportation System Bylaw No. 8500.
Urban Development Institute, Calgary Chapter, Charter.
Urban Research Group, *Decision Making in Plant Site Location,* Saskatoon, Saskatchewan, September 1970.

II: Governmental Sources

A: Federal

Canada Year Book, 1911 to 1967, but especially 1936, 1938, 1946, and 1967.

1. House of Commons:

House of Commons Debates, 1935 to 1970.
House of Commons, Special Committee on Housing, *Report,* Ottawa, Government Printer, 1935.
House of Commons, Standing Committee on Health, Welfare, and Social Affairs, *Minutes of Proceedings and Evidence,* No. 39, June 5, 1969.
House of Commons, Standing Committee on Regional Development, *Minutes of Proceedings and Evidence,* No. 15, June 11, 1969, and No. 16, June 16, 1969.

2. Senate:

Senate of Canada, *Report of the Special Committee on Land Use in Canada,* Ottawa, Queens Printer, 1964.

3. Royal Commissions and Task Forces:

Graver, A. E., *Housing, a Study Prepared for the Royal Commission on Dominion-Provincial Relations,* Ottawa, 1939.
Mackintosh, W. A., *The Economic Background of Dominion-Provincial Relations,* being Appendix 3 to the *Report of the Royal Commission on Dominion-Provincial Relations,* Ottawa, 1939.
1964 Report of the Royal Commission on Banking and Finance, Ottawa, Queen's Printer, 1965.
Report of the Task Force on Housing and Urban Development, Ottawa, Queen's Printer, 1969.

4. Various Government Departments, Councils, and Bureaus:

Federal Services for Businessmen, Department of Industry, Trade and Commerce, Ottawa, Queen's Printer, 1970.
McCrorie, James N., *A.R.D.A.: An Experiment in Development Planning,* Special Study No. 2, Canadian Council on Rural Development, Ottawa, Queen's Printer, 1969.
Monthly Reports, Department of Regional Economic Expansion, Ottawa, 1970.
Stone, L. O., *Urban Development in Canada,* 1961 Census Monograph, Dominion Bureau of Statistics, Ottawa, 1967.

5. Economic Council of Canada:

Anderson, Isobel B., *Internal Migration in Canada, — 1921-61,* Economic Council of Canada, Staff Study 13, Ottawa, 1966.
Buckley, Helen, and Tihanyi, Eva, *Canadian Policies for Rural Adjustment,* Economic Council of Canada, Special Study No. 7, Ottawa, Queen's Printer, 1967.
Economic Council of Canada, *Fourth Annual Review: The Canadian Economy from the 1960's to the 1970's,* Ottawa, 1967.

Illing, Wolfgang M., *Housing Demand to 1970,* Economic Council of Canada, Staff Study 4, Ottawa, 1965.
Illing, Wolfgang M., Kasahaia, Yoshiko, Denton, F. T., and George, M. W., *Population, Family, Household, and Labour Force Growth to 1980,* Economic Council of Canada, Staff Study 19, Ottawa, 1967.

6. Central Mortgage and Housing Corporation:

Andras, Robert (federal minister responsible for housing), "An Address to the Canadian Institute of Public Affairs," Toronto, February 27, 1970.
— Press Release, CMHC, Ottawa, June 10, 1970.
— "Address to the Union of British Columbia Municipalities," Press Release, CMHC, Ottawa, September 17, 1970.
— "Address to the 66th Annual Conference of the Union of Nova Scotia Municipalities," Press Release, CMHC, Ottawa, May 17, 1971.
— "Address to the Conference on Cities, Indianapolis, Indiana," Press Release, CMHC, Ottawa, May 26, 1971.
— "Address to the National Forum of the American Institute of Architects, Detroit, Michigan," Press Release, CMHC, Ottawa, June 23, 1971.
— "Federal Minister Responsible for Housing, Remarks by," Press Release, CMHC, Ottawa, June 28, 1971.
— "Address to The Canadian Real Estate Association, Montreal," Press Release, CMHC, Ottawa, October 20, 1971.
Canadian Housing Statistics, CMHC, Ottawa, 1960, 4th quarter 1960, 4th quarter 1965, 1967, 1970, March 1971.
CMHC Report — Land Values (for year 1971).
Feldman, L. D., *et al., A Survey of Alternative Urban Policies,* Research Monograph 6, CMHC, Ottawa, 1971.
Gillespie, W. L., *The Urban Public Economy,* Research Monograph 4, CMHC, Ottawa.
Housing and Urban Growth in Canada, CMHC, Ottawa, 1956.
Lithwick, N. H., *Urban Canada: Problems and Prospects. A Report Prepared for the Hon. R. K. Andras, Minister for Housing,* CMHC, Ottawa, 1970.
Press Releases, CMHC, Ottawa, November 15 and 17, 1971.

7. Other:

Press Releases, Office of the Prime Minister, Ottawa, November 15-17, 1971.

B: Inter-Provincial Organizations

Atlantic Development Council, *A Strategy for the Economic Development of the Atlantic Region, 1971-1981,* Fredericton (N.B.), 1971.
Canadian Federation of Mayors and Municipalities, *Brief to the Prime Minister of Canada, Ottawa,* April 26, 1971.
The Municipality in the Canadian Federation, Position Paper prepared by the Joint Municipal Committee on Intergovernmental Relations, Canadian Federation of Mayors and Municipalities, August 1970.

C: Provincial (Alberta)

1. Laws and Orders:

Statues of Alberta, 1906 to 1970.
Revised Statutes of Alberta, 1922 to 1970.
Order-in-Council No. 969-53, *The Alberta Gazette,* July 15, 1953, 1126. (Order dated July 6, 1953).
Provincial Planning Board Order 286-M-68, October 16, 1968.
Provincial Planning Board Order, October 27, 1971.
Local Authorities Board Order No. 1234, March 31, 1964, *The Alberta Gazette,* April 30, 1964, 959-997.
— No. 3981, *The Alberta Gazette.* January 15, 1969, 114-120
— No. 4192, *The Alberta Gazette.* May 31, 1969, 1227-1233.
— No. 4804, *The Alberta Gazette.* August 15, 1970, 1582-1589.
— No. 5008, *The Alberta Gazette,* January 15, 1971, 207-222.
— No. 5010, *The Alberta Gazette,* January 15, 1971, 226-231.
— No. 5505, *The Alberta Gazette,* November 15, 1971, 2831-2837.

2. Government of Alberta — Policy Speeches and Statements:

Budget Speeches to the Legislature, 1950, 1952, 1953, 1954, 1955, 1957, 1958, 1962, 1963, 1966, 1967, 1969, 1970, 1971, Edmonton, Queen's Printer.
Government of the Province of Alberta, *The Case for Alberta 1938,* Edmonton, 1938.
Manning, the Hon. E. C., *A White Paper on Human Resources Development,* presented to the Alberta Legislature, March 1967.
— Speech to the Legislature, March 5, 1951, Edmonton, Queen's Printer.
Strom, the Hon. Harry E., "Address to the Town Planning Institute of Canada, 1970 Conference, Edmonton, on July 21, 1970," Press Release, Office of the Premier, July 21, 1970.
— Premier of Alberta, "*A Position Paper* to the Federal-Provincial Constitutional Conference in Ottawa, September, 1970," Edmonton, Queen's Printer, 1970.
— "Address to the Alberta Urban Municipalities Association," Press Release, Office of the Premier, Edmonton, October 30, 1970.

3. Royal Commissions, Special Committees, Task Forces:

The Interim First Report of the Co-Terminous Boundary Commission, Edmonton, Government of the Province of Alberta, 1953.
Report of the Public Expenditure and Revenue Study Committee, Province of Alberta, Edmonton, March 1966.
"Report of the Royal Commission on Taxation," *Sessional Paper* No. 71, 1948, Government of the Province of Alberta, Edmonton, February 12, 1948.
Report of the Royal Commission on the Metropolitan Development of Calgary and Edmonton, Edmonton, Queen's Printer, 1956. (McNally Commission Report.)
Report of the Special Committee Appointed by the Government of Alberta to Study Assessment and Taxation, Edmonton, March, 1970.

Task Force on Urbanization and the Future, *The Role of Regional Planning,* Edmonton, November 1971.

4. Government Departments; Bureaus, and Corporations:

Alberta Bureau of Statistics, *Alberta Industry and Resources,* Edmonton, 1970.

Alberta Housing and Urban Renewal Corporation, *Alberta Housing Profile,* September 10, 1968.

— *A Satellite Community Study for the Edmonton and Calgary Areas,* October 1969.

Alberta Housing Corporation, "Public Housing," Pamphlet, Alberta Housing Corporation Public Relations Department, n.d.

Department of Education, *Thirty-Third Annual Report,* 1938.

Department of Education, *Forty-Third Annual Report,* 1948.

Department of Municipal Affairs, *The Alberta Planning Fund: To Provide Equitable Financing For: Regional Planning, Provincial Planning,* March 1971. (Later draft of *A Proposal* etc., below).

— *Municipal Statistics including Improvement Districts in Special Areas for the year ended December 31, 1969.*

— *A Proposal: To Provide Equitable Financing: City Planning, Regional Planning, Provincial Planning,* August 1970. (Earlier draft of *The Alberta Planning Fund,* above.)

— "The Story of the Industrial Tax Proposal," Unpublished Brief, n.d. (*circa* 1961).

Minister of Municipal Affairs, Statement, January 5, 1972.

Municipal Development and Loan Board, *Annual Report,* March 31, 1968.

Public Accounts of the Province of Alberta, 1939-1941.

The Treasury Department Ledger, Edmonton.

5. Local Authorities Board (LAB) (Alberta):

LAB, Application for Annexation, March 9, 1971. (Concerns the MacEwan Glens application, Calgary.)

— hearings re: Annexation of Jasper Place and other lands to the City of Edmonton, 1963.

— Transcript of Annexation Hearings re: R. Bolster Property (Lot A), March 3, 1969.

Transcript of proceedings, Annexation No. C-20-A, City of Edmonton, re: Alldritt Construction Ltd., held in Edmonton Court House, room 9, March 4, 1970.

Transcript of proceedings of hearings before the Local Authorities Board in regard to the Proposed BACM Annexation of Land, May 19, 20, 21, 1970.

Transcript of public hearings, Annexation C-20-A4, City of Edmonton South-East Development Area, held at Edmonton Court House, room 9, November 24, 1970.

D: Intermediate and Regional Organizations (Alberta)

Calgary Regional Planning Commission, "Guide Sheet as to replies and suggested action resulting from referral of the Preliminary Regional Plan," February 1, 1971.

— *Minutes,* April 14, May 7, 1971.
— *Preliminary Regional Plan,* July 29, 1963, and *Amendments,* May 1, 1964, and October 1, 1965.
Edmonton District (now Regional) Planning Commission, "The Edmonton District Water Supply: A Preliminary Study," 1960.
— *Annual Reports,* 1961-1970.
— Meeting, October 7, 1970, Item XIV.
Edmonton Regional Planning Commission staff, re: *Spruce Grove Development Plan,* August 24, 1970.
Urban Crisis: Alberta Municipal Finance Study, prepared by the Cities of Alberta, The Alberta Urban Municipalities Association, and the Public and Separate School Boards in each city, January 8, 1968.
The Urban Fiscal Problem — Piecemeal or Aggregate Solutions? Position Paper, The Alberta Urban Municipalities Association, 64th Annual Convention, 1970.

E: Municipal (Alberta)

1. Edmonton:

Adams, T. E., Commissioner of Economic Affairs, City of Edmonton, *1972 Current Budget Overview,* January 17, 1972.
Bargen, P., Chief Commissioner, *A Review of Provincial Involvement in the Land Assembly Program,* September 8, 1969.
Gillespie, W. E., Roadway Design Engineer, City of Edmonton, "Progress Report on Edmonton's Roadway Program," presented to the Edmonton Chamber of Commerce Council Meeting, September 16, 1970.
Hanson, E. J., *The Potential Unification of the Edmonton Metropolitan Area,* a Report prepared for the City of Edmonton, 1968.
The City of Edmonton, *City Boundaries and a Unitary Form of Government, A Proposal,* Brief submitted to the Metropolitan Affairs Committee of the Provincial Government, March 1972.
— *Estimates of Capital Expenditures for the Years 1971-1980,* Summary.
— *The General Plan,* Bylaw 3279, adopted May 18, 1971.
— "Capital Estimates — Source of Funds, Summary," 1970.
City Commissioners; Report to City Council, November 3, 1959.
City Commission Board Report No. 8, February 17, 1969.
— March 10, 1969.
City Commissioners' Report No. 4 to the Aldermen of the City of Edmonton, "1971 Current Budget," January 22, 1971.
City Council, *Minutes,* May 27, August 20, 1957; June 26, 1958; May 6, 24, November 28, 1960; February 13, March 13, May 5, 1961; February 19, June 25, July 3, 1962; April 6, 1964; November 14, 1967; February 12, March 25, May 27, 1968; February 2, April 29, October 23, 1969; April 26, 1971.
City Council, Annotated Agenda, July 19, 1971.
— Financing and Budgeting Committee, Report No. 7, April 1, 1969.
— Report of the Public Expenditure and Revenue Study Committee, March 1966.

City Planning Department, "Appendix II," *Amendments to the City of Edmonton General Plan,* May 1971.
— *BACM Proposal,* October 1969.
— *General Plan.*
— memorandum, May 1969.
— *A New Area for Residential Growth for the City,* January 30, 1969.
— Research Branch, *Records of Supply of Vacant Serviced Lots in Developing Residential Areas,* n.d.
— Report to City Council, February 1, 1971.
— *Residential Land Use Staging 1967-1981* June 1967.
— *Residential Land Use Study 1967-1971,* June 1967.
— *Revisions to the General Plan suggested at the Council Meeting held November 16, 1970, February 1, 1971.*
— Submission by the City of Edmonton at the Public Hearing, November 1970.
Edmonton Public School Board, "Accommodation Report and Building Program, 1971."
Re: Staging of Residential Development, Joint Brief by the Public and Separate School Boards presented to City Council, April 16, 1970.
Minutes of meeting with Mr. R. Orysiuk, Alberta Housing Corporation, Mr. P. Ellwood, City Planning Department and P. Bargen, Chief Commissioner, City of Edmonton, July 28, 1969.
Minutes of meeting of Alberta Housing Corporation and City representatives re land assembly, August 26, 1969.

2. Calgary:

City of Calgary, *Annual Report,* 1970.
— Current Budget 1972 Estimates.
— Evidence given before the Hellyer Task Force, November, 1968.
— *The Municipal Manual,* 1920.
— *The Municipal Manual,* 1970.
— Transportation System Bylaw No. 8500, Supplementary Information.
City of Calgary's Board of Commissioners, Submission to Calgary Regional Planning Commission, January 26, 1971.
City Commissioners' Report re MacEwan Glens, June 2, 1971.
City Commissioner's Report to the City Council's Operations and Development Committee, April 10, 1972.
Citizens' Budget Commission, *Report on 1971 Capital Budget,* Part 1, February 22, 1971.
Citizens' Budget Advisory Committee, "Summary of Observations by Citizens' Budget Advisory Committee Regarding City of Calgary 1972 Capital Budget."
Industrial Expansion Committee of the City of Calgary, *Minutes,* February 15, June 17, 1971.
Liaison Committee to Meet With Council Committee of the Municipal District of Rocky View, *Minutes,* April 8, 1971.
Planning Advisory Committee, *Minutes,* November 24, 1971.
Special Co-ordinating Committee on Housing, *Minutes,* November 16, 1971.

Standing Policy Committee on Finance and Budget, *Minutes,* December 22, 1971.
Technical Co-ordinating Committee for Land Use and Transportation Planning, *Minutes,* February 9, 1972.
City Planning Department, *The Calgary Plan: A General Plan prepared on behalf of the civic administration,* March 1970, and *Addendum,* April 1971.
— Director of Planning, *The Proposed Preliminary Regional Plan — 1970,* report submitted to Calgary Regional Planning Commission, January 26, 1971.
— Report (on proposed MacEwan Glens annexation), March 30, 1971.
Director of Planning, Report to Calgary City Council, June 1, 1971.
Calgary School District No. 19, "Submission to the Local Authorities Board . . . ," n.d. ((*circa* May 1971).
Separate Comments of Joseph Yanchula as a Member of Citizens' Budget Advisory Committee Regarding City of Calgary 1972 Capital Budget, January 1972.
(A City Alderman) Report to Calgary City Council "Re: MacEwan Glens Annexation and Development," February 24, 1972.
1972 Residential Development Agreement between the City of Calgary and the Urban Development Institute, draft.

3. Other Municipalities:

Municipal District of Foothills, *Minutes* of Council Meeting, January 1971.
Municipal District of Kneehill, *Minutes* of Council Meeting, January 18, 1971.
Municipal District of Kneehill, Submission to Calgary Regional Planning Commission, January 18, 1971.
Municipal District of Rocky View, *Minutes* of Council Meeting, August 11, 1970.
— Reply to Regional Planning Commission, January 26, 1971.
— "A Brief on Appeal to the Provincial Planning Board Regarding the Calgary Preliminary Regional Plan 1971," June 3, 1971.
"Regional Planning as Designed and Practised in the Southern Portion of the Province of Alberta with Particular Reference to the Region Surrounding the City of Calgary," A Brief by a Representative of the MD of Rocky View. Office files of Municipal District of Rocky View.
Town of High River, *Minutes* of Council meeting, January 13, 1971.
Town of Okotoks, *Minutes* of Council meeting, January 18, 1971.
Town of Spruce Grove, "Brief to the Department of Municipal Affairs: Regarding Finance Borrowing Requirements," prepared during 1971.
Village of Cockrane, *Minutes* of Council meeting, January 1971.

III: Letters

Calgary Assistant Deputy Director of Planning to the City's legal department, December 19, 1971.
Calgary Assistant Deputy Director of Planning to the City Commissioner of Operations and Development, December 28, 1971.

Calgary Commissioner of Operations and Development to Assistant Deputy Director of Planning, January 3, 1972.
Calgary Director of Planning to the City Engineer, re MacEwan Glens, February 1, 1971.
Calgary Director of Planning to Commissioner of Operations and Development, May 31, 1971.
(Memorandum from) Calgary Director of Planning to a member of his staff, December 10, 1971.
Calgary Property Taxpayers Association; letter received by Special Co-ordinating Committee on Housing, November 16, 1971.
Chairman of the Board of Trustees, Calgary School District No. 19, to Minister of Education, April 23, 1971.
Colborne, the Hon. F., Minister of Municipal Affairs, to His Worship, Dr. I. G. Dent, Mayor, City of Edmonton, July 11, 1969.
Dent, I. G., Mayor, City of Edmonton, to the Hon. F. Colborne, Minister of Municipal Affairs, July 16, 1969.
Director of Field Services, Department of Education, to Mr. Cote of Underwood, McClellan and Associates Ltd., January 25, 1972.
Director of the National and Historic Branch, Department of Indian Affairs and Northern Development, to Calgary Regional Planning Commission, December 29, 1970.
Frigon, Charles H., President of Edmonton Home Builders' Association, to the Mayor and Council, City of Edmonton, December 16, 1965.
Edmonton Home Builders' Association to the Mayor and Council, City of Edmonton, October 31, 1967.
Edmonton Home Builders' Association to the Mayor and Council, City of Edmonton, December 13, 1967.
Edmonton Home Builders' Association (signed by the President of EHBA) to Edmonton City Council, January 20, 1969.
Hamilton, J. W., of Imperial Oil Ltd., to Mr. Anthony Adamson, April 26, 1963.
Local Authorities Board to Calgary City Council, May 5, 1971.
Minister of Education to Chairman of the Board of Trustees, Calgary School District No. 19, June 9, 1971.
Minister of Highways and Transport to Calgary Regional Planning Commission, January 27, 1971.
Minister of Lands and Forests to the Calgary Regional Planning Commission, January 25, 1971.
Minister of Municipal Affairs to the Mayors of Edmonton and Calgary, July 11, 1969.
A Representative of Carma Developers to a City of Calgary Commissioner, re MacEwan Glens, March 9, 1971.
A Representative of the County of Strathcona to the City Solicitor, October 19, 1970.
Three Edmonton Councillors on the Edmonton Regional Planning Board to the Executive Secretary of the Alberta Urban Municipalities Association, undated (written sometime before January 29, 1971).